Religion in America

ADVISORY EDITOR

Edwin S. Gaustad

A MEMOIR

OF THE

LIFE AND LABORS

OF

FRANCIS WAYLAND, D.D., LL.D.

FRANCIS WAYLAND AND H. L. WAYLAND

Volumes I and II

ARNO PRESS

A NEW YORK TIMES COMPANY

New York • 1972

Reprint Edition 1972 by Arno Press Inc.

Reprinted from a copy in
The Newark Public Library

RELIGION IN AMERICA - Series II
ISBN for complete set: 0-405-04050-4
See last pages of this volume for titles.

Manufactured in the United States of America

Library of Congress Cataloging in Publication Data

Wayland, Francis, 1826-1904.
    A memoir of the life and labors of Francis Wayland.

    (Religion in America, series II)
    Reprint of the 1867 ed.
    1. Brown University. 2. Wayland, Francis,
1796-1865. I. Wayland, Heman Lincoln, 1830-1898.
II. Title.
LD636 1827.W32   378.1'12'0924 [B]   76-38465
ISBN 0-405-04092-X

A MEMOIR

OF THE

LIFE AND LABORS

OF

FRANCIS WAYLAND, D.D., LL.D.

Yours truly
F. Wayland

A MEMOIR

OF THE

LIFE AND LABORS

OF

FRANCIS WAYLAND, D.D., LL.D.,

LATE PRESIDENT OF BROWN UNIVERSITY.

INCLUDING

SELECTIONS FROM HIS PERSONAL REMINISCENCES
AND CORRESPONDENCE.

BY HIS SONS,

FRANCIS WAYLAND AND H. L. WAYLAND.

VOLUME I.

NEW YORK:
SHELDON AND COMPANY.
1867.

Stereotyped at the Boston Stereotype Foundry,
No. 4 Spring Lane.

THIS MEMOIR

Is Respectfully Dedicated

TO THE

PUPILS, PARISHIONERS, AND FRIENDS

OF

FRANCIS WAYLAND,

WHO HAVE SO OFTEN HEARD FROM HIS LIPS THE LESSON
HEREIN CONFIRMED, THAT NOTHING ON EARTH
IS SO DIVINE AS A LIFE DEVOTED TO
THE SERVICE OF GOD AND THE
WELFARE OF MAN.

NOTE.

In the preparation of this memoir we have been greatly aided by those whose reminiscences form an interesting feature of the work; by those who have kindly placed letters at our disposal; and by those whose contributions, although not appearing in the words of their authors, contained valuable information, of which we have gladly availed ourselves.

For this assistance, always most cheerfully rendered, and for innumerable manifestations of sympathy and friendliness, we return our grateful acknowledgments.

F. W.

H. L. W.

September 25, 1867.

CONTENTS

OF THE FIRST VOLUME.

———

CHAPTER I.

CHAPTER II.

CHAPTER III.

CHAPTER IV.

CHAPTER V.

CHAPTER VI.

CHAPTER VII.

CHAPTER VIII.

CHAPTER IX.

CHAPTER X.

CHAPTER XI.

CHAPTER XII.

CHAPTER XIII.

CHAPTER XIV.

CHAPTER XV.

CHAPTER XVI.

CHAPTER XVII.

CHAPTER XVIII.

LIFE

OF

FRANCIS WAYLAND.

CHAPTER I.

PARENTAGE. — BOYHOOD. — SCHOOLS. — COLLEGE COURSE.

IT is proposed, in the following pages, to present the character and the labors of FRANCIS WAYLAND; to exhibit what he was and what he did. It will not probably be thought that his labors are underrated, if the opinion is expressed that the man was greater than all his works; that the noblest thing which he made was himself. The inquiry into the influences which formed him must, therefore, greatly occupy our attention. Prominent among these influences was the character of his parents and of his early home. These it will be proper to delineate somewhat minutely.

In 1849, shortly after the death of his father, Dr. Wayland, at the request of his sisters, wrote his recollections of his parents and his estimate of their character. These memorials, prepared solely for the family, and with no expectation of any wider publicity, will form our dependence for whatever will be introduced relative to this topic. If apology is needed for the fulness of detail in which he at times indulges, it will be found in the circumstances which gave rise to the papers. They are not the words of one forcing upon the public, narrations in which they have no interest, but of a son and brother reminding his bereaved sisters of the virtues of his and their sainted parents.

FRANCIS WAYLAND was the son of Francis Wayland and of Sarah Moore Wayland.* Of his more remote ancestors it is perhaps sufficient to say that they were persons in the middle station of life, of Baptist sentiments, and, for the most part, of more than usual piety. While they had no immediate agency in forming his character, we are warranted in believing that their piety and their prayers were among the influences which secured for him the blessings promised to the children's children of the righteous.

"My father and mother, shortly after their marriage, emigrated to the new world, and on the 20th of September, 1793, arrived in New York, where he immediately commenced business as a currier.

"Previous to the revolution, leather and manufactures of all kinds had been, to a great extent, imported from the mother country. The change in our political relations opened a wide field for enterprise to artisans in every department of labor. Men thoroughly acquainted with the mechanic arts were rare, and the demand for their products was vast and urgent. My father was perfectly master of his business, and his little capital gave him advantages of great importance in that condition of the

---

* Francis Wayland (son of Daniel Wayland and Susannah Pritchard), born at Frome, Somersetshire, England, June 15, 1772, died at Saratoga Springs, New York, April 9, 1849; Sarah Moore (daughter of John Moore and Elizabeth Thompson), born at Norwich, England, August 16, 1770, died at Saratoga Springs, December 5, 1836. Married at Norwich, May 20, 1793. The following children grew to adult age, and survived the parents : Francis ; Susannah P. (married William L. Stone, of New York), died 1852 ; Sarah T. (married Thomas P. Cushing, of Boston) ; Daniel, died 1861 ; John, died 1863 ; Anne E.

country. He was also emphatically ' diligent in business,' rising early, always at his work, and remarkably
equitable in his dealings. My mother united with him
in every effort necessary to insure success, and they soon
became prosperous to such an extent as satisfied their
ambition."

Both Mr. Wayland and his wife had been members
of the Baptist church in Eagle Street, London. After
reaching New York, they united with what was then the
Fayette Street Church (afterwards the Oliver Street, and
now the Madison Avenue Church), then destitute of a
pastor, but subsequently under the charge of Rev. John
Williams, whose ardent piety and eminent ability they
ever held in reverent and affectionate remembrance. Of
this church Mr. Wayland was early chosen a deacon, in
company with John Caldwell (the father-in-law of the
late Rev. Dr. Sharp), John Withington, and William
Hewitt.

"The other deacons of the church were, like my father,
engaged in active business. At special seasons they
visited each other's houses. Their associations, and those
of their families, were almost exclusively religious. The
only guests I remember to have seen at my father's house
were deacons, ministers, and persons eminent for piety.
Their conversation was almost entirely on questions of
doctrinal or experimental religion. As I look back upon
these events (with the recollection, it is true, of boyhood), my father's associates seem to me to have been
far better acquainted with the Scriptures and with the doctrines of the gospel, and more thoroughly religious, than
we commonly find professing Christians at the present
day. Fuller, Gill, Booth, Romaine, Hervey, Toplady,
and Newton were much more frequently quoted by them
than such writers are by Christians among us. My
father's peculiar treasure was a copy of Cann's Bible,
with marginal references. This he unceasingly studied,
and never relinquished it, until it was actually worn out
by daily and almost constant use.

"With these religious discussions, one other topic—that
of politics—was sometimes intermingled. My father had

felt the oppressions to which dissenters had been exposed
in England, and espoused what was considered the 'popular cause' in this country with considerable earnestness.
At particular times, I recollect to have heard joyful hopes
or fearful forebodings, as one or the other party seemed
likely to be in the ascendant. The particular point to
which their apprehensions turned was the connection of
politics with religion. There was, at this time, if I am
not mistaken, a belief that one party, the 'Republican,'
was more favorable than the other, the 'Federalist,' to
unrestricted freedom in matters of religious opinion.*
With the former party, of course, all the Baptists from the
older country sympathized. In the church to which my
father belonged, I have frequently heard it mentioned
that there was but one member who was not a Republican; and the wonder among his brethren was, how so
good a man could, in so important a matter, err so grievously.

"The arrangements of my father's family were all made
subordinate to his religious principles. Morning and
evening devotions were as regular as the return of the
hours appropriated to those services. So conscientious
was he in this respect, that once, while he was engaged
in teaching, at a later period of his life, my brother recol-
lects that he called the scholars together at about eleven
o'clock, and requested them to keep their seats while
he should be absent for a few minutes. He then took
my brother home with him, assembled his family together, apologized to them for his sin in forgetting morning prayers, read the Scriptures, and prayed, and then

---

* The student of those times will recall the fact that the Federalists favored the continuance of a " standing order," and were
of opinion that the interests of religion required that provision
should be made by law for the maintenance of worship according
to the established usage. The opposing party, in some instances,
from sincere love of religious freedom, and confidence in the
power of Christianity to stand on its own merits, and in other instances from an impartial hatred to all forms of piety, demanded
the removal of these distinctions, and the absolute equality of all
sects before the law. The most pious of the Baptists of that day
found themselves often making common cause, in behalf of
religious freedom, with errorists and infidels.

returned to his school-room. This is the only instance in the memory of any of the family in which this duty was ever omitted.

" On the Lord's day, the rule of the family was for all the children to learn a hymn before dinner, and a portion of the Catechism before tea. The former was repeated to my mother; the latter to my father. It was not his custom to attend the evening meeting. After tea, or at candle lighting, we were all assembled in the parlor; my father, or one of the older children, read some suitable passage of Scripture, which he explained and illustrated, frequently directing the conversation so as to make a personal application to some one or other of us. Singing and prayer followed. Occasionally some little refreshment was introduced, and we retired, at an early hour, to bed. This domestic religious service was never interrupted until my father became a preacher, and spent most of his Sabbath evenings in public worship.

" I remember to have heard, in my youth, frequent conversation between my father and his friends respecting an association, that had been established, by several members of the church, for the purpose of improvement in exhortation and in the study of the Scriptures. Of this association I should suppose my father to have been one of the most active members. He looked forward to its meetings with unusual interest, and spent regularly a considerable portion of time in preparing for its exercises. In this manner his attention was gradually turned to the ministry. Soon after, he applied to the church for a license to preach the gospel. I have an indistinct recollection of the deep interest which this step awakened in the minds of both my parents. On the one hand, my father felt sensibly his want of literary preparation. On the other, a conviction rested with increasing weight upon his mind, that it was his duty to make known to his fellow-men the riches of that grace of which he was a partaker.

" As was the excellent custom of those days, he preached several times before the church, and once, I think, before the congregation, that his brethren might judge of his qualifications to become a religious teacher. His request was granted, and he received a license, June 10, 1805, on the same evening with his Christian brother and life-long friend, Daniel Sharp.

" When my father applied for a license to preach, he had no intention of relinquishing his business and becoming the pastor of a church. He intended merely to become a lay preacher. A number of villages were growing up in the vicinity of New York, and he desired to preach the gospel on the Sabbath to such of them as were destitute of religious instruction, while pursuing his regular avocation during the week. This plan he pursued for three or four years. As, however, he became more familiar with the duties of the ministry, his love for them increased. His aid was sought by feeble churches at greater and greater distances from home. His labors were blessed to the conversion of souls. His secular and his religious avocations became more and more incompatible with each other. To carry on active business under the necessity of so frequent absences from home, was clearly impossible. The question arose, whether he should relinquish the preaching of the gospel altogether, or, abandoning all secular business, devote himself exclusively to the ministry.

" This subject occasioned long and anxious deliberation. On the one hand, provision was to be made for a large and increasing family ; his business, already lucrative, was extending, and a few years would probably, with the blessing of God, leave him entirely independent. On the other hand, his property, well invested, would yield him about a thousand dollars a year — at that time a much more adequate income than at present; and the use of this would enable him to preach in places where the gospel could not otherwise be sustained. He decided to close his business, and to devote himself exclusively to the ministry."

These somewhat copious extracts have been given, in part because of their intrinsic interest, in part because of the insight they give into the influences which surrounded the subject of this memoir, and because it is more than probable that his later views of the standard of Christian and ministerial labor, self-denial, and piety, were in some degree derived from his early impressions.

Mr. Wayland became pastor of the Baptist church in Poughkeepsie in 1807. The church was feeble, disorganized, and destitute of a house of worship. He labored for four years in this field, most of the time without compensation. During this period a house of worship was erected, many souls were converted, and the foundation was laid for the thriving churches that now occupy that field.

From Poughkeepsie he removed, in 1811, to Albany, and from thence, after a settlement of about a year, to Troy. During his residence in Troy, serious reverses befell him. Most of his property was invested in marine insurance companies, which became bankrupt in consequence of the seizure of American vessels under the Berlin and Milan decrees. To these reverses he opposed the force of patience, industry, frugality, and confidence in God. He eked out his scanty salary by teaching a boys' school; and these efforts, united with the wise and conscientious economy of his noble wife, enabled him not only to maintain his family, and to afford them the education which he justly deemed the best earthly heritage, but to exercise, heartily but unostentatiously, the scriptural grace of hospitality toward his Christian brethren.

In 1819 he became pastor of the church in Saratoga Springs, and in that beautiful village he passed the peaceful evening of his pious life. After ceasing from his pastoral cares in 1823, he spent almost his entire time in preaching, in secret devotion, in religious conversation, and in visiting those who were sick or afflicted, or in need of spiritual counsel.

It is the testimony of his son, and of all who knew him, that he was a man of peculiar industry, integrity, and devotion. As a preacher, he was too little endowed with imagination and passion to be largely popular. He was, however, eminently scriptural, religious, and instructive.

" His forte was not the pulpit, but the chamber of sickness; his public ministrations were less successful than

his conversation from house to house. For facility in the
introduction of religious subjects, in his visits among his
acquaintances of whatever station, and of whatever character, and for faithfulness in pressing them home to personal application, I have never known his superior."

It has been seen that the avocations of Mr. Wayland called him often away from his family. This fact
threw the training of the children greatly into the hands
of the mother, and the same Providence that laid this
duty upon her, had imparted eminent qualifications for its
discharge. Her gentleness of temper, her winning manners, her mental activity, and a youthfulness of feeling
unsubdued by care, privation, or sickness, gave her peculiar sympathy with the young. In an especial manner
was her influence felt by her oldest son. His early maturity rendered him in some degree her companion; and
with the reverence due to a parent there was blended the
fondness naturally felt for an older sister. He has mentioned, in illustration of her youthfulness of appearance,
that once when he was travelling with her, after he had
reached twenty years of age, she was supposed to be his
wife. Possibly the tender and devoted attention which
he then, as ever, paid her, had some effect in causing the
erroneous impression.

"Much of my time during my boyhood was spent in
the society of my mother. The time between morning
and afternoon school hours was occupied with dinner
and its attendant avocations. But when I returned home
in the afternoon, I always found her with her needle. I
used to read to her my books, over and over again, and
draw pictures of animals on the slate. I well remember
that she spent much of the time in conversation with me,
relating to me anecdotes from history, the sufferings and
death of martyrs, and the scenes which she recalled of
her childhood. Of these latter, I regret to say, that the
greater part have passed from my recollection. But there
was one class of them, the effect of which upon my mind
I cannot forget. There was a spot in Norwich where

many Protestants had suffered martyrdom in the reign of Mary, and there were also the remains of an old abbey or monastery, in the dungeons of which many pious persons had been tortured for their profession of faith in Christ. The emotion with which my mother used to relate these atrocities I shall always remember. If I have ever cherished a genuine abhorrence for religious intolerance, the sentiment was first awakened by my mother's conversations. Nor was she merely an enemy of persecution for the sake of religion. I have never known a more enthusiastic or more consistent lover of human liberty. For oppression of every kind she felt a true and noble disdain. I was less than four years old at the death of Washington, and his obsequies in New York is the first event of which I have a distinct recollection. I well remember the deep interest which her account of his character awakened in my bosom. When very young, I felt dissatisfied because my parents had not named me after the Father of my country. I wished even then to have it in my power in some way to do him honor."

She possessed a remarkable faculty of rendering her home at once attractive and elevating.

"The excellent taste of my mother was equally apparent, whatever might be our circumstances. Everything under her control was always neat, in keeping, and in perfect order. Whatever might be the furniture of the room, when you entered it, you would have been convinced that a discriminating and cultivated mind presided over all the arrangements of the household."

"From my earliest recollections she was a very assiduous reader. During the early part of her life this inclination could not be fully gratified, for she subjected her tastes habitually to her convictions of duty. After her health failed, and the labor of her hands became impossible, she read extensively. You might call upon her when you would, and if she was not engrossed in some domestic occupation, she was always engaged in reading. With many of the best works on theology she was well acquainted. But she did not confine herself to these. She read with interest every work that conveyed important knowledge or communicated a quickening impulse to the human faculties.   Especially did she delight in tracing the progress of the cause of Christ, the diffusion of knowledge, and the triumphs of freedom in every part of the globe."

A character thus beautiful and benign was perfected and transfigured by the influence of religious principle.

" Her piety was marked by profound humility, a deep conviction of her own unworthiness in the sight of God, proceeding from a clear conception of the holiness of his law, a firm reliance on the merits of Christ for salvation, and an earnest and controlling desire to bring every thought, word, and action into conformity with the precepts of the Savior."

Endowed with such characteristics, it will readily be believed that she engaged the deep affection of her son; and the reader of the following pages will, it is apprehended, find many traces of the influence of her counsels and her example.   It would be quite impossible, without copious extracts, to give any adequate idea of the reverent and grateful tenderness which pervaded his correspondence with her, and indeed with both his parents.   In speaking of them in 1849, he writes, —

" I think that if their children have attained to any portion of success in the present life, or to a well-grounded hope of future happiness, they will ascribe it in no common degree to the precepts, example, and counsels of their parents.   These have been a richer heritage than wealth or worldly honor could bestow ; a heritage which I would not exchange for a descent from princes." *

---

* One or two circumstances in the life of Mrs. Wayland were sufficiently remarkable to merit recital.   No explanation of them is attempted.   At the time of their removal to America, it was the design of Mr. Wayland and his wife to return in a few years, and visit the relatives whom they had left behind, especially the mother of Mrs. W.   This purpose they often spoke of to each other.   But one morning, after they had been some years in this country, she said to him, on waking, " I do not wish to return to England.   My mother is dead."   No previous intimation of her ill health had

Of these parents FRANCIS WAYLAND was born, March 11, 1796, in the city of New York, in a house on the corner of Frankfort and Rose Streets.

Our knowledge of this portion of his life is derived mainly from himself. His sons had often entreated him to commit to writing some account of his own life, and he expressed a willingness to do so. It is probable, however, that he did not feel himself at liberty during the years of health, to devote time to preparing what so largely concerned himself and his own acts, and what would not, in his view, interest or instruct any outside of his own family. But after a severe attack of sickness, in the spring of 1860, he commenced a series of reminiscences, which he thus introduces : —

"October 26, 1860. My children have sometimes intimated to me that they would be greatly pleased if I would write some reminiscences of my own life. Until the present time I have never found leisure for such an undertaking. During the past summer I have been obliged to lay aside active literary labor. I have, however, so far improved, that writing is pleasant to me, though I am hardly prepared for accurate thinking. I

---

been received. He, unknown to her, made a minute of the time of her declaration; and a subsequent arrival brought the news of the event, which had occurred at about the time at which her mind was thus impressed.

When her son — the subject of this memoir — was expected home from New York, after attending medical lectures there, during the winter of 1814–15, Mrs. W., who was sitting with her husband, suddenly walked the room in great agitation, saying, "Pray for my son; Francis is in danger." So urgent was her request that her husband joined her in prayer for his deliverance from peril. At the expected time he returned. His mother at once asked, "What has taken place?" It appeared, that while coming up the North River, on a sloop, he had fallen overboard, and the sloop had passed over him. He was an athletic swimmer, and readily kept himself afloat till he could be rescued. Was it the unspeakable power of a mother's love that imparted a vision more than natural?

have thought that, by undertaking something of this kind, I might the better prepare myself for severer duties, and also give pleasure to those whom I love. I therefore, this day, have commened this rambling autobiography.

" It will at once be evident that I have nothing of special importance to record, for my life has been singularly free from incident. Yet a plain tale of individual history presents a specimen of human life, from which, almost always, some lesson may be gleaned. It is always interesting to personal friends, and for them alone the following pages are written. Without apologizing for the egotism, I shall write almost exclusively of myself; for this, I know, is what those for whom I write would decidedly prefer."

As has before been stated, the first event within his remembrance was the death of Washington, and the funeral ceremonies in New York. He clearly recalled the childish perplexity with which he saw in the parade a coffin and a bier, and the outward semblance of a funeral, while yet he was informed that the person in whose honor all these ceremonies were held had been buried weeks previously in a remote State. He was, it would seem, even then dissatisfied with witnessing spectacles without trying to understand their meaning.

He also gives the following reminiscences : —

" I heard a conversation about some one being *sued*. My oldest sister was called ' Sue ' in the family, and I somehow associated her name with the suing of which I had heard. I asked the meaning of suing, and I remember the answer which spoke of courts, and juries, and constables, all which was perfectly beyond my comprehension. I well recall my childish attempts to understand the nature of civil laws, and of the process which was a subject of discussion ; but the whole matter was beyond my powers. I mention this trifling incident because I think it has been of service to me in subsequent life. I have appreciated the difficulty with which children comprehend any complicated subject, especially the social relations of man ; and I see what was the fault of my instructors.

They told me about judges and courts, while what was meant by these terms was to me entirely unintelligible. Had they laid aside all words pertaining to office, and illustrated the moral nature of the transaction by reference to what might happen in the plays of children, I could have arrived at the general idea. From this incident I have learned to convey a new idea to the young with the greatest simplicity in my power, and not to be satisfied until I see that they are able to comprehend the radical conception without the use of technical terms. There is nothing that a child ought to know, which it cannot be taught, if one will take pains to present the radical idea, and illustrate it by something which is occurring every day in its own experience.

"My father was a man of very fixed ideas of family government, and required of his children implicit obedience. I have no recollection of ever disobeying him deliberately but once. There was a school on the opposite side of the street, taught by a young woman, and it was determined to send me there for instruction. It was, however, a girls' school, and taught by a woman. I resisted to the utmost, and was carried over in arms. It was not that I was opposed to being taught, but I could not consent to be taught by a woman, and in a girls' school. I spent the time in school in loud crying, which was not at all lessened by the threat of the mistress to put me in the oven. After a few trials, the attempt was relinquished, and it was determined to send me to a boys' school. I allude to this incident to mark the difference which fifty years have made in our notions of instruction. At the present day, women are our most esteemed teachers, and they frequently control with ease large schools of the most refractory lads, and sometimes young persons who have almost arrived at majority. I have known them to succeed in the enforcement of discipline where *men*, of their own age, had entirely failed.*

---

* It seems proper to place beside the record of his somewhat immature judgment a later utterance, extracted from the Address before the American Institute, in 1854: " By the gradation of our schools, another most important advantage is secured. A vast field is thus opened for the employment of female teachers. At the present moment, women perform a large portion of the teach-

" I early attended a boys' school in the rear of the old Methodist meeting-house, in John Street. The only thing that I remember of this school is, that no distinction was at that time made in respect to color. A few colored children attended the school, and played with the other pupils without exciting remark. I was not aware that any degradation attached to their color ; and this, I think, was the general opinion of the period.

" The next school which I attended was taught (if I may apply that term to his labor) by an Englishman, a clergyman, who subsequently attained some celebrity in the city. I am unable to say how far he was a fair specimen of the schoolmaster of that day. His school had considerable reputation. He was of venerable, yet severe aspect, and with a strong sense of personal dignity. He used but one motive to obedience — terror. The ferule and the cowhide were in constant use. He never *taught* us anything ; indeed, he seemed to think it below his dignity. I do not remember anything approaching explanation while I was at the school. A sum was set, and the pupil left to himself to find out the method of doing it. If it was wrong, the error was marked, and he must try again. If again it was wrong, he was imprisoned after school, or he was whipped.

" In other studies the text of the book must be repeated without a word of explanation. Geography was studied without a map, by the use of a perfectly dry compendium. I had no idea what was meant by bounding a country, though I daily repeated the boundaries at recitation. I studied English grammar in the same way. I had a good memory, and could repeat the Grammar (Lowth's, I think) throughout. What it was about, I had not the least conception. Once, the schoolmaster was visiting at my father's, and I was called up to show my proficiency

---

ing in New England, and they do it so well that this portion is rapidly growing larger. Women have a much greater natural adaptation to the work of instruction than men. We find only occasionally a man possessed of this peculiar endowment, while among women it is almost universal. Much of the improvement in education in New England is, I believe, to be ascribed to the employment of women, in the place of men, in a large number of our schools."

in this branch of learning. I surprised my friends by my
ability to begin at the commencement and to proceed as far
as was desired ; yet it did not convey to me a single idea.
Years afterwards, when I began to study Latin, and found
the relation of words to each other designated by termina-
tions, and when the matter was explained to me, the whole
of my past study came to me like a new revelation. I
saw the meaning of what I had formerly, in utter darkness, committed to memory.

"Thus I was doomed to spend several of the most
precious years of my life. I do not believe such a school
could exist at the present time in any part of this country
with which I am acquainted. It could not have been
sustained then, but for the fact that the master was a
clergyman, well reputed for piety, and supposed to be
solemn enough to impress boys with awe. The only
pleasure I have in remembering this school is derived
from the belief that boys of the present day are not exposed to such miserable instruction. As, on the one hand,
no such school would now be tolerated, so, on the other
hand, such teaching as is now enjoyed in our public
schools could not then have been procured at any ordinary expense, if at all. Perhaps my experience here was
not altogether lost. It has at least served to impress me
with the importance of doing everything in my power to
bring whatever I attempted to teach within the understanding of the learner."

It was to this portion of his youth that the reminiscence
belongs, given above, of his spending much of his leisure
time in reading by the side of his mother. A surviving
sister, Mrs. C., says of the same period, —

"Although he was but two years the senior of the sister
next him in age, yet, for some reason, he always seemed
much older than the rest of us. When a mere boy, he
was the companion of our mother. While we were at
play, he would sit by her side and converse with her, freed
from all childish reserve. As he grew older, he would
talk with her about his studies, and his various discouragements."

When he was in his eleventh year, his father having
removed to Poughkeepsie, he entered the Dutchess

County Academy. It was here, under the instruction of
Rev. John Lawton (subsequently of Vermont), whom he
remembered with respect and gratitude, that he made
the discovery lately referred to, of the signification of
grammar. Various instructors followed.

"Under one I commenced the study of Greek, with the
use of the Westminster Greek Grammar. The text was in
Latin, and I was required to understand it, at a time when
I could with difficulty construe and parse the simplest narrative sentence in Latin. I learned the declensions and conju-
gations, but the Grammar was of little further use to me.*
With another I attempted to read Virgil, and used to
recite perhaps a hundred lines at a lesson, having read it
over in the most cursory manner with the aid of David-
son, whose edition was then in use. I presume the teacher
could not read it himself, and the only effect of such instruction was to cultivate in me habits of utter carelessness
and of entire neglect of study.

"Towards the close of my father's residence in P. some
public-spirited gentlemen determined to place the Academy
on a respectable footing. They secured the services of
Mr. Daniel H. Barnes, a teacher whom I shall ever remember with affection and gratitude. Mr. B. made
teaching his profession for life, and he chose it wisely,
for this was the avocation for which nature had designed
him. A strict yet kind disciplinarian, ready always
to render all needful assistance, but teaching the scholar
to rely mainly on himself, he possessed in a remarkable
degree the power of instilling his own enthusiasm into
the mind of the pupil. Under him I first learned to study

---

* We have never chanced to fall in with the Westminster Greek
Grammar named above, nor probably have many of our readers;
but the following extract from its pages, which we find quoted by
Sydney Smith, will afford a sufficient idea of its contents. It will
be remarked that the grammatical rules are expressed in hexam-
eter lines: —

"ω finis thematis finis utriusque futuri est
Post liquidam in primo, vel in unoquoque secundo,
ω circumflexus est.   Ante ω finale character
Explicitus δε primi est implicitusque futuri
ω itaque in quo δ quasi plexum est solitu in δω."

for the love of it, and to take a pride in accurate knowledge. The study of languages in this country had not then received the abundant aids now enjoyed; but they were taught by Mr. B. according to the best knowledge of the time, and the spirit which he infused into the work could not be excelled.

"The day on which I first came under his instruction is vivid in my memory. I had been reading Virgil at the rate just now described, and I considered myself quite an advanced Latin scholar. Judge of my surprise when he put the class back into Cæsar, and gave us only one section for a lesson. We came to the recitation with the feeling of persons whose attainments were sadly underrated. But the exercise had not proceeded ten minutes before we were painfully undeceived. We supposed that the section given out for the lesson would be easily recited in a few minutes; but the hour had elapsed before we had completed three sentences. Every word was to be analyzed, and declined or conjugated; its number, person, case, or tense determined; the reason for its present form, and the rule by which it assumed that form, given from the Grammar; the geography of Gaul and of the "tres partes" must be stated, and the Latin text not only rendered into correct English, but the whole matter must be comprehended by each student. We went home humbled and mortified at our ignorance, satisfied that we had been imposed upon by our previous masters, and that now, for the first time in our lives, we had met a real instructor. Our estimate of his superiority was unlimited, and we yielded ourselves with enthusiasm to his guidance."

He has related that while attending school in Poughkeepsie, he used, with his schoolmates, to run down to the bank of the Hudson, and gaze, with wonder and awe, on the creation of the genius of Fulton, the "Chancellor Livingston," as she made her way to and from Albany, achieving the passage in two or three days — little less than a miracle to those who had sometimes been as many weeks in making the voyage by sloop.

Among his fellow-pupils was Hon. Samuel B. Ruggles, now of New York, who writes as follows: —

" I well remember him as my schoolmate in the excellent Academy in Poughkeepsie, under Mr. Daniel H. Barnes, as principal, afterwards distinguished in this city as a successful teacher in connection with Mr. Griscom. He was a good, solid scholar, serious, orderly, and attentive, rather sedate in manner, but of pleasant temper, and a favorite with his teacher. I cannot now recall him as mingling much in the out-door sports and games, still less in the in-door pranks of the school, which occasionally drew down academic justice on some of us. I distinctly recollect his elocution, as a good, strong speaker, and even the fact that he selected for declamation, several times in succession, an extract from an oration on ' injured Africa.'

"But he remains very clearly in my memory from the circumstance that in or near the year 1811, at a public exhibition of the Academy, while the first Napoleon was at the zenith of his power, he and I were set by our ambitious schoolmaster to dispute the political question, then agitating all classes in America (which would now seem to be slightly beyond the ordinary range of boyish exercises), ' if Bonaparte should conquer England, *can* he conquer America.' My father, a good old Connecticut ' Federalist' of the broadest stamp, then practising law at Poughkeepsie, was of course utterly opposed to Mr. Jefferson and Mr. Madison, and their supposed proclivities towards France and its emperor. Of course, also, I took the negative in the dispute. It is my impression that Wayland's family were ' Republicans,' by which denomination the supporters of the Jeffersonian school were then known. At any rate he took the affirmative in the dispute, and maintained it with much force and earnestness. It is among the phenomena of early memories, rendering fugitive words indelible, that I now recollect even the language of one of his statements in that edifying discussion between us striplings, neither of us more than twelve or fourteen years old. ' Canada,' he said, ' stands ready to side at once with the invader. In habits and language they sympathize with France. Their language is already French.' He was not alone in the affirmative. It was the prevailing belief among all our village Republicans. The dread of Napoleon was not dispelled until the disasters of the Russian campaign of 1812, and the final overthrow at Leipsic in 1813, which so filled our village

Federalists with joy, that they not only illuminated their houses, but stigmatized their opponents for refusing to follow their example.

"Meanwhile I had gone to Yale, to learn a little more Federalism from President Dwight, and Wayland, taking an opposite direction, had gone, I think, to Union College. I did not see him again until nearly forty years afterwards, when I knew him as the honored president of Brown University."

We return to the reminiscences : —

"I enjoyed the instruction of this excellent man and remarkable teacher until my parents removed to Albany in 1811. To him I owe much, and I can never remember him but with warm affection. Had I been under the care of such an instructor from childhood, it would have been a blessing, the amount of which I cannot pretend to estimate. He soon raised the Academy to a position of eminence. Many of the leading men of that part of the state were his pupils, and I do not think that there is one of them whose estimate of the late D. H. Barnes would differ essentially from mine.*

---

* After teaching in Dutchess County Academy for several years with great success, Mr. B. removed to Cincinnati, subsequently to Schenectady, and thence to the city of New York. In each of these places he established a high reputation as an instructor, and as a man of science. He died a little past forty years of age. "He had accepted an invitation to attend the annual examination of the Rensselaer Institute, at Troy, which was to occur after the close of his term. It was his uniform habit to improve every opportunity to instil into the minds of his pupils useful, moral, intellectual, and practical precepts. And in dismissing his scholars for the summer vacation, he gave them some advice about travelling. Among other things, he spoke of the wisest course to pursue, if, at any time, the horses should run away. He especially cautioned them against jumping out of the carriage in such a case, and advised them to lie down in the bottom of the vehicle. On his way from New York to Troy, he spent a day or two at Canaan, the place of his birth. As he was going from thence to Hudson, to take the steamboat, the horses of the stage ran away, and the driver was thrown from his seat. Mr. Barnes, from some inexplicable impulse, jumped from the carriage, struck his head against

" I ought here to record my sense of obligation to some gentlemen who coöperated with Mr. B. in his efforts. Rev. Cornelius C. Cuyler * had quite lately been settled as pastor of the Dutch Reformed church in P. Thomas J. Oakley (afterwards member of Congress, and subsequently Chief Justice of the Superior Court in New York city) was just rising to eminence in the profession of law. These, with other gentlemen, would frequently spend an hour in the school, attending with great care to the recitations in progress. At the quarterly examinations, they were sure to be present, and acted as judges when we were examined for premiums. The good that was thus done was greater than either of those excellent men realized. We were accustomed to consider them as in the very first class of men within our knowledge. If they took an interest in our studies, we could not but believe that study was honorable. If they condescended to express pleasure at our success, we felt that the highest of earthly honors had been obtained — *laudari a laudato viro.*"

Of the traits which he exhibited at his home, and among his playmates, his sister, Mrs. C., remarks, —

" Our two younger brothers were mischievous boys, inseparable in all their sports, active, restless, unscrupulous, often wantonly destroying our dolls, playthings, and miniature houses. At such times our oldest brother, Francis, would soothe us and vindicate our rights. He was unlike most boys.† I do not remember that he ever marred or

---

a stone, and never spoke again. The horses, after running a few miles, stopped at their accustomed watering trough, and no injury resulted to any one save to Mr. Barnes. Had he lived, he would have taken his place among the first educators and the first physicists in America."

* Dr. Cuyler was a distant relative of Rev. Theo. L. Cuyler, D. D., of Brooklyn.

† " While I was yet a child, no childish play
    To me was pleasing; all my mind was set,
    Serious, to learn and know, and thence to do,
    What might be public good; myself I thought
    Born to that end, — born to promote all truth,
    All righteous things." — *Paradise Regained.*

destroyed any of our playthings. He had no organ of destructiveness, and the right of property was sacred with him. Even then he was an authority in morals, and a staunch vindicator of personal rights. The least approach to oppression aroused him. When he was but a lad, an older school-fellow was annoying and injuring the smaller boys. After expostulating in vain with the aggressor, my brother resorted to physical force to defend the injured. When he had flogged the lad, there was no further annoyance. The corrected youth became, subsequently, eminent in his profession, and a warm friend of his early antagonist. I have heard mother say that this was the only personal encounter of his school days."

We again extract from Dr. Wayland's reminiscences : —

"After I had been under Mr. B.'s tuition for almost eighteen months, my father removed to Albany, and I entered Union College, in May, 1811, being then fifteen years of age. I had expected to enter the third term of the Freshman year ; but upon examination I was admitted to the third term of the Sophomore year.

"The entrance to college forms an era in the life of a young person, especially if (as in my case) he then for the first time leaves his father's house, and has the care of himself. I was struck with irrepressible awe as I came into the presence of the professors for the purpose of being examined. They seemed at an unspeakable distance from me. It was with an overwhelming thrill of joy that I received the announcement that I could not only enter, but enter a year in advance of my expectations."

In a letter to his father, of May 17, 1811 (the earliest of his letters known to exist), he writes, "I am very glad that I did not enter the Freshman class, as in the Sophomore I am not deficient in anything but mathematics ; this deficiency I hope to make up in vacation."

At his entrance into college, the eminent Dr. Nott was in the seventh year of his presidency. The professors were Rev. Thomas Macauley, D. D., and Rev. T. C. Brownell, D. D., afterwards Bishop of Connecticut.

"Of my college course nothing remains to me but the general impression. The instructors were able, and (for

that time) well informed in their various departments.
Many of them have attained to eminence in their several
professions. But the course was very limited. Chemistry
was scarcely born; electricity was a plaything; algebra
was studied for six weeks; and geology was named only
to be laughed at. I was soon hurried into studies which
I could not understand, and in which I had little interest.
I was a pretty good reciter of what I understood dimly,
or not at all. I studied Kames' Elements, and Stewart on
the Mind, and heard the essays of older students on these
and kindred topics, with a vague notion that if I were
older I could do the same thing, but that at present it was
out of the question for me to understand and reason about
these subjects as they did.

"The social influences about me were bad. The young
men professing piety kept their religion to themselves.
Only one of them ever personally addressed me on the
subject of religion. This was a pious classmate, Rev.
William R. Bogardus, D. D., of the Dutch Reformed
church, now, or recently, in the State of New Jersey,*
who once called me into his room, and faithfully and
affectionately conversed with me in regard to my soul. I
have not seen him since we graduated; yet I never think
of him without an emotion of gratitude and love that I
feel for no other of my college friends. A few of the
students were young men of property, who squandered
their money in eating and drinking. But the greater part
were boys like myself, left to pursue such courses as they
chose, restrained by nothing but fear of college discipline.
I do not think that there was much gross sin in college
at this time, but many habits were forming which would
afterwards harden into open vice. Prevarication and
lying to officers, playing cards, small pilfering, especially
from commons and from the neighborhood of the college,
false accounts to parents, and profanity, especially in
playing games of chance, all sprang up in profusion. A
portion of the students were old enough to understand
and wise enough to appreciate the studies we pursued; but
these mostly associated with each other, and cared little
for those who were uninterested in these pursuits. We
studied, if it might be called study, for recitation merely,

---

* Since deceased.

never carrying our thoughts one inch beyond the page on which our eyes rested. Mental discipline or growth, except so far as the latter was the result of increase of years, was out of the question."

The language just quoted would leave the impression that his discharge of the duties of his college course was very imperfect. While, however, it is unquestionable that he appreciated the advantages then within his reach far less than he would have done in later years, yet it is probable that the account which he gives of his early deficiencies is exaggerated. He always underrated his own attainments, and applying to his college course the elevated standard of maturer years and more exalted motives, he was deeply impressed with a sense of early remissness. It is scarcely conceivable, however, that he would have been invited, a few years later, to assume the office of tutor, had he borne the character of a very negligent student.

Hon. B. P. Johnson, of Albany, secretary of the New York State Agricultural Society, writes, —

"My recollection of him dates back to the time when we met at Schenectady to be examined for admission to Union College. We had a room assigned to us in common, and we continued together for that term. He was fond of athletic sports, and I, too, was much in these exercises, being the son of a farmer and physician, and being obliged to work during the vacations.

"He received a medal, and I, next to him, received a testimonial from the president. We had a large class (of about forty-five), and a large portion of the students were older than we. It required effort to secure a place in the ring of honors, but we succeeded. B. B. Wisner, from Geneva, New York, took the second prize, though we believed that he should have had the first.

"Wayland was a hard student, and I do not recollect that he was ever called up for violation of college laws. He was on good terms with all, and kindly remembered after we parted in 1813."

The late Rev. Mr. Fonda, of the Dutch Reformed church, who was then a Sophomore, once mentioned that not long before the final dispersion of the class of 1813, on some occasion that brought the class and several other persons together, Wayland said, "Boys, we have never done what we could: we have not known what we can do; let us from this time try to make our mark in the world."

The distance from Schenectady to Troy, his father's residence, is but fifteen or eighteen miles, and he often spent the Sabbath at home. When he failed to do so, a letter was generally addressed to the whole family. His sympathy with his home remained unabated, and afforded, no doubt, one of the safeguards that preserved him from any gross vice. But few letters belonging to this period remain. They are the letters of a lad of fifteen, perhaps somewhat more carefully written than are those of most boys of that age, but exhibiting no peculiar interest in study, nor extraordinary depth of feeling.

From his mother: —

"My dear Son: I, or rather we, were rejoiced to have a letter from you. I was uneasy all the day that you left here. The thought of you broke in upon my sleep also; but the coming of your letter has put another song of praise upon my tongue.

"I thought, when you were at home last, you appeared low. Is anything on your mind? If there is, I beg you will not keep it from your mother.

"Whenever I write to you, my dear boy, I must remind you of your duty to God; it is my constant prayer that you may know him in the day of your youth. Sometimes, as I look round upon my dear children, I think, with the apostle, I could wish myself accursed, so that you might be saved. Think of a dying day frequently. I should be glad if you would write me, and give *me* some account of the state of your mind."

In his reply his feelings and his want of feeling are exhibited with candor, and are delineated with that clearness that always marked his descriptions of his own processes of thought and emotion.

" You request me, dear mother, to give *you* an account of the state of my mind. In so doing, I may gratify your curiosity, but cannot give you any satisfaction. The state of my mind, I fear, is awful; and I know it, but cannot help it. I know that I am a lost, condemned sinner, and I do not know how to help myself. I know that I cannot do it. I know that nothing but the blood of Christ applied to my soul can cleanse me; but how can this blood be applied? When I go to church, I am told to examine myself, and see if I am out of the ark of safety, and if I find that I am, I must pray to the Lord. As to examining, there is no need, for I am convinced that I am undone. I try to pray, but I know that I can do nothing to help myself. I think I can say that God would be just, were he to send me to hell; but I know that he alone can save me. I cannot say that this is the state of my mind all the time; but when I do think on the subject of religion, these are my thoughts. I never met with any person who had been in such a state, except a part of Brainerd's experience, and Mr. Hutton, who spoke on his experience one Sunday evening at our house. In this state of mind I have but two sources of consolation (if consolation it may be called) : first, because some who are now Christians were once in such a state of mind; secondly, because God has promised that the seed of Jacob shall not seek him in vain; therefore I think that so many of your prayers must be answered. This is the state of my mind, and I should be glad if you or father (whoever writes first) would tell me what I can do."

He adds in his reminiscences, —

" To what I have said of the college influences, there was one important exception. The recitations of Dr. Nott were of the nature of conversational lectures. After a brief recitation of the text, he occupied the remaining time in animated discussion on subjects connected with the lesson. Sometimes he examined, and either confirmed, refuted, or illustrated the author; sometimes he showed the consequences which flowed from the truth enunciated, and applied it to the various forms of individual, social, and

political life. Sometimes he relieved the discussion by
appropriate anecdotes. On every suitable occasion he
urged upon us a strict adherence to moral principle, and
the necessity of religion in order to true success in the life
that now is, as well as in that which is to come. His recitations were a pleasure which no student was willing to
lose. We then began to think ourselves men, for we had
then first found out how to form judgments for ourselves
on men and things, and on the events which were transpiring around us. I think I do not exaggerate when I
say that attendance upon Dr. Nott's course of instruction
formed an era in the life of every one of his pupils. And
yet, I must confess that I derived from it but half the
advantage it was designed to convey. I was seventeen
years old when I graduated. I think my mind did not
develop as soon as that of boys generally. I was interested; I followed him with avidity; I loved and reverenced
him, but I had not learned to generalize, nor was I, from
ignorance of the world, able to apply his principles as I
should a few years later."

He was graduated July 28, 1813.

CHAPTER II.

MEDICAL STUDIES. — INTELLECTUAL REGENERATION AND
GROWTH. — CONVERSION. — CHANGE OF PROFESSION.

IMMEDIATELY after his graduation he commenced
the study of medicine, entering the office of Dr. Moses
Hale, then an eminent physician and surgeon in Troy.
About six months later he entered the office of Dr. Eli
Burritt.

"He was a man of remarkable logical power, of enthusiastic love for his profession, of great and deserved confidence in his own judgment, and of strong reliance on the
power of medicine. I loved and honored him, and I
believe he was much attached to me. With him I continued until I was admitted to practice, and for several
months afterwards. I was much attached to the study
and practice of medicine. I think that I should have had
reasonable success had I continued in it."

The winter of 1814-15 he spent in New York, attending medical lectures. He once mentioned that, during
this period, he was walking through a street in the lower
part of the city, when he observed two persons coming
out of a ship-yard, conversing together. His attention was
drawn to them alike by their marked appearance, and by
the notice which they attracted from the passers-by. One
was a tall, dark-complexioned man, in the uniform of
the American navy; the other, a slightly-built man, with
olive complexion, dark, curling hair, and a quick, nervous
manner. They were Commodore Decatur and Robert
Fulton, who had been visiting a floating battery that
Fulton was constructing for use in the war then waging
against Great Britain.

He also during the same winter witnessed a thrilling scene, which he has thus described : —

" It so chanced that at the close of the last war with Great Britain, I was temporarily a resident of the city of New York. The prospects of the nation were shrouded in gloom. We had been, for two or three years, at war with the mightiest nation on earth, and as she had now concluded a peace with the continent of Europe, we were obliged to cope with her single-handed. Our harbors were blockaded, communication coastwise between our ports was cut off, our ships were rotting in every creek and cove where they could find a place of security. Our immense annual products were mouldering in our warehouses. The sources of profitable labor were dried up. Our currency was reduced to irredeemable paper. The extreme portions of our country were becoming hostile to each other, and differences of political opinion were embittering the peace of every household. The credit of the government was exhausted. No one could predict when the contest would terminate, or discover the means by which it could much longer be protracted.

" It happened that on a Sunday afternoon in February, a ship was discovered in the offing, which was supposed to be a cartel, bringing home our commissioners at Ghent, from their unsuccessful mission. The sun had set gloomily before any intelligence from the vessel had reached the city. Expectation became painfully intense, as the hours of darkness drew on. At length a boat reached the wharf, announcing the fact that a treaty of peace had been signed, and was waiting for nothing but the action of our government to become a law. The men on whose ears these words first fell, rushed in breathless haste into the city, to repeat them to their friends, shouting as they ran through the streets, ' Peace! *Peace!* PEACE !' Every one who heard the sound repeated it. From house to house, from street to street, the news spread with electric rapidity. The whole city was in commotion. Men bearing lighted torches were flying to and fro, shouting like madmen, ' Peace! Peace!' When the rapture had partially subsided, one idea occupied every mind. But few men slept that night. In groups they were gathered in the streets, and by the fireside, beguiling the hours of midnight by reminding each other that the agony of war was over, and that a worn out and distracted country, was about to enter again upon its wonted career of prosperity." — *Sermon on the Apostolic Ministry.*

He writes, in the reminiscences, —

" My study of medicine at this time and under so eminent a physician has enabled me to observe the changes which have taken place in the healing art within the period of forty years. Dr. Burritt was an able and experienced physician, standing at the head of his profession in Troy and the neighboring region, and a person of high moral character. Yet his practice would at the present time be considered most barbarous. I observed that he changed much during the time of my acquaintance with him. His confidence in the power of medicine greatly decreased, and he administered less and less. While I was a student with him, he frequently bled at the commencement of autumnal fever, and generally salivated, on the theory, then in vogue, that there could not exist two diseases at the same time in the human system, and that the mercurial disease, if established, would extirpate the other. The number of medicines to be daily and hourly administered was surprising. I almost wonder, looking at the matter from my present point of view, that any of the patients survived. Bleeding was a matter of very frequent occurrence on almost every occasion. Salivation, emetics, and drastic purgatives were much in vogue. The ruling idea seemed to be that, when a physician was called, he was to meet the disease like an enemy, and contend with it *pugnis et calcibus, unguibus et rostro.* His weapons were the materia medica, and the body of the patient was the theatre where this contest was carried on. It was a very heroic undertaking on the part of the physician, but a most suffering, not to say perilous condition on the part of the patient. At the present day the same disease would be treated with simple cleanliness, fresh air, and the careful watching of every symptom, to relieve, if possible, any part to which the disease might direct itself. The amount of medicine given has diminished, no one pretends to say how much. Dr. —— (a very eminent authority) prescribes an emetic at the very commencement of the disease ; but even in this he is almost alone. Bleeding is nearly abandoned. Recently one of the physicians at the Massachusetts General Hospital directed one of the house physicians to bleed a patient. He replied that he would cheerfully do it, but he had never seen a person bled. He then called upon the other assistant, who made the same reply, and they requested the older physician to perform the operation, that they might learn how to do it. So great have been the changes in practice since I first knew the profession, and all, without doubt, for the benefit of suffering humanity."

In view of the description which he gives of the medical practice of that day, the reader will perhaps be of opinion that he entitled himself to the gratitude of mankind by turning to a different profession, and that he might rightly claim the civic crown, anciently bestowed by Rome on one who had saved the life of his fellow-citizens.

Though he did not enter on the calling for which he had prepared himself, yet the time spent in his medical course was by no means lost. He began to study with more earnestness than heretofore, from the fact that he had a definite idea of the results to be obtained by his efforts. He understood what he needed to know, and why he needed to know it. He gained an acquaintance with physical science, and a fondness for it, which never forsook him, though the character of his subsequent duties gave him but scanty opportunity for keeping up with the progress of this most rapidly advancing branch of knowledge. It cultivated the habit of observation, alike of nature and of mankind, which through life he possessed and used in a higher degree than most persons were aware of.

It also brought him under the intellectual influence and stimulus of persons who were his superiors in age and attainments, but who discerned in him the signs of promise, and favored him with the fullest and most improving intimacy. While he was a student in college, his intercourse with his instructors had been almost entirely official. Personally he had known as little of them as they of him, and he had caught from them no inspiration. It is probable that even the instructions of Dr. Nott did not, at the time of his enjoying them, exert any special influence on his mind. With Dr. Burritt his personal relations were close, and the influence exerted on him was immediate. When the doctor was called away and did not return till night, his pupil would be in waiting at the office to welcome his return; and then they would stir up the fire and sit far into the night, discussing not merely professional topics, but almost every subject, till the mind of the young man became thoroughly aroused. One of his early friends * observes, —

" I was once riding with Dr. Wayland from Andover to Boston, and I asked him some questions about his early life and the sources of his success. He told me, among other things, that when a boy he was often ridiculed by lads older than himself. This discouraged him. When in college an older student criticised one of his compositions very severely and unjustly. Disheartened and disgusted he unwisely resolved to do as little of study and writing as he could and yet keep in his class. Later, after he had entered the office of Dr. B., the latter said to him, ' Now, Wayland, if you will bone down to it, and give your time and strength to your studies, I will make a man of you.' These encouraging words inspired him with a new life. The condition was performed, and the promise was fulfilled."

Dr. Wayland writes, —

" It was during the period of my medical studies that, as I well remember, a remarkable change took place in my intellectual condition. Upon entering college, I had, for the first time in my life, an almost unlimited command of books. I was very desirous of knowledge, and supposed that in order to obtain it, I had nothing to do but simply to read, and therefore I must read as much as possible. I read everything that came within my reach, without much selection, and with less recollection. Gradually, however, I subsided into reading for amusement. I read travels, novels, and works of humor, with untired avidity. My mind seemed capable of taking

* Rev. Mark Tucker, D. D.

in nothing but narration. I read Scott's Lady of the
Lake for no other purpose than to follow out the story,
and, as this seemed simple enough, I derived from it very
little pleasure. I read the Spectator very much in the
same way, selecting, as I went along, all of the narrative
essays and omitting everything else. I used to wonder
how persons could take so much pleasure in the didactic
essays, and become so much charmed with what they
called ' the beauty of the style.' No abstract thought of
any kind had for me the least attraction. I remember,
with perfect distinctness, the time when I first became
conscious of a decided change in my whole intellectual
character. I was sitting by a window, in an attic room
which I occupied as a sort of study, or reading-place, and
by accident I opened a volume of the Spectator — I think
it was one of the essays forming Addison's critique on
Milton — it was, at any rate, something purely didactic. I
commenced reading it, and, to my delight and surprise, I
found that I understood and really enjoyed it. I could
not account for the change. I read on, and found that
the very essays, which I had formerly passed over without
caring to read them, were now to me the gems of the
whole book, vastly more attractive than the stories and
narratives that I had formerly read with so much interest.
I knew not how to account for it. I could explain it on no
other theory than that a change had taken place in myself.
I awoke to the consciousness that I was a *thinking* being,
and a citizen, in some sort, of the republic of letters.

" I began the Spectator, and read it through, omitting,
for the most part, from choice, the parts which I had
formerly admired. From Addison I turned to Johnson,
and read the Rambler with great satisfaction. My chosen
book, however, for some time, was the Lives of the
Poets, which I read and re-read with delight, transcribing
the passages which struck me as worthy of special notice.
I found that novel reading unfitted me for study, or any
form of improvement, and I abandoned it altogether. I
think that, for ten or fifteen years, I never looked into a
novel. Indeed my taste for this sort of reading was from
that time finally destroyed. For many years past I have
not been able to get through a novel. The interest which
fiction excites in me is painful. I do not like to read of the
horrors of a shipwreck, or of any great disaster, or of intense suffering from any cause whatever. Why I should

take pleasure in narratives of fictitious suffering, I cannot discover.

"My reading henceforth was restricted to works of standard excellence. I found out what was meant by beauty of style, and I derived great enjoyment from it. I now looked back on my college course with unfeigned regret. I saw what I had lost, and I deeply regretted that my education had not been delayed until I should have been capable of understanding, of appreciating, and of loving what I studied.

"I believe that many of our American students, whether in the higher schools or in college, suffer as I did. Parents and instructors often err egregiously. All that is sought is to enable the pupil to repeat the words of the text-book, without inquiring whether he is able to comprehend them, or to form from them any conception whatever. The result is, that we see boys, and even children, pursuing studies that can be comprehended only by adults. The time is worse than wasted; for not only is no knowledge acquired, but the habit is formed of reading without understanding — a habit which, once formed, is apt to continue through life.

"Thus, from observation both of myself and of others, I have been led to suppose that there are several changes in the intellectual growth of the person who is blessed with the benefits of education. At first the human mind can think only by the assistance of sensible objects. The infant can be occupied only with something to play with. Its ball, its toys of whatever kind, are the only things it can think about, or which can form its materials for thinking. As it grows older, it can use pictures, or the representatives of its toys, or of the things which it sees. Hence the intense love of children for picture-books, and the necessity for using them, or something like them, in the education of children. As the mind advances, it can form pictures for itself by the aid of the imagination. This is the era of narrative. Travels, stories, novels, are read with avidity. It is not until the mind is fully expanded, that we can think without an image, either visible or conceived, that is, can use abstract thought in thinking. Until this period has arrived, abstract study is of no possible advantage, but is rather an injury.

"I am aware that this period arrives at varying ages

with different individuals. I suppose that my mind was slow in developing. I have known or heard of persons who said that they read eagerly Stewart on the Mind when mere children. I can pretend to no such precocity. I was in my eighteenth or nineteenth year when I was conscious that the change to which I refer had taken place in myself. I suppose, moreover, that the full development depends very much on education. Savages remain children through life, and can think only of what is addressed to the senses. And of men at large, there are very few who have any considerable power of abstract thought. Hence the folly of presenting abstract ideas to a mixed congregation, in which only one in a hundred is capable of following the speaker. Thus did not Jesus Christ."

The impression naturally made by the passages just quoted, that his mind arrived late at maturity, must be taken with considerable qualification. It has before been remarked that his tendency was to underrate himself. It was indeed a failing that leaned to virtue's side, preserving him from vanity and from a fatal reliance on the power of genius unaided by labor. His maxim, not unfrequently uttered, was, "I always think that I can do what other men have done by taking two or three times the pains they have taken." But as a matter of history, those who remember him in youth, as well as those who have heard older persons express the opinion which they early formed of him, vary widely in their testimony from his language. One who knew him perhaps two years later,* writes, —

" His bright intellect and his strong traits of character interested us very much from the first, and we regarded him as destined to exert a permanent influence upon minds. We remarked especially his high mental standard, his good sense, his wit, his originality, and the almost crystal clearness of his perceptions."

The positions which he filled in very early manhood (often presiding over and instructing those much his

---

* Mrs. Dr. Cornelius.

seniors), as well as his early works, will probably have more weight than his statements given above. Perhaps we should present the matter correctly by saying that though his mind exhibited no traces whatever of early precocity, yet when it began at last to develop, it reached almost at once the vigor and the proportions of intellectual manhood. The following letter, written when he was eighteen, to a sister two years younger, certainly gives no indication of a want of maturity. It may indeed be questioned whether it does not almost painfully impress us as the production of one on whom manhood had come too early. We could wish that there were more of boyishness in it even at the expense of something less of wisdom. The letter is also interesting from the evident proof it gives of his strenuous efforts after self-improvement. In parts it differs but little from an essay, under an epistolary disguise.

"New York, November 28, 1814.

" . . . As I know of nothing new, I will fill my letter with something old; and at this time I will make a few observations on the acquisition of knowledge. The acquisition of knowledge is truly the acquisition of power or influence. People of every description give involuntarily the tribute of reverence to those who are better informed than themselves. But to you, who know the value of information and the superior standing which learning gives, it is needless to argue this point. The question is, How is this knowledge to be obtained? This may, indeed, appear to be a question, but in truth there is no question about it. You and I, and every one else, can obtain knowledge enough to entitle us to respect, if not preëminence, if we only ardently desire it. Books are not wanting. History, chemistry, moral and philosophical essays, you can procure as often as you desire to read. But you complain of want of time. Think of the old adage, ' Take care of the pence and the pounds will take care of themselves.' Believe me, my sister, this is emphatically true respecting time. If all the quarters of an hour were occupied, which you and I spend in looking at our fingers, or in waiting for this thing or that, time would not be wanting: we should not complain of there not being time to read. Now, do think of this, and spend some time, be it ever so small, in interesting or instructive reading. That you have time enough to read I am convinced, from the fact that you once in a while find time to read a novel. Let this little time be spent in instructive reading: do not care so much to read a good deal, as to read well and thoroughly. But this is not enough: not only read, but write: memory is at best treacherous. You can remember but very few particulars (and these very imperfectly) by simply reading. You must also write down, in a book kept on purpose, every striking sentiment, elegant expression, or instructive anecdote. They will by degrees associate themselves in your mind, and tincture your conversation. You would, of course, frequently read over these notes, and every reading will imprint them strongly in your memory. If you want to relate an appropriate anecdote, you will not then, as is often the case with people, stammer through half of it, forgetting the dates, &c., and then break off with saying, 'I have forgotten the rest.' You will become well informed in a short time. This is the way Rush, Clinton, and many others have amassed knowledge that has astonished the world. The moment after Dr. Rush had been in conversation with a friend, he retired to his closet and wrote down every idea which was new or interesting. Do not think I want you to be a pedant. I do not expect you to become a Johnson in conversation. Small talk is necessary: every one who lives in the world must use it, and you must also. But let your small talk be in elegant or appropriate and expressive language; and the means I have advised will produce this effect. Another means of acquiring knowledge is conversation; and to this end, as I told you before, associate with those superior to you in age and reading. I am confident, from your standing in society, that you can associate with persons of learning. Associate with them and profit by it. You can easily find some friend who will read with you, and converse over your history, essays, &c. Improve in knowledge. Do not be afraid of a sneer. A sneer proves nothing; and I am well convinced that when your sex laugh at a girl of reading, it is mostly because they envy her. Write soon, and write a more correct and better letter than this. I would write this over, and very much alter the phraseology, but I must go to lecture immediately. However, you have read the Elements of Composition, and it perhaps would be an instructive exercise to criticise all the bad sentiments and incorrect sentences, and send me your critique on it."

It was during the period of his medical studies in Troy that Mr. Wayland formed the acquaintance of two persons whose influence he regarded as invaluable. The young man is happy, who, in the hour of his mental regeneration, finds friends, that by their intelligent and congenial sympathy nourish into energy the feeble pulsations of his newly-awakened intellectual life. Many a man of subsequent eminence can recall the acquaintance of some one more advanced in years than himself, sometimes of his own, but oftener of the other sex, from whom he feels that he learned, at that particular period, more than books had or could have taught him, or rather, perhaps, who gave to his books and to his past acquirements a meaning and a value that they never had before. If we do not mistake, the person from whom this intellectual stimulus is derived is generally found outside the limits of one's own family circle, perhaps because his mind moves more freely when he is not in the presence of the parents whom he traditionally regards as immeasurably above him; perhaps because strangers are more likely to treat his opinions with respect, and to encourage their utterance, than are those who have heard his childish lispings, and hence can scarcely believe that sentiments of any great value can proceed from the lips which they associate with the babblings of infancy and the petulance of boyhood. He writes,—

"I have spoken of the change which took place in my character as I passed from boyhood to manhood. I began at once to form opinions for myself, to judge of things

from my own point of view, to read works of literature
with a pure appreciation of their beauty, and to become
deeply interested in general views of human nature, and
the biases and tendencies of humanity. The world immaterial seemed to be unveiled to me, and I began to see it
with other eyes and to hear it with other ears. It was
at this time that I became acquainted with Dr. William
Stoddard and his wife, Mrs. Lavinia Stoddard. The former was a graduate of Yale College, who had studied
medicine, and was a well-read and able physician. He
had not, however, practised his profession, but had pursued a literary life, and had devoted himself to teaching,
in which he, with his wife, was engaged when I knew
them. He was a good linguist, and a highly educated
man, of unusual conversational power — a man whom you
could not fall in with by accident anywhere without perceiving that he was a person of decided talent. Mrs.
Stoddard was one of the most remarkable women I have
ever known. Her face was not handsome, and derived
its interest alone from the workings of the soul within.
Her figure was small, and not remarkable for symmetry.
She possessed an intellect, however, capable of any
amount of acquisition, and able to master with ease any
conception. With these endowments were united a power
of expression and an ability to do anything which she
determined to accomplish. A shrewd judge of character;
forming her opinions for herself, and bold in the expression of them; seeing at a glance through all shams, and
loving sincerely whatever was true and good, — she was
withal a perfect woman. All was delicate and refined,
while all was pure, true, and lovable. Coleridge somewhere remarks that in every really great man there are
to be seen some of the feminine elements. I think that
the converse is true. In the most remarkable women
there are always to be found some elements of the sterner
sex. In order to render the intercourse of social life perfect, both parties must have something in common. The
woman cannot confide in the man unless he can sympathize in her tenderness, nor can the man counsel with the
woman unless she can, in some measure at least, look
upon the actual world as he looks at it, or can partake
of his views as to the mode of accomplishing an object.
Mrs. Stoddard had all that was masculine in intellect

without hardness, and all that was tender and humane without a trace of feebleness or sentimentalism.

"Having by some means, I know not how, become acquainted with them, I admired their characters, and was deeply impressed with their powers of conversation. I was surprised to see that they took an interest in me. To be admitted into the intimate society of two such persons formed an era in my life. I began to think that there was some latent power in myself, if such persons treated me as a junior equal, and thought my opinions worthy of discussion, and even of respect. With Dr. S. I discussed medicine, the classics, and whatever in my daily studies seemed of interest; and with both of them I conversed on literature, biography, and all that was then rising into importance before my mental vision. Such an intimacy was worth all the rest of Troy to me, and I so esteemed it. I now look back upon it as one of the most fortunate incidents of my life. I do not know but it was worth more to me than all I had received from my college education. As my mind was emerging from the dim and obscure notions of boyhood, to be introduced to two such persons, of mature age and high intellectual accomplishment, by whom every growing intellectual impulse would be not only stimulated, but, what was of more consequence, rightly directed, was of inestimable value." *

The intellectual regeneration by which he passed from boyhood to maturity had taken place. But a change was at hand, more profound and divine. He writes, —

"In due time I received my license to practise medicine, and was considered, I believe, a promising candidate for professional success. I must now take my position in life. Thus far I had no decided religious impressions; that is, no impressions which resulted in any moral change. My parents took pains to instruct their children in the doctrines of the New Testament, and also to im-

* Dr. Stoddard, with his wife, subsequently removed, on account of her feeble health, to the (then) Territory of Alabama, and there died. Mrs. S. did not long survive him. Dr. Wayland adds to his account of these, his early and valued friends, "If any of my children should ever meet any of their descendants, I beg them to remember their parents' kindness to me."

press these truths on their consciences. Educated in this manner, I of course had a general knowledge of the truths of the gospel. I think, however, that the effect of this teaching was to some extent diminished by the views which my father then held. He was a very rigid Calvinist. The views which he then inculcated were, as it now seems to me, one-sided; and he greatly changed them as he advanced in life, and read the works of Andrew Fuller. In speaking of his views as one-sided, I mean that he dwelt too exclusively on election, and the sovereignty of God, and not enough on the responsibility of man, and the fulness of the gospel. The impression not unfrequently left on one's mind was, that man had only to wait God's time, and had nothing to do until he was born of the Spirit. Such, I think, was the practical effect on my own mind; nor did I completely escape from it, until I had been myself for some years a preacher of the gospel.

"I believed the truths of religion, for aught I know, as fully as I do now. But my heart was unmoved. I had some wish to be a Christian, but I had no true idea of faith or repentance; and all the theological illustrations which I heard seemed to involve the subject in deeper darkness. At times, when my purposes were crossed, my spirit, as I well remember, rose against the government of God. I knew that had there been any universe to which I could have fled, where God did not reign, I would at once have gone thither. But feeling my helplessness, I sank back into forgetfulness. When I reflected at all upon religion, I was miserable. But reading, conversation, and the pleasures of youth generally drove these thoughts out of my mind.

"At times the Spirit of God strove powerfully with me. I saw my danger; I knew that there was but a step between me and death, and that after death was the judgment. Dreadful as were these emotions, I am not aware that I ever sought to repel them, but rather to retain and even to increase them, hoping that thus I might be led to that change of heart which I knew to be essential. But in spite of me, they would go away, as they came, independently of my volition, leaving me in a few days as indifferent as before.

"I do not remember any sermon that did me any good. The preaching, then as now, seemed to me to be too theological, devoted to explaining some doctrine of the gospel according to a particular system, with but little of that warm interest in man's salvation that appears suitable in the herald of a free and finished redemption. Occasionally I heard a plain man who poured out his soul in earnest for the salvation of men, and who affected me deeply; but in general the preaching left me as it found me.

" In this state of mind I continued until the close of my medical studies. It was now necessary that I should fix upon a place for my future residence, and enter on my course of life as a permanent arrangement. I had always had a decided impression that I should be a preacher of the gospel, and had frequently felt that my medical studies were only an incident in my life. After thinking frequently upon these things, it occurred to me that all my life had been spent in studies and labors which had no connection with my eternal destiny. The life to come had been practically ignored. I believed all that the Bible said of my condition and my danger. Jesus Christ came to save sinners; yet I had never sought his forgiveness, nor had I ever made a single honest effort for the salvation of my soul. I had never for a single day in my life laid aside all other business, and earnestly sought of God the renewing influences of the Holy Spirit. This seemed to me most unreasonable, and I could not but think that if I were forever lost, the recollection of it would add increased bitterness to a ruined eternity. I resolved that, dismissing every other thought, I would devote one day to reading the Scriptures and prayer, that I might be able to say that I had at least done something for the salvation of my soul. I at once put my resolution into practice. I retired to my chamber, and spent a day in this way. I perceived very little change in my feelings, save that a sense of the importance of the matter had so grown upon me that I resolved to spend the next day in the same manner. At the end of the second day, I determined to spend still a third day in the same employment; and at the expiration of that day, I determined that I would do nothing else until I had secured the salvation of my soul. How long time I remained in this condition I do not now remember. I was embarassed by ignorance of the plan of salvation — an ignorance all the more embarrassing because I supposed it to be knowledge. I had marked out for myself a plan of conversion in accordance with the prevailing theological notions. First I must have agonizing convictions; then deep and overwhelming repentance; then a view of Christ as my Savior, which should fill me with transport; and from all this would proceed a new and holy life. Until this was done, I could perform no work pleasing to God, and all that I could do was abomination in his sight. For these emotions, therefore, I prayed, but received nothing in answer which corresponded to my theory of conversion. I devoted I know not how much time to prayer and reading the Scriptures, to the exclusion of every other pursuit. This, however, could not be continued always. I recommenced my usual duties, making this, however, my paramount concern. I attended religious meetings, and derived pleasure from them. I read only religious books. I determined that, if I perished, I would perish seeking the forgiveness of God, and an interest in the Savior.

"At the time when I first resolved thus to seek in earnest the salvation of my soul, there was in none of the churches in Troy any religious interest. It was a period of unusual indifference to religion. But while I was in this condition, a very extensive revival commenced. I was deeply interested in it, and attended all the meetings, hoping to hear something which would tend to my spiritual good. I found that I loved the doctrines of the gospel, that I earnestly desired the salvation of souls, and felt a love for Christians such as I never felt before. But I could not believe that the light which had gradually dawned upon my soul was anything more than what was taught by the precepts of men. Everything in religion seemed to me so reasonable, that all which I felt seemed to arise from the mere logical deductions of the intellect, in which the heart, the inmost soul, had no part. I met with the young converts, and with them engaged in devotion, but could not believe that the promises of the gospel were intended for me.

"I remember at this time to have had a long and interesting conversation with Rev. Mr. Mattison, a Baptist minister from Shaftsbury, Vermont. It was of the nature of an earnest argument, in which he endeavored to prove that I was a regenerate person, and I as strenuously contended that it was quite out of the question. I could not deny that there had been a change in me; but the change had been so reasonable and so slight in degree, that I could not be a child of God. Yet the conversation did me good. In looking back upon this period of my life, I perceive that much of my doubt and distrust was owing to the pride of my own heart. I had formed my own theory of conversion, and I did not like to confess that I was wrong. I wished to have a *clear* and *convincing* experience, so that I might never doubt of myself, nor others doubt concerning me. I desired to be the subject of a striking conversion, and was not willing to take with humility and gratitude whatever it should please God to give me. He in mercy disappointed me, and made me willing to accept his grace in any manner that he chose to bestow it.

"Whenever I now have occasion (as I often do) to converse with persons in this state of mind, I do not argue much with them. I set before them the love of God in Christ, the fulness and freeness of the offer of salvation, and the sincerity of God in revealing it to us, and I urge them at once to submit themselves to God; not merely *to be willing* to do this, but to *do it*. If they will do this, I know that God will accept them, and that the evidence that he has done so will soon be manifest. I also urge them without delay to begin at once to serve God, to do what they know will please him, to do good to others, to make sacrifices for Christ, to ask, with Paul, 'Lord, what wilt thou have me to do?' and at once to do it. Only a few days since, a young lady, in this very state of mind, called to converse with me on the subject of religion. The Spirit of God had evidently been granted to her. Yet one of the first things she said to me was, 'O, I am sure I am not a Christian.' She had been arguing the question with herself, and was ready to do so again, instead of turning her whole heart immediately to God.

"About this time (1816) Rev. Luther Rice visited Troy, to awaken an interest in the subject of missions.*

---

* It is not necessary to remind those readers who are acquainted with the history of American Baptist missions, that Luther Rice

He staid with my father, and preached several times
in the Baptist church. The work of missions and the
scheme of subjecting the world to Christ, presented by
one who had just returned from a heathen land, had all
the effect of novelty. To me the subject had an intensity
of interest which has never left me to the present moment.
Mr. Rice was a man of decided ability, and a solemn and
effective preacher. But in addition to this, he was a man
who had given up all for Christ, burning with zeal to
preach his gospel to the heathen, and appearing among
us for the sole purpose of collecting means to carry on
and extend this work. He was the only American who
had gone out into the darkness of paganism and had
returned to tell us what existed there. I remember well
the effect produced on me by a sermon which he preached
from the text, ' The glorious gospel of the blessed God.'
For the first time in my life, I was constrained to believe
that the sentiments of my heart were in harmony with
the gospel; that I loved God and all that God loved;
and that it would be a pleasure to me to devote all my life
to his service.

"An incident occurred which afforded practical confirmation of these sentiments. I had an opportunity to earn
something by medical labor in a small village south of
Troy. It cost me many a mile of walking in the heat
of summer. I was delighted to give all the avails to the
missionary cause. Indeed, I do not know that I ever
derived so much pleasure before or since from the expenditure of money. I felt it to be an undeserved honor that

---

was associated with Dr. Judson in his early aspirations and labors.
He was one of the little band of students in Williams College who
in 1808 consecrated themselves to the work of missions. He was
ordained, in company with Judson, Newell, Nott, and Hall, at
Salem, February 6, 1812, and sailed for India on the 18th. Having changed his sentiments on the subject of baptism, Mr. Rice
was baptized a few weeks after Dr. and Mrs. J., and became connected with the Baptist Convention in America. He shortly after
returned to this country for the purpose of awakening a missionary spirit among American Baptists, intending, as soon as this
object was in some degree accomplished, to resume his labors
among the heathen. Although he was not permitted to carry out
this purpose, his labors in behalf of the cause in which he was
interested, were invaluable.

I was permitted by my labor to aid in any degree the salvation of men."

His sympathies, however, were not expended upon the distant heathen to the neglect of souls near at hand. One who had known him from his boyhood (Mrs. Thompson, of Poughkeepsie) writes, —

"I had a married sister living in Troy, and a younger sister (Rachel) was attending Mrs. Willard's school. When Francis was converted, his first visit was to talk with Rachel; and it was the commencement of a new life with her. She died a few years after, one of the most heavenly minded saints I ever saw. If he had no other precious soul to reward his labors, this alone would be a rich harvest."

Dr. Wayland continues in his reminiscences, —

"Thus gradually I attained a hope that I had passed from death unto life. My pride was humbled, and I was willing to receive any light that God saw fit to give me, and in any manner that he thought best. I observed a change in my character. My mind at one time rebelled against the doctrine of election. It seemed to me like partiality. I now perceived that I had no claim whatever on God, but that if I were lost, it was altogether my own fault, and that if I were saved, it must be purely a deed of unmerited grace. I saw that this very doctrine was my only hope of salvation, for if God had not sought me, I never should have sought him. I had been ambitious of distinction among men, and had been looking for nothing beyond the grave. Now, worldly honors seemed to me trivial, and I desired to serve God. I thought this the highest honor. The cause of religion appeared dear beyond everything else, and I rejoiced in whatever told of its progress. I loved the image of Christ wherever I saw it, whether among the poor and the ignorant, or the rich and the refined. When a Sabbath school was organized in Troy, I at once offered myself as a teacher, and selected for myself out of all the school a class of colored boys, because I thought that they most needed instruction, and because this seemed to me to be following out most closely the example of Christ. Observing all these changes in my feelings and choices, I could not but believe that God had bestowed upon me some of the marks of his children.

" It will be seen, from what I have said, that there appeared to be a want of salient points in my religious history. Everything was gradual, and seemed to have proceeded in the line of logical deduction. The precise time when a moral change took place in my character I cannot determine. I have had many seasons of religious declension and revival; I have been harassed with many doubts of my state before God, and have rarely attained to that full assurance of faith which is the privilege of so many of the disciples of Christ. I have labored and prayed for it. If I know my own heart, I do really with pleasure submit myself and all that I have to God; and yet I ever feel the want of the fervent love and adoring gratitude which I know is promised to the children of God, and which is the earnest of their inheritance. Yet I think that I can perceive in myself some evidences of spiritual growth.

" Perhaps, however, this state of mind, and these somewhat peculiar exercises, may have been of use to others. If this has been the case, I am willing to bear the pain so long as it shall please God to call me to endure it. I have sometimes thought that I was able the more readily to sympathize with, to relieve, and to lead to Christ, those whose feelings were similar to my own, the number of whom is far from inconsiderable. I think also that I have been led to observe more readily the distinctive elements of the Christian character, and to separate them from those which are merely accidental. Of one thing, however, I am certain. I used to think that from one's exercises at conversion, it was possible to determine, without doubt, the reality of a work of grace. I have learned that this is perfectly illusory. I have known several persons, whose exercises seemed of the most marked and satisfactory character, yet who soon fell into open sin, and died the avowed enemies of God and of all goodness. I see the necessity of cultivating with assiduous care the first dawnings of religious feeling, and of insisting strongly on practical obedience to God, ever remembering that this is the love of God, that we keep his commandments."

Feeling that it was his duty to profess his faith in Christ, he was baptized and received into the fellowship of the Baptist church.

" I was much attached to the profession of medicine, for which I had been prepared, and on the practice of which I had in some degree entered. But as soon as I felt a comfortable assurance of my personal piety, I felt that my destiny was changed. The preaching of the gospel seemed the duty to which I was to devote my life. In coming to this decision, I had none of the trials to which many persons are subjected. All my previous reflections, with the education I had received at home, and the example of my father, had prepared me for it. I was ready at once to surrender my medical prospects, and to devote myself to the gospel of regeneration. But I also felt, that even had my inclinations led me otherwise, I could not but give myself up to the ministry, without sinning against God. It mattered not what I should substitute in the place of it; I could not ask the blessing of God on anything else. I felt assured that God would overturn all my plans, and leave me to myself and to the fruits of my devices, unless I obeyed him in this thing. I was thus shut up to one course, and only one. I dared not disobey God, nor could I enter upon any occupation on which I could not ask his blessing. My duty seemed plain, and the providence of God opened the way which I was to pursue."

His change of moral purpose, and surrender of his heart to God, had been the cause of great thankfulness to both his parents, who saw the answer to many hours of tearful supplication. And although his worldly prospects in the profession for which he was prepared were most flattering, yet they gladly saw him abandon them at the impulse of duty and of gratitude to God. The surrender of worldly interests was the more considerable from the fact that at this time the circumstances of his father had become very much straitened, alike by the financial losses before alluded to, and by his withdrawal from the pastoral charge of the Baptist church in Troy.

It was not without great effort and economy that he could provide for the large family which remained at home; and it was quite impossible for him to afford much aid to his oldest son in his further studies.

" But how was I to enter upon the work of the ministry? I had no practice as a public speaker; I was but very imperfectly acquainted with the Scriptures. How should I be prepared for this great undertaking? "

The opportunities for theological study at that time were very limited. No seminary had been established by the Baptist denomination. Rev. Dr. Chaplin, subsequently president of Waterville College, a clergyman eminent for piety and for sound judgment, was giving instruction to some candidates for the ministry, at his residence in Danvers, Massachusetts, as was also the eloquent Dr. Stoughton, at Philadelphia. But Dr. Burritt, and many friends of the family in Troy, urged the advantages of the Seminary at Andover, then just entering on the ninth year of its usefulness; while others suggested the Seminary at Princeton, which had been established four years previously.

While the matter was under advisement in the family councils, Rev. Elias Cornelius visited Troy, for the purpose of awakening an interest in foreign missions. With this faithful minister of Christ, afterwards widely known as Secretary of the American Education Society and of the American Board of Commissioners, Mr. Wayland became acquainted. Upon learning his state of mind, Mr. C. strongly advised him at once to repair to Andover. He assured him that his Baptist sentiments would be respected, and that he would be welcomed to every advantage which the Seminary and its eminent professors could offer. Mr. C. also, on behalf of his own personal friends at Andover, promised to him whatever advice, aid, and sympathy would naturally be desired by a stranger. For these timely words, and for the manner in which these pledges were more than fulfilled, Mr. Wayland never ceased to feel a deep sense of gratitude to Dr. Cornelius. Accepting these kind and providential offers, " I closed," he says, " my little affairs at Troy, and set out for Andover in the autumn of 1816."

Hitherto he had been absent from his father's house only for short journeys, and in expectation of a speedy return. He now left it to go among entire strangers, to a place distant about four days' travel — left it never again to be permanently a member of the household. The scanty facilities for travel and for communication by letter rendered the separation more complete than now takes place when a son removes from New England to Colorado. One of his sisters writes, " Andover seemed a great way off. He took the stage from Troy at one o'clock in the morning. Our parents, and all of the children, even the youngest, were up to say ' good by.' Father's blessing, and mother's emotion, too strong for utterance, and our tears, and his kind farewells, and promises to write to us often — all these are vivid before me. The shutting of the coach door resounds now in my ears ; and I remember our departure to our rooms, and our restless tossings and weary hours till morning, and the vacant seat at breakfast, and the sense of loneliness which our mother's forced cheerfulness could scarcely enable us to overcome."

CHAPTER III.

THE traveller of to-day breakfasts in Troy, and sees the
sun set behind the hills of Andover, a thriving town
of nearly four thousand inhabitants. What the journey
was fifty years ago, is indicated in the following letter to
his parents, dated Andover, November 8, 1816 : —

"Through the kind mercy of an indulgent Providence,
I arrived here yesterday at about two o'clock P. M. On
Saturday morning (having left Troy at one) I left Albany
at two o'clock, and at seven P. M. arrived at West Spring-
field. On the Sabbath I went to hear Dr. Lathrop, but
found in his place a young licentiate, a very indifferent
preacher. Sabbath afternoon I spent in East Spring-
field, about two miles south of the former, and across the
Connecticut River. The stages had altered the time to
begin their winter route, and in consequence I was obliged
to ride to Brookfield on Monday, in a one-horse wagon,
and remain there for the night. On Tuesday morning I
again took the stage, and arrived in Boston at about seven
in the evening of as dreary and rainy a day as you have
ever seen. I soon found out Mr. Winchell's; it was
near the stage-house. The family received me with
hospitality. I staid with them till I left Boston. I
took breakfast at Mr. Sharp's yesterday morning. He
treated me with much friendship, as did Dr. Baldwin.
They all appear well pleased at my coming to Andover.
Mr. Paul, you may have heard, has arrived from Europe.*

---

* Rev. Thomas Paul (a colored man) was a Baptist minister, much
respected in Boston. At the time alluded to, he had just returned
from England, where he had been to take possession of some

I took dinner at his house, with several gentlemen, the day before I left Boston. It was the most sumptuous entertainment that I ever partook of.

"I rode up here in the stage with Professor Stuart. As soon as I reached the stage-house a message arrived from Dr. Woods, that if any gentlemen wished to enter, they were desired to come to his house. I accordingly went, and presented my recommendatory letters. He read them, examined me on a sentence of Greek and Latin, and in a few words on my religious exercises, and said that he should have no hesitation in entering me. I accordingly became a member of the institution in less than half an hour from my arrival in town. The professors are employed in examinations, and have not yet commenced lecturing. They probably commence to-morrow. I have procured a room, and am within the last hour settled. This morning I saw Mr. Cornelius, who introduced me to his friend, Miss H., to whom I had a letter of introduction from Mrs. K. She and her mother treated me with the greatest kindness, and have promised to render me assistance about furnishing my room, which will be a great favor.

"I find one Baptist brother here, Mr. Ira Chase, who appears to be a very pious and excellent man, and one of the best scholars here. I am very much pleased with what I have seen of the institution. Through the merciful providence of God, nothing has occurred of an unpleasant nature since I set out, except the delay, and that was undoubtedly for some wise purpose. I have the greatest reason to bless God for all his benefits. All that I want is a grateful heart. I have found friends whenever I needed them, and have been preserved through every danger in good health."

---

property bequeathed to him by an English gentleman, whom Mr. P. had greatly befriended when the former was a stranger and sick in this country. On the occasion referred to, Mr. P. entertained at his house the leading Baptist ministers and laymen of the city and neighborhood. The son of Mr. Paul has been a successful and esteemed teacher in Providence and in Boston. It was always a source of pleasure to Dr. Wayland to show the son any kindness by which he could evince the respect in which he had held the father.

The Andover of that day was a small and very scattered village, having three stores in the space of three quarters of a mile, and "not even a shoemaker's or a blacksmith's shop that I have perceived." " The institution is a plain four-story brick building, containing thirty-two convenient rooms, or about that. The dining-hall is outside of the house. We board, as students ought to, with the greatest plainness and simplicity."

Upon the catalogue of 1816–17 are the names of sixty-seven students. Among them were Ira Chase, Joel Hawes, Alvan Bond, Pliny Fisk, Miron Winslow, Hiram Bingham, Theodore Clapp, Orville Dewey, Luther T. Dimmick, Jonas King, Henry J. Ripley, Worthington Smith, and Joseph Torrey. With all his fellow-students he enjoyed kind and fraternal relations, and had the pleasure, at times, of ministering to the slighter bodily ailments of some of them, as well as to those of a few families residing near the Seminary. He esteemed it a privilege to repay, in some imperfect degree, by his medical skill, the kindness which he, a stranger, and of another communion, constantly received from the members, officers, and friends of the Seminary.

The faculty consisted of Dr. Ebenezer Porter, Professor of Sacred Rhetoric; Dr. Leonard Woods, Professor of Christian Theology; and Dr. Moses Stuart, Professor of Sacred Literature. With Dr. Porter and Dr. Woods the Junior class came in contact mainly at the "Professors' Conference." This exercise occupied an evening in every week (or fortnight), and was conducted in turn by the several professors. After the regular lecture, opportunity was given for other members of the faculty, or visitors, to speak, and sometimes the students were invited to take part in asking or answering questions, or stating difficulties. We find among the papers left by Dr. Wayland, notes of many of these conferences, and sketches of the remarks of Dr. Woods, Rev. Dr. Spring, and Professor Stuart, upon " methods of becoming more engaged for souls ; " " the mortification of a worldly spirit ; " " heavenly contemplation," and kindred topics. In his reminiscences, he writes, " The value of these conferences was inestimable. I think they did more to keep alive the spirit of piety than any other service of the week."

It was to Professor Stuart that the instruction of the Junior class was mainly committed. This remarkable man had entered six years before on the great work of his life, as an instructor of those who should interpret to mankind the word of God. He was now thirty-six years old. Though he had not attained the renown which attended the publication of his letters to Dr. Channing, in 1819, and of his Commentaries upon Romans and Hebrews, yet it is probable that at no time of his life were his powers of acquiring and communicating knowledge more splendid. There was need of all the enthusiasm he could create, for the inspiration of the teacher must supply the place of text-books. In 1813, he had published a brief Hebrew Grammar without the vowel points. He was now lecturing to the class upon the Grammar with the points ; and these lectures, laboriously taken down by them, constituted their only text-book. The volume containing these lectures is before us. It is written in a clear hand, and the Hebrew is executed with singular care. During all of Dr. Wayland's early life, his handwriting was entirely legible. As he advanced in years, and was forced to write much and very rapidly, one unused to it was obliged to study it attentively. Yet, at the worst, his hand was regular, and one who had mastered it was not troubled with finding the same letter made in a dozen different ways.

In the New Testament, the class used Archbishop Newcome's Harmony of the Gospels, an edition of which had been published in 1814, by the Junior class in the Seminary, under the supervision of Professor Stuart.

The interleaved copy used by our student is filled with notes upon the text, and suggestions taken down from the lips of the professor.

He also wrote, under the direction of the same instructor, dissertations upon many points of biblical criticism. However it may have been while he was at college, not even he, his own most severe censor, could charge upon himself neglect of his advantages while at Andover. Dr. Stuart once said of him to a common friend, " He is an ingrained student."

Of Professor Stuart his pupil never ceased to speak with attachment, gratitude, and reverence. In public and in private he acknowledged the debt he owed to " the instructor of his youth and the undeviating friend of his maturer years." At the semi-centennial celebration of the Seminary, held in 1858, by invitation of the committee he spoke upon the character and services of Moses Stuart. We quote a portion of his words, which exhibit the enthusiastic admiration of youth, confirmed by the matured judgment of threescore.

" You desire me, Mr. President, to speak of the character and services of the late Professor Stuart. It would be impossible for me here to speak on any other subject. Since my arrival in Andover, after an absence of thirty or forty years, I can think of no one else. There were other great and venerable men who occupied the chairs of instruction while I enjoyed the benefits of this institution ; but Moses Stuart was my only teacher, for I left at the close of the first year, and his name is associated with all my recollections of Andover. As I look around me, he is ever present to my mind's eye. I see his long Indian lope as he strode over the plank-walk, on his way to the recitation-room. I gaze upon that ' bending lip that upward curled, and eye that seemed to scorn the world.' I hear the tones of that voice, which, more than almost any other that I remember, opened a way from the heart of the speaker to that of the hearer. I hear that laugh in sportiveness, or exultation, or defiance. I hear and see all this, as though it were but yesterday that I sat at his feet, and drank in instruction from his lips.

"I well remember my first introduction to the man to whom I owe so much. It occurred in the stage-coach, between Boston and Andover, when I was coming to enter the Seminary. Professor Stuart and the late Rev. Sereno E. Dwight were among the passengers. The conversation between these two eminent men turned mainly on the Unitarian controversy, which was then occupying a large share of public attention. It was well worth a journey to Andover to witness the movement of Professor Stuart's mind upon this question. While he spoke with the highest respect of the talents and learning of those from whom he differed, the unshaken, elastic, and joyous confidence with which he held the truth as he believed it, stirred your mind like the sound of a trumpet. He was ready at any moment to enter upon the controversy, and to carry it to the utmost limits of exegetical inquiry. All he wanted was a fair field and no favor. All he wished was the triumph of truth, and he was ever ready to surrender any religious belief which he held, if he could not, on the acknowledged principles of interpretation, show that it was taught in the Holy Scriptures. He had examined the New Testament for himself; he knew what it taught, and he panted for a fit occasion of entering into the conflict. I could compare him to nothing but Job's war-horse: 'He saith among the trumpets, Ha, ha! and he smelleth the battle afar off, the thunder of the captains, and the shouting.' But in the midst of this constant confidence in what he believed to be true, there was not the remotest trace of malice or unkindness; on the contrary, the tone of his mind was joyous, and even sportive. . . .

"If I rightly estimate Professor Stuart, it was not in the more ordinary elements of mental character that he so much differed from other men. Like other men of decided ability, he was endowed with large power of acquisition, great acuteness, wide generalization, a very retentive memory, and unusual soundness of judgment. It was not, however, to his preëminence in these that he owed his power. That which above all things else made him what he was, was an intense, unflagging, exhaustless earnestness, which obliged every faculty to seize with its whole power on every subject presented to it. No matter whether the subject were great or small, if he thought upon it at all, it was with an absorbing interest. Connected with this were instinctive exultation in success and mortification at even the fear of failure. To fail, after he had done all in his power to secure success, troubled him, whether in his garden or in his study. I well remember that on one occasion he needed a little assistance in getting in his hay, and indicated to his class that he would be gratified if some of us would help him for an hour or two. There was, of course, a general turn out. The crop was a sorry one, and as I was raking near him, I intimated to him something of the kind. I shall never forget his reply. 'Bah! was there ever climate and soil like this! Manure the land as much as you will, it all leaks through this gravel, and very soon not a trace of it can be seen. If you plant early, everything is liable to be cut off by the late frosts of spring. If you plant late, your crop is destroyed by the early frosts of autumn. If you escape these, the burning sun of summer scorches your crop, and it perishes by heat and drought. If none of these evils overtake you, clouds of insects eat up your crop, and what the caterpillar leaves, the canker-worm devours.' Spoken in his deliberate and solemn utterance, I could compare it to nothing but the maledictions of one of the old prophets. I trust that both climate and soil of this hill of Zion have improved since I last raked hay here in Professor Stuart's meadow.

"The full tide of this earnestness was, however, reserved for the investigation of truth, as it is revealed to us in the Scriptures. To this every available hour of his life was consecrated. No earthly pleasure would have weighed with him for a moment, in comparison with the joy of throwing some new light upon a passage of the word of God. For this he labored, for this he prayed, for this he lived; and one of the most animating views which he enjoyed of heaven was, that there he should know all divine truth with a spirit unclouded and unembarrassed. . . .

"We should have a very inadequate idea of the earnestness of his love of truth, did we not remember the difficulties which it encountered. Professor Stuart was, through life, a confirmed invalid, the victim of incessant dyspepsia, and of unconquerable sleeplessness. He was enabled to devote to study but three hours a day, and these were granted to him only on the condition that he consumed almost all the remaining hours in the struggle against disease. His sleep was always broken and interrupted, and if he spent an additional hour in study, he could not sleep at all. When the brief period of study was completed, he devoted himself to exercise, reading of books bearing upon his studies, as travels, reviews, &c., or in conversing with his pupils. It was with so imperfect an organization that his intellectual triumphs were achieved. Most men would have considered high effort under such circumstances an impossibility, and would have relinquished the attempt in utter despair.

" I have spoken of Professor Stuart as endowed with great accuracy of judgment. Here I ought, perhaps, to add a word of explanation. Like men of his strongly nervous temperament, the action of his mind was rapid, and his impromptu opinions were frequently erroneous. But when he gave himself time, and really did justice to himself, few men were, in fact, more reliable. This was in part the result of his large and varied knowledge and extensive observation, but more than all, of the noble unselfishness of his nature. I remember to have heard it remarked, that at the convention, some forty years since, for the alteration of the Constitution of this state, when the question was agitated whether the laws for the support of religion, which created an invidious distinction in favor of Congregationalism, should be abolished, nearly all the oldest and wisest of the Orthodox clergy strongly resisted any change. Professor Stuart, almost alone, opposed them manfully, and in so doing suffered somewhat for a time in the estimation of his brethren. He declared that the state had no right to interfere in the matter of religion, and that Congregationalists possessed no rights whatever which they ought not to share equally with Christians of every denomination. After the lapse of a few years, every one was convinced that he was right; his elder brethren became converts to his opinion, and then no one doubted as to the far-seeing wisdom of Dr. Stuart.

" It becomes me more especially to speak of Professor Stuart as an instructor. It was my good fortune, through the latter part of my student life, to enjoy the instructions of two very eminent men. One yet lives, and at the age of nearly fourscore and ten, with his eye not dim, though his bodily force is abated, still presides over the institution of which for more than half a century he has been the most distinguished ornament. *Clarum et venerabile nomen!* Long may he live to adorn and bless humanity, and to temper the brilliancy of eminent ability with the mild lustre of every Christian virtue. The other was Moses Stuart, whose name for so many years was a tower of strength to this institution. If I do not err, he was one of the most remarkable teachers of his age. His acquaintance with his subject in the class-room was comprehensive and minute. There was no sacrifice in his power which he did not rejoice to make, if by it he could promote the progress of his pupils. It seemed as if all he asked of us was, that we should aid him in his efforts to confer upon us the greatest amount of benefit. He allowed and encouraged the largest freedom of inquiry in the recitation-room, and was never impatient of any questioning, if the object of it was either to elicit truth or to detect error. The spirit which animated his class was that of a company of well-educated young men, earnestly engaged in ascertaining the meaning of the word of God, under the guidance of one who had made every sentence and every word in the original languages the object of special and successful study. This alone would have been sufficient to place Moses Stuart in the first class of instructors. But to this he added a power of arousing enthusiasm such as I have never elsewhere seen. The burning earnestness of his own spirit kindled to a flame everything that came in contact with it. We saw the exultation which brightened his eye and irradiated his whole countenance, if he had discovered some new use of *vav conversive* which threw light upon a phrase of the Old Testament; or if, by some law of the Greek article, a saying of Jesus could be rendered more definite and precise; and we all shared in his joy. We caught his spirit, and felt that life was valuable for little else than to explain to men the teachings of the well-beloved Son of God. If any one of us had barely possessed the means sufficient to buy a coat, or to buy a lexicon, I do not believe that he would for a moment have hesitated. The old coat would have been called upon for another year's service, and the student would have gloried over his Schleusner, as one that findeth great spoil. It seemed as though in his class-room we became acquainted with all the learned and good of the past and the present; we entered into and we shared their labors; we were co-workers with them and with our teacher, who was the medium of intercourse between us and them. We hung upon his lips in the lecture-room; we coveted his sayings in his walks or at the fireside; and any one of us was rich for a week, who could report his *obiter dicta*, ever replete with wit, learning, and generous, soul-stirring enthusiasm.

" With all this love of inquiry, his discipline in the recitation-room was strict and exacting. He expected every man to be like himself, *totus in illis*, and his expectation was rarely disappointed. His reverence for the word of God was deep and all-pervading. I remember but one instance, under his teaching, of any trifling with the word of God. The offender, who was odd, opinionated, and constitutionally wanting in reverence, had read an essay which seemed intended to create a laugh. The rebuke which he received was such that we all quailed in our seats. I fancy that many years elapsed before such an experiment was attempted again.

" I do not know that I can better illustrate the effect of his teaching upon his pupils, than by stating my own experience in a single particular. My acquaintance with Professor Stuart continued until his death. He always treated me with peculiar kindness, and was frequently a guest at my house. He invariably addressed me, after my settlement in the ministry, as ' brother.' I, however, could never reciprocate it. I could no more have called him brother, than I could thus have addressed my own venerated father.

" Speaking of the kindness of Professor Stuart recalls another subject, to which I ask leave here to make an allusion. I came from what was then considered a distant part of the country, wholly unknown, and, as some of you may have heard, was then and ever have been a Baptist. Until I came here, there was but a single individual in Andover whom I had ever seen. The lines which distinguished the denominations of Christians were more dis-

tinctly visible then, than now.   Under these circumstances
the question may be asked, Was I treated with entire impartiality?   I feel bound to answer it with truth, and I
must say that I think now, and I thought then, that I was
not treated with strict impartiality.   I think that because
I was a stranger, and a member of another denomination,
I was treated with a degree of kindness to which I had
not the shadow of a claim, and which it would be base
in me did I not here, in this public manner, thankfully
acknowledge.   I hope I have not forgotten the lesson,
and I think I see in this assembly the faces of those who
would testify that under other circumstances I have delighted to put it in practice.   I need hardly add that this
partiality has continued unabated to the present moment,
or I should not have been requested, in the presence of
such men as I see before me, to speak in commemoration
of my instructor and friend."

It will readily be believed that life at the Seminary
afforded but scanty material for narrative.   The daily
arrival of the stage was an incident; the receipt of a letter
from home (after a passage of ten days from Troy), or a
ride to Boston to buy a stove, was an event.   But his
happiness, his real life, was in his study and in the lecture-room.   The day on which he first opened Kuinoel,
or became the possessor of Schleusner, the day on which
Professor Stuart threw new light upon some utterance of
the Lord Jesus, or reconciled an apparent discrepancy
in the several evangelists, or pointed out a new instance of parallelism in the prophets, or enabled his rapt
pupils to see the world of meaning that lay hid in a pat-
tagh furtive, or a daghesh forte, — these were the epochs
of his life.   " It was at Andover that I first learned to
study," he once said.   This statement is not inconsistent
with what he has said of his obligations to an earlier
teacher.   Mr. Barnes taught him to study as a boy; to
know accurately what was contained in the page before
him.   Dr. Stuart taught him to look beyond the page and
the text-book, to inquire, to reason, to gather knowledge

from various sources, and to pour its concentrated light on the interpretation of the revealed Word — to study as a man.

And with his mind, his soul kept pace. The prayers of parents eminent for nearness to God hovered over him; he was studying the Word with the ardor of a heart newly informed with divine love; he was associated with Christian teachers and pupils, and he trod daily the grounds, and entered the rooms, where had been formed and nurtured the lofty purposes of the earliest American missionaries. Although now scarcely a year had passed since his conversion, he exhibited the traits of a matured piety.

Among his papers is one dated " Thanksgiving Day, November 28, 1816." In it he recounts, with gratitude, the mercies bestowed, during the closing year, upon the country, the deliverance from famine, the freedom from foreign war and domestic division, the enlarged liberality and enterprise of the people of God, shown in the formation of the American Bible Society, and in the diffusion of Sabbath schools, the pouring out of the Holy Spirit, the multiplication of revivals, and the blessing granted to missionary labors. He enumerates the divine favors shown to himself personally, the continuance of his life and health, his own conversion and call to the work of the ministry, the continued blessing of " very pious and praying parents," and the conversion of one of his sisters.

"But what return have I made for all these blessings?" He laments his spiritual deficiencies in terms that, to any eye but that of the All-seeing One, might appear exaggerated, and concludes thus: —

" O Lord my God, I now come to thee for purification of this vile nature. Wilt thou be pleased in thy infinite mercy, through Christ thy Son, to purify me. O, wilt thou be pleased to give me greater views of thy holiness, and of my exceeding sinfulness. May I see more of the evil nature of sin, and hate it more thoroughly. I beseech

thee, show me thy glory. Give me such views of thyself as shall effectually detach me from this evil world
and from myself, and make me cleave to thee with full
purpose of heart. I am unworthy of the least of thy favors, and am full of self-righteousness and sin, the greater
part of which, infinitely the greater part, I am totally blind
to. Wilt thou be pleased to make me to examine myself
carefully, prayerfully, closely, sincerely, and, if I am a
hypocrite, wilt thou, in infinite mercy, convert me by thy
grace, and sanctify my heart. O, give me more holiness
of heart. Make me to love thee more, and to serve thee
better than I ever have done. May my soul and all I am
and have be thine forever. Give me greater knowledge
of thee and of heaven. If it please thee, may I have
some clearer evidence of my adoption, if I am thy child.
Wilt thou forgive my coldness and neglect of thee, and
all my sins. O, wilt thou shine into my soul. Give
me more knowledge of the Redeemer, and the way of
salvation through him. O God, thou who art, as I would
humbly trust, my Father, wilt thou hear this prayer for the
sake alone of Jesus Christ, my Redeemer, to whom, to
thee, and the Holy Spirit, shall be the glory. Amen."

The following to William L. Stone, Esq., at that time
editor of the "Whig," Hudson, N. Y., is the first of
many letters addressed to one who afterwards became his
brother-in-law, and a most valued and trusted friend. It
exhibits his fidelity to one then unconverted, who was four
years his senior, and yet more largely in advance of him
in knowledge of the world.

"... The same paper informed me of the death of
Gouverneur Morris. So one generation passeth and
another cometh. Gouverneur Morris is now in eternity.
The place which once knew him will know him no more
forever. His plans, schemes, desires, and aversions are
forever departed. He has gone to answer for the deeds
done in the body, whether they are good or evil. The difference between a good being and a bad one, we were told
by Dr. Woods the other evening, is, that the first lives for
the honor and glory of God, the other does not. This
affords us a very simple test, whereby to try ourselves.
... But whither am I straying? I was almost uncon-

sciously led to this length, by the importance of the topic. If these hints should lead your mind to a serious train of thinking on these momentous concerns, I shall be highly gratified, and, I hope, suitably thankful. I trust, when you write, you will give me your thoughts on these subjects."

To his parents, December 29, 1816; —

"It is now with you Christmas holidays. We know not so much as whether there be any Christmas, in New England. I was busily employed in digging Hebrew roots on the day when you were rejoicing, and knew not, till evening, that it was the 25th of December.

"I feel sensible that there is danger of growing cold in the things of religion. There is danger lest we, in love for science, lose the ardor of love for God. Critical investigation is the same, unless sanctified, whether it be employed on the Scriptures or on any other book.

"When investigating the Scriptures, we are, however, more liable to be off our guard, and, of course, more exposed to temptation. This is the subject on which we have several times been warned by the professors. I pray (and I know that you will also) that God will keep me near to him, that he will give me such views of his glory as will completely abstract me from the world, and fix my thoughts, affections, and whole soul upon him. I have been the subject of many doubts and fears since I have been here; at times ready to give up all hope; when again I have dared to hope, frequently afraid that my confidence was unfounded; equally afraid to offend God, on the one hand, by my unbelief, and on the other, by presumption."

His correspondence with his valued friends, Dr. and Mrs. Stoddard, maintained the intimacy and attachment which had previously been to him a source of so much profit and happiness.

To his younger brothers, after engaging their attention by an account of his journey and a description of Andover, he writes, —

"But the principal object of this letter, my dear brothers, is to give you a warning on the important subject of

religion. . . . Let me then solemnly advise you, first, make
it a point, every morning and evening, seriously to pray
to God that he will preserve your lives and convert your
souls. Do this solemnly, and do not just skim over the
duty, but recollect you are addressing the God who could
crush you in an instant. Second, let no day pass over
your heads without taking up your Bible, and praying
that God would instruct you and grant you his assistance
in reading it. Then read a portion, not more, in general,
than twenty or thirty verses, and try to understand the
meaning of them, and recollect it. Third, strive to recollect constantly, that you are living for eternity. I hope,
my dear brothers, the time is not long before I shall hear
that you have become Christians."

To his parents, January 31, 1817 : —

" . . . As to my medical practice, I gave all the pow-
ders [alluding to some sent him, at his request, by Dr.
Burritt] to a brother who had a long term of rheumatism.
The students (among whom I usually exercise my skill)
are generally poor. The greater number are, like myself,
assisted by the funds of the institution. Of course I
should not think of charging them anything. I would not
think of practising in the town if I could. My time is so
much taken up that I could no more do it than perform an
impossibility. Before I came here I had no idea how
closely my time would be occupied. I am, indeed, glad
that it is so ; otherwise there would be too great a tendency to distract my mind from the grand object of my
pursuits.

" Perhaps it would please you to have a brief account
of the business of the day with me here. I have risen
through the shortest days at six o'clock, nearly an hour
before it was light enough to see to read. That is the
time of the ringing of the first bell through the term.
From six to seven is spent in private and family devotions. At seven the bell rings for prayers, which one
of the Senior class conducts. The exercises are singing,
reading a portion of Scripture, and prayer. Thence we
repair to breakfast. From breakfast till nine o'clock is,
or ought to be, devoted to exercise. At nine we commence study, and study till half past twelve, when we eat
dinner. From one to three, study. At three, recitation.

This generally continues till prayers, at five. After prayers (in the evening by the professors in rotation), supper. After supper, a little exercise, and then study or writing till half past ten. From that time till eleven, devotions; at eleven, bed. Sometimes, however, we go to bed a little earlier. On Mondays and Thursdays, we recite Hebrew; on Tuesdays and Fridays, Greek. There is no skimming over the surface here. A man must go to the bottom, if he goes at all.

" The recitations are not simply recitations of language; that is a very small object. The main thing is to get the meaning, and find out the intent of every passage we go over. O that all my advantages may have a proper effect, and make me more humble, more sensible of my ignorance, and more devoted to God! O my father, could I have that holy faith, that love to souls, which the primitive Christians had, how happy I should be! I hope that God will not suffer me to seek great things for myself, but will make me willing to be anything or nothing, in the wilderness or city, just as he shall appoint.

" O, why should my dear mother be perplexed because clouds and darkness are round about Him? God, my dear mother, is good to Israel. His faithfulness never will fail. What if, in a little anger, he has hidden his face? He has poured out upon us the very greatest of his favors. How great have been his favors to me! Could they have been greater? Have we lacked anything? Has not goodness, has not the greatest mercy, followed us all the days of our life? God, with respect to my dear father, has not yet made his dispensations plain; but that does not belong to us. He has made him the instrument of calling many sons to glory, who will be his crown of rejoicing in another world. Is not this enough? What if his dispensations, in infinite wisdom, interfere in a small degree with our comfort? Should this distress us? Do we not deserve it? What is our humiliation to that of Him who had not where to lay his head? ... I pray you, write frequently. I almost fear I love you, and my dear brothers, sisters, and friends, too much."

To his sister, upon her marriage to Mr. Stone: —

" Permit me, my dear sister, to wish you the greatest happiness, from the bottom of my heart. May you increase, during a long life, in piety, usefulness, and of course in felicity. In few words, may every gift and grace of the Holy Spirit rest upon you and your dear husband, to make you blessings to the world in time, and meet to be partakers with the saints in light in eternity. If I could say more to express my good wishes, I would; but how can I?"

To his parents: —

"... Your letter containing fourteen dollars was received in due time. Permit me to thank you and the other givers for it. It arrived very opportunely. It has cleared me from debt, and brightened my prospects for a short time. I have some work in the library, which will probably bring me in about ten dollars; this, as I shall board myself, will keep me during vacation.

"Your letter conveying the intelligence of the death of my dear friend Mrs. K. was received. While I could not but be deeply affected that God had removed a person whom I had ranked among the most affectionate of my friends, I felt a desire gratefully to acknowledge that unspeakable goodness, which had redeemed her soul from the terrors of the second death. This act of mercy and goodness will afford matter of praise to all eternity. When I left Troy I was much impressed with the situation of my friend, and was enabled to talk to her, the last time I saw her, with seriousness, and I hope with some faithfulness. Her case was very frequently in my mind when I attempted to draw near the throne of grace. When the news of her dangerous illness reached me, it excited afresh my desire and anxiety for her conversion. When I first came on, I wrote to her, among my earliest letters, and endeavored to press upon her the importance of an interest in Christ. When I heard of the goodness of God to her soul, you may imagine with what sentiments of gratitude it inspired me. I could not but return my warmest thanks to Him who had made bare his arm to save her from going down to the pit. May I not hope that the means which God in so much mercy enabled me to use, may have had some effect upon her mind. If he has used me as the least instrument, glory be to his name; if he has not, he has done the work, and equal glory be his due. I have been led to reflect, since this mournful news, upon the goodness of God which enabled me to be faithful, in some small degree, in speaking and writing to her. For whether these means were blessed or not, I had the duty to perform, and should have been criminal, had I neglected it. I hope this will be a solemn warning to me, never to neglect the souls of my friends."

To his parents: —

"With respect to keeping school, I have not as yet determined. I probably shall, when I go to Boston. Possibly a tutorship in some college would be the most eligible situation that I could procure. I dislike to be a burden upon my Pedobaptist friends here for clothes. It is enough that they should furnish me board, and aid me as much as they do. I hope I shall be guided in the path of duty. Though it would be a disagreeable thing to be put back for a year, yet I think that I could look it in the face composedly."

He mentions an opportunity which would offer for sending him a parcel, and adds, —

"I hope you will give all of my friends notice of this opportunity, so that I may not receive less than twelve or eighteen letters. You have no idea of the gratification which a letter from home possesses for me in my isolated situation."

It will be remembered that this was when the old exorbitant rates of postage (eighteen and three quarter cents on a letter from Troy to Andover) rendered correspondence a burdensome luxury, and caused opportunities for inexpensive carriage to be very welcome.

It is painful to remark the evident depression pervading this letter. He was far from his home, and as he wrote, on the last day of the session, all his classmates and associates were preparing to return to their homes for the spring vacation. He was poor and dependent, and, worse than all, had nothing definite to anticipate.

He writes, in his recollections, "I left home with very small means. Although I used the utmost economy in Andover, these means were soon exhausted. Clothes wore out, and I had nothing with which to replace them. Books were needed, and the purchase of them exhausted my limited resources." A Hebrew Bible and Lexicon cost, at that time, from thirty to forty dollars ; * but he expressed a hope of effecting some saving by importing a Bible from Germany. It was not on his imagination that he drew, but on his memory, when he described one of Stuart's pupils purchasing a Lexicon, rather than a much-needed coat. He once showed his sons a copy of Schleusner's New Testament Lexicon, in two volumes, bound in parchment, and said, " While I was at Andover I had ten dollars left. I was very much in want of a coat. I had an opportunity to buy this book for ten dollars, and so I went without the coat."

The scanty supplies which reached him from home proved altogether insufficient; there was no opportunity to earn any thing by labor while remaining at the Seminary. To the members of his own denomination in New England, who would perhaps have aided him, he was unknown.

Though painful, the discipline of the year was not useless to him. It impressed him with the need of depending on his own exertions. It enabled him, in subsequent life, to sympathize with those who, in the face of adversity, were striving after mental culture. He ever held it alike a duty and a pleasure to aid those students who were in need, and who afforded evidence that help would be well bestowed. He thought that such assistance was best rendered, not by the indirect and often indiscriminate agency of an organization, but through the direct, discriminating contact of giver and receiver. An honored minister in a north-western state writes, " About my Junior year in Brown University, I had run myself full length aground, and could see no way of getting over the

---

* It will be remembered that this was not long after the close of the war of 1812.

bar. Short rations in my room took the place of board, and every draft on the treasury was met with, ' No funds.' At about the third watch of that very dark night, President Wayland sent for me to come to his room (not always the most welcome summons). When I entered, he lifted up his spectacles, and said, ' Well, H——, how are you getting along? ' I made some sort of a reply. He varied the question continuously, until he had learned something of the state of my finances. Then he said pleasantly, ' Well, H——, I think we must do something for you. Here are five dollars; take this, and we will try to help you along.' I left, drawing a great deal less water than I had been doing, and soon found myself over the bar. Similar instances were too numerous to make this incident of value to any one but myself. With me it is precious. I knew him as the ' friend in deed ' of the struggling student."

It was probably amid these circumstances that he learned the meaning of the lines he used not unfrequently to quote from Beattie's Minstrel : —

> " Ah, who can tell how hard it is to climb
> The steep where Fame's proud temple shines afar?
> Ah, who can tell how many a soul sublime
> Has felt the influence of malignant star,
> And waged with Fortune an eternal war?"

And the history of that year burned into him a deep and invincible horror of debt. Never again would he place himself in circumstances where he had not the means of meeting his liabilities.

Shortly after writing the letter last quoted, and while weighed down by anxiety, he received a letter from his friend and former instructor, Professor McAuley, of Union College, who wrote, " When I had the pleasure of seeing you last summer, we had some talk of a tutorage. There will be a vacancy here next Commencement. Would you wish me to make application in your behalf? Nothing would give me more real pleasure than to have you here. And I think the thing practicable now."

The correspondence thus opened resulted in his appointment. In his reminiscences he says, " I have received many appointments since, some of which seemed important; some instances of what men call good fortune have happened to me; but I cannot recollect anything of the kind that afforded me so much joy as this. It gave me the means of living; it enabled me to pursue my studies; and it was a sort of recognition of ability and acquisition, which I had never hoped for, but which was all the more gratifying." To his father he writes, —

" I cannot but view this as a peculiar instance of the goodness of divine Providence. I imagine that I shall be much better fitted for the work of the ministry in consequence of the knowledge I shall have the opportunity of acquiring at Schenectady. Besides, every other door for support seemed closed. Want stared me in the face, and not with the most lovely aspect. . . . I think I can save enough to enable me to complete my studies without embarrassment, and to purchase such books as I shall need. I hope also that I shall have something to give away."

At the close of the Seminary year he left Andover, expecting, at some subsequent time, to return and complete his theological course. The year thus completed had momentous bearings on his character and attainments. The instructions of Professor Stuart awakened in him a love, hitherto unfelt, for exegetical study. The study of physiology and medicine he had previously pursued with interest and pleasure; but languages he had studied, only under the pressure of discipline or from a sense of duty. Yet not philological study in general, but the study of the Scriptures, here gained a place in his regard that it never ceased to hold. The matchless expositions of Romans, of the Gospels, and of Ephesians, which he gave during his later years, in the college Bible class, in the university chapel, and in the pulpit and vestry, never could have been given, but for the year at Andover.

We venture to quote a few sentences from Professor Park's admirable delineation of the character of Moses Stuart. It is not difficult, in the lineaments of the teacher, to remark the source of many characteristics of the pupil.

"In his creed the Bible was first, midst, last, highest, deepest, broadest. He spoke sometimes in terms too disparaging of theological systems. But it was for the sake of exalting above them the doctrines of John and Paul. He read the scholastic divines, but he studied the prophets and apostles. . . . When he uttered censure, too severe perhaps, upon the abstractions of our divines, it seemed to be, not that he loved philosophy less, for he aspired after a true philosophy, but that he loved Jesus more."

While ascribing to his year at Andover a great and beneficent influence in preparing him for the destinies divinely appointed him, it would be uncandid to withhold the remark, that, in looking back from an advanced period of life, he was of opinion that there were liabilities attending a course of study in a seminary which needed to be guarded against with peculiar care, particularly the tendency to attach a disproportionate value to the mental, and an inadequate value to the moral, preparation for the ministry. He also thought, that, great as are the facilities offered by a seminary with a learned and able faculty of instruction, there are advantages, by no means slight, scarcely attainable in a seminary, which are afforded by a course of instruction under a settled pastor of solid attainments and eminent piety.

Allusion has repeatedly been made to the kindnesses received by him from all the members of the faculty, and from Mr. Cornelius, as also from Mr. and Mrs. Farrar, and from the daughter of Mrs. Farrar, afterwards the wife and widow of Dr. Cornelius. The fact that these, and so many of his early friends, instructors, and associates, — Dr. Nott, Dr. McAuley, Dr. Yates, Dr. Burritt, Dr. Nettleton, Dr. Wisner, and Bishop Potter, — were outside his own denomination, perhaps demands a single remark. His association with these brethren of other sects was, in one respect, disadvantageous to him. He was not known by the denomination to which he belonged, and with difficulty gained a *status* among them. But this disadvantage was temporary, and had ample compensations.

To these early associations, in part, he owed it, that he was not a Baptist traditionally, nor by sympathy merely, but by conviction and scriptural argument. While no effort was ever made to proselyte him, yet it was unavoidable that he should hear the views of the Pedobaptists stated in the strongest possible form, and as unavoidable that he should inquire into their validity. It is not known that the questions of denominational difference were ever brought to an issue between himself and his exegetical instructor, unless the following may be deemed an exception. Professor Stuart had urged with much emphasis the statement that the form of baptism is entirely immaterial, and that the temper of heart in the subject is the only matter of moment. "If such is the case," asked the pupil, "with what propriety can baptism be administered to those who cannot be supposed to exercise any temper of heart at all, and with whom the form must be everything?" a question, we venture to suggest, which will bear asking a great many times. As a result of the association to which we have alluded, he held to the sentiments of the Baptist denomination, not as the faith of his fathers, but as the effect of conscientious and intelligent conviction.

But another result of this early and most friendly

commingling with members of other sects, was a profound, broad, generous catholicity of spirit. He fully
concurred in the sentiment of Andrew Fuller, that the
points, in which evangelical Christians agree, are more
numerous and more momentous than those in which they
differ. There was not in his nature a single fibre of the
bigot, or of the mere sectarian. To be the leader of a
sect, was a purpose to which he never stooped. And on
the other hand, few men have ever addressed the public
who have had larger and freer access to men of all parties from whom he widely and resolutely differed. "He
called himself, as he was, 'an old-fashioned Baptist.' But
this positive and strenuous nature, with its clear convictions for itself, was singularly liberal and catholic. His
friendship knew no church lines. His hand was joined
with good men of every name, and he was fellow-citizen
with all the saints." *   (Rev. Dr. Caldwell's Discourse.)
This liberality was traceable partly to the breadth of the
nature which he brought from the hand of God, and which
would not bear the confinement of sectarian limits ; in
part, to the positiveness and strength of his own convic-

---

* Scarcely any one, of whatever denomination, more rejoiced
in the success of the missions of the American Board of Commissioners, of which body he constituted himself and his venerated
father, honorary members. A gentleman in Providence remarked,
" I was for nine years chairman of the committee of the ———
Congregational Church, and whenever we fell into any difficulty,
or needed counsel, the first man we went to was Dr. Wayland."
Not many months before his death, he attended the sessions of
the Providence Conference of the Methodist Episcopal Church,
and was deeply impressed with the earnestness of the ministry,
the laboriousness of the bishops, and the many excellences in the
Methodist system of discipline. In 1863 he read with delight and
edification the charge of Bishop McIlvaine, of Ohio, and circulated a large number of copies of that admirable and most evangelical discourse. And his last religious conversation, less than
two days before the fatal stroke, was held with a minister of the
Society of Friends.

tions, which were so firmly, so intelligently held, that they did not need to be reënforced by bigotry, or secluded from the rays of a Christian and catholic charity ; and in part, to his early surroundings.

In allusion to the associations in which he was placed, both at Andover and at Union College, he writes, —

"I was thus thrown into intimate intercourse with Christians of all the most important sects. I think that this has had a material influence upon my subsequent opinions. I saw in the character of these eminent Christian men what is essential and what is incidental in the religious life. It has ever since been my happiness to be on the most intimate terms with Christians of every sect, without regard to denominational differences. I believe most strongly that the sentiments which I profess are, in their peculiarity, the teachings of the New Testament; but they seem to me to be small, in comparison with a temper of heart towards God and man, in harmony with the temper of Christ. I had written above, 'immeasurably small;' I have erased the word 'immeasurably.' This, as it was written, is true of the individual, but not of the church as an organized society. The special peculiarity of the Baptist belief is, that the church of Christ is really composed of none but regenerate persons, and that the visible church should, so far as our imperfect judgment will admit, be formed on this model. Pedobaptism, in all its forms, tends to obliterate this grand truth; and therefore, in this respect, I do not think the differences between us and others *immeasurably* small."

CHAPTER IV.

UNION COLLEGE. — DR. NOTT. — DR. YATES. — RELIGIOUS
AWAKENING. — ASAHEL NETTLETON. — ANXIETY.

DR. WAYLAND writes in his reminiscences as follows : —

" I commenced my labors as tutor with but small literary
capital.   I had passed through college at a very early
age.   My instructors in language were generally tutors
who had themselves been taught by tutors.   I added but
little in college to the knowledge I had acquired at the
academy.   During the study of medicine, I had scarcely
read a sentence either of Latin or Greek.   I had gained at
Andover, but it was principally in knowledge of the Greek
Testament, and in knowing what to aim at in the interpretation of that book.   In such a course as that at
Andover, it was not to be expected that the students
should go back to the study of grammar, though it must
be confessed that this step would, in many cases, have
been advantageous.   But now I was called upon to teach
the languages, paying at first the principal attention to
grammatical forms.   To these I devoted myself.   I could
find, however, but few books to aid me in my labor.
The Westminster and the Gloucester Greek Grammars
were then in general use.   Goodrich's translation of
Hackenberg was just introduced.   The library contained
not even a valuable Greek lexicon, and hardly anything
better in Latin.   I, however, commenced my work in a
good spirit.   The Freshman class was small.   I taught as
well as I could, having three recitations a day.   I read
with the class, the first term, a part of the first book of
Xenophon's Cyropædia ; the second term we finished that
and read the second and third ; the third term we read
five books.   I awakened some interest in my class, and I
trust my instructions were profitable both to them and to

myself. In both my other studies I labored with equal assiduity; and I think that by the close of the first year I had established a reputation for earnest and faithful teaching, and resolute disposition for labor."

In his correspondence with his home, we can remark, increasingly, a tacit recognition of his position as counsellor of the entire family, not in the least assumed on his part, but somehow falling to him spontaneously.

To his brother D., who was employed in a store at Albany, he writes: —

"While I would scrupulously guard against anything like servility or meanness, I would strive to conduct in so obliging a manner to every one, that they should become my friends. The grand principle is, Do as you would, if placed in the same circumstances, wish to be done by. . . . You will probably be a merchant. I hope you will not limit your ideas simply to the buying and selling of cloth. You ought to be well acquainted with the geography, and particularly with the productions, of every part of the earth; where the best of every kind of merchantable produce may be procured; what events are likely to produce a change of markets; and why an article is high at one time and low at another. Every scrap of knowledge, on such subjects as these and a thousand others, should be picked up by you and hoarded like gold."

Of another brother he writes to his parents, —

"What are you thinking of doing with J.? I have been thinking of education for him."

To his brother J., after speaking of study and improvement: —

"If I had had an elder brother to direct me when I was at your age, it would have been of inestimable value to me. I wish to act towards you as an older brother ought, and all I want of you is to consider my advice, and if it appears good, follow it. When you play, play with all your might; when you study, study with all your might. Never be lingering, and waiting, and idly gazing around, while time, and especially while youth, is so short."

To his sister, Mrs. S., who had lately removed to Hartford: —

" You are now, of course, a stranger in H. ; you have no
character. You will understand what I mean. I mean to
speak in the terms of conversation — no one knows what
sort of a woman you are. This state is attended with a
manifest advantage — that it is in your power to establish
just such a character as you shall choose. Ask yourself,
therefore, what is that character. Fix it distinctly in
your mind ; then decide what are the means for attaining
it. For instance, you would wish to be amiable, and to
appear so. For it is not enough that you *are* so ; you
should appear so. Avoid, then, sedulously, all censori-
ousness. Banish from your conversation all *sharp remarks*. An action seems praiseworthy : you may think
you see some selfish motive concealed. Perhaps you only
think so, and think so groundlessly ; would you, then, injure the reputation of an innocent person? But if you are
right, has society committed to you the office of censor?
Are you obliged to perform the unpleasant task of making a disclosure which shall render the individual and her
friends your enemies for life? Ah, my sister, it is much
more difficult to make friends than to alienate them. I am
rather particular on this head, as I think you, from your
natural disposition, would, as well as myself, be likely to
err in this thing. Again, you would wish to be, and appear, discreet and prudent. You would wish to avoid
saying things, which in twenty-four hours you would
desire unsaid. Propriety, it must be premised, is to some
extent a local thing : what would be proper in T. may be
greatly improper in H. Of this you must inform yourself
by close observation of the manners of the people, and
silent remarks on their habits of conversation, and, above
all, by learning to think before you speak. Reflect what
may be the bearing of what you are going to say. Perhaps you may by doing this lose the opportunity of saying
some witty things. But people are not *loved* for their
witty sayings ; and a woman, always recollect, is an
object to be loved, and not to be feared or gazed at. To
be loved is, or ought to be, the ambition of a woman.
. . . I am glad to hear that you like Mr. Hawes so
well. I am pleased to find that he is so pleasantly settled. He is a man of very good mind, and of unquestioned piety."

During the second year, and during all the succeeding years of his connection with the college, he was called upon (in consequence of vacancies existing in the Faculty) to teach every class, and to teach almost everything that was taught in college. "Xenophon, Homer, and Longinus, Tacitus, Cicero, and Horace, geometry, trigonometry, algebra, and the various branches of mathematics, rhetoric, and chemistry, — these I well remember. I was thus enabled to review my college studies, to pursue them more earnestly, and under a much stronger pressure of responsibility, and most of all, to acquire some practical knowledge of mankind, in which I had been unusually deficient."

At a subsequent period of his life, he was conversing with a brother in the ministry, who had held a number of public positions, and who remarked, " Wherever I have been, I have always been thinking of something else, and preparing myself for another position." Dr. Wayland replied, "I have gone on just the opposite principle. Whatever I was doing, I have always fixed my mind on that one thing, and tried not to think of anything else." He proceeded upon this plan while a tutor. He taught Homer as if this were to be his life-long work. Almost forty years afterwards, in speaking to a person engaged in teaching the Iliad, he alluded to Homer's choice of words, and to the importance of accustoming a class to remark the exact shade of meaning conveyed in each instance. "For example," he said, " μῆνιν, in the first line, does not mean wrath in general, but a special kind, a wrath long enduring, unquenchable." While a tutor, he wrote a course of lectures on rhetoric, illustrating all the points discussed by apposite citations from Johnson, Burke, Junius, and many of the classics in prose and verse. During the time he spent as tutor, he read more extensively in literature than he was able to do in later years; for from the time of his entering the ministry until his

resignation of the presidency in 1855, he was engaged in
pursuits so engrossing as to allow him but scanty leisure
for general reading. He also prepared a course of lectures on natural philosophy. In 1852 he wrote to his
son, then a tutor, —

"I would have you lecture to your classes all you can.
I remember, when I was a student, the awe which was
inspired by a lecture. I hardly could conceive how a
man could get to be so great as to make one. But more
than this, much instruction can be best given in this way.
It keeps up the interest in a class. You need not be
deterred because you cannot do it as well as the best.
Those that now do it the best, once began by doing it not
the best."

We quote again from the reminiscences : —

" I think that the greatest benefit I derived was from
my intercourse with the gentlemen with whom I was
associated. Of these, the most distinguished was Dr.
Nott, then in the vigor of his remarkable powers. He
was then, as always, very kind to me, and admitted me in
many respects to a familiar intimacy. I have known him
from that time to the present, as well as persons living at
a distance can know each other. I think him decidedly
the ablest man whom I have ever known intimately. His
mind is in a remarkable degree original and self-sus-
tained. Nothing in books seems to him of any value, unless he has thought it through, and tested it by his own
power of intellectual analysis. He possesses — what I suppose to be the mark of genius — the power of using his
mind for any purpose, and turning it in any direction.
He could have made himself distinguished in any department of science. I have known him to write very good
poetry. He was, when in his prime, the most eloquent
man I ever heard. He had a decided bias towards physical science, and from his own experiments made himself
familiar with the most important laws of caloric. The
number of patents which he has taken out attests his skill
in invention. To him, more than to any other man, are
we indebted for the rapid progress in the use of anthra-
cite coal. His ability as a metaphysician is universally
admitted. His knowledge of men, and of the principles

of human action, is unrivalled. I suppose that no man
ever exerted so great an influence as he in the legislation
of New York. With all this, he was the kindest, the
most charitable, the most forgiving of men. His conversations on religion had the most splendid range I ever
knew, varying from the sublimest conceptions to the tender simplicity of a little child. His executive talent was
unsurpassed. He never seemed satisfied unless he was
carrying on several kinds of labor, any one of which would
have been a full and sufficient task for a single man of
ordinary ability. The attachment of his pupils to him has,
I think, been equalled only in the case of Dr. Dwight.

"When settled in Albany, his reputation as a preacher
was unparalleled. Those who heard his sermon on the
death of Hamilton have always declared to me, that it
was the most eloquent discourse they ever heard. He
always wrote his sermons with care, and committed them
to memory so perfectly that he was able to modify and
vary the train of thought if he chose, though this, I think,
he did not often do. When I once asked him how much
time it took him to commit a sermon to memory, he
replied, 'Just as much time as I have. The intermission
between the services is enough, but I have committed a
sermon by reading it over once.' He frequently spoke of
the memory as capable of almost unlimited improvement,
and said that he had attended a session of the New York
legislature, when he had been able to report the day's
proceedings with more accuracy than they were given by
the salaried reporters for the press.

"I do not think that his voice was remarkable either
for clearness or for power. His gestures were not numerous, but always significant. He had the appearance of
perfect self-possession, and of conscious power over the
audience. So far as I can recall his manner after the
lapse of so many years, the excellency which gave him so
great power, was in the tones of his voice. I would almost say, they were so perfect that a man who did not
understand English would, from his tones alone, have
been able to form an idea of the train of thought which
he was pursuing. I think his style inferior to his ability.
It was frequently involved, the several members of the
same sentence sometimes standing at a distance from each
other; yet when he *uttered* the sentence, the emphasis,

inflections, and tones were so perfect, that every part was distinctly connected with that to which it belonged, and you never failed to *comprehend* his meaning perfectly. A sentence which you would *read* over twice before you understood it, he would so utter that you understood it all perfectly. When to this were joined the tones of emotion adapted to every range of human feeling, you may possibly perceive what must be the effect. He had a short series of sermons on the resurrection, which I heard when I was tutor. I remember at the present time the effect of them. Each sermon seemed to the audience about twenty minutes long, though in reality nearly three quarters of an hour in delivery. I sat all this time perfectly entranced, cold chills running over me from nearly the commencement to the close. When he uttered the 'Amen,' the whole audience experienced a sensible relief. The strain of attention was so great that men hardly breathed, and as soon as it was over every one took a long inspiration, and felt that he could scarcely have endured the effort of concentration much longer. Perhaps we may ascribe part of the effect to my youth, and to my deep veneration for the speaker. I have endeavored to make known the effect of Dr. Nott's speaking on *me*. I can also bear witness to the fact, that those of my friends, who at the time were in the habit of hearing him, had the same estimation of him as a pulpit orator. I confess that no one would receive this impression from his sermons as they are printed. They probably appear stately, ornate, labored, and artificial. But when they were uttered by him, it was as I have stated."

It was, perhaps, in the series of sermons just alluded to, that a passage occurred which Dr. Wayland has been heard to describe as excelling any other to which he ever listened, for dramatic power and effect upon the audience. Dr. N. was exhibiting the absurdity of the supposition that the apostles and early preachers testified falsely in bearing witness to the Lord's resurrection. He supposed them, after the death of Jesus, assembled to frame and carry out the monstrous deception. They consult, they send some of their number to invade the tomb and

to remove the body. Presently the messengers deputed
for this ghastly errand return; they bring with them the
helpless, stark, bloody corpse; they cast it down before
the apostles, exclaiming, in tones of contempt, "There
is your Christ." And then the apostles go forth everywhere, bearing witness to his resurrection, proclaiming
salvation only through his name, sealing their testimony
with their blood, careless of reproach, of danger, ignorant
of fear, welcoming death. The effect, as described, was
overwhelming; and powerful as was the appeal to the
feelings, the argument was equally convincing to the
understanding.

Dr. Wayland adds, —

"With all my admiration for Dr. Nott, I think I am
not unaware of his errors. As the president of a college,
he devoted himself to its material prosperity. Had he
sought more to improve its means of instruction and to
teach its teachers, so that these means might be well
employed, I think his success would have been greater.

"His power of influencing men led him also, I think, into
errors. It led him to delight in doing things indirectly which
might as well be done directly. No one rejoiced more
in entire simplicity of character, or dwelt more eloquently
upon this trait. Yet somehow every one was afraid that
the thing which he seemed to be laboring for, or promoting,
was not that which he really had in view. I speak here
of the general estimation which has been formed of him.
I never experienced anything of the kind myself. I always
treated him with perfect simplicity, and he, so far as I know,
entirely reciprocated it. I have thought, sometimes, that
what seemed to others to be double-dealing and policy
was nothing more than a far-seeing sagacity, which enabled him to look much farther than other men, and to prepare for events of which they never conceived, and that
this sometimes gave rise to the opinion that he had been
laboring to produce, what he only foresaw and provided
for. I think that men of eminent sagacity are frequently
misjudged in this manner.

"An incident which I have often had occasion to remember, will, perhaps, illustrate the singular foresight

of Dr. Nott. Many years ago I chanced to be in New
York, about the time of the disturbances which grew out of
the abolition meetings that had been held in the city.
Similar meetings were held, with similar results, in Boston and Philadelphia. I passed through Schenectady
shortly after, and of course spent as much time as I could
with my old friend and instructor. These meetings naturally became the subject of conversation. I remarked, with
regret, that the meetings had been disturbed, and insisted
on the right of free discussion on every subject, but at the
same time added, that the course of the abolitionists was
such, their language so abusive, their proceedings so calculated to inflame the public mind, that it was scarcely
possible, with any mere police force, to protect them. It
will be remembered that their course was such, on principle, as to inflame the passions of men, and that they
declared that they could arouse the public mind in no
other way. Dr. Nott paused, and after a little while said
in substance, ' Wayland, remember what I tell you. I
may not live to see it, but you probably will. This is one
of those questions that can never die. This agitation will
spread from city to city until it involves this whole country, and becomes the leading political question of the day.'
Both he and I have lived to witness the fulfilment of the
prophecy.

" To this remarkable man I owe very much. To no
one have I applied so often for counsel, and from no one
have I received advice so deeply imbued with Christian
principle and far-seeing sagacity. There is no one whose
maxims are so often recalled for my direction and for
the government of my conduct. I last saw him at New
Haven. He was then over eighty-five years of age.
He had travelled a full day's ride by railroad, and, in
good spirits, was spending the evening with a room full
of friends, who had called to do him reverence. He
preached twice on the following day with much of his
usual vigor, and on Monday by five o'clock A. M. set off
on a journey. His physical health was evidently failing,
and his power of original thought was probably declining ;
but his judgment was as sound as ever, and his friendly
and loving spirit had suffered no abatement.

" These reminiscences seem, I suppose, to savor of the
garrulity of age. It is very possibly so. If it be so, I

cannot help it.   I am writing, for my children, of the
things which I recollect, and which tended to the formation of my character.   It is pleasing to recall them, trifling
as they are, and, without relating them, I could not accomplish the purpose which I have in view."

We do not imagine that any reader will sympathize in
the apprehension expressed in the paragraph just cited ;
yet we have suffered it (not without some hesitation) to
remain, because it suggests the spirit and purpose pervading the reminiscences.   They were written simply when
he felt himself unfitted for severer labor, and when he
could write these sketches only for a few pages at a time,
and with intervals of several days,   Nor were they revised, or in every case re-read.   Yet we venture the belief
that the reader would rather have his words, so far as
the nature of the narrative allows, than any that can be
substituted.

In the passages which we have quoted relative to
Professor Stuart and Dr. Nott, there are to be observed,
on the part of their pupil, traces of a disposition which,
carried to the excess of indiscriminate idolatry, would
deserve the name of " hero worship."   He had a profound admiration for greatness, intellectual and spiritual.
His nature was keenly sensitive to the mysterious magnetism, that goes forth from the divinely-crowned mon-
archs among men.   He delighted to read and repeat their
words, to dwell upon their characters and achievements,
and to study the pictured lineaments of their outward
form.   He paid homage to spiritual kings, unaware, while
he exalted their prerogative, that he too was of the royal
line, and that the reverence he so generously rendered, a
coming generation would lay at his feet.

He continues, —

" One other person, now dead, deserves a distinct token
of remembrance — Dr. Andrew Yates, who was professor
of Moral and Intellectual Philosophy.   He was a member
of one of the most respectable Dutch families of the state.

His brother Joseph was a judge of the Supreme Court, and afterwards governor. His other brothers were men of distinction in their native state. He was educated at Yale College, and was settled at East Hartford, Conn. Removing from that place, he became professor at Union College. He was a most faithful officer, a strict disciplinarian, and a singularly simple-hearted and pious man. During my connection with the college, its steadfastness of discipline depended more on him than on any other person. Always at his post, always prepared for the discharge of every duty, plain in his appearance and unostentatious in his manners, he was a most valuable example to the younger officers. It was my good fortune to live in his immediate vicinity, and we were thrown very much together. He always treated me with great kindness, and to him I am indebted for much religious instruction, and for many of the most valuable ideas which I possess respecting the Christian ministry. He was fond of preaching, and preached well. He resigned the professorship to commence a polytechnic school, designed to teach the higher branches of education to young men in the practical pursuits of life. He subsequently returned to Schenectady, and devoted himself to the ministry, preaching wherever there seemed to be the greatest need. He found on the Sacondaga Mountains a neglected people, who were entirely destitute of religious instruction. He not only preached to them on the Sabbath, but went out and spent much time with them in the week. In one of his visits he was seized with fatal illness, and in the full enjoyment of a Christian hope he entered into rest."

In this connection we may allude to two other men of subsequent eminence, with whom Mr. Wayland was associated. Benjamin B. Wisner, afterwards pastor of the Old South Church in Boston, and at a later day Secretary of the American Board, had been his classmate, and was now his fellow-tutor. They formed an intimate friendship, which continued until the too early death of Dr. Wisner, in 1835. Alonzo Potter, afterwards rector of St. Paul's Church, Boston, professor at Union College, and bishop of the diocese of Pennsylvania, graduated in 1818, and the year after was appointed tutor. Shortly after the death of Bishop Potter, Dr. Wayland called upon the editor of the Providence Journal and expressed his intention of furnishing an article commemorative of his life. But the article was never written. He wrote (Aug. 1, 1865) to Rev. Dr. Skinner, of New York, —

" How sad is the death of Bishop A. Potter! He was the earliest friend whom I recollect. He came to the academy just as I left it. He was in his Senior year when I was tutor, and we were tutors together. He came to Boston just as I left, and we have been always intimate. He was a noble fellow, a devout, earnest, God-fearing man. I saw him just before he sailed, when he was looking forward cheerfully to the restoration of his health. The ways of God are not as our ways. His way is perfect; and when a thing is perfect it can be altered only for the worse."

We may here quote from a letter of Dr. Potter, referring to this period.

" I was brought into daily intercourse with him for two years. We ate at the same table, and were much together. I could not but discern, almost at once, his large and genial heart, his warm sympathy with the suffering, his conscientious, strong devotion to the work in hand, whatever it might be, his tenacious grasp of any subject which came up for reflection and discussion, and his resolute and indomitable industry. During these two years he laid me under personal obligations, which I can never forget while memory holds any trace of the past. During a severe illness he nursed me with the affectionate assiduity of a brother, and with the skill and vigilance of a physician. He seemed to think nothing of broken sleep or interruption to his studies. When in health, I was indebted to him for suggestions in regard to self-culture, for an example of high and constant endeavor after all knowledge and all excellences, and for hours of delightful companionship."

We continue extracts from his letters, yet feeling the propriety of a single remark applicable to his entire correspondence. It cannot be claimed for him that he belonged to the highest rank of letter writers. His mind was rarely in the state best fitted for the epistolary art;

it was usually too earnest, too serious, too little at liberty. His letters are always, of course, sensible, intelligent, manly, and, to his friends, affectionate. But he rarely gave himself up to the play of fancy, or to the indulgence of the lighter forms of thought and feeling. He might have adopted, without change, the language of Dr. Channing: "The chief objection I have to writing letters is, that I can hardly do so without beginning to preach. I exhort, when I should smile. Not that I think a letter should be written without a desire to do good, but instruction should be delivered with somewhat less of formality than from the pulpit."

We venture also the remark, that in his earlier letters the subject of religion is introduced with more of formality, with less of spontaneous naturalness, than in his later correspondence. In his youth he wrote about religion because it seemed to be his duty; in later years, it perpetually found its own way into whatever he wrote, because he could not help it.

The following letter illustrates his way of treating a question of duty; he always tried to go back to the general law, the underlying principle, and to settle each case in such a way that a solution should be afforded for all similar perplexities. A near relative had asked his advice about laboring in the Sabbath school contrary to the wishes of her husband.

"In a letter you wrote me some weeks ago, mention was made of the Sabbath school. In cases of that kind I feel very delicate about giving advice. You know it is a very hazardous business to decide between man and wife. I think, however, if I were to express an opinion, it would be, that you are now in the path of duty, waiting for the moving of the pillar. The person who performs a good action at the expense of domestic tranquillity, does it at a dear rate, though sometimes even at that rate it may be necessary to do it. The duty to perform a good action of this kind is different from the duty which results from a positive command. God has commanded all men everywhere to

repent, and no circumstances can make it the duty of any
human being to do otherwise. Come what will, this duty
is to be performed. Again, God has laid down the precepts of the moral law, and we are bound to obey them,
and no human power should oblige us to break them.
The moment we transgress one of them to avoid persecution, we are seeking the praise of men more than the approbation of God ; and we may rest assured he will frown
upon our servile, wicked, and idolatrous complaisance.
Between these duties to God and duties to men there never
can be any comparison. These immediately swallow up
the other, and no reasoning is by him ever permitted in the
case. But our duties to our fellow-men may sometimes interfere with each other. We may, from some untoward
circumstances into which we are thrown, find it necessary to
abandon one in order to accomplish the other. But such
positions are best illustrated by instances. I hope I shall
not be tedious if I name two or three. You are bound to
support your family. If you provide not for it, you are worse
than an infidel. You are bound to relieve your neighbors'
distresses. You may readily suppose yourself in a situation where to perform both duties would be impossible.
The one must yield to the other. Take another case.
You may suppose a man and woman to commence the
world with nothing, and to have acquired by frugality and
labor a competence. I make the supposition that they
have nothing in the commencement, in order that the case
may be perfectly fair, since then, in point of natural right,
they would both seem to have an equal power over the
property acquired. It is the duty of the wife to bestow
charity upon her neighbors in distress. Suppose in such
a case the husband forbade it. It would then, I should
say, be her duty to acquiesce. And thus I should advise
in any case of a similar kind. God accepts the willing
mind. He is able to raise up others to do what we should
do with pleasure ourselves. We are to consider an object
of this kind as a blessing, of which, from the course of
events in divine providence, we are prohibited from par-
taking. Still we should, and doubtless will, pray that the
prohibition may be taken off. You see immediately that
the reasons of duty in a case of this kind result from the
nature of the marriage relation. The nature of this union
is indissoluble. In this it materially differs from every

other. When two persons are united in business or allied by friendship, should opinions materially interfere, the remedy is at hand: let them part, and each pursue the course which his reason dictates. They can part in good will. Between husband and wife the case is different. *They* cannot part. If one acts in opposition to the will of the other, domestic peace is wounded — I had almost said, destroyed. This, of course, is not to be done unless some greater evil is threatened; and this can rarely, if ever, take place, except in the case of a positive and authoritative command of duty. It follows, of course, that one must yield. Reason and revelation, in this case, decide that it shall be the wife. And in all ordinary cases the wife gains more than she loses. As I have some time before remarked to you, a woman's throne is the affections of her husband. And every honorable means by which she can the more closely entwine herself about his heart, it is lawful that she should use, and she ought to use. Hence, if she gives up one point to-day, she may be able by this means to carry a point to-morrow of ten times as much consequence.

" I have been long on this subject, longer than I anticipated; perhaps I have been tedious. I, however, did not like to give an opinion without giving what seemed to me something like reasons. I thought, also, consequences were involved which might be of importance through the whole of your life, and on which I wished you to have all the light I could give you. If you are angry at my prolixity, I can tell you, by way of alleviation, that I could have written as long again if I had chosen. . . .

" The doubts and fears you mention in your last letter have long been familiar acquaintances of mine. Ah, how often do I doubt whether there ever was the love of God shed abroad in my heart! My evidences are so dark, my practice so contradictory, my heart so hard, my unbelief so strong, my love so cold, I frequently cry out, ' My leanness, my leanness! ' Sure I am, if ever a sinner was saved by grace, pure, and free, and infinite, that soul will be mine, if ever it be saved. O for more grace, more love, more faith! Please accept a volume of Chalmers's Sermons. I call them super-excellent. I trust you will read them with profit."

In connection with the closing words of the above letter, we quote from one to his friend Wisner, of about the same date : —

"I have lately been reading Chalmers. The mind of that man moves like a torrent. Vast, irresistible, overwhelming, it sweeps before it the feeble barriers of infidelity, so that, like the baseless fabric of a vision, not a wreck is left behind. After following his track, you look behind you, and with curious gaze inquire, 'Where could infidelity have had a foothold?'"

It is not a little noteworthy that the youthful admiration thus expressed was not lessened by the "years that bring the philosophic mind." His last published volume was a memoir of the religious and philanthropic labors of Dr. Chalmers.

To his brother-in law, Mr. Stone : —

" . . . You know much more about politics, newspapers, &c., than I do ; but still I will venture one word of advice. I would never, were I you, mention names in a political squib. It takes off the point of the attack, at the same time that it seems more bitter, and malevolent. I should think a painter much sharper, who drew a caricature of me, so pointed and characteristic that every one who looked at it, said, ' That is Wayland,' than a painter who drew one and had to write under it, 'This is Wayland,' for fear nobody would recognize it. The same is true of party thrusts. They pierce deeper and cut the more keenly, the smoother the edge. If a character is drawn with a certain discrimination, he for whom it is designed will soon enough fit it on himself; and then you can, if he complain, immediately retort, ' The galled jade winces.' I am aware you will say these people are so low, they cannot be touched by gentlemanly treatment : I would reply, ' Then let them alone.'

" But, my brother, amidst the turmoil of party, amidst the hurry and bustle of conflicting interests, do you ever have time to look within? Is it peace there? Are the clamors of an accusing conscience hushed by the peace-speaking blood of the cross? This life, whether passed among friends or enemies, in bustle or solitude, is rapidly hastening away. This generation, with all its cares and contentions, will shortly lie side by side in the house appointed for all living, and not one word of rivalry, not one shout of exultation, nor murmur of defeat, will be heard through the silent avenues of that gloomy habitation. This world, the theatre of so many unholy contentions, will shortly be purified by fire. This system, with all its grandeur, will collapse in one universal ruin, and the heavens will be rolled together as a scroll. What will then be of value but an interest in the Savior? In that Savior may we be interested, and the praise shall be to his glorious grace. Amen."

In general he seemed not greatly affected by natural scenery. His mind was habitually too much preoccupied to receive impressions from nature; nor did he possess the "wise passiveness" by which "we may feed this mind of ours." His chief sensibility was to moral grandeur. But the following portion of a letter to his sister shows him by no means destitute of the power of observing and delineating nature : —

" . . . I had a pleasant journey to Ogdensburg. I saw and admired the Little Falls, of which you had given me a description. The solemn and sober majesty of the square pillars of granite which crowd around the approach to them is noble and grand. Here and there a pillar projects from the range of its brethren; and on its head you observe a sturdy little pine entwining its roots among the fissures, and surveying with lordly pride the sublime scenery around. On every side you observe most conclusive evidence that the river, or some more noble stream, of which the present is but the pitiful falling off, once rolled its majestic waters over the rocks, through which the road now passes. The rocks are rounded and smoothed; their sides and tops are full of holes worn by the impetuous action of the water. In one of the rocks in the neighborhood, I found a hole large enough to hold six or eight men. Of all villages, Whitesborough takes the precedence. It combines rural elegance with city refinement, in a degree which I never saw, and scarcely expected to see. From Utica to Ogdensburg, the road is through villages and forests. The trees are thick and heavy, and the elm is the most remarkable. Its trunk shoots up seventy-five or one hundred feet, round, straight, without a branch, and seems nearly of the same size. It divides into four or five branches, which for some time continue close together, and then spread out, forming a fitting crown to this pillar of the forest."

To his sister Mrs. S. : —

" . . . Of your joining Mr. Hawes's church I have only to say, May you be led by the Spirit of truth. The points which you suggest in your last letter I shall not attempt to answer. I would only say, you or I have mistaken the grounds of the question. I did not, I confess, see distinctly the bearing which the texts you suggested, had upon the thing in dispute. If you are happy, as I presume you will be, in that communion, you may rest assured, as I know you do, that I shall never attempt to unsettle your mind.

" I am grateful that your excellent friends think of me. They probably do it out of respect to you, which is certainly kind and flattering to you, and of course to me ; but if you do not wish to injure me, you should be careful how you speak. You may rest assured I am but a very common sort of man. As to acquirements, I am such as I ought to be ashamed of ; as to application, still more so. Your friends, you may depend upon it, would never pick me out for your brother, if you have described me as probably you have.

" You know that it is likely our family will remove to Saratoga. I hope it is for the best. I think the prospect of doing good there is encouraging. . . . God is certainly dealing with our family in much mercy. I, for my part, am frequently led to doubt my title to a heavenly inheritance, I have had so little affliction ; though He, at whose reproof the pillars of heaven tremble and are astonished, knows well how to try me. When he does, may he do it in mercy, and not in judgment."

Meanwhile his friend Wisner had entered the Seminary at Princeton, and was very anxious that Mr. Wayland should do the same. We can imagine the glowing terms in which he excited the almost envying admiration of his friend, as he told of the " prince of preachers," Dr. Alexander, and of the wise and learned Dr. Miller.

Mr. Wayland writes, —

" You have great privileges, and I doubt not you are prodigiously improving them. I know not how one small head will ever carry all your knowledge. I presume that your Seminary is as good as any in our country, or perhaps in the world ; nor do I doubt that you will do honor even to such a Seminary. I pray that with all your gettings you may continue to gain in knowledge of your own heart and of that plan of redemption which it will be our business to preach."

To the letters of Mr. Wisner urging him to repair to Princeton, he replies, —

" I cannot go, for I have not the means. I cannot dig ; to beg I am ashamed. I cannot, for I do not think it my duty. When Providence sees fit to place the means of effecting an object out of a man's power, it seems conclusive evidence that it is not the divine will that he should proceed in its pursuit ; or, more properly, there the question ends. . . . I thank you for the kind and disinterested part which you have taken. I wish I had it in my power to make any return. If the great Husbandman has any work for me to do in his vineyard, I trust he will prepare me, and send me forth. I desire to rely upon him. He has always done for me better than I expected, and infinitely better than I deserved. O that my heart were more melted by his goodness, and more devoted to his praise, and that my faith were more thoroughly placed upon him. I do not dissemble my opnion that I should be a more learned and perhaps useful minister, in the general acceptation of the term, were I with you ; nor do I deny that I have a strong desire once more to grapple with men. I would like once more to come upon the arena of a seminary and measure with my peers. But this is a foolish ambition, and, I fear, not a Christian one."

Several months later he writes, —

" I have been disappointed in some money which I expected to receive for private tuition. I have had to pay a debt which, when I saw you, I did not recollect; and this has dwindled down my resources so far that I know not how to go, without being a greater burden on my friends than I am at all willing to become. Would you, my brother, risk the hazard of becoming the burden of charity? I have once done this, and I have known what it was to remain for weeks without enough to pay the dues of the post-office. I have known what it was to be in debt, and without more than one decent suit of clothes. Though the wound of these things is closed by the hand of time, yet the scar remains. I must inevitably borrow; but when shall I ever repay it? I cannot be a burden to my friends. They are few, very few, and I wish to keep them. . . . For all your kindness, my brother, I am under more obligations than I can express. . . . There is considerable attention to the concerns of the soul in the villages about here. Malta has been visited with an abundant outpouring; principally under the instrumentality of Dr. McAuley. Under one sermon which he preached there, nine, I think, were awakened. The work is still progressing. At Saratoga Springs the work is at a stand."

It was at this time that Mr. Wisner and Mr. William B. Sprague, now of Albany, were speaking, in presence of some of their fellow-students, of a young friend, a Baptist, of extraordinary intellectual endowments, who was anxious to come to the Seminary, but was not able to command the means. This conversation took place in the room of Howard Malcom (afterwards pastor of the Federal Street Baptist Church, in Boston, and subsequently president of the university at Lewisburg, Penn.). He at once said, " I will furnish him with two hundred dollars a year, or more if it is necessary, during his course of study at Princeton." Mr. Wisner immediately wrote to communicate this noble offer, and was happy in the expectation of soon welcoming his friend to the prized privileges of professional study. After considerable delay, he received the following reply : —

" Scarcely ever in my life did I feel so perfectly sensible
of my unworthiness as upon the receipt of your letter. I
am quite undeserving of so much attention and kindness.
But how inscrutable are the ways of Providence ! If the
facts communicated in your letter had been known a few
days sooner, I should by this time have been in Princeton. Your letter was missent to Canandaigua. It did
not return until day before yesterday evening. The session begins in four days. I had to decide whether I
would continue here, so that, if I was to go, my place
might be filled. I decided to remain, and informed Dr.
Nott to this effect; and I cannot honorably withdraw. I
have engaged to teach the Senior class chemistry, and am
now immersed, head and ears, in conflicting theories of
atoms and volumes, and acids and alkalies. There seems
something unusual in this dispensation of Providence.
To Mr. Malcom I am under obligations which I hope
you will be kind enough to acknowledge. I shall write
to him immediately to thank him for his kindness. I
have no way, my brother, to return your goodness. I can
only beseech Him who has blessed me with such a friend,
to shower upon you those gifts of the Holy Spirit which
shall make you an eminent minister of the New Testament,
and fit you for the enjoyment of him in heaven." *

Of the events just alluded to he writes, in his reminiscences, —

"My destiny in life has been materially affected by
the blunder of a postmaster ; and I believe that this blunder was directed by infinite wisdom and love. I could
not but look upon it as a special providence, intimating my
duty in a manner not to be misunderstood. With this
event all my plans for pursuing study at a theological
seminary ended."

Before many months had passed, the providence seemed
to lose something of its mysteriousness. He writes, —

---

* The truly beautiful exhibition afforded in this correspondence, of Mr. Wisner's character as a friend and a Christian brother,
brings forcibly to mind the touching indorsement placed by the
venerable Lyman Beecher upon a letter of Wisner : " That was
the man I loved best of all on earth. I never pass the Old South
but that I think of Wisner."

"The four years which I spent as tutor were of great service to me intellectually. In a religious aspect, the first two years, at least, had no beneficent tendency. I was engaged in study far too exclusively, and religion became a matter of small and distant reality. The idea gained possession of my mind that I was preparing by study, and the discharge of my duties, for future usefulness. I forgot that the love of God is a duty and a privilege of every day and of every moment.

"About this time all that region was overspread by a revival of religion, especially through the labors of the Rev. Asahel Nettleton. It extended to Schenectady, and entered the college. There was a powerful impression made upon the students, and many of them were converted. The occasion was blessed to me in awakening my conscience and recalling me to my duty. I labored as well as I knew how in the promotion of the work, and saw with delight a great change in the moral character of the young men. In the portion of the college which was under my care, a prayer meeting was established, which continued, I think, until I resigned my office. At nine o'clock every evening, all who chose met at my room for reading the Scriptures and prayer. For some time almost every student in my division attended, each one in turn conducting the meeting."

In the following letter * Mr. Nettleton gives a graphic account of the scenes which so deeply affected the character of the subject of our memoir: —

"South from Malta about twelve miles is the city of Schenectady, and Union College, where I now reside with Dr. McAuley. He takes a lively interest in this good work. I first became acquainted with him last summer at the Springs, and more particularly at Malta, where he frequently visited us, and preached, and conversed, and attended the meetings appointed for those anxious for their souls. On a Sabbath, when a number were to be admitted to the church in Malta, he brought with him several students from the college. Some of them became anxious. About this time one of the students was

---

* From Dr. Tyler's Memoir of Nettleton.

called into the eternal world. He was laid out in Dr. McAuley's study. The doctor was anxious to improve this solemn providence to the best advantage. He assembled the students around the lifeless remains of their departed friend, and conversed and prayed with them in the most solemn manner. A number of them engaged to attend to the subject of religion in earnest. From that time many of the students became deeply impressed with a sense of their lost condition. For them were appointed meetings of inquiry. And in this very room, where they lately beheld the breathless corpse of their young companion, and where I am now writing, was witnessed a scene of deep and awful distress. About thirty of the students are brought to rejoice in hope. The revival is now very powerful in the city. Such a scene they never before witnessed. More than one hundred have been converted. Besides these, we had more than two hundred in our meeting of inquiry, anxious for their souls. We met in a large upper room, called the Masonic Hall. The room was so crowded that we were obliged to request all, who had recently found relief, to retire below, and spend their time in prayer for those above. That evening will never be forgotten. The scene is beyond description. Did you ever witness two hundred sinners, with one accord in one place, weeping for their sins? Until you have seen this, you can have no adequate conceptions of the solemn scene. I felt as though I was standing on the verge of the eternal world, while the floor under my feet was shaken by the trembling of anxious souls, in view of a judgment to come. The solemnity was heightened when every knee was bent at the throne of grace, and the intervening silence of the voice of prayer was interrupted only by the sighs and sobs of anxious souls. Some of the most stout, hard-hearted, Heaven-daring rebels have been in the most awful distress. Within a circle whose diameter is twenty-four miles, not less than eight hundred souls have been hopefully borne into the kingdom of Christ since last September. The same glorious work is fast spreading in other towns and congregations. 'This is that which was spoken by the prophet Joel.' "

Mr. Wayland writes to Mr. Wisner, —

"Your very welcome letter was received a few days since. I could not till this evening steal time to answer it. I entered my hall this evening, saying, 'Now for a long letter to brother Wisner.' As I walked up stairs, I heard the voice of praise and thanksgiving. I entered the next room to mine, and found about twenty-three, many of them new converts, engaged in a prayer meeting. I joined with them; and this has delayed me, till now my watch points to ten o'clock.

"The Lord hath done great things for us, my brother, whereof I hope we are glad. But we are not half glad enough. There are now about twenty happy converts, and nearly that number more, under serious conviction. As yet the work has been most powerful among the most moral and religiously educated. You may readily conceive that the aspect of college is somewhat altered. It is no difficult thing to collect a prayer meeting at a moment's warning. In fact, if two or three meet together, prayer seems to be almost the necessary consequence. About a week ago I mentioned to one of the converts, who rooms next to me, the expediency of instituting a section prayer meeting, or more properly a family meeting, at morning and evening. It was joyfully acceded to. They chose to meet in my room. And since that time, at the ringing of the first bell in the morning, and between nine and ten o'clock at night, we offer up our devotions at the domestic altar. This incident expresses, I think, the general feeling about college. I have said that the work was generally confined to those who had been religiously educated. This is not, however, universal. The name of Bob —— used to be proverbial for everything that was lying or mischievous. He is now calling on all who come in his way to repent and believe the gospel."

Of the remarkable man already alluded to, Asahel Nettleton, Dr. Wayland writes, —

"He was among the most effective preachers I have ever known. I never heard logic assume so attractive a form, or produce so decisive an effect. When reasoning on any of the great doctrines in Romans, for instance, election, the utter depravity of man, the necessity of regeneration, or the necessity of atonement, his manner was often Socratic. He would commence with what must be

conceded by every one present; then, by a series of questions, each deliberately considered, and not suffered to
pass away until the speaker and hearer gave the same
answer, his opponents would find themselves face to face
with an absurdity so glaring, that notwithstanding the
solemnity of the scene, the hearer could hardly escape
the disposition to laugh at himself, for holding a belief that
appeared so utterly untenable.

"In other styles of address he was equally successful.
The doom of the sinner, the danger of delay, the condition
of the thoughtless, the vicious, and the blasphemer; the
exercises of the soul from the first moments of conviction,
the subterfuges of the human heart, and the final act of
submission to God, were portrayed by him with a power
of eloquence that I have rarely heard. I suppose no minister of his time was the means of so many conversions.

"He was in an unusual degree obedient to impressions
received in answer to prayer. I believe he never went to
a place, unless he had received an intimation that he had
a duty to discharge there; and he rarely visited a place
where a revival did not follow him. In conversing with
persons under conviction, he exhibited a knowledge of
human nature almost intuitive. Nor was it merely with
awakened sinners that his preaching was remarkably successful. It was his habit (when he could stay long enough
in a neighborhood) to collect the converts and explain to
them the doctrines of the gospel, point out to them their
danger, and then to build them up in the faith, before he
left them.

"In preaching, his countenance beamed with a holy
earnestness, such as befitted one sent directly from God
as an ambassador to men. At this time he very rarely
entered the pulpit, or preached in the daytime. He preferred a vestry or a school-house; and if he spoke in the
body of the church, he addressed the audience from the
deacons' seat, or the platform in front of the pulpit. His
manner was quiet, especially at the commencement; his
voice grave and deep-toned; his whole aspect was that
of a man who had just come from intimate communion
with God. He never used notes (although I believe he
sometimes wrote out some of his sermons), and rarely employed ornament of any kind. He would stand up, throwing a red bandanna handkerchief over his left arm, and in
tones varying but little from those of earnest conversation,

would sway an audience as the trees of the forest are
moved by a mighty wind.

"His manner of life was consistent with his appearance
in the pulpit. His residence was generally with the minister of the parish in which he was laboring. The time
not employed in preaching or conversation with inquirers,
was devoted to secret prayer and the reading of the Scriptures. He was never seen in what is called general society. His whole time seemed devoted to labor for souls.
He was unmarried, and, to avoid remark, he never rode or
walked with a lady alone. He was wholly insensible to
the influence of money. His dress was plain, and well
worn. When money was offered him, he would either
return it all, or would accept only what was wanted for
his present necessity.

"Notwithstanding all this, I have rarely known a man
who was, for a great part of the time, more thoroughly
abused. It was generally admitted that his appearance
in a town was the precursor of a revival. This fact
aroused all the virulence of men at enmity with God.
His mode of conducting meetings was somewhat peculiar,
and his preaching singularly bold and uncompromising.
Thus he greatly excited against him those professors of
religion who did not like anything new in the mode of
preaching. Hence, at first, good men would frequently
turn aside from him, and too readily give heed to the
slanders of wicked men. I knew very well a physician
of eminence, a pleasant, kind man, though utterly destitute
of religion, residing in a village where Mr. N. was laboring, who circulated a falsehood about him, retailing a
conversation, which, he said, Mr. N. had had with him
in his office, when the fact was, that Mr. N. had never
been in his office; and it subsequently appeared that the
doctor was wholly ignorant of his person. To such attacks Mr. N. never deigned to make a word of reply, nor
did he ever intimate that he knew of their existence. He
considered that a man's character is the best defence of his
reputation, and he left it to time and to the providence of
God to refute the slanders.

"A man so unique and so successful was of course
blessed with many imitators. But they could much more
easily imitate his peculiarities, than the spirit with which
he spoke. Some of them preached a very different doctrine from that in which he gloried. Others failed entirely

in moral character. The spirit of revivals declined, and this sort of preaching was made, I fear, a thing of gain. He became involved in controversy with some of the most eminent men in the Congregational church. These differences led to painful results, and it may, I fear, be said that the peculiar type of revival preaching which I remember at this time, rose and declined with this excellent man. I write this in part from general recollection, at the distance of a long intervening period. In some of the facts I may unintentionally have erred."

We need not fear to believe that Providence had wise and gracious designs in so ordering his circumstances that Mr. Wayland should be mingled with the scenes of this revival, and especially that he should form the acquaintance and enjoy the counsels of Mr. Nettleton. " I became intimately acquainted with Mr. Nettleton, and my conversations with him were of great use to me."

His spirit received a quickening impulse whose influence never ceased to be felt, and he gained lessons never to be forgotten in the mode of addressing men on religious subjects. He desired to be engaged directly in laboring for the salvation of men. He writes, —

" I had become somewhat familiar with most of the studies which I was called on to teach, and could devote some time to preparation for the ministry; to this kind of study I now gave all of the time which I could command. Having been licensed to preach by the church at Saratoga Springs, of which I had become a member, and of which my father was at this time (1820) pastor, I began to preach to feeble churches in the vicinity. For some time I supplied the little church at Burnt Hills, a village between Schenectady and Ballston. I began to make skeletons of sermons under the supervision of Dr. Nott. From him I learned all that I ever knew on that subject. He taught me how to make a sermon, by showing me the folly of the plans which I submitted to him, and by giving my mind the right direction in this kind of intellectual labor. His instruction was invaluable to me.

" My preaching was confined wholly to out-stations, and was at first entirely unwritten. Thinking it important not only to make the plan of a sermon, but to finish it completely, I began to write sermons. But it is scarcely possible to realize the labor which writing them cost me. I have been thought to write with more than common readiness. At first, however, it was intolerable labor. It took me weeks — I know not but I might say months — to write a discourse of moderate length. I wrote and rewrote, with endless care and anxiety. How men prepared two sermons a week I could not conceive. I saw, however, that they did it, and at last I settled down into the belief that I could do what I saw other men do, though I could not see how it was accomplished."

These early sermons are valuable chiefly as the comparison of them with those of subsequent years shows that he did not spring into life fully panoplied; that the power of thinking, of expressing, came to him, not by inspiration, but as the result of the most patient and unwearied labor. During the latter portion of his tutorship, he also instructed, in Hebrew, a number of candidates for the ministry, carrying them through a portion of Genesis.

To his brother : —

" You and I are poor. The only patrimony, for which we can hope, is our *pious parents' blessing*. The best fortune we can acquire is, a character above suspicion. By a rigid continuance in virtue, that character may be gained. By one act of infamy it may be lost, lost forever. The gate to infamy is constantly open. We may easily enter it. But to return, — ah, that is next to impossible. Suffer, then, my brother, the advice of one who, a few years ago, was treading the path in which you now are.

" Beware of your companions. I would not be *intimate with any one* who was not perfectly and rigidly virtuous. I had almost said I would be intimate with no one. You have your brother and sisters, and I would spend my leisure time with them. Thus your mind will be enlarged, your information extended, and your manners improved. The society into which they will introduce you will be honorable, and may be useful to you. The chance acquaintances whom you may pick up may be absolutely deleterious. They can do you no good. As you value your character, the character of your family, your future prospects, and your everlasting welfare, I conjure you, hold no intercourse with a vicious man. I speak on this subject from experience. I was once on the brink of ruin. I was intimate with a man of vicious habits, though of unusual mind, and of very entertaining conversation. Intercourse with him gradually diminished my sense of religious obligation, and was leading me on in a course which, if pursued, would have left me at this moment an abandoned and vicious man. Providence interrupted the intimacy, and I never think of it without shuddering at the near approach I made to a total overthrow of all my hopes. For I consider that the hopes of a vicious man are overthrown. Be found in no place of resort to which you would not be willing that I should accompany you. But especially be found nowhere where you would not be willing that God should find you. And find you he will. There is not a word on your lips but he hears. There is not a thought in your heart which he does not mark. There is not a place in which you have been, or in which you will be, where he is not around you on every side. And every deed, every word, and every thought, shall be found registered in that book which a day of judgment will unseal."

We quote further from the reminiscences bearing on this period.

" I had passed nearly four years as tutor in Union College; I was satisfied that I had remained there long enough, and was determined to resign when this year was completed. I suffered from ill health, for I had not learned the value and importance of systematic exercise. In what direction I should turn, I knew not. No prospect was before me. I thought of going to the west, but I was not in a pecuniary condition to travel far. I suffered much from the fear that no prospect of usefulness was open, or likely to open, before me. I was but little acquainted with Baptist ministers, having been for five years associated with men of other denominations. To go about and beg for a settlement seemed hardly what I was prepared to do. I had little experience in preaching, and no power of eloquence, or anything which would be likely to attract attention. It was to me a period of deep and distressing anxiety. I have never since, that I remember, suffered anything comparable to it."

CHAPTER V.

MEANWHILE the First Baptist Church in Boston was destitute of a pastor. The church had enjoyed, under the eminent Dr. Stillman, a high degree of prosperity. " He was probably the most popular pulpit orator of his day. He was a universal favorite." To him and to his church was granted the singular honor of holding up the doctrines of the gospel, when the great body of churches of the standing order had either openly departed from the faith, or, while having the form of godliness, had denied the power of it. When any one became anxious about his soul, it was very commonly said to him, " O, you had better go down to Dr. Stillman's meeting. You will find what you want there." An eminent layman of one of the Congregational churches used to relate, that when a young man, having become aroused by the Spirit of God, and seeking advice suited to his condition, he was referred to Dr. Stillman's church; and at the time of meeting he would steal by retired streets, down to the North End, watching to see that he was not observed, and there would receive into his thirsty soul the words of everlasting life.

Dr. Stillman was succeeded by Rev. Joseph Clay, and he, by the Rev. J. M. Winchell, whose name was long retained in grateful remembrance by his admirable compilation of hymns, Winchell's Watts. Between the resig-

nation of Mr. Clay and the settlement of Mr. Winchell, a
period of more than five years, the church had no pastor;
and during the latter part of Mr. Winchell's settlement,
his failing health had greatly abridged his power of labor.
The house of worship (situated on a narrow alley, that
now, widened and improved, is called Stillman Street)
was old, unsightly, and incommodious of access. It is
scarcely matter of wonder that the church should have
greatly declined in means, numbers, zeal, and unity.
Truth, however, would seem to require the statement that
their sense of the dignity and importance of the church
was all that could be demanded by the most flattering
circumstances. Their estimate of the qualities needed by
any one who should assume the pastoral office among
them, was correspondingly high. " They must have an
able minister, a young man, a scholar. He must be eloquent, like Dr. Stillman, a logician, like Judge Clay. In
their view, there was no man in the ministry quite equal
to so eligible a place as the pastorship of the First Baptist Church of Boston. I have been told that there was
some thought of sending for Andrew Fuller; but he was
the main support of the Baptists of England, the Secretary
of the Foreign Missionary Society, and could not be spared
from the church at Kittering." *

Mr. Wisner, who was now settled at the Old South
Church, urged the deacons of the First Church to hear
his friend Mr. Wayland. On the 8th of January, 1821,
Deacon James Loring, church clerk, writes to Mr. Wayland, stating their destitute condition, and adding, " None
of us have ever enjoyed the privilege of hearing your
public improvements; but having received information
respecting you as an acceptable preacher in our denomination, this church, at their monthly meeting, on the 5th
instant, voted that their committee for the supply of the

---

* Rev. Dr. Neale's Historical Discourse, from which, also, two
sentences were quoted above, relative to Dr. Stillman.

pulpit be directed to request you, in the name of the
church, to visit and preach with them eight or ten weeks,
as might suit your convenience."

The invitation was accepted, and a promise made to
visit Boston in the spring. To a letter of his father, suggested by these circumstances, Mr. Wayland replies, —

". . . Your remarks I have felt to be emphatically applicable to my case. It is my desire not to feel anxious or
sanguine on the subject. I pray that God will enable me
to submit this and all his dispensations wholly to his
will, and that I may be prepared for every and any situation which he may assign me. I have had reason, very
great reason, to be thankful for all the scenes, whether
of trial or prosperity, but especially the former, through
which I have been led. Should the Lord design to teach
me humility by this visit, I pray that he may make me
docile, and willing to learn the lesson. May it make me
more to distrust myself, and lean with more unshaken
confidence upon his guidance and direction. Should he
favor me with prosperity, O that he may keep me humble, patient, meek, and lowly. And if he should place
me in any station of responsibility, may he abundantly
enrich me with every literary and intellectual qualification, but especially with the infinitely richer endowments
of his Holy Spirit, that I may be sincere, wise, pure, holy,
vigilant, and prayerful, and deeply impressed with the
value of souls. In fine, whatever may be my lot in this
world, may I live a life of holiness, and be received at
last to the place where there is no more lukewarmness,
but where they see as they are seen, and know as they are
known. With respect to the course of ministerial study
which you recommend, I am much of your opinion. I
am of opinion that the Bible is the best book a minister
can study; and the next best book is his own heart, and
the hearts of his people: the one without the other will
be ineffectual, or at least imperfect. These are the outlines
of my ideas. I hope, if they are not correct, I may be
instructed better from on high. Should I be located in
Boston, there will be many things pleasant — its proximity
to Andover — and its being the residence of Mr. Wisner,
my old friend. But of this it is needless to talk; we are
not to choose for ourselves. . . ."

In the spring vacation he went to Boston, taking with him his entire supply of sermons, eight in number During this visit, Deacons Snow and Loring spent an evening in conversing with him upon his religious views. He says, —

"I replied to their questions with entire frankness, and when I seemed to differ from them, gave such reasons for my opinion as occurred to me at the moment."

He regarded the course of these gentlemen in holding this interview as eminently judicious, as calculated to prevent misunderstanding, and to secure permanent cooperation. After he had preached four Sundays, and was about to return to Schenectady, it was proposed by some persons that he should visit them again.

"This I declined to do, for they had had a full opportunity to hear and see me. If they did not like me now, they would not probably be changed in their opinion by any further acquaintance, while to return would place me before the public as seeking the situation. I spoke with entire simplicity, and with the distinct impression that by thus speaking I closed forever the prospect of a settlement with them."

During this visit to Boston, Mr. Wayland attended the trial of Judge Prescott, then under impeachment, and heard the speech of Mr. Webster. He says, "I lost, as I suppose, some reputation, if I had any to lose, by saying that I thought Mr. W. a less eloquent man than Dr. Nott." The incident is of little value, except as illustrating his uniform habit of making up his judgments for himself. He could not accept opinions and estimates at second hand. He had but little respect for traditional wisdom. "Every man must sail by his own compass" was an oft-repeated maxim with him.

A considerable portion of the church were in favor of Rev. Mr. E., a clergyman of popular and showy address. But there were a few persons who discerned the force of

character, and the strength of mind and purpose, underlying an unattractive manner.   The weight of their judgment and their personal influence carried a small majority.
Mr. Wayland was called by a vote of fifteen to ten in the
church, and seventeen to fifteen in the society.

"I knew," he says, "that the call was not unanimous
(though I did not then know that the small majority had
been procured with great effort).   But Dr. Nott, whose
advice I asked, treated this as a matter of no consequence,
and insisted that those who opposed me, would soon, in
all probability, become my best friends." *

A few days after forwarding to him the notice of the
call, Deacon Loring wrote urging his acceptance, and
adds, —

"President Messer, who was recently in town, observed,
'If Mr. Wayland is like me, he will not look at numbers,
but weight.'   On Tuesday I saw Professor Stuart.   I told
him I had the pleasure to say to him that our church and
society had requested you to become our stated minister.
'I am glad,' said he, 'your church has so much good
sense.   Were you united?'   'Not so much as I could
wish.'   'Did you unite your principal men?'   This question is so much like Stuart.   'We did, sir.'   Rev. Mr.
Going, of Worcester, says, 'Tell Mr. Wayland, from
me, that the cause of evangelical religion and literature
amongst the Baptists and others says, Come to Boston.'

"P. S.   Permit me to caution you against anonymous
letters.   The communications sent you on Tuesday are
official, and such as you may place confidence in.   In an
anonymous letter you find no responsibility."

Professor Stuart writes to Mr. Wayland, —

"Deacon Loring, of Boston, has recently told me the
circumstances of your invitation to Boston.   He states
(what I thought would be the case) that all the well-
informed and weighty part of the church and society are

* Dr. Wayland once said to Dr. Stow, "I don't think much of
these unanimous calls.   It looks as though people did not judge
for themselves."

in your favor, while the other part would prefer a man who ' could preach by inspiration.' He made me promise that I would write you the result of my reflections on this subject, the first leisure time that I could find.

" On the whole, I am well satisfied that you are better fitted for ' Yankee soil ' than any other. You may not cut a great figure here, with wide-spread branches, broad leaves, and profuse flowers; but what blossoms put forth will be succeeded by fruit, and that fruit will not fall prematurely, but yield a noble harvest. Your society in Boston is the best place in this country to begin the cure of the malady that reigns among your brethren on the subject of educating preachers. I am quite confident, that with prudence and good sense, you will win over the reluctant part of your congregation. Nothing is wanting but a little personal, kind attention, and to preach a few times without notes, so as to let them know that you can be inspired as well as your brethren. And then, the cause here absolutely and imperiously demands a man like you, who has depth of exegetical lore, who can meet the Unitarians on ground where he is not liable to feel his inferiority, or be put to the blush. Besides, Providence College must have such trustees, or it is ruined forever. Radical changes must be made in order to save it. You want more weight, more literature here, to do this.

" All things considered, I am clear that it is your duty to come, and that the opposition to you is of such a nature as can be neutralized by a very little prudent and kind attention, and extempore effort in the pulpit. And, by the way, I say without reserve, you should always extemporize one half the day in your own pulpit."

The call was accepted, and early in August he set out for Boston.

To his mother : —

" . . . At sunset on Thursday I arrived in Boston. I never entered a place with quite such feelings. I had left my home. I had left that part of this earth, which, above every other, was endeared to me by a thousand associations. I was entering the place where I expected to spend the remainder of my life. The people were new to me. Their modes of living were in many re-

spects dissimilar to my own. There were but one or
two persons with whom I felt as though there was any
thorough congeniality. But above all, I was going as an
ambassador of Heaven. I could not but reflect on the
words, 'This child is set for the fall and rising of many
in Israel.' Although in a very humble sense, yet I could
not but reflect that in all human probability, if my life
were spared, I should be the cause of the eternal salvation or damnation of many souls. The doctrines which
I should preach, the behavior which I should exhibit, the
whole course of my life, was to have henceforth a bearing upon eternity. Who was sufficient for these things?
I certainly was not. I shuddered, and was ready to shrink
from the burden which was to devolve upon me. I could
only find consolation in looking to that Name which is
above every name, renewedly dedicating myself to his
service, and praying that he would make me faithful unto
death, that at the end I may render up my account with
joy, and not with grief."

On the 21st of August, 1821, he was ordained. The
services were, — prayer by Rev. William Gammell; sermon by Rev. Dr. Sharp; ordaining prayer by Rev. F.
Wayland, senior; charge by Rev. Dr. Baldwin; right
hand of fellowship by Rev. Dr. Bolles; prayer by Rev.
Joseph Grafton. The text of Dr. Sharp's discourse —
"Now, if Timotheus come, see that he may be with you
without fear, for he worketh the work of the Lord, as
I also do " — would seem to indicate that, in his opinion,
trials awaited his young brother.

Turning for a moment from the publicity, the hurry,
and the confusion of the ordination, let us look (if it be
not too sacred a spot for intrusion) into the heart and
the closet of the Christian woman who sees the fulfilment
of many prayers in the piety and the opening usefulness
of her son.

From his mother : —

"SARATOGA SPRINGS, August 29, 1821.

"My dear Son: Your highly acceptable letter, bearing date August 11, came to hand. I have read it over

and over with tears of joy. I hope my gratitude and love were much increased to the Father of mercies for his goodness to you and faithfulness to me. Truly, God is good to Israel. He has heard my prayer. He has not despised the supplication of his handmaid. Surely the feelings of Hannah were mine, when she said, My soul doth magnify the Lord. I called for all within me and all without to join in praise. I looked around to see if I could find one confidential friend to whom I could say 'The Lord has done great things for me'(and I humbly hope for the church of God), whereof my soul is glad. Come and help me to adore before his throne. And will he open his eyes upon such a one as mortal man, and send him with the glad tidings of salvation to sinners? This is a subject in which I'm lost in wonder, love, and praise.

"The day of your ordination I kept with fasting and prayer, that the Lord would adorn you with all the graces of his Holy Spirit, that you might abound in every good word and work, that you might have many, very many, souls given you, that shall be to your everlasting joy in a coming day. Two things especially were on my mind — that is, that you might be clothed with humility as with a garment, and that your spirituality might appear to all. May these ever go before in all your preaching, and then your education and talents may follow to great advantage.

"The next subject of my prayer was the church over which the Lord has made you overseer, that they might be much blessed, comforted, and edified under your pastoral care. . . ."

On the following Sabbath, August 26, the new pastor preached two sermons from the words, "It is required in stewards that a man be found faithful." The subject, "the duties of the minister of Christ," is considered under three heads: 1. He must deliver to his people, without addition or retrenchment, the truths contained in this holy word. 2. He must deliver each distinct truth to those for whom his Master has designed it. 3. He must deliver the truth in such a manner as his Master has directed.

"He may not add to the word of God his own inferences nor the inferences of other men. . . . Again, he is

forbidden to take anything from the word of God. Some
pastors, from a spirit of timidity, seem to want to preach
less than God has revealed. At one time a doctrine seems
revealed in too unqualified a manner, and in their preaching they guard it by some temporizing paragraphs. At
another, a statement seems not to agree with their pre-
conceived notions, and they modify it to suit their opinions. God commands all men, everywhere, to repent.
One dares not thus to call upon his fellow-sinners, lest
they should imbibe false notions of human agency, or because he does not know that those whom he addresses are
elected. Another will not preach the doctrine of divine
sovereignty, lest men should abandon all concern for their
salvation. But is he a faithful steward who thus mangles
the word of God? Has infinite wisdom revealed more
truth than it is prudent for man to know, and is it the
business of the minister of Christ to becloud it?

" Again, the minister of Christ should preach the truths
of the Scriptures in all their clearness and in all their
obscurity. Some of the truths of the Bible are clearly
revealed. . . . These truths, and others which we might
mention, seem to us distinctly made known in the word of
God, and the minister of Jesus Christ must clearly preach
them, even though by so doing he incurs the enmity of
some and the contempt of many.

" But it cannot be denied, that although the truths are
revealed, yet frequently the manner of their existence
and their relations to each other are not revealed. The
fact God has declared, while its consistence with other
facts he leaves in obscurity ; and with all this obscurity
must the minister of the gospel preach it.

" We find in the Scriptures that Jesus Christ is God,
and again, that he is man. Do you ask how both can be
true? I freely answer, I cannot now explain it. Perhaps
I never shall be able to do so. Nor is it my business,
nor that of any other minister. God has left it unex-
plained, and there I am bound to leave it. Again, God
has clearly revealed the fact of his superintending control.
All things that take place happen under his direction and
by his control ; yet man and all God's intelligent creatures
act freely and voluntarily. Who can show the connection
between these truths? What mortal eye has glanced along
the chain of Jehovah's operations, and fixed upon the link

which connects the decrees of God with the agency of man? Such are some of the obscurities connected with the truths of God's word, and with all this obscurity must the minister of Christ preach them.

"Here it may be asked, Is not God consistent with himself? and if we find one doctrine clearly revealed, and find another which we cannot reconcile with it, is it not evident that the one or the other must be taken with some limitations, and in our preaching, are we not bound to limit it? We answer, God is doubtless consistent with himself, but he has never appointed us judges of his consistency; and until he shall thus appoint us, it were certainly modest in us to decline the office. We answer, again, If two such doctrines occur, — and they may doubtless occur, — the duty of the minister is to preach them both, fully and clearly, as they are revealed in the Scriptures. He has nothing to do with their consistency. If his hearers object on this account, the controversy is between God and their own souls, and there must the minister of Christ leave it."

Usually it is but scanty praise to say of a man that he has not in any degree changed his views during all his lifetime. It is to say that he is no wiser to-day than he was many years ago. And Dr. Wayland would have been the first to declare, that with maturer years his views on many subjects were greatly modified. But the opinions expressed in the paragraphs just quoted he ever adhered to. He had no hesitation in exhibiting the plain teachings of a passage of Scripture, even when they seemed inconsistent with some other truth which he equally believed. Perhaps there could not be a more marked example of this freedom than was exhibited in a sermon preached in the University Chapel, on the college fast day, February, 1852, from the text, " But ye, beloved, building up yourselves on your most holy faith, and praying in the Holy Ghost, keep yourselves in the love of God." In this sermon he shows from the tenor of the command in the text, and from similar passages, that there was a liability that those now " in the love of God" should be found out of it. After a full exhibition of this truth he adds, —

"But I seem to hear many of you exclaim, What, then, is to become of the doctrine of the perseverance of the saints? What does Christ mean when he says, 'My sheep hear my voice, and I know them, and they follow me, and I give unto them eternal life, and they shall never perish, neither shall any pluck them out of my hand. My Father, who gave them me, is greater than all, and none is able to pluck them out of my Father's hand.' You will say to me, What are we to do with such passages? I ask, Are they found in the word of God? Undoubtedly. Then believe them implicitly. They are the words of unchangeable, eternal truth. Heaven and earth shall pass away, but not one word God has ever spoken shall pass away. But are not the other passages which I quoted also found in the word of God? Undoubtedly. And are not they also to be implicitly believed? Are we not with equal authority called upon to believe them both?

"But you will say, How are these to be reconciled? I might say, I do not know; but is this any reason why you should refuse to believe what God has revealed? Dare I, on this ground, refuse to set before you any portion of his holy oracles? Whatever systems, and the makers of systems, and the believers in the makers of systems may say, I must set before you the truth as I find it. Again, I may say, Though I cannot explain this mystery, yet I think I may promise to explain it as soon as you will explain to me how the infinite and the finite unite in any case of human action, or how the sovereignty of God is theoretically reconciled with the free agency and accountability of man. These doctrines all belong to the same class, and to finite minds, like ours, they are hidden in impenetrable obscurity."

The Bibliotheca Sacra for April, 1861, contained an article by the venerable and learned Rev. Dr. Withington, in which a reply is offered to these questions: 1. Why am I a Christian? 2. Why am I a Calvinist? 3. Why am I a moderate Calvinist? Under the last head he says, —

"But you may ask, What is moderate Calvinism? Now, moderate Calvinism consists not in denying any one of the great doctrines, but in mixing these with other truths,

equally obvious and equally important. A moderate
Calvinist knows the magnitude of these speculations,
and the weakness of our moral powers, and therefore he
does not make all the deductions from such high declara-
tions which a rigid logic would seem to demand. . . .
God is sovereign, man is free. God sees no contingency,
man meets scarcely anything else. Now, I must mingle
these truths just as they are mingled in the Bible, and I
have no right to make the one weaker than the other. I
must leave the compound with all its perplexities and
divine contradictions."

Upon reading this article, Dr. Wayland wrote to Dr.
Withington, July 9, 1861, —

"I have lately read your confession of faith in the Bibliotheca Sacra. It is rare (I do not know when it has occurred before) that I have seen my own opinions on these
subjects so clearly expressed. As you say, I can discover
no point of what I suppose to be Calvinism which is not
abundantly taught by Paul. And yet I am a moderate
Calvinist. The sharp angles of Calvinism, which needed
to be filed and hammered out in order to make a system,
I desire to hold no opinion about. It seems to me that
the fault of all theological systems arises from logical
sequences drawn from some revealed truth. Now, for this
kind of logic I have no sort of respect. Human ideas are
the proper materials for the processes of logic. A human
idea I can comprehend. I can know all about it, and
therefore it is a legitimate subject for my limited powers.
I know what is meant by a triangle. I can know all
about it. I can therefore reason about it with confidence
in my conclusions. The ideas of revelation are not human,
but divine ideas, the conceptions of the infinite God. It
seems to me that they are not proper subjects for human
logic, and therefore, by applying reasoning to them, we
are led into absurdity. Take the two opposite ideas, the
free agency of man and the sovereignty of God; how
many men have logically reasoned themselves into absurdity on one or the other of these subjects! Now, when
we take acknowledged truth, and, upon either side, reason
ourselves into absurdity, it is evident to me that we have
passed the bounds set for human reason. I do not know
whether I make myself intelligible, but I have done the
best I could in such weather as this.

" Now, it seems to me, that the points in which uch persons as you and I differ from the out-and-out Calvinists, are precisely those in which they have gone beyond he revealed truth, and inferred from it, logically perhaps, conclusions where we dare not conclude. I stand to whatever God has said ; what men infer from it is merely human, and weighs with me just nothing. As a Christian, I think I can, in my poor way, defend what God has said ; what man has inferred from it, man may defend if he can ; I am not responsible.

" Do not feel obliged to answer this letter, unless it is, in all respects, convenient. I wanted to tell you how much I was pleased with your paper, and I will add, how much I am interested in all you have written."

And now the period of preparation is ended, and the work of life is begun.

On the day preceding his ordination, Mrs. Judson had embarked at Rangoon for Calcutta on her way to America. The Burman mission, reënforced, a year or two previously, by the arrival of Wheelock and Colman, had been bereaved by the death of the one and the rapidly declining health of the other. Dr. Judson, who four years earlier had heard the first acknowledgment of an eternal God from the lips of a Burman, was laboring alone at Rangoon. The missionary enterprise was regarded by men at large with coldness or with contempt, and even by the disciples of Christ, with that lethargic interest which wrung from Dr. Judson the cry, " O that all the members of the Baptist Convention could live at Rangoon one month ! Will the Christian world ever awake? Will means ever be used adequate to the necessities of the heathen world? O Lord, send help ! Our waiting eyes are unto thee." * The Triennial Convention was becom-

---

* During ten months, from July, 1820, to April, 1821, the missionary contributions to the American Baptist Board of Foreign Missions, as acknowledged in the Magazine (exclusive of income from investments), were $4383. A few years later, a committee appointed " on the means of reviving the missionary spirit among

ing entangled in the hopeless embarrassments of Columbian College. George D. Boardman was just entering on his last year at Waterville College, which had been established the year previous.

Newton Theological Institution did not exist even in the hopes or the imagination of Deacon Farwell or of Mr. Cobb ; and Brown University seemed, to the anxious friends of evangelical piety, tending towards the course of its older sister at Cambridge.

Jonathan Going was preaching in Worcester, and the Home Mission Society was unknown ; but John Leland and other apostolic men had gone forth into the Genesee country and into Virginia, gathering in the lost sheep of the house of Israel. A year or two previous Leland had written, " I have travelled distances sufficient nearly to go around the globe three times ; I have preached not far from eight thousand sermons ; I have baptized one thousand two hundred and seventy-eight." The Massachusetts Baptist Missionary Society was sending its laborers into Maine and Vermont, New York and Pennsylvania. There was no " Massachusetts State Convention " for the aid of feeble churches, but every Saturday afternoon Mr. Ensign Lincoln left his bookstore in Cornhill, entered his chaise and drove to Canton or Hingham to nourish some infant church, or to strengthen the things that were ready to die.

Throughout Massachusetts, Unitarianism held predominant influence. While Harvard University imbued the best intellect and the highest culture of the state with animosity to evangelical piety, the decision of Chief Justice

the Baptist denomination in New England," estimated that if the executive seat of the Board was located in Boston, and if public confidence was restored, " we believe that $600 could be collected from the three Baptist churches in Boston; $200 from Salem; $100 from Cambridgeport; and $50 each from Charlestown, Reading, Haverhill, Methuen, Roxbury, Beverly, Danvers, Middleboro', Pawtucket, and Providence, besides $100 at least from the Worcester and from the Old Colony Associations."

Parker threw all church property into the hands of the *society*, to the annihilation of the rights of the spiritual body, leaving many of the Orthodox churches houseless.

In the metropolis of New England these tendencies were intensified. In a city of from forty to forty-five thousand inhabitants, only two Congregational pulpits, the Park Street and Old South, uttered the doctrines of the Reformation. Dr. Baldwin was preaching in the Second Baptist Church, and Dr. Sharp, then in the prime of his powers, at Charles Street. There were also three Episcopal and two Methodist churches. But the wealth, the social influence, the cultured intellect, and the political power of the city were found each Sabbath in Brattle Street, where the echoes of Buckminister and Everett seemed to linger, and where now was heard the scholarly Palfrey, or they were gathered to listen to Dr. Frothingham in Chauncy Place, or to Dr. Lowell at the West Church, or joined in reciting the ritual of King's Chapel, or yielded themselves to the spell of Channing's glowing eloquence and generous sentiments.

Only a few plain people found their way down to hear the awkward young stranger, just settled at the North End. No crowd thronged the long plank walk that led from the street back to the old and unattractive wooden meeting-house, nor did any benches obstruct the aisles, as Mr. Winslow, the sexton, with the dignity of a beadle, gravely preceded the minister, and ushered him into the desk. Nor was the new minister a man calculated speedily to draw a crowded house, and impart popularity to a waning interest. His manner in the pulpit was unattractive; he was tall, lean, angular, ungraceful, spoke with but little action, rarely withdrawing his hands from his pockets save to turn a leaf, his eye seldom meeting the sympathetic eye of the auditor. To those who conversed with him, he appeared abstracted and embarrassed. The work of composition was laborious, and, with his habits of study, consumed so much time as to leave him little leisure to win, by personal intercourse, the affections of the people. They, perhaps, compared him unfavorably with one of his predecessors, who sometimes wrote his afternoon sermon during the intermission on Sunday noon, and naturally could afford to be at ease, and to give much time to social demands.

The minority were determined to make up in activity and persistence what they lacked in numbers. Anonymous letters had been written to a former pastor, of unusually sensitive spirit, with much success. He had taken them into the pulpit and read them in public, showing to the writers how deeply their shots had taken effect. Similar letters now began to reach Mr. Wayland, ridiculing his awkwardness, and enlarging on every fault he had, and on many that he had not. Meanwhile, Rev. Mr. E., the choice of the minority, had been settled in an adjoining town; and his partial friends, refusing to sit under the preaching of Mr. Wayland, would toil out three or four miles to hear their favorite, and then would come into the evening meeting and narrate how they had been blessed, and how glad that good man was to see them, and how he hoped they would come again.

They were anxious, too, that Mr. E. should preach in the pulpit of the First Church, on an exchange with the pastor. But against this the leading members of the church, especially the pastor's official advisers, the deacons, protested. To allow him in the pulpit would encourage the disaffected, and would result in unsettling Mr. Wayland.

It was well for the young pastor that he had not only learned meekness of the Lord Jesus, but had gained worldly wisdom, and knowledge of human nature, under the sage Dr. Nott. Mr. Wayland, from the beginning, steadily refused to be informed who in the congregation were friendly to him, and who were unfriendly. He would not have any obstacle put in the way of his treating all with perfect and impartial friendliness. The anonymous letters, as fast as received, were spread before the Lord, in his closet, and then put in the fire. They were never spoken of, save as in after months the writers came to him, and, with tears of shame and sorrow, confessed their authorship, and begged forgiveness.

The course of the disaffected members in leaving their own church for another, was regarded by many as a violation of the covenant, and was animadverted on in church meeting. It was urged that the offending members should be subjected to discipline. This suggestion the pastor utterly opposed. He was not at all surprised that they did not like his preaching. He was sure he did not like it himself; and he regarded it as their duty to go where they found themselves most edified. As the distance to their favorite sanctuary was considerable, and as many of them were poor, he thought that the church ought to supply them with carriages; and he offered to unite in subscribing to procure them. There was no further complaint on that ground, and the practice ceased.

As for the brother's preaching in the pulpit, the pastor, for the only time in all his ministry, set himself in absolute opposition to the deacons and to all his counsellors. If his relation to the church was of so precarious a tenure as to be affected by the fact of Mr. E.'s preaching in his pulpit, the sooner it was terminated the better. Mr. E. was invited to preach. For some reason he preferred to preach at the Wednesday evening service. Notice was given alike from the pulpit and in the daily papers; the service was removed to the upper part of the meeting-house; the evening came; the pastor occupied the desk with him, and shared in the services. But the people did not come; the audience was small; and the dreaded minister, who depended for his inspiration upon a crowded and sympathizing audience, was greatly straitened. Nothing more was said on the subject, nor was any desire expressed for a repetition of the act of courtesy.

One young man, a member of the church, came to see the pastor, and frankly said to him, "I don't know how it is, but I am not interested in your preaching. I have no doubt it is deep, but I don't understand it, and I do not feel edified by it." Mr. Wayland said to him, "My dear brother, you have done right in coming to me; you have acted a Christian part. I feel that it is my duty to preach the gospel. I studied medicine, and began to practise; but God said to me, 'Wayland, you must preach the gospel.' I came here because God seemed to call me here. But I do not blame you for not liking my preaching, or for not being edified by it. I hope you will go where you find yourself most blessed. I shall not be offended. Go to hear Dr. Baldwin, or brother Sharp; they are both good men." By this time both the pastor and the dissatisfied brother were in tears. The latter henceforth found Mr. Wayland the clearest and most edifying preacher he had ever heard.

In time the pastor learned that one of the minority, an honest and worthy tradesman, was embarrassed in business. He called to see him. The brother opened his heart and his business, and said, "I could go on if it were not for what I owe Mr. John B. Jones" (a wealthy merchant, afterwards of the firm of Jones, Lows, and Ball). Mr. Wayland at once called to see Mr. Jones, and asked him to accommodate the person in question with more time. Mr. Jones readily promised to let him have all the time he wished, and to sell him more goods if he desired. He was saved from failure by this timely interposition, and became a prosperous and benevolent man of business.

Thus by personal kindness, by a regard to the precept,

"Cherish the hearts that hate thee," by obedience to the diviner wisdom of the Sermon on the Mount, and of the twelfth chapter of Romans, he gained the affections of all.* Meanwhile he was growing in confidence and ease of address, alike in public and in private. As he became better acquainted with his people, his sermons naturally were more in sympathy with their circumstances of estate and feeling. In his week-day evening lecture, he adopted a freer and unwritten style of address, and found it in time the pleasantest service of the week. And the evident sincerity of all his words, his avoidance of formal and empty utterances, his deep but unparaded piety, his conscientiousness, his elevated manhood, — all these could not but be seen and felt. The few who would not be won over, went elsewhere, and those who remained, as well as those who were added, found themselves undergoing a process of education, and learned to follow with delight and with profit his consecutive trains of thought, his clear processes of reasoning, his close analysis, his profound meaning, and intense spirituality. "They became Waylandites; not because of any peculiar doctrine taught by him," † but because of the influence which his modes of thought exerted in moulding their mental and spiritual character.

Rev. Dr. Sharp to Rev. F. Wayland, Sr.: —

"My dear and respected Brother: I often reflect with much pleasure on the interview I recently enjoyed with you in Boston. The interesting event which brought you here awakened sympathies which I still love to cherish.

"Your worthy son came here under very peculiar cir-

---

* Rev. Rufus Anderson, D. D., says, "A characteristic remark of his in the first year of our acquaintance became afterwards one of my governing maxims. I was expressing a determination to cut loose from the acquaintance of some one who had disobliged me, when he sharply responded, 'Anderson, never make an enemy!'"

† Rev. Dr. Pattison's Discourse.

cumstances: a previous attachment to another minister, and a little self-will withal, occasioned a larger minority in the church than was agreeable. But I believe they were in such a situation that they would not have been entirely united on any man. I have never had any conversation with any of the minority except one, and when I saw him he expressed much satisfaction with the preaching of his pastor. I believe that is the case with some others. My own opinion has always been, that if he stays with them seven years, they will like him seven times better than they do now.

" It is very much the case at the present day, and perhaps it always has been, that the generality of people are more pleased with sound than sense. Your son has a very respectable share of the latter, and I trust he will have sufficient of the former to please his people. Alas! what false estimates men make of real worth! I remember my old minister in England once inquired of a plain, simple countryman, how his minister got along. ' O,' said he, ' he improves wonderfully; he speaks louder and louder.' "

Mr. Wayland to a younger brother, who was employed as a clerk: —

" I fear lest you should think I neglect you, which I certainly would not do. I feel the deepest concern for your welfare, temporal and eternal, and I assure you I would do every thing to promote it. Nothing would so much delight me as to hear of your success in business, and especially of your soul's prosperity. But I have been very much hurried since I have been here, and have had time scarcely to write to anybody. You people who have so much leisure time, who have only to sell your goods and buy others, and post your accounts, can form but little idea of the toils, the labors, and the anxieties of a man who has every week to make a fresh mental exertion, which must be brought before the public. Especially is this labor oppressive in the case of a minister who enters a new situation. He has friends to make, acquaintances to form, difficulties to surmount, which men in private situations know nothing of. I hope, my brother, you continue in the practice of virtue and rectitude. Beware of your companions. Beware of the first approaches to temptation. Let your eye, ' e'en fixed on vacant space, beam keen with honor.' Lay down for yourself the loftiest principles of mercantile integrity, even those prescribed in the word of God, and resolve never to swerve from them. No matter how frequent the opportunities, no matter how urgent the temptation, be always yourself. And in disposing of goods act on the same principles. Do recollect how base it is, for the sake of a sixpence, to defile your mouth with a lie. Do recollect how awful it is, to gain the favor of an employer, by forfeiting the favor of the infinite Jehovah. I know there are little-minded men who have always at hand a set of cool arguments, by which they endeavor to justify iniquitous dealing. If they charge a man who is ignorant of an article twice as much as it is worth, they cover it by saying, they did not oblige him to take it. If they sell a man an article not worth carrying home, they will tell you that every man must look out for himself; and a thousand such falsehoods. How despicable is all this trumpery! How weak, as well as how wicked! O, how sublimely does the maxim of our Savior tower above all this! — ' As ye would that men should do unto you, do ye even so unto them.' My brother, if you wish to sleep soundly at night, if you wish to enjoy a high reputation, if you wish to please your God, make this your motto. Do you say that this will not allow you to get rich? I do not believe it. I believe honesty will at last be found the best policy. But if not, if you cannot grow rich thus, what then? Who cares? Who would barter away his character for gold? If he did, O, how unspeakably contemptible would be his exchange! I should esteem it a high honor to have it said of any of my relations, He was poor because he could not honestly become rich. And above all, what shall a man gain if he acquire the whole world and lose his own soul? O, how unspeakably awful would be the reflection in eternity, that a man had offended his Maker, had treasured up for himself wrath for the sake of riches, which take to themselves wings and fly away! "

To Mr. Alonzo Potter : —

"November 19, 1821.

" How wise and benevolent, my brother, are the arrangements of Providence! In nothing do I admire them more than in the facility with which the mind adapts itself to change of circumstances. I should have hardly believed it possible that I could so soon have entered into all the duties and feelings of my new calling. I feel now all my soul concentrated in the First Church, Boston. It is to me a little world. I scarcely care about anybody else's folks or anybody else's world. I scarcely care about influence, or popularity, or anything out of it. If I can only see them rise steadily in the tone of their piety, and bring religion more thoroughly out into all their conduct, so that their light may shine, so that they may be as the mountains of Zion where the Lord commanded his blessing, I want nothing more. My salary is, so long as I am unmarried, abundant. It is paid punctually as the town clock, every month. The people are becoming united, if I am not much misinformed. The attention on Sabbath is uniformly good; and I believe that they are not very much elated with the idea of anybody else going into the pulpit. I ought to be thankful to God. I hope that I am. Three have joined the church since I came. Several will, I think, shortly. The congregation is somewhat increased, and I think in some instances a decided moral effect has been produced. It is certainly a cause for great gratitude. I would not change my people for any people in Boston. I have but very little visiting and tea-drinking to do. I know I have more time to read than most ministers in the place. I can, if in good health, write my two sermons without difficulty. My health is generally good. If a man has a grateful heart, what more can he want? My deacons and their families would do anything for me.

" I wish, my dear Potter, that you were settled here. But I suppose it will never be. Do you ever go to Troy? If you can find out anything about my brother J., do let me know of it. My heart is bound up in that fellow. When you can without inconvenience, just look upon him."

To the same : —

" December 3, 1821.

" . . . From lively to severe. — I rejoice, my brother, that you contemplate so soon taking upon you your vows. You will never repent of it. Should Providence open to

you a way of usefulness where you are, I have not a word
to say. Do what seems best, what seems most for the
interest of the church; do as you think you will be most
useful. But, allow me to say, Providence has gifted you
with talents for public life, a head to plan and a hand to
execute, which in such a situation would be lost. You
ought, *me judice*, to be in the ministry. Would God that
you were here! About your health I do not think that
you need to be concerned. I am — I say it deliberately —
in better health than when in S. I have better spirits.
I walk every morning an hour before breakfast, and
unless some bad weather or a cold interrupts, have
clear mental vision generally. I have almost every
week written two sermons. I have not studied much, it
is true. I have, however, done something, and hope to
do more. I really think that you would enjoy better
health in the ministry than you do at present. If you
will come and live under my eye, I will warrant you."

To his sister, Mrs. S.: —

"O, my dear sister, I wish you were here. I wish you
were my hearer. You cannot tell how much I want two
such hearers as you and Mr. S. It would be worth half
my salary. I have no one on whose judgment I can
so safely rely; and then I dare not ask my people freely or
frequently, for fear of appearing vain to them, or really
becoming vain. My society is rather prospering, I hope.
They pay good attention to preaching — very rarely get
asleep. I do not know that I have seen one asleep for
some months; and they very rarely look at the clock when I
preach longer. The most pious and intelligent are my
best friends, and, I believe, think themselves profited by
what they hear. There have been a few instances of
awakening. One young woman — I mention it as a somewhat singular case — was awakened a few weeks since
by a sermon from the text, "Let us go on unto perfection."
It was remarkable that a sermon addressed wholly to
Christians should be the means of awakening a sinner.
It is somewhat laborious to preach twice a week; but,
alas! it is much more difficult to practise habitually the
principles of the gospel than to exhibit them. That is,
after all, the most important part of a minister's duty — to

live near to God, and keep eternity always in view. O
that I had the spirit of Henry Martyn, of Samuel Pearce,
and of the apostle Paul! But God can give it to me.
Sometimes I think I feel a little of it; but a deceitful heart
soon leads me astray. Let us, my dear, go on unto perfection. . . . "

To his brother : —

" . . . I want very much to hear about you and your
business. I hope you are pleased with your situation.
The happiness of situation does not depend upon external circumstances. I could be, I think, perfectly suited
in your place, if it seemed my duty to occupy it. If
it kept me busy, employment would be occupation;
if it gave me leisure, I would occupy the time in profitable reading. A man with a well-furnished mind never
need be unhappy, unless from moral causes. There is a
pleasure in acquiring knowledge. There is a pleasure in
reflecting upon what we have learned. There is a pleasure in communicating it to others. If you want to be a
man of influence in society, you must have information,
real, solid information. You must be able to hold a conversation with men of sense. You must know something
more than the contents of novels. A man never grew
strong, by feeding on whipped syllabub. He must read
works of sense, and he must reflect on what he reads. He
must learn to have a respect for himself. He must feel
that he is able to form an opinion for himself, and that
that opinion is not worthless. Look about you, my brother, and survey the men — especially the young men — by
whom you are surrounded. They can dress. They can
discuss the merits of an oyster supper, or a glass of beer,
or the looks of an actor or an actress, or the dress of
the guests at a party, or perhaps the price of a piece of
goods. If they are not cut off, they float useless through
the world; they lie down forgotten in the grave, having
produced no more impression on the world than the horses
they have driven, and they rise in another world to everlasting contempt.

> ' Ye dreamers of gay dreams,
> How will ye weather an eternal night
> When such expedients fail?'

And are you contented to be such a man? Are you willing to grovel with such grub-worms? O, flee from them. *Look upward.* Think that you are designed for eternity. Cast behind your back all their allurements, and be yourself. Assert the dignity of man. Improve yourself, and place your name among those of the men who have not lived in vain."

To Mr. Potter, upon receiving news of his engagement to the accomplished daughter of Dr. Nott : —

"May 24, 1822.

"My dear Potter: You can conceive better than I can describe the emotions with which I read your most welcome letter. Though the intelligence it contained was scarcely unexpected, yet it sent a thrill through me, which vibrated in every fibre. It affected so nearly two persons for whom I felt so deep an interest, that, stoic as I am, I could not sit still for half an hour. When the rush of feelings had begun to subside, so that the several individual ones were taking each its proper locality, the first which I recognized was most fervent and hearty thanks to the Giver of every good and perfect gift, for the blessing which he had conferred upon you. To him I rendered my feeble tribute of gratitude, that two persons whom I most tenderly loved were made happy for life. You are worthy of each other. In the affections of such a woman, my brother, you have a treasure for which you might well barter away the mines of Golconda or the honors of an empire. I bless God she is yours. But recollect, my brother, *Deus hæc otia fecit.* I need not add, *Sit ille tibi semper Deus.* May this renewed expression of his kind providence bind you still more strongly to love and serve him. O, let not the richest gifts of his providence withdraw you from the Giver. The longer we live, the more shall we be convinced that nothing will make this life happy or death triumphant, but a consciousness that we are living for God. This alone bestows any dignity on the little transitory scene which surrounds us, and makes every action big with consequences of infinite happiness.

"There are a thousand reasons why I want you here.

I always knew your intellectual endowments were more numerous and more excellent than mine. But I thought that in those points where I was best endowed, we had great community of views and of feelings. You are one of the few men whom I have found in my pilgrimage, whom, in all the length and breadth of the term, I could call my friend. It would have been delightful to have had you here: it would have been improving to me. But what is the use of talking? Providence has otherwise ordered it, and he knows exactly what is best. There I leave it. May God grant you grace to be a faithful and successful minister of the New Testament. I long to hear you preach."

To his mother : —

" . . . And first, as my father wrote respecting my health, I assure you my health is better than it was last summer at this time. It has been in general better during the year than during the last year I was at Schenectady; and I also assure you that, should my health require it, I will visit you this summer. I hardly think that otherwise it will be my duty. Still I do not speak with certainty. A very little may alter my determination. You think I am a bad economist. I in part plead guilty. I, however, am improving. Certainly you could desire no stronger proof of the power of my economical principles than their keeping me here when I wish so much to see you. To-day we received one — a very hopeful convert — by baptism. Last communion we received two. I hope on the next we shall receive three or four more. These are, it is true, few; but we have reason to be thankful for any, and I think we have reason to bless God that those who have been received have been so promising. I could not wish them different in character or appearance. May the Lord multiply the number abundantly. We have some who are still inquiring. I hope the spiritual state of the churches is improving. There is an increase of a spirit of prayer and brotherly love.

" As it regards myself, I daily see myself more as an unprofitable and useless servant. If I am at all favored by the assistance of the Holy Spirit, I grow careless, and have to measure back my way with sorrow and mourn-

ing. If I am favored with success in my literary pursuits
or ministerial labors, I grow proud ; and then I am obliged
to be brought down by disappointment and trial. Still I
hope the year I have spent here has not been wholly useless to me in a religious view. I hope I have seen more
of my own heart, and something more of the excellency
of holiness, and have had some desires awakened, to be
made perfect in the image of God. . . ."

   To Mr. Potter : —
                                          "December 15, 1822.

   " You may possibly have heard that I came within a
fraction of seeing Schenectady, the canal, and the hill
folks this autumn. I started on horseback, — by the way,
I am quite an accomplished equestrian, — and had pro-
gressed more than half way, when a variety of unforeseen
accidents — among them the laming of a horse (a valuable and a borrowed one) — made it necessary that I should
return. I had with me, also, a companion whose health
I thought might require it. I shall not attempt to inform you — for it would be a failure — how I revelled
in all the luxury of anticipation, in the thought of
spending twenty-four hours on the hill. I saw Maria,*
and talked with her fifty times. I sat up with Dr. N. in
his study until midnight, was rallied out of countenance
by Mrs. Nott, held a meeting of the triumvirate with you
and Joe, and talked and reasoned until my brain was
almost crazed. O, it was nothing but imagination pic-
turing forth the forms of things unknown, which may
never have a ' local habitation and a name.' I am still
two hundred miles from most that I love. The Connecticut rolls its dark wave, and the Green Mountains lift
their cloud-capped summits between us. Still we are
watched over by the same Providence ; and, what is more
than all, hope we are interested in the same blood of the
atonement. We may all taste of the same promise, and
anticipate the hour when, freed from these bodies of sin
and death, we shall stand around the throne triumphant.
I want very much to see the doctor. There are fifty
questions which I desire to ask him. There are as many

* The daughter of Dr. Nott, afterwards the wife of Bishop Potter.

measures with reference to the church in these parts, and to the Baptist church in particular, that I want to propose. His last letter was worth its weight thrice told in the gold of Ophir. If it were not for plaguing him, I would write often. I received a letter from John a few days since. He is going to enter the ministry. I have good reason to hope that he is a thorough Christian. I know not where to send him to prepare for college."

CHAPTER VI.

DR. BALDWIN. — DR. SHARP. — DEACON SNOW. — DEACON
LORING. — MR. WINSLOW. — CORRESPONDENCE. — HIS
MENTAL HABITS. — CHARACTER OF HIS PREACHING.

DR. WAYLAND always remembered with affection and gratitude the brethren of the laity, and of the ministry with whom he was associated in Boston. He was a young man, a stranger, unaccustomed to the usages of New England, and not greatly versed in intercourse with the world. He always attributed much of whatever success attended him to the sagacious common sense and the judicious counsel of these brethren, and ascribed much of his happiness to their kind and fraternal coöperation.

First among these it is proper to name the honored Thomas Baldwin. Of him Dr. Wayland writes, —

" He was a man of strong native mind, and great sweetness of disposition, and, at the time of which I speak, was, I think, more universally respected than any other clergyman in the city. His appearance was remarkably venerable, his address courteous and winning; he was the oldest minister in town, and every clergyman, of whatever denomination, took pleasure in doing him reverence. The precise place which he occupied in Boston I have never seen filled since his decease. He was always known as a wise counsellor, perfectly honest, always inclining to peace, yet never sacrificing principle."

One circumstance brought Mr. Wayland into peculiarly intimate relations to this excellent man and to his family. Upon reaching Boston at the time of his settlement, it was a matter of no little difficulty to select a boarding-place. To reside with one of the majority would throw obstacles in the way of conciliating those who had hitherto opposed him, and of uniting the church, while to be so closely associated with those who avowedly disliked him and his preaching would be sufficiently unpleasant to all parties. Nor could the fact that he was a young man and unmarried be ignored in his selection of a home. The neutral ground of Dr. Baldwin's house presented a sanctuary from the strife of tongues; and this was his abode for the first eighteen months of his residence in Boston. In the obituary notice of Dr. B. in the Baptist Magazine, February, 1826, Mr. Wayland says, —

" The writer of this feeble attempt to delineate his character was for four years in the habit of seeing him daily, on terms of the most familiar intercourse, and for nearly half of this time was a member of his family, and remarked his deportment under every variety of circumstances; and he can truly say, that he does not recollect ever to have seen him betray a temper inconsistent with the Christian profession."

Of another associate in the ministry, Dr. Wayland says, —

" Dr. Sharp was several years younger. He was of natural strong sense, great simplicity of character, uncompromising love of truth, and unspotted purity of life. To both of these brethren I was greatly indebted for their uniform kindness and courtesy. Never do I remember that a harsh word, or even an unkind look, marred the pleasure of our intercourse. We made it an object to unite our churches in the bonds of Christian affection. For this purpose we had, as far as possible, services together, which were always well attended. Dr. Baldwin was in the habit of being present at my preparatory lecture, and I reciprocated the courtesy. On one Sabbath evening in each month we had a union lecture for the three churches, held with each in succession, each minister preaching in his own meeting-house. Our monthly concerts were, in like manner, united; and it was the duty of the pastor, in whose church the meeting was held, to prepare the intelligence which had been received for the last month from all portions of the missionary world."

Of his lay brethren he writes, —

" I was forewarned by various persons that the church was governed by the deacons, and that their government partook of the nature of a despotism. My friends sincerely pitied me when they learned that I was to be subjected to the rule of men who had controlled the church for twenty years. Never were predictions more falsified. I do not remember that an unkind word ever passed the lips of either of us in conversation with each other. They were honest but thoroughly kind advisers, and were throughout my most intimate and esteemed friends.

" Deacon Prince Snow, a grocer at the North End, was a man of incorruptible integrity, sound-minded and consistent piety, and strong attachment to the doctrines of the gospel. The First Baptist Church was the object of his unwavering and enthusiastic love. Whatever affected its prosperity touched him to the quick. By its prosperity, I do not mean fine buildings or worldly adornments, but its growth in grace, and its faultless adherence to the teachings of the Lord Jesus. During a year of extraordinary and sudden pressure, Deacon Snow was unable to meet his payments. He took counsel with his friends, and, in accordance with their advice, made an assignment of all his property to his creditors. The church at once took action in the premises, and appointed a committee to examine his affairs. After a thorough examination, they reported that there had been nothing unfavorable to his Christian character. In the end, his property paid every creditor, principal and interest, with all the expenses of the assignment, and left a thousand dollars remaining. This is the only failure of this kind that I have ever known.

" Deacon James Loring was quite a remarkable man. He was a printer and bookseller. A close observer of human nature, of great accuracy of judgment, possessing entire control of his feelings, and when once his mind was made up, of unwavering consistency of purpose, he was one to whom, in time of doubt and trial, men instinctively turned. He seemed made for a deacon. Always in his place at all the meetings, his voice was heard on every proper occasion in prayer and conference. He did not speak because it was expected, and evening after evening repeat the same address, but he always presented some one of the distinguishing doctrines of the New Testament, and brought it home to his present hearers. He never spoke unless he had something to say, and he always stopped when he had done. His piety, whether in prosperity or in adversity, was ever the same. He habitually referred everything to God, and seemed pleased with all that occurred, because God had ordered it.

" His reading was extensive, his mind clear and discriminating. He frequently wrote for the public papers, and always with ability. As is often the case with printers, though unacquainted with the rules of grammar, he wrote with entire grammatical accuracy. In company with the late Mr. Weston, he established the Christian Watchman. Whenever the deacons of the churches of different denominations met, to consider modes of action which required the union of all the churches, I doubt if any among them had more acknowledged weight of character than Deacon Loring. He was, from the first to the last, my firmly attached friend.

" No one who remembers the period of my pastorate, can fail to recognize the executive officer of the society, Mr. Samuel Winslow, the sexton. Under his direction everything about the meeting-house, both without and within, was kept in perfect order. He was a man of small stature, but of unusual physical strength and of lion-hearted courage. I was told that on one occasion, when a young man behaved improperly in front of the meeting-house, and replied insolently to a very proper reproof, Mr. W. seized him at once and threw him over the fence. All who remember those times will see him in their mind's eye, with his hair combed back and formed into a long queue, reverently preceding the minister from the meeting-house door to the pulpit stairs. He watched over me with paternal care. When he saw me do anything which would cause unkind remark, he would tell me of it, as he would one of his children. I always thanked him, and, what was better, always took his advice.* He was

---

* Dr. Wayland has related that Mr. Winslow once said to him with considerable concern, " I saw that yesterday, in attending a funeral, you wore white stockings. That would excite remark, and be thought very unbecoming." Mr. Wayland thanked him sin-

a very pious man, the finest model of a thorough Puritan that I have ever seen. 'Peace to the memory of a man of worth.'"

Dr. Wayland sometimes mentioned a fact in the life of Mr. Winslow which he regarded as entitling him to enduring praise. We believe it happened before Mr. Wayland's settlement. The custom had long prevailed of offering intoxicating liquors to the attendants at funerals. Though the gross indecorum of the usage had often made itself painfully obvious, yet no one ventured to disturb it, lest, to omit the customary provision should seem a mark of meanness or (more dreaded still) of poverty. It was reserved for Mr. Winslow to declare, that he would not take charge of a funeral where liquor was used; and in no long time his example and his firm adherence to his resolve put an end to the usage.

Dr. Wayland writes further, —

"Several of the ladies connected with the church were women of eminent piety, full of mercy and good fruits, who aided me more than I can describe, in cultivating the graces of the younger members of the church, and training them for usefulness. Soon after my settle-

---

cerely, and carefully heeded his suggestion. This incident illustrates his readiness to receive advice from whatever quarter. While he trusted greatly to his own meditations for principles and general laws, yet in practical matters he courted advice. One of his friends has said, "I was always afraid to advise him, for he was disposed to give more weight to my advice than I thought it was entitled to."

This incident also illustrates his desire to avoid any needless appearance of eccentricity. In matters of duty, of righteousness, he was willing to stand absolutely alone; but as to the minor details of life, of dress and deportment, he sometimes said, "I have important things which I wish to accomplish, and I will not needlessly do anything that will distract the attention of people to minor matters, or that will create opposition to me, or shake their confidence in my judgment. There is scarcely any reputation which is so valuable to a man, nor any that may so easily be lost, as a reputation for good sense."

ment a female prayer-meeting was established, which
met every week, on Wednesday afternoon, at the house
of Deacon Snow. This meeting was continued without
interruption as long as I remained. They prayed much
for the church and for their pastor, and I believe that their
prayers were heard. In another respect their aid was invaluable. Whenever I knew of a female in the congregation who was at all anxious about her soul's salvation, I
took pains to have her acquainted with some one of these
ladies. They called to see her, and invited her to the
prayer-meeting, gave her suitable advice, prayed for her,
and used all means in their power to lead her to Christ.
I also introduced to them every recent convert whom they
had not before known. Ladies who joined the church,
or proposed to join, from abroad, were introduced to them
in like manner. Thus they all had the blessing of entering at once upon an acquaintance with warm-hearted
Christians. In this manner the plants of grace, nurtured
in a congenial soil, grew rapidly. When there was only
the *appearance*, not the *reality*, of religion, it was also
discovered before the person applied for admission to the
church. All this was a great assistance in my ministry.

"When I became pastor, I found the church meetings
by no means occasions of edification. A few brethren
seemed resolutely to have determined that there should be
no division in the church, and seemed to foresee inevitable
division if their views did not prevail on every occasion.
They could see no hope of harmony unless the large
majority quietly submitted to their dictation. The idea
that they themselves were to submit to reason and to the
will of others, or that others had rights as well as themselves, never had penetrated their minds. They consumed
the time with loud and angry speeches and reiterated forebodings of impending discord, unless the whole church
adopted their sentiments. It was at last determined by
the brethren, in no case to answer them, but to proceed
quietly and resolutely with the business. This put an end
to altercation, and before long an unkind word was never
heard in our meetings. As soon as our little matters of
business were disposed of, the remaining time was spent
in devotion, and the church meetings became our pleasantest gatherings.

"A word in respect to the discipline of the church. I

have referred to the failure of Deacon Snow. The integrity of no man in Boston was more unsullied. As, however, failures frequently brought great dishonor on the cause of Christ, the church felt itself bound to make no exceptions, and to ascertain by their own committee that failure was attended with no loss of moral character.

"I will relate another case of discipline, because it shows the manner in which this duty was then performed. Information was privately communicated to me that a prominent member of the church was in the habit of playing cards, perhaps of gambling, accompanied not unfrequently by partial intoxication. I at once requested the person to call on me, and told him what I had heard. At length he confessed that the accusation was true. I then endeavored to set before him the nature of his sin, and urged him to repentance and reformation. I saw him several times, and at last he seemed penitent, and promised reformation. I then considered the matter settled. But he soon returned to these habits, and the matter, becoming public, was brought before the church. He was suspended from communion, and a committee appointed to bring him, if possible, to repentance. The committee at length reported favorably upon his case; he appeared penitent, and it was voted that he should be restored, after a solemn admonition in presence of the church. This admonition was administered by the pastor, and I think that those are now living who remember it as an occasion of great solemnity. But all our labor proved vain. He relapsed, was excluded, was afterwards seized with a sudden attack while at the gambling table, and in a few moments was in eternity. He was lost; but we had done our duty, and had faithfully labored to reclaim him, and his conduct was no reproach to the church."

Outside of his own denomination Mr. Wayland's personal relations were limited. With Mr. Dwight, of the Park Street Church, whose mental powers he highly appreciated, he enjoyed a pleasant acquaintance. His most intimate friend was Mr. Wisner. They were nearly of the same age, had many interests, associations, and acquaintances in common, and were united by the memory of reciprocal kind offices. They walked together almost daily, comparing their readings and reflections, and debating every topic that interested the mind of either. In the summer of 1822 Mr. Wisner took a journey to recruit his health, and during his absence Mr. Wayland writes to him as follows: —

" I rejoice that your journey, up to the last advices, was so prosperous. My joy was somewhat damped by your remarking, that ' you were as well as when you left.' I had hoped you would have been much better. However, I think that your principal benefit will be derived from the use of Saratoga water. I hope you will try it faithfully and thoroughly, and according to the most approved directions. I am of opinion that your stomach received a shock at Princeton from which it has never entirely recovered. Give it a chance at the Springs. Do not come away until you have made a persevering trial. Let your other arrangements bend to that. Do not get *ennui*. If I were you, I would take an hour or two a day to write sermons, or study, or read, or something which would keep my 'thinkers' agoing; that will conduce much to drive away the blues. Your people are all well. . . .

"You *must* see Dr. Nott. I want to hear his opinon of the state of things here. Do go and see him. Spend a day at least with him. Professor Stuart has gone to the Springs, and will probably be there about as soon as this arrives. . . .

" I watched your carriage as it gradually diminished along the Mill Dam until it was no longer visible. Then, pursuing my journey alone, I thought over the state of the case. I followed you from town to town, put up with you, &c., and carried you even to Johnstown. . . . I should have ' admired ' to be one of your party. But *fata non sinunt*. I am more and more convinced of the propriety of staying. God is pleased, in great mercy, to grant me my health more perfectly than when you were here. My appetite is better, and I can study a little more, though but little. For the last day or two the weather has been refreshing and cool. For the last three Sabbaths I have preached wholly without help. So, you see, I am not on the sick list. I have had some lonely walks, some groans, some hours of dejection; but I have got along better than

I expected. I make out to do something at home, and take now and then a turn in Poplar Street. The air is clear there, you know, and the prospect refreshing. I want very much to see you and shake your honest hand. But it is good for a man to hope and patiently wait. You will have nothing to do at the Springs but write letters. Write frequently, and tell me where to direct to you. I shall inform you immediately if anything should occur of interest. May God, my dear brother, grant you speedily your health, and return you to your labors. May he load you with the blessings of his goodness, and make you useful in your journey; and may we in future preach more faithfully, labor more incessantly, and live more holily than heretofore."

"My dear Wisner: I received your letter this moment, and, although it is Saturday, delay not to answer it. I had been waiting for some time for its reception. Inquiry after inquiry had been made about the Bishop of the Old South, and all were fruitless. 'Who had received a letter?' was the prevailing question. No one but Mr. W., was the answer, and that was dated three weeks ago. Mr. F. came home, but had seen nothing of you. Young A. returned, but no news about you. F. received a letter from my father, but you had not arrived, and he had almost given up the hope of seeing you. More than once I went to Deacon Loring's to know if there was anything for me at the post office. But no response arrived. Yesterday I saw a gentleman who was not personally acquainted with you, who said he had seen you at Saratoga. This removed my apprehensions (which, to tell you the truth, were somewhat serious), that some providential dispensation had arrested your progress. I thank you for your letter. It appears to have been written without any shade of 'blue,' which is rather more than I can say of the other. I am very glad that you are so well. I am confident that the Congress water will be your grand panacea. Do not, by fatiguing travelling, wear yourself down. Travel moderately and rest sufficiently. Everything here goes on as well as usual. P. and B. supplied for you last Sabbath. No deaths have occurred in your parish, that I have heard of. The city is healthy. The prayer-meeting goes on well. I attended it this week. . . . I am rejoiced you saw my brother. I hope you talked freely with him. I have an idea that God will call him to the ministry. If so, he must be educated. This will call me to more sharpness of calculation. I shall rejoice if it be so. . . .

"Do see Dr. N., and talk freely with him about the state of things here. Just ask him whether there could be any harm in my preaching two or three months on the character and offices of Christ, and endeavoring to go as fully as possible into the subject. . . . Say to Maria I love her very much, but I cannot tell how long it will continue, if she does not answer my letter. Remember me to all the professors. I groan in spirit to be with you, but, as I said before, *fata non sinunt*. I am perfectly convinced that it is better I did not go. In this you will doubtless agree when we see each other. I hate to say good by. May God bless you."

From the members of the Unitarian denomination, as he became known to them, he received many acts of friendship and of social courtesy. Indeed, the relations of the Baptists alike to the Orthodox and to the Unitarian churches, were not at this time unfriendly. The Orthodox were disposed to make common cause with the Baptists in behalf of Calvinism, while the Unitarians, never having been of kin to the Baptists, had no ground for a family estrangement, and were disposed to unite with them in opposing the demands of the "standing order." The fact that the Baptist church in Worcester was organized in Dr. Bancroft's meeting-house, was representative of the courtesy which softened the relations of the two denominations.

But it is probable that for the first two years of his residence in the city, there were very few outside his own denomination who knew of his existence. He owed nothing to factitious circumstances, nothing to wealthy patrons or influential friends, or to a commanding position accidentally attained. "I never had any one to boost me," he has sometimes said. It was just as well; nay, better. It was a part of the lesson of life. He learned to leave nothing to good fortune or to friends, but to do his own work each day. "All that I have ever accomplished was by day's works;" and sometimes he would hold up his hands, and tell a story of a minister who said that he owed everything to his two deacons, the two deacons being his right hand and his left. There was nothing that he had of mental acquirement, or of elevated thought, or of position, or influence, or reputation, but had been fairly won. And yet it was touching to hear him sometimes say to young men, "You do not have to struggle up from the very bottom, as I have done."

Of his personal appearance at this time, Rev. Dr. Stow speaks thus graphically : —

"I first saw him at the house of Dr. Baldwin, who then lived at the corner of Hanover and Portland Streets. This was in June, 1822. A little while before the hour for tea, Mrs. Baldwin said, 'Mr. Wayland, pastor of the First Church, is boarding with us, and I shall soon introduce you to him. We think him an extraordinary young man, who will yet make his mark.' 'Yes,' remarked Dr. B., 'he promises to be one of our ablest thinkers and writers.' His personal appearance, as he came down from his study, is very fresh in my recollection. With a large frame, he was very spare in flesh. His face was thin, and the arch of his eyebrows was unlike anything I had ever seen. His complexion was pale, bordering on sallow, and I thought he might be a victim of incipient consumption. When standing, his posture was considerably stooping, and his movements seemed to me not the most graceful; indeed, they were rather angular. The splendid portrait in Rhode Island Hall is the fulfilment of no prophecy of his earlier years. His physical proportions and attitudes, as I first saw him, are truly represented in the portrait possessed by the First Baptist Church in this city."

Mrs. Wisner writes, —

"He was tall and extremely thin; very pale, and often sallow. Indeed he was much of the time far from well, though always active and laborious. I think that he had very little of what is called manner, in the delivery of his sermons, and that you get a better idea of his preaching from reading his sermons than is commonly the case with regard to ministers who have made so deep an impression upon the public. His meeting-house was old, unattractive, and situated in what had become a very undesirable street; and he felt its disadvantages sometimes morbidly. He suffered very much from depression of spirits for a year or two after he was settled. He thought he had not the sympathies of the mass of his people. But there were always some very warm friends among them, ready to sustain and encourage him in his labors. His deacons were devotedly attached to him, and as the young men became more acquainted with him, they rallied around him, and he felt stronger in his position.

"His habits of study, I should say, were very methodical and severe. He took his daily walk of seven miles, with my husband, for more than four years. The two were perfectly united in their aims. No denominational differences seemed to interpose any barrier as regarded the great object of their lives — the promotion of the kingdom of the Redeemer. He was very often at our house, and there he was always perfectly unconstrained."

He was then, as always, very fond of the interchange of thought and feeling. Dr. Stow writes, —

"He once called upon me apparently for no other purpose than to discuss the question, 'When is a thing proved?' I do not remember the answer I gave; but it differed from his, which he gave in form, and then illustrated in various ways: 'A thing is proved, when it must be so, or some law of nature is violated.'"

Rev. S. Peck, D. D., writes, —

"The invitation had not been unanimous. Deacons Loring and Snow and a few of the more intelligent of the church and society had strenuously advocated his election; but a large minority had been merely acquiescent, and some had persistently opposed. It was under this conscious embarrassment that he entered upon his work; and the results, in the edification of his people, as also in the extension of his pastoral influence, were gained through much toil and by slow degrees. He was not a popular preacher in the ordinary sense of the term. There were some, however, who justly estimated him from the first; and their numbers steadily, if slowly, increased.

" His character, as I then regarded it, and as I now recall its unstudied manifestations, was already substantially cast, and it retained its features in later years. There was, perhaps, at that time more of unguarded frankness in the expression of his thoughts and impulses, boldness verging at times on heedlessness; but the elemental texture was essentially one and the same as in after days. He was frank, manly, independent; ready to hear, kind, earnest, forceful in the advocacy of his views, but gracefully deferring at times to the preferences of his older associates; mirthful in seasons of relaxation, and even hilarious; not, however, to unseemly excess; exhaustless in humor and repartee; full of Napoleon and Dr. Nott; holding his own with his early friend Mr. Wisner; fraternal and respectful towards Mr. Sharp and the venerable Dr. Baldwin; while with all alike maintaining the bearing of a recognized equal."

In the delineations given by those who knew him during this portion of his life, the reader has probably remarked an apparent discrepancy. To one person he seems " mirthful, even hilarious; " to another, " depressed, even morbidly." And a similar seeming discrepancy may be observed in his familiar letters. If we may venture an opinion upon the point, we apprehend that by nature his tendency was to depression; that from youth he was more easily dispirited by reproof and failure, than cheered by approval and success. His ideals were high, and his inability to attain to them oppressed him. Mr. Joel Nott, who was very intimate with him while he was a tutor, remarks, " His chief characteristic was extreme nervous diffidence. This was so great and so painful, that it required much persuasion to induce him to preach."

When surrounded by confidential friends, when his mind was inspired by its own successful exertions, and when he was not weighed down with peculiar anxieties and responsibilities, he sometimes threw off this depression. He had entered on the ministry with exalted — perhaps it would not be too much to say with romantic — expectation of immediate success; he anticipated a church growing daily in piety, and unhesitatingly conforming their lives to the precepts which he exhibited; a congregation becoming convinced by his arguments, and giving serious heed to eternal realities. Presently he awoke to the discovery that they were but human, and, worst of all, that he was human also; his labors appeared far less successful than he had anticipated; his utterances perpetually failed to fulfil his ideals; he was suffering from dyspepsia; and he was lonely, for his heart had found no resting-place.

Then, presently, he would experience the soothing influence of the wise Dr. Baldwin's counsels, or he would forget his cares in the amicable conflict of thought with Mr. Wisner, or some new and unexpected evidence of good accomplished would lift the cloud, and he was cheerful, even joyous.

Sometimes humor and sadness combined in the same utterance; as when, in allusion to his failure to attract a large audience, he expressed the opinion that if his head were examined by the phrenologists, then rising into some note, he would be found to possess, in an unusual degree, " the organ of scatteration."

We imagine, however, that the apparent inconsistency between his varying exhibitions of feeling will most readily be reconciled by the reader who shall look into his own nature and remark the twofold personality, and the under-current of seriousness lying beneath the sparkling ripple. It ought to be added, that his feelings, of whatever description, never had the effect to paralyze his energies, nor to interrupt his labors. Rather, it may be presumed that he labored with all the more dogged and conscientious perseverance as circumstances seemed discouraging.

With later years, with a fully matured Christian character, with the abiding trust, the sense of divine nearness, " the faith that looks through death," he was enabled to acquiesce, even to rejoice, in all the dealings of God; and there was less often to be remarked an extreme depression, or a consequent reaction.

Of his sermons he writes to Mr. Potter, May 11, 1822: —

" About sermonizing: I generally select a subject first. Frequently my text modifies it. I like best taking a subject and going through with it. If you hit upon a good one it will last for several weeks; for instance, growth in grace — the nature of it, exhortations to it, means for accomplishing it, &c., have furnished me with several sermons. When I get a subject I do not know how I make a sermon out of it; I think and think, and somehow or other it comes, sometimes head first, sometimes tail first, sometimes *disjecta membra*, neither head nor tail. All I know is, I get it somehow or other."

His sermons at this period are far from perfect. The introduction is often too long, and the temptation to introduce a great deal of matter in the early part of the discourse is not resisted. The application, on the other hand, is too brief and too general. The truth is often left in such a form that it might be received by the candid inquirer, but might without difficulty be resisted or evaded by the careless, self-willed, or hardened. The style exhibits sometimes too much of rhetoric, of ambition, and the less common and intelligible word is sometimes used where the simpler would be as forcible and more clear. There is not in them that profound Christian experience which came with the matured Christian life. He preached about the text, where, at a later day, he preached the text. Thus, from the text " The wages of sin is death," he enumerates the points of analogy between natural and spiritual death. At a later day he would have exhibited spiritual death and its connection with sin, and the fact that the one is the exact desert and the in-

separable consequent of the other. Under the text " I
communed with my own heart," he speaks generally of
the reasons for self-examination ; at a later day he would
have delineated a Christian communing with his soul, so
that every hearer, at least every regenerate hearer, would
have known by his feelings, rather than by formal argument, what self-communion is, how great its excellences,
how desirable the exercise. These defects flowed, in some
degree, from the fact stated in his letter just quoted, that
he selected the subject first, and then the text. Later in
life the text was selected, the subject was deduced from it,
and the sermon became " the text expanded."

We allude to these early characteristics with great
diffidence, and yet with the feeling that he would have
said the same thing. If the style of those days appears
wanting in simplicity, it is because we apply to it the
standard of that absolute transparency, that perfect directness, which characterized his later years. If the
application appears inadequate, it is because he taught
us to press home the truth with such directness that every
hearer should say, " It is I." He had not then renounced
the love of fame ; he had not learned to eschew fine
writing in the pulpit ; he had not gained that victory over
himself, over the love of reputation, position, or emolument, which he subsequently regarded as vastly higher
than all intellectual achievements, and as the only way to
a happy and successful ministry. He had not yet gained
that complete freedom from all fear of man which was
so prominent a feature of his later teachings. Yet his
preaching was always the result of thought, and study,
and prayer. It was always clear, always based upon
Scripture, always solemn and impressive. His hearers
grew in depth of spirituality, and the greater advances
they made in piety the more highly did they prize his
words. And with every sermon, then, as during the
remainder of his life, the faults were fewer and the excellences more marked.

CHAPTER VII.

BAPTIST MAGAZINE. — MORAL DIGNITY OF THE MISSION-
ARY ENTERPRISE. — DUTIES OF AN AMERICAN CITI-
ZEN. — VARIOUS PUBLIC LABORS. — BAPTIST TRIENNIAL
CONVENTION.

IN 1823 Mr. Wayland became associated with Dr. Baldwin in editing the American Baptist Magazine, a pe-
riodical (issued at that time every two months) designed
to communicate intelligence of the domestic and foreign
missions of the denomination, to elevate the standard of
mental discipline and religious attainment on the part of
the ministry, and to further every agency for the evangelization of the world. Upon the death of his venerable
associate, he became the chief editor.

In examining volume iv. (new series), for 1823-4, we find
that in addition to collecting and digesting the extracted
and communicated matter, he wrote about twenty articles,
three of which are made up of material previously used
in the pulpit, the remainder being reviews of recent sermons or volumes, and suggestions looking to the improved
efficiency and increased piety of the denomination. In
one series of articles he considers the Associations, their
objects, their defects, and the means by which they might
be rendered more eminently useful. He entertained the
project — in common probably with many others — of
making the Association the basis of a representative union,
a federation of all the Baptist body. "The Associations
in one state could easily send delegates to a state Convention. This would embody all the information and con-
centrate the energies of a state. These state Conventions

could send delegates to a general convention, and thus the
whole denomination might be brought into concentrated
and united action." " The superintendence of the missionary and educational concerns of our denomination
would be one important business of the general convention." " Another of their duties might be, by delegates,
to correspond with our brethren in England, and thus the
Baptists on both sides of the Atlantic would be united in
a solid phalanx."

A comparison of these early imaginings with his later
utterances, will not only illustrate the constant progress
of his mind, and his readiness to receive new views, but
will exhibit the characteristic frankness with which he
utters those most difficult of all words, " I was mistaken."
In 1855 he writes, —

" To the independence of the churches the vast majority
of our brethren have adhered with a most commendable
and consistent tenacity. Notwithstanding this, attempts
have been made among us to establish some kind of formal representation. When state conventions were first
proposed, it was by many believed (and of them I freely
confess to have been one) that through them we might
establish a general Baptist organization. I now rejoice
exceedingly that the whole plan failed through the sturdy
common sense of the majority of our brethren. We look
back at the present day with astonishment that such an
idea was ever entertained." *

It will be remembered that Mrs. Judson spent a portion of the years 1822-3 in America. She was often in
Boston, where Mr. Wayland formed her acquaintance, and
in common with all who knew her, he was profoundly
impressed by her character. Thirty years afterwards, in
the Memoir of Dr. Judson, he wrote, —

" It was my good fortune to become intimately acquainted with Mrs. Judson during her visit to the United
States. I do not remember to have ever met a more

---

* Notes on the Principles and Practices of the Baptist churches.

remarkable woman. To great clearness of intellect, large powers of comprehension, and intuitive female sagacity, ripened by the necessity of independent action, she added that heroic disinterestedness which naturally loses all consciousness of self in the prosecution of an object. These elements, however, were all held in reserve, and were hidden from public view by a veil of unusual feminine delicacy. To an ordinary observer she would have appeared simply a self-possessed, well-bred, and very intelligent gentlewoman. A more intimate acquaintance would soon discover her to be a person of profound religious feeling, which was ever manifesting itself in efforts to impress upon others the importance of personal piety. The resources of her nature were never unfolded until some occasion which demanded delicate tact, unflinching courage, and a power of resolute endurance, even unto death. When I saw her, her complexion bore that sallow hue which commonly follows residence in the East Indies. Her countenance at first seemed, when in repose, deficient in expression. As she found herself among friends who were interested in the Burman mission, her reserve melted away, her eye kindled, and she was everywhere acknowledged to be one of the most fascinating of women."

Elsewhere in the Memoir he says, —

"As early as the visit of Mrs. Judson to this country, Dr. Judson's demand for books [to aid in his work of translating the Bible] was large; and it was all for the best, for the foundation books. I well remember the pleasure with which I stripped my library of what I considered some of its choicest treasures to supply a part of his most urgent necessities."

To his mother he writes, —

"December 1, 1822.

"She is a most interesting woman. She equals Mrs. Stoddard in many respects, and in some is her superior. She is a woman of ardent piety and a most thorough missionary spirit. I hope you will pray that her health may be restored, and that she may be long spared to be a blessing to the East."

On the 23d of June, 1823, Mr. Wayland writes to Mrs.

O'Brien, a sister of Deacon Lincoln, long known and honored as the treasurer of the Missionary Convention, —

" The vision has passed. The star has set. Many a wave rolls its blue waters and tosses its white foam between Mrs. J. and all in America whom she loves, and by whom she has been so dearly beloved. Ay, and long will those waves roll before she and they exchange the welcoming of lip, or feel the reciprocated throb of affection. Ere that meeting takes place, in all probability, the heavens will be wrapped together as a scroll, and the elements will melt with fervent heat; or, at any rate, heaven and earth, elements and systems, will have faded away to our vision, and nought of this world will be recollected by us with pleasure but the moments of devotion or the acts of piety.

" The vessel, which was expected to sail on the 25th, was hurried away on the 22d, Sabbath. It was evening. The missionaries, Mr. and Mrs. Wade and Mrs. J., had not expected to sail until the next morning. After afternoon service, Mrs. J. stopped a few moments at your brother's, and went to take tea at Mr. Sharp's. A messenger met her to say that the vessel would sail in twenty minutes. We hurried to the wharf. The notice was so sudden that but few persons were there — not more than fifty or sixty; most of them her particular friends. The Edward Newton lay off in the stream near the head of India Wharf. Her topsails were spread, and the flag of the United States, the signal for sailing, floated from her mizzen. A gentle breeze from the west barely kept it from hanging lifelessly. Everything was ready. The men were already heaving the anchor. After prayer by Dr. Baldwin, Mrs. J., Mr. and Mrs. Wade, Mr. and Mrs. Sharp, Mrs. C., Deacon Lincoln, and myself stepped into the boat and rowed to the ship. A few notes from the shore just fell upon the ear as we passed the wharf; but each stroke of the oars rendered them less and less distinct, until they completely died away. On the passage to the ship, Mrs. J. and your brother were much affected; but an effort to recover themselves succeeded, and though but few remarks were made, they were made pleasantly. Your brother drew as near to himself as possible a box of dollars, and scrawled a note to Mr. Judson. We were soon on board, and after a few moments all but the deacon and I returned to the shore. We intended to go out as far as the light-house. The anchor was weighed, and the vessel under easy sail in about twenty minutes after we got on board. In about half an hour or less a fine breeze sprang up, and she walked majestically through the water. The wind freshened so that we were obliged to leave them. We were on deck when we received the information that we must go. We ran down to the cabin, said farewell, and in a moment were on deck, in our boat, cast off, and the water rolled between us. Long shall I see the pallid countenance, the raven hair, and the heaven-directed eye of the missionary as she stood near the centre of the cabin when we ran down and said, 'We must go.' It was the last time I shall ever see her. May God bless her ! "

During the summer of 1823 his health had become impaired, and he travelled on horseback to Saratoga Springs, occupying four or five weeks in the trip. His father most kindly supplied the pulpit, and performed all the pastoral labors during the absence of the son.

Upon his return to Boston Mr. Wayland writes, —

"September 7.

" My dear Mother, Sisters, and Brothers : I wrote to you from Windsor. I left that place on Wednesday morning, and arrived at Hanover at eleven o'clock. I rode alone ; the rest of the cavalcade travelled homewards. Riding alone was not so lonesome as I had anticipated, and when external circumstances were pleasant, it was agreeable.

" I might, however, begin further back, and say that the morning after we left the Springs, we arrived at Glen's Falls. This is a romantic spot, and if I had had any idea of its being so well worth seeing, I would have taken you to see it. It is a beautiful waterfall. Here we parted. Some of us went to Lake George. This is not equal to the descriptions given of it. We were all disappointed. Saturday night and Sunday we spent at Granville. I preached once for Mr. Williams. He is a lovely, humble-minded, Christian man. There has been a considerable revival there, and the assembly was solemn.

" To pass over two days in which nothing material

occurred, I was at Dartmouth College at Commencement. The performances were respectable. On Thursday afternoon I rode to Oxford, on the Connecticut River, where I was most kindly entertained by Mr. Wheeler, the father of one of my friends. On Friday I rode to Littleton, forty miles north, and on Saturday to the White Hills. This is a most dreary spot, and I spent in it the most desolate Sabbath I ever passed. Monday took me to Eaton, and Tuesday to Center Harbor, on Winnipiseogee Lake. Wednesday to Concord, Thursday to Haverhill, and Friday evening to Boston. I travelled pretty rapidly, and improved materially by it. I am now, I think, in better health than I have enjoyed for several months. I am of the opinion that riding does me more good than the Springs.

"Arriving home, I find all things well. Our dear father has been constant in labors, but has enjoyed uninterrupted health. By his kindness and piety he has much endeared himself to the people. They all regret to part with him, and hope that he will soon renew his visit, and bring his wife with him.

"And thus, my dear friends, a kind Providence has carried me safely through all the vicissitudes of travelling, has taken me to you, and has returned me again to my people in improved health, and has suffered no evil to come nigh my path. To the God of all my mercies would I return my most heartfelt acknowledgments. O, how great is the goodness of God to our family! We all enjoy health. Many of us he has, we hope, awakened by his grace, and he is still following us with his loving-kindness and tender mercy. O that his goodness may lead us to repentance. This very day has laid me under fresh obligations to thankfulness. To-day my brother John professed religion, and united with my church. It was solemn and pleasant. O, let us praise God for his goodness."

After returning from his journey to Saratoga, he commenced the habit of vigorous exercise, which he ever afterwards continued, and which added so greatly to his health, his enjoyment, his cheerfulness, and the tone of his mind. To his father he writes, November 10, apologizing for his delay, —

"I am not so punctual as I ought to be. I have been a good deal engaged since you left us. I have taken more sleep, and of course my days have been shorter. My letters used to be written during the hours which now find me asleep. This may furnish some excuse. My health has been better, through rich mercy, than for a year before. Soon after I came back, I took hold manfully of the saw and axe, and have sawed all Deacon Lincoln's wood. I presume I saw a cord every week. I exercise every day until I have produced, and continued for half an hour, a full and free perspiration. It has done me more good than my journey did. That depression of spirits which so much disturbed me has, through a kind Providence, gone — O that it might be forever ! I am able to go through my duties with much greater pleasure to myself, and I would fain hope to the better improvement of my people. My congregation increases gradually. There is an increase of union. Some are inquiring. Mrs. —— has, I trust, obtained pardon, as well as Mrs. ——, although they neither of them believe it themselves."

To his sister, November 10 : —

"I very frequently think of you and your quiet fireside, and wish I were one of your number. My health is much improved since I was with you in the summer. I have recovered my usual flow of spirits. I have been enabled to put forth more energy, for the last three weeks, than at any time for a long while. I pray God that this additional talent may be devoted to his glory.

"And this, after all, my dear sister, is all that is worth living for. There is no such polar star in perplexity, no such solace in adversity, as a strong desire to live to the glory of God. This makes everything peaceful, everything happy.

"I preached yesterday on the means God uses to check the growth of indwelling sin in his people. The subject is interesting. It might, if carefully considered, lead to much knowledge of our own character. We might see what sins he had singled out, and bent the course of his providences to correct."

The daily papers of Saturday, October 25, 1823, contained a notice that the annual sermon before the Boston Baptist

Foreign Mission Society would be preached on Sabbath evening, the 26th, at the First Baptist Church, by Rev. F. Wayland, Jr. The evening came, rainy and chill. The audience, though the three churches united in the service, was small. The text was, " The field is the world ; " the subject, " The Moral Dignity of the Missionary Enterprise." The house was uncomfortable (the preacher wearing his great-coat throughout the service), and there was (if we are rightly informed) but little enthusiasm on the occasion. On Monday morning Mr. Wayland went to Mr. Wisner's, and threw himself on a sofa, in one of his most depressed moods, saying, " It was a complete failure. It fell perfectly dead." * It is not easy to know exactly what impression the sermon made upon the audience ; it is not easy, even for those who were present, to carry themselves back, and to separate their original and unbiassed judgment from the glow of admiration which subsequent events taught them to feel. It is quite certain that they had no conception that they were listening to a sermon which was to mark an era in the history of the missionary enterprise. But there were a very few persons (chiefly Deacon Loring and his son, who were united in business as printers) who insisted that the discourse must be published ; and, says the author, " I was brought, seemingly by accident, into a position in which I was obliged, really against my will, to publish it." It was issued. The first edition, which appeared in December, was almost immediately exhausted, and a second was issued in February. Soon this was exhausted, and another and cheaper edition was published ; which in turn was followed by others. It was adopted by the American Tract Society as one of their permanent series, and has had a place in several published volumes of sermons. In proportion to the population and the numbers then found in America, it is doubtful if its circu-

---

* But he gathered courage to preach it again at Salem, before the Bible Translation Society, a week later.

lation has been exceeded by any American sermon; and certainly no other has held its place so permanently. With the exception of the close of Webster's reply to Hayne, it may be questioned whether any passage in American literature has been more often quoted than the paragraphs which delineate the conquering march of the early church.

Among the Congregationalists of New England, the sermon was introduced by an article in the Recorder, which, while criticising the length of the introduction and the formality of the style, pays a most handsome tribute to the merits of the discourse, and extracts liberally from it. The Richmond Literary and Evangelical Magazine, edited by John H. Rice, D. D., said, " The purpose is nobly conceived and finely executed. A young writer, who, on a hackneyed subject, can produce such a discourse as this, deserves the attention of all who wish to see the standard of pulpit eloquence rise high in our country." It reached the colleges and seminaries of the country, and inflamed the minds of the young with a generous ardor in the missionary cause, as a copy, thumbed and scarcely hanging together, was tenderly passed from hand to hand.

The excellent and venerable Deacon Crane,* of Baltimore, says, " I carried a copy to the Old Dover Association, in Virginia; it was marked, I think, seventh edition. I read it to a few persons, one of whom was Dr. Jeter, now of Richmond. He became so excited by it that he got up and walked the floor, declaring that he could not sit still while listening to that sermon."

It found its way into the hands of readers who were little accustomed to regard with favor any utterance from evangelical pulpits, and in whose eyes the missionary scheme had seemed a needless and fantastic, though well-

* Since the above lines were written, we learn with profound grief of the removal of this venerated, blameless, and benevolent disciple of the Lord Jesus.

meant, extravagance, but who could not be insensible to the splendid conception of the discourse and its impassioned and sustained eloquence. To every candid mind it presented the hitherto despised enterprise in a light so new, so impressive, that it is not too much to say that it very sensibly abridged the number of persons disposed to regard the cause of missions with contempt.

In the course of a year or two it was reprinted in England, with a commendatory introduction by the eminent Dr. Wardlaw, of the Scotch church, and passed through several editions, receiving as hearty admiration abroad as it had done in America. The (British) Evangelical Magazine, July, 1825, says, "This splendid discourse is, beyond doubt, the effort of a highly accomplished mind. It is the burst of genius and of consecrated zeal. Seldom has it fallen to our lot to peruse a sermon in all respects so valuable. Well may America glory in the man who could rear such a monument."

It has been reported — we know not whether with any truth — that Robert Hall, having read it, and having learned that it was by a young man of twenty-seven, said, " The author of that sermon will be heard of again." A few years later the author received a copy translated into German. Of course its reception abroad did not diminish the estimate in which the discourse was held in the land of its nativity.

What was the state of his own mind while all this tide of approbation was flowing in upon him, is a question that will naturally occur to the reader. We have already quoted two of his letters written on the 10th of November, in which no allusion is made to the sermon. It is rarely mentioned in any of his letters. He writes to his father, —

" A second edition of the missionary sermon has been published. It seems to be popular, far beyond anything I had anticipated, and has obtained encomiums which, vain as I am, I can scarcely think it deserves. I hope it may do some good for the missionary cause."

He never seemed to regard the sermon as remarkable, and no one was more surprised at its reception. Deacon Moses Pond relates, " Not long after the sermon was printed, I was standing with one or two others on the plank walk in front of the church, talking of it very enthusiastically. Just then Mr. Wayland passed us. The walk was so narrow that he could not help hearing what we said. He checked us, saying, ' Now do not be talking any more about the sermon; let it go. If it does any good, let us thank God; but do not be talking as if some great or strange thing had been done.' " " The late Rev. Alfred Bennett, of precious memory, once expressed to Dr. Wayland his admiration of the sermon, and said that if he himself could give to the world such a production, he should feel that he had not lived in vain. Dr. Wayland smiled, and said, ' Well, brother Bennett, I suppose every man has one bright idea in his lifetime, and that probably was mine.' " * When one of his sons showed him a newspaper statement, to the effect that the sermon was written thirteen times, he said, " I wrote it just thirteen times — minus eleven; and I wrote two other sermons the same week."

Of course he did not mean to convey the idea that the sermon was the offspring of any sudden illumination, or that it did not cost time and labor. Then, as afterwards, nothing was done — nothing could be done — without a *plan*. After hearing, later in life, a discourse of much elegance of finish, yet without a carefully-digested train of thought, he said, " I could not have written that upon such a plan. The beams were not well laid." When a subject had " simmered in his mind" (to use a phrase he often borrowed from Sir Walter Scott) for days or weeks, until the train of thought was clear, the merely mechanical part was but the smallest portion of the labor.

And the Moral Dignity of the Missionary Enterprise,

* Dr. Stow's Reminiscences.

though consuming no great amount of time in its actual writing, had been the growth of years. Intellectually it was the result of the study and reading prosecuted during the four years of his tutorship at Union College, the study of Longinus and Campbell, of Johnson and Addison and Milton; the result of the instruction of Professor Stuart and of Dr. Nott; and, no doubt, Lake George and the Green Mountains, and the White Hills of New Hampshire, had left an impression which we may trace in the picture of the quiet beauty of a New England village, and in the description of " the autumnal tempest collecting between the hills, and as it advances, enveloping in misty obscurity village and hamlet, forest and meadow." Nor should we forget the humbler agency of the sawhorse, and the weekly conquered cord of Deacon Lincoln's wood ; for these remedies it was, which, in his own belief, drove away dyspepsia and depression, and quickened into action each bodily and mental energy.*

But it is from the heart that great thoughts come ; and the real sources of the missionary sermon were in the closet where Christian parents pleaded before God with strong crying and tears for their first born ; in the divine affection which filled his soul, when, unconscious of the act, he surrendered himself to Christ; in the admiring love for the missionary scheme inspired in him by the eloquence of Luther Rice ; in the weary walks to South Troy, as he sought to gain something which he might offer to the cause of the Redeemer ; in the religious fervor kindled anew by Asahel Nettleton ; in the stirring news from all parts of the mission field, which passed before his eyes as editor of the Magazine, and especially in the glowing letters by which Judson pleaded with Christendom in behalf of the millions of heathenism ; and in the

---

* He once told his sister-in-law, Mrs. O'Brien, that the plan of the sermon was thought out while sawing wood in Deacon Lincoln's cellar.

presence of that noblest of American women, the wife of Judson, whose tireless energy and feminine fascination, inspired by a holy cause and a divine love, had kindled in him a sympathetic fervor, and whose well-remembered face and "heaven-directed eye" lent inspiration as he wrote.

In 1825 Mr. Wayland writes to his brother-in-law Colonel Stone, then editor of the New York Commercial Advertiser, " I am ashamed to tell you that I expect shortly to publish another sermon. I do not see that I can avoid it." He explains that his congregation, not long before, had requested him to publish a sermon with which they were pleased. He declined. They had now made the same request in regard to the sermon under consideration. He adds, " It would create dissatisfaction, and look like disregard to their feelings, if I again refused. I must do it, and will do it as well as I can."

The reference in his letter just quoted is to " The Duties of an American Citizen," two discourses preached on Fast Day, April 7, 1825.

His reluctance to publish was no doubt unaffected, as it certainly was natural. To print a second sermon, when the first had achieved a success so unparalleled, raising the author, at the age of twenty-seven, to the front rank in his denomination and his country, was a hazardous experiment. It could scarcely surpass the former; and yet the inexorable demand of mankind is for advancement, and he who does not perpetually surpass his former self is condemned as having fallen off. We may well believe that a sincere desire to serve his country and mankind, coöperated with the expressed wishes of his congregation, in inducing him to incur this liability.

The previous half century had been crowded with events unparalleled in their importance — the American revolution; the overthrow of monarchy in France; the rise, the conquests, the fall, and the death of Napoleon; the assumptions of the Holy Alliance; the birth of the South American republics; the growth of popular intelligence; and the introduction of steam communication. Many of these had, as they transpired, kindled the imagination of his boyhood, or awakened the hopeful solicitude of his maturer judgment. He had seen and talked with the surviving actors in the scenes of our own struggle. Not many months before, he had seen a nation paying its grateful homage to the champion and protector of our infant independence — the immortal Lafayette. It was not in his nature, he did not believe it to lie within his duty, to ignore the majestic series of events so vitally affecting the interests of America, of mankind. "In the attempt," he says, "to enlighten you upon any of those great questions, in which the well-being of our own country, as well as of other countries, is interested, I seem to myself to be discharging a duty not improperly devolving upon a profession which is expected to watch with sedulous anxiety every change that can have a bearing upon the moral or religious interests of a community." While he never descended to the level of a partisan, and while he ever held to the judgment that "he who uses personalities in the pulpit ought never to enter it again," * he yet felt that men had a right, amid events of a world-wide significance, to expect from the minister of religion, instructions that should guide the course of the disciple of Christ. In the hour of our national agony, in May, 1861, he wrote to his son, a minister of the gospel, "Preach to the times; that is, as one 'knowing the times.' The minds of men are all on one subject, and that not a frivolous, but a grave one, and one that has a thousand connections with the government of God, the salvation of souls, and the encouragement to prayer. Start from any point in

---

* Ministry of the Gospel, p. 101.

the times, but let it ever lead you to the vital and most
solemn truths of revelation."

In the sermons just alluded to, he considers, 1. The
present intellectual and political condition of the nations
of Europe; 2. The relations which this country sustains
to those nations; and 3. The duties which devolve upon
us in consequence of these relations. Some of his utterances, like those of the older prophets, seemed addressed
not only to his own, but to other generations. The
attack upon civil and religious liberty, which we have
seen proceeding from among ourselves, was then anticipated from without; and the counsels of 1825 were equally
apposite to the crisis, when foes, deadlier and more dangerous than foreign despotism could have nurtured, arose
from within our own household.

"Then will America need the wealth of her merchants,
the prowess of her warriors, and the sagacity of her statesmen. Then, on the altars of our God, let each one devote
himself to the cause of the human race, and in the name
of the Lord of Hosts, go forth into the battle. If need be,
let our choicest blood flow freely, for life itself is valueless
when such interests are at stake. Then, when a world in
arms is assembling to the conflict, may this country be
found fighting in the vanguard for the liberties of man.
God himself hath summoned her to the contest, and she
may not shrink back. For this hour may he by his
grace prepare her."

With a similar illumination, and in words, that without
an alteration, might be applied to the armies which he
lived to see gathered in defence of liberty and law, he
says, —

"Should the time to try men's souls ever come again,
our reliance, under God, must be, as it was before, on the
character of our citizens. Our soldiers must be men
whose bosoms have swollen with the conscious dignity
of freemen, who, firmly trusting in a righteous God, can
look unmoved on the embattled legions leagued for purposes of wrong. When the means of education every-

where throughout the land shall be free as the air we breathe, — when every family shall have its Bible, and every person shall love to read it, — then, and not till then, shall we exert our proper influence in the cause of man ; then, and not till then, shall we be prepared to stand forth between the oppressor and the oppressed, and to say to the proud wave of domination, Thus far shalt thou come, and no farther."

The discourses were imbued with a love for freedom, the largest freedom of mind and soul, the liberty that he never ceased to claim as his own right and that of every being. "Better that the earth should revolve without an inhabitant," he once said, "than that it were peopled with a race of slaves." And the sermons glowed with the brightest hopes of human advancement. To think trustfully of the capacity and destiny of the human race, when informed by the gospel of Christ, he regarded as a duty enjoined in the precept, "Honor all men." Those who saw him welcome the stirring news of the European revolutions of 1848, or who heard or read his sermons suggested by those events, cannot forget the hopefulness with which he greeted those popular movements. Dr. Channing's memorable "always young for liberty, I trust," would have found an echo in him. It ought, however, to be remarked, that his hopes were not inspired merely, nor chiefly, by the overthrow of dynasties, or the change in forms of government, but by the enlargement of intelligence, the elevation of moral principles, and the increasing supremacy of the religion of Christ: his confidence was not in man as man, but in man as the abode of the divine Spirit by whom he has been redeemed and renewed.

It was not a little noteworthy, that of his two first published utterances, the one was an appeal for the triumph of religion, the other for the elevation of mankind. Piety and humanity, the love of God and the love of his brother, — it was these impulses which inspired his early energies, and which led him to exertions too arduous for the waning vigor of threescore and ten ; to these appeals he ceased to be sensible only when his latest pulsations were stilled.

The sermons maintained, and even enhanced, the reputation secured by that previously published. They proved that the latter had not been a happy accident, — " his one bright idea," — and that the period intervening since its publication had not been spent in an idle enjoyment of his first success, but in study, self-discipline, and thought, and in the steady growth of all his faculties. Although containing no paragraph so highly wrought as are passages in the missionary sermon, yet they excel it in calm dignity, in breadth of view, in sustained power.

The Boston Recorder, in a notice of the discourses, says, —

" The author of these sermons gained much celebrity by his first production. Few have made a better impression at their first appearance before the public. It has often been said, ' Mr. Wayland must not soon venture his reputation again.' But while the warmth of feeling and the glowing admiration, which his first effort excited, have scarcely begun to subside, he has ventured again ; and if I may judge from the effect on myself, I would say that these last sermons will not only sustain, they will elevate the former feeling. They have fewer faults and more excellences than the first. They evince a profounder intellect, a more classical taste, a richer fund of knowledge. They have finer strains of eloquence, and will be re-perused with deeper interest. There is a vigor of thought, a correctness of ratiocination, a manliness of sentiment, a unity of design, and a steadiness of aim which do equal credit to his industry and talent. The design of his [first] sermon was exceedingly happy. He has struck another popular string. Both are as original as they are felicitous. And I am greatly mistaken if the last do not enlarge the field of his fame."

The North American Review (October, 1825) devotes an article of nine pages to the sermons, awarding to them very high commendation, while taking exception to his remarks on the Romish church, as having been "more applicable three centuries ago than at the present time."

It is proper to add, that, for much valuable information contained in the notes appended to the sermons as published, Mr. Wayland was indebted to Colonel Stone, to whom he was through life united by acts of reciprocal kindness and literary aid.

The publication of the discourses last named, and of the missionary sermon, produced a change in the position of Mr. Wayland; it gained for him the ear of the public. Henceforth, to the end of life, whatever he uttered was sure of an audience, though of course not always of acquiescence, still less of applause. He had now a $\pi o \tilde{v} \sigma \tau \tilde{\omega}$; it was for the future to determine whether he should move the world. He also gained a confidence in himself, in his power to address and to move his fellow-men. And the success of his second publication was of peculiar value in freeing him from that nervous dread of his own former self, of the reputation gained by his maiden publication, which has crippled so many men whose entrance on life was most brilliant.

On the 27th of September, 1825, he delivered the annual address before the Porter Rhetorical Society, of Andover Seminary. The subject of the address was "The dependence of the eloquence of the pulpit upon a deep experience of personal religion."

The Christian Watchman, after a sketch of the train of thought, says, "We do not feel competent to present a correct analysis of this classical oration, which was listened to attentively by a delighted auditory; but we hope it may soon appear from the press." The discourse, with many excellences, partakes of a defect to which all of his more elaborate compositions were in that day liable; the introduction was laid out on a scale suited to the limits of a treatise rather than a discourse. No adequate space is left for considering the real subject under discussion. It was requested for publication, but was never printed.

During the week following the news of the death of the ex-presidents (July 4, 1826), Mr. Wayland preached a sermon appropriate to that event, which afterwards appeared in the volume of Discourses.

For the sake of unity we have thrown together our imperfect notices of some of his public addresses belonging to this period. It would require too much space to enumerate his discourses at ordinations, Associations, and other public religious assemblages.

In November, 1824, the Massachusetts Baptist Convention was formed in Boston, in the First Baptist Church. Mr. Wayland took an active part in its organization, and was appointed its first secretary.

The Newton Theological Institution had its origin in a meeting of ministers and laymen held in the vestry of his church, in May, 1825. He was deeply interested in the movement, was one of the corporate members of the board of trustees, and was the first secretary of the board.

Meanwhile the condition of the missionary enterprise among American Baptists had become such as to give rise to profound solicitude. The Convention, established in 1814 for the expressed and single purpose of " sending the glad tidings of salvation to the heathen, and to nations destitute of pure gospel light," had in 1817 voted " to institute a Classical and Theological Seminary." Such an institution was accordingly established in Philadelphia, and Rev. Dr. Stoughton, the corresponding secretary of the board, was placed at its head. "During the next three years the board turned its attention largely — some thought excessively — to departments for which provision had been made in the amended constitution. The project of founding an institution of learning was started and received with great favor, especially in the Middle and Southern States. . . . But many were rendered anxious by the question if it would be wise in a missionary organization to enter upon the undertaking. It was already

apparent in many minds that this superadded enterprise
was acquiring interest at the expense of the cause of
missions." *

At the next meeting, in 1820, it was voted to establish
a college at Washington, " not, however, without painful
misgivings, in the minds of many, as to results." "It
was feared the enterprise might overshadow the primary
object of the Convention, and divert funds which might
otherwise be available for missions."

In 1821, as we learn from the Magazine for July, the
board voted to loan ten thousand dollars from the mission
funds, to assist in the erection of the Columbian College.†
The next meeting (1823) was held in Washington. Dr.
Baldwin and Mr. Sharp attended, and Mr. Wayland, as
the younger minister, remained at home. Mr. Rice, the
agent of the Convention, reported that his time had been
much occupied by the concerns of the college. He mentions an arrangement, projected by the trustees of the college, that the president should be reëlected corresponding
secretary, and should be enabled to devote one day in
each week exclusively to the business of the Convention.
He states, also, that he (Mr. R.) has made such arrangements with the trustees, as to be able to serve the Convention as agent without charge. " The college, at each
succeeding meeting," says the Magazine, July, 1826, " demanded more attention from the Convention, and the missions received less. The missionary cause lost its place
in the hearts of Christians, until the souls of the heathen
were almost forgotten; and every paper and every report
seemed exclusively devoted to the praises and the suc-
cesses of the Columbian College."

---

* Dr. Stow's " Early History," read at the Jubilee, 1864, from
which, also, further extracts are made bearing on the same topic.

† We learn from Dr. Stow, that this application of the mission
funds created such profound dissatisfaction in New England,
that the money was refunded.

We find among the papers of Dr. Wayland a report, in his handwriting, bearing no date, but exhibiting internal evidence of having been presented in 1823 or 1824. It commences as follows: "The committee to whom was referred the consideration of the question, what means could be adopted to revive the spirit of missionary exertion in the Baptist denomination in New England, beg leave to offer the following remarks, as the result of some deliberation." To what body the report was submitted we are not aware. The report proposes to consider the following topics: 1. The past and present state of missionary exertion among us; 2. If there be a decline, what are the reasons for it? 3. Suggestions as to the means of reviving the missionary spirit, and a view of the difficulties which present themselves; 4. Considerations urging us to the course suggested. The writer delineates the ardor which at one time pervaded the denomination in behalf of foreign missions. Every heart, every purse, was open. In one year, the sum raised was within a few thousand dollars of that received by the American Board. "In the spring of 1818, we actually had twenty-three thousand dollars in the treasury." But now "the mission treasury has been exhausted, no one can tell us how. The receipts have been from year to year diminishing." "Scarcely any missionaries have, of late, been sent out, nor does any one feel the importance of sending them." "The feeling that all is at a stand is becoming universal." "There seems no centre of action." "We hear of the president of Columbian College, we hear of the college, we hear of the debts and embarrassments of the agent, but we hear nothing of missions." "The palsying effects of the system we have felt in our own minds. We cannot feel the interest we wish in our missions. Other missions are going forward, ours are declining." The causes of this decline are stated: 1. The novelty of the undertaking has worn off; 2. The location of the executive department of the missions at Washington — a location for which but one reason could be assigned, that it was the seat of the college and the residence of the corresponding secretary; 3. The want of a suitable person as corresponding secretary. " To the gentleman holding this office is freely accorded the praise of eloquence, learning, literature, unbounded hospitality, and affable good will. Waiving the question, Has he the qualifications needful for his office? it must be asked, Can he discharge the duties, while at the head of the college, and while presiding over several departments of instruction?" "Experience leaves no doubt on this point." " We believe him to be a pious and amiable man, and a man of talent; but we do still consider that both he and his advisers have greatly erred in the conduct of our missionary concerns." 4. The injudicious conduct of the agent. The very valuable qualities of Mr. Rice are cordially recited; " and we do not hesitate to attribute the great success of our first missionary attempts to his high personal and moral endowments." But he has been the means of diverting the public mind from the missionary cause to the concerns of the college, and he has thrown the financial affairs of the Convention into inextricable confusion.

How shall the missionary spirit be revived? We should supply the place of novelty by continually presenting interesting missionary matter before the public, and by continually augmenting our missionary stations. The seat of the executive must be changed. A secretary must be appointed who should give his whole time to the mission, or, at any rate, make that his first business. There must be a competent advising committee. "And finally, each one of us must feel that the missionary cause takes rank of almost everything else."

Upon the obstacles to such a course, and upon the arguments for its adoption as presented in the report, we will not dwell.

The next meeting of the Convention was held in 1826. Of this meeting Dr. Stow favors us with this reminiscence : —

" I met Dr. Wayland at the triennial meeting of the Convention in New York, in the spring of 1826. His sermon on the Missionary Enterprise had placed him in the front rank of the denomination, and secured him a respect and deference accorded to no other man of his years. The session was prolonged beyond precedent, for the subjects under consideration were of unusual importance. In the various discussions, some of which were profoundly exciting, Mr. Wayland earnestly participated, and by his cool, conclusive reasonings, contributed largely to the wise results which were ultimately reached with unexpected unanimity. In fact he did more than any other man to secure the separation of the college from the Convention. Many of his arguments bore heavily upon the policy of the Rev. Luther Rice ; but they were expressed without any bitterness, and gave no personal offence. At the close of one day's warm debate, in which Mr. Wayland had spoken at length in favor of the separation of Columbian College from the Convention as a missionary body, Mr. Rice said to me, ' That Francis Wayland has a very fair mind. He knocked away my foundations, but he did it like a Christian man, and I cannot be offended with him.' "

At this meeting, in addition to the separation of Columbian College from the Convention, the executive seat was removed to Boston, the office of agent was abolished, and Rev. Dr. Bolles, of Salem, was elected corresponding secretary. All the changes made were in precisely the direction indicated by the report from which we have quoted. Of the beneficent results which attended the reorganization thus effected ; of the renewed confidence, the revived missionary zeal ; of the benign impulse that went forth to every remote station ; of the years that followed, full of prosperous labor for the conversion of the world, — it would be needless here to speak.

CHAPTER VIII.

SPIRIT OF HIS MINISTRY. — HIS LIFE, INWARD AND OUT-
WARD. — HIS MARRIAGE. — EMBARRASSMENTS. — CLOSE
OF HIS PASTORATE.

WE seem to have done great injustice to the subject
of our memoir in the view given of his labors.
We seem to have presented the acts which gained him
the largest fame among men as being the most momentous results of his life — as being those by which he would
wish to be judged.   We are aware that he would have felt
— and most justly — that more momentous far in reality,
and in the estimate of angels, was the character of his own
spiritual life and the discharge of his duty to the immortal
ones over whom the Holy Ghost had made him overseer.
Yet it has not been of choice, but from necessity, that we
have made prominent the more public aspects of his life.
It is not difficult to delineate the wide-spread impression
created by a single discourse.   But to describe justly the
daily insensible growth of holiness in the soul; to record
the inward struggles and victories known only to the Infinite
— the ruling of one's own spirit (greater glory than that
of him who taketh a city) ; to follow the pastor out upon
the Neck as he goes to administer consolation to some one
of the Lord's hidden ones ; to record the counsels suited to
the varying spiritual wants of old and young, of tempted
and perplexed ; to trace the progress of conviction in one
soul, the dawning of hope in another, and the noonday of
sanctification in another ; to measure the gradual increase
of seriousness in the body of disciples, of love for the word

of God, of knowledge of self, of spirituality, — all this who may hope to accomplish? And it is rendered all the more difficult, from the fact that during his ministry there was not in his congregation any particular period of widespread and overpowering interest — any revival of religion. Yet he would have told us it was in such results far more than in the production of world-renowned sermons and in the establishment of a transatlantic fame, that his work as a minister of Christ lay.

The following, to his sister Mrs. S., illustrates his longing for the awakening and conversion of his people, and his disappointment when this result was not attained. It was for this result, far more than for any increase of literary fame, that he longed with irrepressible desire. The words of an eminent minister of Christ, "I don't want their admiration; I want their salvation," would have expressed his prevailing feeling. He sought not theirs, but them.

"... I promised Sarah that I would write to you about the work in Boston. There is a considerable revival in Park Street and the Old South. Probably two hundred or more have been seriously impressed in the former place, and a number, I know not how many, in the latter. The attention still continues. It has not, I grieve to say, extended into any of the Baptist churches, though there seems some increasing interest among Christians. I know not that there is any more attention among sinners. A few days since we held a united meeting for fasting and humiliation. It was a pleasant and solemn season. Christians seemed considerably awakened and humbled; but I know not that there was any other effect. When I say *we*, I mean the three Baptist churches. I am sometimes disconsolate, sometimes tempted to sloth and unbelief. But I know this is wrong. I wait for thy salvation, Lord. I hope I may add, ' With strong desires I wait.' I never so much felt the total inefficacy of means to the conversion of a sinner or the edification of a saint. If I learn this lesson it will be of some use. But it is mournful to find no effect produced by our labors, when others so near are reaping so rich a harvest;

not because sinners are better or more deserving in one place than another, but because it looks as though God had a controversy with the people. O, may the blessing at last descend ! . . ."

Difficult as it is justly to exhibit the interior aspect of his life and labors, we must attempt it, availing ourselves of such materials as we may. How was he affected by the new scenes amid which he was placed? Did he retain the simplicity of his nature, the tender reverence for parents, the sympathy with home, the intense love for brothers and sisters, the spirituality of mind, the meekness towards man, the humility before God? The undesigned testimony of his own letters, and the recollection of those who survive, and who recall the tenor of his life, will afford an answer.

His youngest sister — the youngest of the family— he used to call his " scholar ; " for it was he who watched over her studies and aroused her mind to activity. He writes to her, —

" Your letter is very well written ; the lines are straight and the composition very respectable. It does you credit. The studies to which you are attending are very important. I hope you will spare no pains to be thorough in them all. It is better to know one thing well than fifty things badly. If you ever know one thing well you will be a pretty great woman.

" . . . My dear child, make the eternal God your Father. He has said, ' I love them that love me ; and they that seek me early shall find me.' Seek him and find him, and you will be prepared for any event in time and in eternity."

And again : —

" I wish very much that it were possible for you to be with me. I hope Providence will so order it before long. You are getting to be of that age when I can be of more use to you than at any other part of your life. I should like very much to have you near me, where I could have, in some manner, the oversight of your education. But, after all, I think it very probable that I mistake. We are all very likely to overrate our capacity to be useful to others.

"I think your master is putting you forward too fast. I am confident you are not fit to study Virgil; that is, you ought to have read several other books first. You ought to have read Cæsar before reading Virgil. It is wrong to attempt to read Latin poetry before you can read prose."

At his earnest request, his parents allowed his little sister to visit Boston. While she was there, he selected her schools, and watched over her studies, and all her pursuits, with the wise solicitude of a parent. She writes, —

"While I was in Boston, I used always to spend the Sabbaths with him at Dr. Baldwin's; and sweet Sabbaths they were. Dear Dr. Baldwin was my ideal of a lovely, venerable minister of the gospel; he was very kind, and seemed very fond of me. As the twilight of the Sabbath was gathering, dear brother always took me into his study; we read together, and I felt that I could tell him all that was in my little heart, just as freely as to mother. And then we would kneel together. His prayer was not long, but I remember it was just what I wanted and needed for my childish little self. He remembered every one of the family, each of the dear ones *at home.* How I can recall the look of that study! It was calm, quiet, and unpretending. I know I have been better all my life for those twilight evenings. Then he would take me around to Milk Street, to Mr. Wisner's, and my Sabbath was ended."

Surely this was

"one whose heart
The holy forms of young imagination have kept pure."

To his sister, Mrs. Stone, February 6, 1825: —

"My very dear Sister: . . . How singular it is! but so it is; there is no accounting for tastes. You thought your last letter a very poor one. I thought it, on the contrary, one of the best you had written to me for a long time. Be assured I remember, with many a pleasant yet sombre reflection, the hours of our childhood. I well recollect, on Wednesday and Saturday afternoons, our odd amusements, and among them that famous drama, to which, I imagine,

we may advance the claim of prior and undisturbed possession — the adventures of Giant Despair. In those mournful and yet eventful scenes, which probably no one besides ourselves ever enacted, I recollect my favorite part
was the giant, though, I think, M., who was, like ourselves, an amateur, sometimes personated him. I fear that
the effect of those spirit-stirring scenes, in which ourselves
were the sole actors and spectators, may have left some
traces on your imagination; I know not but to this may
be attributed some of that extreme terror of me with
which you are now so grievously oppressed. Be assured
that I have entirely cast off the character, and am absolutely as quiet as a cat, to all which, I presume, Sarah will
bear most ample testimony."

To Mrs. Stone : —

"July 19, 1825.

"My dear Sister: I cannot longer delay to express to
you the pleasure I received from seeing you, and also the
gratification with which I heard that you returned well, and
not displeased with your visit. If God should spare our
lives, I hope these meetings will be frequent. They awaken
a deeper and more hallowed tone of feeling; they give
rise to a thousand endeared and endearing reminiscences
which we look for in vain from other associations. Other
friends may be fast and firm; they may be acute and intelligent; but they can strike none of the chords which
the hand of childhood strung, and whose music falls upon
the ear like the memory of joys that are past — pleasant
and mournful to the soul. I like to revive those things.
I like to recall the little incidents of boyhood and girl-
hood, to tell over their follies and their sorrows, their
pleasures and their pains. Each one, fresh recollected,
seems to add a little to the thread of human existence,
and to give new value to it, too; for it shows how
closely it is entwined with the life of those whom, in auld
lang syne, we loved, and in later years we have honored. 'Rather more poetical than usual, I think,' said
Mr. Shandy."

To his brother John : —

"December 15, 1822.

"I received your letter not long since, and had written to you a few days before. I rejoice to hear the

decision to which you have come. I hope and trust you were led to it by the Spirit of unerring truth. It has long been the desire and the prayer of my heart that you might be associated with me in the gospel ministry, and I now hope to live to see my wish accomplished. May God endue you plentifully with his grace, and make you an eminently useful minister. Cultivate, above everything, my dear brother, the spirit of ardent and constant piety. Seek in the Bible for the nature of true religion. Look not much to the opinions nor to the practice of men, but draw your principles and your spirit directly from the fountain of everlasting truth. There you can never mistake. Seek for the acquaintance of those who are remarkable for wisdom and piety, and let them be your chief companions. Endeavor to get into the habit of acting in everything in the fear of God and for the day of judgment, and you will not be in much danger of acting wrongly.

"I write now especially to say, that about the difficulty of expense in your education you need not be solicitous. I will take care of that somehow. You may make your arrangements to prepare for the ministry, as soon as you have father's permission. As to the place where you shall study, I cannot give an opinion yet. . . ."

To his sister S., accompanied by a watch: —

"I send you a small token of my regard. It is not wholly such as I could have wished, but it is as near as I could find anything. I hope it will please you.

"It will number your days, S., yes, and your moments. Though its voice be weak, it will be impressive. Its monitory finger will point out to you how rapidly time is passing, and how soon you must enter upon that state where duration will no more be measured by sun and moon. Then we shall either inhabit the city where the Lamb is the light thereof, or be shut up in that prison where, when the agonizing inquirer asks, 'How long?' the answer will come back from the gloomy walls, 'Eternity.'

"May this little monitor teach you so to number your days as to apply your heart to wisdom. May it teach you the frailty of man, and the shortness of his probation. It is one of the frailest works of human ingenuity; yet it will keep on its course when she who now owns it, and he who now writes about it, sleep in the dust. When that time shall arrive, my dear sister, may we be found clothed in the righteousness of Christ; and then, though the earthly house of our tabernacle be dissolved, we shall be raised to a building of God, a house not made with hands, eternal in the heavens."

We quote also from a letter of his father, dated March, 1824 : —

"It affords me great pleasure, and at the same time, I hope, excites my gratitude, to notice the great acceptance your sermon met with; I do not think more than it deserves, if a parent may be allowed to express an opinion. But you will allow me to express the whole of my feelings on this subject. I was not without some anxiety lest Satan and a deceitful heart might cause the applause of mortals to prove a snare. It was my prayer, and still is, that our common Friend, who watches over our path, might make his grace sufficient for you. Nothing will afford me so much pleasure as to see you kept humble at the foot of the cross. If you are constantly found there, the talents which God has been pleased to give you will be employed to the good of mankind and to the glory of his holy name. The foregoing remarks, I am persuaded, will be received by you as coming from an affectionate father, whose experience has given him some knowledge of the human heart."

Of his inward temper, of the worship in spirit and in truth which he rendered, illustration is afforded in his letters, many of which have been cited.

We quote from a note written to her who afterwards became his wife : —

"Your note was received, and would sooner have been answered, but it was considered by your kind sister as too precious to remain long in my possession. It was taken away, without my knowledge or consent, very soon after its reception, and was not returned to my table till a few minutes since. It speaks of moral and of physical infirmities, of sickness of soul, and debility of body. . . . For the disease of the soul there is a sovereign remedy, a

remedy which was devised by omniscience, and which has
never failed of success. In the worst cases it has been
tested, and its efficacy is infallible. 'The blood of Jesus
Christ cleanseth from all sin.' This remedy is freely
offered to all the children of men. No one need perish
unless he so will. 'Whoever will, let him come.' It is
offered, and has been offered, to Lucy; and it is the hope
of her friend that she will accept it, if she has not yet
done so."

The piety that was "as a fire shut up in his bones,"
could not but express itself in earnest longings for the
salvation of the souls of which he had, at divine command, taken the care. A Christian lady, at whose house
he boarded, says, "He was a faithful pastor. I have in
mind one person particularly, who was poor and had
many trials. She often came to the house to talk with
the pastor. He was very kind to her, and never wearied
of her coming, however great the interruption. He gave
her his sympathy, and was untiring in his efforts that she
might secure the consolations of religion."

During one summer he boarded, in one of the suburban
towns, with Mr. D., a member of his parish. Mrs. D.
was of a very retiring disposition, and found it impossible to converse freely with any one on personal religion;
but she attributed her conversion to his prayers in her
behalf.

In his "Letters on the Ministry of the Gospel" he
recalls this incident in his pastoral life : —

"I had been preaching on a solemn subject on a week-
day evening, and the audience seemed more than usually
interested. In walking out with one of my hearers, I
was guilty of making some trifling remark, the spirit of
which was wholly at variance with all that I had been
saying. I was immediately impressed with my inconsistency and wrong doing, and I never think of it without
regret, and, I hope, repentance; for that one trifling expression may have wrought permanent injury to an immortal soul."

We may venture to believe that if a single error could thus remain fixed in his memory after a lapse of nearly forty years, his ministerial life must have been unusually free from blemish.

During the first three years of his ministry he boarded, and, during a part of that time, in a portion of the city somewhat distant from the majority of his parishioners. But he was dissatisfied with this course. He felt that by this remoteness he lost much, and failed to hold in his hands countless threads of influence and sympathy. He has remarked, that after boarding out of town for a summer, although he was among the parish almost daily, yet he did not " catch up " with his work for months. He regarded the gospel which is preached from house to house as being quite as efficacious as that delivered more formally upon the Sabbath. Indeed, he felt that next to the Bible there was no other source of sermons so fruitful as the hearts and the conversation of his people. He often in later life quoted the remark (made to him we think by his venerated friend, Rev. Dr. Welch), " Tell the people just what they tell you, and you will find that nothing will interest them so much." We have heard Dr. Wayland mention that he once called upon a mother, who had been bereaved by the death of her daughter. The afflicted mother poured out her heart, and told him how the child had lain in her bosom, had never been absent from her for a day, had been the mainspring and motive of her life, and how utter now was her desolation. Not long after this conversation, the pastor had occasion, in preaching, to allude to a mother's love, and used as nearly as possible the very language of the bereaved mother. The people, in amazement, heard their own deepest emotions delineated, and many of them expressed their wonder that a man so young could know so much of human nature.

Believing that his usefulness would be increased by such a change, in the fourth year of his settlement he rented a house in Hanover Street, and invited his sister (now Mrs. C.) to come and preside over his home. She kindly consented, and had an unusually favorable opportunity to know him in his relations to his charge. She remarks, " He was much in his room, and the hours appropriated to study he was very unwilling to have encroached upon. His house was always accessible to his people, and open to his ministering brethren. His tastes, I suppose, drew him more to his studies than to parochial duties. Of this I think he was sensible, and carefully guarded against any neglect in this respect. The poor, the sick, and the afflicted always called out his sympathy, and I well remember the promptness with which he hastened to such abodes. Having once entered them, any apparent reserve in his manner was lost. He had great tenderness for children, and they approached him confidingly."

We recall his once saying to a minister whom he was visiting, " I was glad to see you speak to those children. Those who are children now, and whose affections you may secure, in a few years will be men and women."

Mrs. C. adds, —

" He seemed to me to have no time for relaxation. The only change was in the character of his work. He did not mix much in society, and was often at a loss for that small change which is always in demand in the social circle. He rarely accepted invitations to dine, and had the impression that he was not fitted for general society. Even in this early period of his life I think he often suffered from a sense of isolation, and had many a hard struggle within. At his own table the flow of conversation was easy, and his humor was irresistible as it scintillated from those deep-sunken eyes. And the attention was often arrested by some striking remark, which to others became the seed of thought. He did not delight in speculation ; his mind was essentially practical. His conversation often turned on the advance of science as contributing to the general well-being of mankind, and to the wide diffusion of the conveniences of life. His aim then, as afterwards, was to raise humanity to a higher level. The ministry of the gospel was the great lever, but subordinate agencies he recognized in their appropriate working."

Of his preaching she remarks, —

"To the young it would not be generally interesting. He was a good deal confined to his notes. The subject was discussed with great clearness, and his power of analysis seemed to me wonderful. He appealed to the reason more than to the emotions, and though exceedingly impressive and always instructive, did not warm and animate his audience as much as some men of inferior powers. The technicalities of religion he avoided. His language was that of common life. His Wednesday evening lectures, at which he never used notes, and which were generally of an expository character, were peculiarly interesting, and were always well attended."

Mrs. O'Brien remarks, —

"As a pastor, his influence was remarkable. Persons were surprised at his insight into the secret springs of their thoughts and feelings, and were led to open their hearts to him in the fullest confidence; nor was their confidence ever misplaced. In conversation he excelled, not only in communicating his own thoughts and feelings, but in drawing out the minds of others, discovering to them their own inward resources, and making them self-reliant and aspiring. If one were involved in perplexity, he had a happy faculty of giving just the counsel needed, often by some pithy maxim, that fastened itself in the memory."

Dr. Pattison remarks, in speaking of his character and labors as a pastor, —

"He sought the conversion of his acquaintances *one by one* — sometimes by private conversation: when he could not see them personally, he addressed, as I know, many by letter, — short, it might be a mere note, — not only serious, but eminently tender and persuasive. I have reason to believe he had ordinarily in mind some one or more outside of his own domestic circle for whose salvation he labored and prayed. Such a habit, nourished by such a spirit, must have made him a useful pastor."

As we have alluded to the character of his sermons

during the earlier years of his ministry, it is but just to add that a marked progress is clearly discernible. Those of the latter half of his ministry greatly excel those of the former in simplicity, in directness, in clearness of style, in effectiveness. Less rhetorical, they are morally much more impressive. We apprehend that the change to which we refer will be noticed by any one who shall read in succession the Missionary Sermon, of 1823, and the sermon on the Duties of an American Citizen, of 1825.

As to the plainness, wisdom, and love which were mingled in his preaching, a single circumstance is a more impressive testimony than the most eloquent eulogiums. He preached a sermon upon intemperance, exhibiting not alone the ruinous effects of indulgence in the vice, but the sinfulness of doing aught that would promote it. The next day, a member of his church called upon him and said, " I have been in the habit of selling liquor at my store. But if what you said yesterday is true, it is wrong, and I ought to abandon it, however much the step may reduce my profits." He accordingly renounced all connection with the traffic. It is a sincere pleasure to record this incident in the life of one of whom Dr. Wayland writes, —

" John Sullivan was one of the older members of the church, an Israelite indeed, in whom was no guile. Humble, mild, amiable, slow of speech and action, he honored his profession by a holy walk and conversation."

We return to the narrative of Mr. Wayland's life and ministry. On the 21st of November, 1825, he was married, by Dr. Sharp, to Miss Lucy L. Lincoln, of Boston. Her brother, Deacon Heman Lincoln, and her sisters, Mrs. O'Brien and Mrs. Haven, had long been, and ever continued to be, among his most endeared and valued friends.

To Mr. Potter, who had just been invited to St. Paul's Church, Boston, he writes, —

"It looks as though the hand of God was in it. I write with a mixture of regret and pleasure. I know so well the painfulness of breaking up long-cherished relations, and entering upon the discharge of new and untried duties, that I cannot but sympathize with you, while I thank God that it is so.

"I pray, my dear Potter, that you may be blessed with that child-like reliance on omniscient wisdom which shall support you, and that clear view of the designs of Providence, that your path may be entirely plain. I will only add, that every day seems to present some new feature, which develops more and more the importance of the station, and the necessity of having here a liberal, and catholic, and evangelical man.

"Should you come, I hope I need not say that you have a home here already prepared. I will only add, that you will drive to 188 Hanover Street, opposite Mr. Ware's meeting-house."

Notwithstanding the growing reputation of the minister, his evident piety, his varied ability, the increasing union and attachment of the people, yet there was a want of prosperity. During nearly every month additions were made to the church, not large in number, yet sufficient to show that labor was not spent in vain. But the congregation remained nearly stationary. The ability of the society did not increase. A debt had for several years been resting on them. This was removed, largely or entirely, through the exertions of the pastor, who, in addition to the labor of personal solicitation, gave one sixth of the amount raised. But even after this removal was effected, the income did not meet the expenses, and another debt was accumulating.

Convinced that the location of the house of worship was an obstacle to the prosperity of the church, he proposed the erection of a new house, on a more eligible site. Apart from a want of confidence in the pecuniary ability of the society for such an undertaking, two reasons were urged against the step proposed. To remove from the present location would put it out of the power of several

very aged members, residing in the vicinity, to attend
meeting (though, indeed, as it was, they scarcely ever
were present). The second reason, which settled the
question, was, that Dr. Stillman had preached in that
house, and walked down that plank walk. Nothing came
of the movement; but after it was too late, it was ascertained that several gentlemen of wealth, attached to other
denominations, who placed a just estimate on the ability
of Mr. Wayland, would have coöperated liberally in the
erection of a new meeting-house.

The salary, which had formerly been sufficient for his
wants, now proved inadequate to the needs of one who, in
addition to his own family, had assumed the whole responsibility of the education of his younger brother. Dr.
Neale says, " He was too humble, or more likely too
proud, to ask to have his salary raised."

He had, too, gradually become involved in a variety of
cares and labors outside of the parish, which consumed
his time and crippled his ministry, yet from which he
scarcely knew how to free himself.

We believe, however, that we shall best satisfy the reader
by presenting Dr. Wayland's own view of his ministry,
and of the causes which led to the termination of it: —

"I had intended to preach without the use of a manuscript. I began by committing my sermons. This I practised for a short time, and should have had no difficulty
in continuing it. My friends, however, especially my
deacons, advised me to read; I followed their advice, and
thus became a reader of sermons. This I conceive to
have been the great error of my life as a preacher. I
had, it is true, little practice as a speaker. I presume I
was awkward in the pulpit. I know that I did not feel at
home there, and I had little confidence in my control over
an audience. I had little power of self-excitement. This
needed cultivation by the intercourse of speaker with audience. My compass of voice needed enlargement. Yet
I had, I think, the elements of an impressive speaker;
and when I have addressed an audience under favorable

circumstances, I think I have frequently been successful.
Had I at this time boldly thrown myself on my own resources, with reliance on the promised aid of the Spirit
of God, I might have been much more useful.

" I saw the absurdity of attempting to conduct the
Wednesday evening service with a written discourse,
and I prepared myself, as well as I was able, to preach
extempore. At first my efforts were sad failures, though
I took a large part of the day for preparation. I resolved
that it must be done. I continued doing as well as I
could. By degrees the work became less difficult, and
at last it became a pleasure. The vestry was well filled,
and I think more good was done than on the Sabbath.
I then acquired some facility in extempore speaking, and
no doubt some vitality was imparted to my written discourses.

" The foundation defect in my ministry was, that I did
not gain victory over myself. I was, I believe, the only
settled Baptist minister in Boston who had received a
collegiate education. I naturally conceived the idea that
more was expected of me than of my brethren. I
preached a missionary sermon, which, upon being published, was highly applauded. Subsequently I preached
a Fast Day sermon, which was also published and well
received. I thus gained a reputation (as I always thought
much above my deserts) which has had a powerful influence on my subsequent course.

" I do not know that I was led from these circumstances
to place a high estimate on my own abilities. I do not
think that this has been my sin. I indeed acquired the
belief that I could do some things (that is, the things that
I had done) ; but there my self-confidence rested. Whatever of success I have achieved may be traced to a dogged
resolution to do my duty, rather than to any other source.

" But I was led to think that plain, simple, unadorned
address, though suitable to other occasions, would not be
appropriate for the pulpit. I could not persuade myself
to carry the Wednesday evening service into the pulpit on
the Sabbath. I never set myself at work resolutely to become *a preacher*, that is, one who, out of a full heart, and
without reading, delivers his message to the people.

" I do not know that I was preëminently at fault above
others. I was, I think, considered direct in my appeals

to the consciences of men. The most religious of my
hearers were pleased with my preaching, and were attached to me, as I was to them. But if I had gained a
proper victory over myself, over my love for reputation,
and desire to be useful to my denomination by raising
their intellectual character,—and if I had, in reliance upon
the Holy Spirit, labored simply for the conversion of
souls, — I firmly believe that I should have been more useful, and I should now look upon the past with far greater
satisfaction.

"In another respect I review my ministry with regret.
I was placed by my brethren on boards of societies, and
took a part in all the measures that were in progress for
the promotion of religion in connection with our denomination; the Triennial Convention, the State Convention,
and the Magazine. I was not employed in secular business. My labors were ecclesiastical. Now, this sort of labor
took up directly, or indirectly, much of my time. Directly,
I was obliged to write much, and to attend a variety of
meetings. Indirectly, I was obliged to see a multitude of
people. Frequently, before I had composed myself to
work in my study in the morning, I was called down,
and was occupied with people until dinner; and sometimes the afternoon was spent in the same way. Thus all
my plans for improvement were broken up; consecutive
study became impossible, and I frequently said that the
Bible and my own sermons were all my reading. When
a man's mind is thus occupied, his interest in his people
will gradually diminish. His outside work seems to be
religious; it must be done to-day: his work for his people
may be done to-morrow, or next week; and in the end it
is not done at all. At last his real work, the work for
which he is paid, — labor for the conversion of the souls
committed to his care, — receives only the chippings and
leavings of his time; and even these chippings and leavings have in them no vitality.

"Another effect of this multiplication of business is, to
break up all habits of devotion, till a man's religion becomes often a dry skeleton of orthodox doctrine, rather
than a living fountain within him, quickening his own
soul, and refreshing the souls of others. But the minister
has the same liability to sin as other people, and some
temptations peculiar to himself. If his religion has be-

come inoperative, the power of temptation is redoubled, and nothing but the especial grace of God can preserve him from falling into sin.

"During my ministry I failed greatly from neglecting to read the Scriptures. I read them in my private devotions, and to find texts to preach from; but I did not study them ceaselessly, as the great source from which to derive all that I was to preach to my people. I fear that this error is far too common. I well remember a conversation which I once had with Professor Stuart bearing on this point. He wanted to see a theological seminary in which nothing should be studied but the Scriptures.

"I also erred, during my ministry, in respect to visiting my people. From the amount of out-door religious business, I had but scant time for this duty, especially during the last part of my settlement. I was not, indeed, much complained of; I felt and acknowledged the obligation. I never regarded it as 'an intolerable bore.' But I did not make it a part of the regular business of every week and every day. I also erred in the manner of it. I did not deal faithfully enough with my people. To the religious, so far as I remember, I was in the habit of talking upon religion; and I made myself so familiar with them, that they would see me in the midst of their ordinary avocations. I remember cases of edifying religious conversation with members of my church over the wash-tub. If I heard of any who were thoughtful on the subject of religion, I never neglected them, and was careful to introduce them to those who would do them good. But with those who were wholly worldly, I fear that I was often found wanting. I did not get them alone and set their danger before them, so that I could say, 'I am free from the blood of all men.' The Lord pardon me, and lay not the sin of blood-guiltiness to my charge.

"And yet I cannot say that I was wholly unmindful of my duty in this respect. One incident I recall with pleasure. One member of my church was a very high Calvinist — higher a great deal, I apprehend, than Calvin himself. He did not consider me 'clear in the doctrines.' He himself was perfectly clear, and was, so far as a good man could be, a thorough fatalist. He was very unwilling to have me invite sinners indiscriminately to repent and believe. His family were amiable and intelligent, but

entirely worldly. I believed it to be my duty to converse
with them on the subject of religion, and did so, but with
very little success. The next time I saw their father, he
plainly, though very kindly, told me that he did not wish
any one to converse with his children on religion; for if
they were elected, they would certainly be converted; if
they were not elected, talking to them would only make
them hypocrites. From this incident I am encouraged
to hope that I was not wholly wanting in the performance
of this part of my duty, for its performance in this instance would seem peculiarly trying to a young minister.
I am sure, however, that I fell very far short of my duty,
both in universality and in earnestness.

" But the source of all my errors may be summed up
in few words: I was not sufficiently religious. I was
greatly wanting in that faith that brings home to the soul
eternal things with the force of an imminent reality. I
was too easily satisfied with employing all my time in
labor (for I was not an idle man), instead of devoting
myself to the work of saving souls, in humble reliance
on the power of the Spirit of God. I see that I had a
sort of idea that I might so construct and deliver a discourse that by its own inherent energy it would produce
a moral effect. Hence my work of preparation was an
intellectual rather than a moral and spiritual effort. I
relied in a certain way, it is true, on the Spirit, and looked
to him for his assistance, but far too inadequately. I was
not habitually devotional. I lived, as I now see, by no
means near to God. I wonder that God did any good
through me, and that he did not cast me aside, as a vessel
in whom he has no pleasure. But in spite of all my
deficiencies, the church became, I believe, more religious,
and souls were given as the seals of my imperfect and
faulty ministry."

We have introduced these remarks, believing that the
estimate which he placed on his ministry in Boston would
not be without interest to the reader. Yet we think it right
to add, that however it may be in the divine view, it is
probable that no human observer would concede in full
the justness of his review. It is certain that he was regarded as in an unusual degree a devotional, faithful

pastor, a scriptural, searching, and eminently evangelical preacher; and the more simple-minded and spiritual of his hearers found themselves the most highly profited by his ministry. The fact that during the latter part of his settlement he was invited to the pastorate of a church then just organized in the city, and that he declined to accept it, from a belief that so many of the principal members of his own people would follow him as to enfeeble and destroy the church to which he had been ministering, — bears testimony to the regard in which he was held by his brethren, and by Christians in the community, as well as to his self-forgetfulness. It is certain too that he underrates the effect of his own preaching. In fact, its full results were probably never known to him. During the year following his removal from Boston, an extensive revival pervaded the city, and the First Church, though at the time destitute of a minister, shared in its blessings. And many who were then converted ascribed their conversion to his labors. A minister * writes, "In supplying the pulpit of that church many years after, I heard one of the members say that a large part of the candidates for admission, since Dr. Wayland left the pulpit, dated their first serious thoughts from his sermons." As he underrated, or was ignorant of, the results of his labors, may we not also believe that he put too low an estimate upon the fidelity, the earnestness, the piety of which his labors were the offspring?

In the spring of 1826, very unexpectedly to himself, he received a letter from Dr. Nott, inquiring if he would accept the Professorship in Union College, recently relinquished by Dr. Potter. After some deliberation he promised to accept the appointment, influenced in this decision by the inadequacy of his income, by discouragement with his supposed want of success, by the apparent impossibility of achieving extensive results in the location then occupied by the society, and by a determination to free him-

---

* Rev. William B. Jacobs.

self from the diversified employments which had rendered his life, of late, so fragmentary and futile.   He adds, " It was never my intention, by accepting a professorship, to relinquish the ministry.   I thought it likely that, within a few years, some opening would appear in the neighbor-hood of Boston, to which place I had become much at-tached, and that I could return without inflicting an injury on my people."

At the monthly meeting of the church in July, Mr. Wayland read a letter addressed to the church, in which, after referring in terms of gratitude to the kindness which they had exhibited during the five years of his ministry, and the charity which they had extended to his imperfect labors, he adds, —

" It cannot, however, brethren, have escaped your no-tice, that my success has, for some time past, been less than you had a right to expect.   It has, indeed, been such as seemed to indicate that Providence designed me for some other field of labor; and after prayerfully reflecting upon the subject, such is the conclusion at which I have ultimately arrived.   This conviction is further strength-ened by the fact that at this time another sphere of useful-ness has been presented before me, which, in the existing circumstances of the case, I feel that it is my duty to ac-cept.   It is painful to me to refer to our pecuniary concerns. You will, therefore, allow me only to remark on this part of the subject, that I feared lest, by longer retaining the office which I hold, I should create embarrassments to you as well as to myself.   Under these circumstances I do hereby respectfully request to be dismissed from the pastoral care of this church and society."

To all the members of the church these words were utterly unexpected, and they were received in amazement and tearful regret.

Dr. Wayland writes, —

" When I resigned my place, it was a matter of great surprise, and, I believe, of sincere pain, to my people. I found that they loved me much better than I had sup-posed ; indeed, had I known, before I was pledged, how sincerely they were attached to me, I think I should never have left them. This attachment has continued to the present day. No member of that church or congregation, now after thirty-five years, ever meets me without the most affectionate recognition; and none love me more than those who at first bitterly opposed me. I was settled in Boston for five years. I did not then understand the value of the element of time in producing results. I supposed that changes might be effected more rapidly than was actually possible. I also underrated the results which had been produced. Many persons, comparing the condition of the church when I left them with its condition when I entered on my ministry, considered my labors more than commonly useful.

" Two questions here arise, as to my resignation and as to the manner of it. As to leaving the ministry, I doubt, at the present time, the wisdom of the step. Were the decision to be made again, with my present knowledge of duty, I think I should not leave the pulpit. My delivery, it is true, was not good. I may well say it was not attractive, since it did not attract. My situation was, in many respects, unfavorable, and there were many disadvantages from without to be overcome. Yet they might have been overcome. With my present judgment I should have remained where I was, corrected my delivery, and devoted myself entirely to my ministry. Determined to deserve success, and relying on the Spirit of God, I might reasonably have hoped for it. As to the manner of leaving my people, I have long looked on it as an error. I pledged myself to go, without giving my people an opportunity to remove the obstacles to my continuance. I should, before making a decision, have laid the case before them, that the claims, both of the college and of the church, might be fairly presented."

On the 17th of September he preached his farewell sermon, from 1 Thess. ii. 19: " For what is our hope, or joy, or crown of rejoicing? Are not even ye in the presence of our Lord Jesus Christ at his coming?" Dr. Stow, who was present, and who had occupied the pulpit during the day, says, " It was not wanting in tenderness, but was eminently instructive and impressive."

We cannot more appropriately close the record of his ministry in Boston, than by quoting a letter written to Dr. Neale, March 18, 1865, in reply to a letter from the latter, inviting him to be present at the approaching two hundredth anniversary of the First Baptist Church, and requesting from him some notices and recollections of the period of his pastoral labors.

"Your letter of the 14th arrived a few days since. With regard to what you say of one of your predecessors, I desire neither to be squeamish nor self-laudatory. I think you know me well enough for that. I have never sought or canvassed for a place among my brethren. I have declined many, really preferring to do the work rather than to seem to do it. I know that as a pastor I had a multitude of deficiencies, but I humbly hope that I *tried* to do my duty. I do not think that I ever endeavored to save myself; but if any good was done, it was all, *all* the work of the blessed Savior. I was at best but a miserable instrument. But in all you say, let this one idea predominate and govern : *All to the glory of Christ.* If it please God, I will endeavor to be with you. Let all be religious, that God may bless it ; let it do good to those that come after us. May God help you and all of us."

The reader will also be interested in a review and estimate of Dr. Wayland's ministry, found in his "Letters on the Ministry of the Gospel." The passage containing this review closes as follows : "If I have any knowledge of the faults of the ministry, the germs, at least, of that knowledge have been derived from my own painful experience."

Of his brief period of labor at Union College, he writes, —

"In September, 1826, I went to Union College. It was intended that I should permanently accept the professorship of moral philosophy, though I temporarily supplied that of mathematics and natural philosophy. I entered at once upon my duties with interest. When a tutor, I had taught most all of the mathematical studies which now fell to my lot. With natural philosophy I was less familiar. I succeeded, however, in putting the apparatus (which had been much neglected) in order, and in giving the class all the illustrations which the subject required. I believe my teaching was considered useful. I also had the opportunity of renewing my acquaintance with my old friend, Dr. Nott.

"About the time of my leaving Boston, Dr. Messer, the President of Brown University, was on the point of resigning. I had been urged to become a candidate for the office. My friends in the vicinity of Boston, especially Dr. Sharp and Dr. Bolles, pressed it. In the course of the autumn Dr. M. resigned. I had now become very pleasantly situated at Schenectady. My feelings, however, turned towards New England, and the hope of doing something for my own denomination had much weight with me. There was some doubt as to the election, as one or two candidates besides myself had been presented. I had but little anxiety about the result, although the uncertainty was annoying. I had left my family for the time in Boston, but I now determined on a day beyond which I would no longer wait in uncertainty, but if nothing decisive occurred previous to that time, I would remove my family and my effects to Schenectady, and would lay aside all thoughts of the other position. Previously to this time, however, I received news of my election. I thereupon resigned my professorship, and returned to Boston, to prepare for the duties of the office to which I had been called."

In February, 1827, he removed permanently to Providence, and entered on his work as President.

CHAPTER IX.

BROWN UNIVERSITY. — THE NEW ADMINISTRATION. — PRINCIPLES OF ACTION. — CHANGES INSTITUTED. — OBSTACLES ENCOUNTERED AND OVERCOME. — TRAITS OF CHARACTER EXHIBITED.

AS early as August, 1826, before Mr. Wayland had left Boston, an article on Brown University appeared in a leading journal in Providence, deploring the decadence of the college, urging the imperative necessity of a change in its administration, and indicating Mr. Wayland as a person eminently fitted, by education, experience, and capacity, to preside over the institution. Similar views were expressed, in subsequent articles, in the same journal, and were echoed by prominent newspapers in New York, Massachusetts, and Connecticut. No one of these presses represented the Baptist denomination, but in every case the favorable opinions expressed of Mr. Wayland were founded on the position which he had already reached, as a man of commanding talent, catholic sentiments, and eminent success in the work of education. In all these utterances the newspapers only expressed a feeling which for years had been growing among the friends of the college.

Our readers will remember that Professor Stuart had already intimated that in his judgment a new regime was demanded, and had alluded to the advantages to be secured by giving to Mr. Wayland a voice in the councils of the institution. Moreover, fears were entertained (how justly it is not necessary at this late day to decide) that

the religious convictions of President Messer had under-
gone a marked change, and that his instructions had a
manifest tendency towards Unitarianism.

In September, 1826, President Messer resigned, and in
December of the same year, Professor Wayland was unanimously elected as his successor. Of the commencement
of his career as president of Brown University, Dr. Wayland writes, in his reminiscences, —

"The condition of the college was not encouraging.
The number of undergraduates was small. Discipline
had been neglected. Difficulties had arisen between the
president and the trustees, and between the president and
some members of the Faculty. In point of fact the
college had not a high reputation in the community, and
probably did not deserve it.

"The first business which I undertook was to frame a
new set of laws for the college. This, of course, involved
the introduction of material changes. It made a vastly
greater amount of labor necessary for both officers and
students. The design was to render study not a sham,
but a reality, and discipline not a form, but a fact. The
previous method of recitation by question and answer was
abolished, and, except in the teaching of languages, neither
officers nor students used a book in the class. Officers
were to occupy apartments in college during the day and
evening, and were to visit the rooms of students at least
twice during the twenty-four hours. Spirituous liquors,
which had been commonly in use, were banished from
the college premises.* A system of marks was devised,
by which a parent could know the standing of his son at
the close of every term. Power was given to the president to send away from college any young man whose
conduct rendered him an improper associate for his fellow-
students, or whose further connection with his class could
be of no use to himself or to his friends. The parent was

---

* Up to this time it had been the custom to provide wine at the
Commencement dinner. Cider was frequently furnished to the
students boarding in college commons, and a barrel of ale was
always kept on tap in the cellar, to which all undergraduates had
free access.

the individual with whom all intercourse respecting the
son was carried on, whereas, hitherto, the dealing had
been mainly with the pupil himself. In short, obso-
lete laws and usages were abandoned, and new duties
were required of both instructors and students. The design
was to render the college a place of real study and improvement; to establish the existence of authority on the
part of the officers, and of obedience on the part of the
students, but all in the spirit of love and good will. The
requirements for admission had been greatly relaxed.
These were raised to the standard of New England colleges generally, and it was understood that they would be
strictly enforced.

" The laws were enacted at a special meeting of the
corporation, after having been approved by the Faculty.
The college, under the new arrangements, commenced
operations in February, 1827.

" At this time, the beginning of my independent labors
as an instructor, I was deeply impressed with the importance of two things : first, of carrying into practice every
science which was taught in theory, and secondly, of
adapting the course of instruction, as far as possible, to
the wants of the whole community. The first seemed to
me all-important as a means of intellectual discipline.
The abstract principles of a science, if learned merely as
disconnected truths, are soon forgotten. If combined
with application to matters of actual existence, they will
be remembered. Nor is this all. By uniting practice
with theory, the mind acquires the habit of acting in
obedience to law, and thus is brought into harmony with
a universe which is governed by law.

" In the second place, if education is good for one class
of the community, it is good for all classes. Not that the
same studies are to be pursued by all, but that each one
should have the opportunity of pursuing such studies as
will be of the greatest advantage to him in the course of
life which he has chosen.

" As I have said, I was strongly impressed with these
ideas from the commencement. I found myself, however,
unable to carry them out in practice. They did not seem
either to the Faculty or to the corporation as practical, but
rather as visionary. The funds of the college were very
small, — hardly more than thirty thousand dollars, — the

interest of which, with the avails of tuition, was all the income that we possessed. To adopt and act upon the principles which I have indicated would have imposed upon the Faculty much additional labor, or would have made necessary the appointment of several additional officers of instruction. In the mean time the experiment, if successful, would not become remunerative until its merits had been demonstrated to the community. For this we had no adequate means, and I saw that for the present, at least, the plan was impracticable.

" All that remained was to raise the standard of scholarship in the college, constituted as it then was, and to improve, to the utmost of our power, its discipline and moral character. In this attempt we were all of one mind, and we labored with earnestness and self-forgetful diligence. The result, I think, was such as to give us cause for encouragement. It was the general impression that the character of the students was materially improved. Intemperance and idleness disappeared. It became an honorable distinction to be a hard student. The examination at the close of the first term was decidedly successful. Gentlemen from the city attended in considerable numbers, and expressed themselves delighted with the evident improvement. The students themselves seemed very much gratified. The Senior class, especially, acted a most honorable part, and were the pioneers of the new movement. Among them were several men of fine talents and highly estimable character. They comprehended their position, and responded promptly to all that it required. To themselves the effort was of great service, morally and intellectually. Hon. John H. Clifford, since attorney-general of Massachusetts, and still later governor of that commonwealth, — a member of the class of 1827, — has, on every occasion, referred to his last collegiate year as the foundation of his future eminence, and the commencement of his brilliant career. Whatever honor is awarded to this change in the condition of the college, a large share of it belongs to the graduating class of 1827. The exercises of Commencement were, I believe, unusually satisfactory, and the termination of the first year was regarded as very auspicious.

" In connection with the changes to which I have alluded, it was necessary to establish one principle of importance, namely, that every member of the Faculty should devote his whole time to instruction, and also occupy a room in the college buildings. Previously, several gentlemen had performed some service, at the same time that they lived at home, and were engaged in other avocations ; while they received, if I remember correctly, nearly as large compensation as those whose whole time was devoted to instruction. The regular officers were competent to perform all the required duties, and by thus dispensing with outside services, they found their means of subsistence materially increased.

" As would naturally be supposed, changes of this kind could not be made without giving offence to the gentlemen whose connection with the corps of instruction had been of the limited nature already indicated. I think I do not exaggerate when I say that no efforts were spared to break down the new arrangements, and to render odious the person to whose agency they were attributed. Public addresses on other subjects were made to bear upon the recent changes in the college, and to cover them with ridicule. Some of the most influential newspapers were used for the same purpose.

" The first class which entered under the new administration was smaller than usual; I think not more than one half the number of the preceding year. It may be inferred that our affairs looked gloomy. Providence had not at that time more than a fourth of its present population. I was not known to the community, and, I presume, was generally considered a rash and headstrong young man, determined to overthrow the works of my predecessors, and having but little respect for the wisdom of the ancients. As is usual in such cases, the community, which had been thoroughly dissatisfied with the previous condition of the college, and had frequently spoken of it as a disgrace to the city, now that the attempt was made to institute a reform, raised a hue and cry, and readily joined the opposition, doubting whether (granting that reforms were needed) this mode of accomplishing a change were wise. The leading members of the corporation, however, coincided with me in opinion, and, assuring me of their cordial sympathy, advised me to continue fearlessly in the course which I had commenced. I cannot omit to mention the name of one gentleman connected with the corporation to whom I was especially indebted for wise counsel and generous encouragement — the late Thomas P. Ives, a man whose quiet opinion carried more weight than that of any ten men in Providence.

" The effect of all this upon the undergraduates may be easily imagined. The students, after the first excitement had passed, began to feel unaccustomed restraint to be oppressive. They became restless, and it was said that they were encouraged in this state of feeling by those gentlemen who had been obliged, by the recent college regulations, to relinquish their offices as instructors. The Senior class was the focus in which these elements of insubordination concentrated. The members of this class made preparation to leave college in a body, and to enter some other institution. They were very nearly anticipated in this design; for on an expected contingency, I had decided to dismiss them all without recommendation or certificate of standing. The expected difficulties, however, soon disappeared, for what reason I do not now remember. I never made any reply to the attack which had been made upon my administration. I relied wholly upon the blessing of God promised to every one who disinterestedly endeavors to do his duty.

" When the income of the college was reduced in consequence of the diminished number of the students, my salary was, by my own suggestion I think, made smaller. I much preferred that it should be so. I was not responsible for the continuance of a college in Providence, but I considered myself responsible for the conduct of the college on correct principles so long as it continued. What income I derived from my position was a secondary matter. I could live on the poorest fare and wear the cheapest clothing, but I must and would do what seemed my duty. Having done this, I was not responsible for the result.

" Year after year the number of students increased. A valuable set of apparatus was presented to the college by Messrs. Brown and Ives. A fund of twenty-five thousand dollars was raised for the increase of the library. Students who had graduated under what was called the ' New System,' were appointed to places of instruction as vacancies occurred, and in a few years all moved on as harmoniously as if no other system had ever been known.

In writing of these affairs I have referred mainly to myself, because I am the subject of this narration ; but I desire, once for all, to say that I only acted one part in the drama. The other officers of the college aided me with entire unanimity, and disinterested effort, and similar sacrifices. If any marked improvement was made, the credit of that improvement should be shared equally by all."

At the dinner which formed a part of the Centennial Celebration of Brown University, September 6, 1864, Dr. Wayland*alluded to somè of the circumstances which attended his entrance on the presidency. Although in some passages he touches upon topics already considered, we are unwilling to destroy the continuity of his remarks by any omissions.

" . . . I was called to the presidency of this college at a time when the corporation supposed that important changes were required in order to promote the best interests of the institution. The college was not deemed to be in a flourishing condition ; through whose fault, or whether through the fault of any one, I cannot say, nor have I ever inquired. It is sufficient to remember that such was generally believed to be the fact.

" They wisely determined to commence their reformation with the officers of instruction. None of them, I believe, had previously occupied a room in college, and their influence was, of course, limited almost entirely to their presence in the recitation-room. Several of them were gentlemen engaged in the active duties of professional life, and, except for a few months of the year, had no practical connection with the college. To remedy this state of things, the corporation enacted that every professor in the college should devote himself exclusively to the labor of teaching, and should also occupy a room in the college buildings during the hours appropriated to study. In consequence of this order, we lost the services of some gentlemen, who, as has been said, were only occasionally connected with the college, and the business of teaching devolved wholly on those officers who made education their life work. We were thus enabled to in-

---

* President Wayland received the degree of D. D. from Union College in 1827, and from Harvard College in 1829.

crease materially the salaries of the resident officers. It was, at the same time, distinctly stated that these salaries were given and accepted on the condition that the professors should comply with the enactments just mentioned.

" The rooms of these officers were so distributed, that each one had under his special supervision a given number of students, for whose conduct he was considered specially responsible, and whose rooms he was to visit once during the evening, and once, at least, during the day. These visits you all well remember, and very few of you, I presume, do not recollect that occasionally the presence of the officer delivered you from the company of unwelcome visitors, and, perhaps, sometimes saved you from the misfortune of wasting the time of others. I think, in my course of visiting, I rarely found you out of your rooms, except from the very reasonable cause of a failure of memory. The common excuse was, ' I only stepped in a moment, sir, to inquire where the lesson was.' This inquiry was promptly answered, and the student was soon in his own room quietly pursuing his studies.

" It was believed by the corporation that the parents and guardians of youth should, at the close of each term, be made acquainted with the standing of those whom they sent here for education. For this purpose the ' Merit Roll ' was established. Every officer took daily notes of the recitation of every student in his class. These notes were averaged at the close of the week; these averages were again averaged at the close of the term, and the result was communicated to the parent, with the regular college bill. Each student thus knew that every recitation would tell upon the account which would meet him on his return, in vacation, to his family and friends.

" It was also determined, that every recitation should be a real trial of strength, and a test of previous diligence. To this end it was enacted that neither professor nor student should ever use a book in the recitation-room, except in those studies where books were absolutely indispensable. The result was, that a knowledge of the subject was so fully acquired, that commonly a large proportion of every class could give, at a final examination, the substance of the whole volume which they had studied during the preceding term.

" To some persons this discipline seemed needlessly

severe. It was real and strict, yet kind; the intercourse
of well-bred men with each other. The young men became earnest in study, and those who were present when
the transition took place, have assured me that during no
part of their residence at college were they so happy as
after these changes had been inaugurated.

"Under these circumstances we commenced the last
term of the college year 1827. The example of the Senior
class, which came more immediately under my instruction, was worthy of all praise. They comprehended their
position, and knew that on the exemplification of the new
system by them depended greatly the future success of
the college. Their conduct, both as students and as young
gentlemen, was high-minded and exemplary. At the close
of the term they greatly distinguished themselves. Of
one of them I would like to speak, but his presence bids
me forbear. [Referring to Hon. John H. Clifford, who
presided on this occasion.] It is enough to say, that he
then gave promise of arriving at that eminence to which
he has attained.

"It had been said that this was, of all colleges, the
easiest to enter and the hardest to leave. This impression, whether it had been true or false, the course adopted
by the corporation tended to reverse. They raised at once
the requirements for admission to the level of the best
colleges in New England, and directed that these requirements should be rigidly enforced. At the same time they
made it my duty, whenever a student, from indolence
or negligence, was doing good neither to the institution
nor to himself, to inform his parents, and desire his immediate removal from the institution.

"It may be supposed that, at first, these regulations led
to a diminution of our numbers. The first class which
entered after the ' new system' commenced was small; it
graduated, I think, but thirteen. There were croakers in
those days, and they predicted the downfall of the college
from such new and unwise regulations. For some time
it was necessary to reduce our salaries. But we were all
in excellent spirits. We did not ' bate a jot of heart or
hope, but still bore up and steered right onward.' I well
remember a conversation with the late Professor Goddard,
now with God, on the subject of our prospects. We both
concluded that whether a college existed here or not, was

none of our concern. Our duty was, so long as it existed, to make it a *good* college.* The vessel might sink, but, if so, it should sink with all its colors flying; we would strive to make it a place of thorough education, and the cultivation of elevated and noble character."

In the foregoing brief recital of his efforts to improve the character, elevate the scholarship, and increase the educational advantages of Brown University, Dr. Wayland has, with his accustomed modesty, made but slight and incidental allusion to the amount of his own labor. But perhaps no period of his life furnishes more forcible illustration of the salient points of his character than the early years of his presidency. His untiring industry; his close attention to details, where moral principle was involved, or the general welfare of the college was concerned; his determination to discharge fearlessly the duty which lay directly before him; his habit of asking what was right, rather than what seemed, for the time, expedient; his keen and ever-abiding sense of personal responsibility; his exalted standard of excellence in his chosen calling, leading him to be satisfied with nothing short of the highest attainable perfection; his love of exact justice; his scorn of all sham, and of every form of deception; his freedom from anything like pride of opinion; his veneration for truth, in reference to every doctrine which he discussed, impressing a conviction, upon all who heard him, of his courage and his candor; the liberal and catholic spirit with which he approached the consideration of every subject; the strength of his moral convictions and the earnestness of his religious faith; his love for the souls of his pupils, and his intense and all-absorbing

---

* It is worthy of note, that in Dr. Wayland's copy of the Life of Dr. Arnold, — a valued gift from the widow of that distinguished instructor, — the following remark of the master of Rugby School is underscored. "It is *not* necessary that this should be a school of three hundred, or one hundred, or of fifty boys; but it *is* necessary that it should be a school of Christian gentlemen."

desire that the young men intrusted to his charge should
be, not only successful scholars, but consistent Christians,
— all these qualities found ample exercise and abundant
illustration from the commencement to the close of his
administration of the affairs of the university.

In this connection we quote the words of one who, as
an undergraduate, was a beloved pupil, and subsequently,
as a member of the Faculty, was an intimate and valued
friend : — *

"He went to Providence at the age of thirty-one, in
the prime of his manhood, with an established reputation, with a commanding personal presence, and with a
capacity for work, and a habit of industry, that made
themselves immediately felt on all with whom he became
associated. His views of education, its objects and its
methods, were already settled. He had formed a high
ideal of what a college ought to be, and of the influence it
ought to exert; and though a stranger at Brown, he resolutely set himself about making it conform to this ideal.
None but those who witnessed the changes he wrought
can fully appreciate what he did for the college in its
standard of scholarship, in the tone of its discipline, in
the increase of its means of instruction, and in the self-
sacrificing spirit which he infused alike into its instructors and its more immediate guardians. Seldom has the
head of a college identified himself so fully with all its
interests and affairs. He built it up anew, and made it
the honored seat of learning it now is. Its departments
of instruction were but imperfectly organized, and in
addition to his own proper work, he taught whatever
there was no one else to teach.† For several years he
held the reins of discipline entirely in his own hands, and
both by day and by night watched over the students with

---

* Professor William Gammell's obituary notice, in the New York
Examiner and Chronicle.

† Mrs. Wayland, writing at this time to a sister of her husband,
says, "Your brother is well, but constantly occupied. Indeed,
he has too much love of work not to be always busy. He never
has any leisure, for if others fail in the performance of their duties,
he supplies the deficiency by additional labor on his own part."

truly parental care. It was his habit to know every one personally; to become acquainted with the character and tendencies of each, and thus be able to caution them against the first wrong step, which, once taken, is sure to cost so much. He seemed to feel responsible for every young man intrusted to his care; and if any one suffered a loss of character, he not only felt the greatest pain, but almost blamed himself. He knew everything that was done, and everything that was left undone, in the whole college; and there is, probably, scarcely one, of his earlier pupils especially, who cannot recall some word of admonition, or some suggestion of encouragement, given precisely at the moment of need by the ever-watchful president. He did not care especially to make the college popular, as it is called; but he labored most earnestly to render it a school of thorough discipline and of sound education. In striving for this, he displayed an ability and devotion that awakened universal admiration. The benefactors and friends of the institution took new courage, and the merchants of Providence, stirred by his appeals on the true uses of wealth, began their contributions for its advancement. During his presidency, and largely through his immediate agency, Manning Hall was erected, the library fund was created, and the library planted on a new basis; Rhode Island Hall and the new president's house were built, the college grounds were enlarged and improved, and the college funds greatly increased. In all this he was not a mere spectator, but an active leader and originator. All his plans, however some of them may be regarded in other respects, were the fruit of liberal and disinterested views, and of a sincere desire to promote the best interests of the college, and to make it as useful as possible to the community."

If we seek to ascertain the cause of the early maturity of his judgment, and his well-defined ideas of education and discipline, we can hardly attach too much importance to the friendly relations, which as pupil and instructor, he had held to Dr. Nott. To have been on terms of intimacy with the president of Union College was of itself an invaluable preparation for the work of a teacher. To learn wisdom from his marvellous knowledge of human nature, to catch inspiration from his electric eloquence, to observe his match-less power of personal influence, and his profound sagacity in dealing with those committed to his care, was of inesti-mable advantage to one called so early in life to assume the charge of an institution endeared to the denominatior under whose auspices it was founded, and already illus-trated by honored names.

Nor should we fail to allude to the influence and ex-ample of another instructor. Mention has already been made of the sentiments which Dr. Wayland entertained for Professor Moses Stuart.

But, while recognizing, to the fullest extent, the advan-tage which the president derived from these sources, jus-tice demands that we should allude to that unconscious preparation for his duties which depended upon his own exertions. His life-long motto, " Whatever is worth doing at all, is worth doing well," was the key-note to his suc-cess in all the departments of labor to which he addressed himself. As tutor and professor in Union College, he had been called upon to give instruction in a great variety of studies. Cheerfully assuming every responsibility which his position imposed upon him, he had endeavored, with conscientious fidelity, to qualify himself for the discharge of all his duties.

Not dreaming of the fields of eminent usefulness for which he was thus preparing himself, he devoted his time to the most thorough preparation for the exercises of the recitation-room. As he was in the habit of saying to his friends, " Nothing can stand before days' works." He avoided every form of social or literary dissipation. He sought the society of persons older and more experienced than himself. He was accustomed, so far as he had the opportunity, to observe carefully the effect which the expressed opinions of those around him had upon their success or failure in life. Writing to a young friend, some years after the commencement of his presidency, he gives the following advice, borrowed, without doubt, from the results of his own experience and observation : —

" You tell me that you are very much alone in your sentiments, both political and religious. This will require good sense in order to wise behavior. I think I should not argue much in the matter. It will make little difference in the state of the nation which way the young gentlemen of the academy think. I should say but little, and think the more. A modest, gentleman-like boy is much more of a man than a great ' argufier.' I do not suppose that your arguments on either side would be very profound. When you are a few years older, it will be time enough to attend to these things. I would not give up what I believed to be right or true. I would hold to my opinions, and let others have theirs. Let them do all the talking. Observe the effect which men's opinions have upon their conduct. This will do you more good, at your present age, than arguing. Always openly avow your opinions, and there let the matter rest."

Again he writes, —

" Let me urge upon you, if you wish to be respected, to be thoroughly master of your studies. I would sit up until midnight, rather than not know them. Never think, ' This will do,' unless it be done as well as you can possibly do it. You will thus acquire the habit of using your faculties to the best advantage, and you will double your intellectual power in a single year. The true way to increase our talents is to employ them to the utmost."

Those familiar with Dr. Wayland's modes of study will not fail to recognize in this last quotation one secret of his success.

And yet with all the self-respect and self-reliance which the consciousness of acting from pure motives could not but engender, there was a distrust of his fitness and capacity to meet the demands of his new position, amounting almost to diffidence. This feeling, and his consequent dependence upon divine Providence for guidance and support, will appear in the following letters, written in February, 1827 : —

To his wife : —

" What an eventful year this has been to both of us! It has seen me a pastor, a father, a professor, and the president of a college. In rapid succession new and important duties have devolved upon me, and multiplied interests have been confided to my care, which might well teach a wiser man to tremble. It is my prayer, and I know that it will be yours, that I may become more humble, childlike, and dependent, and may act in every situation as is meet for a Christian and an heir of heaven. This world is all vanity. I feel this more and more. I hope that I may learn to love. it less, and to be habitually prepared for another."

To his parents he writes, —

" I need not say that my position here is arduous, difficult, and responsible in no ordinary degree. Much will be expected of me ; much must be done, or comparatively little good will be accomplished. Had I sought the office, or had I not believed that divine Providence directed me to it, I should be unhappy, and, I think, discouraged. I know, however, that God never calls us to situations which he will not enable us to fill, if we look to him in humble sincerity. In this frame of mind I desire to go to him for wisdom and guidance. I am aware that the best of all qualifications for this or any other station are moral qualifications ; a heart right with God, and a spirit prepared and waiting to obey every command and trust every promise of the Savior. I desire to recognize my reliance upon him for all needed gifts and graces, and I make these remarks now, particularly, in the hope that you will pray for these things in my behalf. I do, indeed, feel that they are what I especially require. If I please God, I am sure that he will order everything aright. He will bless me and make me a blessing. If I do not please him, I know that he will confound all my projects, or else he will cause even my apparent success to result in my destruction."

To the same : —

" I am tired of this wandering life, and hope soon to be settled in my own house. My prospects here, so far as I can discern, are good ; but I dare not promise much."

Again he writes to his wife (February 23, 1827), —

"Nothing unfavorable has yet occurred here. God only knows how soon it may come, and he only can prevent it."

To a friend : —

"I am worrying along here, doing what I can ; but that is very little."

CHAPTER X.

REMINISCENCES OF GRADUATES. — THE FIRST COM-
MENCEMENT. — REPORTS OF THE FACULTY TO THE
CORPORATION. — DR. WAYLAND'S REVIEW OF HIS
METHODS OF INSTRUCTION. — ADDRESS OF HON. B. F.
THOMAS. — DR. WAYLAND'S LECTURE-ROOM A PREP-
ARATION FOR LEGAL STUDIES. — HIS INTEREST IN
JURISPRUDENCE.

FOR an impartial estimate of the success of Dr. Wayland as an instructor, it may be well to introduce the
recollections of gentlemen cognizant of the previous condition of the college, and of the results accomplished
under the new administration.   A member of the class of
1826,* and a leading scholar of that year, after alluding to
the various causes which had conspired to lower the intellectual standard and impair the moral influence of the
institution, says, —

"Such were some of the circumstances under which
President Wayland commenced his official duties at
Brown University.   But unpromising as these circumstances were in one point of view, they were in another
aspect quite favorable, if rightly used, for the inauguration of a new administration.   There was room for great
improvement, and the friends of the college were ready
to second every suggestion which seemed adapted to that
end.   The reputation of Dr. Wayland had preceded him.
His missionary sermon had gained for him a wide celebrity, and had prepared the way for a most effective

---

* Hon. John Kingsbury, LL. D., late commissioner of public
schools for Rhode Island.

influence in moulding the characters of young men. The plans which he adopted and carried into full effect, were minute, exact, and thorough. They were, moreover, as comprehensive as the limited time and resources at the disposal of most of the students would allow. Order, discipline, and study took their appropriate place, and it was soon found that a new *régime* had commenced.

" The larger part of the pupils not only acquiesced in the change, but rejoiced in its beneficial results. There are now living men in high positions who ascribe their success in life to the influence of President Wayland in recalling them from the worse than waste of their time, and inciting them to assert their manhood by a different course of conduct. The favorable change in college, consequent upon President Wayland's induction into office, was very happily illustrated at prayers in the college chapel. Previous to his coming, this occasion had been usually selected by students to show their insubordination. All this soon passed away, and an attentive and serious demeanor was manifest. So great was the change, that it was not an uncommon thing to answer the inquiry of former graduates in respect to the success of Dr. Wayland, by introducing them to chapel at the hour of college prayers. No one came away without acknowledging that he had received a satisfactory answer."

Hon. John H. Clifford writes, —

" You are aware that when Dr. Wayland assumed the presidency of the college, my class (1827) had nearly completed its course. We enjoyed, therefore, a smaller measure of his invaluable instructions than our successors. Yet the single year of our intercourse with him was worth more to us than all the previous years of our connection with the university.

" He found us, when he came, drifting through the most perilous part of the voyage of life without rudder or compass, and with a reasonable prospect of making shipwreck of the precious freight with which we were laden. The disorganized, almost chaotic state of the college, the government a sort of *locum tenens*, without authority and devoid of discipline, and the undergraduates destitute of high aims and aspirations, — all this presented a dismal

prospect to one who felt, as he did, the full weight of the
burden he had assumed. Fortunately for us, Dr. Way-
land· was endowed with precisely the qualities to enable
him successfully to encounter this condition of things, to
the discouragements of which most men would have suc-
cumbed in helpless despondency. He took the helm with
a firm but parental hand, and piloted us safely through
the perils to which we were exposed. He possessed a
degree of personal magnetism unsurpassed by any one
I have ever known. And although an apparent severity
of discipline was indispensable to a successful administration of the duties of his office, the great quality of justice
was so conspicuous in all that he did and in all that he
said, that we were all in his hands ' like clay in the hands
of the potter.' It is due to him, under God, that some of
us were saved from being ' fashioned into vessels of dishonor,' to which, at that time, we seemed to be predes-
tined. So complete was the moral revolution which he
effected, that the class of 1827 became at once, from the
unpromising materials which I have described, most enthusiastic in the support of his policy, and took an
especial pride in the designation which he gave us of
' Pioneers of the New System.'

"Instead of contenting himself with a mere personal
oversight of the police and economics of the institution,
he assumed at once, in addition to these sufficiently oner-
ous duties, the arduous labors of a teacher in the highest departments of science. And here, in the recitation
and lecture room, his power was unequalled. He entered
it, as he required the students to enter it, without text-
books ; his purpose being to instruct his class not merely
in the contents of the volumes which treated of the science,
but in the science itself, in the teaching of which he regarded the text-books but as auxiliaries. Indeed, his own
oral instruction, independent of the accepted treatises in
use at that period, was so much more copious and exhaustive than the books themselves, that in a few years it
was elaborated into volumes of higher authority for students, superseding the older text-books upon the same subjects. It was quickly perceived by us that he was, in
truth, the ' master,' and far in advance of the books from
which he taught. This was one great source of the new
spirit with which he inspired his pupils, namely, that he

was thoroughly the master of his subject, and not a mere conduit of another man's thoughts.

"Moral and intellectual philosophy, rhetoric, criticism, and political economy were the departments of instruction to which he addressed himself. To these he required the student to apply a rigid system of analysis. This he regarded as the great means of intellectual discipline, and the only mode of enabling the pupil to acquire the power of self-culture. His theory was, that the college curriculum was not designed primarily to make learned men, but to train and invigorate the intellectual powers, and thereby prepare the students for their efficient exercise in the acquisition of knowledge upon any subject to which he might devote himself for the work of life.

"This brief retrospect of a turning period of my own life revives so many associations that are precious to me, that I could go on until your patience was wearied with my reminiscences of one whose memory I shall never cease to love and honor."

Another member * of the first class that graduated under Dr. Wayland contributes the following reminiscences:—

"The new system introduced by Dr. Wayland was the exact antipode of that which it displaced. It was in harmony with the spirit of the age, and yet sufficiently original to be correctly called 'Wayland's.' The excitement throughout the college and the town was great. The change was believed by many to be too sudden and too radical. As the man addicted to lying was advised to speak the truth and discontinue his old habit gradually, for fear of too severe a shock to his moral nature, so it was thought by some that the prompt abandonment of the old routine and the introduction of new measures would prove injurious to the interests of the university.

"The first Senior class that came under his immediate charge was charmed with him and with his 'new system.' Any member of the class of 1827 will gladly testify that the last year of his college life was worth all the other three. Dr. Wayland may have been disturbed by the opposition which he encountered in certain quarters, but I never detected any outward manifestation of it. He

---

* Hon. Charles Thurber.

quietly pursued the even tenor of his way, and before the callow Freshman became the dignified Senior, he thought himself much more fortunate than the members of the upper classes, in that all his four years were moulded by the hand of Wayland. Although, as I have already intimated, there was some outside opposition to the change in the discipline and mode of instruction, I do not believe that a single individual was disaffected to the altered condition of affairs when he saw and understood its actual workings.

" I am satisfied that no one who candidly examines and rightly comprehends what a revolution was effected by Dr. Wayland, can fail to be amazed at the wonderful executive ability of the thorough and self-sacrificing author of such great improvements in college education. Indeed, I think Dr. Wayland entered upon the presidency of the college at a time when to discharge its duties faithfully and efficiently required more nerve and courage and greater capacity than had been required at any previous period in its history, or perhaps than will be required at any time in its future career.

" The management of the college library had been singularly devoid of system, and by no means adapted to the wants or conducive to the convenience of students. I do not believe that one quarter of the undergraduates derived any considerable benefit from it. It was kept in one of the projection rooms of University Hall, and was almost a *terra incognita* to many of the students. A member of the Junior class once informed me that he had never taken a book from the library, and had been in the room but once. What Dr. Wayland accomplished for this department of college education is already well known to all the friends of the university.

" Commencement dinners were at this time dinners merely. No speeches were made, and graduates lingered over the wine, which was always furnished. I need not say that all this was soon changed. Again, physical training had never been thought of or alluded to. Our attention was called to this important department of education immediately after Dr. Wayland's induction into office.

" Heretofore, members of the Faculty had not been required to spend any portion of term time, excepting during recitation, within the walls of the university; but the new system made it a *sine qua non* that every officer of the institution should have a room in college, and be there every day during certain prescribed hours. To this was added the duty of regularly visiting the rooms of the students.

"Theatre-going was prohibited, and a late supper was no longer considered a valid excuse for an imperfect preparation for a recitation. Fixed hours for study became the rule rather than the exception, and indeed it was soon evident to all, that the requisite preparation for the recitation-room could not be made without careful and conscientious study. Up to this time we had always been accustomed to carry all our text-books with us into recitation. When we were compelled to leave these behind, we were of course deprived of the aid which an occasional glance into our books had formerly furnished. And in addition to this, that utter stranger to us, an exact analysis of the lesson, now required, made it a still harder task to deceive our instructors and wrong ourselves. Still, although all this increased our labors, I am satisfied that we were grateful for the addition to our burdens."

Another graduate, who was a pupil of Dr. Wayland during the early years of his presidency, writes as follows: —

"When President Wayland assumed the charge of Brown University, discipline was lax. In fact, the students did pretty much as they pleased. Instruction was entirely from text-books. These were used in recitation, always by teachers, and often by pupils, and were closely followed.* Officers were not required to occupy apartments in the college buildings, and the rooms of the undergraduates were almost never visited by members of the

---

* It is related that one of the instructors of this period was accustomed to have the text-book open before him, and, as the student recited, to move his finger along the lines, striving to keep pace with the progress of the pupil. From time to time, as the recitation of the student outstripped the reading of the professor, he would look up — keeping his finger at the point which had been reached — and say, in a tone of mild reproof, " Not so fast; not quite so fast."

Faculty. There was no such thing as discussion in the class-room ; recitation was only an exercise of the memory.

"But with the administration of Dr. Wayland all this was changed. The non-residence of officers was abolished. Every instructor was required to occupy a room in the college buildings, and to visit the students every day. Strict discipline was enforced, and the idea inculcated that young gentlemen came to college to study, and that all other considerations must be subordinated to that purpose.

"The personal example and influence of Dr. Wayland at once infused a new spirit into the university. The power of a great mind, and the energy of a controlling will, were immediately felt. He taught without a text-book, encouraged discussion and inquiry, introduced the important element of analysis, and imparted a novel interest to every recitation which he conducted.

"Improvement in the discipline of the university marked a new era in the life of the institution. The president spent in the college all the hours appropriated to study, and made daily visits to the rooms in his division. It was soon understood that a college usage, or tradition, could not be pleaded as an excuse for the violation of established rules. Raids upon adjacent gardens and poultry-yards were no longer tolerated. Disturbances of the quiet and order of the college premises were prohibited and punished. The students ceased to be a nuisance to the neighborhood, and began to appreciate the high duties and grave responsibilities of their position."

All these changes and reforms commenced with the new administration of affairs. It was evident that Dr. Wayland had a distinct and clearly-defined idea of what a college should be, and could be made, and he did not delay an instant to apply to his theory the test of practice.

There was no mild and moderate transition from lax discipline and unchecked license to strict enforcement of law. The reins of government were not loosely held in hesitating hands. There was no early adoption of temporizing expedients, to be succeeded in due time, and

when the safe moment arrived, by bolder and more vigorous measures. The reform was instant and radical.
President Wayland had not been in his new office twenty-
four hours before it was apparent to everybody that a new
régime was already instituted.

It cannot be denied that this sudden change in the
discipline and mode of instruction awakened opposition
among some of the students ; but it was confined to those
who, from indolence, indifference, or perversity, were indisposed to improve their advantages, and their connection
with the college was soon dissolved.

The prevailing feeling was pride in the ability, and
respect for the zeal and enthusiasm, of the new president.
The fresh stimulus given to study, and the new interest
imparted to the exercises of the recitation-room, were
most manifest. Especially was this true of the branches in
which instruction was given by the president. The fact
that he invited, and even urged, free discussion on all
subjects germane to the topic under consideration, the
lively interest which he displayed in the mental improvement of all his pupils, the wealth of illustration with which
he enriched his teachings, — all these quickened the intellects and sharpened the faculties of the student.

As has already been stated, Dr. Wayland spent in his
room in the college all the hours assigned for study. It
should be added, that he rarely left his study before ten
o'clock P. M. For years he invariably conducted two
daily recitations, and often more. He frequently supplied
the place of any officer, who, from sickness, or absence, or
any cause, was unable to attend to his classes. He gave
instruction, as it became necessary, from time to time, in
the ancient languages, in rhetoric and the natural sciences.
During the Junior and Senior years of 1829 and 1830, he
taught Campbell's Rhetoric, Kames' Elements of Criticism,
Physiology, Stewart's Mental Philosophy, and Paley's
Moral Science. The exercises of Commencement by the

graduating class of 1827 were pronounced by the public journals of Providence " an occasion of unusual interest," and the audience was said to be " larger than at any previous Commencement."

The editor of a leading newspaper in New York city, writing from Providence at this time, says, —

" For a number of years past, Brown University has seemed to be somewhat on the decline. Its affairs languished until last autumn, when,

'Discipline at length,
O'erlooked and unemployed, fell sick and died.'

The consequence was a change in its head, and a speedy and thorough revolution in its affairs. The course of studies prescribed under the new *régime* was such as to raise the requirements of the institution to as high a standard as any other ; and a code of laws was formed and adopted by the Faculty, which, it is believed, may be considered a model for the government of academic institutions. The salaries of the acting professors have been increased, and the non-resident professors, whose places were little more than sinecures, have been dispensed with.

" Arrangements are also making to add to the studies already prescribed, a course of popular instruction in English and the modern languages of Europe. In fine, under the administration of President Wayland and his able assistants, it is believed that the reformation has been such, that the university will assume a proud rank among those of greater age and more richly endowed."

Additional evidence of the increased prosperity of the college, under the new administration, is contained in official documents.

At the annual meeting of the corporation of Brown University held September 30, 1829, President Wayland, in behalf of the Faculty, presented a report embodying the results of their observation and experience as instructors during the two preceding years. The report specified the studies pursued by each of the classes for the past year, alluded to the recent alterations made in the course of

instruction, described the condition of the several departments, and recommended an important change in reference to vacations.   The president deprecated long vacations, as tending to dissipate the mind of the pupil, and as
interfering materially with the true objects of a college.
He urged the importance of devoting the winter months
to study, contending that the design of affording facilities
to the students to teach school during this portion of the
year was inconsistent with the duty imposed upon the
Faculty of devoting to collegiate exercises those months in
which study could be most profitably pursued.   He alluded to the fact that no regular annual appropriation had
ever been made for the purchase of books for the college
library, and recommended that definite and stated provision should be made for this object.   He further reported
that several important branches of instruction, including
the Evidences of Revelation, and Political Economy, had
been added to the collegiate course of study, and, generally, that every effort had been made to give to the pupils
largely increased educational advantages.

The whole report furnished abundant evidence that the
president would be satisfied with nothing less than the
adoption of such measures as should put the university on
an equality with the foremost institutions in the land.

In the report of the Faculty, presented to the corporation at its annual meeting in September, 1830, due prominence is given to the fact that "the behavior of the young
gentlemen of the college has been, during the past year,
in the highest degree commendable.   Very few instances
requiring the exercise of discipline have occurred."   After
alluding to the manner in which instruction had been
given in the various departments of learning embraced in
the college curriculum, the president adverts to the principles which have governed him in the discharge of his
own duties.

This part of the report presents so tersely and truth-

fully his views as to the mode in which instruction should
be imparted in the recitation-room, that we make no
apology for quoting the passage without abridgment.

" I have endeavored to teach, not any particular book,
but the science itself of which the text-book has treated.
I have aimed, so far as I have been able, to determine the
nature and objects of the science, its elementary principles, and the order in which they should be presented to
the mind. This knowledge, thus, as I have hoped, sim-
plified, and more completely analyzed, I have desired
to communicate to the pupil. The text-book has been
used to invite and stimulate inquiry, rather than to re-
press it.

" In conducting the recitations of my class, I seek to
inculcate the necessity of the greatest exactitude of knowledge in all that belongs to definitions and general principles. With this in view, I accustom them to extemporaneous illustration of every principle of importance.
When I differ from the author, I give my reasons. I
endeavor to show where his doctrines are false, or where
they require to be limited or extended. I encourage free
discussion on every important subject, either in the lesson,
or connected with it; always asking my class, after a
series of remarks, or after a lecture, whether they wish to
make any inquiries or to urge any objections. Of this
privilege they always avail themselves; nor have I, except
in a very few, and those very trifling instances, seen it
abused. It has been my desire to render the recitation-
room attractive, not merely by the communication of
knowledge, but by exciting inquiry and eliciting talent;
by giving exercise to logical acuteness, and refinement to
moral sentiment. I am aware how imperfect has been
my success in this important work. I speak rather of
what I have desired, than of what I have accomplished.
In connection with this daily course of study, I have accustomed my class to continual review from the beginning
of the work. In this manner the relation of the principles already acquired to those which may hereafter be
presented, is easily discovered; and the whole science
may thus, at any moment, be surveyed in totality as well
as in detail. I have aimed so to conduct this exercise,
that a pupil, at any period of his study, can easily recall,

from the commencement, the outline of the whole, so far as he has proceeded.

" In addition to the daily discussions of the recitation-room, I have delivered a series of lectures on the Elements of Political Economy, another on the Principles of Rhetoric, several lectures on Intellectual Philosophy, and a brief course upon the General Principles of Animal Physiology."

It is surely not surprising that such constant and conscientious discharge of duty should have been crowned with unequivocal success ; and we feel confident that the president was warranted in closing this interesting report with these words of good cheer to every friend of the university : —

" I have endeavored to present to the corporation a plain and intelligible account of the objects which the Faculty have kept in view during the past year, and the manner in which they have sought to attain them. With gratitude to God, we are enabled to entertain the pleasing conviction that our labor has not been in vain. We believe that we can discern visible improvement in intellectual power and mental discipline, since the date of our last report, in every class under our charge."

President Wayland adhered to the mode of imparting instruction, just described, until his connection with the college terminated. Not long before his death, on a thoughtful review of his experience as a teacher, he deliberately recorded his conviction that his system of instruction had been correct in its principles, and serviceable to both teacher and pupil. We quote from his reminiscences : —

" As so long a portion of my life, and that portion in which I have been known most widely to the world, has been spent in the labor of instruction, it may be well for me to record briefly the principles by which I have been guided in the discharge of this part of my duty. Very much that I have done is, of course, wholly forgotten, and I can only refer to those general rules of action which occur to me as I endeavor to look back upon the past.

Many of the events of my life, already alluded to in these reminiscences, I have not recalled even so often as once in twenty-five years or more. Much that might have been of interest has faded from my memory. I have no documents to consult, and I may possibly have erred in my recollection. I think, however, that I have no reason to remember what did not occur, and that, therefore, my memory may be considered trustworthy.

"I may here observe that I have never considered myself, in any manner, peculiarly adapted to the work of an instructor. It seemed my duty to undertake the labor, and I honestly attempted to discharge that duty as well as I knew how. When, however, I compare myself with Pestalozzi, Dr. Arnold, and other teachers, who have apparently been endowed with every faculty needed for their calling, and animated with an intense love for it, I am compelled to feel and confess my vast deficiency. If this remark shall provoke the inquiry, 'For what, then, were you intended?' I am really unable to answer it. I do not know that I have ever had any special predilection for any one pursuit. I had promising prospects as a physician, and, when young, was fond of natural science. My position as a clergyman was above mediocrity. I labored with some success as an instructor; but the station upon which I have ever looked with peculiar admiration and reverence is that of an able and upright judge.[*]

"With reference to teaching, I may say, in general terms, that my governing principles were few. I suppose that everything that is to be taught may be resolved into certain elementary truths. These are usually simple, and if presented in a simple form, may be easily apprehended by persons of sufficient age and common understanding. I say of sufficient age, for the mind, at successive periods of its growth, makes distinct progress in its power of comprehending abstract truth. It can be taught merely to remember the way in which an idea is expressed, without any knowledge of the idea itself. To such an extent

---

[*] Writing, in 1856, to his friend Hon. Ellis Lewis, then Chief Justice of the Supreme Court of Pennsylvania, Dr. Wayland says, "The only position the world could offer me, which I have thought I should like, is that of a judge of a court whose decisions involved grave questions of right."

is this true, that I have known a young person to receive
a truth, which he has not been able heretofore to comprehend, as an entire novelty, when in fact it was the very
same truth, the expression of which, in words, he had
committed to memory several years before.

"But to return: I endeavored always to understand,
for myself, whatever I attempted to teach. By this I
mean that I was never satisfied with the text, unless I saw
for myself, as well as I was able, that the text was true.
Pursuing this course, I was led to observe the principles
or general truths on which the treatise was founded. As
I considered these, they readily arranged themselves in a
natural order of connection and dependence. I do not
wish to be understood as asserting that I did this with
every text-book before I began to use it in my class. I
generally taught these subjects during a single year.
Before I had thought through one subject, I was called
upon to commence another. Yet, with every year, I
made some progress in all. I prepared lectures on particular subjects, and thus fixed in my mind the ideas
which I had acquired, for use during the next year. The
same process continued year by year, and in this manner,
almost before I was aware of it, I had completed an entire
course of lectures. In process of time I was thus enabled
to teach by lecture all the subjects which I began to teach
from text-books.

"I have always aimed, as I have already intimated, not
only to understand a subject for myself, but to make my
pupils understand it. There need be no difficulty in
detecting by the expression of a listener's eye whether he
catches and understands the idea which the instructor
seeks to communicate. If I saw that what I said was not
comprehended, I repeated and illustrated until I was
convinced that I had succeeded. I also caused it to be
understood that our subject was one in which they and I
were equally interested. Therefore I not only allowed,
but encouraged, my pupils to ask questions with reference
to any portion of the lesson recited, or of the lecture
delivered. They very soon began to avail themselves of
this privilege. Pursuing this method, our recitations consisted not merely of the repeating of passages from the
text-book, or answering questions framed from the text-
book by the teacher, but were really animated discussions

on the subjects under consideration. From this course I derived great benefit, in common with the class. The students were stimulated to a considerable degree by the consciousness that they were independent seekers after truth. I rarely passed through such a discussion without great advantage. Sometimes I was convinced that I had been in error. At other times I became satisfied that I had presented the idea obscurely, or without proper limitations or sufficient generalization. It not unfrequently happened that when the subject under consideration was especially interesting or important, two or three days were consumed upon a single lesson.

"It may be said that this method is liable to abuse. This is undoubtedly true: I have seen it abused. Young men would now and then ask frivolous questions from thoughtlessness. At other times, by collusion among themselves, they would ask questions with the design of arresting the progress of the recitation, when their friends, who were unprepared, were in danger of being exposed. This, however, may be easily prevented by an instructor. It is only necessary to answer a fool according to his folly, in order to make the experiment too dangerous to be repeated.

"There were two other modes of giving instruction, to which I adhered, which were, in my opinion, of essential service to my pupils — they were analysis and review. As to the former, our practice was, in all recitations from text-books, to accustom the student to make out the analysis, skeleton, or plan of the lesson to be recited. He was expected to commence, and, without question or assistance, to proceed in his recitation as long as might be required. The next who was called upon took up the passage where his predecessor left it; and thus it continued (except as there was interruption by inquiry or explanation) until the close. It is, of course, understood that the knowledge of the instructor enabled him to correct any error, and suggest any deficiency or inaccuracy in the analysis. It was also customary to commence the recitation by calling on some one to give the entire analysis of the lesson. Every one was expected to be able to do this, as it was a regular part of the daily exercise. This practice, introduced at the beginning of a term, became very easy before the next vacation; and to be able to give an exact and distinct analysis of a lesson was made a special mark of good scholarship. In general, no man could do it well who was not a clear-headed and diligent student.

" The advantages of this mode of study I have supposed to, be several. Whether a similar plan is adopted in other colleges, I have no means of knowing. My first experience of it was while in Union College, under Dr. Nott. I have observed that students, coming to Brown University from other colleges, have spoken of it as new to them.

" This mode of recitation is of advantage to the instructor. When he conducts an exercise of this kind, and such a knowledge of the subject is required of the pupil, he is compelled, unless he is willing to lose the respect of his class, to be himself thoroughly prepared. He must (no matter how often he uses the same text-book) take pains to qualify himself for every recitation. This will impart a deeper interest to the subject; will, from time to time, restore its freshness ; and in this manner, a recitation, instead of being a bore, will become an agreeable and improving exercise.

" It may be objected that this is imposing unnecessary labor upon an instructor. It certainly calls for additional, but by no means unnecessary, labor. Without intellectual exertion, a teacher is in danger of wearing out and becoming a mere machine. An indolent teacher will soon degenerate into a very stupid man. His pupils will discover this, and in almost every class some of his students will, by common consent, be considered superior to their instructor. Such a change of relations can only be prevented by the absolute prohibition of all inquiry. This expedient will inevitably render the recitation a dull formality, irksome to both parties, until it becomes a contemptible mode of spending time under the guise of instruction.

" To the student, also, the advantages are no less obvious. He is obliged, in preparing in this manner for a recitation, to make himself master of each daily lesson. More than this, he *knows* that he has mastered it. He can lay aside his book, go through the analysis by himself, and then take up and complete the train of thought,

not using, with servile exactness, the language of the author, but in his own words. When called upon to recite
in the presence of his class, he knows that he understands
his subject, and soon learns, with confidence, to give expression to the ideas of which he has possessed himself.
Not until he can do this is he prepared for recitation.
It soon becomes a matter of emulation in a class for a
student to recite with accuracy, in good language, and in
such a manner as to interest his fellows. Indeed, I have
rarely taught a class which could not furnish two or three
members whose recitations were listened to with evident
gratification by all their auditors.

"The effect of such an exercise in cultivating ease of
delivery, and in promoting the power of extemporaneous
speech, is manifest. He who has thus learned to prepare
himself on a given subject, and then to express himself in
the presence of his instructor and his classmates, has laid
the foundation of success as a public speaker. Nor is this
all. Let a young man accustom himself to frame a careful and correct analysis of what he is about to recite, and
resolve never to speak or compose until this analysis is
completed, and he will have made decided progress in
mental discipline. He who has learned never to address
his fellow-men, either orally or by written language, without forming a definite plan which shall tend to produce a
particular effect, has acquired a most valuable habit. By
pursuing this course habitually, he will soon be able to
continue it with scarcely a perceptible effort. In fact, he
will find it so much easier to use his mind in this way than
in any other, that he will soon do it spontaneously, even
while he is commencing an unpremeditated address. Instructors in law schools, and lawyers in the preparation
of their arguments, have frequently referred to this method
of study as of essential service to them. I have been told
that a late distinguished professor in the law school at
Cambridge was accustomed to say that he could at once
distinguish a graduate of Brown University by the facility
with which he was able to analyze a lecture or a legal
argument. The power which this practice would naturally give to a clergyman in constructing a train of thought
for the pulpit is apparent.

"Accompanying the habit of analyzing every lesson,

and making this analysis a distinct feature of the recitation, was that of frequent review. It was my custom in the class-room to require, first of all, the lesson of the previous day, whether that consisted of a lecture or a portion of a text-book. This fixed every lesson in the mind of the pupil. As we advanced, I would begin the book, and call for the analysis of several portions of what we had gone over. When we had overtaken our advance, we commenced anew from the beginning. In this manner we were enabled to review the whole book frequently during the course of a single term, thus strengthening materially the habit of generalization.

"The result of this training was, that all the best scholars of a class could, without prompting, go through the entire book which they had studied, at the first examination. The more moderate scholars would do the same with little prompting. No man, however, would make any claim to good scholarship who could not readily do it. At examinations, the chapters or sections of the text-book were written on separate slips of paper, and drawn out for every student by lot. The time occupied in examining a pupil was allowed to the one who was to follow, for the purpose of recollection. An exercise conducted in this manner would proceed for three hours, and if the class were a good one, a failure would rarely occur. If a student were unable to proceed, he was allowed to draw again, and thus often recovered his standing.

"I am satisfied that nothing enabled me to escape the danger of mental indolence and stagnation to which I have already alluded, but the manner of conducting recitations which I have described (in distinction from the more usual mode of question and answer), and the habit of lecturing from time to time on every portion of the text-book. By adhering to these practices I was soon able to form text-books for myself, and amidst constant attention to details, and the incessant interruptions consequent upon my office, to make, year by year, as I hope, some progress.

"So far as the student is concerned, it can hardly be denied that there are manifest advantages in such a mode of giving instruction. If the object of the teacher be to impart knowledge, and to fix it in the mind of the pupil, certainly this object can be more successfully accomplished

in this way than in any other.   Nothing tends more surely
to implant knowledge in the mind.   If the object be the
cultivation of the mental powers, by daily effort and by
comparing the relation of various truths with each other,
this will be most certainly attained by uniting the view of
the whole subject with perfectly free discussions in the
class-room.   The object of an education is not, as many
parents would seem to believe, to get a student through
college by going over a certain number of books, but to
impart knowledge which shall be remembered, and to increase the intellectual capacity of the pupil by habitually
calling into exercise as many of his powers and faculties
as the circumstances of the case will permit."

Many graduates of Brown University have, in subsequent life, borne their testimony to the value of this system
of instruction.   Upon the occasion of Dr. Wayland's resignation of the presidency, Hon. B. F. Thomas, of the
Supreme Court of Massachusetts, thus addressed the
retiring president, in presence and in behalf of his assembled pupils ; —

"I rise, Mr. President, for the discharge of a painful
and yet a grateful duty.   The alumni of the university,
having heard of your resignation of the office you have so
long held with signal honor to yourself and signal advantage to her, met yesterday to give utterance to the feelings
which that event awakened.   They passed resolutions
(would they were worthier) expressing their sense of the
value of your services to the college, and of the loss she had
sustained by your retirement.   They instructed their committee (Governor Clifford, of New Bedford, Hon. Mr. Bradley, of this city, and myself) to present these resolutions to
you to-day, the last time we shall have the pleasure of
meeting you in this near and interesting relation.

"It is but little to say, that these resolutions were passed
unanimously, — there was but one mind and one heart in
the assembly, and that mind and heart were but one, —
for the calmest result of the judgment was in harmony
with the warmest feelings of the heart.   We did not, however, forget that we were speaking of and to the living,
and in avoiding what may be said to be the natural

warmth of eulogy, — that, we trust, far distant service to come from the trembling lips of some later pupils, — we may have assumed a tone too subdued.

" One of these resolutions comes from those whose privilege it was to have been your immediate pupils. Of that resolution, as one of the earlier of those pupils, I will say a word. I should be sorry if I thought myself capable of making a formal speech in an hour like this. You are, Mr. President, too largely my creditor for me to judge calmly and wisely. I cannot pay the debt. I do not ask you to forgive it. I can and will confess it. More than twenty years ago it ripened into a judgment, and yet no lapse of time will bar it. Hundreds around you owe the like debt. It grows ever. It is an investment for all time. If you see in it, as I know you do, the true riches, more than the wealth of an Astor is yours. Its bonds are stronger than those of the railroad, its pulse is quicker than that of the telegraph. It is the tribute of loving hearts. It is the debt of filial gratitude.

" I came here to-day, Mr. President, to say now what I have often said at home and to my own pupils, and what this seems to me a fitting occasion to say more publicly.

" It has been my privilege for three years to be your pupil. I have seen and have had other eminent masters : Joseph Story, whose name is identified with the jurisprudence of his country; John Hooker Ashmun, who, an invalid for years, and dying at the early age of thirty-three, as a lawyer left behind him no superior in Massachusetts, whose mind had the point of the diamond and the clearness of its waters; Pliny Merrick, who graces the bench on which I have the honor to sit, but of whom my near relation to him forbids me to speak as I would. A quarter of a century has passed since I left these walls with your blessing. I have seen something of men and of the world since. I esteem it to-day the happiest event of my life that brought me here, the best gift of an ever-kind Providence to me, that I was permitted for three years to sit at the feet of your instruction.

" Others may speak and think of the writer and scholar, my tribute is to the great teacher; and he is not the great teacher who fills the mind of his pupil from the affluence of his learning, or works most for him, but who has the rarer faculty of drawing out and developing the mind of another, and making him *work for himself.* Rarest of all God's gifts to men. Great statesmen, great orators, great jurists, are successful and useful in the degree that they are great teachers. Office of unequalled dignity and worth, — even our divine Lord and Master we call the 'Great Teacher.'

"Mr. President, if I have acquired any consideration in my own beloved commonwealth, if I have worthily won any honor, I can and do, with a grateful heart, bring them to-day and lay them at your feet — *Teucro duce et auspice Teucro.*"

Another graduate * has observed, —

"To those designing to enter the legal profession, his instructions were invaluable. This is the uniform testimony of every one of his graduates who has since distinguished himself at the bar. The singular rapidity with which he seized upon the strong points of whatever subject was under discussion in the class-room, the tenacity with which he held all the disputants to the precise issue, brushing aside the rubbish of irrelevant and inapposite details, and obliging the pupil to deal with the vital principles which lay at the foundation of the immediate topic under consideration, and, above all, the constant habit of exact and exhaustive analysis which he counselled and even compelled the pupil to pursue, — all this was an admirable preparation for the profitable study and successful practice of the law."

It may not be inappropriate to allude, in this connection, to the interest which Dr. Wayland always manifested in the science of jurisprudence, and his earnest desire that those of his pupils who entered upon the legal profession should be guided by high-minded and generous views of duty. Writing to a young friend and pupil, who had recently commenced the practice of the law, he says, —

"If you are in ' the full tide of successful experiment,' you

---

* Hon. C. S. Bradley, Chief Justice of the Supreme Court of Rhode Island.

must beware that nothing interferes with its legitimate result.   Prosperity renders weak men careless, and strong
men more careful.   Old Jeremiah Mason was as exact and
cautious in the height of his reputation as when he was a
young practitioner.   It must be so with every man who
would arrive at eminence.   The higher a lawyer rises, the
abler are his competitors, and the greater need he has of
the full exercise of all his powers.   Nothing can exceed
the intensity of mental action necessary to the discharge
of the duty of an eminent practitioner in Westminster
Hall.   The same is true, *mutatis mutandis*, of other
places.   You remember the dialogue between George the
Third, I think, and the elder Pitt.   ' Mr. Pitt, deserve my
confidence, and you shall have it.'   ' Sir, give me your
confidence, and I will deserve it.'   The king had the best
of it.   It is so with the public.   If a man deserve confidence, he is sure, sooner or later, to have it."

To the same : —

" I am not sorry that you have perplexing cases, for
thus only can you learn to manage them.   Always seek
to find the governing principle which underlies them, and
then every case you determine settles the rule for a class.
As these rules multiply, you will discover that the perplexities diminish in number, and soon, what would puz-
zle another will be easy for you.

" I am glad that you are applying yourself closely to
the law, and that you are diversifying it with the classics.
Read over and over again the best passages, and, if you
please, commit them to memory.   You will soon find
that such knowledge will place you in a different class
from those who do not possess it.   It will serve, moreover, to enlarge your range of illustration, and to give
energy to your thoughts.   This will be vastly more profitable than spending your time in amusement.   In the one
case, you are laying the foundations for future professional
success ; in the other, you are pulverizing the very stones.
But, above all, establish rules for study.   In no other way
can you have any just notion of the value of time.   If time
be used miscellaneously, and no task be assigned for every
day and hour, it will glide away, — no one knows how, —
and with no practical result.   The only way to eminence

is to love labor, or, at the least, to be perfectly willing to
expend all the labor necessary to accomplish a given object. Besides, we can never govern others until we have
learned to govern ourselves.

" I am glad to hear that you are devoting your evenings
to the law. Every evening's study squares, or helps to
square, a stone which you may lay aside to put in the
building whenever a client gives you an invitation. I
would always keep this idea in mind. Study with an
object, that is, with a distinct point or principle in view.
As fast as you settle a principle, pause and frame, or discover, a case to which it will apply. Make your notes
and references, and pass on to another. Thus, day by
day, you will be able to mark your progress, and to say,
' I am prepared to-day on what I did not know yesterday.'
The real cases will come along in due time, and you will
discover that you are ready to meet them."

To another pupil : —

" Leave nothing to chance. Remember that the smallest amount of labor necessary to do anything, is all the
time and labor necessary to do it well. You may sometimes find yourself not so thoroughly prepared as you
could wish, but you ought always to be able to say, ' I
did all that I could to deserve success.' Always do as
well as you can, and you will do better every day."

In the opinion of Dr. Wayland, the high-minded and
conscientious lawyer has it in his power greatly to promote the welfare of civil society. For the low cunning
of the pettifogger he had an abhorrence which he never
sought to conceal. He urged upon all his pupils, who
designed to enter the legal profession, the importance of
placing before themselves an elevated standard of excellence, seeking always to establish correct general principles, never being satisfied with simply carrying a point,
but aiming rather to secure a result in harmony with
sound jurisprudence. He would say, —

" Do not accept any recognized doctrine for no better
reason than that it has the authority of decided cases, nor

keep in view only the facts of the particular question under consideration. This was the weak point of Lord Eldon. Examine the precedents carefully, and see if they rest on the principles of eternal justice. If you believe them to be wrong, labor to refute the fallacious reasoning, and contend earnestly for what is right and true. Do your work in a manly, straightforward manner, remembering that your business is not to gain, by any means, a victory over an opposing counsel, but to settle the matter in dispute in the fear of God and for the good of man." *

Those who were familiar with the favorite studies of Dr. Wayland will not need to be reminded that, while the biographies of men distinguished in all the departments of art, science, and literature, or devoted to practical philanthropy, had for him a peculiar charm, he read with especial pleasure and profit the recorded lives of those great lights of jurisprudence, who, in every age, have illustrated their profession, and established important principles in constitutional or municipal law. Not only was his acquaintance with the history of English jurisprudence exact and thorough, but he readily recalled the leading incidents in the career of every eminent English lawyer, whether his distinction had been earned by his decisions from the bench, or by the ability of his arguments at the bar. He delighted to hold up, for the admiration and imitation of his pupils, the shining examples of Sir Matthew Hale, Lord Hardwicke, Lord Ellenbor-

---

* It may not be out of place to state, in this connection, an incident illustrating his love of justice and his active sympathy with the suffering poor. Having been informed, that, in one of the inferior courts of Providence, innocent persons arraigned for alleged misdemeanors were sometimes convicted and sentenced because they were unable to employ counsel, he conferred with a competent lawyer on the subject, and requested him to appear for the defendant in any such case that came to his knowledge, promising to assume the expense of such professional service.

ough, Lord Erskine, and Sir Samuel Romilly, Chief
Justice Marshall, Alexander Hamilton, Jeremiah Mason,
and Daniel Webster. He was accustomed to point to
Lord Erskine as the model advocate, and to his reported
arguments as the finest specimens of forensic reasoning to
be found in the English language. He had read them
critically, and analyzed them again and again, and could
readily quote, from recollection, some of the most eloquent
passages. From these sources, also, he derived many
appropriate illustrations and apposite anecdotes, with
which he diversified and enriched his instructions.

CHAPTER XI.

THE LECTURE-ROOM. — DR. BAILEY'S REMINISCENCES. —
ILLUSTRATIONS. — DR. WAYLAND'S CHARACTERISTICS
AS A TEACHER. — HIS RULING PRINCIPLE.

WHAT has already been said, in general terms, of
the peculiar features of Dr. Wayland's mode of
teaching, will, after all, fall far short of conveying a correct conception of his manner of conducting a recitation
in the class-room. While those who have enjoyed the
benefits of his instruction will not need to be reminded
of the hours so rapid in their passage and so profitable in
their results, still to others of our readers a brief sketch
of the president, as he appeared before his classes, may
not be without interest. We quote from reminiscences
kindly furnished by Rev. Dr. Silas Bailey, professor of
Theology in Kalamazoo Theological Seminary, Michigan.

"In September, 1830, I entered Brown University. I
am now unable to say whether any one pointed out to me
the president. There was certainly little need. He was
then in the thirty-fifth year of his age and the fourth of
his presidency. His step was elastic, his form erect, and
his bearing manly and dignified. Altogether he was the
most perfect man in physical and intellectual development
that my eyes had ever beheld. Who the president was,
had no place among the difficult problems which the new-
comer would be called upon to solve. Indeed, a stranger
in the college halls, or even in the city, soon discovered
that he was within the sphere of influence of a profound
thinker and an earnest man.

"The student who had been for a year in college
seemed to the new pupil to have ' Dr. Wayland on the

brain.' The president was the prolific theme upon which all dwelt. This topic once reached, the conversation would not flag for an hour. By this means the curiosity and expectation of the new-comer were raised to a high point, and everything subsequently proved in keeping with his first impressions. Having seen the president in the college chapel, or in his private room, or in his cap and gown proceeding to the First Baptist Church on Commencement day, and there presiding over the exercises of the graduating class, or conferring the degrees, the student was prepared to believe that whatever the university might lack, it certainly was not without a head.

"Nor did these impressions abate as he advanced in his studies, and came nearer to the president's recitation-room. There were, indeed, other instructors in the several departments, whose subsequent career has more than justified the expectations then entertained of them. Yet all the while there was but one Dr. Wayland. He had not even a second. His recitation-room was the goal towards which every student turned his eye. As the distance lessened, his eagerness increased. When he had at last passed through the preliminary years, his joy was full, because he would now be under the 'old doctor.' This silent influence, this unconscious tuition, was of unspeakable value. Although not directly unfolding any science, or evolving any principle, it imparted inspiration. The president threw over his pupils the spell of his own genius, and many of them still feel the enchantment, although the mighty spirit which imparted it has been withdrawn.

"At the time to which I refer, his recitation-room was on the first floor of the middle hall of Hope College, and in the rear of his own study. It had been a dormitory, but was afterwards furnished with benches, and what served for writing-desks — narrow pine boards upheld by pine uprights. We were obliged to use these with great care, lest we should be left without any support for our papers and our arms, during the severe trials of skill in handling our pencils. The entire furniture of the room did not exceed ten dollars in value.

"Entering by a door connecting the recitation-room with his study, he was in his chair at the moment, and he required the same promptness of each pupil. A second or third instance of tardiness was a dangerous experiment. The form of penalty could never be anticipated. Sometimes it was a look not likely to be soon forgotten; sometimes there was a painful pause, if the recitation had commenced; sometimes the delinquent was formally introduced to the class.

"All being present, and subsiding instantly into silence, the work began. He had no table, but sat with his manuscript for the lecture of the hour resting upon his knee. At this period none of his text-books had been published. The members of the class, in succession, recited the lecture of the preceding day, or perhaps one still farther back in the series. The recitation proceeded in this quiet manner until the lecture or lectures had been recalled to the minds of the pupils. Occasionally a question was asked by teacher or student, until everything obscure or ambiguous had been not only cleared up, but made as definite as language could render it. At the same time no irrelevant discussion was permitted, no argument for the sake of argument was encouraged. The class and the instructor were there for a definite purpose, and that purpose could not be thwarted by any art or subtlety: meanwhile — as all his pupils will readily remember — a silver pencil-case was passed from end to end between his thumb and finger. The compressed lips were moved slightly, but nervously. The small dark eye, through which, even in repose, his whole nature spoke, was resting, steadily but kindly, upon each student as he rose and recited.

"This exercise concluded, there was a rustling all around the room; papers were adjusted, and preparation made for writing. The president's manuscript was opened, and the well-known *a-hem* was the signal for all to be ready, and for the work of the hour to begin. He read slowly, and the class copied, each member following his own method; some using short-hand, others abbreviating words, or omitting some altogether. All were intent to catch the thought, at any rate, and the exact phraseology, if possible. The lecture was written out in full by the students at their rooms. What one failed to catch, he gathered from another, and thus by 'comparing notes' a correct copy was secured.

"These lectures seemed to us more wonderful than anything we had ever heard. They carried all the conviction of a demonstration. To have believed otherwise would

have seemed absurd. Some of us at a later day found
reason to modify the views then received and accepted.
But at the time the conviction was complete.

His definitions were clear, simple, and easily remembered. His analysis of any obscure but important part
was exhaustive, omitting no essential element. His progress through either of his favorite sciences was that of a
prince through his own dominions.

" At intervals, not regular in their occurrence, yet sure
to occur somewhere, he suspended his reading for a few
minutes, and, waiting for a short time, until each member
of the class could complete his notes and give his attention,
he would relate some incident or anecdote strikingly illustrating the point last made. In this department he was
always most happy. The confirmation imparted to the
argument was often unexpected, and even irresistible.
These anecdotes were drawn from any source that offered
the richest supply; from history, from romance, from poetry, from common, unrecorded, every-day life. Often they
were mirthful, sometimes ludicrous. Frequently statistics
would be given, conclusively verifying the position which
had been assumed. Illustrations, anecdotes, and statistics
came at his bidding, and always did capital service. They
were ' as arrows in the hands of the mighty.'

" Hands and arms having been rested, the reading was
resumed, and the lecture advanced to the stroke of the
bell. It was concluded as promptly as it commenced,
closing abruptly, even if in the middle of an argument or
a paragraph. Those were short hours. We wondered
whither the sixty minutes had flown, and how it was that
we had taken no note of their flight. Half in doubt of
the correctness of the bell, we left the recitation-room.

" Whether in these exercises Dr. Wayland stirred up
the intellect of his pupils, it was not difficult even for a
stranger to determine. As they issued from the lecture-
room, and went by twos and threes to their own apartments, the subjects which had just been discussed became
the theme of most earnest conversation. Nor did the
momentum thus acquired expend itself during the next
twenty-four hours. The mental machinery was still in
motion, when, on the following day, the class was again
summoned to that unpretending room.

" I have said that on most points the conviction produced was perfect. Yet sometimes an individual, perhaps from peculiarity in his mental constitution, perhaps from pre-occupancy, did not yield his assent. And sometimes nearly the whole class would, in the review or recitation of the lecture, express disagreement with the positions taken. If (which was seldom the case) the second effort of the instructor did not succeed in producing conviction, the dissentients were required to present the grounds of their dissent in writing. This custom often called out papers of marked ability. In one or two instances the weight of argument was, in the judgment of the class, with the pupil. The discussion closed with these words: 'I have given you, young gentlemen, all the light I now possess on this subject. If you are not satisfied, I can say no more.' We all felt that even a 'drawn battle' with such an antagonist was not a result of which we had any reason to be ashamed.

"I never knew an instructor who was so perfectly master of the subject he handled, or who left the impress of his own mind so ineffaceably upon the minds of all susceptible of receiving it. He was free from all pedantry. His movements in the realm of science and thought were quiet and unostentatious. His manner was simple and child-like. There was no indication of special concern that others should assent to his views. Yet the mind that was not quickened by contact with his, that did not gird itself for more strenuous and elevated endeavors under the inspiration of his presence and teachings, must have been hopelessly dull. The recitation-room was his empire, and he reigned with imperial dignity."

Although patient to a proverb of all discussions in the recitation-room which promised to benefit the class, or to develop, in any degree, their love of truth; and although singularly tolerant of dullness and slowness of comprehension, if there were also any evidence of a sincere desire to improve, yet he never encouraged unprofitable debate.

He seemed, by an almost unerring instinct, to know when questions were asked from a desire to save some unfaithful classmate from exposing his want of preparation, or to afford the inquirer an opportunity for personal display. He had also unusual sagacity in detecting the prospect of useless discussion, and in such cases never hesitated to avoid debate. But the terms in which he declined the challenge were often equivalent to an argument.

A sceptical student, promising himself the pleasure of a prolonged controversy, once informed the president that he had been unable to discover any internal evidence that the Old Testament was inspired. "For instance," said he, "take the book of Proverbs. Certainly it needed no inspiration to write that portion of the Bible. A man not inspired could have done it as well. Indeed, I have often thought that I could write as good proverbs myself." "Very well, my son, perhaps you can," was the prompt reply. "Suppose you make the experiment. Prepare a few proverbs, and read them to the class to-morrow. *The next.*" It is hardly necessary to add that the attempt to rival the wisdom of Solomon came to an abrupt and inglorious termination.

Again, when asked if "he considered dancing wrong," he answered, "Not much time for that sort of thing in this world, my son. *The next.*"

On another occasion, when he had been impressing upon his class the importance of avoiding all literature which was licentious in its character and demoralizing in its tendency, and urging his little audience to keep their hearts pure and free from all taint of evil thoughts, he was met with the inquiry, "Was Dean Swift wrong, then, when he said, 'A nice man is a man of nasty ideas'?" Looking at his young friend with that pleasant and almost quizzical expression of face which all his old pupils so well remember, he asked, in return, 'Well, my son, what kind of a man was Swift? Is he a very safe guide to follow in such matters?"

At another time he was lecturing on the weight of evidence furnished by human testimony. He was illus-

trating its authority and sufficiency even for the establishment of miracles. A member of the class, not entirely
satisfied of the correctness of the teaching, suggested a
practical application of the doctrine: "What would you
say, Dr. Wayland, if I stated, that, as I was coming up
College Street, I saw the lamp-post at the corner dance?"
"I should ask you where you had been, my son," was the
quiet reply in the instructor's gravest manner.

Now and then some undergraduate, who, during the
first three years of his collegiate course, had acquired a
high reputation among his associates as a debater in the
literary societies of the university, would, upon commencing the studies of the Senior class, boldly enter the lists,
and invite the president to a verbal encounter. Fluent in
speech, and not unpractised in the fence of words, the
ambitious youth would confidently assail the positions of
his instructor, summoning to his aid all those graces of
rhetoric and felicities of speech which had so often secured
for him the admiring applause of his fellows.

On such occasions, Dr. Wayland would listen patiently,
frequently with a kindly, but never with a contemptuous
smile, now and then interrupting the pupil only to say,
in a tone of encouragement, "Keep to the point, my son,
keep to the point," until the speaker had concluded.

He would then, first of all, recall to the recollection of
the class the exact issue involved in the discussion, relieve
the subject of all extrinsic considerations, point out the
fallacies in the argument of his young opponent, and then,
by apt illustration and natural analogy, seek to enforce
the central principle on which the whole question hinged.

In these and all kindred cases, however, he never ar-
gued for victory, but always for truth. Whenever he
became satisfied that his own positions were unsound, he
was prompt to acknowledge his error. If, in the progress
of discussion in the class-room, he received, from any
source, valuable information, or learned important facts

with which he had been hitherto unacquainted, he never failed to manifest his interest and express his gratitude. No man was ever more free from pride of opinion, or from obstinate adherence to his recorded sentiments. Not unfrequently, while discussing before his class some topic suggested by his own text-books, he would say, " There I differ from the author ; " or, " I have come to the conclusion that the author's views on that point should be modified." He constantly regretted that the pressure of his daily duties gave him no opportunity to revise his text-books, with such alterations as experience or reflection, or the " discussion of the lecture-room," had suggested.

From first to last, every one of his pupils was profoundly convinced that his only object was to arrive at truth, and to communicate that truth as simply and as intelligibly as possible. To the successful accomplishment of this purpose, he cheerfully consecrated all his mental powers, and all the earnestness of his moral nature.

In the preface to the revised edition of the Elements of Moral Science, written August 30, 1865, — his latest literary labor, — he says, —

" In using the following volume as a text-book for many years, I have derived great benefit from the free discussions of the lecture-room. Some of the principles, I thought, needed modification, and others might be presented in a form more easy to be understood. As soon, therefore, as I was released from the labor of instruction, I commenced the work of revision of what I had so long taught. My progress was arrested by an attack of illness, and for two or three years I was obliged to lay it entirely aside. With returning health I resumed my labors, and I lay the result before the public."

It was certainly characteristic of his long and laborious career as an instructor, that he should have devoted the closing months of his life to the revision and improvement of his earliest text-book. The candid and thorough revision of this, the earliest of his text-books, formed certainly a fitting conclusion to his life-long labors as a teacher.

Considered as an instructor, perhaps no quality of his mind was more striking than its freshness. He never repeated himself. He had no traditional anecdotes, handed down from class to class, and looked for as certain to be related, when, in the stereotyped programme of instruction, the time had arrived for their natural and appropriate introduction. While the text-books which he taught were of necessity the basis of the exercises of the recitation-room, the principles which those books inculcated were illustrated and enforced by apt analogies borrowed from every department of science and from the whole range of human knowledge. Here he derived incalculable benefit from the extent and variety of his educational labors before he became president. We have seen that he had been called upon to give instruction in very many branches of study, and, governed by that conscientious view of his duty which was ever the controlling principle of his life, he had spared no pains to become familiar with the details of every department which was committed to his charge.

His intellect was essentially progressive. He thought nothing beneath his notice which tended to promote the welfare, or conduce to the comfort of the race. His generous mind received, his rare analytical powers classified, and his retentive memory cherished, every important fact and principle in ethics, science, literature, or art, which came under his observation. And all this wealth of information was lavishly expended for the benefit of his pupils. He delighted to see them not only industrious, but interested in their studies. He never chilled them by any formality of manner, nor intimidated them by any needless display of personal dignity. While his discipline was strict, and his authority absolute and undisputed, he never, for a moment, forgot that his duty as an instructor required him to present truth in its most winning and attractive aspect to the minds of his pupils. Keeping this obligation constantly and conscientiously in view, he infused a life and spirit into the all too brief hour devoted to his recitations, which made them the most agreeable incidents of college experience.

A marked peculiarity of the teachings of Dr. Wayland was his profound conviction of the absolute truth of what he taught. He was never satisfied until he had ' thought through' every subject within the legitimate scope of his instructions. Each principle, so examined and embraced, became a part of himself. To quote the words of one of his pupils, —

" I think the most striking feature of Dr. Wayland, as an instructor, was his intense and remarkable personality. Whatever he taught, he taught not out of books, but out of himself. Whatever he derived from books was, as the Prayer Book hath it, ' inwardly digested,' and in the process made fairly a part of himself, and then enforced and impressed upon his pupils, in such a manner, aided by his commanding presence, that they never went behind him for authority, and had no need to do so."

He had, moreover, in the highest degree, that element of character which is indispensable to success in any employment — professional enthusiasm. An ardent desire to develop to the utmost the mental and moral powers of the young men intrusted to his care inspired all his efforts and stimulated all his energies. His mind was ever on the alert to devise means of creating fresh interest in the department which he taught. To this object all his reading, all his researches in science, all his study of the Scriptures, were made tributary.

Up to the last day of his official connection with Brown University, his preparation for the exercises of the recitation-room was as careful and conscientious as when, a tutor in Union College, he commenced the work of instruction. For a teacher who neglected his duty, or who discharged that duty listlessly or mechanically, he had no respect. Indeed, it was his constant endeavor to prevent " the customary separation of salary and duty — the grand principle which appears to pervade all human institutions, and to be the most invincible of all human abuses." The desire of making money, as the leading motive for entering the profession, excited his stern contempt. He considered it disloyal to an exalted calling, and always predicted mental bankruptcy as its inevitable result.

He was very far from believing that teaching had a natural or necessary tendency to dwarf the mind of the teacher. He maintained, on the contrary, that, if properly pursued, it could not fail to expand and ennoble the intellect, and to quicken into new life and increased activity every faculty of the faithful instructor. As early as 1830 he writes to his sisters, who had just commenced a school for young ladies in Saratoga Springs, New York, —

" It is, I assure you, a noble business. You will find that your minds will gain more in one year than they ever gained before in five years."

He urges them, however, not to neglect proper preparation for their new duties.

" You will, for the first year, be obliged to devote a great deal of time to study. This you will discover to be both advantageous and pleasant. You had better divide the branches, and each pay particular attention to the department in which you propose to give instruction. It is one thing to know a subject as others do, and quite another thing to know it so as to be able to teach it properly. The latter requires much patient and original thinking; the former does not."

His own example, however, furnishes more conclusive evidence than can be found in any words, of the sincerity of his convictions on this subject.

Steady, unflinching earnestness in the work immediately before him, was the rule of his life. In a letter to a friend, he says, " I have much writing to do, but I shall always write to you when I am able, and when I can do you any service. I may not, in every case, be a punctual correspondent, but I will always be in earnest." Sometimes, in seasons of mental depression, he may have doubted if, in devoting himself to the work of instruction, he had not mistaken his destiny ; but he never allowed any such misgiving to diminish his professional enthusiasm. He subordinated all his tastes and inclinations, all the energy of his nature, all the well-disciplined faculties of his mind, to the one business of fulfilling, to the best of his ability, the trust reposed in him as the head of Brown University. Upon this point his own testimony will be read with interest.

" In reviewing that part of my life which has been devoted to teaching, I see much that I could wish had been otherwise. That I applied myself to the duties which devolved upon me with an honest and earnest purpose, I think I may without vanity assert. I believe I have been generally considered a laborious man. I allowed myself no recreation, except physical labor for the preservation of my health. My mind was occupied continually, either upon the studies which I was called upon to teach, or else upon the government of the college, or the details relating to its increased efficiency. All my reading was directed to the subjects immediately before me. From the beginning to the end of the collegiate year, whether in term time or in vacation, the interests of the college were almost never out of my thoughts. I cheerfully undertook any labor by which its welfare might be promoted.

" Perhaps I erred in this respect. Such continued concentration of the mind upon one subject tends to diminish its elasticity, and leads to premature mental decay. It would, perhaps, have been better if I had allowed myself more recreation ; but for this I had no aptitude. And, besides, considering myself, more than anybody else, responsible for the success of the college, I could not be satisfied unless I did everything in my power to promote it. Therefore, to be thus ' *totus in illis* ' became to me a sort of necessity. I could not neglect the present for the sake of the future. I felt obliged to do what seemed to be the duty which pressed upon me for the moment. This mental habit rendered my life, to a considerable extent, fragmentary, by reason of frequent interruption. Whether I should have succeeded better with another view of duty, I cannot now determine. Considering the condition of the college at the time, I do not see how I could have taken a different course."

Undoubtedly a wider range of studies would have gratified his eager thirst for knowledge. Certainly a greater indulgence in social recreation would have lightened his labors, and given increased elasticity to his often overtasked mind. Travelling, and the familiarity with men and their modes of life, which the frequent traveller can hardly help acquiring, might have given him more ease of manner, and made him more accessible to his casual acquaintances. But all this was inconsistent with his stern views of duty. Whenever a conflict arose between desire and obligation, he never asked himself, "What will be agreeable?" but rather, "What will be right?" In every instance self was left out of the question.

Thus, in the fall of 1834, when many of his friends urged him to visit Europe for the benefit of his health, and as a change which he very much needed, he writes to a relative, —

"Since you left there has been more talk about my going to Europe. It seems to strike those who have spoken of it, more favorably than I had anticipated. I am rather more disposed than before to think of it seriously. If I am ever to go, now is the time; and probably such an opportunity will never occur again. I am endeavoring to collect facts and materials for forming an opinion. I pray that God may direct the decision according to his will."

Further reflection, however, satisfying him that it was his duty to remain at his post, the project was abandoned.

In fact, to deny himself for the good of others, and for the benefit of the cause in which all his energies were enlisted, had become so completely the habit of his life, that any personal sacrifice demanded of him was made without apparent effort. He recognized no other rule of action. A serious estimate of his accountability to God and to his fellow-men for the full and faithful exercise of all the faculties with which his Creator had endowed him, was the standard by which he tested every question of personal duty.

CHAPTER XII.

FEELING OF PERSONAL RESPONSIBILITY. — VIEWS OF
DISCIPLINE. — RESPECT AND AFFECTION OF PUPILS. —
RELIGIOUS CONVERSATIONS. — COLLEGE CHAPEL. —
SERMONS TO UNDERGRADUATES.

IN his relations to the college, as everywhere, conscientious devotion to duty was the key-note to all his conduct. He could be satisfied with nothing less than the consecration of all his powers to the profession which he had chosen as his life-work.

A keen sense of the responsibility which he had assumed in undertaking the mental and moral training of the pupils committed to his care, was never for a moment absent from his mind. He looked upon them, not as so many young men whose names would appear on the catalogue, and whose bills for tuition would be duly collected during a period of four years, but as immortal beings, whose usefulness in life, and whose eternal welfare, must be materially affected by their connection with the institution over which he presided. He recognized in every young man who entered the university a new trust imposed upon him, and held himself personally accountable to the student, to his parents, and to his God, for the faithful fulfilment of so serious an obligation. This abiding conviction of personal responsibility continued, in unabated force, to the close of his official connection with the university. In 1844 he writes to a friend, —

" . . . I thank you for your cautions. I should be very glad to obey their pointings if I knew how to do it.

It is not really that I do hard labor, but that my situation allows of no relaxation, and is one of invariable responsibility. Were I my own man, with power to arrange my time for myself, and to throw off care at intervals, or so that I could have a day in a week, or a week or two every three months, I could do twice what I do, and be as elastic as need be. But these alleviations do not belong to the lot which has fallen to my share. The harness is buckled on, and I cannot get it off without quitting the service. If I find that I have not the health to go through with it, I shall quit it, and leave it to some better dray-horse. You may think me dull or discontented. I trust that this is not the case. But I have seen much of college life. I knew the peculiar position and its necessities. I do not believe that this calling can be made to succeed unless some one does as I do, if he have not much more talent than I have. I am constituted, perhaps, peculiarly. Official responsibility presses steadily, I do not say heavily, upon me. To see a thing go wrong for which I am responsible, without doing everything in my power to set it right, is impossible. It is against my nature. It is not obstinacy; it is not ambition, but a dogged feeling of duty, that I cannot get rid of. So much for my position. I think it not improbable that I shall leave it, should my life be spared a few years longer. But of this I need not predict. I have generally seen that when Providence has placed a man in any situation, and designs him to leave it, there are two kinds of indications — the first, that his work there is done; and the second, that there is work for him to do somewhere else. Since I have been here, the first has been given several times, but not, as I have thought, the latter. It may be that the latter will be given here. But I am ashamed of prosing to you, at this rate, about my affairs.

He fully sympathized with Dr. Arnold as to the individual accountability of an instructor, and especially approved, and frequently commended, these sentiments of the master of Rugby School: —

"It is a most touching thing to me to receive a new boy from his father, when I think what an influence there is in this place for evil as well as for good. I do not know anything which affects me more. If I could ever receive a fresh boy from his father without emotion, I should think it high time to be off."

The discipline of an instructor holding such opinions, and binding himself to so severe a standard of duty, could not fail to be always thorough, and often severe. While he did not probably expect of his pupils undeviating obedience to every college regulation, he was particularly careful to watch their moral tendencies. If they were frank, candid, and outspoken, he was slow to censure and prompt to pardon. Confession of wrong doing, and an evident desire to amend, gave him an opportunity, which he gladly embraced, to forgive the offender, and to set before him the moral consequences of his misconduct. He appreciated the evil results of defective training in early life, and was ever ready to make due allowance for errors in home education. At the same time, while the natural kindness of his heart always inclined him to mercy, he never forgot the importance of maintaining those general principles of discipline which are essential to the wise administration of college government.

As the views of Dr. Wayland, in regard to discipline, were in some respects, perhaps, peculiar to himself, and certainly had a marked effect in giving character and individuality to the college, we quote, on this point, from his reminiscences.*

" With respect to the discipline of a college, it is, perhaps, proper that I should give my experience. I may say that my views on this subject are very simple. So far as I know, it has been generally supposed that the head of a college can only succeed by understanding the peculiar temperament, habits, disposition, &c., of every pupil, and, on the basis of this knowledge, making out a distinct mode of treatment for each undergraduate. In

---

* The reader should bear in mind that the reminiscences from which the following extract is made, were written for his sons, and not for publication.

strict accordance with this theory, parents without number, when entering their sons in college, have come to me, and at great length have informed me of the peculiarities of their children, stating that their dispositions were excellent if they were only governed in some particular manner. I always listened with due attention to such statements, but paid to them no regard whatever. Indeed, I very soon learned that these *peculiar* young men were in fact, in almost every case, spoiled children, with whom I was likely to have more than the usual amount of trouble.

"It seemed to me that such a view of the proper method of governing a public institution for instruction would greatly impair, if it did not entirely destroy, the value of any college in which it should prevail. If it were the business of instructors to study the character of every pupil, and in each instance to modify the course of discipline to suit the peculiarities of every individual, sound judgment would, from the very nature of the case, be impossible. A college would then fail in one of its most important designs, namely, as an intermediate place between the family and society, to prepare the student for entrance upon the practical duties of life. I came, therefore, to the conclusion, that the laws of a college should be simple, just, kind, and of such a character that they could be shown to be right and salutary, both to parents and pupils. These laws, having been established, were to be rigidly observed, and, by making every young man feel that he must be accountable for his own actions, prepare him for becoming a member of society, where this rule is to be enforced under more severe penalties. The more peculiar a young man is, and the more his peculiarities have been suffered to gain strength, the more important it is that he should be subjected to the same restraints as his fellows, without making any allowance for his eccentricities. If a young man be rude, arrogant, passionate, untruthful, indolent, unpunctual, it is far better, after one admonition, that no allowance whatever be made for these evil habits, than that they should ripen into confirmed biases, which a whole lifetime might be insufficient to correct.

"It was therefore my aim to have no laws which could not be shown to be perfectly reasonable, and then to execute those laws with all possible strictness and impartiality. Of course, in saying this I assume that it will be understood that the government of impulsive, thoughtless young men is different from the government of adults. It must, of necessity, be kind, conciliatory, persuasive, or, in a word, parental. Penalty must be visited only after other means of restraint and correction have been tried in vain. But it must be distinctly understood that when these have proved ineffectual, punishment will inevitably come, and come on all alike, without the shadow of partiality.

"In the government of a college, every case becomes a precedent; and if the precedent be a bad one, it will never be forgotten, but will be pleaded without fail, as though it established a law. I always, therefore, considered it a matter of prime importance to decide every new case correctly. It was my habit to take time for deliberation, to examine each case in all its bearings, and to see what would be the result of a decision if generally adopted as a rule. I endeavored to ascertain the principles on which a decision should be founded. I appreciated the fact that a case settled on true principles would harmonize with every other case that might subsequently occur, whether nearly or remotely connected with the one before me. The laws of college, and the results of violating them, became thus perfectly well known. When the younger students were disposed to combine in perpetrating some violation of law, their seniors would tell them distinctly what would be the inevitable consequence, and their predictions rarely failed of fulfilment. The principles which governed in such cases were well understood, and it was known that by these principles all cases of discipline were to be decided.

"I know that all this seems easy to be understood and easy to be accomplished; and yet it is not exactly so. What needs to be done may be readily perceived. But when the doing it may destroy the prospects of a young man, and scatter to the winds the long-cherished hopes of parents, that measure of discipline, which one knows to be right and unavoidable, is attended with the severest pain. I never attempted an important case of discipline without great mental distress. I took every means possible to escape it, and to maintain the government without harming the young men. When, however, all other means had been tried, and action became necessary, I nerved myself to the work. From that moment all the distress was over, and I went through it so coolly, that I believe I acquired the reputation of being a stern, unfeeling disciplinarian, who was determined to carry out college regulations regardless of the pain which he caused. In this respect I suppose I must be classed among those unfortunate men who think themselves misunderstood.

" My notions of college discipline differed, I believe, in another particular, from the general opinion of my time. It was formerly supposed — and to a considerable extent the opinion continues to be entertained — that an undergraduate is amenable to no other laws than those of his college. He may do what he pleases ; he may violate, almost at pleasure, the laws of society, and yet be liable to no other punishment than college censure. I have known college officers to take very great pains to shield students from the consequences of their violation of municipal regulations. My view of the matter was the reverse of all this. For simple infraction of the rules of academic society, college censure is the suitable and appropriate punishment. For violation of the laws of the community, the penalties which society has decreed in such cases are as justly to be awarded to the student as to any other young man. His connection with the college should afford the wrong-doer no sort of protection. The sooner a student discovers that he is amenable to the laws of society, like any other citizen, the better it will be for him.

" It always seemed to me absurd that two brothers, entering together upon their preparatory life, the one choosing the course of active life, the other devoting himself to intellectual and moral cultivation, should speedily find themselves under systems of law so opposite in their nature. If the former breaks his neighbor's windows, or steals his fruit, or disturbs his peace, he is arrested, and held accountable to repair the damage he has done. The other may commit any or all of these offences, and only be thought to have played a 'college trick,' which will be winked at by the community, while the officers of his college are considered as bound to stand between him and the deserved penalty. If I am not mistaken, President Quincy, of Harvard, was the first man who reversed the process. He taught the students under him that they were responsible, in all respects, to the laws of Massachusetts. President Felton, as I am told, has pursued a similar course. Both of these gentlemen, however, for doing what was plainly right, were subjected to considerable animadversion.

" I recall two cases in which I was compelled to call upon the civil authorities. On one occasion two students had robbed the philosophical cabinet of several valuable instruments. I caused a warrant to be issued for their apprehension, but gave them time to leave the state. The other case was of one student drawing a pistol on another. Here also the offender was suffered to escape. The principle, however, was established, and this answered my purpose."

While the discipline of Dr. Wayland may have seemed to many of the undergraduates strict, and even at times severe, they rarely failed, before the close of their collegiate course, to appreciate the moral elevation of his motives, and the soundness of his principles of government.

In fact, his dignity of manner, the purity of his moral character, his unremitting industry, his intense earnestness, his independence of thought, his professional enthusiasm, his exact and impartial justice, his enlarged and progressive views of college education, his freedom from narrow and sectarian prejudices in "religious concernments," and his loyalty to truth, could but secure the respect and command the confidence of his pupils.

They saw that he exacted nothing of them to which he did not cheerfully conform. If he insisted upon punctuality, he set the example of never being behind time, without an excuse, the justice of which commanded universal assent. If he urged the importance of fixed hours of study, they knew that he was governed by the same rules which he applied to them. If he cautioned them against frivolous amusements, and every species of mental and moral dissipation, they felt that his advice was conscientiously given, and was enforced by his own constant practice.

In a word, it was impossible to escape the contagion of his example, and the more closely the undergraduates were brought into contact with the president, the more profound was their respect for his character, and the higher their appreciation of his ability.

Yet this was not all. With the better class of pupils he not only inspired sincere reverence, but he created strong attachments. It has been truly said of him, " There was so much kindness in his stern justice, so much that was generous and noble in his severity, that the students generally loved him as much as they respected him."

Indeed, such sincere, exclusive, and self-sacrificing devotion to duty, was peculiarly fitted to touch the feelings and enlist the sympathies of all right-minded young men. While the members of the younger classes may have been sometimes deterred from approaching him from a natural awe inspired by his presence, and a traditional fear of entering his study, every feeling of this kind was quickly dissipated, when, in the Senior year, they became in a more exact sense his pupils.

We quote once more from the interesting reminiscences of Mr. Kingsbury : —

" I have had in my Bible class about two hundred and fifty young men connected with Brown University, most of them, of course, undergraduates during his presidency. They often visited me to converse about matters concerning their relations to the college. I invariably observed that they entered the institution with a good degree of awe of Dr. Wayland. But when they had once come under his immediate instruction, their uniform testimony was, that there was no other member of the Faculty in whose presence they felt so free from constraint."

They then learned to appreciate the degree of his interest in their individual welfare, and his absorbing anxiety that they should be not merely proficient in their studies, and correct in their external deportment, but qualified to be valuable members of society, and, above all, Christian young gentlemen. Many a wayward pupil, reclaimed from vicious courses by the untiring efforts of Dr. Wayland, will bear cheerful testimony to the timely admonitions and the kindly counsels of his revered instructor. He will recall, not without emotion, the tender and touching appeals drawn from a father's anxiety and a mother's love, the serious enforcement of moral obligation, the constant reference to the teachings of Christ as the only infallible guide to duty and criterion of conduct.

In the words of Dr. Bailey, —

"Often, when an undergraduate entered the doctor's study, he was invited to be seated. Then followed a conversation of great tenderness, rich in gospel truth, and prolific in motives, urging him to the salvation of his soul. He was entreated to read his Bible daily: he was shown its treasures, and its influence upon his character and his destiny. He was called upon to consider his standing in the sight of God. He was affectionately urged to suffer no delay; to peril no longer interests so momentous, but to commence at once a life of piety. The interview was closed with prayer — a prayer so humble, sincere, and affectionate, that the young man felt convinced, as he rose from his knees, that at least one soul, second to none in greatness, believed his moral danger to be real and imminent, and yearned for his salvation.

"These personal interviews were never regarded as of secondary importance. In all conditions of religious feeling, amid the most engrossing academic labors, they were not forgotten or neglected. While they did not always result in the speedy conversion of the pupils, the impression (I speak here from personal experience) was ineffaceable. They led to the Bible and the closet, hedged up the path of scepticism, and frequently produced ultimate consecration to Christ. Many a man, now serving God and his fellow-men in a Christian life, was first arrested in his course of selfish ambition, and turned to God by these seemingly accidental interviews. Many a young Christian, weary, faint, and despondent, has been reinvigorated in his faith and purpose, by words spoken in the retirement of the president's study. Many a young man, doubting and hesitating in respect to his duty, has been rendered resolute in his determination to live for Christ, by the timely counsel of those lips, now silent in death. Whoever else was indifferent, the president never was. Whoever else was careless in respect to the wants of Zion, there was one who did not cease to labor and plead for her, and who might at all times truly say, ' I prefer Jerusalem above my chief joy.' "

The following extract is from the Congregationalist : —

" I was a free-thinker ; read Rousseau and Lord Byron, and believed in them. Religion I judged of by the long stereotyped prayers and ascetic looks of some ill-bred Christians. I hated Orthodoxy as I saw it from the stand-point I had, in my proud imagination, taken. In this mental status I took my seat in the lecture-room of Dr. Wayland. He was then discussing the powers and functions of ' the moral sense.' His course of argumentation was so keen and clear that I soon began to listen. I began to question, to argue, to present objections in order to drive him from his position. It was like damming up the waters of the Nile with bulrushes. His logic, unfolded in his perspicuous, yet laconic style, quite overwhelmed, confounded me. I saw that I was a miserable sinner in the sight of an offended God.

" I went to my room to pray ; my knees were stubborn ; the load upon my heart was crushing me. What must I do to escape the wrath of the Almighty? Hope seemed to have taken its everlasting flight.

" I arose and went into the presence of Dr. Wayland. He was in his study, reading his old, well-worn copy of the sacred word. He received me kindly, and I at once made known to him the anguish of my soul. I felt and said, ' My sins are so great and so many that God cannot pardon me.'

" Fixing his keen black eyes, beaming with tenderness, on me, this good man said, — and never till my dying day can I forget the earnest solemnity, the eloquence of the tone, — ' When he was yet a great way off, his father saw him, and had compassion on him, and ran, and fell on his neck, and kissed him.' I felt that the case was mine, and Hope, reviving Hope, came to me. Dr. Wayland then knelt down and prayed with me and for me ; and on leaving him, he lent me his well-thumbed copy of Bishop

Wilson's Sacra Privata, advising me to read that, and the Life of Brainerd, instead of Byron,

> ' And if I met with trials and troubles on the way,
> ' To cast myself on Jesus, and not forget to pray.'

I never knew till then the full meaning of that great English word *friendliness*. I never before knew Jesus Christ."

But in addition to the moral power of personal intercourse with his pupils, and the facilities furnished by the daily meetings of his class in the recitation-room, Dr. Wayland did not overlook the somewhat wider field afforded by the regular morning and evening religious exercises of the college chapel. It was his habit, when the students were thus assembled, at the conclusion of the reading of the Scriptures and the subsequent prayer, to address the undergraduates upon any matter of college discipline which had recently occurred. On such occasions he always sought to refer the case of misconduct under consideration to some general principle, and to impress upon his youthful audience some salutary lesson suggested by the moral bearings of the misdemeanor.

A member of the class of 1833 * has kindly contributed the following reminiscence in illustration of this subject : —

"I remember on one occasion, after some of the neighbors had been despoiled of their turkeys, that the doctor addressed the students on the subject, after evening prayers, substantially as follows : Undoubtedly you will say that this appropriation of turkeys which did not belong to you is a venial offence. I believe you call it ' hooking' turkeys, as the idea of ' stealing' turkeys would be offensive. But, young gentlemen, I beg you to bear one thing in mind. Those of you who have thus ' hooked' turkeys have taken the property of another, without right, and in violation of law. I do not say that those who have been guilty of this offence may not hereafter become good citizens and worthy members of society ; but I do say, that

---

* Hon. H. B. Anthony, United States Senator from Rhode Island.

there is a decided difference between the man who has committed such a misdemeanor and the man who has not; and that the fact of the wrong-doing can never be undone nor recalled. It is not wise or safe to tamper thus with our moral nature, and to lose sight, even for a moment, of the distinction between right and wrong. The extent of the injury which you may be inflicting on yourselves by persisting in such a course of conduct is beyond your power to estimate. I implore you not to trifle with your moral sense. Do not, I pray you, dull the edge of your conscience."

From another eminent alumnus of Brown University we learn that

" Dr. Wayland had rare power in referring (in his frequent addresses to the students after evening prayers) every incident relating to college discipline and the general subject of university education to some general principle, the importance of which upon the character and future career of the undergraduates he always enforced by apposite illustrations and telling appeals."

We quote from the address of Professor Chace: —

" Another means employed by President Wayland for awakening impulse, and correcting, guiding, and elevating public sentiment in college, was addresses from the platform in the chapel. These were most frequent and most characteristic in the earlier days of his presidency. They occurred, usually, immediately after evening prayers, and took the place of the undergraduate speaking, which at that time formed a part of the daily college programme. The occasions which called them forth were some irregularity, or incident, or event which seemed to render proper the application of the moral lever to raise the standard of scholarship or character. We all knew very well when to expect them.

" As the students then, with few exceptions, lived within the college buildings, and took their meals in Commons Hall, they constituted, much more than at present, a community by themselves. They were more readily swayed by common impulses, and more susceptible of common emotions. When gathered in the chapel, they formed a unique, but remarkably homogeneous, audience. President Wayland was at that time at the very culmination of his powers, both physical and intellectual. His massive and stalwart frame, not yet filled and rounded by the accretions of later years, his strongly-marked features having still the sharp outlines and severe grace of their first chiselling, his peerless eye sending from beneath that Olympian brow its lordly or its penetrating glances, he seemed, as he stood on the stage in that old chapel, the incarnation of majesty and power. He was raised a few feet above his audience, and so near to them that those most remote could see the play of every feature. He commenced speaking. It was not instruction; it was not argument; it was not exhortation. It was a mixture of wit and humor, of ridicule, sarcasm, pathos, and fun, of passionate remonstrance, earnest appeal, and solemn warning, poured forth, not at random, but with a knowledge of the laws of emotion to which Lord Kames himself could have added nothing. The effect was indescribable. No Athenian audience ever hung more tumultuously on the lips of the divine Demosthenes. That little chapel heaved and swelled with the intensity of its pent-up forces. The billows of passion rose and fell like the waves of a tempestuous sea. At one moment all were burning with indignation; the next they were melted to tears. Now every one was convulsed with laughter, and now as solemn as if the revelations of doom were just opening upon him. Emotions the most diverse followed one another in quick succession. Admiration, resentment, awe, and worship in turn swelled every bosom. At length the storm spent itself. The sky cleared, and the sun shone out with increased brightness. The ground had been softened and fertilized, and the whole air purified."

Any sketch of Dr. Wayland as a teacher of young men and the head of a college would be imperfect, if it did not describe somewhat in detail his manner of conducting religious exercises in the college chapel. It was a manner peculiarly his own, and as much a part of himself as any feature of the daily life of Brown University, with which his memory is associated. In the words of Dr. Bailey, —

" In the chapel service he was always brief. Part of a chapter was read, and the morning prayer was in the spirit of the passage selected. If it related to the attributes and perfections of God, the prayer was a humble expression of adoration. If it described man as degraded and ruined, the prayer was a penitential confession of weakness and guilt, and an earnest petition for divine assistance. He had a moral sensitiveness which readily responded to any phase of truth which the lesson of the hour presented.

" In the evening we generally went from the lecture-room to the chapel. The prayer at this time was often suggested, not by the selected Scripture, but by some form of moral truth which had occupied our attention during the preceding hour. Perhaps it was a thanksgiving to God for rich revelations of science, or for the increase of happiness which these great general truths had brought to our sinful, suffering race, or a fervent supplication that by thoroughly understanding them we might be fully prepared for the work of life before us. I was not at that time a Christian, but I was often deeply impressed with the influence which Christian faith had over him in everything which he thought or did.

" While a student, and wholly inexperienced in respect to the difficulties of this religious exercise, I was frequently struck with the prayers of President Wayland; with the absence of repetition, with their variety and richness. And when called to a similar service for more than twenty years, what was before only striking has seemed to me truly wonderful. The appropriateness impressed me strongly at the time; but subsequently I found occasion to recall what I could, and to inquire, for my own benefit, upon what the success depended, and how the requisite interest was maintained. I soon became convinced that it was not a matter of mere accident, nor was it left to the feeling or impulse of the moment.

" I do not mean to say that the public devotions of the late president were faultless. His attitude was frequently careless. There was also, at the time of which I speak, too much brevity. Perhaps this apparent brevity was owing to a conscientious apprehension that time might be expended in prayer, which ought to be devoted to study, or that some who were required to be present might be wearied. Yet for all this, I have heard few men, perhaps none, whose public devotions presented so little to which impartial criticism could object. His conceptions of Deity seemed to me vast, his reverence profound, his love filial and deep as his own great moral nature admitted. Evidently he approached the throne of God with an awe such as I imagine angels and glorified spirits must feel. Sometimes he offered adoration and praise in language so exalted that it seemed inspired by a rapt vision of the Holy One.

"But when his own moral nature, and its deep, pressing wants, were the burden of his prayer, there was visible a humble and patient feeling, absorbing and subduing. His whole soul seemed pervaded with a sense of the exceeding sinfulness of sin. He lamented the stains of guilt, and sought relief alone in the blood of Christ. He mourned over the insubordination of the passions, and prayed that grace might be given to bring them into captivity to the will of the Master.

"Before preaching, his prayer for aid was most earnest. One was reminded of the wrestling of the patriarch at the fords of the brook Jabbok. There was a timidity and self-distrust which seemed almost unsuitable to his position in the church. Admiring as I did his genius, and feeling that nothing required of the human intellect was beyond him, I used then to listen to these pleadings with wonder.

"A prayer offered by him at the opening of a term of the U. S. Circuit Court, Mr. Justice Story presiding, is to this day vivid before my mind. It was an invocation of the presence of God as the Author and Source of all justice, and the Being before whom the judges of the earth would all stand to give an account of the manner in which they had administered the laws among men. An allusion to the omnipresence of God made me tremble. 'Hell is naked before thee, and destruction hath no covering.' I recall no passages in his sermons or addresses that surpass in sublimity some portions of that prayer. Spectators, jurors, advocates, and judges were hushed into perfect stillness during its utterance; and I asked myself who, during that session of the court, would dare to connive at injustice, or to devise or award anything which would not be approved at the final judgment day. The court seemed to me but a faint and poor imitation of the great tribunal before which we must all appear."

But the president was by no means contented with these modes of approaching the hearts and consciences of his pupils. He longed to discover yet other avenues to their moral natures. Therefore, although already over-tasked by the arduous labors and grave responsibilities of his position, he commenced a series of Sabbath services in the college chapel. In 1832 Mrs. Wayland, writing to Dr. Wayland's mother, says, —

" I wish to inform you what is your son's present course of religious instruction in college. He has every Saturday evening a conference meeting, which he holds with the Senior class; and for three Sabbaths past he has preached to the students and to the officers and their families in the college chapel. His Bible class continues every Sunday evening. I think too much devolves on him, but he says, ' it is his dispensation always.' "

These sermons were continued, with only such inter-missions as the pressure of his duties made absolutely necessary, until nearly the close of his presidency; and who shall measure and estimate the influence which these discourses, addressed to so many successive classes of young men, may have exerted upon their future career in life? How have those pointed, personal sermons moulded the Christian belief and stimulated the piety of hundreds of students!

At a meeting of graduates, October 3, 1865, A. Payne, Esq., said, —

" If I were to speak of the things done by him, which I think were most remarkable, I should not fix upon any of the great works by which he is known all over the Christian world. I should recall some of the sermons which he preached in the old chapel, on what was called the Annual College Fast — some of those occasions upon which he laid himself alongside of the young men in college, and, with all the earnestness of which he was capable, tried to bring them to his way of thinking upon the subject of religion. I have never heard anything in human speech superior to passages in some of these addresses. And I am very much mistaken if, when that sifting process has been performed upon his works which has to be performed upon the works of every author, some of those University Sermons, as I believe they were called, will not survive everything else that he has written or spoken."

And yet, whatever of spiritual power or of impressive eloquence these discourses contained, was borrowed, not from the momentary excitement caused by a crowded house, but from the love of the preacher for the souls of his hearers. Says a member of the class of 1838, — *

" On one occasion, in my Senior year (1838), Dr. Way-land preached on Sunday afternoon in the college chapel. Through some mistake, notice of the service had not been given to the students. Hence only three were present.

" The text was, 'I have heard of thee by the hearing of the ear, but now mine eye seeth thee,' &c. The subject of the discourse was the nature of genuine repentance. He spoke without notes, and with singular clearness and power. It was a most convincing, eloquent, and impressive sermon, and as animated and earnest in delivery as if preached to a crowded audience. His inspiration was drawn solely from his sacred theme."

We cannot better illustrate his diffidence and self-distrust than by quoting his expressions of surprise at the cordiality of the reception by the public of his volume of " University Sermons : " —

" . . . I heartily reciprocate your wish that the author was as good as his sermons, without, however, claiming much goodness for them. It is easier to preach than to practise. I seem to be striving to do better, but I come lamentably short in everything, and I can get no higher than ' God be merciful to me a sinner.' The Sermons have been received far better than I expected. The first edition is exhausted, and a second is already published. This is encouragement which I had not anticipated. May God command his blessing on them, and make them useful in his cause."

---

* Rev. E. G. Robinson, D. D.

In order that our readers may be able to form a more correct estimate of the sermons addressed by Dr. Wayland to the undergraduates than can be afforded by any mere sketch, however graphic, and because the "University Sermons" do not adequately exhibit the parental tenderness of his personal appeals, we present in full one of his discourses, hitherto unpublished, preached in the college chapel, July 18, 1847, at the close of the collegiate year.*

"*A wise son maketh a glad father, but a foolish son is the heaviness of his mother.*" — Prov. x : 1.

"It is interesting to observe, young gentlemen, how admirably all the relations which we sustain are intended to promote our virtue and well-being. Every one of us stands connected with the society of which he forms a part, in ways too numerous to admit of a ready specification. We are citizens of a common country; we are fellow-townsmen of the place of our residence; we are members of a particular social circle; we are intimates with those of our own age; we are co-workers with those in our own profession; we are kinsmen of those descended from the same ancestor; we are brothers and sisters in the same family; we are parents or children in the same household. In all these, and a hundred relations beside, our happiness or misery is of necessity affected by the conduct of those with whom we are thus, with so much complexity, associated.

"Now, one of the results flowing from these associations is the consciousness of a peculiar responsibility for the good conduct of others. We feel disgraced in the eyes of the world if an American citizen dishonors his name, forfeits his word, is false to his engagements, or becomes a traitor to his country. We feel an additional pride in

---

* It is worthy of note that for these Sabbath services in the chapel, Dr. Wayland almost invariably wrote new sermons, not availing himself of the ample supplies accumulated in the course of former parochial labors. The preparation of these discourses, occupying Friday afternoon and Saturday, consumed the hours which might have been claimed for rest and relaxation.

our citizenship, if our brethren, in cases of emergency,
display the evidences of high integrity, unsullied faith,
unshaken bravery, and disinterested benevolence.   Nor is
this feeling at all confined to ourselves.   It is the reflection of a sentiment which others, whether we are aware
of it or not, entertain towards us.   A few years since it was
believed that this whole country was about to disavow its
solemn obligations.   What American did not feel humbled
when he contemplated the prospect?   And there was reason
for this feeling of humiliation.   Wherever an American
travelled over the face of the earth, he heard of nothing
but Repudiation.   It mattered not from what part of the
Union he derived his origin; it was of no consequence
whether he had or had not been a party to the acts in
question.   He was an American citizen, and he must bear
his part of the odium, and suffer his part of the social
punishment which was inflicted on those who were believed to be the ill-doers.   And who of us has not breathed
more freely, who of us has not looked a foreigner more
calmly in the face, as this reproach has been from time to
time wiped away, and the good faith of our country has
been, in many instances, so nobly maintained?   Again,
when these very nations, who thought ill of us, were suffering by famine, and their poverty-stricken populations
were perishing by thousands and hundreds of thousands,
who has not exulted in the spontaneous liberality with
which our people moved to their relief?   It was a noble
spectacle to behold this whole country, from the Gulf of
Mexico to the distant Aroostook, — once almost a battle-
ground, — from the Mississippi to the Atlantic coast, —
so lately almost threatened with bombardment, — hastening to pour out their offerings for the sustentation of a
starving peasantry.   It was a proud sight to look upon,
when our national vessels, originally designed to accomplish nothing but the purposes of vengeance, were sent
on this errand of mercy.   It was glorious to behold
them, dismantled of their armaments, every destructive
engine laid aside, the white flag of the Prince of Peace
floating from every mast-head, loaded with provisions for
starving thousands, enter the harbor of a famine-stricken
land.   It was reserved for us, in the kind providence of
God, to be the first people upon earth who should thus
commence the fulfilment of that prophecy, 'Men shall

beat their swords into ploughshares, and their spears into
pruning-hooks.' And who of us does not exult in this deed
of national mercy? Who does not feel that he himself
is exalted in the eyes of the world, in this honor that has
been done to the American name? Who does not feel
conscious that in the presence of a holy universe, and of
God, the Father Almighty, the acts of Palo Alto, and Mon-
terey, and Buena Vista, and Vera Cruz, and Cerro Gordo
are covered with blackness, in contrast with the mission
of the Jamestown and the Macedonian, and the fleet that
accompanied them, bearing succor and life to millions
who were dying for lack of bread?

"But this illustration has carried me farther than I
intended; so far, I fear, that I may seem to have lost
sight of its original design. You will, however, all observe the point to which it tends. It is to show that in
this, the most general sense, we all feel responsible for
the acts of those with whom we stand connected, even in
the most common relations. We rejoice in their well-
doing, and are pained at the sight of their folly and their
sin. And you will all perceive at once that this feeling
of responsibility is stronger, and its action is more decided,
as the relation which gives rise to it is narrower and more
exclusive. We are more sensitive to the good or evil conduct of a native of our own state than of one who is
merely an American citizen. We are more strongly
moved by the acts of a townsman than of a native of the
same state. We are still more deeply affected if he who
has done well or ill is our kinsman, our friend, or our
brother. To be even remotely related to one who has
deserved well of his country, is a heritage more valuable
than wealth, and we hand down to other ages the evidences of our relationship, —

'And dying mention it within our wills,
Bequeathing it as a rich legacy
Unto our issue.'

"But it will be obvious that to none of the relations
which exist among us are these remarks so applicable as
to that of parents and children. There is here not a
seeming, but a positive responsibility. The parent is
intrusted by God with authority over the child. To him
is committed the duty of forming the character of his off-

spring, of correcting his defects, of fostering his virtues, and of instilling into his mind those principles which must lie at the foundation of his future manhood.   The life of the man is generally held to be the exponent of the education which he has received from his parents.   No one speaks of the Gracchi without, at the same time, remembering the mother of the Gracchi.   No one mentions Washington without also honoring the mother of Washington.   Indeed, so far has this sentiment been carried by some nations, that they have held the parent legally responsible, during his whole life, for the actions of his children ; rewarding him, and not them, if they have acted well ; punishing him, and not them, if they have acted unworthily.

" Now, to meet the demands of this relation, there have been implanted in our nature all the needful propensities. In infancy the care of the child devolves almost exclusively upon the mother, and the manner in which she discharges this duty has passed into a proverb.   Her self-denying care for her babe has ever been, among all nations and in all ages, the highest conception which we can form of disinterested affection.   She will toil till life itself is exhausted that she may furnish sustenance to her little ones.   When gasping in the deadly faintness of famine, she will pass the untasted morsel to her babe. Shivering in the winter's storm, she will strip herself of covering to save her child from freezing.   In shipwreck she will beseech with tears a place for her infant in the long-boat, and go down, without a murmur, in the foundering bark.   Nor are we ever astonished at beholding such scenes of self-devotion.   We look at them as the expected and ordinary workings of a mother's heart.   Were it not so — did she act otherwise — did she seek her own safety at the expense of her offspring, we should look at her with horror, and declare that, in not loving her child better than herself, she had proved herself false to the primary instinct of her maternal nature.

" As the child grows up to boyhood and youth, the care of him is devolved more directly upon the father. And here you behold the same impulse carried into action with almost similar results.   The object of the father is to prepare his son for manhood, and to give him every advantage for performing his part in life with success.

That he may be enabled to do this, what labor is too exhausting, what care too corroding, what self-denial too severe? You behold around you on every side the putting forth of ceaseless toil. In all the departments of life, whether agricultural, commercial, manufacturing, or professional, from early dawn to drowsy twilight, muscle and sinews, body and mind, are strained to their utmost point of tension. The results of all this activity are most carefully husbanded. The dollar and the cent are scrupulously laid aside and thoughtfully invested. When gains begin to accumulate, the man still toils on with undiminished energy; his raiment scarcely less coarse, and his relaxations hardly more numerous. He has all that he needs for himself, but he chooses to be still bending over his task. He looks forward to no release until death, and expects no other end than to die in the harness.

"Now, if you were to go among these busy multitudes, who are laboring on the wharf, or in the counting-room, in the field, the factory, or the office, and ask them why this ceaseless exertion, what think you would be their answer? Would it be, that they were endeavoring to secure for themselves ease, or rank, or pleasure? Far from it. They would tell you of the family at home, who were growing up, and who were depending on them for the means of support, and the opportunity of preparation for future usefulness. It matters not how hard the parent may toil; he bears it patiently, that so he may render the life of his child less irksome. It matters not how neglected may have been the education of the father; he will see to it that the education of his son be not neglected. He may have been cast off in boyhood to buffet with the storm, and struggle with it as for life, but he will labor without ceasing that his children may commence their career under happier auspices. In fact, this feeling, as we all see, is liable to be carried to excess, and men are commonly disposed to do more for their children than they really need; forgetting that the lesson of self-reliance can only be learned in the school of anxiety and hardship, and that it is taught us only by the severe discipline of personal responsibility and mortifying failure.

"It is a most interesting sight to behold one who has attained to some consideration among his fellow-men, watching with paternal solicitude over the education of his offspring. He will undergo the severest professional labor, and task his intellectual energies until they sink benumbed with paralysis, for the sake of placing his children under the most favorable and costly conditions of improvement that his country can afford. Nor is he satisfied when these are exhausted. He will toil on in solitude, at midnight, that his son may enjoy the advantages of European instruction. Every mail, with its frequent remittances, carries with it his lessons of wisdom and incitements to improvement. Gladly does he peril even life for the sake of enabling his child to commence his career from a more advantageous starting-point than he himself enjoyed, and to hand down unsullied to another generation the name which he has with so much effort rendered illustrious.

" But a still stronger case than this is yet more frequently seen. Amidst the families of restricted means in our land, it is not uncommon to observe talent of unusual promise; for in this gift the poor share as liberally as the rich. The natural feeling of which I have spoken leads the parents to wish that the child thus endowed may enjoy fit advantages for developing that talent which, to them at least, seems to have been so largely bestowed. The course, however, is long, and the outlay such as must bear heavily upon every resource that has been placed at their disposal. Still, they and their other children resolve to make the sacrifice. The labor of the household is increased. Every expense is curtailed. The table is shorn of its slender luxuries, and the wardrobe is rendered plainer and more scanty. Thus year after year of self-denial — honorable, noble self-denial — is endured, that the son and brother may wear clothes such as they do not wear, eat from a table such as they do not spread, devote himself to quiet study while they are exhausted with toil, and enter upon a sphere of professional eminence where they know that they can never follow him. It is in such unobtrusive examples as these that we see the true nobleness of man; and no country on earth presents them in greater number than our own.

" And what is the reward which the parent hopes to receive from all this lavish expenditure? Does he expect that it will ever be repaid? Far from it; for the parents lay up for the children, and not the children for the parents. Does he anticipate that in his declining years the self-denial which he has suffered will be repaid by similar self-denial, in his behalf, by his child? Far, very far from it. This thought never once enters his mind. All that he desires is, that his son may wisely improve the advantages which are purchased for him at so great cost. If that son, with honest and faithful assiduity, devote himself to the acquisition of knowledge; if he resolutely form those habits of honorable and virtuous self-government which are absolutely necessary to success; if he spurn from him the examples of the bad, and turn away his ear from listening to the principles which lead to shame; if, while doing this, he act from motives of piety, and set the Lord always before his face, that he sin not against him, — then is every wish of a father's heart gratified. Then, as, from time to time, he welcomes home his son, and observes the evidence of improvement in his expanding faculties and enlarged knowledge, in his principles more firmly fixed, and manners more decorous and gentleman-like, in judgment more matured, and affections more confiding and grateful, — then it is that the heart of the parent leaps for joy; then do all his self-sacrifices seem over and over repaid, and the sentiment of the text is fully illustrated, A wise son maketh a glad father.

"But what shall we say if all this picture be reversed? What if the son, as soon as he has escaped from under the eye of his parents, become forgetful of all filial obligation? What if every opportunity of improvement be neglected, and the time which is thus dearly purchased for him be spent in dreamy idleness, in frivolous or vicious reading, or in the company of the impure and profligate? What if the funds wrung, it may be, by ambiguous representations, from the self-sacrificing earnings of parents, be consumed in boyish sport, or sensual gratification; what if the young man who was early taught to fear God has learned already to scoff at religion and to make a mock at sin; what if, as he returns home at the close of every term, a more and more decided testimony of his worthlessness follow him; if, as his ignorance becomes more apparent, his arrogance become more insufferable; what if the contagion of his example begin to corrupt his younger and more virtuous brothers at home; and finally, what if it be needful to remove him from an insti-

tution to which his character has become an offence no
longer to be borne? Then is it that the cup of a parent's
misery is filled. Then is a foolish son a heaviness to her
that bare him.

"It has been my lot to witness most of the ordinary
forms of human sorrow, but never have I been called to
sympathize in any so hard to be endured as that occasioned by filial ingratitude. I have heard the father re-
count his sacrifices and those of his family for his son,
and then narrate, what I too well knew, the manner in
which these sacrifices have been requited. I have seen
tears coursing down the sun-burnt cheeks of a gray-headed
man, while sobs that choked his utterance told of a grief
which language could not unfold. I have felt at such a
time that earth had no consolation for such a mourner.
I could do nothing but mingle my tears with the broken-
hearted man, and commend him, from my inmost soul, to
God, who is the Comforter of those that be cast down.

"It will, I know, be said that these are extreme cases;
that few are as thoughtful as the former, and few as reckless as the latter, of these instances suggests. I am perfectly aware of this. There are not many who wring
their parents' hearts with anguish such as I have described;
but, on the other hand, the praise which we bestow on
the young man who is ever thoughtful of his parents'
feelings, and grateful for his parents' sacrifices, teaches
us that such examples of filial duty are also rare. But
why, I ask, should they be so rare? Is it a very remarkable attainment of virtue for a young man to embrace the
opportunities of attaining to honor and distinction which
are freely placed before him? Is it an act of preëminent
goodness to requite kindness with affection, to be grateful for favors purchased by labors, self-denials, and priva-
tions, which are endured for you, and have no other object
than your own well-being? If a man be thoughtful and
grateful, reason itself teaches us that he does no more
than his duty; while to fail in this cardinal point exposes
him justly to our severest reprehension.

"Now, I by no means intend to affirm that an utter
disregard of the happiness of parents is common among
young men. It is, on the contrary, quite uncommon. A
portion of filial affection is frequently an element in the
character even of the most reckless. It may be overlaid

by a variety of bad habits and vicious sentiments; but any violent disruption of ordinary relations is likely to bring it to the surface. When a young man falls into disgrace, it usually happens that the pain which he thus inflicts upon his parents is the bitterest ingredient in his cup of sorrow. This always affords reason for hope. It shows that the man has not become wholly worthless. And not unfrequently have I seen this strong principle of our nature the means of recalling a young man to virtue, when hope from every other source had long been abandoned.

"It is not, then, from deliberate and heartless ingratitude that the young so frequently inflict pain upon their parents. It is from thoughtlessness and utter want of consideration. They do not think of consequences in respect to themselves, and they do not think of them in respect to others. They have no idea of the joy which they can create by doing well, nor of the misery which they must occasion by doing ill. It is on this very account that I have taken occasion, young gentlemen, to set these things plainly before you. I do it now that you may go home with these considerations distinctly before you. I do it because you will have the opportunity, very soon, of judging from your own observation whether I have said truly. It is on this very account that our college vacations occur so frequently. We wish you to be as often as possible brought under the influence of home, and to be at short intervals reminded of the obligations which the filial relations so manifestly impose upon you. Permit me, in closing this discourse, to suggest a few reflections which may tend to deepen these convictions, which I cannot but hope already exist in your minds upon this subject.

"1. Regard to the feelings of parents has a manifest tendency to cultivate refinement of character. It teaches us to act continually from the most amiable and praiseworthy impulses of our nature. We thus learn to do, or to refrain from doing, not for ourselves, but for others. We acquire the habit of acting for the happiness of those who love us best, in the place of seeking our own ease, or pleasure, or sensual gratification. He who has formed these habits is surely developing in himself every disposition that can render him estimable among men, or prepare the way for his future success. As he enters into life, and takes his place in society, he will only need to transfer to his friends, and to the world at large, the sentiments which he has cherished towards his parents, and he can scarcely fail to become an amiable and accomplished man.

"2. The habit which he cultivates lies at the foundation of all moral attainments. You all know that to regard the feelings of parents, while we are absent from them, is to place ourselves under the control of an *unseen* law, written on our hearts, and read there only by ourselves. Now, this is the very principle from which all virtuous conduct proceeds. He who has learned to obey such a law in one case, will the more readily obey it in another. And hence it is, that, in all ages, obedience to parents has been considered the germ of all honorable conduct in after life, and the unfailing augury of future success. And I think that all observers of human nature will bear me out in the assertion that the future career of a young man can be more certainly predicted from this single element of character, than from any other that can be mentioned.

"3. Remember that the relations which you sustain to your parents must soon, in the order of nature, terminate. It may reasonably be expected that they will die before you. Then it will be impossible to remedy the errors or supply the defects of the past. When this sad hour shall arrive, no one can estimate the alleviation which it will prove to your sorrow to reflect that you have never given needless pain to the venerable form that lies cold in death. Nor can any one tell how exquisite will be your grief, if, as you behold that countenance that can never again reciprocate your look of love, you recollect that your conduct has forced tears from those sunken eyes, that your misdoings have wrung that heart with anguish, and that your thoughtless ingratitude has brought those gray hairs with sorrow to the grave. As you would secure peaceful composure in that trying hour, and as you would avoid the anguish of remorse to which it may consign you, I beseech you now to remember that ' a wise son maketh a glad father, but a foolish son is the heaviness of his mother.'

"Again, let us observe that success in any of our pursuits is ever the gift of God. 'A man's heart deviseth his way, but the Lord directeth his steps.' You can expect to attain to no success without his blessing. You must inevitably fail in all your undertakings, if you act under his displeasure. Now, you all very well know that of the moral laws which he has given us, this is the only one to which he has affixed a definite promise. ' Honor thy father and thy mother, as the Lord thy God hath commanded thee, that thy days may be prolonged, and that it may be well with thee in the land which the Lord thy God giveth thee.' This is not a commandment to the Israelites alone, for the apostle repeats it as a commandment and promise to us. We have, then, the law of God to each one of us. If we obey it, we may claim the promise of his gracious protection. When you can so easily and honorably obtain it, would you go forth into life without such a guarantee?

" In fine, let us all look back over the year which is now drawing to a close. There is not one of you who does not stand in this relation, and who is not under these obligations, either to parents now living, or to those already with God. In many things you have all, I doubt not, come short of your duty. Your diligence might have been more earnest, your self-government more exemplary, your regard to your parents more constantly in exercise, and your affection to them more thoughtful and respectful. I trust you all regret a failure in these respects, even in the least degree. Let us then recall the past with penitence, and look forward to the future with sincere resolutions of amendment. May you all return to your homes bearing evidence of such improvement in intellect and character as shall gladden the hearts of those who love you. May God preserve you and yours during this approaching season of relaxation, and by his blessing may we meet here again, earnestly resolved to spend the next year in a manner worthy of the advantages which God in his mercy has bestowed upon us.

" I cannot close these chapel discourses for the present term, young gentlemen, without a brief reference to the time which we have spent together. When we first assembled in this place, on our return from vacation, I took occasion to offer to you such advice as our situation seemed to demand. It is therefore proper that I should express to you the pleasure which I feel in believing that my advice was useful to you, or, what is still better, that your own correct principles rendered this advice unnecessary. I think I may say with truth, that in no collegiate term since my connection with this institution have we done more work, or in a more scholar-like manner. Your instructors, young gentlemen, bear united testimony to your punctuality, successful application, and gentleman-like deportment. Unless all the indications with which I am acquainted have proved fallacious, you have all made decided progress in intellectual and moral character. It is most delightful to us to bear this testimony. It cheers us in our labor. We thank God and take courage.

" Since we first assembled here, at the commencement of this term, several of us have been visited with sickness : one is now seriously ill, and one of our number has been summoned to the bar of God. We part in a few days ; but shall we all meet here again? How easily are our plans frustrated by the approach of sickness or the touch of death ! All these events should remind us of the uncertainty of everything earthly, and the importance of being reconciled to God, and ever living in preparation for our last change. Let not, then, the joys of a return to your friends render you thoughtless respecting your immortal interests. Remember you are everywhere forming character for eternity. Everywhere you are consuming the time allotted by God for your probation. See, then, that it be not spent in vain.

" Before the opening of another term the present academic year will have closed, and a new one will have commenced. This little era in our existence should suggest to us thoughts that should make us better. It is a suitable season for a review of the past. We should examine the history of the year just closing, and ask what report it has borne to heaven, and how it might have borne more welcome news. It is a suitable season for resolutions of amendment and progress. Time past is beyond our power. Neither prayers nor tears can recall the moment that has flown. The future will receive its character from our decision. Let us then, if we are spared to enter upon a new year, commence it with a solemn determination to spend it in the fear of God, and in seri-

ous preparation for eternity. Let us look up to God for
his grace to assist us, and this grace is never wanting to
those who seek for it aright. Thus commencing the year
in the fear of God, we may confidently look up to him for
his blessing; and whether we see the close of it or not,
will be a matter of indifference to us, for, ' absent from
the body, we shall be present with the Lord.' "

CHAPTER XIII.

BIBLE CLASS. — RELIGIOUS INTERCOURSE WITH PUPILS
REVIEWED. — RELATIONS TO FACULTY. — TENDENCY
OF HIS TEACHINGS.

POWERFUL for good as were the daily religious
exercises of the college chapel, the Sabbath services,
and the frequent opportunities of personal conversation,
they were far from satisfying Dr. Wayland's anxious concern for the spiritual welfare of his pupils. Early in his
administration he commenced a Sunday evening Bible
class. The careful and critical study of the Scriptures, to
which he had already devoted so much of his time, and
the invaluable treasures of biblical lore which he had
derived from the teaching of Professor Stuart, were an
admirable preparation for such an exercise. The manner
in which this class was conducted, and the salutary influence which it exerted among the undergraduates of the
university, are happily presented in the reminiscences of
Dr. Bailey.

"Dr. Wayland's Bible class became somewhat famous.
It met on Sabbath evenings in the old chapel. He commenced with the study of the Epistle to the Romans.
The examination of this portion of the Scriptures proceeded slowly. Each verse, and, when necessary, each
word, was closely scrutinized, and its exact meaning and
force determined. What the apostle affirms in regard to
man's moral nature was made a topic of special investigation.

" With unfaltering step Dr. Wayland conducted his pupils over the ground traversed by the apostle. He listened
patiently to all inquiries, heard and considered all objec-

tions, and discovered a reply to both in that wonderful
utterance of inspiration.   What it declared, he repeated;
when it was silent, he did not seek to supply the omission.
Although I was not myself a Christian at the time to
which I refer, and did not often attend the ' doctor's
Bible class,' yet I could not associate with the religious
undergraduates without hearing frequently of the wonderful things said on Sabbath evenings in the college chapel.
My room-mate, a pious young man studying for the
ministry, was laborious in preparing for this exercise, and
constant in his attendance.   He always entered our room
on his return with some expression of admiration.   When
we conversed on the subject of religion, my dissent from
his views was frequently met with a wish that I had heard
what the ' old doctor' had said on that subject in the
Bible class.   I soon found that I had to grapple not alone
with my room-mate, a young man of respectable promise,
but, in the last resort, with the president himself, and with
the wonderful institution of which he was the presiding
genius.   In visiting other rooms, I discovered that the
subjects discussed on the Sabbath were not forgotten during the succeeding week or weeks, but continued to give
rise to interested and animated conversation, and usually
to conviction.

"This Bible class, in his hands, became a power, and
gained a reputation extending far beyond the walls of the
college.   It even excited, it was rumored, the jealousy of
a theological institution then struggling for a place in the
affections of the churches.   It was hinted that the student
preparing for the ministry at Brown, after attending the
instructions given in that class for four years, did not feel
that he greatly needed a course of lectures from a professor in didactic theology.   It was hinted, indeed, that
those who pursued their theological studies in a seminary, sometimes annoyed their instructors by too frequent
allusions to the views and opinions which had been
advanced in the chapel of their *alma mater*.

" By these varied and prolonged efforts, as well as by
his labors in the pulpit, soundness of faith was secured to
the university.   Yet what he most of all desired was for a
considerable time withheld.   Year after year he prayed,
labored, and watched for a revival; but it came not.

" Some time during the year 1833, Mrs. Wayland, then

in feeble health, invited several pious ladies to join her, at her house, in special prayer for a revival of religion in college. For a long time they sought this great blessing apparently in vain. At last, however, soon after the commencement of the winter term of 1834, there was a cloud, which, though small, sustained their hopes. There was increased interest in the weekly college prayer-meeting. Religion became more and more the subject of conversation. Christians gave evidence of new activity and quickened zeal. The impenitent were visited, and prayed for and with. Each class met by itself in a private room, and untiring efforts were made to secure the attendance of all. Christians confessed with tears their unfaithfulness, and entreated those with whom they had been intimate, no longer to neglect salvation. Soon new-born souls added their appeals to those of older Christians.

" This revival — the first under his administration — occurred after years of anxious labor, and was the consummation of his desires and hopes. During it all, his state of mind was truly heavenly ; humble, tender, prayerful, solicitous now for this one and now for that one, and incessant in his efforts to persuade all his pupils to be reconciled to God. His conversations, his exhortations, his sermons, his prayers, seemed to me more eloquent and melting than anything I had ever heard from mortal lips.

" Meanwhile, at his home, one who had shared with him the toils and the trials of faith was rapidly sinking into the arms of death. Constantly he was expecting to be called from his lecture-room, or from his study, or from the prayer-meeting, to hear her last words and to bid her a last farewell. I have seen him start, almost convulsively, when his little son entered the recitation-room, supposing that the child had come to bring tidings of the near approach of the final hour. Throughout the weeks of that eventful term, amid all these conflicting emotions, he was calm, subdued, affectionate, sad, cheerful.

" We shall never see his like again. His mantle has not descended upon any of us."

Notwithstanding the extent and variety of Dr. Wayland's efforts to promote the spiritual welfare of his pupils, he by no means believed that he had done his full duty in this respect. While to others he seemed, even tested by the most exalted standard of moral obligation, to have labored to the utmost limit of his mental and physical capacity, his rare modesty, and his severe criterion of duty led him to put a very low estimate upon what he had accomplished. In the sight of his Maker he even felt convicted of moral delinquency. Upon this point the following extract from his personal reminiscences will be read with deep and affecting interest: —

"So far as labor is concerned, I cannot charge myself with dereliction of duty. In another respect I am conscious of serious cause of regret. I did not rely, as I ought to have done, upon the blessing of God, without which no amount of exertion can succeed. I did not make my labors the subject of earnest prayer, but depended too much upon personal effort. I had, of course, a general sense of dependence on God, and of reliance on his goodness in the discharge of duty. I did not make this sufficiently special, in view of the fact that all my efforts were utterly valueless without the divine blessing.

"I did not pay suitable attention to the cultivation of the religious character of my pupils. I am aware of the influence which an instructor is capable of wielding in this respect; but I did not adequately exert it. It is true that I frequently joined the young men in their religious meetings, and endeavored to speak to them directly and solemnly. This I did as often as they desired. In times of particular attention to religion I gave myself up primarily to their spiritual instruction. For several years I preached regularly in the chapel for their special benefit, preparing a sermon every week. But this was not enough. I should have allowed no student to leave college, especially those under my particular instruction, without having a private, earnest, faithful conversation with him on the subject of his eternal interests.

"Year after year I resolved to do this; but I did it only in part. I sometimes appointed evenings for conversation with those who desired an interview for this purpose. I often sent for individuals with this express design; but it turned out, at the close of each year, that many left me, perhaps forever, on whom I had never urged attention to religion, and before whom I had never set forth their danger of eternal destruction. If I had plainly and resolutely done this, I should probably have been of more real service to my pupils than I accomplished by all my other labors in connection with the college.

"In this respect I fear that officers of colleges greatly err. They are, in most colleges in New England, and in the Northern States (and I am acquainted with no others), professors of religion, and often clergymen. They are expected to exercise a positive religious influence upon their pupils. But I apprehend that such expectation is frequently disappointed. For the most part, they set before the students a proper example, and sometimes refer to religion, when such a reference is manifestly demanded by the subject under immediate consideration; but the reference is rather such as would be made by any observer of the historical laws of cause and effect, than what would naturally be expected from those whose distinction is, that they are ' the salt of the earth,' ' the light of the world.' If every instructor in every college in our land felt himself personally responsible for the spiritual well-being of every young man under his charge, a collegiate life would cease to be a season of danger, and frequently of sore temptation. God would crown with his special blessing all honest efforts for the religious improvement of the undergraduates, and an academical society would become a nursery for heaven."

We have thus far considered Dr. Wayland only in his relations to his pupils. The following letter from Professor William Gammell describes the nature of his intercourse, official and social, with those gentlemen who so efficiently aided him in the labors of collegiate education : —

"You request me to give you some account of the relations, both official and social, which Dr. Wayland, while president of Brown University, was accustomed to hold with his associates in the Faculty of instruction. I was with him there for twenty-three years. Entering the Faculty soon after my graduation, I grew up in it from being the junior tutor until I was at length one of the senior professors. My mind is so full of recollections of the president, who was first my teacher, and afterwards through life my associate and friend, that I hardly know how to arrange and state them so as to set forth his character as it used to present itself in our daily intercourse. His relations to those connected with him changed somewhat, as a matter of course, with the progress of his life; but I will attempt to illustrate them as they existed in the vigor and noonday of his career, and, for the most part, without reference to any one period rather than another.

" 1. No one feature of his official character, I am sure, is more conspicuous in the recollections of his associates, than his pervading sense of the responsibility of his position as the head of the college, and especially as the guardian and teacher of young men. This feeling he used constantly to express; and he always desired his associates to share it, as a condition, so to speak, of their own success, as well as of the prosperity of the college. He was in the habit of referring very frequently to the property which, for the time, we were using, and to the duty of guarding it from injury and loss, to the dignity of an instructor's work, to the moral trusts involved in the care of young men, especially when away from home, and to the hopes and expectations of parents.

" If any of us officially mentioned to him the case of a student who was not doing well in his studies or in his conduct, he would almost invariably inquire if we had used our best endeavors to keep him up to the mark and save him. He would often remind us that if it should become necessary to send the young man home to his parents, he must be able to say that the college had done its utmost to benefit him. He always sympathized most deeply with the pain which a measure of extreme discipline would be likely to produce in the family circle to which the student belonged; saying that nothing was more trying than to be obliged to tell the truth to a parent about an idle or wayward son.

" This feeling of responsibility arose in part from his profound estimate of the transcendent importance of character, as compared with even the most advantageous gifts of fortune, and in part from his religious views of human life. He believed in it as an opportunity given to us for work and for culture, as a season of probation, as the spring-time of the immortality to come. To have the best portion of it wasted by any of those for whose training he was in any degree responsible, gave him the utmost concern. If anything occurred in the conduct of a student, or in the general course of the college, indicating a low moral tone, he seemed always to blame himself that it had not been anticipated and guarded against. In the earlier part of his presidency, his standard in some of these respects was, perhaps, an unattainable idea ; but its existence in his own mind gave a sort of heroic energy to his administration of the college, which we were all obliged to share. He constantly admonished us to give attention to the first wrong step in any young man, and to seek to prevent its repetition. *Obsta principiis* was a motto which he always had in mind.

"2. He was himself, as all his pupils will remember, an enthusiastic teacher. He was a great master in the art of imparting knowledge and discipline to the minds of others. He also possessed, in a remarkable degree, the power of awakening thought and kindling aspirations after excellence. On assuming the presidency of the college, he had introduced a system, both of instruction and discipline, far more thorough and exact than had before prevailed there, or was common in any of our colleges fifty years ago. The younger officers, in my time, had been trained to this system while they were undergraduates ; and I well remember the lively interest which Dr. Wayland used to manifest, when I was a tutor, in all our efforts to maintain it. He perfectly appreciated the difference between genuine teaching and all its manifold imitations, and he would never tolerate anything that aimed to substitute the appearance for the reality. He detested *shams* of all sorts, and had no respect for those who were willing to resort to them. On the other hand, he held work in very high esteem, whether in officer or in student ; and he wished to have that work done by both as thoroughly and as liberally as possible.

"The system of instruction which he introduced made it necessary, not only that the general subject, but also the particular lesson of the day, should be in the mind both of the teacher and the pupil. He paid particular attention to all the examinations, and judged of the success of every instructor, and also of his style of instruction, very much by the manner in which the members of a class acquitted themselves on these occasions. By pursuing this course, the college soon came to have a standard of its own, which was always before us, and attended us as a perpetual presence, from term to term, and from year to year. It was a standard, moreover, which at length came to be as distinctly recognized by the students as by the instructors themselves.

" 3. The laws and usages of our college have placed a larger authority in the hands of the president, and have made him personally responsible for its management in a greater degree than is true of most other colleges. But, at the same time, it was the habit of Dr. Wayland to consult very freely with members of the Faculty respecting every measure of importance relating either to the internal or the external affairs of the institution. The changes inaugurated in 1850, and known as the ' new system,' sprang from his own reflections and inquiries concerning the proper functions of higher education, and, as such, were submitted to the corporation, and received their sanction. But until that time I do not recall a single instance in which the nomination of an officer, whether professor or tutor, was made to the corporation without the advice of the Faculty, or in which any measure of importance that concerned the interests of the college was decided upon without their sanction and coöperation. He regarded our common position as, in some sort, a partnership, in the management of which all should have a voice, at least in the way of counsel, if not of legal authority.

" 4. In matters of discipline in our respective spheres, he favored the fullest exercise of personal authority on the part of every member of the Faculty, and he invariably gave his own official support to what another had found it necessary to do. He encouraged no appeals from professors or tutors to the president. No fear was felt, on the part of either, that he would ever seek to promote his own popularity or comfort at the expense of that of his associates. His standing direction, even to the youngest officers, invariably was, that they should first exhaust their own resources in every case of discipline which arose in their classes, and bring it to his attention only when they had failed to adjust it for themselves. Whenever it became necessary, he bore unflinchingly and magnanimously the odium of every measure, no matter what was its origin, which the good of the college seemed to require. He especially deplored a bad precedent in administration, and had a genuine dread of the vicious example and the contagion of idleness among students. He often told us that we should be ashamed to meet our pupils in after life, if we had suffered them to waste their time without restraint, or to ruin themselves by unreproved dissipation.

"5. Dr. Wayland was at no period of his life what is called a man of society. His habits were those of a man of thought and of recluse study. But he possessed in an unusual degree the endowments and the resources which are required for the fullest enjoyment and the largest influence in cultivated society. His conversational powers were of a high order. He had a vast fund of wit, anecdote, and interesting knowledge; such as have often given celebrity to literary men as Table Talkers,' or as prominent members of social circles. I have seen him when he appeared to the greatest advantage in the company of distinguished men and brilliant women; but he lived too habitually apart from such scenes to mingle in them with the fullest zest. It is possible that his constant devotion to work, and his earnest views of life, may have been somewhat unfriendly to the perfect development of his rare social powers. His attachments and sympathies, however, were very strong, and they constantly prompted him to seek the genial intercourse of other and kindred minds. He was also, at all periods of his life, much given to having intimate friends, with whom he freely counselled and communed. Most of his social intercourse was probably at his own home, where he was accustomed to dispense a liberal hospitality, and where he frequently gathered around him those in whose society he most delighted. He was, moreover, very mindful of the social duties incident to his position as president. He entertained, in some way or other, most of the persons of literary distinction who visited Providence from abroad, and constantly invited to his house his brethren in the ministry, and those who came to consult him in connection with matters pertaining to the college.

" But it is of his social relations with the officers of the university that you desire me more especially to write.

To them all, I may say, his house was a place of frequent and familiar resort, although his relations to them differed with different persons in their degrees of intimacy. To the younger members of the Faculty, I remember, he was particularly attentive, and ever mindful of the solitary life they led, residing, as they did at that time, within the walls of the college.

"In those earlier days we dined with him almost always on Saturdays. Very often, after evening meetings of the Faculty, which, I believe, are everywhere considered the most stupid of conclaves, he would invite us to remain at his house, and share in some extemporized entertainment, as an offset to the weary routine of college affairs. In many other ways, also, did he bind his associates to him in the daily intercourse of life. Even in his busiest days he was always accessible for consultation in every professional perplexity. Indeed I have never known a man so full of generous sympathies and ready consolation for every personal trouble or sorrow.

"In the summer season his early morning hours, and sometimes those at the close of the day, were spent in his garden, among the vegetables, and flowers, and fruits, which he cultivated very largely, with his own hands, with a skill and success that awakened universal admiration. He took great pleasure and pride in these products of his industry, and was always delighted, when, as very often happened, he excelled any of the professional gardeners of the neighborhood. His familiar friends, and especially members of the Faculty, were in the habit of visiting his garden very frequently; and he was never happier or more genial than when narrating passages of his horticultural experience, or calling attention to some curious process of nature which he had observed, or pointing out the prospective yield which promised to reward his labors. He usually had, according to the progress of the season, some beautiful flower, some luxuriant vegetable growth, or some ripening fruit, to commend to the notice of the visitor. He never failed to embrace such an opportunity to illustrate the bounties of nature. Sometimes also the traces of noxious insects would naturally suggest to him reflections concerning the origin and purpose of evil in the world. Those persons who never visited Dr. Wayland in his garden in the summer or autumn, have

failed to see him in one of his most interesting and characteristic moods.

"At other seasons of the year he was exceedingly fond
of walking in the country, always seeking companionship on such occasions. The evening prayers of the college, until they were abolished in 1850, were invariably
at five o'clock. On the dismissal of the students, he
would very commonly summon some of us to join him in
the walk to the Seekonk River, going by one road and returning by the other. This had always been the favorite
walk of academics, both young and old, and the banks of
the Seekonk are associated with the college memories of
every generation of students. Although now, for much of
the way, lined with houses, and the popular drive of the
wealth and fashion of the town, this ancient road, five and
twenty or thirty years ago, was rural and secluded, full
of attractive scenery of meadow and grotto, of wooded
hill and flowing river, and pervaded throughout its whole
extent with the tranquillity always so grateful to reflective
and studious minds.

"In these walks, which were continued through many
years, he would often do all the talking himself, especially
when accompanied only by his juniors; sometimes on a
question suggested by a companion, sometimes opening
the results of his own recent reading, or perhaps recalling,
in connection with the public incidents of the time, anecdotes, stories, and reminiscences of well-known characters,
with which his mind was largely stored. Grave as were
his daily studies, and serious as was his habitual tone of
thought, those who mingled thus freely in his society
amidst the scenes to which I have alluded, knew him to
be exceedingly fond of both humor and of wit, and to
be capable of a mirthfulness that was in singular contrast
with other moods of his mind. He had a remarkable
memory of anecdotes and incidents, of passages of literature and images of every kind which savored of the ludicrous; and the slightest occasion would often call them
forth in long succession, with the utmost merriment to
himself, as well as to others. He had read, in his day,
a great deal of light literature, although he had no fancy
for such as is now most in vogue. I remember being
much with him, long ago, at a time when he was suffering from an affection of the eyes, and being surprised at

his extensive and varied acquaintance with the English poets. He not only knew all that was worth remembering in Young and Cowper, but he could repeat from memory many of the best passages of Goldsmith, Burns, and Scott. He was also unusually familiar with the sonnets of Milton and Shakspeare, as well as with their grander works. A little later than this he wrote and presented to a friend a brief critique on the minor poems of Milton, which, if it could now be found, might be ranked among his best executed pieces of composition. His familiarity with such literature, although not very extensive, was yet so thorough as to be available alike in conversation and in the work of instruction; and it added greatly to his resources in both, while at the same time it revealed to his familiar associates a class of tastes and a phase of character which those who knew him only as a moralist and theologian did not imagine that he possessed.

"But I must close these reminiscences of my early instructor and life-long friend. I might greatly prolong them, for I delight to recall the earnestness and genuineness which made themselves felt in every circle in which he moved, the richness and instructiveness that marked his conversation, and the varied phases of his many-sided character that seemed to have touched human life at so many different points. It is, however, far easier to recall all these than it is to describe them; and I fear that, after all, I have done but little towards making him understood by those who did not know him before."

At a meeting of the graduates of Brown University, on the occasion of Dr. Wayland's decease, Dr. Caswell — a member of the Faculty from 1828 to 1864, said, —

"I was associated with Dr. Wayland for nearly thirty years; and, during that time, perhaps no day passed without our meeting and chatting upon some subject connected with the college, or with the church, or with the missions, or with the charities in our community. And though there were subjects, religious, political, and scientific, wherein we differed, yet I may say that, during that whole period, there never was an interruption in the confidential relations existing between us.

"So far as I can recollect, there was but one occasion on which I felt in the least hurt by anything which Dr. Wayland did, or in which I felt that there was any want of kindness or consideration. There was one such occasion. I did not understand his course. Our intercourse had been such that I was unwilling to allow any misunderstanding without seeking an open explanation. My own nature would not allow me to hold any position that was ambiguous; and I went to Dr. Wayland and told him how I felt. He turned to me and said, 'Caswell, I never meant it. I would not hurt your feelings for the world.' Never have I had so intimate intercourse with a man, continued with such uniform kindness. I have been with him in his own deep affliction — he has been with me in mine; and his spontaneous sympathy was always that of a brother, and I feel this day as though I had lost a brother."

We should do obvious injustice to the character of Dr. Wayland, as an educator, if we did not make some allusion to the tendency of his teachings. From what has already been said in reference to his peculiar method of instruction, our readers will have no difficulty in believing that he encouraged and inculcated independent and exact thinking on the part of his pupils. He constantly cautioned his classes against extensive reading, if unaccompanied by serious and patient reflection, frequently quoting the saying of Dr. Arnold to his scholars, "Young gentlemen, you come here not so much to read, as to learn how to read."

One of his pupils, a young man of fine abilities, was in danger of contracting habits of moral and mental dissipation, from a fondness for social indulgence and desultory reading. The president went to his room one day, and said to him, "C., you seem to be fond of poetry. Now, here is a volume of poems which I think you will enjoy. Suppose you read it." The young man, appreciating the attention thus paid him, and touched by the interest in him which it indicated, willingly followed the advice of his instructor, and a literary taste was awakened which had a powerful effect in leading him to a high standard of scholarship and character.

Several years later a student, who had not yet come under Dr. Wayland's personal instruction, was wasting his time in idleness, or in worse than useless reading. The president, after conversing with him kindly, said, "Here is Boswell's Life of Johnson. Take it to your room, read it carefully, write out your impressions of it, and then come and see me again." When the pupil returned the volume he was a new man. His mental reformation had commenced. Works of fiction had lost their attraction for him. He devoted himself to his studies with earnest purpose, and left college with an enviable reputation as a scholar. He became eminent alike in his profession and in literature, and has ever ascribed his intellectual salvation to the timely and parental counsels of Dr. Wayland.

He did not seek to put certain views into the mind of the pupil, but to call out and develop his original powers; to make each one a man of independent thought. A member of the class of 1845 observes, "Six words which Dr. Wayland once said to the Senior class were worth more than any words ever addressed to me — 'Young gentlemen, cherish your own conceptions.'" The closing words of the chapter on "Taste," in his Intellectual Philosophy, are in a similar spirit: —

"In studying the works of others for our own improvement, one caution is to be observed. They are the production of fallible men, like ourselves. We are, therefore, to bring to the examination of every work of art the exercise of a calm, discriminating judgment, prepared to distinguish beauty from deformity wherever they exist. We must exercise our own taste, if we would cultivate our sensitive nature. When we study the works of others to awaken our own sensibilities, to correct our errors, and to arouse ourselves to emulation, we develop our own faculties. But if we study only to bow before a master as we would worship our Creator, we become servile copyists and degraded idolaters. It is not impossible that our veneration for the ancients has in some degree produced this effect upon modern literature. . . . To study the works of others that we may be able to equal them, cultivates the power of original creation. To study them only that we may learn how to do feebly what they have done well, is fatal to all mental development, and must consign an individual, or an age, to the position of despairing and wondering mediocrity."

The following letters to a former pupil have a similar tendency: —

" . . . The difference between a man who uses his own mind and the man who merely deals out what he has learned is as great as the difference between putting your hand into the fire and taking it out again. I do not wish you to go over the course as a well-trained charger, but like Scott's stag, —

' Stretching forward free and far
Seek the wild heaths of Uam Var.'

Where Uam Var is, I neither know nor care; but if a man stretches 'forward free and far,' he will surely come out somewhere."

" . . . You have now entered upon that portion of your life when every day counts. Your mind should by this time have attained to a good degree of ripeness, and you ought to be preparing to go alone; to form your own judgments on events and conduct, and to be daily increasing in all sound knowledge. I say sound knowledge, as the time for frivolous pursuits is surely past. You should strive to cultivate your own mind, not merely by acquisition, but by so learning as to call forth and strengthen your original powers. You must not aim merely to use your intellectual instrument, but to perfect it by use; the latter being by far the most important consideration."

His fondness for the analytical method of teaching arose, in large measure, from his conviction that in no other way could the habit of logical thinking, and the power of concentrating all the mental faculties upon a given subject, be so surely and so speedily acquired.   He was unwearied in urging his pupils never to write or speak until they knew precisely what they wished to say, and in what order they could say it with the greatest possible effect.

Counselling a young friend upon this point, he,once observed, —

"Were I to advise you on this subject, I should say, Study your plans thoroughly, sketch them out briefly, and reflect upon them carefully, before you write. Do not begin the work of composition until you have thought the matter well through, and so revised and corrected as to be well satisfied with it.   Then, and not until then, write."

His experience as an instructor had given him abundant opportunities of observing how readily young men form the habit of speaking and writing without any definite purpose or well-defined aim, and it was his constant effort to counteract this unfortunate tendency.   "Always have some distinct point in view," was an injunction which he often and earnestly impressed upon his pupils.

So much importance did he attach to this element of a thorough education, so essential did he consider it to eminence in any profession or calling in life, that he never hesitated to recommend it, not only to those under his immediate instruction, but to all in whose success his personal attachment inclined him to be peculiarly interested.   Among these, was a clergyman long and favorably known in Providence, who says, —

"Dr. Wayland frequently walked to church with me, and often sat with me in the pulpit. On such occasions he usually made the opening prayer. Before this exercise he would invariably ask me, 'What is the point of your sermon?'—designing to make his prayer appropriate to the theme of my discourse. If I could not give him a clear conception of what I proposed to say to my people, he would seem disappointed. And this led me, in time, to seek in each sermon for some definite idea to be presented, some systematic and logical plan of the subject under consideration. If I have had any success as a preacher, it has been mainly due, under God, to the suggestions, in regard to the construction of my sermons, which I received, from time to time, from Dr. Wayland."

In his criticisms upon the sermons and other public addresses of his former pupils, he never lost sight of this cardinal principle of all his teachings. Speaking of a young divine, whose sermons rarely presented any consecutive train of thought, and were sadly wanting in directness of application, he once remarked, with a good-humored twinkle of his eye, " The great difficulty about the preaching of —— is to discover precisely what he is after."

Clearness of expression was, in his view, hardly less important than clearness of thought. His own style was certainly a model of simplicity. He always sought to convey his ideas in the fewest and plainest words possible. Both his example and his precepts were opposed to obscure and involved modes of expression. Criticising a composition of one of his pupils, he once said, " Avoid long and complicated sentences. I had sometimes to read over a sentence twice. No man has a right to ask this of another."

At the commencement of his professional career he evidently cultivated his powers of imagination with much care. At this time his efforts towards his own mental development plainly pointed to æsthetics. Some of his early published discourses are characterized by a rare grace of diction, frequently rising into the regions of the grand and sublime. There are paragraphs in his writings, at this period of his life, which for rhetorical beauty and genuine eloquence can hardly be surpassed in English literature.

His work as an instructor, however, was necessarily of such a nature as to withdraw his attention more and more from the graces of style and the cultivation of the imaginative faculty. He found that the only text-book then accessible in the department of ethics was defective and unsound. Incapable of teaching a system that was at variance with his convictions, he sought to place the system of morals on a truer basis and in a clearer light. This labor he accomplished with such eminent success, that, in the words of a gentleman who was under his instruction during the third year of his presidency, "the Senior class seldom left his recitation-room, during the term when ethics was their study, without expressing their admiration at the skill and clearness with which he unfolded to them the elements of moral science."

Such labors, as a matter of course, removed him each year further and further from the walks of elegant literature, and confined him more and more closely to subjects embraced within the domain of practical science and vigorous action.* It resulted naturally that all the weight of his example had its inevitable effect upon the minds of his pupils. They also gravitated towards analysis and abstract thought, and away from æsthetics. While it would be incorrect to say that the legitimate tendency of his teachings was to discourage the careful cultivation of style, it may be safely asserted that his pupils received a peculiarly strong impulse in the direction of clear statement and robust thinking. The vigorous logic of that renowned lecture-room gave tone to their intellectual efforts.

Regarding the discipline of the faculties, rather than the acquisition of a given amount of knowledge, as being the object of a collegiate education, Dr. Wayland constantly aimed to call into active exercise every mental power of his pupils.

---

* To this cause may be added the constant pressure on his time, created by the ever-present necessity of maintaining the temporal interests of the college, which left him little leisure for mental luxury, or purely æsthetic culture.

If the graduates of Brown University left their *alma mater* with minds trained to exact and logical thinking, accustomed to habits of patient and systematic industry, and inspired with a generous enthusiasm to improve to the utmost every opportunity for moral and intellectual advancement, these results were greatly due to the impulse imparted in his lecture-room. In the homely and expressive phrase of an eminent graduate, " He would hold a man right down to the subject, until he had brought his mind to an edge."

Another marked effect of his instruction was to inspire in his pupils an ardent love for truth. He was always seeking to discover some general principle in accordance with which every material fact in ethics should be classified. Such a fundamental truth, when once found, he followed fearlessly to its legitimate consequences. At an age when most men are satisfied with collecting isolated facts and recording individual experiences, he had formed the habit of dwelling long and frequently in the regions of abstract thought. Convictions which had not passed through the analytical process, opinions which he could not refer to some general principle, had little weight with him. What is expedient, what is popular, what will be likely to succeed, — did not long occupy his mind. But a train of thought proceeding from correct premises and carried forward by strictly logical connections, he willingly embraced with the independence which belonged to his generous nature. Sound moral reasoning had for him the force of mathematical demonstration. He was as certain that free trade is the great economical law of commerce, as was Galileo that the earth turns on its axis and revolves around the sun. That slavery is a moral wrong and a political blunder, was as clear to his mind as the plainest proposition in Euclid. How much he valued, and how earnestly he set before his pupils, " the glorious privilege of being inde-

pendent" in the cause of truth, not one who enjoyed his
instructions can have forgotten. Resting securely on fixed
and immutable realities, as defined by the laws of God
and the moral nature of man, he gave little heed to the
hasty decisions of irresponsible majorities. Scarcely a
volume did Dr. Wayland publish, scarcely a course of
lectures did he deliver, which did not excite opposition in
some quarter. His sentiments in regard to slavery were
severely criticised by a class powerful, and even prepon-
derating, at the time when he gave to the public his "Elements of Moral Science." He commenced his lectures on
political economy when party strife ran high in regard to
some of the fundamental principles of this science ; and yet
he seemed unaware that the public mind was excited on
such questions. For some of the positions taken in his
"Limits of Human Responsibility," he was fiercely as-
sailed in the public press and in his personal correspondence. But he submitted in silence to all these complaints,
at least so far as any public reply was concerned. Conscious of the rectitude of his motives, and of his simple
and sincere desire to inculcate only what he believed to
be true, he was willing to await the deliberate judgment
of his fellow-men.

It is not surprising that this ardent and fearless attachment to truth gave him great moral influence with those
who came under his instructions. Young as they were,
they rarely failed to appreciate the earnestness of his convictions, and his disinterested devotion to the principles
which he had embraced. In the words of one of his pupils, —*

"It was not necessary to follow Dr. Wayland, to be his
admirer. It was not necessary to accept his opinions, to
have the utmost reverence for him. A graduate a year
older than myself, whose views upon theological and
public questions were entirely diverse from those of Dr.

* Hon. C. S. Bradley.

Wayland, and whose experience and observations in life have been as mature, perhaps, as those of any of us, told me that he had never seen so great a man as Dr. Wayland. Many of us, having found ourselves in distant countries, in some strange city, every person around us unknown, with no pleasant surrounding of friends to keep us on our course, facing the world alone, as it were, have found the precepts and the ideas of life which Dr. Wayland had given us, to be nearest to the core of our hearts. They were the truths upon which we rested.

"And what were those truths which we recall now from the lecture-room and the chapel? Were they not principally these — that life was a place where work was to be done 'as ever in the great Task-master's eye,' and that such work could not fail, although no signs of victory appeared in this life?

"Do we not always feel that his simple purpose was to get at the truth upon every subject which he presented to us? Was not that the central idea of the man in teaching us not to look for enjoyment, but for the truth? Would he not say, as he met us, 'I ask not, my son, what fame or position you have acquired; but have you sought the truth?'"

Another pupil has said, — *

"We think that one principal source of Dr. Wayland's personal power was the fact that his mind seemed to be, and was, *in more direct contact with truth* than is the case with the minds of most men. He appeared to be seeking for nothing else. Nothing seemed to intervene between his mind and the truth, to warp his vision or bias his judgment?"

Holding this allegiance to truth, and ever seeking to attain to it in theory and in action, he could not content himself with asking what has been said, what have men thought and believed. Everything must be brought to the standard of perfect rectitude. Regarding absolute goodness as the goal of human progress, he was eminently progressive.

---

* Professor G. P. Fisher, in New Englander, January, 1866.

" In that struggle which is ever going forward between the *retiring* and the *coming* under the banners of conservatism and progress, in that ceaseless war which, from the very elements of human character and condition, must be waged, in one form or another, between the past and the future, on the battle-ground of the present, Dr. Wayland was always found, no less in his later than in his earlier years, in the advance of the party of progress. No man had a sublimer faith in the destinies of the race. No man, in anticipating those destinies, clothed them in the drapery of a more gorgeous imagination. The failures of the past could not shake his confidence in the future. From the mournful teachings of history even, he gathered an inner lesson of encouragement and hope. At no time had anything been really lost. The best forms of civilization which the world had seen, had, indeed, fallen into decay, or yielded themselves a prey to violence; but out of their ruins had emerged new civilizations, embodying all the best elements of the old, together with some higher principle, which in them was wanting. The thread of progress, which for a time seemed broken and turned backwards, reappears to guide our steps anew through the historic labyrinth." *

It belonged to Dr. Wayland's nature to be intensely in earnest about everything which he undertook. Life with him was a serious business, and time was of inestimable value. This spirit governed his daily labors, and inspired his daily teachings. He could not himself be idle, nor could he tolerate idleness in others. Upon instructors and pupils alike he ever inculcated the importance of patient and persistent industry He discouraged all relaxation which tended to dissipate the mind, or to unfit the student for the profitable employment of the hours which should be devoted to serious study. How often have we heard him quote those memorable words addressed by the first Napoleon to the Polytechnic School: " Young gentlemen, never waste a half hour: if you do,

* Commemorative Discourse of Professor Chace.

the time will come when you will be embarrassed, and perhaps will fail of your destiny, for want of what you might have gained in that half hour." In private conversation, in his occasional addresses in the college chapel, and often in his sermons, he was accustomed, as we have seen, to remind the undergraduates of their obligations to those parents who had furnished them with the means of acquiring an education, and of their accountability to that Creator who had endowed them with faculties capable of indefinite improvement.

He never wearied of urging upon young men the vital importance of continuous, conscientious study — of forming the settled habit of close attention to the work in hand. Thus he writes to a young friend and pupil: —

" Seek to acquire the power of continuous application, without which you cannot expect success. If you do this, you will soon be able to perceive the distance which it creates between you and those who have not such habits. You will not count yourself, nor will they count you, as one of them. Thus you will find yourself emerging into the higher regions of intellectual and earnest men ; men who are capable of making a place for themselves, instead of standing idly gaping, desiring a place without the power to command it. Keep on striving to accomplish more and more every day, and thus enlarge constantly the range of your intellectual ability. If you learn to do as much work in one day as you used to do in two or three days, you are as good as two or three such men, as you formerly were, boiled down to one."

These earnest views of human life and of moral accountability had their natural effect not less upon his theory of college discipline, than upon his system of instruction. If his discipline seemed severe, it was only because he never lost sight of the grave responsibilities of his position. He could not consider any case of misconduct, any violation of college laws, without, at the same time, weighing the moral tendency of the offence.

He could not forget how much the four years spent in college contribute to form the character and determine the destiny of a young man. He was keenly alive to the injurious effects of evil example, and knew, by a certain rare and instinctive knowledge of human nature, how and when these dangerous influences could be most effectually counteracted or removed.

He felt that he had a duty to perform as well to the offending pupil as to his innocent comrades; and when there seemed to be no reasonable hope of reclaiming the culprit, he did not hesitate to terminate his connection with the college. And it naturally resulted that, —

" As his moral power predominated over his intellectual, he was more successful both in investigating and in teaching moral than intellectual philosophy. The laws of conscience; the heinousness and the fatal results of sin; the unchangeableness of the divine laws; the immutableness of right; the power of habit; the right of every man to himself, and the consequent wrong of human slavery; the paramount duty of every man to develop his faculties to the utmost, and to live to the glory and honor of God, — these and kindred topics were discussed with such clearness and force, and illustrated so variously and so aptly, that we believe it to be literally true that no student, however thoughtless, ever pursued the study of moral philosophy under Dr. Wayland without receiving positive moral impressions which remained through life. You can hardly find one of his pupils who cannot repeat memorable utterances of the teacher, which have been to him maxims throughout his career. His original mind naturally coined striking and sententious expressions, which clung to the memory of his hearers. How many of the graduates of Brown University have we heard say, with grateful hearts, that they owe their success in life more to the intellectual and moral training they received from Dr. Wayland, than to any or all other causes! To his exalted standard of duty he held others with a strenuousness which sometimes seemed too severe. But he held himself as rigidly up to the same standard. Like all

strong men, he maintained his beliefs with such positiveness, that his opponents sometimes deemed him unjust to
them. He was by no means lacking, as some have supposed, in sensitiveness to the approbation of his fellow-
man. But he loved truth and duty better than human
praise. Having carefully determined what he thought to
be right, he would cling to that in the face of the whole
world. He pursued his course so eagerly that he sometimes jostled, rather rudely, those who crossed his path.
But it was only because he was so intent upon discharging
his duty. No man was more desirous of doing full justice
to the opinions of others. No one was more ready to acknowledge his error, and to change, when convinced that
he was in error." *

In a review of Stanley's Life and Correspondence of
Thomas Arnold, in the North American Review for October, 1844, Dr. Wayland eulogizes the characteristics of
that eminent educator in language which sets forth with
singular exactness his own ideal of a successful teacher
of youth : —

" When he went to Latham he adopted education as
his profession. This determination effected a great change
in his character. It brought upon him definite intellectual and moral responsibilities, which he strengthened
himself to the utmost to sustain. He took large and very
grave views of the field of duty upon which he had entered, and he resolved to occupy it without shrinking.
He devoted himself without stint to the intellectual cultivation of his pupils. He sought to improve in the highest degree every one committed to his charge. Hence he
was employed with great industry in enlarging his own
mental resources.

" But, above all, he deemed it his duty to prepare his
pupils for heaven. He felt that he must teach them by
example as well as precept, if he desired his instructions
to have any salutary effect. Hence all his moral powers
received fresh energy from the circumstances in which he

* President J. B. Angell, of the University of Vermont, in Hours
at Home for December, 1865.

was placed. He was always setting before his boys the highest motives of Christian conduct; and these motives had the more commanding efficacy from the fact that their instructor was himself striving to be the exemplar of all that he inculcated."

We are but too well aware that we have most imperfectly presented the characteristics of Dr. Wayland as an instructor, and that those who never enjoyed the benefit of his teachings, or have never been themselves engaged in the work of instruction, may still find it difficult to discover the secret of his influence over young men, or adequately to appreciate his labors in the cause of education. The daily trials and perplexities incident to such a calling; the difficulty of dealing wisely and justly with indolent or wayward pupils; the importance of deciding every case of discipline in such a manner that, while due allowance is made for the inexperience of youth, a dangerous precedent may be avoided; the frequent and often painful interviews with parents and guardians; the labor of preparation for the exercises of the recitation-room, keeping pace with the progress of science, and embracing the ever-widening area of human knowledge; the varied and often delicate questions, which must arise from time to time, involving the respective rights and duties of associate instructors; and, above all, the vast responsibility of preparing the young, not only for usefulness in this life, but for happiness in the life to come, — all these and many kindred duties and cares of the teacher who labors in the fear of God, can be estimated at their true value only by the honored few who have devoted themselves with faithful and conscientious zeal to the cause in which he spent the best years of his life.

And yet it cannot be doubted that the graduates of Brown University, during the administration of President Wayland, will most heartily respond to the sentiments with which he concluded his remarks at the centennial anniversary, to which allusion has already been made.

"Let me say, in a word, that I cannot express the pleasure I feel at seeing myself surrounded by such a number of my former pupils, in every one of whom I recognize a friend. I know, as I look upon your faces at this moment, that there is not one of you who does not believe, that, notwithstanding my many imperfections, my paramount motive was an honest intention to promote your highest and best good."

CHAPTER XIV.

THE " LIBRARY FUND." — MANNING HALL. — THE COMMON
SCHOOLS OF PROVIDENCE. — THE AMERICAN INSTITUTE
OF INSTRUCTION. — THE PROVIDENCE ATHENÆUM. —
THE SMITHSONIAN INSTITUTION.

WE have already referred to the earnest efforts
which Dr. Wayland made, from the earliest
years of his presidency, to improve the quality of the instruction imparted in the university, and to increase the
facilities for acquiring knowledge. As we have seen, he
found the institution poorly equipped for its work, with
a small, ill-selected library, rarely used by students, and
furnishing little assistance to the occasional visitor; with
chemical and philosophical apparatus ludicrously inadequate (even tested by the low standard of that day) to the
just requirements of a New England college.

He at once undertook to remedy these grave defects.
By correspondence, by personal solicitation, by communications to the press, and by every legitimate method, he
sought to interest the friends of the university and the
public generally, in a subject so vital to the true interests
of the college. At a meeting of the friends of Brown
University, held in the summer of 1832, for the purpose
of seconding the efforts then making to secure a permanent fund for the benefit of the library, and to provide
suitable apparatus, addresses were made by several gentlemen in behalf of the proposed object. The remarks
made by President Wayland, on this occasion, exhibited
so broad, generous, and far-sighted a view of the kind of

education adapted to the wants of this country, and stated so clearly the general principles which should lie at the foundation of all schemes for providing this education, that we make no apology for quoting the address in full.

" All efforts for intellectual improvement are comprehended under two classes: first, efforts for the advancement of science; and, secondly, for its universal diffusion. In the first instance, we enter the domain of knowledge, and discover the laws of the universe; and in the second, we put the knowledge thus attained within the reach of every grade of society. It is to the second of these objects that the labors of this country have been directed. We have established common schools in every portion of the older states, and by means of them the facilities for acquiring elementary education have been abundant.

" For the actual advancement of science, however, we have done almost nothing. We import our learning scantily from abroad. Even our universities have employed themselves in the diffusion, rather than in the advancement, of science; and even for this comparatively humble effort they are but ill prepared. Our universities and colleges are, at present, known principally by the number and magnitude of their edifices. If the student wishes to push his inquiries beyond the ordinary routine of instruction, where shall he go, in our country, for the means of information? If he enter our college halls and ask for books, he is shown long rows of lodging-rooms. If he inquire for instruments for philosophical research, he is pointed to large piles of brick and mortar. If the teacher desire to investigate truth for himself, and coöperate with the learned men of Europe, where, in this country, can he go to avail himself of the researches of past ages?

" The humiliating answer is found in the fact that in each of the learned professions the most valuable books with which we enrich our libraries could not have been written here, because the knowledge which they embody could not have been found in America.

" And besides, instructors cannot furnish themselves with libraries; their incomes do not admit of it; nor can such a library as the cause of science demands, be collected in a single lifetime. It must be the accumulated wisdom of past ages added to our own. Such a library can be procured only by public munificence, and by that munificence so directed as to collect from time to time the rich results of the intellectual labor of man.

"It is, however, cheering to observe that other institutions of learning are aware of the importance of the subject, and are employing all the means in their power for the substantial advancement of science. Harvard University is appropriating five thousand dollars per annum to the increase of her library, already the most valuable of any possessed by any university in the United States. Yale College is raising a fund of one hundred thousand dollars for these and similar purposes. Is it not time that we followed such noble examples, and, as citizens of the Republic of Letters, contributed our portion towards the intellectual advancement of our country?"

Allusion having been made by a subsequent speaker to the importance of making the college library accessible to all, Dr. Wayland further said, —

"That he had heard with great pleasure the allusion of Judge P. to the importance of having the library, under proper restrictions, perfectly accessible both to professional men and to all persons who wish to consult it upon scientific subjects. Science was in its very nature diffusive. A library should be a source of intellectual illumination, not to one class of men only, but to all men who were disposed to profit by it. The only laws regulating its use should be designed to prevent its abuse and extend its utility. Such had always been his sentiments, and such, so far as his power had permitted, had been his practice. He pledged himself to coöperate cheerfully with his friend Judge P. in such arrangements as would render the present effort the most efficient means possible for promoting the scientific and professional advancement of the city." *

The amount obtained in response to this application, and to the untiring efforts of President Wayland, Dr. Caswell, and other ardent friends of the college, was nearly twenty thousand dollars. This sum was put at in-

---

* Providence Daily Journal, June 16th, 1832.

terest until it had increased to twenty-five thousand dollars; constituting what has since been known as the "Library Fund." The interest of this fund (which we believe has never been increased) has been devoted to the purchase of books and to the improvement of the chemical and philosophical apparatus.

Dr. Wayland believed that it was the business of a college to furnish the best, and not the cheapest, education. While, therefore, he never hesitated to appeal most earnestly to the community in which he lived, and to all persons on whom the college might be supposed to have a claim, for funds to be expended in such a manner as to increase the facilities for acquiring knowledge, he never encouraged the foundation of scholarships, nor any of the numerous devices for bribing young men to accept a collegiate education.

In a letter to a friend, written during the second year of his presidency, he says, —

"You may have seen that I have been attacked in the newspapers. Some very untrue statements have been made in these attacks. To all this I answer, I acknowledge not the jurisdiction.* A few matters of fact have been so stated, that I may, perhaps, in due time, enter a denial; but of this I am not certain. We shall have as many students as I care for at present, and meanwhile the college is gaining ground abroad. If we get the students, and teach them well, we can afford a little abuse of this sort. I have caused notice to be published that provision has been made for defraying the tuition of thirty-five beneficiaries in this institution. It is a mode of operation gen-

---

* In illustration of his indifference to the attacks which from time to time were made upon Dr. Wayland by the press, we give an extract from a letter written to a friend, in allusion to an unfounded and even calumnious charge against him, which had some currency in the newspapers of that day: "I had repeatedly seen the article which you sent me, but I really did not think it worth an answer. I assumed that those who knew anything of me would not believe it, and that it would sooner die away by being let alone."

erally, or rather universally, resorted to nowadays. I am strongly opposed to the policy, but I yield to the present emergency, and I hope only for the present. A college education ought to be good enough to be worth having, and not such that you are glad to give it away." *

Fortunately for the welfare of the college, the zeal of Dr. Wayland quickened the liberality of one of its most generous friends. In 1834 the Hon. Nicholas Brown, of Providence, to whose enlightened benevolence and intelligent interest in education Brown University owes so much of its success, caused an appropriate and tasteful building to be erected at his own expense, designed to be used as a library and chapel. To this edifice the name of Manning Hall was given, in honor of the first president of the university.

The dedication discourse was delivered by President Wayland, February 4, 1835. Ever controlled by a profound conviction that all mental training which does not fully recognize our moral obligations, and does not inspire the soul with sentiments of devout gratitude to the Author and Source of knowledge, is fatally defective as a preparation for the duties of active life, and for the future destiny of an immortal being, — that the most costly appliances of education, and the most untiring industry expended in scientific research, must fall far short of producing their noblest results, unless sanctified by a humble reliance upon omniscient wisdom, — Dr. Wayland selected as the theme of his discourse, the " Dependence of Science upon Revealed Religion."

We quote the concluding paragraphs of the address.

---

* In the opinion of Dr. Wayland, if a man has such intellectual and moral qualities as promise to render his high culture a blessing to himself and to the community, it is a duty to see that he has the means of procuring education. What he objected to, if we rightly apprehend his meaning, was making poverty the sole qualification for aid, without regard to mental and moral endowments.

"If I have succeeded, even though imperfectly, in the illustration which I have attempted, I have shown that revealed religion, so far as the individual is concerned, is the warmest friend to the cultivation of science, the most strenuous advocate for the universal promulgation of truth; and that, in so far as society is concerned, it has given existence to that state of civilization in which alone science can exist; and that only by its aid can society be so carried forward as to allow of indefinite scientific progress.

"The result from all this, so far as it respects the present occasion, may be stated in very few words.

"If such be the fact, a large portion of the duty of every instructor of youth must be the inculcation of religious principles upon the minds of those committed to his charge. He would be wanting in the discharge of his obligations to science, not less than in the discharge of his obligations to God, if, while he stimulated, by increasing knowledge, the impulsive powers of man, he did not also strengthen the restraining principles by which alone that knowledge can be made a blessing, either to its possessor or to mankind. Specially imperative is this obligation at the present time, when in our own country, as well as in others, the social fabric is already tottering under the assaults of passion, I fear, too strong for the barriers that surround it.

"And, again, if all this be so, how appropriate is it that we daily commend to the protection and blessing of Almighty God the youth committed to our charge, the welfare of this university whose servants we are, and the interests of science throughout the earth! And especially is it seemly, that, while in devout gratitude we acknowledge every additional means of usefulness which we receive from his hand, we should, first of all, consecrate whatever he has given us to the glory of Him who is the sole and underived author of good to everything that exists. This is the purpose for which we are assembled. Let us, then, unite in prayer while we dedicate this edifice to the service and glory of Almighty God."

The educational labors of Dr. Wayland were by no means confined to Brown University, or to the cause of collegiate instruction. Every department of teaching awakened his deep and earnest interest. Nor was this interest. theoretical only, confined to general statements, but leading to no practical results. With him to feel was to act. Consequently the common school, the high school, and the academy, all found in him a sympathizing friend, a wise counsellor, and a most efficient helper. He had held his presidential office but about a year, when he was appointed chairman of a committee of citizens, " to whom was referred the consideration of the present school system of the town of Providence." This committee were " directed to recommend such alterations and improvements as they might deem necessary." In April, 1828, the committee made a report prepared by Dr. Wayland, which is printed in the American Journal of Education for July, 1828. In the remarks introducing the report to the readers of the Journal, the editor says, —

" We have already had occasion to mention it as one of the most valuable expositions hitherto made of a system of public schools adapted to the actual circumstances of society. The report has been drawn up after a careful inspection of the school system of Boston, both in respect to the gradation of the schools, and the methods of instruction adopted in them. It forms, accordingly, a useful document for reference, whether for information relating to plans of arrangement for public education, or for direct assistance in teaching. School committees and teachers will derive equal benefit from a perusal of it.

" We would recommend to the particular attention of our readers the just and practical observations on the true policy of communities in relation to common education, and, especially, the remarks on elementary and high schools. The comparative view of methods of instruction is also worthy of peculiar notice, as presenting the results of close observation and judicious reflection on topics about which there still exists a diversity of opinion among teachers. In the leading name of the committee (whose signatures are appended to the report), our readers will recognize that of an ardent and distinguished friend to popular improvement, whom they will, with increased pleasure, observe devoting himself, with his accustomed energy, to one of the most useful labors of an enlightened benevolence."

In this report the attention of the municipal authorities was earnestly directed to the principles which should control a system of public schools, the expenses of which were to be defrayed by a general taxation of the property of the community. The report also considered the character and quality of schools demanded by the nature of our republican form of government; the defects of previous and existing systems of public education, with reference to the gradation of schools; the measures proper to be adopted with a view to the removal of these defects; the mode of instruction suitable to such schools; the beneficial results to be anticipated from a system of rewards; the kind of text-books required for the wise instruction of the young; and the importance of maintaining a careful and constant supervision of the schools by a competent board of visitors.

The report was accepted, and its recommendations were favorably received and promptly put in practice. While we cheerfully accord to the gentlemen, who united with Dr. Wayland in this effort to improve the system of public schools in Providence, the praise to which they are most justly entitled, it may yet be said, without disparagement to any of them, that the controlling influence of the chairman of the committee in devising a plan for the permanent elevation of the system of schools to a higher standard, and in stimulating the public to adopt and sustain it, was gratefully acknowledged by the entire community.

In 1827 he laid before the General Assembly of Rhode Island a plan for organizing a system of free schools throughout the state. Other gentlemen gave most efficient aid in the same direction, and at the January session of 1828 the proposed design received the needed legislative sanction. Dr. Wayland's interest in this cause continued to the close of his life.

"In the diversified plans and agencies by which the

commissioner of public schools (Hon. Henry Barnard) labored, from 1843 to 1849, to interest parents, teachers, and school officers in the great work of organizing an efficient system of public instruction for Rhode Island, Dr. Wayland gave his active counsel and coöperation. He was as ready to assist in a meeting of the Rhode Island Institute of Instruction at Kingston, or at the dedication of a school-house at Chepachet, as to address the American Institute at Boston, or to take part in the celebration of the founding of a college or a theological seminary." *

The generous interest which Dr. Wayland felt in the cause of education was not confined to the limits of his adopted state. Education, in its best and highest sense, he regarded as cosmopolitan. He aimed at nothing less than the mental and moral elevation of the whole human race. By his life-long devotion to the cause of home and foreign missions, he gave abundant evidence of his love for the souls of his fellow-men; and by his untiring efforts to promote the diffusion of general education, he manifested his anxiety for their intellectual development.

He was one of the founders of the " American Institute of Instruction " — an organization which has been exceedingly useful in promoting education, not only in this country, but throughout the world. He delivered the opening address at the first public meeting of the " Institute " — a discourse " which produced a deeper impression on the friends of education than any which had ever been pronounced on the same subject in America." He was chosen the first president of the association, and for some years not only presided at its annual meetings, but took an active part in all its deliberations.

At the annual meeting of the Institute, held in Boston, August 22, 1833, Dr. Wayland resigned the presidency of the organization for which he had, from the commencement, manifested such a deep and abiding interest. That his efforts in the cause of national education did not fail to

---

* Barnard's American Journal of Education.

receive appropriate recognition from those with whom he had so efficiently labored, is evident from the recorded action of the Institute on the occasion of his resignation : —

"*Resolved*, That the 'American Institute of Instruction' entertains the highest respect for the character of their late president, Dr. Wayland, and the deepest gratitude to him for his early, continued, and efficient efforts to promote the objects of this association. And while they regret that they are to be deprived of his services as a presiding officer, they confidently rely upon his future coöperation in prosecuting the great objects of the society which he has contributed so essentially to place before them."

In further illustration of the desire of Dr. Wayland that the benefits of education should be universally enjoyed, and should be adapted to the growing wants of our country, we may refer to an address which he delivered on the 11th of July, 1838, at the opening of the "Providence Athenæum," the design of which was to furnish to the community the advantage of a large and well-selected library. In this address Dr. Wayland developed the object which the founders of this class of institutions should keep constantly in view, viz., "to provide the means for the universal diffusion of knowledge in its most extensive signification." Alluding to the design of the donors, he said, —

"They have determined that this library shall be a repository for the standard English works, in every *science* with which an intelligent community would desire to become acquainted. They believe that such an institution should contain the intellectual aliment by which the genius of a Davy, an Arkwright, a Franklin, a Rittenhouse, or a Bowditch, might be nourished. God has scattered the seeds of preëminent ability as profusely among the poor as among the rich. When such gifts perish through the want of cultivation, the loss is suffered by mankind. It becomes us, then, as philanthropists and as citizens, to provide for the whole community the means of cultivating, in the most perfect manner, all of the talent with which the Creator has enriched it.

" Having thus provided the means for attaining a knowledge of the *laws* of the universe, their next endeavor will be to collect the *facts* which its history has unfolded. It is their design here to provide the student with the means of investigating the *history* of man, as he is seen in every stage of his transition from barbarism to civilization, under all the diversified influences of climate and situation, of political and religious institutions, of poverty and wealth, of prosperity and decline. But *history* would be imperfectly understood without a knowledge of *biography*. Hence it is their intention to furnish the reader with a collection of the lives of those who, in any age, have distinguished themselves either by profoundness of knowledge, brilliancy of achievement, or splendor of discovery. They mean that we should here have the opportunity of holding communion with the warriors and statesmen, the philosophers and scholars, the poets and orators, the civilians and divines, who have made their names illustrious by the changes which they have wrought in the current of human thought, or feeling, or action. We may thus be enabled to trace the most stupendous effects to their elementary causes, and to behold what responsibility God has conferred upon genius, and to observe how signally it is in the power of individual man to bequeath happiness or misery to the entire race of which he forms a part.

" But the facts which respect man alone form but a small part of that knowledge which it becomes us to acquire. Our globe itself has been subjected to accurate observation, and the changes through which it has passed during the long period of its existence have been traced with scarcely less than philosophical accuracy. The *vegetable* productions which cover it have been examined and classified, their characters described, their uses ascertained, and their modes of cultivation carefully illustrated. The *animal* kingdom in all its varieties, whether inhabiting the air, the water, or the land, has, from the time of Aristotle, attracted the attention of the naturalist, until now, at last, by the labors of Cuvier, its whole extent has been brought within the view of the philosopher. Of the utility or of the attractiveness of these studies it is superfluous here to speak. I surely need not tell you how greatly the knowledge which they unfold conduces to the development of national resources, nor how admirably

calculated are the classifications to which they are subjected to discipline and invigorate the human understanding. Aware of this, it is the intention of the directors of
the Athenæum to enrich their collection, as far as may be
in their power, with works on natural science.

"But the laws of nature, and the facts which have
transpired, and the beings which *actually* exist, are far
from being all that is comprehended within the domain
of human knowledge. The wonder-working power of
the imagination has created forms of awful grandeur and
of surpassing loveliness. By the contemplation of these,
the love of the beautiful is cultivated, the taste is refined,
and the social sympathies are purified and ennobled.
Hence it is the intention of the directors of this institution to render it rich in everything, whether in prose
or verse, whether in didactic literature or the literature
of fiction, with which genius has ennobled our mother
tongue.

"Admittance to its privileges is designedly rendered so
easy, that, for all practical purposes, it may, in effect, be
declared free. It is, moreover, the design of the proprietors that it should be useful *to all*. While they look at
the treasures of human thought *in general*, they do not
forget that they are collecting books for men *in particular*. Hence they wisely adjust the general principles of
their selection to the case of the community in whose behalf they act. They intend that there shall be no occupation, whether professional or industrial, which shall not
here find the means both of instruction and relaxation.
They mean to open a fountain of living water, at which
the intellectual thirst of the whole community may be
slaked.

"We have arrived at a crisis in the progress of civilization such as, I believe, has rarely, if ever, been witnessed.
Those nations of modern times, which have felt the impulse of the Reformation, have directed all their efforts to
the simple object of widely disseminating the elements of
education. Their highest aim has been to see that 'the
schoolmaster be abroad,' and thus to enable every citizen
to read in his mother tongue. But in New England all
this has long since been accomplished. The schoolmaster
here has always been *at home*. There is scarcely a native-
born man, or woman, or child among us who is not able

to read, and write, and keep accounts. The book of the English language, with whatever it contains of life or death, and whatever of these it may hereafter contain, is spread open before the whole community.

"If we desire to reap the benefit of all our previous exertions, it must be done by carrying out the plan which the proprietors of the Athenæum have adopted. We must render knowledge — valuable knowledge — accessible to the whole community. We must collect the treasures of science and literature, and throw them open to all who are disposed to avail themselves of their benefits. We must provide the means by which the light of intellect shall shine into every house, and pour its reviving beams into the bosom of every family. And, still more, we must act for the future. In our present state, no great object can be accomplished, unless we act for posterity. We must, therefore, lay the foundations of this institution in such principles that it will grow with the growth of intelligence, widening and deepening the channels of its influence, as it passes on from age to age, more and more thoroughly imbuing every successive race with admiration of all that is great, with love for all that is beautiful, and with reverence for all that is holy."

In July, 1838, the avails of the Smithsonian bequest having been received by the United States, and Congress having pledged their faith for the performance of the trust involved in the acceptance of the legacy, letters were addressed by the Secretary of State to several gentlemen prominent in the cause of education, asking their views "as to the mode of applying the proceeds of the bequest which shall be likely at once to meet the wishes of the testator, and prove advantageous to mankind."

Dr. Wayland replied as follows, October 2, 1838: —

"Sir: In reply to your communication dated July last, requesting my views respecting the Smithsonian Institution I beg leave to state as follows: —

"1. It is, I suppose, to be taken for granted that this institution is not intended for the benefit of any particular *section* of the United States, but of the whole country;

and also that no expense which may be necessary in order
to accomplish its object will be spared.

" 2. I think it also evident that there is no lack in this
country of what may be properly termed *collegiate* education; that is, of that education which may be given
between the ages of fourteen or sixteen, and eighteen or
twenty. All the old states, and many of the new ones,
have as many institutions of this kind as their circumstances require. And, besides, since persons of the ages
specified are too young to be for a long period absent from
home, it is probably better that a large number of such
institutions should be established within convenient distances of each other. The age of the pupils in these institutions would also render it desirable that very large
numbers be not associated together.

" 3. It is probable that professional schools — that is,
schools for divinity, law, and medicine — will be established in every section of our country. Divinity must be
left to the different Christian sects. Law will probably
be taught in the state, or at least the district, in which
it is to be practised. The same will, I think, be true of
medicine.

" 4. If the above views be correct, it will, I think, follow, that the proper place to be occupied by such an institution would be the space between the close of a collegiate education and a professional school. Its object
would be to carry forward a classical and philosophical
education beyond the point at which a college now leaves
it, and to give instruction in the broad and philosophical
principles of a professional education.

" The demand for such instruction now exists very
extensively. A considerable portion of our best scholars
graduate as early as their nineteenth, twentieth, or twenty-
first year. If they are sufficiently wealthy, they prefer
to wait a year before studying their profession. Some
travel, some read, some remain as resident graduates, and
many more teach school for a year or two, for the purpose of reviewing their studies. These would gladly
resort to an institution in which their time might be
profitably employed. The rapidly increasing wealth of
our country will very greatly increase the number of such
students.

" The advantages which would result from such an institution are various. It would raise up and send abroad in the several professions a new grade of scholars, and thus greatly add to the intellectual power of the nation. But, especially, it would furnish teachers, professors, and officers of every grade, for all our other institutions. As the standard of education was thus raised in the colleges, students would enter the National University, better prepared. This would require greater effort on the part of its professors, and thus both would reciprocally stimulate each other.

"The branches which should be taught there, I suppose, should be the same as in our colleges (only far more generously taught, — that is, taught to men, and not to boys), and the philosophical principles of law and medicine. This would embrace lectures on Latin, Greek, Hebrew, and the Oriental languages; all the modern languages of any use to the scholar, with their literature; mathematics, carried as far as any one would desire to pursue them; astronomy; engineering, civil and military; the art of war, beginning where it is left at West Point; chemistry; geology; mining; rhetoric and poetry; political economy; intellectual philosophy; physiology, vegetable and animal; anatomy, human and comparative; history; the laws of nations; and the general principles of law, the constitution of the United States, &c.

"5. Supposing such an institution to be established, something may be added respecting the mode of its constitution and organization.

"I suppose, then, that an institution of this kind is a sort of copartnership between the instructors and the public. The public furnishes means of education, as building, libraries, apparatus, and a portion of the salary. The professors do the labor, and provide for the remaining part of their income by their own exertions. Hence there arises naturally a division of the powers and duties of the parties. To the corporation, or governors, or trustees, or by what name they may be called, would belong the management of the fiscal concerns of the institution, and the control of that portion of its affairs which depended specially upon its relation with the public donation. The government of the institution, the conferring of degrees, and the appointment of professors, would be performed jointly by the officers of instruction and the corporation.

In the English universities, the government of the institution is vested in a general meeting of the former graduates. This forms a literary public, which exercises ultimate jurisdiction in most matters requiring deliberation. How far such an institution might be constructed upon this principle, may be fairly a question.

" 6. If the above-mentioned views should be adopted, it will be perceived that no funds will be required for dormitories. The young men will provide for themselves board and lodgings wherever they please, and the professors will be responsible for nothing more than their education. It is to be supposed that they are old enough to govern themselves.

" Hence the funds may be devoted to the following purposes : —

" 1st. A part would be appropriated to the creation of a library, cabinets, and for the furnishing of all the apparatus necessary to the instructors.

" 2d. A part to the erection of buildings for the above purposes, together with buildings for professors' houses.

" 3d. A fund would be established for the endowment of professorships, giving to each so much as may form a portion (say one third, or one half) of his living, and the rest to be provided for by the sale of the tickets to his courses.

" 7. If the institution is governed by a board, this board should be appointed by the president and senate, or by the president alone ; and they should hold their offices for a period not longer than six years, one third of them retiring, unless reappointed, every two years.

" 8. Graduates of the university should be allowed to teach classes and receive payment for tickets, upon any of the subjects on which instruction is given in the regular course. This will prove a strong stimulant to the regular professors, and will train men up for teachers.

" Degrees should never be conferred as a matter of course, but after a strict and public examination. They should never be conferred either in course, or *causa honoris*, unless by the recommendation of the Faculty.

" I have thus very briefly, but as far as my avocations would allow, thrown together a few hints upon the subject to which you have directed my attention. That I should go into detail, I presume, was not expected.

Whatever may be the plan adopted, I presume it will
not be carried into effect, until an extensive observation of
the best universities in Europe has furnished the government with all the knowledge which the present condition
of science and education can afford.

I have the honor to be, Sir,

Respectfully, your obedient servant,

F. WAYLAND.

" Hon. J. FORSYTH, *Secretary of State.*"

CHAPTER XV.

PUBLIC LABORS. — TRACT AND SCHOOL SOCIETY, RHODE ISLAND. — CHILDREN'S FRIEND SOCIETY. — RHODE IS- LAND BIBLE SOCIETY. — AMERICAN BIBLE SOCIETY. — PROVIDENCE DISPENSARY. — FIRST BAPTIST CHURCH. — REV. DR. PATTISON. — MISSIONARY CONCERTS. — LADIES' BIBLE CLASS. — MURRAY STREET DISCOURSE. — ADDRESS BEFORE THE SUNDAY SCHOOL UNION. — DUDLEIAN LECTURE. — THE PHILOSOPHY OF ANAL- OGY. — DISCOURSE ON TEMPERANCE. — ORDINATION SERMONS. — DESIGNATION OF MISSIONARIES. — PHI BETA KAPPA ADDRESS AT HARVARD UNIVERSITY. — MORAL LAW OF ACCUMULATION. — AGRICULTURAL ADDRESS.

WHILE Dr. Wayland was thus indefatigable in his efforts to advance the general interests of educa- tion, he neglected none of the duties of a good citizen. From the commencement of his residence in Providence, he identified himself with every enterprise which sought to promote the prosperity and sound morals of the com- munity. Especially did he aim, from the outset, to incul- cate, by precept and example, a spirit of enlightened be- nevolence. It was remarked of him, even then, that in proportion to his means, he was the most liberal man in town. Up to the time of his arrival in Providence, the amounts contributed to public charities had been small. They were mainly in the form of annual payments, of from one to three dollars. It is stated that one gentleman of ample means, who was prominent in religious affairs, considered it a matter of self-gratulation that, once a year, he was in the habit of giving half a dollar to the cause of foreign missions. When, on one occasion, a wealthy citizen of Providence made a donation of twenty dollars to a deserving charity, it was proposed at the next annual meeting of the society, whose funds had been thus unexpectedly increased, to present a vote of thanks to the donor, in grateful recognition of such unusual benevolence.

Dr. Wayland was soon convinced that the painful contrast between the sums contributed and the pecuniary resources of the contributors was due, not to the indifference or stinginess of the people of Providence, but to the fact that their minds had never been suitably awakened to the paramount duty and blessed results of systematic charity. He availed himself of every opportunity, in public and private, to disseminate throughout the community correct views upon this subject. His voice, and purse, and pen were ever at the service of any meritorious public enterprise. By judicious and well-timed personal appeals, by liberal donations from his scanty income, and by public addresses, he succeeded in stimulating into increased activity the charitable and benevolent institutions of Providence.

In 1828 he preached a sermon in behalf of the Tract and School Society — an organization designed to establish schools for the poor in all parts of the state. The collection taken up at the close of this discourse amounted to two hundred dollars, which is believed to have been the largest contribution ever made, up to that time, in the town of Providence for a similar object.

Of the part which he took in the formation of the Children's Friend Society, which for more than thirty years has provided a home for destitute children, a Providence lady, ever forward in all good works, has kindly given the following account : —

" It was at the close of one of our Bible-class meetings,

that Dr. Wayland requested Miss —— and myself to wait
until the class had retired, for the purpose of hearing
from Miss Harriet Ware a statement of her efforts to aid
the children of the vicious poor of the town, and of her
plans and wishes for their future benefit. Dr. Wayland
was exceedingly interested in her narrative, and in the
quaint way in which she described her labors and the
obstacles which she encountered. Having heard her touching story, he requested Miss —— and myself to make an
effort to collect money enough to enable Miss Ware to
carry on her praiseworthy enterprise. He drew up the
heading to a subscription paper, was himself the first to
contribute, and the result was, that we raised the three
hundred dollars with which that excellent charity, now
established on so firm a foundation, commenced its beneficent career."

For several years, and until the permanent success of
this organization was fully assured, Dr. Wayland attended
its meetings, shared in its counsels, and actively aided in
all measures adopted to increase its resources and add to
its efficiency.

On the death of Miss Harriet Ware he was selected as
her biographer, and in a short and deeply interesting memoir, paid a merited tribute to the Christian virtues and
rare ability of this remarkable woman.

In 1828 he became a member of the board of trustees of
the Rhode Island Bible Society. This position he retained
until 1843, discharging all its duties with fidelity and zeal.
In fact, any scheme designed to secure the distribution
of the Scriptures could not but enlist his warmest sympathy.

The Rhode Island Bible Society is auxiliary to the
American Bible Society. With this venerable and catholic organization Dr. Wayland coöperated throughout his
life. He was of opinion that all Protestant Christians
may, without any sacrifice of their distinctive principles,
unite in circulating the English version of the Scriptures,
as well as those versions which are commonly received

among Christians in Protestant Europe. Where it is found needful to make new translations into the languages of heathen nations, and when the different sects could not agree upon a common rendering, he was of opinion that the existing missionary organizations afforded all needed facilities for the work to be accomplished. Their missionary laborers were the persons best fitted for executing the translations, and the circulation of the Scriptures, thus rendered into the vernacular, was a part of the legitimate missionary work of the several societies. This course seemed to him in accordance with a wise economy, and well calculated to promote in the largest attainable degree "the unity of the Spirit and the bond of peace" among all the followers of the Redeemer.

Perhaps no local charity interested him more deeply than the Providence Dispensary, formed in 1829, for the purpose of furnishing medicine and medical attendance gratuitously to the poor of Providence. While the benevolent aims of such an organization appeal most strongly to the heart of every friend of suffering humanity, with what peculiar power must they come home to the faithful disciple of that Savior whose richest rewards are promised those to whom He can say, "I was sick and ye visited me"! Dr. Wayland was from the first a contributor to the funds of the society, was for many years a member of its board of managers, and presided, July 5, 1865, at the last quarterly meeting held before his death.*

An extract from the resolutions passed at a meeting of the Dispensary will be read with interest: —

"*Resolved*, That, in common with our fellow-citizens, we shall hold in grateful remembrance and respect the

---

* The following statistics, from the annual report for 1865, furnish gratifying evidence of the amount of good accomplished by the Dispensary. During this year the number of patients relieved was 1248; number of house visits made, 2881; number of office consultations, 1596.

name of one who has so long been prominent in promoting the interests of benevolence, learning, and religion in this community, not only by his varied official labors, but by the pervading influence of his personal character."

Dr. Wayland's labors for the good of the community in which he lived, suffered no abatement with his advancing years. To quote from the funeral address of Dr. Caswell, —

"In every assembly of citizens, whether for deliberation upon grave public affairs, or for the founding and endowment of hospitals, or providing shelter for orphans, or homes for the aged and infirm, his presence was felt as no other man's was. All waited to hear the utterances of his voice. In every enterprise amóng us for the moral and religious improvement of the community, in every charity for the relief of the poor, in every effort to succor the fallen and reclaim the wanderer, his counsel was sought as an almost indispensable condition of success. It may justly be said that he stood among us as the first citizen of Rhode Island."

But Dr. Wayland never forgot that, while he was called upon to discharge to the utmost of his ability his obligations as a citizen, he had a higher and more imperative duty to perform as a follower of Christ. Although he believed that he had obeyed the manifest indications of divine Providence in abandoning the pastoral office for the position of an instructor, he did not cease to feel a deep and ever-increasing interest in the work of the ministry. He never declined an invitation to preach, or to perform any kind of religious labor, unless prevented by his college duties or some indispensable engagement.

On the 3d of April, 1828, he became a member of the First Baptist Church in Providence. Dr. Stephen Gano, long the respected and beloved pastor of this church, died in August, 1828. Nearly two years elapsed before his successor was installed. During this period Dr. Wayland devoted to the spiritual interests of the church all the time which he could spare from his regular duties. He frequently preached on the Sabbath, took a prominent part in evening meetings, visited the sick, attended funerals, and conducted the communion services. After the lapse of nearly forty years, his addresses and his prayers, particularly at the sacramental table, are distinctly in the remembrance of many who were his hearers.

His active coöperation in advancing the interests of the church did not cease when the pulpit was no longer vacant. In 1830 Dr. Gano was succeeded by Rev. R. E. Pattison, whose eminent personal qualities and varied excellences as a minister of the gospel Dr. Wayland ever held in high esteem. In the discourse from which we have already quoted, Dr. Pattison says, in allusion to this period, and to a second settlement over the same congregation, —

" Though less than five years my senior in age, yet *as a graduate*, having graduated so young, he was thirteen years my senior. During nearly eight years that I was his pastor, I never ceased to feel that he was the teacher and I the pupil. As a preacher of the gospel, and as the pastor of my flock, of which he was a member, I felt that I must acknowledge but one Master. Yet in our almost daily intercourse I ceased not to draw from his well. It was rarely book knowledge. Sometimes the topic was my own sermon, to which he was to listen on the next Sabbath, or which he had heard on the preceding ; but more frequently it was some one of those subjects of investigation about to be incorporated into his imperishable works. . . . With such relations to Dr. Wayland, I can fully appreciate his reverence for Dr. Nott." *

During the pastorate of Dr. Pattison, an extensive and

* We trust it may not be improper to add that the sentiments, expressed in the above extract, towards Dr. Wayland, his sons have never ceased to cherish for Dr. Pattison ; and one of them, as the pastor of Dr. Pattison, has felt that the debt of counsel and kindness, which was due to the subject of this memoir, has been abundantly repaid to the second generation.

powerful revival of religion occured. We think that
we speak the sentiments of those members of the church
who remember those days of the right hand of the Most
High, when we say that the counsels and labors of Dr.
Wayland at this time were of incalculable value.

We cannot forbear quoting, in this connection, a further
passage from Dr. Pattison's discourse, strikingly illustrative of the character of Dr. Wayland : —

" The ease with which a personal difficulty could be
settled with him, arose not merely from his quick perception of the reason of the thing, and freedom from prejudice, but chiefly from his habitual religious feelings. . . .
In the early part of my ministry, my congregation being,
as I thought, peculiarly insensible to the claims of religion,
I resolved on producing a sensation ; that I would preach,
for several weeks in succession, exclusively on the claims
of the divine law, and the certainty and solemnity of its
retributions. This series was to be followed by another,
exclusively on the way of life. Before the completion
of the first division, I perceived a sensation ; but whether
favorable or unfavorable I was not assured. With much
hesitation, however, I persevered. The doctor, ignorant,
with the rest of my congregation, of my motive, on our
way to our homes at the close of a Sabbath morning
service, betrayed dissatisfaction with my continued selection of such subjects. I commenced a reply with the
expression that it was an experiment. He interrupted
me, saying, with a severity of which he was capable, ' I
do not wish to be experimented on.' Exactly what reply
I made, I cannot say ; but it was one prompted by self-
distrust, and by feelings wounded by his severity. He
added nothing further. But in a few minutes after reaching my home, a messenger handed me the following
note : —

" Dear Pastor : * I regret sincerely my manner and
spirit in our recent conversation. I hope, as a sinner, to

* It was illustrative of the relations subsisting between them,
that up to the close of his life, Dr. Wayland never ceased to address Dr. Pattison by the designation " pastor."

be cleansed in the blood of Christ. Forgive me. Love
me, pastor, though I am unlovely. I hope Christ does.

Your affectionate brother,

F. W."

During the vacancy which followed the resignation of
Dr. Pattison, and at various periods of peculiar need in
the history of the church, the post of responsibility and
labor was either tacitly or by formal vote assigned to Dr.
Wayland. It was he who supplied the place of a pastor
when the office was vacant, and it was on his counsels
that reliance was mainly placed when the pastoral office
was to be filled. In the language of an honored member
and office-bearer in the body, " the doctor took the church
on his shoulders, and carried it right over every difficult
place."

In none of the exercises of the church was his presence
more sensibly felt than in the missionary concert, held on
the first Sabbath evening of each month. The concert in
the college chapel was held at an early hour in the evening, and was a scene of deep interest. It cannot be
doubted that, of the graduates of Brown University who
have labored for the salvation of the heathen, very many
found their zeal quickened, or, perhaps, first awakened,
by the influence of this service. It was a delightful and
characteristic feature of these meetings that members of
all denominations took part; that intelligence was communicated from the Missionary Herald and from the
Spirit of Missions, as well as from the Magazine; and that
the collections (with the entire approbation, and, perhaps,
at the suggestion, of the president) were sometimes bestowed upon agencies outside the denomination to which
most of the contributors belonged.

From the college concert the president went to the
vestry of the church. The tidings found in the leading
missionary journals were communicated by intelligent
laymen, who regularly held themselves responsible for

the discharge of this duty. After the missionary intelligence had been spread before the audience, Dr. Wayland's voice was usually heard. Perhaps he would communicate some striking fact or anecdote which he had learned from the brethren at the missionary rooms, or at the mission house in Pemberton Square. Perhaps he would carry out the reflections suggested by some feature of the intelligence found in the magazines. Perhaps he would trace the course of God's providence through the centuries in vindicating righteousness and punishing oppression. At one time, when the continent of Europe was the scene of tumult and bloodshed, he reviewed the course of these nations, in a former day, in rejecting the light and persecuting the saints. " And now," he said, " God is giving them blood to drink in great measure." His language and manner were exceedingly simple; but all who remember these meetings will probably coincide in the remark, which was not unfrequently made, that " nowhere else was Dr. Wayland so truly eloquent as in the missionary concert." And even more impressive were his prayers, as he spread before Jehovah the condition of the world, and pleaded all the divine promises and perfections; as he invoked the interposition of God in behalf of his oppressed people, in behalf of his servants and ministers who were exposed to persecution and violence from wicked men and rulers: " Rebuke kings for their sakes. Say to them, Touch not mine anointed, and do my prophets no harm."

These meetings (which many persons now recall as having been the most interesting and delightful that they ever attended) exerted an incalculable influence in arousing a spirit of liberality and of enlightened missionary zeal. It will be remembered that in 1823 (or 1824) it was estimated that, under favorable circumstances, not less than fifty dollars might be expected from the churches in Providence. At the close of these monthly concerts it was not uncommon for the collection, in a single evening, to reach twice that amount; and (if we are not in error) the church at one time held the first place among the Baptist churches in America in the amount of its missionary contributions.

The religious labors of Dr. Wayland were very far from being sectarian in their character. He earnestly sought to promote the spiritual welfare of all whom he could bring within the sphere of Christian influence. In 1833 he commenced a ladies' Bible class, inviting the attendance of members of every denomination. The following, from his journal of that time, exhibits the feelings with which he entered on this undertaking: —

"*April* 7, 1833, Sabbath. I have, during the past week, made arrangements for commencing a Bible class in town. So far as I know, I have intended to obey the intimations of the Spirit of God. I have always observed that I deeply regret having neglected such intimations, and thinking that this might be one, I dared not let it pass unimproved. I do not know that I desire anything else than to promote the cause of Christ and the interests of holiness. To the Spirit of all wisdom and holiness do I commend this effort. May it be the means of promoting the knowledge and the love of God; may it be blessed to every one who attends. Wilt thou direct, O God, the best and proper way in which to conduct it! Wilt thou call in the most suitable persons! Wilt thou enable me to direct it in such manner as may please thee! On thee I rely. In thy strength would I carry it on. Grant me health, strength, piety, illumination, and enable me to drink deeply into the spirit of religion, that I may thus teach others. Hear me, O God, for Christ's sake! Amen."

Of this Bible class (which met every Saturday afternoon, and was continued for several years) Mrs. Professor Chace has furnished the following reminiscences: —

"The circumstances which led to the formation of Dr. Wayland's Bible class for ladies were these: Mrs. Wayland was one day calling at our house, and, with the earnest interest which she always took in the religious welfare

of the young, invited my sister and myself to attend, with
the ladies of her own family, the young men's Bible class
in college. How well I remember the gloomy hall, the
low, ill-lighted chapel, with Dr. Wayland's noble figure
looming up grandly against the dark background! What
a new thing to me was that wonderful power with which
he took the confused, half-uttered thoughts of the students,
and by short, clear explanation, or by some illustration,
sometimes quaint, always striking, poured a flood of light
upon the hidden truth which they were groping after,
bringing it out with such distinctness that every one beheld
it with the delight of a new discovery! This was my first
knowledge of Dr. Wayland as an instructor, and it was
the commencement of my own education, in the true sense
of the word.

"When it was known that the attendance of ladies was
permitted, the number became so large as to embarrass
the young men, and prevent that freedom of discussion
which is the life of any Bible class. The ladies were
then banished from college, and gathered into a class of
their own. Its first meeting was on the 13th of April,
1833. I was at that time in a sick-room, but am told that
the number present was about thirty. I judge that later
there could not have been less than sixty members, with
an average attendance of about forty. They were from
all the different churches in the city, of all ages, and of all
degrees of intelligence and culture, from the old dame,
who, in her fear of mere human teaching, asked, 'If the
Lord wanted a man larned, wouldn't he give him larn-
ing?' — to the most carefully reared and instructed.

"Dr. Wayland was equally attentive to all. He was
never wearied by questions, whether wisely or unwisely
put, but always patient in his explanations and in his replies to the good but ignorant woman, whose opinions, very
complacently held and very freely expressed, were sometimes too much for the gravity of the listeners. He
' checked with a glance the circle's smile,' and gave us a
valuable lesson in Christian courtesy.

"The first book was the Gospel of Matthew. I was
only occasionally present during the examination of this
portion of the New Testament, and my recollections are
chiefly confined to the study of the Epistles of Romans and
Hebrews. His habit was to give us a carefully-prepared

analysis of the epistle. I have that of Romans now, and am using it in the instruction of my own scholars.

" The exercises of the class were always commenced with prayer; and few who were present will ever forget those prayers. There were times when the veil which conceals the spiritual world seemed, for him, to be lifted, and his soul to stand in the open vision of the infinite glory. By the strength of his faith he bore us with him; and when it was over, it was like coming back to earth after a glimpse of heaven. The prayer ended, he required of some one — choosing quite at random — the analysis of the chapter as given in the previous lesson, afterwards taking it up verse by verse. He never lectured, but conducted the recitation by question and answer, striving to lead the student to think for herself, rather than blindly to follow his explanations. He always encouraged the expression of opinions even when they were not in harmony with his own, and discussed them with fairness and a thoughtful regard for the feelings of others. He held us, however, closely to the subject, checking us decidedly, although not ungently, when we wandered too far. Among the most interested members of the class were a large number of young ladies who had just left school. I think they will all remember and acknowledge the great intellectual benefit which they derived from these instructions. He never allowed us to imagine that we understood a passage of which we could give no intelligible exposition. He taught us that half-knowledge is no knowledge. He inspired in us an enthusiastic love of truth, and a feeling of responsibility as to its attainment. He made us conscious that there may be an inner life richer and fuller than the outer one. He once said to me in later years, 'You know that to elevate the standard of character among women has been a constant aim with me all my life.'

" The striking features of his teaching in the Bible class — as everywhere — were its clearness, its simplicity, its directness, and its wealth of illustration. He never lost sight of the important distinction between what may be known, and what in its very nature is beyond human comprehension, and he always repressed speculation as to the latter. Young souls, earnest and thoughtful, but bewildered by the great mysteries of life, and losing themselves in a maze of doubts, he never sought to extricate by argument, but led them by the holier and gentler affections to the sure faith and quiet peace which the gospel only can give.

" Dr. Wayland's personal influence, which was not confined to the class-room, was controlling, helping to mould many a character at the age when it takes shape for life. The tone of society, among its younger members, was materially affected by the graver views of life which he inculcated; and it is a striking proof of his power, that while many young ladies, who received their religious training in his Bible class, were reigning belles, dancing, of which he disapproved, was rigorously excluded from their parties.

" It may be that I have reached that period in life in which one begins to glorify the past. But it seems to me that society in our city was never more charming than in those days when the highest subjects of human thought, and that eternity, which, near or far, awaits us all, were frequent themes of converse in ordinary social gatherings.

" The closing meeting of the Bible class was held October 29, 1836. Dr. Wayland found his engagements so numerous that he could no longer spare the time necessary for it. Nearly twenty years afterwards, in 1855, it was resumed, and continued three years."

Another member of this Bible class says, —

" When we assembled for the first time, Dr. Wayland told us, among other things, that he must insist upon punctuality of attendance. If we had not this habit now, we could not form it too soon. He added, that punctuality did not consist in arriving at the class-room several minutes before the hour, but only so early as to enable us to be in our seats precisely at the time appointed. Here, as everywhere, we should bear in mind the value of time, and avoid consuming needlessly the time of others as well as of ourselves. He had no occasion afterwards to allude to this subject. I have never known punctuality to be so uniformly observed as in Dr. Wayland's Bible class."

That the ladies who enjoyed the benefits of his teachings did not fail to appreciate his labors in their behalf is evident from the following note, dated " November 25,

346 LIFE OF FRANCIS WAYLAND.

1834," and found, after his death, preserved among his most valued papers : —

" The ladies of the Bible class return a vote of thanks to Dr. Wayland for the unceasing exertions which he has made for their spiritual improvement.

" A note can but inadequately express the heartfelt gratitude with which many have received from his lips the truths of the gospel ; and the amount of good done can be known only to the Searcher of all hearts, who will abundantly reward his labors.

" To that Master, whom they believe he has thus faithfully served, they would commend him and all who are dear to him, beseeching him to add his prayers to their own, that, of those who have attended the Bible class, not one may be missing in that day when the Savior shall ' make up his jewels.'

" By request of the ladies of Dr. Wayland's Bible class."

During the years 1834 and 1835, Dr. Wayland conducted a somewhat similar exercise every Tuesday evening, at his house, to which ladies of all denominations and of every age were cordially welcomed. On these occasions, the attention of those present — numbering usually from thirty to forty — was not directed to any particular portion of the Scriptures, but free conversation was encouraged respecting all topics of religious inquiry. In order that no one should be prevented by diffidence or reserve from seeking information, Dr. Wayland suggested that any one who chose should put on the table unsigned papers, containing questions to which replies were desired, statements of doubts to be solved, or subjects to be discussed. Not unfrequently the consideration of these papers consumed the entire evening. The teacher and the taught derived mutual benefit from this exercise, and parted with minds greatly quickened by the unrestricted interchange of religious sentiments. It should be added that these meetings were always opened and closed with prayer.

But while thus actively engaged in the work of instruction, and exercising a careful and constant supervision over the internal management and the external interests of Brown University, framing new laws for its government, and collecting funds to promote in every right direction its increased efficiency, and while, as we have seen, ever mindful of his duties as a public-spirited citizen, and more solicitous for the souls of his fellow-men than for the success of any merely temporal enterprise, however deserving of encouragement, he yet found leisure for much additional labor.

In the spring of 1830, a series of sermons was preached in the Murray Street Church, of New York city, by eminent clergymen representing several denominations. These sermons were subsequently published in a volume, entitled Murray Street Discourses, and in this form received a wide circulation. Dr. Wayland was one of the clergymen selected to perform this service, and his discourse on "The Certain Triumphs of the Redeemer" takes rank among his happiest public efforts. It is an earnest, able, and manly defence of the truths of revealed religion, enforcing the authority and inspiration of the Holy Scriptures, and predicting, in language of surpassing power, the glorious results which will follow the final and blessed reign of the Redeemer on earth.

On the 25th of May, 1830, he addressed the American Sunday School Union, in Philadelphia. Assuming that, on such an occasion and before such an audience, "the importance of inculcating upon the young the principles of the gospel of Jesus Christ may be taken for granted," he invites their attention "to an illustration of some of the encouragements which the present state of society offers to an effort for the universal diffusion of Christianity." After a brief allusion to the nature of the Reformation in the time of Luther, he considers "the physical and intellectual changes, very similar to those which characterized the Reformation, which are at this moment going forward in this country." He discovers in the increased value of labor, in the progress of science as applied to the useful arts, in the rapid improvement of the means for cultivating the human mind, and in the peculiar facilities for intellectual development furnished by the character of our political institutions, all the encouragement needed by the enlightened Christian to induce him hopefully to persevere in the work of religious reform.

We quote a single paragraph from the conclusion of this discourse, to illustrate his earnest interest in the cause of Sabbath Schools: —

"Time will barely suffer me to allude, in the briefest manner, to that species of religious effort which has given occasion to this address. You cannot, however, have failed to observe, that, if ever the gospel is universally to prevail, it is by some such means as this, under God, that its triumph will be achieved. By furnishing employment for talent of every description, the Sabbath school multiplies, almost indefinitely, the amount of benevolent effort, and awakens throughout every class of society the dormant spirit of Christian philanthropy. It renders every teacher a student of the Bible, and thus, in the most interesting manner, brings divine truth into immediate contact with the understanding and the conscience. All this it does to the teacher. But, besides all this, the Sabbath school is imbuing what will, twenty years hence, be the active population of this country, with the principles of the gospel of Jesus Christ. It is teaching that class of the community into whose hands so soon the destinies of this country will fall, the principles of inviolable justice and eternal truth. But more than all, it is implanting in the bosoms of millions of immortal souls 'that knowledge which is able to make them wise unto salvation, through the faith which is in Christ Jesus.' How transcendently glorious are the privileges before us! Who will not embark in this holy enterprise?"

He delivered a discourse on "The Moral Efficacy of the Doctrine of the Atonement," February 3, 1831, at the installation of Rev. William Hague, as pastor of the First Baptist Church in Boston. There is something peculiarly touching in the solemn, earnest, and affectionate tone of this sermon, addressed to his former flock.

In May, 1831, he gave the Dudleian Lecture at Harvard University, upon Natural Religion, taking as his text Romans ii. 14: "When the Gentiles, which have not the law," &c.

On the afternoon of Commencement day, September 7, 1831, occurred the first anniversary of the Rhode Island Chapter of the Phi Beta Kappa Society. President Wayland deliverd the oration, selecting as his theme "The Philosophy of Analogy." This discourse " is remarkable for a rare felicity of conception and treatment, for the fine vein of original thought which runs through it, for the grace and beauty of its illustrations, and for the classic finish of its style. It is pervaded throughout by a highly philosophic spirit, and contains passages of the loftiest eloquence." *

On the 20th of October, 1831, he addressed the Providence Temperance Society. The discourse was characterized by his usual force of reasoning, pungency of personal appeal, earnestness of expostulation, sympathy with suffering humanity, and elevation of moral sentiment. It produced a profound impression upon his audience, and, when published, gave a fresh and powerful impulse to the cause of temperance in Rhode Island, and throughout the whole country.† Its most striking passages were extensively quoted. The spirit and tone of the discourse

---

* Commemorative Discourse of Professor Chace.

† The fact that a recent riot in the suburbs of Providence, fomented by a few drunken sailors, had resulted in the destruction of several buildings, and the loss of several lives, was made the subject of indignant comment, and served to illustrate the evils of intemperance in a manner calculated to arrest the attention and awaken the apprehensions of the community in which the incident occurred.

were universally commended, and the soundness of his conclusions was everywhere conceded by all right-minded men.

The people of Providence were peculiarly gratified to find Dr. Wayland manifesting so lively an interest in their welfare, and a new and strong bond of sympathy was created between him and his fellow-citizens.

September 27, 1832, he preached a discourse at Portland, at the ordination of Rev. John S. Maginnis, on "The Objections to the Doctrine of Christ crucified, considered." December 17, 1832, he performed a similar service at the ordination of Rev. W. R. Williams. The services took place in the Oliver Street Church, New York. We quote a single paragraph : —

" This occasion is, in a degree unusual even to such services, interesting to myself. On this spot I first heard proclaimed the gospel of Jesus Christ. My parents are among the earliest members of this church. The first minister whom I remember was the immediate predecessor of the present pastor of this parent church, and the father of the candidate for the ministry in that which has just been constituted. Many years have elapsed since I waited upon the instructions of that venerable man. Since then I have seen many meek, many holy, many humble, many able, many peace-making ministers of the New Testament ; but I have yet seen no one that has reminded me of JOHN WILLIAMS."

Among his other occasional public discourses at this period were a sermon on " The Abuse of the Imagination," and an address before the Howard Benevolent Society of Boston on " The Motives to Beneficence."

On the evening of Sunday, June 29, 1834, a large body of missionaries (Mr. and Mrs. Comstock, Mr. and Mrs. Dean, Mr. and Mrs. Vinton, Mr. and Mrs. Howard, and Miss Gardner) being about to embark for Burmah (in company with Mr. and Mrs. Wade, who were returning to their field of labor) were publicly designated to the

work before them by appropriate services held in the
Baldwin Place Church, in Boston, On this occasion Dr.
Wayland gave an address, upon "The Moral Conditions of
Success in the Propagation of the Gospel." The Magazine
remarks, —

" While listening to his lofty, bold, beautiful, and, we
may add emphatically, *scriptural* delineation of the
objects, qualifications, and duties of a Christian missionary, — a delineation that made every other object and
character than that of the Christian dwindle into utter
insignificance in the comparison, — we felt as did Peter
on the mount of glorious vision : ' It is good to be
here.' And the thought more than once occurred to
us, How would the venerable BALDWIN have enjoyed
the scene?"

The following extract from Dr. Wayland's address to
the departing missionaries derives a peculiar and touching
interest from the circumstances of the speaker, whose
home had recently been desolated by bereavement : — *

" You will pardon me if I say nothing to you respecting
the pains of that separation which is immediately before
you. Sympathy, under such circumstances, can do little
else than aggravate our natural sorrow. And, yet more,
we have all learned enough of the mutability of the things
which are temporal, to be convinced that, in a world
where death reigns, there exists no tie which could permanently bind you and your friends together, even if you
remained at home. It seems, at first view, as though
loneliness were connected solely with your residence in
Burmah. But God could in a single hour render the
dwelling-place of your fathers as solitary to each one of
you as Ava or Tavoy. If Christ be with you, you will
have, in every event, an unchanging source of consolation ;
if he be absent, the thronged city may, at any moment, be
made, by a single act of his providence, a solitary wilderness."

On Thursday, September 1, 1836, Dr. Wayland delivered
the Phi Beta Kappa address, at Harvard University, select-

* Mrs. Wayland died April 3, 1834.

ing as his theme, " The Practical Uses of the Principle of Faith." He considered it, first, in its relation to our intercourse with created beings ; and, second, in reference to those circumstances which arise from our relations to the Deity ; and, lastly, the practical influence of the principle of faith in our relations to the life to come. The discourse was able and impressive ; if somewhat more grave in its subject and its tone than is usual upon the occasion of a literary anniversary, the force of thought and of language was well fitted to secure the attention of an intelligent audience.

The year 1837 is memorable in the annals of our country as a time of almost unparalleled financial embarrassment. A spirit of reckless speculation had been followed by universal bankruptcy. On the 14th of May of that year, Dr. Wayland delivered, in the First Baptist Church in Providence, two discourses on " The Moral Law of Accumulation." In the first discourse he enumerated and illustrated the moral causes which had produced this wide-spread disaster, and in the second suggested some of the lessons to be learned from the history of this crisis. He explained and enforced the scriptural doctrine as to the accumulation and expenditure of wealth, dwelling upon the manifold evils of making haste to be rich, the habit of unscrupulous dealing which it encourages, the wasteful and often licentious extravagance to which it tends, and, above all, the neglect of religious duties, which is its almost inevitable result.

Discourses so well adapted to the times could not fail to attract public attention. Their " lessons of wisdom and piety " were gratefully recognized in the request which was at once made that they might be published. The sermons passed through several editions, and were widely circulated.

Dr. Wayland not only labored to disseminate just views on education, and to elevate his fellow-men to a higher plane of intellectual culture, but, as an ardent lover of his country, he desired to see her physical resources developed to the utmost. He had, moreover, a natural taste for agriculture and horticulture, and derived peculiar pleasure from his own success in these pursuits. He discharged, therefore, a congenial duty, when, on the 6th of October, 1841, he delivered the annual address before the Rhode Island Society for the Encouragement of Domestic Industry. On this occasion he inquired, " What are the capabilities of our present condition as farmers of Rhode Island, and in what manner can those capabilities be improved and extended? " He spoke of the importance of agriculture, of the opportunities which the cultivator of the ground may have for mental improvement, and of the climate, soil, and products of the state. He offered valuable suggestions as to the means of increasing, by intelligent labor and the application of the laws of chemistry, the natural advantages which Rhode Island farmers already enjoyed. In conclusion he said, —

" I beg to assure you of the deep interest which I feel in all your pursuits, and to express the ardent wish that it were in my power in any manner to be of service to you. If I, or the gentlemen associated with me, can in any way promote your interests, it will give us at all times the greatest pleasure to do it. The commercial, the manufacturing, the agricultural, and the literary interests of this community are one and indivisible. May they all unite in rendering this little state the brightest star in the constellation of the Union."

CHAPTER XVI.

HABITS OF STUDY AND EXERCISE. — HOME LIFE. —
DEATH OF MRS. WAYLAND. — HER RELIGIOUS CHAR-
ACTER. — LETTERS TO HIS PARENTS. — HIS DEVOTION
TO HIS CHILDREN. — DEATH OF HIS MOTHER.

WE may well pause here to inquire how it was possible for any man, without the neglect of any known
duty, to respond to so many and so varied demands
upon his time. An answer to the inquiry involves some
allusion to his daily habits at this period of his life.

That he was conscientiously industrious, and that his
industry was systematic and methodical, might be taken
for granted, in view of the amount of labor which he
actually accomplished. But in addition to this, he had,
in a rare degree, the power of concentrating his mind
upon any subject which for the time engaged his attention. He often quoted with approbation, and he certainly
illustrated in his own instance, the characteristic saying
of Dr. Johnson: "A man may write at any time, if he
will set himself doggedly about it." He never asked
himself whether he was in the best mood for this or that
kind of mental effort. He never humored the passing
fancy of the moment. He had some duty assigned for
every working hour of every day, and he compelled himself to undertake the allotted task with unflinching determination. He patiently prepared his mind for the labor
of composition by the slow process of close and logical
thought, carefully writing out an analysis of the discourse,
or lecture, or treatise on which he was engaged. This

accomplished, he was ready for what remained. To clothe
with flesh and blood the skeleton so perfect in all its parts,
and to inspire the whole with the vital energy of his own
earnest nature, was comparatively easy. While so employed, he was impatient of interruption, and frequently
denied himself to all visitors. An incident related by
his pastor* happily illustrates his habits of study : —

  " During eight years I was his pastor, with an intimacy
peculiarly free ; and yet never but once did I venture to
intrude on his morning and choicest study hours. Knowing the annoyance he felt at the briefest interruption at such
times, — that he often studied with locked door, or did not
respond when solicited, — I had invariably regarded his
wishes. But necessity knows no rule. I rapped at the
door of his study when he was most secluded. There
was no response. I then gave the ' Faculty rap.' Still
no answer. Satisfied that he was within, and that, if he
knew my errand, he would welcome me, I addressed him
by name, saying, ' Dr. Wayland, I must see you.' To this
he replied in a gentle tone, ' Come in, Pastor.' I opened
the door. Crossing the threshold, I found him, pen in
hand, standing with his back to the little light which crept
through the shutters nearly closed. In this room, thus
darkened, he was *thinking*. It was at the time, I well
remember, when he was making the analysis of his work
on political economy — not one of his most difficult treatises, but requiring a large generalization, as well as a
minute analysis. Everything at this period of his life
was made tributary to his mental dicipline. I never
knew the scholar so rarely interrupted in ' study hours '
as he, and to this, in no small degree, is his success to
be attributed."

  It was Dr. Wayland's habit to qualify himself for such
continuous and exhausting mental application by vigorous
physical exercise. For many years this was his sole relief from study. Indeed, his only idea of relaxation was
exercise in the open air. He enjoyed nothing so much

---

* Rev. R. E. Pattison, D. D.

as laboring in his garden, and it seemed to him that his favorite amusement must be equally attractive to all. Thus he writes to one from whom he expected a visit: "Come, and stay as long as you can. Bring your working clothes: there will be an opportunity to use them." He always preferred that his exercise should take the form of productive labor. If the weather was unfavorable for gardening, he resorted to sawing and splitting wood. When a clergyman once asked him to suggest some species of recreation not inconsistent with clerical propriety, he said, with a smile, "Walk." He rarely left his home, unless summoned by some immediate call of duty. Travelling for the sake of travelling was not to his taste, and not in accordance with the severe standard of daily duty to which he habitually conformed. It was only with great reluctance that he ever consented to make visits which did not combine with the pleasure of seeing friends and relatives, some useful labor to be accomplished. January 1, 1834, he writes, —

"Your kind invitation is by no means slighted; but what should I do in Boston? Could I find my room, my fire, my books and papers there? I should be a mere hanger-on, in the way of other people, hindering them, and of no use to them or to myself. I should feel like the boy who played truant, finding neither the dog, nor the horse, nor the bee willing to play with him, and very glad to get back to school again."

He was ill at ease when not actively employed; as he once said, "I find doing nothing a most laborious and time-consuming business." It was, moreover, a marked peculiarity of his mental habits that he could never perform any literary labor with satisfaction to himself, except in the seclusion of his own study. Later in life he may have regretted that he had never learned the art of innocent recreation; but at the period of which we speak, he found his chief happiness in exerting to the utmost all the faculties of his mind.

At times he seemed aware that he was overtasking his strength. Thus he writes to his mother, June 3, 1831 : —

" I have for a long time been aware that I owed you a letter, and have several times been on the point of paying the debt; but various circumstances, which I could not control, have prevented. Before my last term closed, I prepared a discourse on natural religion for Harvard University. This required much time and reflection. I was then obliged to go and deliver it, and afterwards to remain a week in Boston to preach for Mr. Malcom's congregation. When I returned, I had the writing of the term to finish. Subsequently my eyes showed symptoms of weakness, which, in these days of the sickness and breaking down of clergymen, I considered an admonition to use them less."

To his sister, 1832 : —

" I am, my dear A., a perfect dray-horse. I am in harness from morning to night, and from one year to another. I am never turned out for recreation. Our term closed yesterday. To-morrow I go (D. V.) to New Bedford to prosecute college business, and raise some money for our library. Thus I shall be engaged all the vacation. Next term, the same thing is to be done over again. I want rest and ease for a little while. I barely seize a moment to write to you, out of the time which I have set apart for answering college letters. God, however, is pleased to smile upon our labors. We have a good entrance, and have done a good term's work, and are, by the blessing of Providence, making friends."

To Colonel Stone, March 14, 1832 : —

" I rejoice that your labor is so nearly completed. I wish I could say the same of mine. I am pained to add that I cannot do what you request of me. By too close attention to writing during the last vacation, I have lamed my chest, and have not been able to write a page a day for weeks. I may be obliged to take a journey on horseback to recover. Even writing what I am obliged to do in correspondence affects me."

He could not, however, be persuaded to seek that

relief from excessive labor, which those who were familar
with his daily life frequently recommended. His wife
writes to a friend, March 20, 1833, —

"The anxiety of my husband to complete his work on
moral science has led him to spend the vacation in writing, when he needed recreation to recruit his health, already much impaired by the severe and engrossing labors
of the preceding term. His daily exercise of sawing and
splitting wood has failed to keep him in good physical
condition; and he needs a journey, but he will not allow
himself this indulgence."

Yet while often exerting himself beyond the just limits
of his capacity for labor, he did not fail to impress on others the importance of obeying the laws of health. He
writes, June 3, 1831, to a relative engaged in teaching, —

"You will be in great danger of forgetting the necessity
of exercise both for yourself and for others. Remember
that you are to look to nature and natural tendencies for
lessons. A child loves play, and finds even simple motion
agreeable. The Creator meant it should be so. Let it
have play then; let its limbs be thoroughly and habitually
exercised. Thus only can it have a sound and healthy
constitution. Thus will you be able to counteract the
sensitiveness acquired by study."

And again, —

"I regret that you go to bed tired, and get up tired.
This is not right. Sleep ought to do away with *tired*.
You need, and must take, some sort of physical exercise,
and get more sleep. Every twenty-four hours should
take care of themselves, and provide for their own re-
cuperation. To be tired on getting up, casts the burden
of yesterday upon to-day."

While he delighted to receive his friends at his house,
and welcomed them with generous hospitality, his studious habits were always rigidly maintained. All business
engagements, and particularly his college appointments,
were kept with exact and unvarying punctuality. Indeed,

he never failed to recognize the paramount importance of his official obligations. On one occasion, when invited to preach in a neighboring city, he replied, —

"I cannot preach for your people, as you request. I could not do it consistently with my views of duty. Could I feel that it was right, few things would give me greater pleasure. This, I trust, you know, and therefore I need not multiply words to assure you of it. I cannot leave home in term time, except for an extraordinary case."

The following letter written at a later period exhibits the same spirit: —

"PROVIDENCE, July 15, 1845.

"Rev. and dear Sir: I have the honor to acknowledge the receipt of your letter of July 13, inviting me to be present at the Semi-Centennial Anniversary of Union College.

"Nothing could give me greater pleasure than to revisit once more the scenes of my early education, to renew those friendships, which, more than thirty years since, I formed within the walls of Union College, and to hold communion, although it were but for a day, with those teachers to whose instruction I owe whatever of success has attended my professional career. I fear, however, that my engagements will render it impossible for me to indulge my strong inclination. Our examinations, during the next week, will not allow me to be absent from home even for twenty-four hours. I learned long since, from the president of Union College (a name never uttered by his pupils without the most filial reverence and the most enthusiastic admiration), that the most powerful allurements of pleasure must bow to the requirements of duty. And I should hardly dare to appear in such a presence in disobedience to those instructions, which it has been the business of his life to exemplify. Should I not, therefore, be found in my place on Tuesday next, to answer to my name when the roll of the class of 1813 is called, I trust that my *alma mater* will allow me to plead, as my excuse, the principles with which she has imbued me."

Those leisure moments which he was able to snatch from the constant pressure of his steadily increasing cares,

he gladly spent with his family. He was a man of tender affections and quick sensibilities, ever studying how
best to promote the happiness of his wife and his children,
and ministering to their comfort with prompt and delicate
forethought. Of his only daughter, who died in 1829, at
the age of fifteen months, he was especially fond, and the
child warmly returned his love.

Mrs. Wayland writes, —

"It was delightful to observe her father's increasing
fondness for her. She was overjoyed whenever he entered
the house, and always, when I told her that her papa was
coming, she would run across the hall, holding out her
little hands to embrace him."

A few years after the loss of this dear child, he was
again called to pass through the furnace of affliction. On
the 3d of April, 1834, death once more entered his little
family and took from him his beloved wife. His feelings
under this sore bereavement, his firm reliance upon the
promises of God and the consolations of religion, his spirit
of Christian resignation, and his all-absorbing desire to
learn and profit by the true lessons of this mysterious
providence, are fitly set forth in his letters to his parents
and other relatives.

In view of the fact that the life and example of Mrs.
Wayland, and the reflections suggested by her sickness
and death, had an important influence in moulding the
character and directing the aims of her husband, her sons
do not feel that they are precluded by their relationship
from presenting a brief estimate of her moral qualities,
condensed from reminiscences prepared by Dr. Wayland,
for the perusal of her children.

Her type of piety was earnest and active, leading her
— notwithstanding her constitutional timidity — to make
untiring efforts for the conversion of souls. She was
greatly interested in the young, particularly those who
were students in college, and improved every opportu-

nity to direct their attention to the way of salvation, or,
if they were professors of religion, to urge upon them
entire consecration to Christ. There were, probably,
very few of her young friends with whom she did not
have personal and serious conversation on the subject of
preparation for eternity. She assisted in the formation of
the "Maternal Association," in the church with which she
was connected, and her labors to promote the success of
this society undoubtedly hastened her final illness.

But her efforts to benefit those with whom she came
in contact were not confined to any age or condition in
life. She lost no opportunity — whether within her own
social circle, or among her casual acquaintances, or in
her frequent ministries of consolation to the afflicted and
bereaved, or in her charitable visits to the poor and friendless — of manifesting her deep concern for their spiritual
welfare. She had great faith in prayer, and was accustomed to seek divine direction in every undertaking, not
only of parental government and religious effort, but even
of domestic detail.

"Her maternal character was peculiarly worthy of
imitation. It is rare to see a mother who appeared to
enjoy her children with so deep and tender an emotion.
She seemed perfectly happy to witness their innocent
playfulness, and especially to reciprocate their opening
affection. Her care of their bodies and minds was incessant, amounting to a sort of limited omnipresence. Whatever else engaged her attention, she could not forget her
children. But with all this strong attachment, she permitted no fault to pass unnoticed or uncorrected. She
never suffered them to disobey her, but blended with her
love a most persuasive, yet always efficient, authority."

The illness of Mrs. Wayland, although not of long duration, was painful and distressing in the extreme.

Dr. Wayland writes to her brother, March 4, 1834, —

"Lucy is exceedingly feeble. I know not what more
to say. If she be spared, it will be a special and peculiar mercy. She suffers less than when I last wrote, but

is greatly prostrated.   I can sometimes look up with faith ;
but when I see her extreme debility, I hardly dare to hope.
I can only say, ' If it be possible, let this cup pass from
me ; ' and then leave her with the gracious and merciful
Savior.   Pray for me and for us all."

To his parents : —

"PROVIDENCE, March 12, 1834.

"I observe that it was Leigh Richmond's practice to
write to his mother annually, on his birthday.   It struck
me as a very appropriate custom, and I resolved to
adopt it.   Yesterday, however, which was my birthday,
I was too unwell to write.   My letter of to-day is the
best evidence I can give of my intention to follow so good
an example.

" Since I last wrote, Lucy has been on the border of
the grave, where she still remains.   I fear you will never
see her again.   She seems to be growing weaker and
weaker, and from one day to another her departure is
expected.   She frequently speaks of you, and desires an
interest in your prayers.   This I know she has.   I hope
that I may soon receive a letter from you containing some
words of consolation for her.   She is remarkably patient,
although in great distress ; and while she has not that
sense of pardon for which she longs, she gives to her
friends clear evidence that she is a child of God.

" You will, I know, desire to know my feelings under
this affliction.   It is the severest stroke I have ever been
called upon to bear.   I can, however, say, if I do not
mistake, that I lay my wife at the feet of Jesus, praying,
' If thou canst do anything for me, help me ; but if not,
glorify thy name.'   I needed this affliction.   There is
not a single bearing of it that I have not needed.   I hope
it is the correction of a Father, and that he in faithfulness
afflicts me.   Although his hand presses me very sore, I
think I would not have a finger removed unless as God
wills.   I believe that my prevalent desire is, that this sorrow may be sanctified to me, to my family, to the college,
to the church, and to the world.   Let me entreat you to
wrestle with me in prayer that this correction may not be
in vain.

" I did not, however, intend to write as a husband, but
as a son.   This day reminds me of the solicitude you

have both felt for me, of the self-denial you have practised for me, of the prayers you have offered to God for
me, of the exhortations, the warnings, the reproofs, you
have been obliged through my sinfulness to administer
to me.

"For all these, my dear parents, I am glad to have this
opportunity of thanking and blessing you. And this day
also reminds me of my disobedience and thoughtlessness,
of my waywardness and obstinacy, of the thousand times,
in boyhood, and youth, and manhood, when I must have
wounded your feelings. For all this, I would here with
tears implore the forgiveness of my heavenly Father, and
of you, the best of earthly parents. Never have I ceased
to be sensible of your goodness, and always have I delighted to attribute whatever little success I may have had,
more to you than to myself.

"My paper is almost filled, but I must make room to
add that God is doing a glorious work in college. Nearly
half — certainly more than a third — of those who were
thoughtless at the commencement of the term, have expressed a hope in Christ. We look forward to still greater
triumphs of the Holy Spirit. Help us to pray for it, and
although our earthly comforts wither, may God still visit
us with his rich salvation. Remember me most affectionately to the family. Lucy frequently speaks of you all.
May we be prepared for a sick bed and a dying hour."

To the same : —

"PROVIDENCE, Friday, April 4, 1834.

"It has pleased God in his holy providence to take
dear Lucy to himself. She was released from her great
distress last evening, at about half past five o'clock. Her
sufferings were severe ; but, so far as we could discover,
her mind was clear, and her last word was, 'Pray.' I
cannot say more at present, but will soon write to you all.
I can only beg a renewed interest in your prayers that I
may be sustained, and especially that I may be sanctified
and made more humble and holy."

To his father, April 17, 1834 : —

"Your very acceptable letter reached me on my return
from New York, whither I was called by business. I
should have gone to Saratoga Springs to visit you, but
I felt that my little family needed my presence ; and

also it seemed to me that when God afflicts us, it is not pleasing to him for us to run away from his dispensation. Where his hand is upon us, there I suppose he means us to be. I have thought that one of the most important considerations connected with afflictions is, that they are a special and very costly means of grace. Is not this evident from David's remark, ' Precious in the sight of the Lord is the death of his saints'? This has been to me one of the most solemn views connected with my bereavement. I never so much felt the need of the prayers of those who love me, as for this one thing—that this affliction might be sanctified to me. I see that afflictions, of themselves, are by no means sanctification. They are only means, and are useful only as they are attended by the influences of the Holy Spirit. For these I have not ceased to pray, and I beg you to pray not so much for present support, as for great and peculiar sanctification. Your remark that you have found afflictions blessed to you is a great comfort to me. I pray God that I may have the same rich experience."

To his parents : —

"PROVIDENCE, June 6, 1834.

"Your very acceptable and consoling letter was duly received, and I have ever since been seeking daily for an opportunity to answer it. But the fact is, that, in addition to my college duties, there seems a special door opened in several ways to be useful in the dissemination of religious truth ; and I have been thus so constantly occupied that I have been obliged to take every moment I could get for sleep and exercise. As it is, although my health is good, yet it is barely sufficient for the accomplishment of what I have to do.

"You refer to my apparent depression of spirits. Perhaps it is so. The affliction is continually present with me, and casts a gloom over everything. It is not the acute anguish that it was, but rather like the dull, heavy, continued throbbing after a grievous, lacerating wound. You will say this ought not to be ; the Lord hath done all things well ; has glorified his name, and will glorify it again. I believe and know this, and hope that this pain will work in me the peaceable fruits of righteousness. I would not alter the Lord's doing, and am sometimes melted at his goodness. I would not but have drunk the cup. Still it is very bitter, and the rod is very heavy, and it requires a strong effort of faith and hope to receive it as I ought.

"I know that it is the Christian's privilege to rejoice in the Lord always, and to be exceedingly joyful in all tribulation ; but I cannot say that I have as yet attained to this. I think, however, that I can truly say that I have sought consolation nowhere else, and desire it from no other source. My prayer has been, and is, that God would glorify his name in this event, cause me to be sanctified by it, and make me habitually heavenly-minded. I have a comfortable hope that he will do this, although I have not the evidence of its actual accomplishment which I could desire.

"I wish that I could give you a more cheering account of my feelings. Perhaps the cold and wet weather, which has in a measure deprived me of exercise, has had some effect. I do most sincerely thank you for your tender sympathy and your prayers, which I believe will be answered."

He writes to his mother, September 28, 1834, —

"I know that I want nothing but a large effusion of the Holy Spirit, and the presence of Christ in my own soul, to render me perfectly happy. There are sad reminiscences everywhere around me, and everything which I hear or see recalls them to my mind. But they ought to point me to heaven, and bid me reflect how those who have gone before are spending their eternity, and how we, who expect to follow them, ought to be spending our time. I seem to myself to be feebly striving after more holiness, and longing to be more conformed to the image of Christ. But I make, at the best, such tardy, such almost imperceptible progress, I am so frequently overcome by temptation, that I am at times ready to give up all for lost. God has bestowed upon me abundant means of grace. The situation in which I am placed, the responsibility of so many young men, the various opportunities which I enjoy for making others better, should call me to the very highest attainments in holiness. Besides this, he has laid upon me an affliction which comes upon me daily, and which is in its nature peculiarly fitted to lead the mind to heaven.

When I consider all these things, and my own sin and unfaithfulness, I am almost overwhelmed. My only refuge is in that blood which cleanses from all sin. I hope, my dear mother, that you can tell me some way of making more rapid progress in divine things, and of gaining more deadness to the world and more close and vital union to Christ.

" I can hardly say how much I thank you for your late visit. It was very kind in you to travel so far to see me in my loneliness. I pray God to reward you, and in some way or other to make your coming a blessing to us all."

To his sister, October 27, 1834 : —

" . . . I am daily working at my Moral Philosophy, carrying on the business of the college, and endeavoring to do my duty as best I can. My little boys are doing well, and I have much to be thankful for. Still my house is lonely, my avocations without stimulus, and I go on in a steady, monotonous sort of way. I try to live religiously; to maintain a temper of faith, and hope, and resignation. Sometimes I trust that I succeed; but I am very frequently far off again, and need the use of every means to bring me back. How blessed a doctrine is the intercession of Christ to such poor sinners ! How strong is the ground of hope ! How near it brings us in union with Christ and heaven ! "

Writing, in 1834, to a relative, he says, —

" . . . I am constantly employed, and suffer mainly from a sort of dulness, a steady monotony of occupation, affording no play to the feelings to which I have been accustomed, combined with a sense of sadness and lacerated recollection which meets me in everything I see and surprises me in everything I do. Yet this is a portion of the cup which has been poured out for me by my Father in heaven, and I feel happy whenever I can bow in submission to just what he appoints."

To his parents : —
" PROVIDENCE, November 18, 1834.

" Your very kind letter was duly received, for which accept my warmest thanks. I rejoice to hear of the improving health of my mother, and that when you wrote, everything was going on so pleasantly with you.

"It has pleased our heavenly Father to enter your pleasant circle by death. I know what it is by sad experience, and thought of you much and often during the Sabbath day of your trial, and since that event. Though your consolations in this case abound, yet there is a deep and awful sadness in the death of those we love which nothing can remove. Indeed, I am not sure that it ought to be removed. It seems as if the veil which separates time from eternity were for a space withdrawn, and we almost became inhabitants of the other world. I trust that as your affliction has abounded, your consolation has yet more abounded, and that you have already seen, and may still more see, its good effects upon the other members of your family.

"How sweetly and how fully was the dear child prepared, and in how short a time! I have thought that a brief account of her conversion, sickness, and death might be very profitable to the young, and might be a valuable addition to our narratives of pious children.

". . . I am quite alone, but this very loneliness may be of service to me. It is a path that I have never trodden before. I think its tendency is to wean the mind from creatures, and, if sanctified by the Holy Spirit, must also tend to fix the affections upon God. I hope that it renders the truths of religion more precious to me, and the doctrine of the atonement more my companion than formerly. We need to have our wills subdued to the will of Christ in all manners and by all methods. It is necessary to learn to do his will, to suffer his will, to make him our trust and confidence; and he knows best the methods which will most successfully accomplish this holy purpose.

"Occupied so continually as I am and have been for a long time in worldly business, perhaps this is the only way in which I could be taught the lesson. If he will only sanctify it to me, I think I am willing to bear it so long as he shall lay his hand upon me. That is, I shall be willing so long as he grants me grace to subdue my will to his. Otherwise I shall rebel and repine in a moment, and say with Jonah, 'I do well to be angry.'"

" My dear Parents: A year since I wrote to you under the immediate visitation of the chastening of God. In one room lay dear Lucy on the bed of sickness unto death, and in the other I had been confined for some days, with barely sufficient strength to write to you. How many the changes which have been meted out to me since then! After three weeks more of most afflictive suffering, dear Lucy was released, to join, as I doubt not, the general assembly and church of the first born. What a glorious year has it been to her! What attainment in holiness has she made before this! How must our sluggishness in the cause of Christ seem to her now! and how precious every self-denial for the Savior's sake, every sigh of penitence, and every breathing after holiness! Let us learn how to live here, by reflecting how the saints above must, at the present moment, look down upon our actions.

" As for myself, I have to sing of mercy and of judgment. I hope that this affliction has been sent by the chastening hand of a covenant-keeping God. It seems to me, if I do not deceive myself, that my will is somewhat more subdued than formerly; that I long more for holiness, and see more desirableness in the Christian graces. I hope that I have some clearer views of the holiness of the law of God, and of the way of salvation by Christ, and a more prevalent desire to go out of myself, and to be found alone in Him who loved me and gave himself for me.

" If these are the fruits of affliction, it surely ought not to be grievous, but rather joyous. And although these blessed results are infinitely less than they should be, and much less than others have enjoyed, yet I would bless God for his faithfulness in answering my poor supplications in the day of my trial.

" But besides these, I have many other mercies to record. The lives of all the rest of our immediate family have been spared, especially that of dear mother, of late brought very low. This is a cause for fervent and united thanksgiving from one and all of us. Let us praise his holy name for this, and also for the comforts of his presence which he granted both to mother, when sick, and to you, my dear father, when you were threatened with so severe a bereavement. For so many kind brothers and sisters, who, with you, have been permitted to visit me, I would also thank the Lord. It was a great mercy to me in my loneliness and sorrow. For the kind provision which God has made for my dear little boys, I ought to be very grateful. I give thanks to God that I am able to have them with me, instead of seeing them scattered abroad, as some children have been under similar circumstances. I desire also to be thankful that God inclined me to take the charge of them myself, rather than intrust them to the care of others. This has been, I think, a blessing to them and to me. They are more attached to me, and I am to them; and I believe that they have improved in character and conduct, notwithstanding their irreparable loss.

"For the health which we have all enjoyed, I would also return thanks. I do not think that we have passed any year with so little sickness, or one in which my children would not have suffered more severely for the want of the attentions of their dear mother. Then God has enabled me, notwithstanding all my domestic cares, to accomplish more study and writing than in any previous year. He has, since you were here, brought me nearly to the close of my work on moral philosophy, which has cost me a good deal of labor. And this in addition to my other labors in college, and as many extra duties as usual.

"Thus you see that I have abundant reason to speak well of his name. What an infinite mercy is it to be called by his grace! still more to be chastened for our good, and still more to have the chastisement attended with so many unmerited and peculiar blessings.

"I sometimes feel lonely, although not so much so as I feared. I think that God has ordered my present arrangements in mercy, and that they are the best which, under the circumstances, could have been made. It is a most grateful recollection to look back and see that when we knew not what to do, and committed our way unto the Lord, he directed our steps. Especially has this been the case when we had no experience to guide us, and could not possibly tell, of two ways, which was the better."

"PROVIDENCE, March 11, 1836.

"My very dear Mother: I am again reminded of my promise, made some time since, to write to you on my birthday. I fulfil it with great pleasure, in the hope

that whenever your health will permit, — but not otherwise, — you will send me a few lines in return.

"I cannot think of this period without again calling to
mind the scenes through which I was passing two years
ago this day. The bitterness of that season I can never
forget, although time has somewhat blunted the edge of
the pain. Throughout the period which has since elapsed,
God has graciously supported me, and in mercy led me
along all my path. My bread has been given me, and my
water has been sure. All my wants have been richly
supplied. My house has been in peace, and my children
in health. . . . They are very fond of me, and, I believe,
try, especially of late, to obey me from love. They got
through the whole of last week without a single reproof.

"It has also pleased God to give me unusual success
in my labors since he saw fit to afflict me. I think I have
never done so much writing, nor, so far as I can judge,
with so good success. I hope that what I have published
during the past year may be useful, both to the more advanced and to the young. For all this I have unspeakable
reason to be thankful, and, yet more, to be prayerful. It
seems to me of not so much importance what we do, as
what we do prayerfully. We have little reason to hope
that our efforts to do good will succeed, unless they be
sanctified with prayer; and if they succeed, we shall
derive only so much blessing as belongs to a right temper
of mind. In this, I find myself, most of all, deficient.
There is a restlessness about me which demands employment. As soon as I have done with one thing, I must be
engaged in another, or I am miserably downcast and unhappy. When my Moral Philosophy was finished, I was
uneasy until the Political Economy was commenced; and
now that this is under way, I cannot willingly do anything
else until it is completed.

"But to carry on the spiritual work which ought to
accompany and sanctify these things, and make them
really sacrifices to the blessed Savior, — this I find to be
a very different and vastly more difficult work. I discover in myself no tendency to holiness. Whatever in me
is holy, is the work of the Spirit, and of him alone. Yet
I strive, if I do not mistake, to maintain a spiritual mind.
I pray, and, I think, labor, to live near to God. Sometimes I seem to gain some little nearness to Christ, and

feel a temper of submission to his commandments; but soon I find myself again longing for the sources of this world's happiness, or murmuring against the dispensations of Providence, or else so engrossed in my studies that all I have gained is lost, and I am once more the sport of wild affections, unreasonable desires, and all the corruptions of the human heart.

"I hope, however, that the Savior does not leave me entirely desolate. He brings me back again at times, and fills me with confusion at my own waywardness and sin. I hope the result of all his dealings with me will be to show me more than I have ever before known of the wickedness and deceitfulness of the heart of man, of my own utter helplessness by reason of sin, and of the absolute necessity of relying on the Savior for strength as well as for pardon. I think I see more of my need of the righteousness of Christ, and that I am only complete in him. But I am reminded of what Fuller, or Cecil, — I forget which, — calls a 'dry faith.' I see these things. I think I can rest my soul upon them. At times I mourn over my sins, but I am confounded when I reflect upon my want of affection and love to the Savior. I know that in Christ is all that is calculated to draw out the warmest love and desire for his person — the same fervor of attachment which we feel for a near and beloved friend, only infinitely purer and more intense. But here I feel my great deficiency. My affections seem paralyzed. I long for the love which I ought to feel, but I do not feel it. I desire to be like him; I desire to obey him. I lament my waywardness and folly. I think I would part with everything for more holiness. But still my heart is unwarmed; my affections are unmoved; yet I long, and pray, and trust I may yet feel his love shed abroad in my heart.

"I will not apologize for writing so much about myself, for, knowing so well your kindness and forbearance, I am sure that you will willingly read anything even on such a subject as this — my poor, miserable, and sluggish feelings, and my hard, rebellious heart.

"I rejoice, my dear mother, that you have been spared during the past winter, and have got through it so much better than the last, although it has been violently cold and severe. The river here is still frozen — a thing that, I presume, has not occurred for a great many years. I

bless God that he has spared you to counsel, guide, and
pray for us for another year. I believe that we have all
been greatly assisted in our various employments by the
prayers of dear father and yourself. Doubtless it sometimes seems to you trying that you are confined to your
chamber and unable to render much active assistance to
your family. But, my dear mother, you little know how
much you are doing. Probably no part of your life was
ever spent so profitably. Think how many of us are engaged in, I hope, not useless duties. If the labor of any
one of us is made more effectual through your prayers, —
and of this I have no manner of doubt, — you are working,
not with one pair of hands, but with several; not in one
place, but in many places; not in one sphere of duty, but
in various, and all of them interesting spheres of duty. Be
not, then, discouraged or disheartened, inasmuch as your
labor is not in vain in the Lord."

April 7, 1835, he writes to a relative, —

". . . I bless God for what you write respecting young
——. These are the unmerited rewards which God
sometimes gives us. It is, I believe, greatly in answer to
the prayers of that sweet saint who now sleeps in Jesus.
I have felt that, so far as I am concerned, it was worth
going through all the affliction I have suffered during the
past year, to have been made the instrument in the hands
of the Savior of being useful to one soul — especially of
one who is likely to be so useful to others."

It will have been observed that he counted it as one of
the crowning mercies vouchsafed to him by a compassion-
ate and covenant-keeping God, that he was permitted to
have his surviving children with him, " instead of seeing
them scattered abroad, as some children have been under
similar circumstances." For his sons, deprived at so early
an age of the constant care and fostering love of a mother,
his parental solicitude was manifested in many ways. He
devoted himself with renewed zeal to their mental and
moral training. He joined in their childish sports, and
sympathized with their youthful feelings. Many a visitor
was surprised, when, calling upon the president at his

residence, to find him stretched at full length upon the floor, engaged in a frolic with his boys, and abundantly enjoying their wild delight when they were allowed to believe that they had conquered their father. Often, as they met him on the college green returning from his study, he would carry them home on his shoulders, much to the amusement of those who witnessed this exhibition of parental affection. He made them his companions in his walks, in his exercise in the garden or the wood-shed, and took them with him during his brief journeys, whenever his engagements did not conflict with the care and oversight which their youth and inexperience required. Writing to a relative, February 20, 1835, he says, —

"My few leisure hours are almost all spent with my children, and I always feel guilty when I neglect them. They need all my time and attention."

But there were hours for study as well as for relaxation. The efforts of the faithful teacher to impart instruction suited to their tender years were efficiently aided by home discipline. Reports from school of good conduct and diligent attention to lessons were always rewarded in such a manner as to encourage obedience and industry, while idle or wayward habits were promptly but kindly corrected. Dr. Wayland was fond of entertaining his children with stories of his own invention, or founded upon incidents in his early life. These were frequently continued from evening to evening for weeks, and were eagerly anticipated and intensely enjoyed by his little hearers. From time to time he read to them books combining amusement with instruction — such as Sandford and Merton, Robinson Crusoe, Swiss Family Robinson, and the Parents' Assistant.

On Sabbath evenings it was his invariable custom to give them biblical instruction in the form of Scripture narrative. The lives of the Old and New Testament worthies — especial reference being had to the recorded incidents

of their boyhood — were presented so simply and with
such frequent enforcement of the practical lessons to be
learned, as to render the hours so spent not only full of
interest, but rich in the inculcation of religious truth.

Thus did he teach his sons to look upon their father as
their best earthly friend, while seeking, at the same time,
to fasten their affections upon that Savior who took little
children in his arms and blessed them.

Time had not blunted the edge of his great sorrow before he was visited with a fresh affliction. On the 5th of
December, 1836, his mother, so fondly loved and so tenderly revered, was taken to her eternal rest. He writes
to his bereaved father, December 8, 1836, —

"· · · Of the bitterness of your sorrow I can form some
conception. I know you will say that before this you had
hardly known the meaning of affliction, and had scarcely
felt the chastening hand of our heavenly Father. Rarely
has any husband lost such a wife, rarely have children
lost such a mother. You have felt that the light of
your tabernacle is put out, that the glory of your house
is departed, that you have been cleft in twain by a single
stroke, and that the bleeding wound is exposed to pain
from even the touch of your nearest friends.

" But while all this is so, let us look to the hills from
whence cometh our help. When my spirit is overwhelmed
within me, *Thou* knowest the path that I take. No affliction for the present seemeth joyous, but grievous ; yet afterwards it worketh the peaceful fruits of righteousness to
those that are exercised thereby. Whom the Lord loveth
he chasteneth, and scourgeth every son whom he receiveth.
Let us, then, endeavor to look upon this dispensation in the
light of the sanctuary, and survey those points in which it
may melt and humble our hearts in gratitude. This I
have found to be the best balm to a wounded spirit. When
we can look up to God in gratitude and love, we can say,
almost in exultation, These light afflictions, which are but
for a moment, work out for us a far more exceeding and
eternal weight of glory.

" How thankful should we be to God for giving to our
dear mother so superior a mind, so accurate and discrim-

inating a judgment, so strong and expansive a thirst for
knowledge, such tender and enduring affections, so warm
and self-denying a charity, and, above all, that he sanctified
all these excellent qualities by calling her so early to a knowledge of himself! How can we be sufficiently grateful to
him for that grace which he bestowed upon her in causing her path through life to be that of the just that shineth
more and more unto the perfect day, and throughout her
whole course rendering her so bright, so illustrious an example of the excellency of his grace, so that, wherever she
lived, wherever she was known, in public or in private,
among Christians or men and women of the world, among
the young or old, every one loved, every one venerated
her, every one was willingly constrained to confess that
she was an Israelite indeed, a chosen and much beloved
disciple of Christ! How great reason have we to be thankful that she has been spared to us so long, and has been in
so many cases our guide and counsellor, that all her children have grown up to love and honor her, and that we
have all had for so long a time the blessing of her advice,
her example, and her prayers! How great reason have we
to be thankful that her mind was spared to the last, that
so many of those she loved were around her bed, that
Christ was with her, and that, as she was entering into rest,
she was permitted to look back upon us, and to say to us,
'All's well'! And all is now well with thee, beloved saint.
That aching head now rests upon thy Savior's breast; that
heaving bosom shall throb no more with sorrow, or anguish, or regret, or repentance. Thou art now a pillar
in the temple of thy God. Thou hast eaten of the hidden
manna. Thou hast washed thy robes and made them
white in the blood of the Lamb. He that sitteth on the
throne hath wiped away all tears from thine eyes. Thou
art now forever with the Lord. We have seen thee ascend
as in a chariot of fire. O that thy mantle may rest upon
us who remain!

"My dear father, let us comfort each other with these
words. I pray God to be with you, to strengthen, comfort,
stablish you, and make you to come out of this fire, as
gold seven times purified.

Your affectionate and sympathizing son."

To his sister in a letter of the same date: —

"That I am with you in spirit, my dearest sister, I need not say. I feel indeed as though I were really with you. I go from room to room. I gaze with you on that form which so lately moved among us, on those lips from which we have received our best instructions, on those eyes which always beamed on us with love, and which, I fear, we have often caused to fill with tears: and I witness that calm, heavenly composure shining upon the tabernacle from which a glorified spirit has so lately departed. I feel deeply the loss which I have sustained in not being with you, to hear the last words and catch the latest exhortations of so blessed a saint.

"What a treasure have we, in the recollections of such a mother! What a blessing to have such an assurance, such a consciousness even, that she is now present with the Lord! It seems almost as though we had seen the chariot of fire in which she ascended, and heard her song of glory coming back to us after she had left the house of her bondage.

"I pray God, my dear sister, to be with you and help you. The chasm in your circle can only be filled by the presence of God himself. No arm can sustain you but the arm of omnipotence. House, and home, and earthly happiness are words of which the signification has wonderfully departed, and affliction has acquired a meaning which it never before possessed. Yet let us look up to God as our Father, and cherish more fondly our love for the Savior as earthly affections are dried up."

To his father, January 3, 1837: —

"I have thought much of you, my dear father, and my dear sisters, at the return of these anniversaries. I know how different they are to you from any which you have before spent. I know by experience how they bring with them all the thronging recollections of years past, and the contrast between what is and what has been seems at times too much for the heart to endure. Such, I know, have been your feelings at the present time. But even to this there is a bright side. We may look beyond the grave, and think on the contrast which must be experienced by souls in heaven. How different their Sabbaths, their anniversaries, from ours! I have thought frequently of our Lord's remark to his disciples. 'And now I go my way to him that sent me, and none of you asketh me, Whither goest thou? but because I have said these things, sorrow hath filled your hearts.' 'None of you asketh me,' as though he had said, If you were to ask me whither I am going, and were to reflect upon the exaltation to which I am to be raised, you would sorrow no more, but your sorrow would be turned into joy. Thus, I suppose, it should be with us. We should remember the crowns that our beloved ones wear, the palms of victory which they carry, the robe of righteousness with which they are clothed, the rewards which God has given to all their labors, and sorrows, and self-denials, and thus we should the less grieve at their departure.

"I bless God, my dear father, for the special and peculiar support which he has granted you, and for the abundant manifestation of his presence with which he has cheered you. At such an hour as this, what could you have done without him and the light of his countenance? Let us be thankful for all that is past, and even over the graves of those we love, erect our Ebenezer, saying, Hitherto the Lord has helped us."

To his sister : —

" Your very welcome letter came duly to hand. I bless God that he supported you through that trying scene — the most trying that a child can ever witness. But, my dear S., what a blessing it is to have had such a mother! I do not know anywhere so perfect a character. She looks to me not merely bright, but spotless. How expansive and universal her love to everybody, but how tender, how endearing to us ! How boundless, and how full of forethought her self-denial ! How meek and how gentle her spirit ! How pure and heavenly her thoughts, and how strong and unwavering her faith ! As you say, we ought to have been, and we ought to be, very different from others. We should be specially grateful to the Savior for all his goodness to her, and specially for his goodness to her at the last.

" We must collect all of her letters. I regret that they were so few, but they are invaluable. The letter she wrote to me on the death of Lucy, and all that she has ever written to me, are perfect of their kind, and breathe the very spirit which animated her.

" I hope this week to look over my letters and select
hers from them. If we all do this, we may be able to
form a delightful little memorial of her. She wrote me
on my birthdays, and occasionally wrote also with dear
father at different times. What a blessed testimony she
left everywhere to young and old, at home and abroad!
What do we not owe to her prayers and her example! It
has frequently seemed to me, that whatever success any
of us has had, has been much more the result of the
prayers of our parents than of our own exertions, or anything in ourselves. Let us all strive to be like her, and
then we shall be with her. But especially would I imitate
her lovely humility, her child-like meekness, her touching
self-denial and disinterestedness, and her tender and affecting charity. These were her peculiar graces, and she
seemed to have learned the art of imitating the Savior
most successfully. It was a type of character to which
very few attain. And, blessed saint, how little did she
believe that she possessed it!

" I feel most deeply for dear father. I praise God for
the support which he is receiving. Nothing but help
from on high could hold him up, severed, crushed, as he
is. But I see that in the furnace one walks 'with him
like unto the Son of God, and the smell of fire shall not
even pass upon him.' Yet no one who has not gone
through this furnace can tell how hot it is; and it is impossible that any can be more severe than that which
now surrounds him. There have been few such unions;
so long, so harmonious, so entirely happy. May God be
with him yet. We will be all to him that we can, and
will unite to render his sorrow as light as possible. And
let us remember the voice of the dear departed saint, and
be drawn closer together by this overwhelming stroke."

CHAPTER XVIII.

"ELEMENTS OF MORAL SCIENCE." — ITS RECEPTION. —
TRANSLATIONS. — "ELEMENTS OF POLITICAL ECON-
OMY." — "LIMITATIONS OF HUMAN RESPONSIBILITY."
— SECOND MARRIAGE. — RHODE ISLAND HALL AND THE
PRESIDENT'S HOUSE.

DURING these years of affliction, Dr. Wayland's devotion to his official duties never abated. He
wasted no time in unprofitable grief. While with Christian resignation he bowed meekly under the chastening
hand of his Maker, and sought to learn the true lessons
of these providences, he did not overlook the importance
of preserving a healthy mental tone by constant occupation. Writing, in 1837, to a relative who had recently
suffered a severe bereavement, he says, —

"May God support you, my brother. Be engaged in
duty as much as possible. If you are for a moment
unemployed, you may not be able to bear your sorrow.
Prayer and duty are the supports which we must seek in
such afflictions. If I had not labored to the utmost limit
of my strength, it seems to me that I must have sunk."

We have already seen that he did not content himself
with following the text-books which he found in use when
he became president, and that he very soon began to
deliver lectures to his pupils upon moral philosophy and
political economy. The increased interest imparted to
the exercises of the class-room by this mode of instruction naturally suggested the idea of publishing these lectures in the form of treatises upon the subjects taught.

He first prepared for the press his Elements of Moral Science.

With what motives and in what temper of mind this labor was commenced, will appear by an extract from his journal, December 22, 1833 : —

" I have thought of publishing a work on moral philosophy. Direct me, O thou all-wise and pure Spirit. Let me not do it unless it be for thy glory and the good of men. If I should do it, may it be all true, so far as human knowledge at present extends. Enlighten, guide, and teach me so that I may write something which shall show thy justice more clearly than heretofore, and the necessity and excellency of the plan of salvation by Christ Jesus, the blessed Redeemer. All which I ask through his merits alone. Amen."

He writes to his sister December 26, 1834 : —

" . . . I have wrought at my work with only tolerable success. It is slower labor than one would suppose ; but if it proves to be true, and does anything towards settling points in ethics which were before considered doubtful, it matters not how long it takes. The shortest time in which anything can be done is precisely the time necessary to do it well. This saves subsequent labor, and it is better to aim at correctness than to repair incorrectness."

To the same, February 28, 1835 : —

" I am getting towards the close of my moral philosophy, which, if it proves of any value, will be a good work done. It has cost me a great deal of time and thought, for which I hope the world will be better."

To the same, May 14, 1835 : —

" . . . My book (Elements of Moral Science) is out to-day, and you will soon receive a copy. I want you all to read it through as soon as your other duties will permit, and let me know candidly what is the first impression it makes upon you. If I can get the honest criticism of a few candid persons, I can easily judge how it will strike the rest of the world. I suppose it is natural and innocent to desire it to succeed, and right to wish that, if it be the will of God, it may be useful."

June 6, 1835, he writes in his journal, —

" During the year succeeding my affliction, God enabled me to prepare and publish my work on moral philosophy, a labor on which I had long been meditating. I have endeavored to make known the ways of God to man. Lord God of Hosts, I commend to thee, through Jesus Christ thy Son, this work. May it promote the cause of truth, of peace, and of righteousness. I lay it before thee, and cast it at thy feet. I humbly pray that thy good Spirit may cause whatever of it is true to be believed, received, and practised, and whatever is false to be discovered, refuted, and confounded, so that it may do good and no harm to thy cause. But when I consider the greatness of such an undertaking, and the good it may accomplish, if successful, what am I, that I should hope for so much favor? I dare not; only, my God, if it should please thee for thy Son's sake to condescend thus to use me, make me humble and grateful, and let me give all the glory to thy holy name."

In the preface to the first edition of the Elements of Moral Science, Dr. Wayland explains at some length the design with which the volume was prepared, and the reasons which induced him to publish it as a text-book.

" When it became my duty to instruct in moral philosophy in Brown University, the text-book in use was the work of Dr. Paley. From many of his principles I found myself compelled to dissent, and at first contented myself with stating to my classes my objections to the author, and offering my views in the form of familiar conversations upon several of the topics which he discusses. These views, for my own convenience, I soon committed to paper, and delivered in the form of lectures. In a few years these lectures had become so extended, that, to my surprise, they contained in themselves the elements of a different system from that of the text-book which I was teaching. To avoid the inconvenience of teaching two different systems, I undertook to reduce them to order, and to make such additions as would render the work complete in itself. I then relinquished the work of Dr. Paley, and for some time have been in the habit of instructing solely by lecture. The success of the attempt exceeded my ex-

pectations, and encouraged me to hope that the publication
of what I had delivered to my classes might in some small
degree facilitate the study of moral science.

"From these circumstances the work has derived its
character. Being designed for the purposes of instruction, its aim is to be simple, clear, and purely didactic.
I have rarely gone into extended discussion, but have contented myself with the attempt to state the moral law, and
the reason of it, in as few and as comprehensive terms as
possible. The illustration of the principles, and the application of them to cases in ordinary life, I have generally
left to the instructor or to the student himself. Hence,
also, I have omitted everything which relates to the history of opinions, and have made but little allusion to the
opinions themselves from which I dissent. To have acted
otherwise would have extended the undertaking greatly
beyond the limits which I had assigned to myself; and it
seemed to me not to belong to the design which I had in
view. A work which should attempt to exhibit what was
true appeared to me more desirable than one which should
point out what was exploded, discuss what was doubtful,
or disprove what was false.

"In the course of the work I have quoted but few authorities, as in preparing it I have referred to but few
books. I make this remark in no manner for the sake of
laying claim to originality, but to avoid the impression
of using the labors of others without acknowledgment.
When I commenced the undertaking, I attempted to read
extensively, but soon found it so difficult to arrive at any
definite results in this manner, that the necessities of my
situation obliged me to rely upon my own reflection.
That I have thus come to the same conclusion with many
others, I should be unwilling to doubt. When this coin-
cidence of opinion has come to my knowledge, I have
mentioned it. When it is not mentioned, it is because I
have not known it. . . ."

The success of the treatise, the origin and design of
which are thus modestly described by its author, has long
since become a matter of history. The clearness and independence of its teachings, the elevation of its moral
tone, the candor and ability of its discussions of practical
ethics, and the humane and catholic spirit with which it

is imbued, have given it a celebrity hardly less than world-wide.

The first edition was soon exhausted, and in September, 1835, a second was published. " It was almost immediately adopted by a large number of the colleges, academies, and high schools of the country; and although thirty years have since elapsed, it still holds its place, almost without a rival." *

Meanwhile, the labors of the author were commended by those whose approval could not fail to afford him the highest gratification. Professor Moses Stuart writes, July 23, 1835, —

" Thanks for your excellent book on morals. I have as yet found time to read but few chapters. *Sed ex ungue leonem.* Brother Woods says, ' It is the first entirely Christian book of this kind that we have had.' "

Chancellor Kent writes, —

" NEW YORK, July 25, 1835.

" Dear Sir: I have just finished the perusal of your work on the Elements of Moral Science. I have read it carefully and with deep interest. The first half of the volume, on theoretical and practical ethics, was by far the most interesting to me. The residue of the work, on the duties of man to man, led me over ground with which I have been familiar, and most of the topics are discussed at large in my Commentaries. Your views, however, on that branch of the subject are just and striking, as well as remarkably clear and sound.

" Take the volume together, I do not know where to look for its equal. The results of natural religion are strikingly displayed. The chapters on Virtue, and on Love to God, or Piety, are masterly. I never read a discussion more interesting or affecting, or one that set forth my own imperfections in a more impressive light. Such discussions affect me more than a thousand sermons, because the arguments are addressed so fairly and so rationally to the judgment and conscience of the reader.

" Permit me, my dear sir, once more to return you my

* Professor Chace's Commemorative Discourse.

grateful and humble thanks for your admirable work, and
to assure you of the high veneration and esteem of
Your friend and obedient servant,
JAMES KENT."

His early and attached friend, Rev. R. Anderson, D. D.,
secretary of the American Board, wrote as follows: —

"BOSTON, May 30, 1835.

"My dear Brother: . . . I desired to thank you in person for your invaluable work on moral science. How
exquisite your satisfaction must have been in rearing the
fabric of that noble science upon the foundation of the
prophets and apostles, Jesus Christ himself being the chief
corner-stone! Be assured, my dear brother, that you have
not lived in vain. I have not yet had time to commence
the reading of the volume in course, but I have examined
it carefully in those parts of the system which I deemed
vital, and in others which have, at present, a great practical importance in our community, such as slavery, war,
&c.; and the whole appears to me to be founded upon a
rock which cannot be moved. What strikes me very
forcibly is, the very obvious relations of the different parts
of your system to each other. This strengthens the edifice
exceedingly.

"The existence of these relations is, indeed, no new
thing; but nowhere, to my knowledge, have they been
rendered so obvious. This may be owing, in part, to the
conciseness of your statements, but is far more to be attributed to your full and hearty recognition of certain great
scriptural principles which lie at the foundation of morals.
My dear brother, I rejoice, I give thanks to God, that I
see nothing in you of that parleying with the world which
is so fatal in Paley. You are bold and uncompromising,
but not unreasonable, nor wanting in candor. I am not
sure that your work will be, at once, received with general favor, though it will be generally read; but I cannot
doubt that it will ultimately carry the day, and exert a
most auspicious influence, not only in the church, but on
the politics of our nation, and on the whole structure of
society. We needed a treatise on this subject which should
become authority, and this will become such. . . ."

Far more gratifying to the author than such testimonials was the evidence which was furnished, from time to time, until the close of his life, of the influence which, by means of this work, he had been permitted to exert in leading souls to Christ. This was a most welcome answer to his earnest prayers that his labors might be sanctified to the glory of God and the good of his fellow-men. A single fact which comes to our knowledge as these pages are preparing for the press is representative of many similar instances. A young lady of great intelligence, but destitute of all faith in religion as a personal reality, was a member of the State Normal School at ——, qualifying herself for usefulness as a teacher. While so employed, she studied Wayland's Moral Science as a part of the prescribed course. The teachings of this book removed her spirit of scepticism, and led her to place her reliance upon the work of the Redeemer. She is now one of the heroic band of laborers in the foreign missionary field.

The Moral Science has reached a circulation of ninety-five thousand copies, and an abridgment (prepared for the use of the younger class of pupils) a circulation of forty-two thousand. The work has also been republished in England and in Scotland.

In this connection the following letters from honored missionaries of the American Board will be read with interest: —

> "HONOLULU, SANDWICH ISLANDS,
> December 2, 1841.

"Dr. Wayland: The accompanying volume contains so much of the matter and form of your small work on moral science that it may be properly called a translation of it. A few new topics have been introduced, and the discussion in some cases modified by a variety of illustrations adapted to the people of these islands; but in the form and basis it is the same as your compend. I have thought that it would be gratifying to you to know this, and to receive a copy of the translation in the Hawaiian language. That it will be of great use in our schools,

and especially in our seminaries, there can be no doubt.
I am now going through it with a class of fifty adults, including the governor of the island of Oahu and his principal magistrates. The subject of conscience is entirely
new to them, and deeply interesting. They have no word
for it in their language, but they readily perceive that
there is such a faculty, and they are delighted with the
discovery.

"On all moral subjects their minds are yet very much
in the dark, and such a work as this has been long and
loudly called for. It is now adopted by the resident committee of the Tract Society here, and printed at their expense.

Very truly yours,

RICHARD ARMSTRONG."

"CONSTANTINOPLE, September 14, 1847.

"REV. F. WAYLAND, D. D., President of Brown University.

"My dear Sir: I have forwarded to the Missionary
House (care of Dr. Anderson) two copies of your Elements of Moral Science, translated into Armenian, which
I beg you to accept as a proof that the book is appreciated
here, and that you have become a co-laborer in the great
work of regenerating the East.

"The volume is admirably adapted to be useful among
the awakened and more intelligent class of Armenians,
and is read by many of them with a freshness of interest
resulting in part from their previous erroneous ideas of
moral science.

"I have sent a copy of your Elements of Political Economy to the secretary of the grand vizier, a gentleman well
versed in English, and I hope his master will order its
translation into Turkish or Armenian. Should he do so,
I shall send you a copy as soon as it is issued from the
press. I have very carefully revised the translation I now
send, and should the Political Economy be published here,
I shall endeavor to see that it comes out in such a form as
you would approve, although the prejudices and ignorance of the East may call for some changes or omissions.

With sentiments of high regard,

I am, my dear Sir,

Yours truly,

C. HAMLIN."

A similar version of the Moral Science was also made in the modern Greek language, by the missionaries of the Baptist Missionary Union, and we learn that a translation has appeared in the Nestorian language.

For an adequate explanation of the success of the text-books of Dr. Wayland, we must look not only to the motives by which he was governed, but to the spirit which animated his educational efforts. He kept constantly in view the importance of imparting to his pupils that kind of mental and moral culture which should prepare them to become Christian citizens. He relied on the Scriptures as revealing, with divine infallibility, the highest wisdom.

" He was a constant student of the Bible, and believed in its sufficiency for all human guidance. How often have we heard him say, as he would hold up his well-worn Greek Testament, ' All that a man need to know is to be found within the covers of this book ' ! and he never expected anything in which he was engaged to succeed, save as it was in accordance with the principles there unfolded." *

Dr. Wayland published his Elements of Political Economy in 1837. As the author informs his readers in the preface to this work, when " his attention was first directed to the science of political economy, he was struck with the simplicity of its principles, the extent of its generalization, and the readiness with which its facts seemed capable of being brought into natural and methodical arrangement."

He found, however, that " the works on this subject, in general use, while they presented its doctrines truly, yet did not present them in such order as would be most likely to render them serviceable either to the general reader or to the practical merchant." He aimed accordingly " to write a book which anybody who chose might understand." He therefore " labored to express the general principles in

---

* Professor Gammell's obituary notice.

the plainest manner possible, and to illustrate them by
cases with which every person is familiar." It was not
his purpose to prepare a learned and philosophical treatise
for the use of a few, but to bring the cardinal doctrines of
the science within the easy comprehension of the many.
He believed that the great truths of political economy
were simply the maxims of common life and every-day
experience in private life applied to the regulation of the
affairs of communities.

He sincerely regretted that the course of discussion
unavoidably led over ground which had frequently been
the arena of political controversy, but asserts that in all
such cases he had endeavored to state what seemed to him
to be the truth, without fear, favor, or affection. He was
conscious of no bias towards any party whatever. While
cherishing for those of his fellow-citizens who were engaged in political warfare every feeling of personal respect,
he entertained for party itself, whether political or ecclesiastical, the opinion which befitted him, " as an American,
a Christian, and a gentleman."

He once said, " The great study, at present, of every
thoughtful man is the social improvement of the human
race." This was, in his view, far more important than
the temporary success of any political party or any political
measure.

He entertained a high estimate of the educational as
well as the material benefits likely to flow from a generous
study of political economy. In writing to Rev. Dr. Anderson he expressed the opinion that scarcely anything
would be more calculated to arouse and stimulate the
minds of persons emerging from barbarism than the study
of the elementary principles of this science.

That this text-book was less popular than the Elements
of Moral Science, is undoubtedly to be attributed, in a
large measure to the cause to which we have just referred
— the inevitable discussion of subjects already involved in

partisan warfare. Prominent among these was the question of free trade and a protective tariff.

At the same time such were the fairness and candor which were brought to the consideration of every topic, so plain and perspicuous was the style, so simple and logical was the treatment, so familiar and attractive were the illustrations, and so elevated was the moral tone, that it speedily secured, and has ever since maintained, a popularity in our country which no text-book on this important subject by any American author has ever attained. The circulation of the larger treatise has reached the number of fifty thousand copies, and of the abridgment twelve thousand.*

In the spring of 1838, Dr. Wayland published a small volume, entitled "The Limitations of Human Responsibility." He thought that he perceived a strong tendency, more particularly among persons engaged in philanthropic and religious enterprises, to assume and to urge upon others, exaggerated views of the extent of man's responsibility for the ills that afflict his fellows. The result of this excessive estimate was, sometimes to produce a morbid sense of guilt for responsibilities not discharged, and sometimes to lead the persons who were oppressed by it, to feel themselves justified in resorting (if not indeed morally obliged to resort) to extreme and questionable measures, for the promotion of the ends which they sought to compass.

* "When we remember what multitudes of youths he instructed during the nearly thirty years of his presidency, and how his text-books have been scattered broadcast over the continent, and when we reflect how those principles of which he was so illustrious an expounder have been silently assimilated into the mental and moral structure of the nation, who can compute the number or the energy of those elemental forces of American society into which Dr. Wayland's thoughts and tuitions have been metamorphosed?"—*Rev. Geo. D. Boardman, D. D.*, in his remarks before the Pennsylvania Historical Society.

In the volume referred to, the design of which is sufficiently indicated by its title, he held the view that there
are limits to man's responsibility; that he is responsible
for results only up to the extent of his power over them;
that no man is responsible for evils which he cannot
prevent without transcending the means with which
Providence has endowed him; and without violating the
relations which he holds to his fellows, and the duties which
grow out of these relations.

After an exhibition of these principles, which few candid readers could fail to regard as just and timely, the
author considered, in the closing chapter, their bearing
upon American slavery. The question was not, as he
expressly stated, whether slavery was or was not right.
It was, what were our responsibilities and duties in regard
to slavery.

It is possible that, in his effort to be perfectly just, he
unconsciously conceded too much.

Rev. Dr. Cutting writes, —

" I once took the liberty to say to him that I thought
the work open to criticism at this point; that, written to
protest against a disposition to crowd men beyond the
limit of their duties, he had failed to bring them fully
up to that limit. After a moment's thoughtful consideration, he assented to the criticism as perhaps just."

Later events made it obvious either that he mistook the
temper of the southern leaders, or else that their spirit and
aims had so far changed as to place them in a totally
altered aspect to the northern people and to the Constitution.

Dr. Wayland never varied in his view of the essential
nature of slavery as an indefensible violation of personal
liberty. But there was a change in his view of its practical workings, and of the relation which the northern
people sustained towards it. For a long time the existence of slavery was deprecated by southern Christians

with apparent sincerity. They said, " We find ourselves encumbered with it, we see its evil, we desire as rapidly as possible to rid ourselves of it, and we beg our northern brethren not to embarrass us in this effort by untimely interference." Eloquent voices at the south urged emancipation, and there seemed good reason to hope that, acting upon the dictates of justice and of a wise public policy, the southern states would follow the example of those northern states that had eradicated the curse from within their borders. A wise, humane man, trusting in the professions of his southern brethren, might very reasonably think it proper to leave the evil undisturbed, to find the natural death towards which it seemed hastening.

When called on, in his Moral Science, to test slavery by the absolute standard of rectitude, he pronounced it at variance with the revealed will of God, disastrous in its effects upon the morals both of master and slave, and condemned by the principles of a sound political economy. And as time advanced, and as the practical character of slavery became more manifest, as the demand was made on its behalf, first for an equality of power in the government, then for predominance, and then for unquestioned and universal supremacy, still more when the slaveholding states, by their own act, freed the United States from all constitutional obligation in the matter, — he felt that his practical duty was largely changed.

" A man," says Macaulay, " who had held exactly the same opinion about the [French] revolution in 1789, in 1794, in 1804, in 1814, and in 1834 would have been either a divinely inspired prophet or an obstinate fool. Mackintosh was neither. He was simply a wise and good man, and the change which passed over his mind was a change which passed over the mind of almost every wise and good man in Europe." We may apply the same just principle to the views which a wise and good man might take of his duties towards slavery, as its aspects varied with the lapse of years.

But it is not needful to go back so far as the days of
Mackintosh for illustrations of the principle.   The Abraham Lincoln of 1861 was the Abraham Lincoln of 1863 ;
nor did the Emancipation Proclamation condemn the first
Inaugural Address.

To his sister : —

"January 31, 1859.

" . . . However, on all these questions you seem to me
to devolve upon yourself too great a responsibility.   Have
you read a work on that subject by your much abused but
most meek and patient brother?   If you have not, you
had better do so at once, as it may enlighten you on these
points.

" We have a duty to perform where we are responsible ;
but that being done, our responsibility terminates.   That
being ended, nothing is to be gained by anxiety or self-
reproach.   I think you should strive against these things.
They wear out your nerves for no purpose ; or rather they
unfit you for other occupations.   I know it is difficult to
control ourselves in such cases, but it is a duty."

On the 1st of August, 1838, Dr. Wayland was married
to Mrs. H. S. Sage, of Boston.   The fact that she yet sur-
vives, and a regard for her known wishes, will prevent the
biographers from speaking in such terms as would be
most gratifying to their feelings, as well as true to their
childish memories of the joy which her graceful and loving presence brought to that little household.   But they
cannot, in justice to the husband whose life she made so
happy, refrain from saying that he was ever grateful to
the "Giver of every good and perfect gift" for the light
which once more illumined his long desolate home, and
for the congenial companionship which gladdened the remaining period of his earthly experience.

The year 1839 is memorable in the annals of Brown
University.   The friends of the college had for a considerable time been of the opinion that the interests of
learning demanded additional facilities in important departments of education.   Unsuccessful efforts had been

made to procure the requisite funds, and the improvements so much desired seemed beyond the reach of the institution. At this critical moment the following letter was received by the treasurer : —

"In common with a number of the friends of Brown University, I desire the erection of a suitable mansion-house for the president, and likewise of another college edifice for the accommodation of the departments of natural philosophy, chemistry, mineralogy, and natural history. As it is highly important that these buildings, so necessary to the welfare of the institution, should be erected without delay, I hereby tender to the acceptance of the corporation two lots of land as a site for the president's house, and the lot of land called the Hopkins estate, on George Street, as a site for the college edifice ; and I hereby pledge myself for the sum of ten thousand dollars, viz., seven thousand dollars for the president's house, and three thousand dollars towards the erection of the college edifice, the suitable improvements of the adjacent grounds, and the increase of the permanent means of instruction in the departments of chemistry, mineralogy, &c., provided an equal amount be subscribed by the friends of the university before the first of May next.

"I am, with affectionate regards and great personal respect for all the friends and patrons of the university,

Respectfully,

NICHOLAS BROWN."

The response to this generous offer was prompt and satisfactory. Within the indicated time a sum amounting to more than twenty thousand dollars was subscribed, and the success of this most important movement was secured. A suitable building devoted to the pursuit of the natural sciences was speedily erected. In the summer of 1840 Dr. Wayland removed to what has since been known as the "President's House."

CHAPTER XVIII.

HIS HOME. — HIS SOCIAL LIFE. — CONVERSATIONAL
POWERS. — VARIED INFORMATION. — KINDNESS OF
HEART. — PARTISAN VIOLENCE DEPRECATED. — WEST
POINT. — POLITICAL FORECAST. — PUBLIC HOLIDAYS.
— FAMILY AFFLICTION. — CONSCIENTIOUS EXPENDI-
TURE. — LETTERS TO THE YOUNG. — MISCELLANEOUS
CORRESPONDENCE.

DR. WAYLAND was now in the full maturity of his
powers. His acknowledged eminence as an educator, the popularity of his text-books, his successful labors
as " a Christian philosopher, displaying more love for the
truth than for mere symbols and creeds, more love for the
world than for his country, and more devotion to the
church than to any sect," and his reputation as a wise
counsellor in all matters affecting the temporal or spiritual
interests of his fellow-men, had placed him in the front
rank of American citizens. In the city of Providence, and
in the State of Rhode Island, his name, associated with every
public enterprise, whether designed to extend the benefits
of education, or to relieve the sufferings of the poor, or to
increase the facilities for religious instruction, had become
familiar as a household word. Meanwhile, although there
had been no diminution in the number or importance of
his daily duties, yet he had made himself so completely
master of the studies which he was called upon to teach,
and, with the efficient aid of a Faculty of instruction in
full sympathy with his views, and sharing his professional
enthusiasm, had brought the college into a condition of

such correct discipline, that he had probably more leisure at his command than at any previous or subsequent period.

Enjoying these welcome results of many well-spent years, once more happy in his home life, and provided by the liberality of the friends of the university with a residence worthy of the office which he held, he could indulge, in a manner most congenial to his tastes, his love of social intercourse. Those who knew Dr. Wayland only in his official relations, or as a casual acquaintance, saw but one phase of his character. It was reserved for those who were admitted to his closer companionship to learn, that beneath that grave and thoughtful exterior there lay concealed a fund of humor, an inexhaustible store of interesting and entertaining anecdote, and an extent and variety of useful information, which made his conversation as delightful as it was instructive. He had been a careful student of human nature, and his estimate and analysis of character were original and striking. He abounded in quaint expressions, usually embodying some general principle in such apt, idiomatic language as not to be easily forgotten. For the singular shrewdness of observation, and sharp insight into the motives of human conduct, embalmed in so many popular maxims peculiar to our Yankee dialect, he had an especial fondness, and often used these homely proverbs of the people with great effect. We should be glad to give some examples of these features of his conversation; but deprived of the aroma of the occasion which called them forth, and wanting the expression of countenance which characterized his mirthful moods, they would lose their chief attraction, and convey but too feebly the lively interest which they imparted to his unstudied utterances.

It resulted from the simplicity of his character that he never talked for effect. He shrank with instinctive modesty from anything like a display of learning. He was

as willing to receive as to communicate information. His
natural kindness of heart and his love of knowledge made
it impossible for him to fall into the habit — common with
good talkers — of social despotism. He delighted to gain
important and interesting facts from those whose occupations were far removed from the natural direction of his
own studies, and he had singular skill in selecting subjects
with which they were familiar. " He held dialogues with
common men, farmers and mechanics, by the way, wherever he met them, with as much ease and good understanding as if he had been of every man's guild and
society all his life." *

Writing to his son, then a boy, he says, —

" Neglect no opportunities of gaining useful information while visiting ——. Mr. D. is a great teacher in the
art of fishing, the management of a boat, &c. These are
worth learning thoroughly, and I advise you to acquire all
the knowledge you can respecting them. The art of becoming familiar with a practical matter is of inestimable
importance."

A distinguished officer in the United States navy, after
spending some hours with Dr. Wayland, remarked to a
friend, —

" I called on the doctor, expecting to be greatly improved by an interview with a man of his reputed learning ; but he made me do all the talking. He squeezed me
like a sponge."

The writer remembers that Dr. Wayland once directed
his attention to the following extract from the " Fortunes
of Nigel," as containing much practical wisdom : —

" Experience and knowledge of the world soon teach
every sensible and acute person the important lesson, that
information and increase of knowledge are to be derived
from the conversation of every individual with whom he
is thrown into a natural train of communication.

" For ourselves, we can assure the reader, — and per-

* Rev. Dr. Bartol's Discourse.

haps, if we have ever been able to afford him amusement, it is owing in a great degree to this cause, — that we never found ourselves in company with the stupidest of all companions in a post-chaise, or with the most arrant cumbercorner that ever occupied a place in a mail-coach, without finding that, in the course of our conversation with him, we had some ideas suggested to us, either grave or gay, or some information communicated in the course of the journey, which we should have regretted not to have learned, and which we should be sorry to have immediately forgotten."

One of the president's pupils says, — *

" On one occasion, after having spent several weeks in the most intimate daily intercourse with an accomplished naval officer, I called to see Dr. Wayland. Thinking to surprise him with my knowledge of what belonged to naval science, I contrived to introduce this subject, and discoursed upon it at some length, and, as I flattered myself, with some learning I soon discovered, however, that he knew vastly more about it than I did ; and I retired in confusion, carrying with me two books which he had recommended me to read — Collingwood's Despatches, and Letters to his Daughter."

We are indebted to the same gentleman for the following reminiscence : —

" In the early part of the recent rebellion, one of my friends, who had been for a few years captain of a first-class merchant vessel, was anxious to secure some appointment from the naval department, in which his seamanship might be of service to his country. I introduced him to Dr. Wayland, thinking that a recommendation from such a source would materially assist my friend in his patriotic purpose, and then, after some words of explanation, retired, leaving them in earnest conversation. When I next saw this aspirant for naval promotion, he said, ' What sort of a man is Dr. Wayland? I supposed he was only a clergyman ; but I never passed so severe and searching an examination about everything that be-

---

* E. H. Hazard, Esq., of Providence, R. I.

longs to my profession as a sailor. He seems to know everything about a ship.' "

It was significant of the practical tendency of his mind that he was careful to surround himself with the best maps and atlases which could be procured. His accurate knowledge of the geography, not only of the United States, but of foreign countries, was often a matter of surprise to those who were most familiar with his habits of study. When he first heard of the commencement of the Crimean war, he was able to predict, with singular correctness, what would be the important strategical points to be occupied by the allied armies. He was very fond of studying, even to the minutest details, the military operations of modern history. Profoundly impressed with the genius of Napoleon, he had followed him through all his campaigns with the deepest interest, and, aided by such maps and diagrams as served to assist him in these investigations, had acquired a knowledge of the career of the great emperor possessed by few men not professionally interested in the art of war. He was hardly less familiar with the campaigns of Wellington, Sir William Napier, Frederick the Great, and the Duke of Marlborough.

He read English history with never-failing delight. When a Sophomore in Union College, he devoted all the leisure hours of the long vacation to a most careful and critical reading of Hume's History, taking copious notes of whatever he thought worthy of future reference. In after life he frequently referred to the benefit which he had derived from the studies of those weeks, both in laying a foundation for future historical researches, and in cultivating and confirming the habit of serious reflection. Nor did he confine himself to those sources of information which commonly supply all the knowledge needed by the casual student of history. In connection with those eventful epochs in the annals of our mother country, when great constitutional principles were settled, deciding not only the destinies of the British empire, but most materially influencing the condition of the whole human race, he read the biographies of the master spirits through whose agency these all-important results were accomplished. He made himself familiar with the history of the leading families in England. Perhaps no secular book in his library was more frequently consulted than " Burke's Peerage." One who knew him well writes, " When any question relating to ancient lineage was the subject of conversation, he was able at once to supply any broken, or rather forgotten link in the pedigree, and assign to each the proper place in English history." At the same time, we presume it is hardly necessary to observe that there was nothing aristocratic in the temper of his mind or in the direction of his tastes. Indeed, his prime favorite was Cromwell. He had made the character and career, military, administrative, and diplomatic, of the Protector, an especial study. As one of his friends has said, " Long before Carlyle's famous work on Cromwell came out, Dr. Wayland knew all about it."

His kindness of heart was nowhere more conspicuous than in his social intercourse. He could be witty, and was often ironical. But his wit never gave offence, and his irony was always good-natured. He could not bear to wound the feelings of others. It was a matter of conscience as well as of inclination with him to be charitable in his judgments. Though severe in his condemnation of social evils and public wrongs, he was slow to censure the motives of individuals. His anecdotes or observations about the absent were never in an unfriendly spirit. To hear another spoken of harshly gave him pain. When he detected any tendency to fault-finding, he would say, with a pleasant smile, " Let us talk of things rather than of persons," and turn the conversation into another channel. He once wrote to a young friend, —

" Cultivate kindness of feeling. When we become faultless ourselves, we may learn, if we please, to speak harshly of the infirmities of others."

To the same : —

" He who is displeased with everybody and everything, gives the best evidence that his own temper is defective, and that he is a bad associate."

To one who proposed to criticise with some severity a recently published book of travels, —

" I do not think of Mr. ——'s book as you do. It is well enough, and does not call for any castigation. It is gossiping and very good-natured. If you cannot speak kindly of it, you had better let it alone."

He had an especial dislike for controversy conducted in a spirit of recrimination and unfriendly criticism. He once said, " My instinct teaches me always to avoid a quarrel." Where he differed in opinion from another, he was content to state briefly and clearly the grounds of his own belief, and his objections to the principles of his opponent. While he felt that he owed so much as this to the cause of truth, he had no desire to press a discussion beyond the bounds of courtesy and good feeling. His letters to Dr. Fuller furnish an excellent illustration of this feature of his character.

Cherishing an ardent love for his country, proud of her free institutions, and intensely republican in all his feelings, he was profoundly grieved by the tone of acrimony and vindictive bitterness so common in our political discussions, and ever sought — both by personal appeal and in his correspondence — to assuage the virulence of partisan warfare.

Writing to a friend connected with the press, he says, —

" I hope you will adhere to your resolution to leave the war of mere party politics, and devote more time and space to European affairs and general questions of statesmanship. These will transcend in interest and importance

all petty, local issues. Lead in this, and you will be the
leader in all."

During the fierce excitement in New York on the question of slavery, culminating in the " abolition riots" of
1834, he wrote to one of his intimate friends — a prominent editor in that city, who had been especially earnest in
advocating the aims and objects of the Colonization Society, and had vehemently denounced the abolitionists, —

"Your duty at the present time must be very trying.
Let me urge upon you a word of advice.

" 1. Decide in your own mind what your precise situation and responsibility are. You are not responsible for
what you cannot help. You cannot prevent the proceedings of the general government. Your most important
office is to state the facts as they exist. You are not under
obligation to excite the people. We have excitement
enough, and the very appearance of it renders men sus-
picious of the truth of facts. This is the case at present.
The press has been so generally devoted to party, that
now the truth is not believed, and has lost its power. If
you talk of Caligula and Nero, you will not be believed.
The facts are stronger without the comparison.

" 2. Strive to keep your feelings from being embittered.
Unless you do this, you will be miserable. Do your duty,
and leave the result with God. You can be happy in no
other way.

" 3. I pray you, do not call ' the people' by hard names.
Do not say they are ' fools,' and ' knaves,' and ' idiots.'
If you speak of men in this way, who will believe you?
We are all fellow-citizens. Let us treat each other as
such. Who are you and I but the people? We should
not like to be called idiots by those a little higher than
ourselves.

" 4. Abandon partisan and personal feeling. If one
who has hitherto differed from you now agrees with you,
do not chide him for his change of opinion and want of
consistency, for the sake of showing that you have always
been right. Rather rejoice that he is at last convinced.
Welcome him as a fellow-laborer, and commend his candor. We should not labor for party, but for truth.

" 5. Seek to be a peace-maker. The country is very much agitated. The passions of men are aroused, and they have not the fear of God before their eyes. The day of our retribution seems at hand. There will be great pecuniary pressure, much distress, and perhaps division. Let us strive to allay party violence and to calm the passions of men."

A little later he writes again to the same, —

" I think you mistake your position. Because you are the conductor of a public journal, you greatly err if you suppose the community care a rush about your private quarrels. Indeed, why need you get into a quarrel? You are not called upon to be a gladiator, or a Don Quixote, to run about the city attacking every one who speaks against the Colonization Society. Yours is a public journal, for the statement of facts, and for general discussion ; and its design is perverted when you make it the medium for the display of your private feelings and your personal grievances.

" Besides, you are a disciple of Christ. By this shall all men know that ye are my disciples, if ye love one another. But you may say, If I am attacked I must defend myself. I have not so learned Christ. When he was reviled, he reviled not again. Paul said, ' I will spend and be spent for you, though the more abundantly I love you, the less I be loved.' We must learn meekness, and patience, and forbearance in the school of Christ.

" If you continue in this course, I fear that you will lose all comfort in prayer, and all evidence of religion — that you will sink into gloom, and perhaps go back into the world. I know that the Spirit of God will not shed abroad his love in the bosom of one who is so ready for contention. He is a peaceful Spirit, and resides only with those who bear even injuries with meekness and in silence.

" You will perhaps reply, My situation is peculiar, and these rules do not apply to it. Is it so? If it be a situation to which the rules of Christ do not apply, then a Christian cannot hold it. You must either give up Christ or the situation. But in all this there is a sad mistake. There is too strong a desire for the glorification of self. Leave self out of the question, and the difficulty will be greatly diminished. . . . In a word, unless you love the cause of Christ better than the Colonization Society, you will have only such comfort as the Colonization Society can give you.

" I beg you to forgive my plainness of speech. I love you, and desire to see you a happy, peaceful Christian. For this reason I have written. May God grant you his grace and wisdom."

To the same, in reference to the preceding letter : —

" . . . I wrote from my own experience, and this may not correspond with that of others ; but I have found that if I allow myself to be much interested in worldly matters, my enjoyment of religion is gone, and my consciousness of the presence of God departs. This is peculiarly the case when my feelings are awakened to anything like controversy. It was my earnest desire for your growth in grace that led me to write as I did. I am feebly and most imperfectly attempting to live more religiously than heretofore, and I felt deeply anything which I thought might be injurious to your soul. Pardon any improper warmth or harshness of expression, and if any part of my advice was good, try and make use of it."

In the summer of 1837, Dr. Wayland was appointed a member of the Board of Visitors for the annual examination at West Point.

From this place he writes as follows to Colonel Stone : —

"June 8, 1837.

" . . . The members of the Board of Visitors are mostly strangers to me, and I believe there are not many with whom you are acquainted. Yet the scenery is as beautiful as ever, and Cozzen's hotel is, as usual, attractive to *bons vivants*. I have a room with one of the professors while I am engaged in the study of the art of war. I have not yet received a military appointment ; but, as I learn that I am getting into favor with the Jackson Van Buren patriots, there is no knowing what may happen. In case I should receive anything valuable, I shall, of course, remember you. Of the news of the day I know nothing. Should anything important from Europe transpire, I wish you would be good enough to send me a paper. The ordinary party intelligence I do not care about. I forwarded to you some sermons recently, but presume that you have not yet had time to read them. They are intended to moderate the violence of party feeling. I am sure that this will please you.

" However, the fashion of this world passeth away ; all these vehement desires, and loves, and hatreds will very soon be silent in death. Let us look forward to something better and more valuable than this world can give, and let us seek to quiet the peevish restlessness of the present existence by drinking at the fountain of eternal life."

That Dr. Wayland was not indifferent to the political questions which, from time to time, agitated the country, and that his political predictions, carefully considered and temperately expressed, were confirmed by future events, will appear from the following letter to a friend, written immediately after the presidential election of 1852 : —

" I had intended to write to you before the election, and give you my opinion, but could not command the time. I am not surprised at the election of Mr. Pierce, but I am surprised at the greatness of his majority. I gave the Whig leaders more credit for forethought and common sense than they deserved. They surrendered principle, and tried availability. They have lost election, principle, honor, and all. I consider that there is now no Whig party. They have no principles to which they adhere, and profess none of any power in opposition to the Democrats. They cannot make another stand. The next move will be a division of the Democrats ; and this will again give an opportunity for choice. I think you may safely look upon the Whig party as defunct. You will have, therefore, an opportunity to leave all parties, or to select from those that will hereafter be formed which one you will join. For my own part, I prefer to be of no party. If I were in your place, I should deliberate long before making a choice. When Jefferson was elected, Hamilton advised the Federalists to disband, and unite with the best part of the Democrats. They did not follow his advice, but died by inches, until the very name became a word of reproach."

To the same, November, 1854 : —

" You will learn, before long, that politicians are generally among the stupidest and most mole-sighted of men. It must be so, for they are preëminently selfish. Because, like the mole, they burrow under ground, they suppose that, of course, they go right; which is no more true of under-ground than of over-ground movements. You may remember my regret that certain prominent politicians, instead of seizing upon the great principles which were agitating the community, were determined to keep up the Whig party, or, in other words, to cling to an organization of which the only advantage was, that it benefited a few leaders, and kept the rest at work for them. The result has been the same in both parties. The chains are broken, and in New York the administration candidate is nowhere. You are very fortunate in being out of the whole affair. You will now, I trust, imitate the example of the man, somewhere in the northern part of New York, who succeeded very well by minding his own business."

Dr. Wayland's political sympathies were always with that party which, for the time being, sought to elevate humanity, and to promote the cause of equal rights.

He was, however, too wise to bind himself to follow the dictates of any party organization. To quote his own words, —

" I do not wish to be connected with politics. Indeed, I dare not commit myself with politicians. No one knows what they will be next year by what they are this year."

He could never give to party " what was meant for mankind."

" He was of the people ; every drop of his blood was in fellowship with the mass of mankind. He was democratic to the core — in his manners, habits, and thoughts. He never talked *down* to the community, or to any audience. He knew nothing of better blood, but only of the *one* blood. By his instincts he hated, as by his vows he opposed, all tyranny and caste. He was an advocate of freedom and free trade. It was this wide communion with humanity which moved him to open collegiate degrees, not only to the learned professions, but also to the useful arts." *

Dr. Wayland's views about society were characterized by the utmost simplicity. Few things gave him greater pleasure than the informal intercourse of congenial companions; but late hours, costly entertainments, or any form of social dissipation, had no attraction for him. To this day many of his surviving friends are fond of recalling the pleasant memories of evenings spent in his society. They delight to dwell upon the evident gratification with which he welcomed them to his home, the unaffected interest which he exhibited in everything that concerned their welfare, his playfulness of manner, the contagion of his hearty laugh, his shrewd but kindly comments on men and manners, and the spirit of Christian courtesy which pervaded and sanctified these memorable interviews.

At this period of his life, somewhat relieved, as we have seen, from the engrossing occupations of former years, he seemed to recognize not only the advantage to himself of occasional relaxation, but our national need of regularly recurring holidays.

He writes to his friend, Rev. Dr. Hoby, of Birmingham, England, —

"December 25, 1837.

"My dear Brother: When I last wrote to you, I thought it not improbable that at this time I should be joining in the rejoicings which, from time immemorial, have gladdened the homes of England on this festive occasion. I have, by the by, a great love for these national, universal merry-makings. They tend to abate the ferocity of party strife. They blend together the different classes of society. They attach children to their parents and to each other. They bind together the various collateral branches of kindred. They allow every one to throw off the load of care which more or less presses upon every bosom; and the

* Discourse of Rev. Dr. Bartol.

man goes forth with a somewhat lighter heart to meet the exigencies of his peculiar calling. Such I suppose to be the effect of these days with you. We in this country pay too little attention to them. We toil, and fight, and talk politics, and make money, to the end of the chapter. I should very much like to spend Christmas holidays in Old England."

His fondness for family meetings seemed to increase with his advancing years. As, one by one, the playmates of his boyhood passed into the " silent world," he clung more closely to those of his relatives who survived.

He writes to his sister, September, 1837, —

" I am very thankful that we were permitted to meet together so pleasantly this summer. Such little family gatherings are good and lovely while they last; they are delightful in retrospect; and the results which they leave on the spirits are most cheering and refreshing. They brighten the chain of affection, and rivet its links the closer. We understand one another better, and sympathize with far greater freshness in each other's joys and sorrows. Surely whatever has this effect is among the best as well as pleasantest medicines to the soul."

With his serious estimate of life, and testing all questions involving the expenditnre of money by the severe standard of conscientious duty, he habitually practised self-denial as to all social indulgences, which did not take the form of healthful relaxation, or furnish the means of mental quickening. In this spirit he writes to a friend, August 13, 1840, —

" Mr. Audubon is here, and I have screwed my ornithological courage up to the sticking-point of one hundred dollars. I had great misgivings as to the matter of duty. One hundred dollars is a considerable talent, and I doubted whether I had a right thus to appropriate it. However, I made out a view of the case that satisfied me. It seemed to me that so complete and beautiful an exhibition of this portion of the works of God ought to be procured, and on this ground I thought I was justified in purchasing the work. I am much pleased with Audubon's moral temper.

He seems habitually to refer what he sees to the wisdom and goodness of God. I think he would hardly agree with the notion of our friend B., that creation is no proof of the being of a Creator. Talking to him of animals, I said, 'The buffalo is certainly very stupid.' 'Stupid!' said he; 'man is the only stupid animal I ever saw.' It is delightful to see such enthusiasm in any profession. Would that we could imitate him in our own pursuits."

We cannot remember another instance in which Dr. Wayland made a costly addition to his library not called for in the prosecution of his chosen studies. His was emphatically a working library. Perhaps a score of volumes would cover all it contained in the departments of fiction and light literature. In addition to books religious and devotional, comprising a large proportion of the whole, there was a considerable collection of standard biographies, works on English and American history, books of travel, scientific treatises, dictionaries, and works of reference. Nothing was for show, all for use. The library correctly indicated the man and the bias of his mind. It should be added that the books which bore the marks of most frequent perusal were his Greek Testament, Baxter's Saints' Rest, Wilson's Sacra Privata, and Leighton's Commentaries.

The interest which Dr. Wayland never ceased to manifest in the mental and moral development of his young acquaintances, his unwearied efforts to give a right direction to their expanding intellects, and his anxious concern for their spiritual welfare, are deserving of especial mention.

To a lad at school, the son of one of his dearest friends, he writes, —

"You ask me about self-government. It is a very proper question. I wish I had more time to write about it. I will, however, say a few words in reply. You must have observed that when a man or boy is about to perform any action involving character, there are two sorts of impulses operating upon him, one urging one way and the other another way. Suppose a boy saw some apples in a neigh-

bor's field. Appetite would say, 'They are good; help
yourself.' Conscience would say, 'No; it is wrong.'
Suppose you had an opportunity to get an advantage over
a comrade by a mean trick. Selfishness would say, 'Do
it; look out for yourself.' Conscience and nobleness of
soul would say, 'Be above doing a mean thing for any
advantage.' Suppose you were tempted to play truant in
violation of the rules of your teacher; the love of pleasure
would say, 'Go; no one will know it.' Conscience would
say, 'I would not do wrong, although nobody knew it.'
Self-government consists in accustoming ourselves to obey
these higher and nobler impulses of our soul, rather than
these lower and meaner impulses of our body. This is
the nature of the thing. How to do it, I will tell you
when I write again. . . ."

To the same: —

"In my last letter I wrote to you about self-government,
and what it was. It consists in subjecting our conduct to
some rule, and accustoming ourselves to obey a higher,
rather than a lower propensity. For instance, idleness is
a low and mean propensity; industry is respectable and
honorable. We exercise self-government when we act
industriously, in opposition to the strongest impulses of
sloth. To illustrate: If you were tempted to lie in bed
when you ought to be up, it would be an act of self-
government to start out of bed, although the cold was as
biting as Jack Frost could make it. So in the case of
learning a lesson, or of any other duty. So, if you were
tantalized by another boy, passion would urge you to
scold, or quarrel, or fight, or return evil for evil. It
would be an act of self-government to restrain your anger,
and keep perfectly mild and good-natured.

"But you naturally ask, 'How shall I acquire this desirable habit?' I do not know that I can tell you; but I
will do the best I can. In the first place, then, you must
be thoroughly in earnest about it, and really desire to succeed. You know it is of no use to give a man medicine
unless he is willing to take it. If you are then seriously
desirous of acquiring a habit of self-government, you must
resolve, in general, that you will always act from conscience and reason; and, in particular, resolve against
any actual errors into which you may have fallen. It is

important to guard against passion on the one hand, and against procrastination on the other. When you are in danger of yielding to laziness, resist it on the instant. When your passions begin to be excited, either calm them immediately, or go away from temptation. In all cases you must strive to do right.

"But, in the next place, if you have done wrong, always go and confess it. This is one of the best ways to gain self-government. A boy will soon break off from wrong if he will form the habit of apologizing for every wrong action. No matter whom you have injured, young or old, I would always apologize when I had erred.

"And lastly, we must seek divine assistance. In the morning, ask yourself, 'Wherein am I likely to fail?' and pray God to keep you from failing. In the evening, recall your wrong doing; be penitent, and resolve to do so no more. Do you not think that if any boy would act thus, he would learn self-government? Well, then, try it, and see how it answers for yourself."

To the same: —

". . . You wish me to tell you something about character. Character is from χαράσσω — which means, I scratch, or make marks, as an engraver does. It is what is perfectly wrought into a man. A man's character is his principles, his habits, his nature. Reputation is, as you say, from *reputo*, and means what our fellow-men think of us. The first is by far the most important. Suppose you were going to make marks upon a piece of wax; would you do it when it was soft, or when it had become hard? How could you seal a letter with hard, cold wax? You will say, of course, we must do it when it is soft and yielding. What should we think of a man who would not put his seal on the wax when it was soft, but determined to wait until it was cold? You would call him a stupid person. Now, apply this opinion to ourselves. When should we be more careful to form character — when we are young, or when we are old? Tell me what you think of this when you write again."

To the same: —

"Let me urge upon you ever to set before yourself the highest standard of character, and aim to reach it. Be not satisfied with the notion that you are as good as this or that boy, but say to yourself, ' I will try to emulate the character of the greatest and the best of men.' This will give you something to strive for. It will, moreover, make you humble, and this very striving will tend to make you good and great. Had Washington desired to be nothing more than those around him, he would have lived and died a plain Virginia farmer. Begin, then, at once. Resolve that you will do everything well. Spare no pains or effort, and by thus aiming at excellence you will develop and improve whatever is good in your character, while you will diminish whatever is bad.

" Now, in order to accomplish this, you need to exercise self-government. This is only to be gained by practice. For instance, your appetite frequently enslaves you. Begin at the table. Select that article of food of which you are most fond, and abstain from it for a week. You will be surprised to observe how much power of self-control this will give you. You are indisposed to mathematics. Take half an hour, or whatever time is necessary, every day, and study mathematics, hard or easy, and select the hard in preference. Never leave a proposition, whether it requires a longer or shorter time, until you have mastered it. You will thus gain confidence in yourself. An army that is always beaten can be beaten without effort; while one that has acquired the habit of victory is invincible. Thus is it with mind. If we acquire the habit of success by resolute effort, we can rely with confidence on our ability. You remember what Virgil says — ' *Possunt, quia posse videntur.*"

To the same : —

" It is of great consequence to our moral life to spend our Sabbaths well. I hope you have begun aright. I would have a fixed plan for the day ; a time for rising, for reading, meditation, self-examination, and prayer, as well as for public worship. I would never allow myself to read secular books, or to do any secular business whatever. I would be, so far as possible, alone. No one can estimate the value of a well-spent Sabbath as a means of moral culture. It arrests the course of worldliness, brings us near to God and to ourselves, and strengthens us in all good resolutions. . . .

"You ask me about Miller's doctrines. I have not read anything he has written. It can make but little difference to you or me when the end of the world comes, if we are prepared for it. Death, which is the end of the world to us, may come, as we know, at any moment. To be in readiness for this event is all that need concern us.

"... I do not know precisely the difference between biography and memoir. It may be correct to say that biography is simply a life of the person. A cat or a dog may have a biography. Memoir combines with the life, important transactions in which the subject took a part. You would feel that a memoir of a cat would be ludicrous. This I suppose to be about the distinction."

To a young relative on his birthday: —

"... Another year upon earth! How solemn the thought! I suppose, throughout the universe, there is not a world in which time is so inestimably valuable. Ours is a world in which God became incarnate to save us from the most awful destruction, and to raise us to a glory like his own; in which he offers to every one of us this infinite mercy; in which his Spirit is everywhere present, urging us to accept of his freely-offered pardon, — and all this limited to the few and uncertain moments of this present life. We lie down to sleep. We may awake glorified spirits, or souls lost forever. We commence a sentence; before it is ended we may have completed our probation. And yet God waits. His compassion is boundless, even while we are rejecting his infinite mercy. He gives us days, weeks, months, and years in which to secure our eternal salvation.

"You are commencing another year. Shall it be like the one just closed? What have all your labors amounted to in comparison with securing the salvation of your soul? Will you spend the year before you in pursuing objects which, considered in the light of eternal truth, are all vanity? Do not rely upon doing certain things, in the hope that a change will come over you gradually. Has this plan succeeded up to the present time? If not, what reason is there to suppose that it ever will? Agree with thine adversary quickly. Now is the accepted time. The blessed Savior waits. O, let him not wait in vain.

"Do not think this advice obtrusive. With my sincere interest in your temporal and eternal welfare, I could not suffer this opportunity to pass without seeking to impress upon your mind these important truths."

To a young friend about to travel in Europe: —

". . . As I shall not probably see you before you go abroad, I shall try to think of a few of the things which I wish to say before you leave. I shall begin and go on at random, stopping when recollection, or time, or paper is exhausted.

"Take care, in the first place, of your soul. The fact is, whether you think of it or not, that the issue of this whole concern is in the hands of God. He will give you all the success you enjoy, and inflict every chastisement you suffer. He will introduce you to every acquaintance, prepare the way for every expedition, and be the Author of whatever improvement you make from every occurrence. He will shield you, if you are shielded, from every temptation, and cause you to grow, if you do grow, in virtue where most men fail. He therefore should be your daily confidant; look to him not only when you are in trying emergencies, but before you enter upon them; and as you never know when this will happen, look to him habitually. Strive ever to maintain a devout spirit; take time for it, and be resolute about it; and if you find yourself growing thoughtless, take a day for this alone, putting aside every other business, and make it your sole concern to recall your thoughts and get your heart right.

"Make up your mind on the moral questions which will probably come before you, and on the courses of conduct likely to be matters of moral trial. Hold firmly to your resolutions, whatever may oppose. For instance, you believe in the Sabbath; you will go where it is a day of pleasure. Keep it as you believe it ought to be kept, though you are alone and lose ever so much by keeping it. God will abundantly reward you, and you may be sure that nothing you may gain will be sufficient to compensate you for displeasing him.

"In observing, beware of a rustic or puerile curiosity to see the shows or lions. You cannot see everything. Select, therefore, what is most worthy your attention, and, though it may cost most money and most labor, be willing to undergo labor and pains to do your work well. Therefore be careful to cultivate, as far as possible, physical hardihood. This will give you better health, a higher zest in seeing, and will increase your total amount of conscious existence.

" Claim no precedence, but take just the place that is given to you, and make no fuss about it. Louis XIV. wished to ascertain whether the Earl of Stair was, as he was reputed to be, the most polite gentleman in Europe. He therefore invited him to ride in his carriage, and when they came to it, the king asked him to get in first. The earl bowed most respectfully, and obeyed. The king said that any other man would have stood bowing, and scraping, and refusing to enter for a quarter of an hour.

" Every country has its peculiarities, and its disagreeable ones; we Yankees have our share, as the world reports. I would observe particularly those which English writers remark respecting us, and be careful to avoid them; not at all because I am ashamed of my nation; but the best manners are of no country; they are the manners which belong to all well-bred men; they are the manners collected from what is good in every country, with what is peculiar thrown away.

" Have your objects as much as possible marked out before you, or else you will be looking for a needle in a haystack. Do not attempt everything; but find out what is most desirable, and do that well. Get facts, and be sure that they are facts, not guesses, blunders, and mistakes. Certain knowledge alone is worth having, for it is the only knowledge that in a year any one will care a fig about remembering.

" Write down names, dates, and everything that you want to remember. Never trust to your memory; always treacherous, it will, in travelling, be doubly so. *Quod scriptum manet.*

" September 18.

" I had filled the preceding sheet before your letter arrived. I am glad that you are going in such spirits, and that you have so agreeable company. All, thus far, seems well. You feel like a young man, feeding your hopes on your imagination, and rejoicing in happiness which you will never realize, and expecting bliss from

sources which will tire, rather than satisfy you. But still
go on. Keep yourself as cool as you can, and try to be
useful, or at least to prepare yourself for being so. I
should like to be with you, and almost wish I was going;
but it is now too late.

To the same : —

" Some time has elapsed since I received your letter ;
and where to imagine you at present, I know not. I
trust, however, that wherever you are, you gain knowledge, improve in adroitness of mind by intercourse with
the world, see more of its vanity and littleness, and thus,
by becoming better acquainted with it, become better prepared to leave it.

" Before I proceed to things in general, I will answer
your letter. You ask me if a copy of Hall's works, hand-
somely bound, is what I would buy, were I there. I reply,
no — not for myself. My circumstances do not allow of
literary luxury. But it is not so with you. You have
the opportunity and the means of laying the foundation
of a good library. Whatever you can afford to expend,
you had better expend in this manner. Get good and
handsome books, so as to furnish a small room for your
personal and private reading. By doing this you will
give a tinge to the whole character of your life, and at
least once a day you will be reminded that there is something valuable in the world besides invoices, notes of
hand, orders, and balance-sheets. Get all the British
classics in suitable style — Milton, Cowper, Johnson,
Goldsmith, Shakspeare, Burke, Scott, &c. Buy books in
your own calling — on political economy, statistics,
money, exchange, &c., and every thing you can find concerning the manufactures with which you are connected.
Also get Hume, and whatever illustrates English or
American history.

" . . . I trust you are improving your time. Not that
I doubt your seeing enough, which you will do, of course,
from the very principles of your nature. But this is not
all. See to remember, and judge, and generalize. This
will render you a well-informed man, and give richness,
scope, and precision to the operations of your mind. And
do not forget to look at everything with the eyes of a
Christian. I feel a very deep interest in all your pursuits,

and hope to see you greatly benefited by this period of absence."

To a young friend about to travel in this country : —

" . . . I want you to remember all you see at the south and west, and be able to give me an account of it. Observe carefully the modes of thinking, and especially the points which are taken for granted. The things men take for granted without affirming are frequently of much greater importance than all that they affirm.

" By all means, see what you can of the west. As, in all probability, I shall never be able to go there, I must look at it through the eyes of others. I want the elements of sound opinions. Note down your observations and the incidents which happen to you."

To a young friend intrusted with important business interests : —

" . . . It is at some risk that so much confidence is reposed in a young man. But this only furnishes the stronger reason why you should deserve this confidence. Remember one thing. Never make up your mind *instanter*. People will seek to commit you, and will then feel sure that they have carried their point. Always say, ' I will think of it, and let you know ; ' and then make up your mind out of their sight, and out of hearing of their persuasive eloquence. If possible, resolve upon no important matter without a night's sleep. If you will only take time, you will make as few mistakes as other men. The difference between young and old men is this : young men are ashamed to be thought obliged to take time for deliberation, and old men are willing to be so esteemed. Consent to be an old man, and you may have an old man's wisdom."

For the sake of preserving the continuity of the narrative, we have hitherto inserted only such letters of Dr. Wayland, written between the commencement of his presidency and the year 1840, as had especial reference to the particular topics under consideration. The following letters, although introduced without special regard to chronological order, are deemed worthy of publication, as affording additional insight into his character and opinions. Upon hearing that his father had suffered pecuniary reverses, he writes to his sister, January 1, 1828, —

" The change which has taken place in father's circumstances, rendering you the poorer, has many sources of consoling, as well as of afflictive reflection. It is afflictive that it should have been occasioned by human rather than directly by providential agency. It is afflictive that the loss is associated with impropriety of moral conduct, and that the money has tended to make mankind worse, rather than better, by its expenditure.

" On the other hand, it is consoling to reflect that whatever was wrong, was not by our or by our parent's design.

" So much for the loss of the money. What effect has it produced upon you? It has made you poorer. But has it diminished your intellect? Has it taken away your education? Has it deprived you of any rational or moral means of happiness? Has it made you less estimable in the sight of God? Certainly not, unless it has caused you to murmur, and charge God foolishly. If it has made you humble, grateful, child-like, penitent, and faithful, God esteems you infinitely more. This loss, therefore, cannot be a matter of much importance.

" But it may be necessary for you to earn your own support. Well, what is there humiliating in this? What is there more humiliating in earning our own support than in having some one else earn it for us? Into these two classes all mankind must be divided. Other things being equal, — that is, moral character remaining the same, — I consider the class of supporters more respectable than the class of supported. It is to the former that I always expect to belong.

" It is impossible to decide at present whether this change is for the better or for the worse ; whether it is an affliction or a mercy. It surely will be the latter, if we improve it aright. All that you or any one can understand, is, that God has seen fit to turn you into a different path from that in which you were walking. Whether it will lead to a more or less pleasant prospect than that which you leave, he only knows. Our sole business is to follow him, and seek, first of all, to obey him. He knows what will conduce to our best interests. It all proves that there is nothing certain or valuable but religion. God has promised this to all who seek for it. He has promised nothing else. He has secured that, and that alone, to us. It is the only treasure which we can make our own."

To Mrs. O'Brien, December 21, 1829 : —

"My dear Sister: Your last letter was duly received; and few things of an epistolary nature could have given me more pleasure. In Mrs. R. I have always felt a deep interest, which was increased by the tidings of her recent affliction, although I knew not how it had affected her. To hear of the supports of divine grace which she has received, to know how good God has been to her in the hour of her calamity, to be assured that in this furnace of affliction she was even joyful, is refreshing beyond the ordinary incidents of this changeful life. Mrs. R. is, in my opinion, no common Christian. She certainly wields the weapon of prayer with more skill in the Christian warfare than almost any one whom I have ever known. It seems never to fail her. I was peculiarly struck with this in the last visit I made to her. I have not often seen any one breathing so elevated and invigorating, and yet so bland, an atmosphere of piety. It is delightful to see how God prepares his servants for the service to which he calls them, and how he takes them by the hand before he leads them through the fiery furnace."

To his sister : —

"November 13, 1832.

" . . . What sad havoc has death made in the ranks of the leading minds of England during the past year. The names of Sir James Mackintosh, Robert Hall, and Sir Walter Scott will at once occur to you among the list of those whom the world has lost. How wide was the intellectual empire, how powerful the sway, how undisputed the literary eminence, of the great novelist! In these respects we shall hardly find his equal in the history of modern times; and yet how mean are the fictions of this gifted mind, compared with the contemplations of the devout saint upon God, and the communion of the soul with the Savior of sinners. Let us remember that this is not our home, and live daily in preparation for heaven.

"You have undoubtedly heard of the death of Dr. Spurzheim, the celebrated phrenologist and physiologist. He was a man of rare endowments, vast information, singular acuteness, intimate knowledge of the world, uncommon candor, persevering industry, searching observation, and truly philosophical spirit. His death will be widely felt and sincerely mourned both in this country and in Europe. I saw him in Boston, and heard him lecture with much pleasure."

To a friend : —

"October 23, 1833.

"I rejoice to hear of your improved health. . . . Let me entreat you to pursue the course which I recommended to you when we were last together. Put your feelings into action, and you will recognize their importance. Engage in works of benevolence and usefulness. Especially would I once more suggest to you the benefit to be derived from the charge of a Bible class. Consider how delightful would be the task of training young minds for heaven! Meanwhile, you had better commence housekeeping, and have some command of your time. Spend as many hours as possible in retirement. You will enjoy it, and it will do you good."

To his father : —

"January 10, 1834.

" . . . I entirely agree with you as to the treatise of Mr. Gurney. I have never seen the great doctrines of the gospel presented in a manner so simple and scriptural. The book is written, as you are probably aware, by a Quaker; and yet I presume that Episcopalians, Presbyterians, Methodists, and Baptists, would unite with him in every sentiment which it contains. This results from the fact that he confines himself closely to scriptural statements. One thing, at least, is thus made manifest — that Christians differ from each other, not so much respecting what the Bible teaches, as about their own glosses and deductions, from it. How much wiser, happier, and more united should we all be, if we were willing to be simple-hearted disciples of the Holy Oracles! I sincerely hope that such a union is advancing. I think I observe, that, in the character of the religious literature which is getting into cir-

culation, we find more unction, a stronger leaning towards experimental religion and 'heart-work,' than has
been seen heretofore.

"In my last letter to S., I alluded to Mrs. Fry's recent
work — 'Christ our example.' It is written in an admirable spirit, and should be widely circulated. I hope you
will read it carefully, and get several copies to lend where
such a book is needed. It is adapted to the wants of all
Christians."

On the death of his early friend, Rev. Dr. Wisner, he
writes to the bereaved widow, —

"PROVIDENCE, February 10, 1835.

"My dear Friend: I have just heard the melancholy
tidings. I fear to break in upon the depth of your sorrow by writing, and yet I can do nothing else until I have
mingled my grief with yours. But what shall I say? and
how shall I comfort you? I know in part what the
world, and the church, and the missionary cause have
lost, but what you have lost, no one but yourself can appreciate.

"'Verily thou art a God that hidest thyself, O God
of Israel, the Savior.' 'I was dumb. I opened not my
mouth, because thou didst it.' 'As for our God, his
way is perfect.' These and similar passages of Scripture
are in my mind continually, and I know that with such
consolations you are staying yourself in this hour of your
awful visitation.

"I feel as though I had lost a brother. You know
how long we were associated together, and how, almost
from boyhood, we were united. I do not think that there
is any one left on earth, out of my own family, with
whom so much of my life has been spent. We sat on
the same seat in college, we were tutors at the same time,
and for five years we labored together in Boston. All
now comes up before me — his frankness, his generosity,
his steadfast and unchanging piety, his soundness of judgment, his sagacity in counsel, his faithfulness in advice.

"But why do I speak of my feelings? When I think
of you, my heart bleeds. I have gone through such a
scene, and I know something of its sorrows. I can at
this moment sympathize with you in your bereavement;

and day after day, as though I were with you, I shall bear your grief, and go with it to the throne of grace. I trust you have the presence of Christ. I am sure he will not leave you at such a time. I pray that he may abundantly comfort you, and lead you to rest upon him.

"Can I do anything for you? Can I in any manner alleviate the bitter distress with which you are overwhelmed? I beg you to consider my house as one of your many homes. May the blessed God be with and sustain you. Yours affectionately,

F. WAYLAND.

"Save me a pen, or whatever you can spare without robbing yourself."

A few months later, he lost, in the death of Thomas P. Ives, Esq., of Providence, one of his wisest counsellors, a life-long friend of the college, and a most useful and valued citizen. In reference to this sad event, Dr. Wayland writes to his sister, May 14, 1835, —

". . . I came home, as you are already aware, to a scene of deep affliction and most sad and affecting bereavement. I left Mr. Ives in health: his was the last house at which I called. It was the first which I visited on my return, and I found him in the chamber of death, after a sickness of scarcely seven days. I did not know that he had been ill until I was informed of his death. There is reason to hope that his end was peace. He was always, from my first coming here, my steadfast, sincere, kind, and sympathizing friend; a prudent counsellor, a most upright merchant, a man of unerring sagacity, of instinctive benevolence, and great natural and cultivated courtesy. I have rarely known a man whom I esteemed more, or whom every one considered so thoroughly worthy of esteem. The loss to the college and to me is, so far as man can see, irreparable."

November 20, 1837, he writes to a friend who had suffered serious losses in business, —

"Your last letter has given me great pain. I sincerely regret that you should be thus involved, and can hardly imagine how it has happened. I presume that your pecuniary difficulties must have been caused by some specula-

tion. What my views on this subject are you already
know. Still, what has been done cannot be recalled. All
that remains is to act wisely under existing circumstances.

"The condition in which you find yourself is one which
sorely tries the character of men. How many, when thus
tried, utterly fail! You can now lose either property
alone, or both property and character. See to it that you
lose only the former. Look at your affairs calmly, with
the advice of judicious friends. Ascertain at once what
property you have, and make every sacrifice to pay your
debts. If possible, discharge every obligation to the utter-
most, and give up everything to accomplish this result.
I would glory in being poor for the sake of being strictly
just. This is called for by correct principles of conduct,
and is still more strongly demanded by your Christian profession. You have now a better opportunity to demon-
strate the value of religious principle than you may ever
have again. Resolve to pursue such a course as I have
ventured to indicate, and you will at once feel a peace of
mind which nothing else can give. Let me urge you to
act as promptly as is practicable, for suspense in such a
case is always peculiarly painful.

"You are abundantly able to make yourself independent by your own exertions, and therefore need not be concerned about the future. Be not discouraged. Be just,
and fear not. Cast all your care upon God, who careth
for you, and he will deliver you in due time."

To the wife of this friend, Dr. Wayland writes, —

"The simple loss of property, when one is able to earn
his own support, is very bearable. You do not, I am confident, feel apprehensive of coming to want. You may,
indeed, be compelled to live less expensively. But this
will diminish your domestic cares, and may result in your
living quite as comfortably and much more pleasantly.
You will need fewer servants, and will be subject to fewer
interruptions. Do not fear a disclosure of the change in
your circumstances. See to it that you act right, and you
will gain the respect and love of all the good; for the
opinion of the rest you do not care.

"In such cases there are some duties especially devolving
upon a wife, of which I beg leave to remind you. Never
say, 'I told you so.' Seek to be cheerful, and to look at

things precisely as they are. Show by your conduct that
you are not concerned about the loss of property. Endeavor, at once, to reduce your expenses to the lowest
point. Do for yourself what others have hitherto done
for you. Practise entire plainness in dress. If I am not
mistaken, you have a large investment in jewels. Pardon
me if I suggest that it may be your duty to dispose of
them. Under existing circumstances, would it not be a
reproach to you to wear them?

"Encourage your husband to sacrifice everything rather
than abandon a single point of high Christian integrity.
Let it be seen that, although he may have made an error
in judgment, he is still determined to pursue a strictly
honorable course. No matter how unjustly he may have
been treated by others, he is now called upon to act for
himself. Others may have involved him in purse; let
them not also involve him in reputation. I am particularly
desirous that you should both show the elevation of character which becomes you as Christians.

"I know you will not for a moment doubt that I sincerely sympathize with you in your present distress, or
that the advice which I have given has been dictated by
affection. I do not see that you have anything to reproach
yourself with. You could not have prevented what has occurred, and therefore you are in no manner responsible
for the result. This being the case, do not 'borrow trouble.'
Endeavor to act like a Christian woman and a Christian
wife. Save all you can, and be willing that all should see
that you are saving. Uphold your husband in doing right.
Do not pine or repine; but 'bear up, and steer right onward.' I pray God to support and comfort you. Try to
leave all with him. We see at present but in part, but we
shall see fully in the end. You do not know how rich
this cloud may prove to be in blessing."

A call to the Federal Street Church, in Boston, which
he received in the fall of 1838, was the occasion of the
following letters to Deacon Heman Lincoln : —

"PROVIDENCE, November, 1838.

"My dear Brother : ... Your letter of this morning
is just received. It is, of course, a serious matter, demanding grave and prayerful reflection. It does not ap-

pear to be my duty, but it deserves examination. Were I to be settled in a city, I should prefer Federal Street Church to any church I know of. I love the ministry; and were the choice an open one, I rather think I should decide for it. But I will not prejudge the matter, or even write about it. Ask the direction of God in my behalf."

A week later he writes, —

"Yours of yesterday was received in the evening. The case you present shows that the door is fairly opened to go to Federal Street. It, however, does not show that it is open for me to leave the college. These are two different questions. The one by no means includes the other. I am prepared to hear all that can be said in the case, but, as yet, see no reason to think that it will be my duty to leave.

"While I write thus, I beg you to be assured that I feel a deep sense of gratitude for this instance of the confidence of my brethren. I shall cherish a peculiar interest in them, and a strong desire to serve them. If I do not go, I will labor with the utmost zeal to procure a pastor for them, and shall not rest until it is accomplished."

The following letter to Rev. Dr. Bartol contains an allusion to the same subject: —

"November 15, 1838.

"My dear Brother: I cannot resist the impulse to answer immediately your kind and excellent letter of yesterday, which has been this moment received. I thank you for your clear and distinct views, and for the candor with which they are expressed. I am peculiarly gratified, inasmuch as they entirely coincide with my own.

"As the case was a grave one, and I felt that I might misjudge in my own calling, I was sincerely desirous to know how the matter was looked upon by unprejudiced observers who saw it from a distance, and would take in its whole bearings perhaps better than I. The fact is, I am partial to the ministry; it is specially good for a man's soul, and I never intended to abandon it for life when I commenced teaching. But God has given me so much greater success in teaching than in preaching; my labors have seemed so much more effectual; the number of those who succeed in teaching appears so much less than in preaching; my health is so much better; and, so far as I see, the present situation is so clearly preferable for H., both in climate and duties, — that I should not feel authorized to leave unless there were a manifest intimation of Providence. . . ."

To Rev. Dr. Hoby: —

"December 25, 1838.

" That you did not see more of Dr. Potter, I regret as much as you. He was one of my earliest friends, and we have been intimate since the commencement of our acquaintance. I scarcely know a more excellent, amiable, or able man. His time abroad was limited, as he was obliged to be at home in September. I presume he remained in Birmingham as long as he could. I would most gladly have been with him, and do not yet quite give up all hope of following him. I yearn to visit the graves of my ancestors; the tombs of the mighty dead, of whom I have read from childhood; the homes of England, both of high and low degree; to look upon that land where civilization has reached a higher point than any other country has ever attained; and to see the eminent men who are doing honor to our language and to our nature."

To Rev. Dr. Bartol: —

"January 3, 1839.

" . . . I have read the article on Cromwell in the Westminster Review. It has many fine passages, and is written by a strong man. As Robert Hall said of Owen, though he dives deep, he sometimes comes up muddy. In his endeavor to be far-reaching and profound, he is sometimes, if not frequently, obscure. He has a better knowledge of the character of Cromwell than any one whom I have read. I should have liked the article better if it had been more historical and less philosophical. Still I rejoice to see it. There have been very few men with whom Cromwell could be compared. As was said about Napoleon, we must search centuries for his parallel. The world has seen few such men, and to few has it been more flagrantly unjust. Literature owes Cromwell much, for she has robbed him sorely. I rejoice to see one instalment of the debt paid. As to the death of Charles I., I consider it rather an irregular proceeding, but it was really with

Cromwell very much a matter of necessity. If he had not killed the king, the king would have killed him; and it would be difficult to prove that the king had a better right to the throne than he. . . ."

To a clergyman: —

"January 12, 1839.

". . . I am pleased to learn that my services seem likely to be useful. I like the work of the ministry, and sometimes doubt whether I ought to have left it. I have no time now to write sermons, or I should preach oftener. I am not quite sure that you are correct in the notion that a man can write sermons to better purpose when out of the ministry. Dr. Stillman once said that the oftener an oven was heated, the easier it was to heat it. I used to find that I wrote more readily, and I think more effectively, the more I wrote. Fox was in the habit of speaking every night when he first entered Parliament. It is perfectly amazing to perceive the amount of speaking done by men who accustom themselves to it in Parliament and in the courts of law in England. Erskine's speeches make two thick octavo volumes, closely printed; and yet it is stated, in the preface to the English edition, that they comprise the labors of only *three weeks* out of a life of *thirty years'* service at the bar. What an inexhaustible volcano such a mind must be. The same must be true of other men, especially of almost any of the chancellors of Great Britain. Indeed, I rather suppose that the human mind does not improve so much, in advancing life, in power to do great things, as in the power to do the same things with less labor. I doubt whether Canning could speak better at fifty than at thirty; but he could speak as well on the instant at the former age, as by a week's preparation in the latter. Hence I conclude that the oftener a man preaches, the easier and the better he will preach."

To his sister, December 22, 1839: —

". . . You ask me about the state of the soul after death and before the resurrection. The Scriptures are almost silent on the subject, and on such topics, where they teach but little, we cannot know much. What they have taught us seems to me substantially as follows: The human being may exist as body and spirit united; as spirit disconnected from the body; and as spirit united to what the apostle calls a glorified or spiritual body. The first is our state here. The last will be our state after the second resurrection, as I suppose St. Paul teaches in the 15th chapter 1st Corinthians, and in the Epistle to the Thessalonians. The second, I have thought, will be our state after death and before the resurrection. It will, I suppose, be a state of inconceivable joy to the righteous, and of sorrow to the wicked, but still inferior to the final state of both. Our Savior, as I have always believed, passed through all that we are to pass through. He lived as we live; was a man of like passions as we are. He died as we die. He existed, as to his human soul, separate from his body; and on the third day he was clothed in a glorified or spiritual body, being thus the first fruits of them that sleep. Such are my views, briefly and without argument. Where I derived them, except from the Scriptures, or who believes as I do, I do not know."

To the same, February 16, 1840: —

"Your inquiries respecting self-examination are not so unusual as you might suppose; nor do they betray a state of mind to which a religious friend should show no quarter. They (that is, your representations of your own feelings) indicate a state of mind in which the knowledge of duty is superior to the performance; the conscience, aware of the discrepancy, occasionally stimulating the performance, so that the two do not lose sight of each other, yet not quickening the soul to such habitual action as shall keep them near to each other. If such be a true exposition of the case, the result to be feared is, that the knowledge of duty and the performance may gradually lose sight of each other altogether. The thing to be desired is, to bring them into more immediate communion, and establish between them the relation of steadfast cause and effect.

"Now, if we inquire into the cause of this state of mind, I think we shall find it to be this: We do not allow our moral faculties a fair opportunity. The soul of man is a stage, on which is carried forward a daily contest between the powers of the present world and the powers of the world to come. The soul herself holds the balance between them. As she yields to the powers of the world, they gain strength and the others decline ; as she governs the passions and strives after holiness, the reverse takes place. In such a state of mind as you describe, the balance is not evenly held. We must give more scope to spiritual things. To be more specific, we shall generally find, upon looking into the matter, that reading, study, business, or something else, has crowded out religion, and that we do not allow ourselves sufficient time for prayer and reflection. We must then turn over a new leaf, and permit the duties of religion to resume the ground they have unrighteously lost. By portioning out your day, and adhering to the resolution, you will find where the difficulty is, and also the remedy. Time devoted to calm reflection will recall us to ourselves. A season of special humiliation is frequently useful ; but this will only be of temporary advantage if our daily arrangements are not so made as to give their due share to religion and to God. But perhaps as good a way of knowing our hearts as any other is, to do our duty. Goethe says, as I am told, ' Do your duty if you would know what is in you.'

" You speak of a tendency to deify abstract holiness, instead of being practically holy. This must be so if our hearts are by nature deceitful. We are very prone to do anything rather than our duty. But this tendency we must strive against, knowing that it is a part of ' the body .of sin and death.' . . .

" That you cannot by searching find out God is not remarkable, it having been observed as long ago as the time of Job. Nor is it wrong, so far as I can see, for you to love the image of God reflected in nature. He has said, ' Because they regard not the works of the Lord, nor consider the operations of his hand, he will destroy them.'

" . . . As to the personal reign of Christ, I have no knowledge. I have never found anything to warrant belief in it. I see no reason to suppose that Messiah will come to this earth until he comes to judgment, and then the world and the things of it will be burned up. I believe, however, that his gospel will triumph, and this earth be wholly subject unto him.

" . . . Free toleration in religion is attended by (I do not say causes) bad enough preaching ; but I have not discovered that the absence of toleration has been attended by better.

" . . . If the Head of the church had no more patience with preachers than they deserve, I am sure that their condition would be a sad one. My sympathies are, I must confess, with the people rather than with the clergy. There are not very many who do as well as they can. Old Dr. Ryland, a very irascible man, once heard a miserable choir sing. He stopped them in anger, saying, 'If the angels in heaven should hear you, they would wring your little necks off.' How much better would some ministers fare?"

END OF VOL. I.

Engraved by J.C. Buttre.

FRANCIS WAYLAND.

From a bust executed in 1860
by Thomas Ball of Boston.

A MEMOIR

OF THE

LIFE AND LABORS

OF

FRANCIS WAYLAND, D.D., LL.D.,

LATE PRESIDENT OF BROWN UNIVERSITY.

INCLUDING

SELECTIONS FROM HIS PERSONAL REMINISCENCES
AND CORRESPONDENCE.

BY HIS SONS,

FRANCIS WAYLAND AND H. L. WAYLAND.

VOLUME II.

NEW YORK:
SHELDON AND COMPANY.
1867.

Stereotyped at the Boston Stereotype Foundry,
No. 4 Spring Lane.

CONTENTS

OF THE SECOND VOLUME.

————

CHAPTER III.

CHAPTER IV.

CHAPTER V.

CHAPTER VI.

CHAPTER VII.

CHAPTER VIII.

CHAPTER IX.

CHAPTER X.

CHAPTER XI.

CHAPTER XII.

LIFE

OF

FRANCIS WAYLAND.

CHAPTER· I.

DR. WAYLAND had long desired to enlarge his knowledge of the most approved modes and systems of instruction by visiting the world-renowned seats of education. In 1840 the corporation voted him leave of absence for the purpose of visiting Europe, and requested Professor Caswell to discharge temporarily the duties of the presidency.

Professor Stuart, in a note accompanying a letter of introduction, remarks, —

"I need not say to you that a voyage to Europe has made a dunce of many an American who had some sense before he went. I believe it will not influence you in that manner. You do not go to see the *lions*, but to know more about men, and to advance your own resources. Peace be with you and yours.

"Glad should I be to hear from you when in England or Scotland, if you find any literary or religious phenomenon that will interest me, as no doubt you will. *Vive et vale.* The God who rules the seas protect and guide your way."

Atlantic steam navigation was then an experiment; and probably this consideration, combined with a hope of gaining in health from a prolonged voyage, led him to embark in a sailing packet. The voyage was long, rough, and every way unpropitious. He suffered greatly from sea-sickness; his digestion became deranged, and the physical and consequent mental depression seemed to cling to him during almost his entire absence.

To his father and sisters he writes, —

"... A more uncomfortable twenty-three days I have rarely experienced. A sea life is anything but agreeable, let them say what they may. It was peculiarly otherwise to me, in consequence of the absence of all religious society. Still I hope that it was not wholly unprofitable. I never was thrown so much on my Bible and on God. Never have I so much felt the excellence of prayer, and I trust also so many answers to it. I could not but believe that the prayers of my friends were on various occasions answered in my behalf."

During his journey Dr. Wayland maintained a somewhat full correspondence with his home, and also kept a diary for Mrs. Wayland. From these materials we shall make a few extracts that peculiarly illustrate his character, or explain his subsequent views. But for the most part the letters and the diary are either entirely of a personal nature, or have been robbed of their interest by the lapse of twenty-seven years, and by the vastly increased travel between America and Europe.

"*Liverpool, November* 1, *Sabbath.* Attended Dr. Raffles' church. The singing was more general throughout

the house than with us; it was softer, but seemed to me
rather careless. In prayer Dr. R. was delightful; devotional, calm, earnest, but solemn; particular, but not familiar. It raised the souls of the people to God, and kept
them near to the throne. His voice is soft and musical,
though not of great compass; his manner animated, yet
not boisterous; his diction chaste, and sometimes ornate.
He is, by the tone of his thought as well as his voice,
rather calculated to produce admiration than conviction;
to awaken feeling and gratify taste rather than to arouse
the conscience and subdue the heart. On the whole, I was
greatly pleased. I was never so much melted in any services of the sanctuary, unless it may have been at some
communion seasons. The contrast between this and my
last three Sabbaths, the voice of praise from the assembled multitude of Christian worshippers, the united prayers and thanksgivings from so many who loved the Lord
Jesus, all came on my spirit with thrilling effect; and when
the stanza, ' My God, how excellent thy grace!' was sung
(a stanza which I have always greatly admired), and when
I remembered the preservations of the voyage just closed,
the answers to prayers still fresh in my recollection, my
heart, in the language of Fisher Ames, ' grew liquid' while
I sung, and I ' could pour it out like water.' ...."
   " I find it to be the common impression that the Tory
interest is strengthened. I am told that when the reform
bill passed, many of the reformers, elated by their success, determined to make it merely the commencement of
a much more extensive and radical change. They declared at once for a dissolution of the connection between
church and state. This had the twofold effect of arousing the dormant but enormous power of the Establishment, and of cooling the ardor of many of the most judicious reformers, who were satisfied with what they had
gained, at least until they should see how it would work.
By this means the Tory and Church party have gained,
and are at this moment more powerful than they have
been for many years.
   " *Monday Evening*. I took tea at Dr. Raffles', in company with the dissenting ministers of Liverpool, who meet at
each other's houses in succession on the first Monday of the
month, and go from thence to the monthly concert. They
were generally young, and seemed greatly oppressed by

secular religious business. Every charity is governed by
a committee, and these ministers form the committee, — a
very time-consuming arrangement.

"I am struck with the great difference between an old
and a new country. Here everything is fenced around
by precedents; you cannot move without infringing on
vested rights. If you attempt any reform, you are called
upon to consider how it will affect the landed interest, or
the aristocracy, or the church. It is taken for granted
that everything must remain as it is, in so far as the powerful and the men of rank are concerned, and then, what
is left may be managed for the good of the lower classes,
provided you will give all the management into the hands
of those whom 'God has made responsible for power.'
I may be wrong. This is a first impression, and I so record it, that I may compare it with my subsequent views.
With us everything stands on its own merits. There are
no constitutional embarrassments. And in another respect there is a vast difference. I had no idea of the variety of grades and degrees which are marked below zero in
the social scale. In addition to the various grades of titled
rank, there are, below these, the rich and independent,
the independent though not rich, the various ranks of re-
tailers and artisans, the laborers and servants, and all
those who are able by ordinary effort to procure food and
clothing. This is with us as low as the scale usually
goes. But here, I fear, there are many lower grades down
to absolute starvation; and these grades comprise so large
a portion of the population, that a benevolent mind shud-
ders to think of it. It seems to be conceded that there is
necessarily so much poverty, that the idea of doing away
with it is not to be even entertained. I presume it is so
to a very considerable extent in the large cities of our own
country. But such is not, I think, the feeling of our people. We have much stronger confidence in social per-
fectibility.

"*Friday.* Made calls and dined at 'Green Bank' with
Mr. Rathbone. The cottage, as it is called here, is of
stone, beautifully built and delightfully situated. I do
not know of anything of the kind in America — all the
conveniences of a city, all the luxuries of living, all the
elegances of literature, combined with the retirement of
the country. There were present Mr. and Mrs. Rathbone,

Mr. Roscoe (son of the historian) and his wife, Mr. Booth, a gentleman distinguished for knowledge of mechanics, and manager of the B. and M. Railroad, Mr. Smith, Mr. Heady, Dr. Raffles, Mr. and Mrs. Thom, the latter a daughter of Mr. Rathbone. Conversation turned on phrenology, animal magnetism, politics, &c. It was free, perfectly good-natured, and animated. The party separated at about ten o'clock.

"Mr. R. accompanied me to my bedroom, and we talked, standing before the fireplace, for nearly an hour. He is a delightful man, very quiet, very intelligent, and guileless as a child. He reminds me in social intercourse of Dr. Bowditch, more than any other person whom I remember. He has the same love of justice, the same impulsiveness, the same gleefulness. Mrs. R. is a very intelligent woman. Mr. R. quoted a remark of Jeffrey : ' He did not object to blue stockings, provided the petticoats covered them.' I apprehend the remark could be applied to but few persons with more justice than to Mrs. R.

"*November* 7. Took the train to Birmingham. The road passes through a very level country ; the soil, in general, a stiff clay, at present saturated with water. The hedges, of which we hear so much, were very often broken down, and the hawthorns straggled and interrupted. The climate is so moist that the brick and stone soon become dark-colored, and the roofs in a few years are covered with green moss. Everything looks old. The fields are small and well cultivated, of course, since the price of land renders this indispensable. The cattle are better than ours, but I did not see one cow equal to mine. The grass is still green. There has been no black frost, and the cattle are yet in the fields. They have rain instead of cold.

" This railroad is smoother than is common with us. The journey (ninety-eight miles) is made in four and a half hours. Saturday evening arrived at Birmingham, where my friend Rev. Dr. Hoby lives in a very pleasant style, and preaches the gospel without compensation. I have received from Dr. and Mrs. Hoby the utmost Christian hospitality.

" *Sabbath Morning.* Dr. Hoby's chapel. Was unwell, and did not hear to advantage. Preached in the evening, still unwell.

"*Monday*. Went out with Dr. Hoby. Bible meeting. The king's printer receives ten thousand pounds a year from the printing of the Scriptures — a shocking monopoly, which to this amount, for no reason whatever, increases the price of the holy oracles. . Rev. J. A. James visited us, and took tea. All the talk about abolition, &c. It is amazing to perceive how this question seems to absorb every other among the dissenters, and to what extent they carry out their notions. A man who does not adopt their opinions is, it would seem, excommunicated from church and society. I have already had some reason to observe this. May God grant me grace to act like a Christian, and the more abundantly to love them the less I be loved. I respect their motives and their love of freedom, although I have small sympathy with their modes of expression. I have suffered intolerably from low spirits. I apprehend that this arises partly from ill health. I pray God to restore me to health, and to enable me diligently to employ the time which he has allotted to me here, that I may be the means of promoting the cause of education, and of doing good to my country and to the church of God.

"Birmingham has been remarkable for the strength, I may say bitterness, of its political animosities. Here Dr. Priestley's house was torn down by a mob. Here was formed the famous union which drew together two hundred thousand people to petition for reform. It is still the centre, to a considerable degree, of all radical political action. The same temper seems to be carried into religious, and even into benevolent, associations. Here, at present, all is in agitation and ferment among the dissenters about abolition. It is assumed that these gentlemen are to decide not only whether slavery be right or wrong, but also in what manner it is to be abolished, and that they have a right to treat as they will whosoever does not, under all circumstances, do as they see fit. They decide what is the duty of the northern states and of every citizen thereof, and they excommunicate, without reserve, every one who does not agree with them to the utmost. Here, then, we see in dissenters the admission of the very principles which they abhor when put in practice by the Establishment. It is an assumption of the power and right to inflict disabilities or exclusions on those who differ from them in points on which every man may justly claim to entertain an opinion of his own. They know not, as it seems to me, what manner of spirit they are of. And, besides, this spirit of exclusion, let it exist where it will, is anti-social. If the claim on which it is founded be allowed, where is it to end? One party excludes another for disagreement in respect to the slavery question. By the same principle they should proceed to exclude each other for disagreement on the question of temperance, or of peace, or of woman's rights. Thus exclusion begets exclusion *ad infinitum.* The result is party spirit, bickerings, seclusion from each other, and all its natural attendants — the indulgence and the cultivation of the evil passions of the human heart. Is it a wonder, then, that the best — and these are always the peace-loving — are attracted to the Establishment, where such feuds are less known, and where, at least, this exclusive tendency is, from the nature of the church, unable to take effect? Is it strange, then, that, with all the errors, and faults, and weaknesses of the church, and even in spite of the false position in which it is placed, it should not only maintain its ground, but even make head against its opponents? . . ."

We quote from the reminiscences of Dr. Stow : —

"When I was in England the following summer, I was informed of an incident which I could well understand. Dr. Wayland, in the course of his visits to the English institutions of learning, called to see the Baptist Academy in ——, where many eminent Baptist ministers had been educated. The principal, who was also the preacher at —— Chapel, after giving Dr. Wayland all facilities for examining the institution, said, ' Sir, I am sorry that I cannot invite you to occupy my pulpit next Sabbath. Personally, I have no objection ; but some doctrines in your treatise on " The Limitations of Human Responsibility" have rendered you unpopular in England, and, were I to do it, I should incur reprehension.' Dr. Wayland replied in one sentence : ' Sir, when I ask for your pulpit, it will be time enough for you to refuse it.'

" Several times, while I was in England, I heard that story related, and the severity of the rebuke justified. In a few other places he encountered supercilious treatment from small men, and several of his replies to discourteous words were quoted as proofs of his power of disposing effectually of such annoyances."

From Birmingham he went to Bassingham, where he was a welcome guest in the accomplished and cultivated family of his uncle, Rev. Daniel S. Wayland, rector of Bassingham. His acquaintance with this gentleman, which was subsequently maintained by correspondence, and by the interchange of frequent kind offices, was one of the most pleasing incidents of his journey. There was something not a little remarkable in the mutual attachment subsisting between two men, of whom one was an Englishman, thoroughly loyal to church and state, the other the sturdiest of republicans; one a conservative in religion and politics, the other in the front rank of progressives; one an Episcopalian, the other an Independent and a Baptist. But a common appreciation of all that is excellent in the world of letters, and a common loyalty to the Redeemer, afforded them a broad ground of sympathy, a strong bond of attachment.

From Bassingham he proceeded to Lincoln.

"Until I had seen Lincoln Cathedral I had no conception of the power of architecture. As you survey its exterior, you are struck with its vast size. Yet, owing to the perfect proportions, the great height, the profusion of ornaments (ornaments, however, so light and graceful, so in keeping, that all seems precisely in the right place, and never too much nor too little), you forget its magnitude in admiration of its beauty. The great tower is immensely high, and is the most impressive part of the exterior. It looks like the work of fairy hands. You would not believe that stone could ever assume a form so fragile, much less that it could retain that form unhurt for centuries.

"But all this impression is deepened when you enter the building and look up the nave of two hundred and eighty feet. Here you see the power of the Gothic pillar and arch. You pass to the transept, and gaze upon the painted windows, the stone compartments of which look as though cut out of paper. You proceed to the choir, and examine the carved work which adorns it so profusely on every side. You visit the chancel, where repose the ashes of the builder, the bishops of the Cathedral, and other eminent dead. You walk through the side aisles ; you gaze upon the arch supporting, with infinite ease, the mighty mass of the central tower ; and at every step you are filled with wonder, which you strive in vain to express. It is the epic of architecture. It is certainly one of the most wonderful efforts of human talent. I do not remember ever to have seen any work of art which impressed me so powerfully. Grecian architecture — a simple, beautiful, and sublime conception, but all external — fades away before it. The greatest power of the Gothic is within. The sense of beauty is in the highest degree gratified in both, but in Gothic the effect is more various and more inexhaustible, with a vastly deeper tinge of sublimity. It accomplishes its purpose — a more difficult one — with greater skill, and more perfectly. The Grecian merely suggests to you that this was the work of man. The Gothic is all so light, so strong, so flexible, so rich in ornament, and yet so consistent with itself, that the idea which constantly presents itself to you is, that it grew ; that it is the work of nature, and not of art ; and yet, when you reflect that this is all the work of man, that man designed, conceived, and planned it, knew the difficulties, and how to overcome them, and did actually overcome them, you are overwhelmed at his genius, and cannot fail to perceive that he must have been one of the most able men of any age.

"The Roman Arch is remarkable for its associations. What events have transpired since it was erected ! What generations have passed away ! Lincoln was once an important Roman station. Here works were erected to keep in check the hordes of barbarians whom Rome was subduing to her sway. And now those barbarians are able to cope with the world in arms, and Rome, ' lone mother of dead empires ' — what is she ? . . ."

After crossing the Channel, he writes, —

"Everywhere in France we found soldiers in great numbers. The milita are detailed to serve in the army, I believe, from nineteen to twenty-six. Thus the flower of the nation, at an age in which character is forming, are obliged to learn the habits of the camp and barracks.

Such a shocking waste of human beings I had never conceived. The soldiers whom we saw were all young, and
seemed to have nothing to do, with one exception. At
St. Omers we saw a detachment returning from work
with shovels on their shoulders. But this was merely
military labor. It added nothing to the means of human
subsistence or human happiness. These men were taken
from the plough, the workshop, and the mart of business.
I do not, however, blame the government. What could
they do better? Such a government is infinitely better
than anarchy. Yet why will man not learn that self-
control is wiser than force? that religion is cheaper than
muskets? that the proper cure for human evils must begin
with the heart? O God, send forth thy light and thy
truth, and illumine with the rays of the Sun of Righteousness the dark places of the earth, and reclaim this
world, which the Savior has purchased with his blood!
Never before did I realize the necessity of strong faith,
and never before did I conceive of the immensity of
power which is involved in the fulfilment of the promises
of God. Look at this nation, advanced in civilization,
bowing down in form to the Romish ceremonial, yet
without God in the world. 'By whom shall Jacob arise?'
How shall this kingdom be subdued unto Christ? we ask;
but wé can make no reply. Faith alone looks to the
promises of God, and, relying upon them, knows that
what God has spoken he will certainly fulfil. But this
is one of the nations denominated *Christian;* what are
we, then, to say of the millions and hundreds of millions
of Heathendom and Mohammedanism? How great is
the work which is to be accomplished before Jesus Christ
takes to himself his power, and reigns King of nations!
Hasten it, O God, in thy time, and let me, though most
unworthy, in some manner conduce to the good of thy
chosen, the prosperity of thy heritage!

"Every step and every moment impress me more
strongly with the fact that Americans know not their own
mercies, nor how to conceive of them. The blessings of
true religion, of equal rights, of being each one allowed
to take care of himself, of not being over-governed, — all
throng upon an American abroad with a depth of meaning
of which at home he knew nothing.

"*Friday, December* 11, *Paris.* Visited the prepara-

tions making for the reception of the remains of Napoleon.
It is said the ceremony will be the most imposing that
modern times have witnessed.

" . . . Nature and art have united to grace with their
loveliest offerings this city of taste. Much of this is owing
to Napoleon. He intended to make Paris the centre of
the civilized world. In part he has succeeded, but only
in part. No city or nation can be central to the world
without surpassing all others in wealth and mental energy.
These can only exist under free government, enlightened
by universal education, and by the religion of the gospel,
with its benign and ennobling effects. Of these he had
no conception. He aimed at results which physical
means could not accomplish, and thus he signally failed.

" I expect, during this week, to behold more of the
glory of man than ever before. Grant me, O God, a wise
and .holy temper! Enable me to survey everything in a
kindly spirit, willing, nay, desirous to be pleased, yet as
a Christian and as an heir of immortality. Grant me
health, if it may please thee, that I may accomplish something for myself, and especially for the cause of education
and of religion. May I be seriously in earnest. May my
faculties be aroused, my observation awakened, and may
I thus obtain knowledge which shall be of permanent use
to me. May I never forget the lessons which thou art
teaching me. May I be strengthened to confide in thee,
and may I, by every vicissitude through which I pass, be
enabled the better to glorify thee both here and hereafter.
All this I ask for Jesus Christ's sake. Amen.

" *Monday, December* 14. The whole city seems in
motion. Every part is crowded. A vast number of
strangers is said to be present. Yet I saw nothing that
looked like disaffection or unkindness to the government.
All seemed pleased and satisfied. There were no knots
of persons consulting or criticising. I apprehend the fears
of an outbreak are groundless.

" In the afternoon returned and wrote to friends at
home. After dinner attended the conversazione of M.
Coquerel, a distinguished Socinian Protestant preacher,
and one of the most effective pulpit orators in France.
He is also a voluminous writer. He seemed exceedingly
quick, learned, eloquent in conversation, and polite. He
is strongly impressed with the belief that Protestant senti-

ments are gaining ground in France. His church — an
established Protestant church — is crowded. Many of
his hearers are distinguished men; among them is Guizot.
Whence his hopes arise I know not. He thinks that a
reformation will proceed from the Catholic clergy themselves. I learn from him that all the lectures here by the
most eminent men are gratuitous. He said that, no matter
what might be the subject, be it science, or the arts, or
languages, you would find it taught gratuitously. Yet
among the people in general education is at a low ebb.

"*Tuesday, December* 15. The pageant is over. I
presume that from fifty to one hundred thousand troops
were present. Besides these the crowd was immense.
Everything seemed well conducted. The houses were
deserted, the shops shut, and all was in motion; yet I
have not heard that any accident occurred. The pageant
in line of motion, aside from the car and the personages
immediately near it, was not impressive; there was almost
nothing except the body of troops, and from a single station you could see but little of the long line. It was very
cold, and a sheltered situation was worth a great deal, and,
I may add, cost a great deal. The people seemed but
little affected. They cheered when the car approached,
but nothing was funereal; and, upon the whole, the impression on my mind is that of a splendid, vain show.
Such is human glory!

"Americans say — and 'The Guide to Paris' seems not
to deny it — that the people of Paris are totally devoid of
honesty to foreigners. Such, however, might be expected
to be the condition of a country without God. Yet, with
all this, there is intense love of knowledge among scientific men, great self-sacrifice in advancing it, and an intense love of truth, that is, scientific truth. The ardor in
this cause is such as we have no conception of in our
country. All catch the enthusiasm; but then it is remarkable that it is but slightly connected with benevolence.
Men study diagnosis, and are willing to do anything to
diagnose; but whether a patient live or die is almost a
matter of indifference. I say *almost*, but this is hardly
true. They rather prefer that the patient should die, as
this enables them to determine the truth of the diagnosis.

"Visited the Louvre again, and walked through the
gallery of Spanish pictures purchased lately by the pres-

ent king. The number is very considerable, but I should think the value could not be great. I saw few that struck me pleasantly but Murillo's. These were almost universally fine. A picture of Joseph and the Savior was, I think, the best picture I have seen in Paris. The others seemed hard and dry, the outline fixed, and the coloring a dead level, without relief or any gentleness of shading. I have a very clear idea of what I mean, but I know not how to express it. I have not the language of the art, and hence, if my meaning cannot be guessed, it will probably be unknown.

" *Saturday.* Hotel des Invalides. The chapel and the approach to it are hung with black cloth studded with bees in silver paper, and lighted with innumerable chandeliers. In the centre is the catafalque, an immense gilded structure, containing various emblematical figures, and bearing on its top the black marble coffin, in which are the remains of the emperor. Its appearance is imposing, but everything has been done for parade and in a hurry, and already the frail fabric begins to show signs of decay. Such is human grandeur! O God, why should we fix our affections on earth? It is all deceitful, vain, and more fleeting than a shadow. Suppose we add to this, what is infinitely better, the pure affection of upright souls; still what is this to thy love, to the consciousness of thy favor, to the indwelling of thy Spirit! Whom have I in heaven but thee, and there is none upon earth that I would desire in comparison with thee. Reveal thyself to me, O God. Make thy face to shine upon me. Fill me with humble and adoring views of thy character and work; and may I here and everywhere, and through time and eternity, glorify thee in my body and spirit, which are thine.

" *Wednesday, December* 23. Visited the gallery of modern sculpture, at the Louvre. Louis XIV. is a great favorite with the genius of France. His likeness is seen everywhere in stone or on canvas. His praises have been sung by poets, and his deeds recorded by historians. Men and women — I had almost said kingdoms — bowed before him. And yet, when weighed in the balance of justice and truth, what was Louis XIV.?

" Sunday morning I spent at home, afternoon preached at Chapel Thaibout, from Rom. viii. 1. I felt it a privilege to be permitted to lift up my voice for God in the midst of this city. May the Holy Spirit render it a blessing to some immortal soul.

Monday. Attended the Chamber of Deputies. The speakers were animated, but monotonous; the attention about as good as in our House. Rather more were present; fewer were engaged in writing, more in talking, and there seemed more noise. The speaker was frequently employed in rapping on the desk with the handle of his paper-knife, and in ringing his bell. This occasioned a little variety, but I did not perceive that it had any effect in diminishing the rattling of tongues. The representatives are, in general, an intelligent company of men.

" *Monday Evening.* Went to Monsieur J.'s soiree at the Royal Library. It was numerously attended. Moderate refreshments, coffee, some sort of spirits and water, hot, in small glasses, and little pastries and tea, made up all that I saw of the material part of the entertainment. Mr. J.'s rooms, three in number, lined with books, engravings, and curiosities, were open, and the visitors looked at the one, read the other, or talked together, as suited them, without restraint, and came and went as they pleased. Mr. J. was dressed as usual, having a green shade over his eyes, and seemed a happy, cheerful old gentleman. He was with Napoleon, attached to the scientific corps in Egypt, and is the last survivor of that body. It is the custom in France for gentlemen whose society is at all sought after, to have an evening which they appropriate in this way to the reception of company. They send to their friends a general invitation. In this manner various parties and numerous individuals are brought together, and the social bond is strengthened throughout all the walks of literary and well-bred society. It could, I think, be well introduced into our country.

" Last evening I went to General Cass', to see Marshal Soult. I arrived, through the indolence and stupidity of the coachman, just as he had left. Such is the fate of a traveller. You traverse thousands of miles to see persons and places, you have but a fixed time to devote to each, and some accident occurs which puts it wholly out of your power to accomplish your purpose.

" *Friday, January* 1. Mr. S. proposes to accompany me to Italy if I will go. I am strongly tempted. I know that many of my friends will expect me to go. I know there is much to be seen there, and I should be pleased to travel with Mr. S. But, after all, I am a husband and a father. I am under the obligation of these relations. I doubt my right to spend this time in pleasure. Besides, I am no longer young. My time, to the church and the world, ought to be valuable. I doubt whether I have a right to spend it in this manner. Life is too short to devote much of it to sight-seeing.

"I have been here a month. I have not been idle, and yet how very little have I gained or learned which I did not know before! and of what small value is that which I have learned! A man who does not speak the language of the country in which he is, can see nothing but buildings, trees, &c., the mere external forms; and these in winter are not very beautiful or very attractive. Besides, several matters in my own country seem to demand my attention — the Convention, at which I might possibly be of use, the meeting of my brethren in May, where I hope to be present. Indeed, I feel more than ever the importance of laboring for Christ while it is day. This sort of life does not suit me, and I had better return, as soon as Providence permits, to my labors. My conscience intimates to me that this is the path of duty, and my feelings unite in the decision."

To Deacon Lincoln he writes, —

" . . . I hope by the blessing of God, and in answer to your prayers and those of my brethren in America, to return in April. I have seen enough of the Old World, its church and state, its blessings and its curses, to make me long inexpressibly for home. I feel as I never felt before the utter vanity of everything earthly, and the supreme desirableness of living at all times and in all places for God. Never before did the church of Christ seem half so precious, or the communion of saints half so lovely. Never before did I so clearly recognize the importance of laboring to spread the gospel at home, or desire so strongly to live for Christ alone. I want to be at home at the meeting of the Convention, to say to my brethren, 'Love one another,' and to strive with them to keep the unity of the Spirit in the bonds of peace. You cannot imagine the advantages we enjoy until you see the condition of others. Our country, bad as it may be, is simple, virtuous, moral, and religious, in comparison with other countries. God bless her, and lift her up forever. . . ."

To another friend he writes, —

" You well know how sweet to the travelling exile is the package of letters from the land of his fathers. One thing, however, you do not know, and that is how delightful it is to hear from that land, of the welfare of wife and children, from whom you have been absent. May you never be thus separated. No one who has not made the trial can be at all aware of the pain which it involves and the care through which it leads. All London would not tempt me to repeat the experiment."

" *Monday.* Jardin des Plantes. This magnificent establishment, nearly two hundred years old, is upon a scale more grand than I had conceived. I learn that travelling professors are continually exploring every corner of the globe, and sending home, from time to time, all that they can collect of whatever has not yet been treasured up in the Garden of Plants. Lectures, on an average of four a day, are delivered by the most eminent men in France or the world, on all subjects of natural science. And all this is open to the public in the freest sense. Any one who chooses may avail himself of these advantages. It is difficult to imagine a more attractive mode of recommending science to an intelligent community. Here is one of the most delightful spots to be seen on earth, possessing everything that can gratify the eye or please the taste, and all this devoted to science and made to minister to knowledge.

" *Saturday.* Visited Versailles. The gardens form the most remarkable feature of this place. The whole gave me a conception, such as I had never before formed, of royal magnificence. It also raised my conception of the talent of Louis XIV.

" But it cost, as is supposed, forty millions sterling. This sum would have constructed thirteen canals, each as expensive as the Erie Canal, and would before this time have doubled or trebled the wealth of France. I am well satisfied to be without such monuments, and specially without the power in a government to make such a use of the money of the people.

" I hear my countrymen sometimes lament that we have

no monuments to taste and the arts, no palaces like those
which we see in Europe. I do not participate in their
lamentations. It may be said that these things foster love
of country. But what is love of country? Is it the admiration of splendid palaces, of magnificent paintings, of
gilded domes, of lofty columns, of spacious gardens, of
powerful fleets, and numerous armies? These may tend
to exaggerate what is called the love of glory, the love of
national supremacy, but it is far different from what I call
love of country. I love the cities, and far more the fields,
the woods, the rivers, the waterfalls, the clear blue sky,
the interminable horizon of my native land. And I love
them, I trust, as sincerely as a Frenchman loves his old
chateaux or his splendid Paris.

"But more, far more, I love her free institutions, her
universal education, her spiritual liberty and her religious
observances, her moral purity and her simple manners,
the perfect freedom with which mind is there suffered to
develop, and the means afforded to foster that development. These are the attributes which awaken my love
of country.

"I see that here no revolution would be produced by
enlarging or abridging either the means of education, or
by increasing or diminishing religious freedom. But I
presume a serious murmur would arise if the sums appropriated to the theatres and operas were restricted, or
if the public squares were allowed to decay. I believe
in the beauty of public places. I believe in sacrificing to
taste as much as taste is worth. But supposing a given
amount of money is raised, in what proportion shall it be
devoted to the intellectual cultivation of a people, to improving their condition physically and mentally, and what
proportion to buildings, palaces, and splendid but useless
edifices. I must say I go for the useful. Palace after
palace has been raised in Paris, million upon million has
been expended in adorning the capital, but there is no
railroad yet from Paris to the sea, nor any railroad in the
kingdom, except from Paris to Versailles — a railroad to
see a show. I am more and more a Puritan. I love
simple manners, simple tastes, a simple government,
which has very little to do, which leaves everything possible to be done by the individual, and which stimulates
talent of every kind, not by patronage, but by giving tal-

ent free exercise, and leaving it to its own resources; a
government of which the constitution may remain firm
as adamant, while the men who administer it may be
changed every year by the popular will. This is the
country for me, and may it be the country for my children ; and may it please God that such a country long may
be the United States of America.

"Here are books, libraries, lecturers, all the means for
learning, and here is learning itself. We have neither
books, libraries, nor learning. But we have institutions
which develop mind, which unfold and invigorate the
faculties, and give action and energy to whatever knowledge we possess. This, at least in some degree, counter-
balances the defect in learning. An American mind of
the same native strength is, I apprehend, a match for a
European. Learning does not give a European the same
advantage when compared with us, that it does when
compared with his own countrymen. We are benefited
by our training, he is not. So, at least, it seems to me.
It may be nothing but Yankee prejudice; but this is my
opinion, and there is the end of it.

"On Thursday left Paris in the diligence for Boulogne.
We had taken passage in a particular line, because we
were informed that it was fitted up expressly for winter.
It was cushioned in some peculiar way to promote the
passengers' comfort, and warmed by vessels of hot water
placed under the floor. When I looked at the coach, and
inquired for the warm water, I was told that this day was
so warm that it would be uncomfortable. When Mr. B.
inquired of the agent, he was told that they were out of
repair, and would not be used at this time. When we
had proceeded half the journey, we asked the conductor
about it, and he laughed at our credulity. The whole
story was a humbug. The consequence was, that one of
our party suffered most severely from cold. From first to
last, all my dealing with Frenchmen has shown me more
and more their disposition to lying and dishonesty. I left
Paris without a single regret, nay, with a feeling allied to
exultation. Why it was so I can scarcely say. I had
seen many interesting things there; I had learned something of men and manners; I had experienced in some
cases hospitality, and in one or two cases, especially, the
most devoted friendship. But I was glad to be out of a

city without a God, a city of frivolity, of heartless gayety, of thorough selfishness, and of sensual appetites and savage passions. I know that all this is glossed over by much that is attractive, and much that is fascinating. There is in Paris an unusual degree of taste, rather than refinement, of civility, if not of politeness. But there seems to be among the people at large no moral basis. Their feeling seems no deeper than a shrug of the shoulders. But I had better stop here. I like them not, and may be prejudiced against them. They treat Americans better than they do Englishmen. The one they cheat kindly, the other surlily; but both are considered, I think, in the nature of victims."

Dr. Stow favors us with the following: —

"When I first entered Paris with my wife and Mr. and Mrs. G., while on our way to our hotel, we met Dr. Wayland, and were welcomed by him with warm cordiality. He was often at our rooms, appearing greatly to enjoy the society of those whom he knew, and who could speak English. He was suffering from depression of spirits, occasioned partly by the physical effects of an uncomfortable sea voyage, and partly by a feeling of loneliness among a people of whose character he had not a high estimate. At different interviews he made remarks expressive of his state of mind, such as, 'This crossing the Atlantic is no joke.' 'This visiting Europe is not what it is cracked up to be.' 'You have come here for your health: that is well enough; but I do not think any minister has a right to spend six months for the mere purpose of sight-seeing. All the talk about mental improvement is the merest fudge. Life is too short to justify the waste of such a fraction of it. If I live to return, I shall set my face against the practice as wicked.' One Sabbath evening he came in deeply affected by what he had seen of the desecration of the day, and expressed a desire to join with us in some religious service. After tea he gave us a rich exposition of Romans viii., and then offered prayer — such a prayer as only he could make, and such as seldom ascends from that city of frivolity and sin. That evening was one of the greenest spots in our tour.

"While he was in Paris, General Cass, then our minister at the French court, made arrangements to 'present' a number of Americans to the royal family. In that number Dr. Wayland and the Hon. Isaac Davis, of Worcester, were included. When the company was collected and duly arranged in the audience-room at the Tuileries, they had to wait some time, standing in a semicircle for an introduction to his majesty. The doctor was ill at ease, and at length expressed his regret that he had suffered himself to be placed in such a position, and made strong remarks indicative of a feeling of humiliation. Subsequently he declared to me his conviction, that such homage to a man, mortal like himself, was ' unworthy of an ambassador of the King of Kings.' "

Returning to England, he writes, —

"*Saturday, London*. Breakfasted with Sir R. H. Inglis.

"At breakfast Sir R. and Lady Inglis, Lady Raffles, and two gentlemen. Sir Robert is a fine specimen of an old English baronet, intelligent, straightforward, with firmly fixed opinions, yet tolerant, frank, and I should think very consistent and religious. It was a very pleasant occasion. Lady Raffles is a most interesting woman, subdued with grief, yet cheering up in conversation.

" In the evening, dined at Mr. Bates'. There were there Dr. Milman, prebendary of Westminster (the poet), and his wife, Mr. and Mrs. P. Butler (Miss Kemble), Mr. Baring, &c. Dr. Milman is not externally very much of a poet. His appearance is heavy, and his manner slow. In conversation he evinces good taste and much kindness of manner.

" *Evening.* Dined at Mr. J. Parkes', a distinguished barrister. Conversation on state of country, political and religious. Mr. Parkes is, I think, the most remarkable man I have ever seen in England — cool, sagacious, unruffled, bold, determined, yet willing to bide his time. He will rise to eminence, and if ever trouble comes, he will be a man to be looked up to.

" *Monday.* Called to see Miss Edgeworth, with Mrs. Sigourney. Miss Edgeworth is a woman far advanced, small, not handsome, affable, but with nothing that would betoken the authoress. She has evidently all the kindness which ordinarily attends high and successful intellectual accomplishments.

" Dined at Sir R. H. Inglis'. There were there Hallam

(Middle Ages), the Dean of Chichester, Mr. Palmer (a distinguished Cambridge scholar and barrister), Lady Raffles, Sir Demetrius Balsamachi and his wife, and the late Bishop Heber's widow. I had much conversation, principally on religious subjects, with Lady Raffles. She is a very intelligent, pious, and lovely woman.

"*Thursday, January* 26. The queen opened Parliament, and through the kindness of Mr. Bates I was furnished with a ticket. This merely gave me access to the gallery or corridor along which the royal *cortége* and the peers and peeresses passed. There were present the guard, a common looking troop, the yeomen of the guard, and the beefeaters, dressed like harlequins. The peeresses and peers' daughters were passing me for an hour and a half. They are not so fine looking an assembly of ladies as I had expected. I saw no one whose bearing was as noble as that of Lady Raffles. I saw none of that baronial aspect of command, none of that bewitching charm of loveliness, or that majestic self-reliance, which we have been taught to expect in the descendants of ancient families. They acted just as our own women would have acted. They felt as awkwardly in awkward positions, and presented as great a variety of manners and behavior, as well-bred women among us. None of them were strikingly handsome. The queen, preceded by the chancellor, prime minister, and high officers of the crown, passed close by me. Prince Albert led her by the hand. Her robe was borne by two ladies, followed by two gentlemen and four pages. She is a small, pale, girlish-looking young woman, with nothing peculiar in her countenance, at least under the circumstances in which I saw it. Prince Albert is a moderate-looking young person. I could not perceive any marked indication in him, though this could hardly be expected for the moment I saw him. Both he and the queen really looked like persons who were thinking of something else (as was probably the fact), and made you suppose that they were two young and innocent persons who were unable to comprehend the nature of the transactions that were going on around them.

"I know not how it is, but all I see renders me more doggedly a Democrat and a Puritan. I say this wholly without unkindness. I have no objection to these forms, for those at least who like them. I had supposed that such spectacles would be impressive, and would convey some feeling of awe or reverence to my mind or to that of the people. But I confess such was not the fact. It seemed to produce no impression upon anybody, and appears on reflection to be merely a matter of puppet-show. It is nothing but acting, and the mind falls off from it. The peers, if they intend to keep up the thing, should themselves pay more attention to it. If they mean to impress the nation by a spectacle, everything must conduce towards it. If they treat it as a slip-shod matter, it will soon lose all respect among the people, and they may as well give it up altogether. Such, at any rate, is my impression. I am new in these matters, but I believe little in the effect of such things upon the human mind, and I return with more and more complacency to our plain manner of doing things.

"I forgot to say that, before the arrival of the Queen, I went, in company with R. Ingham, Esq., M. P., a Serjeant of Queen's Bench, to visit the several courts. We called at the Chancellor's and Vice-Chancellor's Courts, the Court of Exchequer, the Court of Common Pleas, and Court of Queen's Bench. It was a thing remarkable to look at. I do not now speak of the robes, &c. In the pictures these seem far more august than in the reality. I saw all these in passing from one court to another, and before I had seen them all, I hardly observed them, so readily does the mind lose all power of being impressed with what is merely a matter of form. I say, this did not look particularly venerable. But when I remembered that before me, on every bench, were men who were the lights of the world, men whose authority on any question of law or justice would be respected to the remotest limits of Christendom, and that these men were there devoting themselves, with the full power of their faculties, to the administration of justice throughout this realm,— this, I must say, impressed me. Here I beheld the majesty of law. Here I saw a temple erected for the habitation of Justice. Here I saw a barrier to the encroachments of aristocracy, and a rampart against the waves of popular fury. I felt that the voice of law uttered there was heard and obeyed throughout the land, and I knew that I was in a region of civilization, of justice, nay, of Christianity; for out of the limits of Christendom, where shall all of this or any of it be found?

"I was much pleased to perceive with what freedom the counsel addressed the bench on a point of law. The judge and the counsel differed; and the counsel pushed his lordship as closely and as freely, though with entire respect, as he would have done one of his brethren, and, as it seemed, without offence.

"The whole bearing of the assembly was that of several men of eminent talent and learning, striving, to the best of their abilities, to arrive at law and justice, in the cases submitted to their jurisdiction. It was a more impressive sight, I must say, than the scarlet robes of the peers, the ermine of the bishops, the crown of state, the robe of her majesty, or all the pomp and circumstance which I witnessed an hour or two afterwards.

"*Wednesday.* Breakfasted with N. W. Senior, Esq., a gentleman well known as a writer on political economy, and the author of the present poor law system. He was formerly professor of political economy in Oxford. Two other gentlemen were present.

"*Thursday Evening.* Met, at Mr. Kenyon's, Mr. Rogers, the poet, and his sister, Sir George Staunton, and many others. Mr. Rogers is a rather stout-built old gentleman, with a very short neck, somewhat stooping, and looking as though a mistake had been made in setting his head on his shoulders.

"*Friday.* Went to Stepney, to Dr. Murch's, to dine. Here I met Rev. Messrs. Dyer, Cox, Angus, Stovel, Crow, Steane, and Greene, and possibly some others. They are all Baptist clergymen, and seem intelligent men. They are generally rather young, a good deal interested in abolition, but good-natured in all their intercourse with me. I was pleased with the interview. We had some conversation on slavery, on the Bible question, the condition of dissenters, and the manner of organizing congregations. I believe that not a word was said that gave any offence, and the whole thing passed off very pleasantly. Mr. ——, who had been represented to me as the most bitter, as I presume he is, after a good deal of conversation, walked with me to the omnibus, and evinced a very pleasant and candid temper of mind.

"*Saturday.* Dined at Sir James Clarke's. There were present Sir J. Lubbock, a banker, and president of the Royal Society, a very able mathematician, Dr. Arnott,

Dr. Key, Professor Wheatstone, Professor Madden, Dr. Forbes, and some others, all men of science. Their dress and manners were plain. I believe I was as much dressed as any of them, which rarely occurs when I am in company. Sir J. Clarke lives in a plain and not very commodious house, not richly furnished, and seems to bear his elevation with the utmost meekness and the most unassuming good nature. It is delightful to observe a man basking, as he is known to do, in the sunshine of royal favor, carry so little of the appearance of it in his outward bearing. His dress and manners are plain, and I presume royalty has rarely had so respectable and worthy a medical adviser to rely upon. It would be interesting to know how it happened that so unpretending a man — not at all an old man; not over fifty, as I should suppose — has attained to a station, and an influence in that station, which it is commonly believed can be arrived at only by the possession of very different qualities.

" *Sunday.* Heard Rev. B. W. Noel, text Matthew xxv. 24, seq. The whole discourse was pervaded by a lovely Christian spirit, good taste, good sense, absence of all exaggerations, and a winning ease of manners, that could not but interest all that heard it. After service I conversed with Mr. N. He is a tall, slender man, with light hair and a lively expression of countenance. From all I learn, he must be an excellent pastor and exemplary Christian. He preaches in the church where preached Cecil, Pratt, and Daniel Wilson (now Bishop of Calcutta).

" *Monday.* Spent the greater part of the day at London University. With Professor Madden, professor of Greek and Latin, I visited the preparatory school, and was present at the recitations in Latin, geography, French, and mathematics. These were similar to those with us, in the main. The geography the boys studied from a map, and the master examined them from a large skeleton map — a very excellent plan. In mathematics, I observed the master drew the figure; this seemed to me a mistake. In the French class, the boys were correcting exercises which had been handed to the master previously. One of them wrote the corrected exercise on the blackboard, and the others corrected theirs from it: the peculiarity was, that they in no case had their own exercise, but each one that of another: this secured accuracy. I

noticed that the boys all took places for excellence, and
that one common reason for change of places was the better choice of an English word by which to render the
Latin or Greek. I did not perceive that the master made
it a point to construe the lesson after his boys. I next
attended Professor Madden. First the Juniors or Fresh-
men in Xenophon's Cyropædia, and second the Seniors in
Thucydides. The manner of doing it was essentially the
same as with us, only the instructor lectured more extensively on every point of difficulty, and analyzed words, and
phrases, with much greater accuracy. In order to do the
same, we want nothing but men able and willing to adopt
this plan."

"*Wednesday.* Dined with the club of the Geological Society, on invitation of R. Ingham, Esq., M. P.,
to whom I am indebted for a succession of favors for
which I shall ever be grateful. Nothing could exceed his
thoughtfulness or his kindness. At the club meeting were
Dr. Buckland, Professor Whewell, Colonel Mudge, and
several others well known to fame. The dinner was
good, the company in excellent spirits, and all seemed
well pleased with each other. In fact, a delightful temper
prevailed. After dinner, attended the meeting of the society. There were present Mr. Lyell, Mr. De la Bouche,
Mr. Murchison, Professor Sedgwick, besides those before
named. Dr. Buckland was in the chair. A member,
Mr. Hopkins, delivered a discourse on the *modus* of the
formation of the hills in the south of England, with reference to a general theory of such formations, where the
crust of the earth has been for a large district heaved up.
After the discourse, Mr. Lyell, De la Bouche, Sedgwick,
and Buckland, all spoke in respect to particular parts of
the discourse, some offering objections, and others confirming its doctrines. A love of truth seemed to pervade
every speaker, and no one appeared to consider anything
personal, how far soever it might oppose anything which
he had advanced.

"*Thursday.* Westminster Abbey. I followed the beadle around, and heard him describe the various groups of
statuary, with which the interior of the building is lined.
The Abbey is incomparably superior to anything and
everything in it. The sculpture is but moderate; much
of it in bad taste, and much of it in no taste at all. The

statues of Watt, Canning, Sir S. Raffles, Wilberforce, and
some others, struck me pleasantly; but few of the rest
gave me any satisfaction. But how impressive is all this
from its mere failure! This is human glory. This is sublunary immortality. Nelson said before one of his battles,
'Victory, or Westminster Abbey.' He had both, in effect;
and what are they? To have a stone or marble image
of yourself put up to be looked at and criticised after your
name has been forgotten, or, if not forgotten, in fact un-
heeded, — this is the whole. Such is the object for which
men consider life, honor, virtue, the cheap reward. O,
what madness is in their hearts! O God, impress this
lesson on my mind! May I never ask for any record of
my actions but the record of thy remembrance, and seek
for no other reward but thy favor, which is life, and thy
loving kindness, which is better than life.

"*Friday.* Dined with the Political Economy Club, on
invitation from Mr. Senior. There were present Mr.
Senior, Colonel Torrens, Mr. Tooke, Lord Monteagle
(Spring Rice), and others. After dinner, when the fruit
was brought on, the questions for discussion (printed)
were handed round the table. The discussion was opened
by Colonel Torrens, and continued until ten o'clock, when
I came away.

"*Saturday.* Went to Camberwell, to the residence of
Mr. Gurney, a leading Baptist, and short-hand writer to
the House of Lords. Mr. Gurney mentioned to me a
singular fact in his own history, worth recording in a
metaphysical point of view. He was engaged in taking
minutes of evidence on one occasion from four P. M. to
four A. M. It was on the inquiry relating to the Wal-
cheren expedition. At two o'clock he fell asleep, and was
aroused by some one asking the reporter to read the evidence of the last witness. It was the evidence of Sir
James Erskine, and was a description of the fortifications
of Flushing. Mr. G. said to the witness, who was standing near him, 'Sir James, I fear I have not written it all.'
'Never mind,' said the other; 'begin, and I will help you
out.' The evidence consisted of nearly two pages of short-
hand, and Mr. G. read it through, recognizing perfectly
all of it but the last four lines, of which, after a particular
sentence, he had no recollection whatever. These last
lines were written to the full as legibly as the rest, and he

read them without any difficulty. When he ceased, he turned to Sir James, and said, ' Sir James, that is all I have.' ' That,' replied the other, ' is the whole of it.' While asleep, he had continued writing as steadily and correctly as before.

" *Monday*. Dined with Rev. Dr. Harris (author of Mammon, and The Great Teacher) at the Spread Eagle Tavern. Present, Dr. Styles, author of Essay on the Stage, Mr. Jenkyn, author of a work on the Atonement, Mr. Belcher, and Mr. Ward, publisher. They all seemed sensible and good men. The conversation was in many respects profitable. The habits of the English are more convivial than ours. I saw no effect whatever of wine, yet more was used on this occasion than as many New England ministers would drink at a dozen dinners, if, indeed, they drank any. Dr. Harris is, I should suppose, between thirty and thirty-five years old, small, of a good countenance, evidencing strong determination, decision, and quickness. He appeared well, and in everything acted like a Christian and a gentleman. Mr. Jenkyn is a very sound, serious, and sensible man. He is the principal of the college which was formerly Dr. Doddridge's Theological School.

" *Tuesday*, *February* 9. Dined at Mr. Kenyon's. Present, Rev. Mr. Raymond, Mr. Hawthorne, Mr. Robinson, Captain Jones, R. N., Professor Babbage, and others. Mr. Babbage is a man about medium size, or rather less, compactly and firmly built, yet constructed for great activity. His head is remarkable for size, and, I should think, for symmetrical development; his eye deep-seated; nose aquiline, and rather crooked; mouth large and determined; and whole face indicative of strong feeling, easily excited. The eye, however, is the most remarkable feature in his face. It has a vividness that is almost scorching. It is restless, changing, yet always intense. It has the effect upon you of the eye of insanity. Indeed, that intensity of mental action is commonly nearly allied to insanity, and frequently is, for a while, on its very brink. The evening was very pleasant; I came away at a few minutes after eleven o'clock.

" *February* 11, *Thursday*. Dined with Sir J. Clarke, and went with him to Dr. Forbes', to the meeting of the Royal Society. The meeting was full, all the seats in the room being occupied, and several members standing. The Marquis of Northampton in the chair. Sir J. Lubbock proposed Sir H. Vivian, Master of Ordnance, as a member, and moved that according to the custom of the society in cases of persons of distinguished rank, he be balloted for without the usual period of nomination. He was elected immediately. I was informed that in the case of noblemen, bishops, privy councillors, &c., this rule is always adopted. Presently Mr. C. was proposed, and the names read of those who had recommended him at a previous meeting. He was balloted for and elected. I learned that this gentleman was a dentist, in large business. To me, I must confess, all this looks odd. I have nothing to say about hereditary legislators. I enter no protest against an aristocracy of rank. This may be a question of taste. Let those who like such a form of society establish it and maintain it. But I do not see why it should not be restrained within its own limits. Why should it invade the aristocracy of science or of talent? Why should not each be independent within its own sphere? Why should the aristocracy of talent bow down before that of rank? Why should not a peer be treated, in matters of science, like any other man? Why should science assume that its respectability must be supported by rank? These may be useless queries, but to me they seem very natural. It may be said, that, in this manner, the benefits are shared by both parties. I think not quite so. The peerage does not extend its rank to the philosopher. All England would stand aghast were a man to be raised to the peerage on account of scientific merit. Why then should the peerage of intellect be conferred on a lord, on account of his rank? Let both parties blend in social intercourse, where those courtesies may be reciprocal, but let each rank stand for its own order.

"*Sunday*. Dr. Leifchild; a good sermon. Afternoon at home, reading Scriptures, and hymns, and prayer. I have generally spent the afternoon thus, since I have been abroad, and find it, I think, more profitable than the public service.

"15*th*, *Monday*. Purchased various articles for ——, and others. Nothing has seemed to bring home nearer than this occupation. I know not when I have enjoyed any time more.

"*Friday.* Anniversary dinner of the Geological Society. I attended as a guest of Mr. Murchison, the newly elected president. There were present about one hundred persons. The dinner table is set in the room next to that in which the company is assembled. Before dinner every one goes in and ascertains where is to be his place. This is known by his name on a card placed opposite his plate. There were present the Russian ambassador, Baron B.; Marquis of Northampton, president of Royal Society; Bishop of Norwich, president of Linnæan Society; Bishop of Litchfield; and Earl of Selkirk. After dinner, the Queen, royal family, &c., were toasted; the Geological Society and Dr. Buckland, late president; the Royal Society and Lord Northampton; the Linnæan Society and Bishop of Norwich; the Zoölogical Society; the Astronomical Society; the British Institution and President Whewell. The speeches and replies were all good, and some very happy. I observed that the fellowship of science was thus admirably cultivated. Every one who had done anything in any department felt that he was a member of the fraternity, and that his claims were recognized. We need something of this sort very much among us. Our lights are not very brilliant, but if collected in a focus, they would make a much better figure, and throw abroad a much wider illumination, than now.

"*Monday.* To Cambridge with Professor Whewell.

"Evening at Cambridge. Philosophical Society. Professor Whewell explained the principle on which oblique arches should be constructed, and read a paper to prove that all matter must have weight. I confess that I could not see the force of his argument. ·He evidently took for granted some principles which did not seem to me self-evident; but this was probably my ignorance of the higher mathematics. With the reasons, however, I have not so much to do. I only record the fact. I was not convinced, nor am I now.

"*Tuesday*, 22*d.* Breakfasted with Mr. Carus, Dean of Trinity, a pious and excellent man, the successor of Simeon, of whom he mentioned several anecdotes. Mr. S. was, when he first entered the university, vain, thoughtless, and wicked. He was required to take the sacrament. His unworthiness roused him to reflection, and for weeks he was miserable almost to despair, until he obtained a view of the atoning sacrifice of Christ; and then he began anew to live. He became fellow of the college and rector of a church in the city. At first he was bitterly persecuted. His church doors were nailed up. Dead cats and dogs were thrown at him in the streets. Every one avoided him as though he were infected with the plague. One day, as he was passing through the college grounds, a student touched his cap to him. This act of kindness so affected him that he went directly to his room, and poured out his soul to God, with thanks and tears, at the thought that there was one person who did not despise him. The story of his opening to the passage, 'They found one named Simon, and him they compelled to bear his cross, &c.,' is confirmed by Mr. Carus; only it occurred in his room as he rose from prayer.

"I attended Professor Whewell's lecture. About sixty or seventy persons, most of them graduates, were present. It was on the character and doctrines of Hobbes. It was well done. The points were brought out clearly, and the view given was lucid and distinct. He traced Hobbes' doctrines to the ancient Greeks, and I was surprised that he did not refer to Plato's notion of a republic, which seems to me very analogous to Hobbes' Leviathan.

"*Friday.* At one o'clock, to Dr. Whewell's lecture on the writers that opposed Hobbes. It was well done, but scarcely as interesting as the preceding.

"From Cambridge to Earlham, near Norwich. I was received with the greatest friendship by my friend and the friend of all good men, J. J. Gurney. I immediately felt that I was at home, and this little period has been an oasis in my wilderness of journeyings.

"The governing principle of this family is love. Mr. Gurney is loved most devotedly, and he as devotedly loves and seeks the happiness of all. It is the most delightful Christian family that I have ever seen. The house of our friend is situated on the side of a gentle slope, commanding quite an extensive view in this generally flat country. It is flanked on both sides by a grove and walks. In front and rear, a vista is opened to the country beyond. The house is quite ancient, the oldest part being about three hundred years old, and a newer part two hundred. The entrance-hall is lined with specimens in natural history, in fine preservation. Similar ornaments are seen throughout the stairway, and upper halls and galleries. The rooms are almost everywhere covered with books, to the number of about eight thousand. Mr. G.'s study is filled with books, principally theological; among them are some of the most valuable and rare of the Fathers, some of the best Lexicons in Greek and Hebrew, and many of the best commentators in various languages. The house, the place, the books, the ornaments, are such as express the idea of an English literary Christian gentleman. When I arrived, it was nearly nine o'clock in the evening. I was ushered into the drawing-room, where I was introduced to the family. Tea and coffee, and other refreshments, were ordered; and, as I was not quite well, every attention was paid to my comfort. After hearing the arrangements for the next day, I retired.

" *Saturday.* I arose much better for my night's repose. At half past seven the bell rings for rising, at half past eight for reading the Scriptures. Mr. G., Jr., reads from the New Testament or Book of Psalms; then some remarks or a prayer is offered. Mr. G., while the breakfast is coming, takes a turn round the garden. After breakfast each seems to retire to his or her own business for the day. Mr. G. proceeds with his literary work, or what may require his attention, until he goes to town. The carriage was ordered for me, and with Mr. Taylor, a young friend of the family, I went to Norwich. In the carriage I found a copy of the Holy Scriptures, which, I presume, is always kept there. I called on Rev. Mr. Alexander and Rev. Mr. Brock, the former the Independent, and the latter the Baptist clergyman. Both received me with great kindness. From them I learned whatever was to be known of my mother's relations. We returned in the carriage with Mrs. Opie, the authoress, an intimate friend of the family of Mr. G. She is one of the most remarkable persons I have ever seen. Though now more than seventy years of age, she appears only forty or fifty, with the activity of a girl. Her mental energy seems not in the least diminished. Her conversation is as rapid, her apprehension as quick, and her wit as brilliant, as ever. She has a full recollection of almost all the great men of the time of Pitt and Fox. She was the intimate friend of Lafayette, of whom she entertains the highest opinion. She once had a very good view of Napoleon, reviewing his troops.   She gazed on him as long as it was possible, in a sort of amazement.   As she returned through the garden of the Tuileries, such was her emotion that she burst into a flood of tears.   She said, ' It seemed as if I should die if I could not thus give way to my feelings.' It was a feeling of dread, of indefinable awe, mixed with the conviction that she should never witness such a sight again.

"*Sunday*. Rode into town ; heard Mr. Brock.   'I can do all things through Christ, which strengtheneth me.'   It was an excellent sermon, showing that Christ knows all our conditions internally, all our circumstances externally, has all power to order everything for our good, and has promised that he will do so.   Grant, blessed Redeemer, that I may be enabled thus to rely upon thy strength, and confide in thy power, and be made perfect by thy righteousness.   Lunched with Mrs. Opie, and attended worship at the Friends' meeting in the afternoon.   Mr. G. spoke briefly and prayed.   An aunt of his, a most excellent lady, eighty-four years of age, had died during the week, after a short illness.   It affected the whole assembly, and the meeting was for the most part spent in silence.   This is the twenty-first Sabbath from home.   After six more, if it pleases my God, I hope to see my native country.   In the evening at about eight o'clock the servants and immediate neighbors assemble in the dining-room, and Mr. G. reads the Scriptures, with remarks on what has been read.   On this occasion the portion was the first three chapters of Ephesians, and his remarks were pious, judicious, and pertinent.

" At breakfast, Monday, we were joined by Mr. Alexander and Mr. Brock, who staid until noon.   They are very sensible and religious men, and our intercourse on subjects connected with the ministry, &c., was instructive.

" *Tuesday*. An ordination occurred to-day in Norwich. Mr. A. Reid, son of the Rev. Dr. A. Reid, was to be ordained over the oldest dissenting church here.   I had just set out to walk, when Mr. Brock met me in a gig, which he had brought out to take me to Norwich.   Mr. Alexander delivered a discourse on the nature of a Christian church.   The candidate was asked several questions touching his personal evidence of religion, call to the ministry, views of doctrine, &c., to which he replied by reading from a manuscript in full. This was nearly an hour's exercise. The father then preached from the text, ' He that goeth forth and weepeth,' &c. The subject of the discourse was an analogy between the work of the husbandman and that of the preacher. It was exceedingly well done. The address to his son at the close was very touching, and the assembly was generally moved. I was invited to close the exercises by prayer. It was a very interesting occasion, though too long. It occupied from half past ten till nearly three."

In Edinburgh Dr. Wayland visited the lecture-rooms of many eminent men, with some of whom he enjoyed agreeable interviews. No portion, probably, of his journey afforded him more pleasure than the time spent in this city. He remarks, —

" Everywhere we perceive a strong feeling of kindness towards America, and a dread of war, which is truly delightful to every Christian sentiment."

Of Dr. Chalmers he writes, —

" Dr. C. entered at once into the subject of non-intrusion, and we had a very interesting discussion. If I mistake not, he will soon relinquish his sentiments on religious establishments, and become essentially an Independent. He seems to me now, within a step of it. Dr. C. is a stout, strongly-built man, of middle height, with a very large cerebral development, rather passing into years, but of vigorous and active mind, buoyant with hope, full of benevolence, and, I should think, remarkable for candor and ingenuousness of mind. He walked with us to the Botanical Garden, and we had an hour of animated discussion.

" On Monday we proceeded to the university, where we attended Dr. Chalmers' lecture. The room was well filled by students, of the age and appearance, in general, of our theological students. The doctor wore the gown of a doctor in divinity. He lectures from a pulpit, and the lecture-room contains a gallery for occasional attendants. He commenced with prayer; after this was the calling of the roll, and then the lecture. The subject was the divinity of Christ, proved from the various texts with which we are familiar. He insisted strongly on the following point. The first Christians were originally idolaters. The worship of Christ, if he be not God, is idolatry. The apostles would have guarded their disciples with peculiar care against this idolatry, if it were idolatry. This idea presents the passages in a stronger light than they could otherwise have. His manner is earnest, but his accent was the broadest Scotch I almost ever heard. He seems to have no idea of any distinction in vowel sounds, and frequently the same word will be sounded in several different ways. Yet his earnestness bears him on, and carries you along with him. I was strongly impressed with the opinion that the pulpit is his proper place, and that he erred in leaving it. We dined at Dr. Abercrombie's, so well known by his works on intellectual and moral philosophy. He is a stout, well-built man, with a pleasant, benevolent face, though it has something the appearance of a Jew, using the word in its good sense. It was a delightful visit. We went with him to the meeting of the Royal Society of Edinburgh, Dr. A. in the chair. The papers were mostly controversial, for which the secretary apologized, and assured us that such was not their usual character.

" The meeting was well attended, and much more interest was shown than in the Royal Society of London.

" The papers were by Sir T. Dickland on the parallel roads of Glen Roy, and by Dr. Forbes on his discoveries in the polarization of light. After meeting there was tea, as in the Royal Society of London. We closed the evening by supper at Sir W. Hamilton's. The conversation was interesting, and it was one o'clock before we arrived at our lodgings.

"·*Tuesday Morning*. Breakfast with Dr. Chalmers. None but his family and sons-in-law present. Conversation on the voluntary system, non-intrusion, &c. It is a delightful family. It was cheering to see a good man so happy in his domestic circle. From Dr. Chalmers' we hastened to town, and took stage for Glasgow. In the coach were several intelligent people, and I found the topic of universal interest was the non-intrusion doctrines. I am strongly of opinion that the voluntary principle will yet become the doctrine of the non-intrusionists. It would almost be so now, but for the erroneous statements which have been made by Dr. B. and others respecting our country."

Returning from Scotland, Dr. Wayland again visited Liverpool, and at the house of Mr. Rathbone met Rev. J. Blanco White. His interview with this remarkable man made a deep impression upon him, and was often referred to in subsequent years.

From Liverpool he proceeded to Oxford, taking on his way Kenilworth and Stratford-on-Avon. At Oxford he visited the leading objects of interest, and was indebted to the eminent scholars of the university for many courteous attentions. He writes, —

" Of Oxford, what shall I say? Its buildings are magnificent, the surroundings beautiful beyond description. Its foundations are princely. Its colleges are palaces, its grounds all that the eye could desire. The officers are, so far as I saw, thorough-bred gentlemen, highly intelligent, and, I presume, finely educated. It is a place where you would love to dwell, and about which you cannot but wish to linger. But when one reflects on the immense wealth of its establishment, and remembers that this was designed to promote the prosecution of science and the advancement of learning, and not for the cultivation of luxurious ease ; when one remembers that it was for the education of the people of England, and not a part of them, and that it is now used for the good of a part, and is the avenue to all social and professional standing, I cannot think of it with unmixed respect. It seems to me a monstrous perversion. I do not speak of the present incumbents, — I know not how far they are responsible, — but of the system. Of this I can hardly speak in terms of too great disapprobation. It is in the main the same as Cambridge, though in detail it is more restrictive, and is more inclined to theology. It seemed to me to be cultivating narrowness rather than expansiveness of mind, and to be conferring rather a fragment of education than an enlarged view of human knowledge. Authority appeared to be the *ultima ratio;* and hence they must, I think, continue year after year to proceed in interminable discussions, without ever making any satisfactory progress.

I may judge them severely, but I must say that I think
them too rich, too close a borough, and too much interested in the social system of England, to do anything valuable for the cause of science, or at least anything that shall
correspond to their great advantages.

"From Oxford to Frome. Frome is an old town, formerly the seat of extensive wool manufactories. These
have migrated to the coal districts, where machinery has
taken the place of hand-loom weaving, and Frome is a
place of minor consequence.

"We were entertained at Mr. John Shepherd's, a distant
connection of mine, a gentleman of leisure, a writer, and
a poet. We were treated with great hospitality, and saw
much of the environs, which are very beautiful. The
country is assuming the dress of spring. The meadows
are greener than any I ever saw, and the trees are bud-
ding as ours are in May. I saw the house of my father's
parents, and traced out some of his relations.

"From Frome to Bristol; and thence to Stapleton, to
visit John Foster. He is now an aged man. He wears
an old gray surtout, yellow bandanna neckerchief, and old
shoes. He talks with all the vivacity of youth, is a most
ardent friend of civil and religious liberty, and is better
acquainted with America than any man whom I have
seen in England. He is oppressed with the infirmities of
age. His teeth are almost gone; he wears a wig; and
everything reminds you that this, the last Baptist light of
England, is at no distant day to be extinguished."

We find no record of his visit to Rugby, nor of his interview with Dr. Arnold.

Dr. Wayland returned to America in April, 1841. Not
long afterwards he writes Colonel Stone, —

"As to my coming home too soon, &c., I am well
aware that it may seem a mistake; but the fact is, my
health was so poor that I was unable to travel until the
time for visiting the south of Europe had passed. I had
scarcely a well day, a day free from fever, until March.
During almost the entire period of my residence in Paris,
my pulse was above ninety, and my whole system was
very much disordered. Travelling under such circumstances was utterly useless to me."

Undoubtedly Dr. Wayland shared the not uncommon experience of tourists in the feeling that it is very pleasant to *have travelled*. Upon the knowledge acquired while absent he was accustomed to put a low estimate, perhaps lower than was justified by the facts. Probably his observation of the institutions of the old world, alike social, political, educational, and religious, emancipated him from any undue and superstitious veneration. He became convinced that, in common with his countrymen, he was as likely to attain success by cherishing his own conceptions, and by applying his independent judgment to the means of reaching results, as were the men of the old world by worshipping the wisdom of the past. To have learned this was worth a voyage across the Atlantic. If there were other results, if there were, in addition, valued acquaintances and friendships acquired, these were clear gain.

At this point we take pleasure in introducing the following interesting reminiscences, for which we are indebted to Hon. Isaac Davis, LL. D., of Worcester, Mass. : —

"In February, 1841, I returned from the Continent to London, where I met Dr. Wayland. He was unwell and much depressed in spirits, longing to return to his home and family. I had then completed my travels in Europe, and made my arrangements to take the next steamer for America. He urged me to accompany him to Scotland and some parts of England, and to postpone my return to America for two months. After some hesitation I consented, and we left London for Edinburgh, stopping, however, on our way thither to visit his uncle, Rev. D. S. Wayland, who resided at Bassingham. He was a clergyman of the Established church, a ripe scholar, and a Christian gentleman. His household realized my ideal of an English home circle. I have seldom known a family of greater mental culture or more genial social qualities.

"During our journey I took the whole charge of our arrangements, and, so far as was practicable, relieved Dr. Wayland of all care and annoyance. His health soon improved, and his enjoyment of travel increased proportionally.

"When we arrived in Edinburgh, one of the first places which we visited was the university. Dr. Wayland was at once received with marked attention by Dr. Chalmers, Sir William Hamilton, Professor Wilson, Dr. Abercrombie, of the Royal Philosophical Society, Lord Murray, and other distinguished men. The officers of the university very courteously afforded him every facility for examining all its departments.

"We next visited Glasgow. Here, as was natural, the university was the earliest object of attention. The president and professors were unwearied in their courtesies, assisting him in every way to understand the practical workings of their system of education.

"In Liverpool we remained several days. The mayor was very courteous in showing us all places of interest in and around the city. I well remember that Dr. Wayland had more invitations to dine with distinguished men in Liverpool than it was possible for him to accept. Dr. Raffles was especially attentive.

"From thence we went to Oxford. Here he was most cordially welcomed by the magnates of the university. I need not tell you with how eager an interest he visited the chapels, libraries, and printing establishments of this ancient university, or with what patient attention he examined the discipline, courses of study, and educational advantages thus fully open for his inspection. More than a week was most profitably spent in this city of colleges.

"From Oxford we went to Frome, stopping at intermediate places which contained objects of interest. Frome was the birthplace of the father of Dr. Wayland. We were received with great kindness by Mr. Shepherd of that place, and invited to his house. We found him a most estimable man, a lay preacher, 'going about doing good,' like his Lord and Master. He was a distant relative, I believe, of the Wayland family, and a Baptist.

"At Frome there was a Baptist church, where the senior Wayland had worshipped. It was pleasant to discover that he was remembered by several citizens. In this church Dr. Wayland preached. The congregation listened to him with attention, and were more than once moved to tears.

" From Frome we went to Bristol, visited the Baptist Theological Institution in that city, and the Broadmead Chapel, of which Robert Hall was once the pastor. Many interesting reminiscences were collected of that great man from those who had heard him preach, and were on terms of intimacy with him.

" We passed a day with John Foster, at Stapleton, near Bristol. In a letter which I received from Mr. Foster after my return to America he alludes to that day as the most interesting he had spent for many years with friendly strangers. For Dr. Wayland's purity and simplicity of character, as well as for his talents and acquirements, Mr. Foster expressed his most profound respect.

" From the time I met Dr. Wayland in London, until I parted from him in New York, several elements of his character particularly attracted my attention. His humility in all cases and under all circumstances, whether he was among the common people or in the most literary and polished society, his wisdom and learning, were discovered rather than displayed. His benevolence was wide as the world. He pitied all whom he saw in distress, and did all in his power to relieve their wants, often giving indeed more than he could well afford.

" His religious character stood out in bold relief, on all occasions. However late at night before we retired, a portion of Scripture was always read, and prayer offered. So also every morning before commencing the labors of the day. When we had opportunities for being present at any exhibition or place of entertainment, he would say, ' Davis, if Christ were on earth, and present here, would he attend this exhibition?' If he believed Christ would not, he would not. He tested duty ever in this way. Christ-like and striving to obey all the commands of the Master, he lost no opportunity to labor for his Savior and in his cause. Withal, he was cheerful, relishing timely flashes of wit, and enjoying refined merriment. In his interviews with the learned men of England he exhibited a good command of nervous English, and was remarkable for the lucidity of his explanations."

CHAPTER II.

DISCOURSE ON NICHOLAS BROWN. — DEATH OF COLONEL
STONE. — PROFESSOR GODDARD. — DEATH OF REV. F.
WAYLAND, SENIOR. — RHODE ISLAND REBELLION. —
DEBTS OF THE STATES. — ANNEXATION OF TEXAS. —
MEXICAN WAR. — "DUTY OF OBEDIENCE TO THE CIVIL
MAGISTRATE." — FULLER AND WAYLAND ON SLAVERY.
— IRISH FAMINE. — DR. JUDSON. — MISSIONARY UNION.
— UNIVERSITY SERMONS. — REVIVAL IN COLLEGE. —
PRAYER MEETINGS. — PARENTAL AUTHORITY IN RE-
LIGIOUS AFFAIRS. — "THOUGHTS ON THE COLLEGIATE
SYSTEM." — TOWN LIBRARY SYSTEM.

RETURNING to his home, President Wayland resumed his labors, not only cheerfully, but eagerly.
He was weary of the pursuit of relaxation, and to be
again at work was rest.

The first duty of a public nature to which he was called
was the Discourse on the Life and Character of Nicholas
Brown, delivered November 3, 1841. While sharing, alike
on public and on personal grounds, in the general grief
at an event which had dried up a fountain of charity, he
willingly undertook, at the request of the authorities of
the university, the task of exhibiting before the citizens
of Providence an example of boundless benevolence, tender sympathy, and enlarged public spirit. In one passage
of the eulogy it is not difficult to trace the influence of his
recent journey: —

"If such be the relation which this life sustains to another, and if such be the influence which we must exert

over those that come after us, it is manifest that we can accomplish in no signal degree the purposes of our being, unless we act for posterity. We can associate our names with succeeding ages only by deeds or by thoughts which they will not willingly forget. And thus it is that everywhere man seeks to attain to a sublunary immortality. The crumbling tombstone and the gorgeous mausoleum, the sculptured marble and the venerable cathedral, all bear witness to the instinctive desire within us to be remembered by coming generations. But how short-lived is the immortality which the works of our hands can confer! The noblest monuments of art that the world has ever seen are covered with the soil of twenty centuries. The works of the age of Pericles lie at the foot of the Acropolis in indiscriminate ruin. The ploughshare turns up the marble which the hand of Phidias had chiselled into beauty, and the Mussulman has folded his flock beneath the falling columns of the Temple of Minerva. But even the works of our hands too frequently survive the memory of those who have created them. And were it otherwise, could we thus carry down to distant ages the recollection of our existence, it were surely childish to waste the energies of an immortal spirit in the effort to make it known to other times that a being whose name was written with certain letters of the alphabet once lived, and flourished, and died. Neither sculptured marble nor stately column can reveal to other ages the lineaments of the spirit; and these alone can embalm our memory in the hearts of a grateful posterity. As the stranger stands beneath the dome of St. Paul's, or treads, with religious awe, the silent aisles of Westminster Abbey, the sentiment which is breathed from every object around him is the utter emptiness of sublunary glory. The most magnificent nation that the world has ever seen has here exhausted every effort to render illustrious her sons who have done worthily. The fine arts, obedient to private affection or public gratitude, have embodied in every form the finest conceptions of which their age was capable. In years long gone by, each one of these monuments has been watered by the tears of the widow, the orphan, or the patriot. But generations have passed away, and mourners and mourned have sunk together into forgetfulness. The aged crone, or the smooth-tongued beadle, as now he hurries you through aisle and chapel, utters, with measured cadence and unmeaning tone, for the thousandth time, the name and lineage of the once-honored dead, and then gladly dismisses you, to repeat again his well-conned lesson to another group of idle passers-by. Such, in its most august form, is all the immortality that matter can confer. Impressive and venerable though it be, it is the impressiveness of a solemn and mortifying failure. It is by what we ourselves have done, and not by what others have done for us, that we shall be remembered in after ages. It is by thought that has aroused my intellect from its slumbers, which has ' given lustre to virtue, and dignity to truth,' or by those examples which have inflamed my soul with the love of goodness, and not by means of sculptured marble, that I hold communion with Shakspeare and Milton, with Johnson and Burke, with Howard and Wilberforce."

To his sister : —

" . . . I am glad that you liked the discourse on Nicholas Brown. It gave me a great deal of trouble, and I feared that it might seem stiff and formal. What you say of the paragraph about Westminster Abbey is certainly true. Everything in an old country reminds you of the past, of its changes, and of the shortness of human life. Here everything looks towards the future. In a country that bears the marks of two thousand years, an individual or a race appears exceedingly insignificant, and one is continually reminded of the instability of everything but religion. I felt it constantly."

Dr. Wayland had now reached that period of life at which he must expect, if he himself survived, often to lament the removal of the friends of his youth and the counsellors of his manhood. In the summer of 1844, in the decease of his brother-in-law, Colonel Stone, he experienced one of the severest bereavements of his life. For nearly thirty years the strongest affection and the freest intercourse had subsisted between them, conjoined with the unity in essentials and the diversity in non-essentials, that rendered such intercourse in the highest degree pleasing and profitable. They had discussed in the fullest manner every topic that could interest either of them, whether in the field of education, politics, or morality. And for many years their sympathy had been rendered more absolute than before by an entire agreement of sentiment in regard to the realities of religion.

To Mrs. Stone : —

"August 18, 1844.

" My very dear Sister : Amidst your overwhelming sorrow I scarcely know how to address you. I am too well aware of what you have lost, I feel too deeply my own bereavement, not to understand that at such a moment almost any voice must seem intrusive. Earthly consolations, I know, can offer but little comfort. At such a time ' the proud helpers do stoop under us,' and our only hope is derived from taking hold of things unseen.

" For the greater part of my life I had known your dear husband intimately ; more intimately, indeed, than any one of my own brothers. During all this time not a word of unkindness ever passed between us. His temper was so sweet, his affections were so generous and lively, his desire for the happiness of others was so active and untiring, that we soon became intimate, and have always continued so. I feel that a brother at my right hand has been stricken down, and I am left alone.

" And it has, at last, been unexpected. Only by the papers have we learned the mournful event. I had always persuaded myself that he would recover. Everything had seemed to be gradually tending to his restoration. But God has destroyed our hopes, and has recalled our treasure to himself.

" But herein, my dear sister, is our only consolation — God, God in Christ has done it. It could only have been done at his bidding. ' As for our Rock, his way is perfect.' Nothing could be added that would render what he has done wiser, better, or more holy. Nothing could be altered. ' What we see not now, we shall see hereafter.' He will yet teach us that all is right, and that he has in faithfulness afflicted us."

To the same : —

"December 8, 1844.

"I have thought much of you for some weeks past. The change of the seasons, the Thanksgiving last week, all brought home to me recollections of which I would say to any other member of the family, but dare not to you. It would only open afresh those sources of sorrow that bleed sufficiently without being probed. It is very, very sad, and nothing will explain it, but ' even so, Father, for so it seemed good in thy sight.' This is our only support. When we look at home or abroad, at the daily or the literary press, at politics or the history of our country, it seems as if a chasm had been made that could never be filled. At every turn I am reminded that one has left my side with whom I had walked in sweet converse for nearly thirty years, with whom I could always advise, and who would always look at my interest as though it were his own. What, however, is this to your loss? But I will not go on. Such, my dear sister, is this world of sin. ' In the world we must have tribulation ;' it is in Christ alone that we can have peace. What a blessed book the Bible is to a bereaved and crushed spirit. Did it ever occur to you to reflect, what affliction and bereavement must have been to the heathen, to whom the grave was a starless midnight? Their affections were, as we know, frequently as strong as ours ; and when every hope was destroyed, and every support stricken down, where did the crushed soul look for consolation? It was all the darkness of despair. What do we owe to Him who by the sacrifice of himself brought life and immortality to light! He not only revealed to us the unseen world, but gave himself to render it possible that the world should be heaven, instead of hell, to us. I pray that you may be enabled to stay yourself on God ; and even in your sorrow may your peace be as a river, and your righteousness as the waves of the sea. I hope that you will not allow yourself to look back upon second causes. I do not believe that you have the remotest reason to refer to them with pain. I do not know, if the past could be recalled, how we could do better or differently. If dear brother could, six months or a year before, have been taken off from all business, this might have produced, with the blessing of God, a different result. But in this respect it pleased our heavenly Father to spread a veil before the eyes of all of us. We thought that with some modification of labor he might improve ; but the veil was the thickest over the eyes of the dear sufferer himself. Yet it was God who did it, and this was his chosen way of accomplishing his purposes."

After Mr. Stone, there was perhaps no one with whom the president held more intimate relations than with Professor Goddard. This gentleman (who was but two years the senior in age) was the first member of the Faculty with whom Dr. Wayland became acquainted, and the friendship continued to grow in strength until the sudden death of Professor Goddard, in 1846. At the request of the Faculty of the university, Dr. Wayland delivered a discourse, afterwards published, upon the character of his deceased friend, in which he paid a generous, or more properly, a truthful tribute to the memory of a man of singularly elegant taste, rare scholarship, and high character.

Three years later, in the spring of 1849, Rev. Francis Wayland, Senior, was removed by death, bequeathing to his children a priceless legacy. The event was not indeed unexpected, for he was within three years of fourscore. But it brought the end of life nearer at hand, and made his son feel that the outposts were driven in, and that none now stood between himself and the advance of death.

To Deacon Lincoln : —

" . . . My dear father's end was most blessed. I arrived twenty-four hours after his decease. During his whole sickness his soul was filled with joy. He always spoke of death as ' going home,' and said he had ' a desire to depart and to be with Christ, which was far better.' ' Yes,' added he, ' a thousand times better.' Mr. K., who was with him, said that if he had spoken two minutes before his death, he would have spoken as calmly as at any hour of his life. May God give us grace to follow in his steps. I think I can truly say, that I would prefer the heritage of his life and death to that of all the honors this world could confer. I cannot conceive of any comparison between being the son of such parents and being the son of any whom the world calls great or noble." *

To his brother-in-law, Rev. Dr. Bartol: —

"There is in the death of friends who have on earth realized something of heaven, a remarkable power to draw the mind upward, and teach it communion with eternal things. We seem to be looking through a veil which has been made transparent. The joys that we saw on earth seem merely continued in eternity. The one appears to be a sort of measure of the other. It was thus, in a peculiar manner, with my father. His sickness was one continual longing to depart and be with Christ."

The following letter of Dr. Wayland was written to a niece who was then suffering from illness, which soon proved fatal.

"My very dear Niece: We had been waiting for many days, in great anxiety, for a letter from the Springs. We had heard that you were unwell, and daily remembered you in our prayers, but we knew not the extent of your illness. The letter which we have received to-day has awakened our serious apprehensions. I lose not a moment in writing to you.

"I need not assure you, my dear child, how deeply we are grieved at such accounts of your sickness. You have been a great comfort to us all, and we all feel towards you the affection which belongs to a daughter or a sister. We have tenderly loved you for your gentleness, your disinterestedness, your self-sacrifice, and your undeviating yet mild conscientiousness. I do not say these things simply to praise you, but I want you to feel how much you are beloved, and to know that we all have appreciated your constant desire to render those around you happy.

* "My boast is not that I deduce my birth
From loins enthroned and rulers of the earth;
But higher far my proud pretensions rise —
The child of parents passed into the skies."

"These things make us lovely, my dear child, in the eyes of men; but you know, as well as I can tell you, that they form no ground of acceptance with God. In his eyes we are all sinners, under just and solemn condemnation. Judged by his law, we are wholly without excuse. But, blessed be his name, our helpless sinfulness is no ground for despair. 'God so loved the world that he gave his only begotten Son, that whosoever believeth in him should not perish, but have everlasting life.' The gate of heaven is thrown wide open through the atoning mercy of Christ. 'Whosoever cometh unto him he will in no wise cast out.' 'This is a faithful saying, and worthy of all acceptation, that Christ Jesus came into the world to save sinners.' All this is the simple truth. The blessed Savior says precisely and exactly what he means; only, human language cannot reveal the extent of his love.

"Strive, then, my dear child, to go in simplicity of heart to the Savior. Suffer nothing to interpose between him and your soul. If any objection arises in your mind, take the objection to him, and lay it at his feet. Look to him to strengthen you in weakness, to raise your eyes that you may look up to him, and to direct your hands, that they may take hold on him. Endeavor to cast aside everything, and ask him to help you to do so. Lie down at his feet, and touch the hem of his garment. May his grace assist you!

"Your aunt and I are very desirous to do everything for you which is in our power. Should you become able to leave your home, we shall be delighted to have you come to us. I do not expect you to write. I know you are too feeble for this. But let me hear from you, and tell me as much of your feelings as you are willing to dictate. . . ."

In the letters of Dr. Wayland, written during years of intense political excitement, the reader has probably noticed but few allusions to the party strife then dividing the country. Whether one set of men or another should occupy the offices of government, was a matter to which he was indifferent. He frequently urged his friends not to become too much absorbed in questions which did not turn on great principles. In his correspondence with gentlemen largely interested in politics, he sought to assuage the violence and rancor of party strife, and to urge the cultivation of friendly and fraternal feelings.

But he did not seek to withdraw into a literary seclusion or clerical neutrality when the country was imperilled. In the year 1842, the State of Rhode Island was the scene of profound and painful agitation. A portion of the inhabitants, becoming dissatisfied with the restrictions upon the right of suffrage imposed by the existing charter of the state, attempted to overthrow the government by force of arms, and, in the attempt, resorted to means that were as abhorrent to morality as their purpose was subversive of social order. Upon the Sabbath following the suppression of the first outbreak, and again upon the day of Thanksgiving appointed by the state authorities after the final restoration of order, Dr. Wayland preached two discourses (afterwards published), in which he unfolded the true principles of constitutional government, and exhibited the duty of the citizen to the commonwealth. As he incurred unmeasured abuse at the time for these utterances, and as attempts have been sedulously made to misrepresent the question at issue, it seems proper to remark that the question was not in the least whether the privilege of suffrage should or should not be extended, but rather whether a company of men, without the semblance of law, could overthrow all social order, and put the property and the life of every citizen at the disposal of an armed and irresponsible mob.

Two years later, when some of the states were repudiating their obligations, he wrote two articles, for the North American Review and for the Christian Review, upon the Debts of the States, urging, with all the power of argument and appeal of which he was capable, an adherence to the dictates of honesty and national honor.

It needs scarcely be said that he was profoundly hostile to the annexation of Texas; regarding it as a measure utterly needless to a nation already possessed of more territory than it could profitably occupy, calculated to involve us in war, and, above all, tending to increase the extent and power of slavery. At the election of 1844 he voted for Mr. Clay, designing by this act to protest against the annexation scheme.

The Mexican war he regarded with unfeigned abhorrence, and never ceased, in public and in private, to urge the cessation of a wicked invasion, and to pray for those whom we were, by cruel hands, reducing to widowhood and orphanage. In 1847 he preached, in the chapel, three sermons upon " The Duty of Obedience to the Civil Magistrate," * suggested by the events of the war then transpiring. The citizen, in his view, is under obligation to obey the voice of the magistrate, so long as the commands are such as he can obey without a violation of conscience. But if the state directs the citizen to do a wrong act, if it bids him go forth, causelessly and needlessly, to murder his innocent fellow-men, then the obligation to obedience has ceased; the citizen may not at its command engage in an iniquitous war, nor may he derive profit from any complicity in the wrong-doing.

To Rev. Dr. Cutting (then editor of the New York Recorder) he writes, —

" I read your article on the war, in the main, with pleasure; but I thought that it did ¬ot take high ground enough. The whole war is so bad, that arguing on the conduct of it is a compliment, take what view you please. It is, *ab origine*, wicked, infamous, unconstitutional in design, and stupid and shockingly depraved in its management. Were I you, I would have a few short articles, setting forth, first, the causes in their naked deformity; second, the cost of the war in blood and money; third, the guilt of it as resting on the nation."

---

* Afterwards published in " University Sermons," and in " Salvation by Christ."

To his sister : —

"December 16, 1847.

"It is a long time since I wrote to you; but I am not wholly without excuse. The fact is, I cannot use my eyes in the evening (I am now transgressing the law). I have been at work for the press as fast as I was able. The results you have seen. I had written the introduction to the 'Recollections'* in the vacation, but was dissatisfied with it, and wrote it again. The sermons I had preached long since; but they required re-writing. In the mean time rheumatism came on, and broke me up for three weeks. I grew cold in my affections towards the sermons, and the more so, as I was obliged to work by snatches, as I could. However, after much delay, they at last reached the press. At first I apprehended that they were destined to blush unseen; but within a day or two their chance of obtaining a hearing has somewhat improved. I never felt more anxious about anything I have published; not, I trust, on my own account (for necessity was laid upon me, and I could not but bear my testimony), but on account of my country. I see not what is to be the result if the moral sentiment of the nation cannot be awakened. I should rejoice to see my sermons die and be forgotten, if this would arouse some one to undertake the task who is better fitted for its accomplishment."

* We have seen how agreeable an episode, in his experience of foreign travel, was his visit to Bassingham Rectory, the residence of his uncle, Rev. D. S. Wayland. His aunt, to whom he was strongly attached, died December 22, 1846. In 1847, a collection of reminiscences of incidents in a country parish, prepared by her at his solicitation, was published in America, under the title of "Recollections of Real Life in England," with an introduction by Dr. Wayland. This little volume was designed to illustrate the condition of the laboring classes in an agricultural district, and especially the relation which exists in more favored instances between these classes and the parochial clergy.

The graphic description which Dr. Wayland gives of English rural life under its most attractive aspects, and his vivid and truthful picture of the varied and invaluable labors of a faithful clergyman and his family, occasion a feeling of regret that he could not find time for a more extended narrative of his observations in England.

In 1844, Rev. Richard Fuller, D. D., then of Beaufort, S. C., had addressed a letter to the editor of the Christian Reflector in reply to arguments that had been urged against slavery. In the course of his letter he appealed for confirmation of his sentiments to some of the principles laid down in the Elements of Moral Science. The circumstances seemed not only to invite, but almost to demand some reply from Dr. Wayland. And he was more than willing to embrace the opportunity afforded him. He had long felt that he had a testimony to bear in behalf of his brethren who were in slavery, as well as a duty to discharge towards those who were holding in bondage the little ones of Christ. In an interview with his pastor, Rev. Dr. Granger, Dr. Wayland entreated him to pray that he might be so guided by wisdom from above as not to say anything at variance with the spirit of the gospel, and that the discussion might tend to the promotion of piety and the interests of humanity.

In a series of letters addressed to Dr. Fuller, Dr. Wayland exposed the fallacy of the arguments that had been drawn from the Scriptures in defence of domestic slavery. These letters, together with those of Dr. Fuller in reply, were collected in a volume, and published under the title " Domestic Slavery considered as a Scriptural Institution." The arguments of Dr. Wayland, weighty in themselves, derived additional force from the temperateness and courtesy with which they were urged. The letters tended to form and confirm the Christian public sentiment that twenty years later was to remove slavery from the nation. How far the correspondence circulated at the south we are not informed. We have no knowledge, however, of its having changed the opinions of any who, from interest or education, were defenders of slavery. The time for that had passed, and everything was hastening the inevitable and final appeal. Yet whatever the reception of his words, it never ceased to be, on his part, a

cause of gratitude to God, that he had been permitted to
lift his voice in behalf of human liberty.

Holding the views which he did, there could be little
room for doubt as to Dr. Wayland's action, when the question arose upon the admission of slavery into the territories of the United States. He favored the adoption of
the Wilmot proviso, and voted in 1848 for the candidates
of the Buffalo Convention.

But while a citizen of America, Dr. Wayland was no
less a citizen of the world, and his sympathies, though intense, were not narrow. Upon the breaking out of the
Irish famine, he was among the first to urge the people of
Providence to exhibit their wonted liberality towards a
suffering nation. As a member of the soliciting committee, he labored personally in collecting money, and at his
suggestion the means which were raised were transmitted
for distribution to his friend William Rathbone, Esq., of
Liverpool, whose personal kindness, practical wisdom,
and enlarged benevolence had deeply impressed Dr. Wayland while visiting him in 1840. It may with confidence
be asserted, that no portion of the contributions forwarded
from America were more productive of good, than were
the moneys intrusted to Mr. Rathbone.

Dr. Wayland writes to his sister, —

" . . . This morning I have been out in behalf of the
Irish. In less than two hours we raised here sixteen
hundred dollars. We hope to increase it to seven thousand dollars, and send it by the next steamer. The amount
received by Great Britain from this country will be large,
and I hope will set a new example of national intercourse.
It is noble to see such efforts in behalf of humanity, for
the sake of Christ, and even for the sake of general benevolence. It shows that the gospel of Christ is influencing nations. It is a bright spot in the darkness that in
many directions seems so closely to envelop us."

We have alluded in a previous chapter to the part which
Dr. Wayland took in the reorganization of the Triennial

Convention in 1826, and the success which attended the missionary operations of the Baptist denomination for a number of years after the changes there inaugurated. Gradually, however, it became evident that other modifications were needed, and that a new impulse must be imparted to the work of missions. The withdrawal of the Baptists of the Southern States seemed to render prompt action needful, and in November, 1845, a special meeting of the Convention was called, for the purpose of effecting such changes in the constitution of the body as were demanded by the exigencies of the times.

Peculiar interest was imparted to this meeting by the presence of Dr. Judson, who, after more than thirty years' absence, had been compelled, by his own declining health and that of his family, to return to America. Dr. Wayland had invited Dr. Judson to visit Providence, the scene of his collegiate education, on his way to the meeting of the Convention in New York. It is needless to repeat the account of this visit, as the narrative is fully given in the Memoir of the missionary, the author of which has recorded the profound impression made on him by the apostle to Burmah; but we quote the following from Dr. Wayland to his sister : —

" . . . We had a pleasant visit from Dr. Judson : he staid with us from Saturday to Monday evening, and accompanied us to New York. He is a most modest, meek, and heavenly-minded man. He is, to all appearance, wholly unmoved by the adulation he receives, and seems to wonder, with unfeigned *naïveté*, why any one should be so much interested in him. I went to Boston to accompany him here. I met him there, and he asked me when I should return to Providence. I told him, whenever he was ready, as I came to accompany him. His simple reply was, lifting up his hands, ' Why, I am ashamed.' I really think that this is a specimen of his feelings and temper. It is most delightful and edifying to see a man on whom the eyes of the whole country are turned, so entirely destitute of self-consciousness. When he was at

our church, a large congregation was present, for the purpose of seeing him. He did not rise during the services,
and almost every one was disappointed. You never saw
anything so remarkable as the veneration in which he
seems to be held. It was a difficult matter to get him out
of the church, such was the press to shake hands with
him."

Dr. Wayland presided at the meeting of the Convention
(having been elected its president in 1844), and introduced the honored missionary to the body, with the memorable words, " Brethren, I present to you ' Jesus Christ's
man.'" The address of Dr. Wayland on this occasion,
with other interesting proceedings at the Convention, are
found in the Memoir, which is undoubtedly in the hands
of all who will read these pages.

In reference to the changes in the constitution of the Convention, which were proposed and adopted at the meeting,
we are happy in being able to quote the words of Dr.
Stow.

" In 1845, after the disruption of the General Convention by the secession of the southern wing, a committee
of nine, of which Dr. Wayland was one, was appointed to
prepare a new constitution for the body, to be submitted
at a special session. As the members of the committee
were widely scattered, and could not conveniently meet,
it was agreed that Dr. Cone should draw up one, and Dr.
Wayland another, and that a Boston member should, as
secretary, construct one out of the two, for final consideration. The two forms prepared by Drs. Cone and Wayland, and their letters to the secretary, are now in my possession, and contain materials for a chapter, showing an
equal fervor of interest in the missionary enterprise, but a
wide diversity of opinions as to the shape of the organization for carrying it forward, the views of Dr. Cone being
eminently democratic, those of Dr. Wayland insisting on
greater power in the executive agency. As the instrument
was finally adopted, it embraced all that Dr. Wayland regarded as essential in preserving the organization from
harm by any sudden irruptions of popular excitement.
In the compromise effected between Drs. Cone and Way-

land, on that occasion, there was a beautiful exhibition
of their strong elements of Christian character.

"In the debate upon the constitution, one member was
apprehensive lest the door was not sufficiently closed
against the admission of slaveholders, and reflected with
some severity upon the motives of the committee in leaving
thus unguarded the entrance to membership. Dr. Wayland,
then presiding over the body, felt keenly the insinuation,
and made some remarks, repelling it with a force which
none who were present can have forgotten. His words
were few, but they were crushing, and showed a manly
indignation, that made impossible a repetition of the
offence."

Alike under the old organization of the Convention, and
the new organization of the Missionary Union, Dr. Wayland was frequently present at the anniversaries. He had
studied the whole subject of missions thoroughly; he read
every missionary biography or narrative of interest, that
appeared; he was familiar with the geography of the regions which were the scene of these self-denying labors
for Christ. When he spoke, there was little of rhetorical
ornament. But there were a sincerity, a clearness, a
moral earnestness, an unselfish devotion to the object in
view, and, mingled with all, a courtesy and a freedom
from personality, that commanded attention, and rendered
his presence a power. At this point we may with propriety again quote from Dr. Stow.

"In 1848 there was a conference at the mission-rooms
in Boston, to adjust some difficulties that had arisen between the executive committee and prominent individuals
outside, respecting some questions of missionary policy.
The difference of views had generated considerable personal feeling, and the parties came together under a heavy
burden of solicitude. Dr. Wayland was requested to open
the conference with prayer. As he knelt, the first sentences were uttered with a solemnity that was impressive,
almost awful — 'O God of eternity, this is not our cause;
it is thine. We are nothing. Thou art all.' That prayer
gave the key-note to all that followed, and the final result
was favorable to harmony and earnest coöperation."

But amid all these public labors for the regeneration of
the world, he did not forget that his first duties were to
the college, and peculiarly to the moral welfare of its members. He sought to avoid the ground of self-accusation,
found in the recollection, " My own vineyard have I not
kept." The series of Sabbath afternoon sermons, which
had been for a few years intermitted, was resumed in
1845. A portion of these discourses were published in
1848, under the title of " University Sermons," although,
as has before been intimated, the contents of this volume
give but an inadequate idea of the tenderness, the yearning
of heart, the personal wrestling of soul with soul, which
often characterized the services in Manning Hall.

The work alluded to provoked criticism from theologians. By some persons there was thought to be too
much latitudinarianism in the Sermon on the Unity of
the Church. Others were of opinion that disproportionate stress was laid on the obedience and holiness of
Christ, as a part of the work of the Messiah, and they
could have wished a stronger presentation of the sufferings of Christ, as an equivalent for the merited punishment
of mankind. Others, still, were dissatisfied with his view
of human sinfulness, and thought that his definition of
depravity did not answer the demands of the symbols.
But, on the whole, the book met an exceedingly favorable
reception, and its circulation (which, including the edition
subsequently published, as " Salvation by Christ," reached
four thousand copies) was much larger than is usually
accorded to a volume of sermons.

To Rev. Dr. Bartol : —

" December 25, 1848.

" . . . I am greatly obliged to you for reading my sermons through, and am gratified to learn that they impress
you favorably. Newspaper notices I have no confidence
in. They are usually written without looking at the
book beyond the title page, and are considered a remuneration for sending the book and advertising in the

paper. When a person capable of judging correctly reads a book through, his opinion counts. In any case of this kind I seek for the opinions of a few persons, each representing a class, and from them, taken together, make up my own mind. When this has been done, I let the matter rest, and think but little more about it. Until I have got so far, I am always a little solicitous, for all this is a matter of experiment, and no one can pretend to be a judge of his own work; and I am not so much of an old stager, as to look upon failure and success with perfect indifference.

"You say that my views are preferable to Calvinism. I am glad of it; but I did not know that they differed from it. I have never read any of Calvin's works, or anything on controversial theology. . . . A *happy* Christmas to you. I cannot say *merry;* if Christmas means anything, *merry* does not seem the epithet that belongs to it."

He was far from feeling that he discharged his whole duty to the souls of his pupils by delivering these discourses. No means of moral influence were left untried. Nor were his cares always fruitless. Early in the winter term of 1847, it became known to the president that a student, a young man of fine abilities and scholarship, hitherto prone to scepticism, had become anxious about his soul.

The gentleman to whom we refer says, —

"The president met me, and desired me to call at his study the next Sabbath morning at nine o'clock. I went very unwillingly, for I did not care to have any one know how I felt. He talked with me most kindly, and cited several passages of Scripture very apposite to my condition. Then he said, 'I should like to pray with you before you go.' He knelt down near me, while I, looking at him, really lost all apprehension of what he was saying, so struck was I with the moral beauty of his appearance, his profound humility, mingled with dignity. That was the first of many interviews. His wisdom was as great as his kindness. I was at first troubled about the evidences of Christianity. So I got from the library Paley, and Chalmers, and Butler, and pored over them until my head was weary. The president said to me, 'You had better go and take a walk. Now, to-morrow is Saturday. Go off and walk. Be in the air all day.' This was the wisest advice that he could have given me, and I found the benefit of it. It was not long before every doubt and difficulty was removed, and I was rejoicing in a Christian hope."

Meanwhile, a few students, each unaware of the feelings of the other, were agitating the questions that deal with eternal realities. In no long time religion took precedence of all else within the walls of the university. The annual Fast-day deepened and extended the prevalent seriousness. The president spent almost the entire time, not demanded by his prescribed duties, in his study, conversing with young men who desired to open their hearts to him. Carrying the spirit of these personal and familiar interviews into the prayer meetings, he seemed to speak to each heart while he was addressing a hundred. Fearing lest his presence should prove an embarrassment, he usually did not enter until half the time of the meeting had expired. The heart seemed aware of his coming before the eye or ear had discovered it. He occupied always the same seat. His tone was familiar and conversational; his words were with power from above. We give an incident — though it is already familiar, and though it belonged, chronologically, to an earlier period.

A member of the class of 1839 has related, that, in one of these meetings, the president said, in substance, " Do not, young gentlemen, throw away your souls without trying to save them. Make *one honest effort* for their salvation. Even if you are lost, it will be something *to have tried*." Profoundly impressed with these words, the young man went to his room, determined that he would follow the advice which he had heard. Soon he was rejoicing in the forgiveness of sin. He subsequently became a clergyman of eminent usefulness in the Baptist church.* A brief and touching narrative of his conversion, written by himself, after appearing in the columns of the American Messenger, was published as a tract by the American Tract Society, and widely circulated. A few months since, in an account of a revival which took place in the parish of Rev. T. L. Cuyler, of Brooklyn, particular mention was made of the good which was accomplished by the tract, " One Honest Effort."

Of course among the young men who resorted to the university were the members of families holding a wide diversity of religious opinions. The question will naturally arise, on what principles did President Wayland proceed in giving religious instruction to the representatives of these varying faiths. While believing with the fullest conviction in the truths of evangelical Christianity, and in the distinctive doctrines of his own communion, he yet recognized the right of every man to follow the dictates of his own conscience, and the right of every parent to choose what religious instruction shall be given to his children, so long as he is charged with their support, and intrusted with their management.

In 1842, in the court of Lycoming County, Pennsylvania, Hon. Ellis Lewis, president judge, and more recently chief justice of the state, delivered a decision in which he upheld the right of a parent to control the religious instruction which should be imparted to his minor children. In the course of his decision, he cited a passage from the Elements of Moral Science, and in doing so, paid a high tribute to its author. A copy of the opinion having been sent to Dr. Wayland, he wrote to Judge Lewis as follows : —

* It is an interesting fact that this gentleman is the son of the clergyman who, as we have seen, at an early period in Dr. Wayland's history, proffered him generous aid in the prosecution of his studies.

October 14, 1842.

"My dear Judge Lewis: I received and read, with great pleasure and attention, your decision in the case of the Commonwealth *vs.* Armstrong. It was my intention to write you immediately, but I have been prevented by ill health. I seize the earliest opportunity of performing this agreeable duty, and of thanking you for your letter, which a day or two since came to hand.

"I thank you for your decision upon one of the most delicate and important questions which has ever come before a court. I believe it to be correct in principle, impartial in spirit, and lucid in statement; and I rejoice to see truths of so much importance thus set forth by so high authority. I presume that we should not differ upon any point of it. That we may compare our views with the greater certainty, I write for your consideration such thoughts as have occurred to me on the subject. I do this with the greater pleasure, inasmuch as I know you will correct me if I err.

"The Creator has established it as the law of our being, that the parent must be an adult. This law was manifestly established in order that the child may receive the benefit to be derived from the experience and wisdom of the parent, directed by strong natural affection. But this wisdom and experience would be useless to the child, unless there were conferred upon the parent the authority to enforce his decision. This authority continues during the period of the child's minority, and no longer. When the reason for the authority terminates, the authority terminates with it.

"The next question which arises is, Does religious instruction come within this rule? I think that on this point there can be no diversity of opinion. If the parent is bound to care for the soul of his child, he is bound to superintend its religious education; and he must possess all the authority necessary to the carrying on of that superintendence. This I understand the law to give him.

"But it sometimes happens in the education of children, that the child comes to entertain different religious sentiments from the parent. The parent conscientiously requires the child to do, or to abstain from doing, and the child's conscience forbids it to obey. Now, inasmuch as both parties, in the absence of evidence to the contrary, are to be supposed equally conscientious, the question cannot be decided upon this ground. It must, therefore, be decided by the general principle above stated; and as the parent is older and wiser, the law would confer the authority upon him, and give him reasonable means of enforcing obedience. In this case, since the law at the period of the child's majority relinquishes its power, it acts merely to postpone an action, which in a few years, at most, may be done without offence.

"While, however, I suppose this to be the legal right of the parent, I by no means would assert that it is always wise or just to enforce it. When a child has arrived at such maturity that it is able to judge of its duty by reading the Scriptures for itself, and has thus formed its opinion on questions of religious duty, it is very difficult to decide in how far the parent is morally bound to interfere, provided it be a *bona fide* case of religious belief. He should doubtless advise, and teach, and persuade. He may use his authority to oblige his child to reflect maturely on the subject, and decide without the interference of interested persons. But having done this, I think that he should allow the child to obey the honest dictates of its own conscience.

"But suppose the parent were disposed to press the subject further, and command a child to do what it could not, without, as it believed, disobeying God, or the contrary. What in such a case is the child to do? This is a most trying case, and would be decided by a variety of circumstances. The parent has the legal right to control the child, but if the child, from an honest sense of duty, disobeys, and meekly suffers the consequences, I do not know that we could blame it.

"But another question arises. How far does the law undertake to protect the parent in the exercise of his authority? It certainly gives him the right to teach his child at home, to direct the reading which it shall pursue, and the person who shall visit it. No one has a right to interfere with these parental privileges. But suppose a parent allows his child to mingle in society, to go where it pleases, how far does his authority then extend? Is every person bound to ask a parent on what subject he may talk with his child? And again: suppose the child honestly desires religious instruction, and comes to me to ask for it.

I may not go to the parent's house to proffer it; I may not in any manner obtrude it upon his child; but if the child come to me and ask for it, am I obliged, or at liberty, to refuse to impart it? I think not. Or suppose a child of a full age for religious responsibility came to me for my professional assistance, to enable it to perform a service which it supposed commanded by God, am I at liberty to refuse? I should urge upon the child to delay — to set the reasons of the act before the parent. The law gives the parent the power of prevention if he choose to use it; but if he does not use it, and the child comes to me to perform this religious service, I do not know that I am at liberty to refuse. Nor has the parent, that I see, any ground of complaint against me, provided I have acted on the principles above specified. Were it otherwise, every religious teacher, and every other man, would be almost forbidden to speak; and if I were preaching, and a child came in, whose parents were of a different opinion from my own, I must stop, and in fact I must perform an ordinance of religion not according to the will of the subject, but of its parents. In fact, if every parent has the power of dictating to every person what he shall say to his child, all conversation must cease, for in a mixed company you could say nothing that would not offend somebody.

"This is the way in which it strikes me. I wish very much to know how far you agree with me; I am ashamed to be giving opinions of this kind to a learned and experienced jurist; but I know that you will forgive my presumption. I have always acted on these principles myself. Whenever I know the parents of my pupils to differ from me, I studiously avoid, in conversation, allusion to the points of difference. If they come and ask me what they shall do to be saved, I tell them as well as I am able. Whenever I am liable to discuss points where there may be difference of opinion, their attendance is perfectly voluntary.

"I do not know how to refer to the very kind manner in which you have spoken of me. I can only say that I do not deserve it, but that I know of no man whose approval I should be more glad to receive. I will send you a pamphlet or two. Let me hear from you soon."

To these principles, so far as we know, he always adhered. It was not that he had a slight estimate of the importance of the points in which the several denominations differ from each other. But he felt that there were limits to his responsibility, and that he had no right to violate, on any plea, the rights of another.

Alike from the reminiscences quoted in Chapter IX. of the preceding volume, and from the tone of all his addresses and communications, it has, we presume, been evident that Dr. Wayland regarded education as a question open to argument, subject to inquiry and change. At a later day (perhaps in 1855 or 1856) he wrote to Rev. R. Anderson, D. D., —

"I consider that a great step is made in a reformation when it has been granted that the present system is open to examination, and not stereotyped for all ages. Wherever this is done, light will break in. All my labor about education 'hath this extent — no more.' It begins to be admitted that college systems may *be examined*. When this is done there is hope of amendment."

This feeling found expression in his little volume, published in 1842, entitled, "Thoughts on the Present Collegiate System in the United States." In this book he is rather occupied with defects than with their remedies. He was not satisfied with the kind or the degree of education imparted in the American colleges. He ever sought to elevate the standard of instruction, and to enlarge the number of those to whom the blessings of education should be extended. Though not pointing out in detail any line of policy, the volume now referred to, or at least the state of mind which gave rise to it, was the parent of important movements in the future.

In reference to this work he writes to Rev. Dr. Anderson, —

"I cannot tell you how much I am obliged and encouraged by your kind letter. I wrote with fear and trembling, apprehending that I might very likely stand alone and be considered a disturber of Israel, a sort of Dorr in the literary camp of New England. I, however, felt so strongly convinced that I was in the right that I concluded to venture; and your letter encourages me to hope that I may do some good. As it is, we are multiplying little men and forming no great ones; and the community, having no leaders, is tossed about with every wind of ultraism."

To John N. Wilder, Esq., of Albany, who had written in regard to the movement then on foot to establish a university in Western New York, he wrote: —

"What I want you to think of is, first of all, not to erect dormitory buildings for students. It leads to half, or more than half, of the trouble in colleges, and besides absorbs money that might be much better employed. If you start on this principle, it will save you from much expenditure.

"But pray observe another thing. Try to establish an institution that shall teach what people will pay for learning. As it is, colleges are merely making lawyers, ministers, and doctors; and these will not support one half of the colleges at the north. Try the application of science to the arts. I think that this will support itself, and aid the professional school."

It has already been remarked that President Wayland desired so to aid those who were in pursuit of an education as in the highest possible degree to elevate the standard of scholarship. With this view he proposed to the corporation to devote the income of certain funds, bequeathed by Hon. Nicholas Brown, to the establishment of premiums for excellence in various branches of study. And he himself founded the "President's Premiums," for the purpose of advancing the scholarship of those entering the university. The Rev. Henry Jackson, D. D., also established premiums for excellence in the studies pursued by the Senior class. Among those who competed successfully for the various classes of premiums named above, are many persons who have since attained the highest eminence in literary and professional life.

We have more than once alluded to the labors put forth by Dr. Wayland for the advancement of popular education. He, however, did not feel that it is by schools alone that this object can be promoted. He regarded popular libraries as indispensable to the cultivation of a fondness for reading and of general intelligence. The town of Wayland, in Middlesex County, Mass. (formed from portions of several adjoining townships), had received its name in honor of the president of Brown University.

"On commencement day at Brown University, in the year 1847, President Wayland, in an informal manner, expressed a desire to do something, according to his humble means, to help the inhabitants of the town of Wayland to a town library. He said that he wished not only that the inhabitants of the town might enjoy the advantages to be derived from such a library, but also that other towns in its vicinity might be induced by this example to establish for themselves similar libraries. He proposed to make a donation to the town, of five hundred dollars for this purpose. At the suggestion of Judge Mellen, the donation was tendered upon the condition that five hundred dollars should be obtained in the town by subscription or otherwise, — the whole amount of one thousand dollars to be devoted to the purchase of books for a town library.

"Five hundred and thirty-four dollars were quickly raised by subscription, and President Wayland immediately placed his donation in the hands of Mr. Mellen." *

The free library, thus originated in the town of Wayland, was opened for the delivery of books, August 7, 1850, and has ever since been in beneficent action.

"After the Wayland Library was in successful operation, the suggestion was made to have a 'Library Celebration,' in which every one could participate, the expense to be borne by the town. This suggestion at once re-

---

* For the facts relating to the Wayland Library we are indebted to a pamphlet by Rev. Jared M. Heard (a graduate of Brown University), entitled, "Origin of the Free Library System of Massachusetts."

ceived the approbation of the inhabitants. The wish was universal to invite Dr. Wayland to be present upon the occasion, as the guest of the town.

"All the necessary preparations for such a celebration were made with great cheerfulness and promptness.

"The 'Library Celebration' took place August 26, 1851, and will long be remembered by those who witnessed it. The writer hopes that an effort will be made at an early day to publish an account of these exercises. A most interesting occasion it was for several reasons. First, from the cause that originated it, which was most justly stated in the following words by Dr. Wayland to Judge Mellen, the president of the day, while seeing the people, old and young, crowding the church in which the celebration was held : ' This gives me a higher idea of New England character than anything I have before witnessed. Your inhabitants have assembled without distinction of age or sex, to celebrate, with joyful festivities, not any great victory, not any great political event, but *the founding of a library.*'

"Another reason for the interest of this occasion was the unanimity and heartiness with which it was entered into by the inhabitants of the place.

'"The exercises at the church consisted of an address by Judge Mellen to Dr. Wayland, in which he thanked him in behalf of the people for his generous donation, and extended to him a cordial welcome. This address was followed by one from President Wayland, which it is hoped may one day be published.

"In his introductory remarks, this gentleman stated the whole idea from which sprang his wish to have free public libraries established. He said, ' Our fathers founded schools where we are taught to read ; when we know how to read, we want something to read, — we want books.' And from this simple idea in his great mind originated the movement which has resulted in giving to our state the free public libraries so successfully established in various parts of it."

But the benefits of Dr. Wayland's act of true liberality were not confined to a single town. As the immediate result of the events above alluded to, an Act was passed by the legislature of Massachusetts, in 1851, which empowered all the towns of the state to raise money by taxation for the support of free town libraries.* From this law, and from the action of Dr. Wayland which gave rise to it, have sprung the magnificent free libraries which now enrich Boston, Worcester, New Bedford, and a great and constantly increasing number of towns, and which have already conferred a degree of intellectual benefit that we in vain attempt to estimate.

The following letter from Rev. E. H. Heard, of Concord, Mass. (the adjoining town to Wayland), affords illustration of the influence of the system thus inaugurated:

"CONCORD, MASS., November 24, 1851.
" F. WAYLAND, D. D.

" Rev. Sir: Since you were the prime mover in the free library movement which is now going on in this state, I thought I would write and inform you what progress has been made in the work. The people at Wayland were never more interested than now in their library. At their last town meeting they voted to put the books belonging to the school districts into the town library. And you can hardly find a house in town in which there are not some of these books. They also voted to raise sixty dollars for the library this year.

" And there is to be a town library in this village. The proprietors of the circulating library voted to give it to the town, provided they would raise the largest amount of money allowed by law, every year, with which to increase it. The town accepted it, and voted the required sum. There are six or seven hundred volumes, and the tax will amount to about one hundred and fifty dollars. Many of the adjoining towns are also taking measures to establish libraries. And the time is not far distant when there will be a library in every town in the commonwealth. And other states will not only adopt our common school but our town library system.

" Thus, by your foresight and benevolence, the town of

---

* This act was prepared by Rev. John B. Wight, a member of the legislature from the town of Wayland, who was also allowed, by the courtesy of the house, the honor of reporting it, without reference to a committee.

Wayland has been enabled to take the lead in a work which will affect the moral and intellectual condition of the people, not only of this state, but of the whole country. And many will yet regard the establishment of town libraries in this state as the crowning benefit which, through your instrumentality, has been conferred on the country. For this, like other acts of benevolence, will be inspiring and creative, and will excite others to rank themselves in the same fellowship by deeds of kindred benevolence. And thus, ages after you shall have passed from these transitory scenes, the offspring of your own benevolent action will be multiplying in numbers and shedding ever-increasing blessings on our happy country.

"Long may you continue to reap the reward of your labors, so vast and of such surpassing value, in the heartfelt gratitude of the people of the whole country.

I am, sir, with the highest respect,
Your obliged servant,
EDWIN H. HEARD."

The following letters of Dr. Wayland belong to the period embraced in this chapter, 1841–1849 : —

"Rev. Dr. Anderson: I hear you are going to the Mediterranean ; and being in town on business, I snatched a moment to see you, to tender to you again my best wishes, and to assure you of my warm personal attachment, and my love to the work in which you are engaged. May the blessed Savior be with you by sea and on land, among men barbarous and civilized, Christian or pagan. May he prosper your way in the manner best suited to his infinite wisdom, and give you the desire of your heart. May he grant you that wisdom which He who sees the end from the beginning alone can impart, and return you, in due time, to your family, your labors, your country, and the church of Christ. If in anything I can secure your pleasure, command me."

To Rev. Dr. Hoby, Birmingham, England : —

"The last packet from England brought the sad news of the death of John Foster, *clarum et venerabile nomen*. The last great Baptist light on earth is extinguished. The greatest man in our Israel is fallen. I do not think that you have lost so fine a mind in England since Canning.

Southey was learned, classical, a thorough master of English, a poet, and an historian; but he fell immeasurably short of the vigor of Foster. Robert Hall was, I suppose, surpassingly eloquent, a writer almost without fault, and a classic in the language, vying with almost any who have ever written it. But none of them approaches the massive cubic sense of Foster. No one appeals with such irresistible effect to the conscience and common sense of mankind, and neither of them ever has had a transforming effect on so many minds as Foster. He drives his weapon to the hilt at every blow. Were I to characterize his style by any terms I know of, it would be, '*Britons, strike home.*' He never fails to strike home like a true Briton. And then he was so simple in manner, so thorough and heart-felt in piety, so unaffected in his greatness, so apparently unconscious of his power, so humble, that I presume he really thought much less of himself than any one that knew him thought of him; in fine, he was in every respect so remarkable a man that we are filled with despair at the thought that we can never expect to see such another raised up among us."

To Baptist W. Noel, London: —

"Rev. and dear Sir: I know that you will not consider as an intrusion a letter from one who can claim no other personal acquaintance with you than that derived from a few moments' conversation at your chapel, Bedford Row, some years since.

"I have just completed the reading of your volume on the Union of Church and State, and I should do injustice to my feelings did I not embrace the earliest opportunity to express to you the sentiments with which it has inspired me. I do not remember ever to have read a work on any subject with such profound and delightful emotions. Every sentence which it contains seems to me pregnant with most important truth — truth that must tell on the interests of the church in all coming time. I bless God that he has put it into your heart to write and publish it; and that his Spirit has guarded you in so remarkable a manner from acrimony and unkindness, while it has led you to adopt a faithfulness which cannot be surpassed.

"But I well know the penalty which you must pay for all this. I cannot measure the storm which will be raised against you from those whose worldly interests are attacked. But, my brother, be of good cheer. God has pledged himself to sustain you, for you have held forth his simple truth. You have left everything worldly for the sake of that truth, and he cannot forsake you. A multitude of those who love Christ will bear you on their hearts before the mercy-seat. Whatever hosts of earth surround you, the mountain will be filled with chariots of fire and horses of fire, which will be your sure defence.

"Nor is this all. Free churches and ministers need your words of rebuke, caution, and encouragement. Their piety will be increased by the efforts to which you incite them. You will behold now, or in heaven, millions blessing you for every sacrifice; and, above all, the Savior will accept it as done for himself.

"One idea alone has occurred to me, which I do not see that you have noticed. It is the injustice done to the supporters of the Establishment by the union. They pay for religious instruction five, eight, ten, or twelve hundred pounds, and are frequently served by a curate at one hundred. They receive only a tenth of what they pay for, and the rest is often spent in dissipation or vice.

"Excuse me for thus extending to you the hand of fellowship across the water. I have taken the liberty to send you a copy of some sermons which I have lately published. I hope they may reach you. You will see that our thoughts have partly been directed in the same channel."

To Rev. Dr. Hoby : —

" I rejoice at the position assumed by your government in relation to protective duties. If Sir R. Peel carries out his plans, as I think he will, it will do more to advance the cause of civilization than any measure that has been accomplished for centuries. It will be followed, from choice or necessity, by all other nations, and being followed, will bind nations so thoroughly together, — it will render them so necessary to each other, — that wars will be almost impossible. This will be specially the case between your country and ours. We shall be but one in fact, one in language, in religion (saving Puseyism), and we shall be able together to keep the peace of the world. May God of his infinite mercy grant it. I hear of many of your world's conventions that are to be held this year in London. What they will effect I do not know. I, however, believe that the mild, dignified, and forbearing manner in which you have treated this country, will do more to bring about peace and take away the war spirit than anything else that has been or that can be done."

To his uncle, Rev. D. S. Wayland, Bassingham, England, May 22, 1848 : —

" . . . I see no objection to the course of the government, as I understand it. To be sure, I would not live under such a system ; but this is another matter. If the Queen is the head of the church, and responsible for its management, as much as for the administration of justice, there is no reason why she should not appoint bishops as well as judges. I do not see any use of bishops, or the whole of your hierarchy. I think Christianity would be better without it. But, were I an English prime minister, with my present views, I would appoint such men as I believed to be for the good of religion and in favor of religious freedom, to the extent of the royal prerogative.

" But these perplexing questions belong to the nature of the union of church and state. The only wise course is to separate them forever. I am glad of the appointment of Dr. Sumner to the archbishopric, and of Bishop Lee to Manchester. I knew the latter in Birmingham, and took to him very much.

" We are receiving, with every steamer, most stirring news from Europe. The movement of the Chartists is very like that of the insurrectionists in Rhode Island a few years ago. I feel, therefore, as if I understood your position better than I should otherwise have done. I fancy that the revolutions on the Continent are more gratifying to me than to you. I am an untamed republican, but not a sectarian one — a lover of representative governments, in opposition to dynasties and every form of absolutism. I believe that freedom of opinion in matters civil and religious (our old Roger Williams doctrine) will come out of this trouble ; that soul liberty will advance towards universal acknowledgment, and thus the race will have a chance, at least, for development. I know there will be a flood of error, but this must be met by a flood of truth. For Louis Philippe I have no regret, except as for an unfortunate man. He has been selfish, absolute, and treacherous. I hear that our Sovereign Lady Victoria says openly that he has lied to her, as I believe he has always done when he thought he could gain by it.

"The indications in France and Germany are good. I shall not live to see the results of all this, but my children may. I cannot but believe that a new era has dawned upon the race, that another seal has been opened, and another page in history commenced. You have no idea of the energy instilled into a human being by individual self-reliance, and the feeling, that, under God, every man depends upon himself. But I know this is heresy, and I will not add another word. Let us unite in prayer that God will overturn and overturn until he brings in the desire of all nations, or at least that amid this overturning, he will direct all events to his own glory."

CHAPTER III.

THE REORGANIZATION OF THE UNIVERSITY.

THE college Commencement of 1849 passed off successfully; the exercises of the graduating class were of the usual degree of interest; the dinner was held in Rhode Island Hall, whose ample and well-lighted apartment afforded a grateful contrast to the low, dim, dingy Commons Hall, where the dinner had usually been served. The after-dinner speeches expressed a warm attachment on the part of the graduates to the institution which had nourished their intellectual life. The next day, at the meeting of the corporation, the president read his annual report, which contained these words : —

" The undersigned deems this a suitable occasion to carry into effect a purpose which for some years he has had in contemplation, and to devote the remainder of his life to pursuits which require the uninterrupted command of his time. With this view he respectfully requests to be relieved from his present engagements, and hereby resigns the office of President of Brown University and Professor of Moral and Intellectual Philosophy. . . . He asks that this resignation may take effect at the earliest practicable period within the present collegiate year."

These words were a surprise to all who heard them, — a surprise as painful as it was profound. And the emotions experienced by the members of the corporation were but representative of the feeling of the entire community, academic, commercial, and industrial.

The corporation at once appointed a committee to express their desire that he would withdraw his resignation ; and he consented to continue in the discharge of his office for the current year.

The step that he had taken, however unexpected to others, was the result of deliberation on his part. Four or five years previously, he had mentioned his purpose in his correspondence with Dr. Nott. It is not impossible that the act, long contemplated, had been deferred until he should have witnessed the graduation of his two older sons.

He desired to have leisure to prepare for the press several works not yet published, and to revise, with the aid of leisure and of a matured judgment, those hitherto issued.

This, however, was not the only reason. The college for fifteen years had shown a steady decline in the number of its students.* Its income from all sources fell short of its expenses, and the inevitable tendency was towards bankruptcy.

But it might be said, let an appeal be made to the public for an increase of funds, in order to afford the college the support that it cannot derive from pupils. To this course there were strong objections. The college evidently was not answering any public demand. It was doing only what a great number of colleges, all over New England, could do just as well. To appeal to the public for money was, in reality, only to ask them to contribute for the support of the officers. To do this, while he felt able to maintain himself, did not accord with the president's self-respect.

But there was no reason to suppose that the public

---

* The number enrolled on the catalogue for

1835–36,	is	195.	1842–43, is	167.
1836–37,	"	196.	1843–44, "	169.
1837–38,	"	187.	1844–45, "	157.
1838–39,	"	188.	1845–46, "	140.
1839–40,	"	177.	1846–47, "	146.
1840–41,	"	172.	1847–48, "	141.
1841–42,	"	175.	1848–49, "	150.

would respond to such an appeal. Indeed, an effort
which had recently been made to raise fifty thousand
dollars for the college had been entirely futile.

To Rev. Dr. Bartol, October 5, 1849: —

" . . . I was much obliged by your letter, specially
because it touched the precise nerve of the question, and
presented the point on which, in my opinion, it all hinges.
The question I have asked myself in this matter has been
simply this: Have I that power of available labor that
will enable me to be more useful with the full command
of my time, than with the command of a portion of it
only; or, in other words, have I strength enough to stand
alone, or do I require official position to support me? I
must admit that, after considerable doubt and serious
hesitation, I have with diffidence come to decide in the
way which perhaps indicates undue self-confidence. I
know that this is an experiment; but I prefer to make it.
I know that I am liable to overrate my own powers; but I
am encouraged by this fact in my past history, that I have
been supposed to do what I have done, better than, when
I undertook it, I supposed myself capable of. This gave
me confidence, perhaps unwarrantable, in my own decision. The event must decide.
" In this, I know I am considered, by many persons,
unwise. There are those who speak of the importance
of position and official influence, and the folly of abandoning it. My view of the matter is this: if a man is equal to
a place such as this, the place confers on him no honor or
power. If he is unequal to it, he may as well leave it to
others. Besides, I do not think so highly of official station,
and the fuss there is about it, as many men. It is in many
respects a trammel, and a man's power is very much in
the ratio of his freedom. With such views I have acted,
and I more and more believe I acted wisely; and I think
most men, who are competent to judge, agree with me.
" Still there is a remote possibility that my plans may
be counteracted. Should men here wish to do something
noble and of great use to the state, and should the carrying it out depend upon me, I may feel obliged, against my
will, to remain for a time. This is the only contingency
which I see which can alter my views."

The expression of the wish of the corporation that he should remain at the head of the university prepared the way for a full communication of his views; and on March 28, 1850, he presented his "Report to the Corporation of Brown University," a pamphlet of which it is not, probably, too much to say, that its eminent ability was recognized by those who approved and by those who opposed its conclusions, and that its appearance constituted an era in the history of collegiate education in America.

Without aiming at an exact analysis of this pamphlet, we shall seek to present concisely his later views of education, availing ourselves, for this purpose, of the Report, of his Address at Union College (1854) on "The Education demanded by the People of the United States," and of his Lecture before the American Institute of Instruction (1854), and of other published works, as well as of the manuscript reminiscences from which already the most interesting portions of this memoir have been derived. While, for the sake of brevity, we shall not throughout employ his exact language, every sentiment will be such as he has expressed.

We find the number of students in Brown University steadily diminishing. It is not urged by any one that this decrease results from a want of ability on the part of the officers, or from any inferiority in the instruction imparted, to that afforded in other colleges. It is the unsolicited testimony of the officers of the professional schools, that our graduates hold at least an equal rank with the alumni of other institutions. The diminishing number of our students, as compared with the attendance at other colleges, is due to the fact that we have no means of reducing the cost of tuition, and giving education away. If funds were provided by which education might be rendered nearly or quite gratuitous, and pecuniary assistance afforded to the pupils, young men might be attracted from other colleges or allured from the active into the learned professions, and thus the number of students be increased. But whether the real interests of education would be thereby promoted is scarcely a question.

"And it may be doubted whether this would be more than a temporary expedient. The reduction of tuition might avail so long as our terms were lower than those of other colleges; but so soon as theirs were reduced to the same level, we must provide the means for still further reduction. It seems undesirable that the colleges of our country should, by any contingency, be enlisted in a competition of this nature." — *Report.*

But we find that in all the colleges of New England the number of students is decreasing relatively to the population, and that each year the colleges are compelled anew to appeal to the public for the support which they confessedly cannot derive from the pupils whom they are able to attract; and this, too, amid a population constantly increasing in numbers, and increasing yet more rapidly in wealth and intelligence, and universally thirsting for education. These amazing facts seem susceptible of but one interpretation — that the colleges are not meeting the educational wants of the community. The facts justify, nay require, a reëxamination of our collegiate system.

"It would seem that our whole system of instruction needs an honest, thorough, and candid revision. It has been for centuries the child of authority and precedent. If those before us made it what it is, by applying to it the resources of earnest and fearless thought, I can see no reason why we, by pursuing the same course, might not improve it. God intended us for progress, and we counteract his design when we deify antiquity, and bow down and worship an opinion, not because it is either wise or true, but simply because it is ancient."—*Address.*

The earliest colleges of America were modelled as exactly as possible after Oxford and Cambridge. Designed, like those ancient universities, primarily for the education of the clergy, they established a four-years course of study, filled up almost entirely with Latin, Greek, and mathematics. As new colleges arose in America, they copied, with undeviating fidelity, the exact organization of their seniors. "There seems a fatal tendency, in the formation of systems of education, blindly to follow precedents, without examining the laws on which they are founded, or the results which they have attained." We have all "copied the universal model, without considering how entirely unsuited to our condition must be institutions founded for the education of the mediæval clergy, and modified by the pressure of an all-powerful aristocracy." Thus the college of the later half of the nineteenth century aims to imitate the college of the early half of the thirteenth; and the American college, whether founded amid the learned leisure of the oldest form of New England society, or among the farmers of Illinois, or the miners of California, offers to all but one unvarying type of education.* No regard is had to the infinite variety existing in human minds, nor to the progress of man during the centuries, nor to the demands growing out of the changing aspects of human society.

It is true that some changes have been grafted upon the original model. While a predominance is still given to the classics and mathematics, yet a great number of new branches have been introduced into the system, until the four-years course now includes twenty or more studies. Attempting to pursue all these in the limited time spared from the classics and mathematics, the student finds himself unable to do more than feebly grasp the rudiments of each; he makes himself master of nothing; he is not "taught in college anything with the thoroughness which will enable him to go safely and directly to distinction, in the department he has there entered, without returning to

---

* And it may be added, that where our American missionaries propose a college for the youth just rescued from barbarism and heathendom, they seem to aim at the precise reproduction of the old-fashioned New England college.

lay anew the foundations of his success." * However strongly marked are the indications that God has designed him for excellence in some one branch of knowledge, yet he is compelled by the requirements of the college course to spend so much time upon studies which are repugnant and comparatively useless to him, that he gains but a meagre knowledge of his chosen department, and purchases superficiality in the studies which he loves, at the expense of a toilsome but almost complete ignorance of those which he dislikes.

The effect on the instructor is scarcely less disastrous. "He has no motive to increase his knowledge. He already knows more than he has any opportunity to communicate. There is no stimulus to call forth exertion. There is no opportunity for progress."

"It has already been remarked that the first and most prominent place is held by mathematics and the classics. Of the former of these it need, perhaps, only be said, that we do not so teach them as to make mathematicians. I suppose that the acquisition of an abstract truth in mathematics is almost valueless, unless it is carried out into its applications, and the student, by such applications, is enabled to use it for himself. If this is done, there is a probability that the principle will be remembered. If it is not done, it will be speedily altogether forgotten."—*MS.*

As to the classics, " I observed that nearly half of the time occupied in the college course, as well as two or three years of preparatory study, was spent on the Latin and Greek languages. I observed that this knowledge was very soon forgotten, and that every year we graduated young men who could not construe their diploma, and that in a few years afterwards not one in twenty could read a sentence of Tacitus or a line of Homer. The sentiments of these authors could have no effect on the mind, for the sentiment evidently was not appreciated.†

---

* George Ticknor, Esq., as quoted in the Report.

† The writer was present when a lady said to President Wayland, with an appearance of considerable solicitude, " Dr. Wayland, I should think that the morals of our young men would be very much injured by reading the classic authors, in which drunk-

This was obvious from the bald and unintelligible translations which disfigured our examinations. I observed also
that those who were the best linguists among us were
by no means deeply imbued with the sentiments of the
classic writers. This kind of learning did not seem to
have imparted richness to their minds. They very rarely
quoted their most admired authors, or uttered sentiments
which indicated that by reading the classics they had im-
bibed the spirit of the objects of their idolatry. With no
other language than English, Burns had approximated
more nearly to Horace than men who had spent years in
the study of the Roman bard.

"Again, when the present course of education was
established, all the knowledge which the human mind
had acquired was contained in these languages. The
nations of modern Europe had, at best, but a language
without a literature. But how great the change produced
by the last four centuries, or even by the century which
dates back from the present year! All the most important
knowledge or thought of our race is found outside the
classic languages. The world has awaked as from a long
sleep, and invention and discovery from every part of the
globe press upon us with a rapidity that amazes and con-
founds us. Yet not a word of all this is to be found in
the classical languages. Surely such a change in the
knowledge of our race would indicate the necessity of a
change in our plans of education.

"If it be said that the study of grammar and of con-

---

enness and every form of vice are celebrated and made attractive."
He replied, "Madam, it might, at first sight, appear so; but, in fact,
the young men understand so little of the classics, and enter so
little into their spirit, that I do not really think that such studies
do them much harm."

It will, of course, be understood that Dr. Wayland had no disposition to ignore the benefits that may be derived from a wise and
generous pursuit of the classics. What he designed to urge was,
first, that the place assigned to these studies in the system of modern education, and the amount of time allotted them, should be
determined by a view of their educational value as compared with
other branches of learning; and further, that they should be so
pursued as to secure, in the highest attainable degree, all the advantages which they are adapted to confer.

struction is a valuable discipline for the student, it may be replied, this is true, but it is by no means the only one. And if the construction of language be the only valuable form of youthful discipline, why should we not also study Sanscrit and Arabic, and most of all, the old Gothic languages, which are sufficiently difficult and have the additional advantage of being the fountain from which flowed the noble English tongue?

" But supposing that this form of study has advantages for confining the attention, strengthening the memory, and (if properly pursued) for sharpening the powers of discrimination, are there not other studies which seem capable of conferring equal advantages? The works of God, in nature, animal and vegetable, in history, in geology, are all formed upon a plan, and are the mere realization of the ideas of God. Their classifications, their relations to each other, and their relations to time, are indications of wisdom with which no classic can compare. Why should we suppose that the thoughts of man are more appropriate food for the human mind than that which we may know of the thoughts of God. In morals the mind enlarges by conceptions of God — his perfection, his love, mercy, kindness, and truth, and by training our minds into harmony with his character. Why should it not be so with the human intellect? Why should we not study the laws of God in creation, the relations of these laws to each other, and the magnificent generalizations which they suggest, that so we may learn the modes of operations of the divine Being; that so we may (I speak it with reverence) train ourselves to harmony with the divine mind?

" I submit whether the study of the ideas of God is not likely to elevate and expand the mind as much as the study of the ideas of Virgil, Horace, or Homer. I would add, of Plato ; but not one in a hundred, perhaps in five hundred, of our students, ever enters into the ideas of Plato."— *MS.*

" The knowledge of facts leads at once, by the principles of the human mind, to generalization. Hence the mind at a more advanced stage would desire to understand the classifications of physical science. The more simple principles of animal and vegetable physiology might be comprehended at a much earlier age than is generally supposed. The structure of plants might be so far unfolded by living specimens, that every walk in the fields would be to a child a miniature voyage of discovery. The classifications of animals and insects, their habits and modes of life, would form another most interesting line of investigation. I apprehend that this kind of education would be an admirable preparation for more abstract study. . . . And besides this, we should thus spread before the youthful mind the volume of the works of God, and render the world we live in a source of ever-renewed wonder and delight. I know of no part of my early education that I would not thankfully exchange for the ability which, under good instruction, I might possibly have acquired, of understanding and interpreting the ideas of God in creation, and of thus being brought into daily and intimate relation with my Father, who is in heaven." — *Lecture before American Institute.*

" The power of forming conceptions which shall lead to discovery in science, or to the practicable in action, is clearly of vast importance. Can this power be cultivated? On this question there can be no doubt. It steadily increases with the progress of the human mind. We naturally inquire whether the cultivation of this element of intellectual character has been regarded with sufficient attention by those who form our courses of higher education. A large part of the studies which we pursue add very little to our power of forming conceptions of any kind whatever. A larger infusion of the study of physical science, not merely as a collection of facts, but as a system of laws, with their relations and dependences, would be of great value in this respect. We thus study the ideas and conceptions of the Creator. We become acquainted with his manner of accomplishing his purposes, and learn in some measure the style of the Author of all things. Surely this habit of mind must be of unspeakable value to a philosopher in the discovery of truth, or to a man of affairs in devising his plans, since these can only succeed as they are in harmony with the designs of infinite wisdom and benevolence." — *Intellectual Philosophy.*

It appears, then, that the existing system of collegiate education is open to serious objections. It gives to classical studies an amount of time utterly disproportionate to their real value; it has no adaptation to the diversities of mind and genius, to the age, to the country, or to the demands of the people to whom it is offered; it compels the student to study much that he does not want, and does not allow him to go beyond the rudiments of the pursuit on which his livelihood and his usefulness are to depend; and it tends to produce a superficial habit of mind in those who yield themselves to its influence. It is adapted mainly to candidates for the learned professions, especially for the ministry. It excludes the great body of our population — the productive classes — from its advantages; for if they come to our colleges, they do not find the knowledge that they want, or they find it held at so high a price in time as to be beyond their means. But most of all does it rob those who repair to the colleges, and who, when youth is gone, and manhood, with its demands, is upon them, find that though they have paid the price, in time, they have received only an education not thorough in itself, and not suited to their needs.

To remedy these defects, the Report proposes to abolish the four-years term of study, and to lay aside the effort to teach within the period of four years a round of studies requiring a much longer time; to teach thoroughly every study that is taught, and to afford the student the opportunity to prepare and perfect himself in the branches of knowledge which he pursues; to throw open the college to all who desire knowledge, and to allow each person to study what he wants, without compelling him, as a condition, to study what he does not want; and to establish such new departments as may be demanded by the present state of human knowledge, and by the wants of the productive classes.

It was further proposed, not as a necessary part of the reorganization, but as promotive of a high education, that the emolument of the instructor should be made in some degree dependent on his success in imparting knowledge, and should be, in part at least, graduated by the number of his pupils; * and further, that the academic degrees should not be given in course, but should represent a definite amount of attainment, rather than the mere lapse of time since the candidate entered college, or since he graduated.

The statutes of the university enacted in 1850, embodying the practical applications of the principles of the Report, state, " In order to become a candidate for the degree of A. B., the student, having been regularly examined for entrance, must have been proficient in nine courses of one year each. . . . It is the design of the corporation to require for the degrees of Bachelor of Arts and of Philosophy an amount of study which *may* be accomplished in three years, but which may, if he pleases, occupy the student profitably for four years; and to require for the degree of Master of Arts an amount of study which *may* be accomplished in four years, but which, if generously pursued, may occupy the student with advantage a considerably longer time.   And the Faculty have the power to direct in all cases the discontinuance of a third study, or the addition of a third to two already pursued, if such diminution or addition of labor will, in their opinion, be for the advantage of the student."

The object of these provisions is obvious.   The degree was conditioned upon the amount of attainment rather than upon the time consumed in securing the attainment. Many pupils, perhaps the majority, would be unable to pursue with proper thoroughness three studies at a time. For example, how many young men could carry on a course

---

* It is, perhaps, worthy of note, that President Wayland urged this feature of the plan from a conviction of its importance, although he of course knew, as the event proved, that as his own department of ethics and metaphysics was remote from the line of popular studies, he would be the first to suffer pecuniarily from the new provision.   But his watchword was, " I go for the human race."

of history, metaphysics, and Greek tragedy, and perform the reading and independent investigation required by these studies? The Faculty, using the power wisely put in their hands, would restrict the pupil to two studies, and his faithful pursuit of these would insure more mental maturity than the superficial study, without original thought, of three branches. Thus it would seem that the provision elevates instead of lowering the standard of education. The same remark applies with yet greater force to the requirement for the degree of A. M. It need scarcely be said that the carrying out of these provisions would require a large amount of conscientious fidelity on the part of the Faculty of instruction.

In favor of the change of organization above proposed, the Report urges three arguments. First, it is just. All classes of the community are alike entitled to the benefits of high education. Second, it is expedient. The number of students now in attendance will not be reduced; the standard of education will not be lowered; large numbers of the classes now excluded from the college will seek its benefits, and the blessings of high education will be universal throughout the community. Third, it is necessary. The present system cannot maintain its place. If unable to find in the college the education they need, the productive classes, the mechanic and the manufacturer, will establish institutions for themselves, to which the body of the young will be attracted, and the colleges will " become very good foundations for the support of instructors, but few will be found to avail themselves of their instruction."

If it is objected to the proposed plan of organization, that it would diminish the attention paid to the classics, —

" The reply is easy : If, by placing Latin and Greek upon their own merits, they are unable to retain their present place in the education of civilized and Christianized man, then let them give place to something better. . . . But is there not rather reason to hope that by rendering this study less compulsory, and allowing those who have a taste for it to devote themselves more thoroughly to classical reading, we shall raise it from its present depression, and derive from it all the benefit which it is able to confer?"

If it is objected that such a change is opposed to the wisdom of all our ancestors, it may be replied, —

" This is a question which cannot be settled by authority. We are just as capable of deciding it as the men who have gone before us. They were once like ourselves, men of the present, and their wisdom certainly has not received any addition from the slumber of centuries. God gives to every age the faculty for perceiving its own wants, and discovering the best means of supplying them, and it is, therefore, desirable that every age should decide such questions for itself. We cannot certainly decide them by authority."—*Address*.

As the plan proposed would involve the establishment of several new professorships, and the extensive modification of the college buildings, it was deemed needful for the inauguration of the experiment, that the sum of one hundred and twenty-five thousand dollars should be added to the funds of the institution.

Such was the spirit of the Report presented to the corporation. The corporation ordered it to be printed, with a view to its being finally acted upon at their next meeting.

During this interval, the president, wishing to gain all possible aid from the light of experience, travelled with his friend Mr. Zachariah Allen, of Providence, to Charlottesville, Va,. for the purpose of observing the condition of the University of Virginia, in which a system had been adopted somewhat similar to that proposed in the Report. The result of his observation, so far as it related to the practicability and efficacy of the system, was highly favorable. He was particularly impressed with the earnestness and enthusiasm of the officers of instruction. It would be wrong to affirm that the impression made by the

young men assembled at the university, and by the general
aspect of society in Virginia, was in a high degree pleasing. A single circumstance affected him deeply. One
evening a number of students came to the house of one of
the Faculty, by whom Dr. Wayland was entertained, and
desired to see the president of Brown University, and to
hear a short speech from him. He accordingly addressed
to them a few words, as they stood on the lawn before the
house. They listened respectfully, and with a gratified
curiosity, yet with a manner in which a close observer
might see an air of hostility and suspicion towards the
speaker. After they had retired, his host said to him,
" Not long since, one of the professors, who was my dearest
friend, had incurred the ill will of some of the students ;
and upon the spot where those young men stood this evening, I saw him lie in the agonies of death, murdered by
the hands of his pupils."

The corporation met May 7, and adopted the Report
and its recommendations, with the condition that the
amount named above should be subscribed by or before
the 5th of September, 1850. It is probable that there was
not in the corporation a majority who fully approved of
the plan ; yet they were unwilling to take the responsibility of opposing a measure which, in the judgment of the
president, promised the only means of saving the college
from decline, and of opening to it a field of enlarged usefulness.

The author of the Report had no occasion to offer the
complaint uttered by Dr. Johnson after the publication of
one of his pamplets — " Sir, it has not met with opposition
enough." Perhaps no pamphlet upon education ever published in America was more severely criticised. In New
England, the North American and the New Englander
reviewed it adversely ; the North American conducting
the criticism with an absence of personalities, and in the
tone and manner in which educated gentlemen of liberal

views are accustomed to discuss questions of high public concern. The tone of the Reviews generally was unfavorable. From a great many sources came elaborate defences of the old system, and particularly of the classical course of study.

The Bibliotheca Sacra for 1851 contains an article on College Education, by one of the most eminent and truly scholarly divines of America (Professor B. B. Edwards), which is almost entirely devoted to a defence of the classics, and which, though not mentioning the Report, has obvious reference to it.

The newspapers, truer exponents of popular thought and feeling, were almost unanimous in welcoming the movement, and in looking hopefully for its success.* And the people, the mechanics, for themselves and for their sons, hailed the approach of a brighter day. On the railroads, by the wayside, at the work-bench and the forge, men talked of the enlargement of education, and saw in him who had suggested the change a benefactor of humanity.

The author of the Report did not deem it necessary to reply to the animadversions of critics ; and we shall not undertake to do imperfectly what he might have done conclusively had he thought it needful.

To Rev. Dr. Bartol : —

"I have no doubt that the doctrines set forth in the Report will meet with opposition. It is somewhat disagreeable to be held up personally before the public, but I suppose it is necessary to success. The other view cannot be taken without unfolding and really laying bare the ground on which it rests. When this is done, I think that its condemnation at the bar of public opinion is certain. A philosopher who believes the middle ages to be the glory of Christianity, must be opposed to my notions, as most surely I am to his. The real opposition, I almost fear, proceeds from a desire of maintaining the exclusive-

---

* It would be scarcely pardonable to omit mention of the valuable aid rendered by the Providence Journal.

ness and rank of what are called the learned professions, and a corresponding indisposition to render science and liberal culture universal. All I can say is, that I believe myself to be working for man in all his relations — for man universal, as created by God, entitled to the right of equal and liberal culture. I think that men will so understand it. . . ."

He felt, probably, that it was a matter not to be determined by theory nor by argument, but by experiment, fairly tried. The hearty subscription of a sum considerably beyond the required one hundred and twenty-five thousand dollars, almost entirely by the citizens of Providence, insured the inauguration of the experiment ; and accordingly, in September, 1850, the college was opened substantially upon the principles of the Report. Of the system which was then adopted, the author, at a later day, writes, —

" It did not go so far as I would have chosen, and did not, with sufficient freedom, carry out the principles on which it was founded. It was partly a compromise between the old ideas and the new, and was, perhaps, the best arrangement that could be adopted." — *MS.*

But, at any rate, the " new system," as it was popularly called, was a great advance upon the ancient plan of collegiate education. It continued in operation during the remaining five years of his presidency ; and with what result ? Did it extend to an enlarged number the blessings of high education ? Did it maintain, and even elevate, the standard of intellectual attainment ? Under its auspices, was the general character, social and moral, of the college preserved ?

The number of students enrolled on the catalogue of

1848–49, is 152
1849–50, " 150

Upon the adoption of the new organization, the number was, in

1850–51, first term, ...	174
" second term, ...	195
1851–52, ...	225
1852–53, ...	243
1853–54, ...	283
1854–55, ...	252

The little State of Rhode Island furnished ninety students — a number larger than proceeded from any other state, and amounting to two thirds the entire number that had been enrolled on the catalogue under the old organization.

But it had been darkly predicted that with the liberty of choice given, the severer studies would be neglected, and ease of attainment alone would influence the student in his selections. It appeared that, instead of thirty-nine who had studied geometry in 1848–9, the class, in 1851–2, numbered sixty-three, and in the following year seventy, and in the next year seventy-four. The class in trigonometry, which had numbered forty-two, rose to sixty-five. "But the classics, the type and summit of liberal and humanizing influences, would be utterly neglected: not a student would pursue these, unless forced into them by a kind, but rigid authority." For a year or two there was a falling away, but the catalogue soon showed that one hundred and seven were studying Latin; * and the number of candidates for the degrees of A. B. and A. M., for which classical study was required, was one hundred

---

* And of this number, it will be remembered, every one was pursuing the study because he deliberately chose it, and the instructor was not compelled to keep back the really forward and studious, that he might bring into something like an alignment those who, forced into the study, asserted their manhood by a faithful and conscientious indolence. He had only to guide the hearty enthusiasm of those who *wanted* to learn.

and sixty-one, while the candidates for a degree in 1848–9 had been but one hundred and forty-five. The class in rhetoric, which had numbered forty-two, rose to sixty-four. The class in chemistry from thirty-five rose to eighty-two.

From 1851 to 1858, inclusive, two hundred and forty-one graduated with the degree of A. B. or A. M. This afforded an average of thirty and a fraction annually, not counting, of course, those graduated with the degree of Bachelor of Philosophy. The number of graduates with the degree of A. B., from 1830 to 1850 inclusive, was five hundred and seventy, an average of twenty-seven and a fraction annually. Thus it would appear, that facts justified the language of the Report, " There is no reason why this class of pupils [those preparing for the learned professions] should be diminished."

As to general demeanor under the new organization, we may quote briefly from the annual report of the executive board to the corporation, for 1851 : —

" During the year ending September, 1850 [the last year of the old system], the absences averaged thirty-three to each student; during the year 1850–51 [the first under the new system], seventeen to each student. And it is to be remarked, that, owing to the absences being reported daily to the president, a much greater degree of accuracy is attained than under the previous system.

" During the first term of the present year (1850–51), the total number of demerits incurred was two thousand and twenty-five; during the second term, with an increase of students, the number of demerits was one thousand and twenty-five. During the first term, eighty-nine incurred no demerit, during the second term, one hundred and twenty incurred none."

The last paragraph is quoted not as affording any ground of comparison between the old system and the new, but as exhibiting the improvement made by the new system upon itself.

During the first term of the following year, owing to temporary and incidental causes, the standard of demeanor was low, and much disorder prevailed. But during the second term, the executive board reported that the college was in as good a state of discipline as it had been at any previous period.

At the close of the year ending September, 1853, the board report to the corporation, —

" The conduct of the students has been in general commendable. Since the middle of the first term, no case has occurred requiring public censure."

The board also state, —

" From the account of the register, it will be seen that the collections have never been made so satisfactorily as within the last two years, and that the loss by bad debts for this period will be very small if there be any. The finances of the university are in a prosperous condition. Should the number of students continue to increase, or should the number of entrances maintain its present rate, the corporation will have the means of making important additions to the number of courses taught in the university. It is by thus using our prosperity as the means for attaining still greater prosperity, that we shall be able to accomplish the purposes which should ever be had in view by one of the oldest universities in our country."

For the year ending with September, 1854, the executive board report, —

" The whole number of students in attendance during the past year has been two hundred and ninety-six. The attendance and conduct of the students have been, on the whole, satisfactory. During the first term, the number of absences and of demerits was such as evidently to require special attention. Several young men were advised to return to their friends, and two were dismissed for cause. The second term manifested a decided improvement, and the conduct and attendance became perfectly satisfactory."

The report concludes as follows : —

" The present condition of the university is full of hope. The principles which we have adopted seem to receive the approbation of the community. Our income is sufficient to meet our expenses, and to leave a small surplus. When our lands become available, considerable additions may be made to our means. An opportunity will then be afforded of enlarging our courses of instruction, and carrying out more perfectly the principles which we have made the basis of our present system." *

To President Manly, of the University of Alabama : —

"August 9, 1851.

". . . The year before the experiment we entered forty-seven. The past year we entered ninety. . . . Every prophecy of evil has failed ; and the college never before stood in the public estimation as it does at present. It can be carried through ; if it fails, we are the persons in fault.

" We make no difference in our young men. All study alike in the same classes, and all could room in the college, if there were accommodations. We prefer to break up the distinction among classes and courses, and to consider every young man who comes to study, and who conducts himself correctly, as being as good as any other young man. Our young men studying for A. B., B. P., and select courses, are in every respect as deserving and as good scholars as any we have. There is every encouragement, so far as I can see, for trying the experiment."

To the same : —

"March 15, 1852.

" I think our prospect good. New cases are coming daily to my knowledge, where we shall be able to do good to men, who, otherwise, would have stopped at an academy."

It has already been seen that the number enrolled upon the catalogue was nearly doubled under the new system. But it was by no means designed to limit the advantages

---

* The Report of the Executive Board for 1855 we have been unable to find among the documents on file in the university.

of high education to those who had leisure to enter upon regular courses of study. Desiring to make the university a blessing, not alone to the candidates for a profession, and to the children of affluence and leisure; feeling that it had not yet discharged in full its mission in behalf of the creators of wealth, — the productive classes, — the president and those associated with him devised other and wider plans of usefulness. In 1852 a course of lectures was given by Mr. W. W. Pearce (instructor in Analytical Chemistry) upon the Principles and Processes employed in Calico Printing."

In 1853 Professor Chace (to whose able coöperation, it is but justice to say, the successful working of the new organization was largely due), having been appointed to the chair of Chemistry applied to the Arts, determined, in accordance with the original design of the department, to render it as available as possible to the mechanics, manufacturers, and artisans of Providence. The number of persons, and the amount of capital, employed in the manufacture of jewelry in the city, naturally suggested the class to be first addressed. Having, by patient and widely-extended observation and experiment, made himself acquainted with the subjects to be discussed, he announced a course of eight lectures upon " The Chemistry of the Precious Metals," addressed to the jewellers and other workers in those metals. The course embraced the following subjects: —

The relation of the metals to oxygen; the relation of the metals to the more important acids; the composition and properties of the acids and salts chiefly employed in acting upon metals; the formation, constitution, and properties of metallic alloys; the composition and action of solders and fluxes; the tempering of metals; the refining, parting, and coloring of metals; electro-silvering and electro-gilding.

An audience of about three hundred and thirty-five

assembled, filling Rhode Island Hall.* The lecturer
explained to them the laws and principles governing the
processes of their art, pointed out numberless ways of
avoiding failure, waste, and loss, and showed the steps
necessary to conduct each operation to a successful result.
They listened with profit, and, it seems not too much to
say, with delight. One said, " I see why it is that I have
so often failed. I have been doing, or trying to do, these
things all my life without ever knowing *why*." Another
said, " if I had known these things years ago, it would
have saved me thousands of dollars." At the conclusion
of the course, the jewellers presented to Professor Chace
a beautiful and significant token of gratitude for the benefit they had received from his instructions — a large silver pitcher, of elegant workmanship, made by the hands
of those who presented it. Upon its sides were engraved
scenes taken from the workshop and the lecture-room.
The testimonial, designed to commemorate the alliance
now inaugurated between science and industry, was itself
an event, and afforded an illustration of the true mission
of knowledge, and of one of the functions of a university.

These courses of lectures were intended as but the commencement of a series of similar movements, to diffuse
among the laboring and productive classes the knowledge
appropriate to their several callings. The new system
included, among its features, courses of lectures on all the
prominent applications of chemistry to the arts of life —
on the working of the different metals, on the principles
of combustion, the laws of heat, the most approved methods of warming and ventilating buildings, on the prin-

* Affording almost an exact realization of the anticipation expressed in the admirable address of Professor J. W. Draper (1853):
" I heartily join in the sentiments recently expressed by an eminent clergyman, and trust that the time is not distant when we
shall see the New York mechanic passing up the steps of the
university, and depositing the tools he has been using behind the
lecture-room door."

ciples and methods of dyeing and bleaching. It included also within its scope similar lectures on the applications of science to the mechanic arts, on the construction of machinery, the economy of power, the strength of materials, and on mining and engineering. It further proposed the establishment of an amply-furnished laboratory, open to mechanics of every class, who could there perform experiments and make analyses. Thus, with every year, the college was gaining in popular favor, and was conferring its blessings on every class. While no less useful than formerly to the candidates for the learned professions, it was also giving to the people of Rhode Island, and to their sons, an education which should fit them for whatever calling they might choose to pursue ; which should lighten their toil, lessen their hours of labor, and render more safe their often perilous processes ; which should make their daily life no longer a drudgery, but elevated, heroic, and promotive of their own and of the general wealth and happiness.

In 1854 Dr. Wayland delivered an address at Union College, upon " The Education demanded by the People of the United States." In no one of his many utterances did his powers do themselves ampler justice. His mind had worked itself clear on the subject of education, and the experience of the past four years had fully justified his convictions. In this address, while taking the same general direction as that followed in the report, he speaks with greater confidence and with a higher inspiration. Without attempting an analysis, we quote a few paragraphs.

On the assertion that useful, practical knowledge is destitute of disciplinary power : —

" Is it, then, to be supposed that God has made for our brief probation two kinds of knowledge : one necessary for the attainment of our means of happiness, but incapable of nourishing and strengthening the soul, and the other tending to self-culture, but leading to no single practical advantage ? Shall we believe that the God and Father of all has made the many to labor by blind rules for the good of the few, without the possibility of spiritual elevation ; and the few to learn nothing that shall promote the happiness of the whole, living on the labors of others, selfishly building themselves up in intellectual superiority? . . . We might surely suppose that that, which God had made most necessary to our existence, would be, in the highest degree, self-disciplinary. . . . We cultivate our powers of every kind by exercise, and that study will most effectually aid us in the work of self-development, which requires the original exercise of the greatest number of them.

" There are two methods by which we can determine the truth in this matter. First, we may examine any particular study, and observe the faculties of mind which it does and which it does not call into action. . . . Or we may ask, What are the results actually produced by devotion to those studies which are allowed to be merely disciplinary? We inquire, Are mathematicians better reasoners than other men in matters not mathematical? Are classical students more likely to become poets or artists than other men? or does their style, by this mode of discipline, approach more nearly to the classical models of their own, or of any other language?

" It is by such considerations as these that this question is to be answered. We have long since abjured all belief in magical influences. If we cannot discover any law of nature by which a cause produces its effect, and are unable to perceive that the effect is produced, we begin to doubt whether any causation exists in the matter."

Mental culture designed to be universal : —

" Skill in invention, united to the miraculous power of steam, is removing from human sinews the most laborious parts of every operation. . . . God is thus lifting off from us that oppressive severity of toil which paralyzes intellect and benumbs the power of emotion. The mind is thus rendered physically capable of thought and reflection. . . . We see here a tendency to realize the beneficent designs of the Creator. It is evident that God intended all men to think, and to enjoy all the advantages of intellectual culture, for he has given to all men all the powers adapted to thought and culture. It is equally evident that he intended all men to labor, for labor is essential to physical health and enjoyment. And, moreover, men think the better for working, and they work the better for thinking. He, however, never intended that labor should crush the power of thought. His design concerning us will not be accomplished until every man shall be able to secure a competence by an amount of labor which shall leave his spiritual nature free and unembarrassed, nay, the better prepared for its work, on account of the physical labor in which it has been engaged."

We may suppose the following words to have had their origin in the successful endeavor, lately mentioned, to carry the blessings of science into the workshop : —

" The practice of every art depends for success on a knowledge of some social or physical law. To such a community as ours, knowledge is, then, a matter of imperative necessity. Without it, unless by accident, man must labor in vain, and consume his capital without remuneration. But if it be said that, after all, the men who avail themselves of the laws of nature in their daily pursuits, do not resort to our colleges, the reply is easy: If they resorted thither, would they find what they want? Our teaching of nature's laws is designed not for men who expect to use their knowledge, but for those who expect immediately to forget it. Let, however, instruction be given, adapted to the wants of the community, on any scientific subject, and the instructor, wherever he can find men, will rarely want for hearers."

The discussion of the main subject of the address closes as follows : —

" Is it not imperative on us to set an example for ourselves? In a free country like our own, unembarrassed by precedents, and not yet entangled by the vested rights of by-gone ages, ought we not to originate a system of education which shall raise to high intellectual culture the whole mass of our people? When our systems of education shall look with as kindly an eye on the mechanic as the lawyer, on the manufacturer and merchant as the minister ; when every artisan, performing his process with a knowledge of the laws by which it is governed, shall be transformed from an unthinking laborer into a practical philosopher; and when the benign principles of Christianity shall imbue the whole mass of our people with the spirit of universal love, — then, and not till then, shall we illustrate to the nations the blessings of republican and Christian institutions."

In 1856, at the dedication of the Norwich Free Academy, he said, —

" I regard with special interest the announcement that young men are here to be fitted for the practical employments of life. . . . I look upon the practical arts as a great triumph of human intellect.   Our admiration for this sort of talent is legitimate.   We do well to revere the genius of Milton, and Dante, and Goethe.   But there is talent in a cotton mill as well as in an epic.   And I have often been deeply impressed, as I have stood in the midst of its clattering machinery, with the thought, How great an expenditure of mind has been required to produce these spindles, and looms, and engines !

" Besides, we shall do well to remember that the agencies which have revolutionized society and advanced civilization have been inventions in the mechanical arts.   I rejoice, therefore, that the studies in this school are to be, in part at least, of a practical cast.   It will do a great and noble work if it shall foster and develop practical genius to be engaged upon practical things."

In 1861, after alluding to the principles which have been dwelt upon above, and the results aimed at, he wrote in his reminiscences, —

" The college commenced, accordingly, to act in conformity with these views, and, so far as I am able to discover, justified their truth.   Difficulties were indeed experienced, but they arose not from any inaccuracy or want of wisdom in the plan.   So long as I was connected with the college, it continued to be thus carried on, and satisfied my expectations."

Again, in 1864, at the centennial dinner of the university, he said, —

" It was upon such principles as I have thus briefly stated that the new arrangements of this college were commenced. Of their adaptation to the present state of civilization, and especially to that of our own country, it is, perhaps, premature to speak. Time will decide upon their truth or their fallacy. It is worthy of observation, however, that the changes in collegiate organization of late, so far as I know, have all been in this direction. Nor is this true of this country alone. The Universities of Oxford and Cambridge are adapting their courses of study in such a manner as to meet the demands of the different classes of the community, and are becoming accessible to classes who were formerly not allowed to enter their sacred enclosures. . . .

"I hope that you, gentlemen, may yet see these views 'familiar as household words' to the whole civilized world, so that every seminary of higher education shall scatter broadcast over the whole community, over every rank and every class, over every profession and every occupation of life, 'the benefits of knowledge and the blessings of religion.' Rhode Island gave to the world the first practical example of a commonwealth founded on the principles of 'perfect liberty in religious concernments;' and this principle is now making the circuit of the civilized world, and awaking the nations from the slumber of ages. It will be a pleasing matter of reflection for us, gentlemen, if we shall be permitted to see this little college taking the lead in another glorious reformation, and being the first to offer to our brethren, in every walk of life, all the blessings of broad, generous, universal intellectual cultivation."

Shall we, then, hesitate to say that the system of education pursued in the university from 1850 to 1855 was successful? And if so high a degree of success was attained notwithstanding many disadvantages, — was attained when to an organism not new was applied a new principle, when the impulse went forth from one man almost alone, without the coöperation, and with the opposition of many, upon whom absoluteness of success greatly depended, — shall we not say that the system has demonstrated its practical value, and has shown that under favorable or even under fair auspices, the result would have been as benign as the humane aspirations of its originator could desire?

Many facts show that he rightly estimated the demands and the tendencies of humanity. The University of Virginia (already alluded to), continuing upon its enlarged and liberal courses of instruction, became the leading institution in the south, containing in 1861 not far from seven hundred undergraduates. Very many of our colleges have made provision for a generous scientific culture. The United States, by act of Congress, has granted munificent endowments for the support in each state of " at least one college, where the leading object shall be, without excluding other scientific and classical studies, and including military tactics, to teach such branches of learning as are related to agriculture and the mechanic arts, in such manner as the legislatures of the states may respectively prescribe, in order to promote the liberal and practical education of the industrial classes in the several pursuits and professions in life." The Massachusetts Institute of Technology, endowed by the public and private munificence of the immortal Commonwealth to whose name it at once owes and imparts renown, has entered, without any period of immaturity, upon a career of broad and almost unlimited usefulness. It offers to the members of every class the privilege of a high education, at once liberal and productive, without exacting as a condition the study of the ancient languages. In addition to its regular and its special courses, it has established evening classes for the free instruction of persons of both sexes above the age of eighteen.* Among these evening classes were, last winter, the elementary class in French, numbering one hundred and sixty, and the class in grammar, rhetoric, and composition, numbering one hundred and twenty, besides smaller classes in mathematics, navigation, anat-

---

* These evening classes are established by a grant of money from the Lowell bequest.

omy, and physiology. The whole number of applications
for tickets to these evening classes (exclusive of the
students in the regular course, who are not admitted),
was between five and six hundred. On Wednesday and
Friday afternoons forty-eight tables in the laboratory are
occupied by teachers in public and private schools, for
instruction in chemical manipulation.

In these steps towards a universal and a truly liberal
education, in the pamphlets of Professor Atkinson, Dr.
Bigelow, and President Barnard, in the address of Dr.
Hedge before the Alumni of Harvard University (1866),
and in numberless other utterances of the advancing age,
is to be found the true rejoinder to the adverse criticisms
upon the " Report."

And the same tendencies, less marked, perhaps, but
unmistakable, are visible in other lands.

Such was the position of the university in the summer
of 1855, in the twenty-ninth year of the presidency of Dr.
Wayland — the fifth of the new organization. He might,
with humble gratitude to the Author of every noble work,
review the changes since he entered on his office. He
found the college with less than ninety students. He had
seen its numbers rise to two hundred and ninety-six.
Eight hundred and thirteen had graduated under his
presidency. He found it with three professors; it now
had eight. It then had no library, nor apparatus worthy
of the name, no laboratory, nor cabinet, nor any means
of securing any of these. It now had an admirable apparatus for philosophy and chemistry, a good laboratory, a
valuable cabinet, a library of thirty thousand volumes, and
a fund of twenty-five thousand dollars, by which the library was increasing at the rate of one thousand volumes
annually. It then had two public buildings; it now had
four. It then had about thirty thousand dollars of funds;
it now had one hundred and fifty-six thousand dollars, in

addition to the library fund. It then conferred its benefits on a few members of privileged classes and professions; it now was irradiating every workshop with its benign light, and was blessing mankind.

And its future seemed as bright as its recent history had been progressive.

CHAPTER IV.

IN June, 1850, Dr. Wayland wrote to Deacon Lincoln, —

"You must be patient with me about letters. I am pressed beyond measure in things which do not allow of haste. I am in the most laborious part of the year for me in college without any relief. I am working at my plan of organization, attending to what I can of the subscription, and harassed by a multitude of anxious cares and delicate arrangements."

And again, in July, —

"Last night, at about eleven o'clock, the committee had its last meeting on the Report [embracing the laws of the college]. . . . Then comes the meeting of the corporation ; then the preparation for commencing the course ; and then, if I live, a year of responsibility such as I have not yet seen."

After speaking of the point thus far reached in the subscription, —

"This is all that we know of. The time presses heavily, and I wonder sometimes that I can sleep o' nights ; but it is all in better hands than mine."

Of the labors and cares of the years 1849–55, from the hour when the first suggestion of a reorganization was

made, to the close of his connection with the university,
it is impossible to convey any just idea. His ordinary
duties as president and as instructor must be discharged.
Then the plan for the reorganization must be created,
objections anticipated, and the report written. Upon
the adoption of the report, there arose the work of the subscription, to which he gave time, and labor, and correspondence. Then came the draughting of new laws. Upon the
opening of the new year, each member of the college —
those formerly members as well as the recent entrances
— was personally examined by the president, that his
studies and courses might be assigned. The president
was the centre of everything. If any complaint was
made, if any difficulty needed to be obviated, recourse
was had to him. The executive board, between May,
1850, and July, 1851, held thirty-five meetings, at each of
which he presided. Some of these were exceedingly
laborious and of great length, extending far into the night.
During the following year (1851-2) nineteen meetings
of the board were held. Besides these, there were the
meetings of the Faculty. And the public attention, which
had been attracted to the new system, led to a vast amount
of correspondence.

To his sister : —

"June 26, 1851.

". . . The fact is, I have, for a year, written nothing but
business letters, so that I hardly know how to write anything else. I have inquiries of all kinds about college,
and have had an amount of official duty thrice as much, at
least, as ever before. I have lectured daily, and examined
weekly essays for my class. This has taken a large part
of my time, so that I do not know when I have made
a visit. I sometimes feel disheartened with the life I lead,
but it seems appointed to me, and the rule of our life
should be, that man must not live by bread alone, but by
every word that proceedeth out of the mouth of God;
that is, by whatever God sends us. For two years I have
not known what relaxation means. After Commence-

ment I shall, probably, have a little more time. But all depends on business which I cannot control."

And throughout, if any work seemed so unusually difficult that others shrank from it, it either fell to him, or he, of his own accord, assumed it. It was apprehended that the preparation of the catalogue for the first year would involve extraordinary labor, as it must contain a great amount of new and explanatory matter, and as the old arrangement of classes was entirely abolished, and the names must be classified on new principles. The president said at once, " I will do it; " and he did it.

To Rev. Dr. Hoby: —

"July 22, 1851.

" I am obliged to confess that I am a bad correspondent. For two years I have not known rest or leisure until within a few days. We have commenced important changes in our college arrangements, adopting some new principles, and cutting loose from your old university plans. To do this it was requisite to raise one hundred and twenty-five thousand dollars. The work has begun, and it has now gone through one year of its course. We have thus far been successful, and the prospect is, that we shall be able to carry it through with great advantage to the cause of education. But the care and responsibility have been exceedingly oppressive. If it had failed, on me would have fallen all the reproach. Through the great mercy of God, however, it now looks prosperous — and to him be all the glory. But I would not, for any earthly consideration, go through the same work again.

" I have not seen any of your friends. I have been, and am generally, so confined at home, that I rarely see any one, unless some one, in passing this way, calls upon me. My lot is to turn grindstone and work steadily in one place."

He was so made that it was an impossibility to see anything with which he was connected go wrong; he must either relinquish it, or he must, at whatever cost, make it right. At this time he felt even an enhanced sense of responsibility. The eyes of the public were on him. The system was of his creation and proposal. On his recommendation it had been adopted; in confidence in his capacity, and often on his representations, the means for its establishment had been contributed. It *must* succeed. During the first term of the second year, under the new arrangement, his cares and anxieties were greatly increased by certain annoying circumstances, purely incidental in their origin, and in no manner connected with, or growing out of, the natural working of the system.* He preserved perpetually an undaunted front. Probably the absolute certainty of physical prostration and death would not have moved him till the system was fairly established. Indeed, such was his iron will, that neither to himself nor to others was the draught on his strength apparent. Yet how these things told upon him, is shown, in some degree, in the following letter, written during the vacation succeeding the term recently alluded to.

To his sister : —

" It is true I have been unwell for some time — not from disease, but from over labor and mental anxiety. My work and care have been for some time rather too much for me, and I have, almost for the first time, spent as much of the vacation as I could in doing nothing. I was so worn out that the writing of a letter was a burden to me, and I have hardly written one but from sheer necessity.

" Your fear of my suffering from homœopathic treatment was groundless. I did not need, and I did not take, medicine. I wanted nothing but mental rest. You are, perhaps, in danger of thinking too highly of medical treatment of every kind. The most accurate researches show that people get well as certainly without treatment as with, if well cared for in other respects. This holds true, at least in very many diseases. I observe that all the best physicians give but little medicine ; and the older they grow,

---

* It was the opinion of his physician that he never ceased to experience the effects of the strain to which his brain was at this time subjected. Indeed, the varied, and, to a considerable extent, unshared responsibilities which rested on the president, might well have destroyed the health of a younger man.

the less do they give, and the less is their confidence in
medicine. Such is my belief, or rather my want of belief,
as to this matter."

Meanwhile his care for the moral and religious culture
of the college was unwearied, nay, was deepened, as the
numbers for whom he felt himself responsible were increased. During much of the time he preached on the
Sabbath in the chapel. And never, certainly, did he with
more eloquent earnestness pour forth his soul for the conversion of his pupils. One occasion — the Annual College
Fast Day of 1852 — was memorable. On the evening preceding, he received, by telegraph, news of the sudden death
of his early playmate and tenderly attached sister, Mrs.
Stone. His heart yearned to look on her features once
more, before they were concealed in the grave. But the
divine voice seemed to say, "Let the dead bury their dead,
but go thou and preach the gospel." He preached from
the words, "But ye, beloved, building up yourselves on
your most holy faith, and praying in the Holy Ghost, keep
yourselves in the love of God." The sermon was mainly a
warning expostulation addressed to those who, having professed religion, were in danger of failing to keep themselves in the love of God. It was an occasion of profound
solemnity.* During the same year, also, he instituted
among the officers a weekly meeting for prayer in behalf
of the students. And he was frequently at the Wednesday evening prayer meeting. He desired to attend, as often
as he could without detracting from the familiar character
of the meetings.

In his own home, too, there were claims upon him of
peculiar tenderness. His youngest son, for many years an
invalid, was, during the years 1850–51, in a condition so
critical, that at times his life was endangered. He required

---

* The late Rev. Bradley Miner, of Providence, a man of singular
correctness of judgment, said to the writer, "It was one of the most
awfully solemn sermons I ever heard."

ceaseless attention, and on his account the president slept
on a lounge, ready to rise and minister to his wants.   It
is probable that he had not, during that winter, one night
of unbroken sleep.

His public labors outside of the university were never
more arduous.   At the invitation of the legislature of
Rhode Island, he addressed that body, explaining the
features of the new system, and securing their approval.

In 1849–50, a course of lectures having been proposed
before the Association of Mechanics and Manufacturers, he
was asked to open the course, and consented, feeling a
strong sympathy with the objects of the Association — the
elevation and culture of the mechanics of Providence.
His subject was, " The Elements of high Civilization existing in Rhode Island."   The lecture was written expressly for the occasion, and was never used again.   Indeed, it
was so special in its character, that to employ it elsewhere
would have been almost impossible.   It bears the marks
of haste in composition ; but it contains thoughts worthy
of fixing the attention, not alone for the hour, but for all
time.   The definition which he gives of civilization is
profound and radical, and the address is imbued throughout with his characteristic public spirit and large humanity.   How inspiring is the delineation of a community
whose members should have realized the idea of a high
Christian civilization !   " Upon such a nation, God himself, according to his invariable law, would shed down
his richest blessings.   The land tilled by industry and skill
would yield its largest increase.   Its waterfalls would pour
down wealth.   Its mines would unveil their treasures.
Its harbors would be loaded with the riches of every
clime.   Piety would gladden every fireside, and the consolations of the gospel would watch beside every death
bed.   Happy is the nation that is in such a case, yea,
happy is that people whose God is the Lord."   As was
to be expected in addressing a Rhode Island audience, he

did not forget a tribute to one of his favorite heroes, the eminent founder of the first commonwealth that established absolute spiritual freedom.

In September, 1851, he gave the annual address before the Rhode Island Society for the Encouragement of Domestic Industry. This, too, was prepared especially for the occasion, and aimed to direct the farmers and manufacturers of the state to the means by which they might render the industry of Rhode Island in the highest degree productive. The familiarity which he exhibited with the subjects discussed, illustrated the breadth of his intelligent sympathy. To the farmers especially he spoke from the heart. If he had a passion, it was the culture of the soil. The address breathes throughout his desire to see every man, whatever his class or trade, raised to a higher level of knowledge, goodness, and happiness.

In 1852 he received from Harvard University the degree of Doctor of Laws. While he set a very low value upon titles as such, yet the assurance thus afforded that his labors in behalf of education were held in favorable estimation by gentlemen of high character and enlarged public spirit, afforded him unaffected pleasure.

During the winter vacation of 1852–3, he acceded to the request of a number of eminent gentlemen who were interested in the movement for establishing a National University, and attended a meeting, for this purpose, at Albany. He made an address in the State Capitol, upon the principles of university education. Many members of the legislature, then in session, were present, to whom the address was a revelation. They had hitherto regarded high education as something remote from popular interest, calculated only to aggrandize an intellectual aristocracy. Now they saw its relation to the elevation and enfranchisement of universal humanity.

Upon the death of Dr. Judson, the feeling was universal that a life so peculiarly devoted to the glory of God and the welfare of man should not be left without a suitable record; and, after the return of Mrs. Judson to America, the executive committee of the Missionary Union, having consulted her wishes in the selection of a biographer, voted to request Dr. Wayland to prepare the Memoir. The request found him already overwhelmed with labor, and purposing to devote such hours as he could with difficulty snatch from the college, to a revision and re-writing of his Moral Science. But to exhibit for the imitation of mankind the life and character of this most noble of men, especially when thus he could repay to the widow and orphan a portion of the debt that humanity owed to Judson, was a duty to which all else must be postponed. If his brethren who had been associated with the missionary, and if she who knew him best, and to whom his fame was very dear, regarded Dr. Wayland as the most suitable person to discharge the duty, he would not gainsay the decision.

The work was attended by peculiar difficulties. He was to write the memoir and delineate the character of one whose life had been spent on a remote continent, whom he had scarcely known personally, having seen him but for a very few days, and having never, so far as we are aware, enjoyed any correspondence with him. For nearly forty years Dr. Judson had been prominently before the Christian world; the leading events of his history had become as household words; his published journals and those of Mrs. Judson had been widely read. On the other hand, by far the greater part of his private correspondence, with his family at home and with his missionary associates, had, from a variety of causes, perished. There was little material accessible to the biographer, except such as had for many years lain open to universal observation. Dr. Wayland writes to Rev. Dr. Peck, —

"The want of all material for the Life of Dr. Judson is

pressing and painful. I do not see what can be done about it. Fire and water have done their worst with regard to all his letters and manuscripts, and what is in print has been made public in every form. I hope you have something for me at the Rooms. Pray cause all your correspondence to be examined, and send me everything you can get. From all the circulars we have, as yet, received nothing; I believe not a line."

To present the subject in a light that should be fresh and impressive, and at the same time truthful, was not a work of easy accomplishment.

The presence and aid of Mrs. Judson were of inestimable service. He writes, —

"I saw her very frequently, and was in the habit of conversing with her with the utmost freedom respecting missions in general, and the missions to the East in particular; and, in fact, on almost every subject connected with the progress of religion in the world."

In the preface to the Memoir, Dr. Wayland ascribes to her aid a large share of whatever value the work may possess. During its preparation she spent several months in Providence, in his immediate vicinity, and was for some time a member of his family. The high estimate which he formed of her character (expressed in his letter to her biographer), and her sincere regard for him (which was touchingly exhibited in her request that he would preach the sermon at her funeral), remind one of his striking remark, found in an early chapter of this Memoir, that, in order to render the intercourse of social life perfect, each sex must have something in common with the other. To outward view, no two persons could be more unlike than the great, robust, practical man, capable of "toiling like an ox" (as his friend Dr. Pattison has sometimes said), braving almost unconsciously the buffetings of the world, and the woman, inexpressibly fragile, sensitive, imaginative, filled with genius. Yet, in reality, they had much of sympathy. Her frail nature was inspired by a heroism and a sense of duty as strong as his; and in him there were a vividness of sentiment, a tenderness of feeling, scarcely surpassed in woman. Since his death, a lady who knew him well, and to whose religious life his words had been blessed, said, —

"There was one remarkable trait in him that I never heard spoken of. I never knew any one who understood women as he did, or who could influence and control them like him. He sympathized perfectly with all their weaknesses and trials. It was easy for them to open their hearts. They had no difficulty in confiding absolutely in him; and this confidence was always safe. I have often told him things that I told to no other being, knowing that they would die with him and with me."

The assistance of Mrs. Judson aided greatly in removing the embarrassment growing out of the scantiness of material for the Memoir. But the needed time he could gain only by devoting his Saturdays and his scanty vacations to the labors of examination and composition.

Early in September, 1853, the Memoir was published. It is probable that rarely has a religious biography been issued which has secured the approving opinion of critics so diverse in character. The ordinary reader found himself carried on by the interest of the narrative; the pious experienced a quickening of devotion from its deep spirituality; and those who had no sympathy with evangelical views could not but admire the simplicity of the style and the lofty heroism of the life which was recorded.

Theodore Parker writes, —

"It contains less information about the Buddhists than one might look for, but the noble Memoir of Mr. and Mrs. Judson is beyond all praise. Yet they carried absurd dogmas to the Burmans, who had a plentiful supply of their own. Had the same pains been taken at home to remove poverty, ignorance of natural laws, to abolish slavery, drunkenness, and prostitution, and to teach piety and morality in general, what a good result would have come from it! Bigotry must be expected in a missionary.

He says to one he tried to convert, ' A true disciple inquires not whether a fact is agreeable to his own reason, but whether *it is in the Book*.' The ' Creed for his Burman Church ' is a dreadful document. Judson's character is truly noble. If the only results of missions were to raise up such men, it were enough ; for one such man is worth more to mankind than a temple like the Parthenon."

Of course it was not to be expected that the book would escape adverse criticism. By some persons it was objected that too much space was given to the journals and letters of Judson, and that the hand of the biographer was not sufficiently seen. By others it was urged that the views of Dr. Judson upon matters of missionary policy had taken a tinge in passing through the mind of the biographer, and that in some instances he presented his own opinions rather than those of Judson. This impression, perhaps, was not absolutely unnatural, for so coincident were the views of both, that the one might well seem to be presenting his own when he was most faithfully delineating the opinions of the other. It is within the recollection of the writer of these lines, that, while Dr. Judson was a guest at the house of Dr. Wayland, in November, 1845, the formation of the American and Foreign Bible Society having been alluded to, Dr. Judson said, " Dr. Wayland, that is the only subject on which I ever differed from you in opinion." Mrs. Judson, after reading the manuscript, writes, April 12, 1853, —

" Dear Dr. Wayland: . . . You have made me your debtor for evermore. It does not of course become me to speak, except to one point of your work, however much I may enjoy its eloquent simplicity and perspicuity ; but from the mere beauty of truthfulness, it has given me such genuine satisfaction as I never expected to feel in the management of this one subject. I believe that language is incapable of a more faithful daguerreotype. I am more than pleased. I am deeply grateful to you, and to the great Power who, I believe, has guided your pen. I have no suggestions in regard to your conclusion, and but a very few trifling ones in matters merely verbal."

Mrs. Wade, who, with her husband, had been associated in missionary labors with Dr. Judson since 1823, writes to a friend, from Maulmain, —

"How do you like the Memoir of Dr. Judson? We think it remarkably truthful. It is thought by some that Dr. Wayland has made the book express his own views of missionary work, rather than those of Dr. Judson. But the truth is, two great minds, looking carefully into the work of evangelizing the heathen, would come to very nearly the same conclusions, though little acquainted with each other's views, and residing on different sides of the globe. We, who knew Dr. Judson so long and so intimately, well know that his views of missionary labors are remarkably well expressed."

We cannot avoid inserting, alike for its appositeness at this point, and for the great value of its general views, the following letter from, confessedly, the highest living authority on the whole subject of foreign missions (of whom Dr. Wayland once said, "Anderson is the wisest man in America").

"MISSIONARY HOUSE,
BOSTON, November 7, 1853.

"My dear Brother: Your Memoir of Dr. Judson I have read with more interest and profit than any other missionary biography since Henry Martyn's. Indeed, it is unique in value for men of my cloth. The volumes are exceedingly suggestive, and all the more so and more valuable for your not concealing the eccentricities, peculiarities, defects, whatever they were, of the great subject. I have not had much time for general reading since our annual meeting, and I cannot read you as fast as I can most others, and I have marked certain points for recurring to them again. Our missions have been supplied with the Memoir, and I wish all our brethren may read it with the care and thought it deserves. Dr. Judson's firm rejection of all work preparatory to preaching the gospel, except learning the idiomatic language, is admirable, and so is your unequivocal sanction of his views. Blessed that heathen people whose first missionaries begin their work as he did. . . . Dr. Judson appears to me to have

been made for just the position he occupied. He was
great as a pioneer. He had, perhaps, all the strong
qualities that were needed in his sphere. In some of
these he resembled the apostle Paul. Whether those
high qualities that fitted the apostle for the ' care of all the
churches' could have been developed strongly in Dr.
Judson, we may not know. He is an original. In some
respects he is a fine model. But it is in connection with
the development and illustration of some fundamental
principles in missions, that he especially interests me. I
think that he was right in the main, and that the Christian
world will at length come substantially to his way of
thinking, and that you have done a great service to the
cause of missions by your impartial development of his
proceedings and character. Few would, or perhaps
safely could, have been as bold as you have been in some
points of importance. You have purchased the ' good
degree' which gives you boldness to speak with authority.
Yours truly,
R. ANDERSON."

It need scarcely be stated that Dr. Wayland presented
the copyright of the Memoir to Mrs. Judson. He also
paid all of the personal expenses incident upon his connection with the work, and paid for the greater number
of the copies of the book which he presented to his personal friends. He counted it, he once said, a high honor
to have the opportunity of doing this act, and he would
not, in however slight a degree, mar the satisfaction it
afforded him.

Fidelity to history perhaps demands mention of the fact
that, under these circumstances, in October, 1853, a publisher in New York, acting (as he alleged) under the
" written approval of some of the wisest and best of Christians," advertised as in press a " cheaper and more popular " Life of Dr. Judson ; designed, of course, to take the
place of Dr. Wayland's work. For a sufficiently full
narrative of the events connected with this publication,
and for Mrs. Judson's correspondence on the subject, we
refer the reader to Dr. Kendrick's deeply interesting

Memoir of Mrs. Emily C. Judson. It is sufficient to add here, that although the volume alluded to never emerged from the obscurity into which it was born, yet the promise of its appearance had the effect to check considerably the circulation of Dr. Wayland's work, and of course to impoverish in the same degree the widow and orphans of the man who had poured his little patrimony, and all his scanty earnings, into the mission treasury, who " bore in his body the marks of the Lord Jesus," and who, after a life spent in the service of Christ, had left to his family only his name and his prayers. It would be false to deny that these events were a source of profound painfulness to Dr. Wayland. That such purposes should find a lodgment in the hearts of men called by the Christian name, distressed him more deeply than words could express.

The Memoir was republished and copyrighted in England simultaneously with its appearance in America. Although its circulation was naturally less considerable abroad, it took a place at once in the first class of biography. Several years afterwards, a member of Dr. Wayland's family, while visiting England, found himself the recipient of many acts of courtesy and kindness from those who knew him as a relative of the author of the Memoir of Judson.

To a personal friend, in reply to an invitation to lecture : —

"November 18, 1852.

" I am really very much obliged to the people of ——— for thinking so well of me ; but it grieves me to think how sadly they would be disappointed if they were to hear me. They would say with Solomon, ' As a fining pot to silver, so is a man to his praise.' But, in fact, I could not go without a dereliction of duty. I am engaged in Dr. Judson's Memoir, which takes all my time. I am doing it for the widow and the orphan, and they need it. And, besides, I do not think my talent, whatever it is, lies in this direction. People go to these occasions to be amused and astonished. I can neither amuse nor astonish. I have never been very successful in this line."

To Mrs. O'Brien: —

"June 2, 1853.

"The Memoir is done, so far as I am concerned. It has taken all my time since September; and this morning I feel relieved of a pressure that has not left me since I commenced it. I think it will be useful and interesting. Indeed, I feel a more than usual confidence in it. Mrs. Judson thinks it truthful. If it should prove otherwise than useful, I shall regret it, for it has taken a year of my time when years begin to grow few. Still, I have done it for the Master. My time is his; and I trust that I have given this to him, and have done it as well as I could. If he is willing, in his great compassion, to receive it, I shall have reason to rejoice, and I will rejoice. I presume it will be liked and disliked, as is the fate of most that I have written. I have made several efforts to see you, but 'have been let hitherto.' The fact has been, that when I got hold of this work, and the work got hold of me, I could not leave it without feeling that I was wasting time. This is the only way of doing anything, exposed as I am to interruptions."

To his son: —

"October 21, 1853.

"As to Guyonism and the 'threefold cord,' I have indicated my general views. I do not believe in any one's taking the modes of moral improvement indicated by others. This runs into the rites and austerities of the Romish church. I do believe in a man's taking the New Testament and applying it to his own practice in such way as he finds to edification. The rout made about Judson, on this account, was absurd and very weak. It indicated a sick and puling appetite in the moral character of the churches. Christians may be covetous, fashionable, attend balls and waltzes, and it is looked at kindly; but if a man takes unusual means to make himself better, the saints are in commotion."

In June, 1853, he was suddenly summoned to preach at the funeral of Rev. Dr. Sharp. It would be gratifying to quote from this tribute to his early friend and the friend of his father. But this pleasure will not lie within the reach of the present generation, as the manuscript of the sermon was deposited beneath the corner-stone of the First Baptist Church in Boston.

He had accepted an invitation to preach the annual sermon in July before the New York Baptist Union for Ministerial Education, and he prepared for this occasion the discourse afterwards known as " The Apostolic Ministry." This sermon received in its preparation more than usual labor, and was twice written. It was preached at Rochester, on the day preceding the Commencement of the university. The discourse was two hours in length, and was relieved by a brief intermission and the singing of a hymn. By its singular clearness of style, vigor of thought, and earnestness of feeling, it commanded the attention of the audience throughout. A Unitarian clergyman, who was present, said, " Some might call it a long yarn, but I call it rather a long cable." It was shortly afterwards issued in two editions of four thousand each. Subsequently, it was included in the " Sermons to the Churches." It has also been republished in England.

He remained for some days in Rochester, and attended the Commencement of the university, the anniverary of the Theological Seminary, and the inauguration of his former pupil, Rev. E. G. Robinson, D. D., as professor of theology. After spending a day or two in the wheat-growing country south of Rochester, he went to Niagara, and returned to his home by way of Saratoga, where he passed a few days. The journey afforded him a little much-needed rest, and was almost the only relaxation he had enjoyed for several years.

To a candidate for the ministry, then engaged in teaching : —

" September 26, 1852.

" I am glad that you are interested in your work. Do it well, and do it on system. But never let it be absent from your mind that you are preparing for the ministry. Make that always your end and aim. You should, therefore, always have a portion of your time set apart for this work. Have some ministerial study ever going forward, that you may be making progress in this direction. You had better preach, — once a fortnight, for instance, — to improve yourself and others. Do not, however, preach until you are prepared. Study your sermon and the delivery of it. Make plans; keep making them; write sermons as you can; make a most prayerful effort to deliver them well. Learn to do this, and leave the rest to God."

To the same: —

"I would commit some Scripture every day, and have always some book of devotional character in reading. I am greatly delighted with Neander on John. I have almost completed the second reading, and shall read it again. This is more than I can say of any book that I have read for years. I would advise you to read and study it carefully. It treats of the great and essential relations between man, the Messiah, and the Father. They are relations frequently taken for granted by the writers of the New Testament, and underlie and determine the most solemn and important ideas. Hence to have them clearly developed in our own thoughts, will give us great aid in understanding the Word. I cannot tell you how much I thank Mrs. Conant for translating it so well. It is worth a cart-load — I hope I may be pardoned — of German philology."

To a son, who had written to congratulate him on his fifty-seventh birthday: —

"March 13, 1853.

"I thank you for your expressions of gratitude and filial love. With countless imperfections I have endeavored to do my duty to my children, without any conscious desire of anything but their good. I have endeavored to encourage you in the pursuit of whatever was independent, virtuous, self-reliant, and disinterested, and have labored and prayed for your salvation and usefulness in the cause of Christ. I bless God that my labors, through his boundless grace accompanying them, have not been wholly in vain. Every birthday reminds me of the lessening portion of life, of which a year is annually a larger part. I feel more and more that what I do I must do quickly ; and yet my opportunities for doing good are but imperfect. But above all things I would always bear in mind how much inward work there is to be done, how much sin to subdue, how much heavenly affection to acquire, before I can be meet for that world towards which I am so rapidly tending. Pray for me, that I may be permitted to finish my course with joy."

An article had gone the rounds of the papers stating that Dr. Wayland was engaged in investigating the phenomena of the so-called spiritual rappings, and anticipated very important results from these developments. A friend wrote to him, suggesting the propriety of denying, through the public journals, this absurd statement. The circumstance is utterly without interest, except as his reply illustrates his manner of dealing with similar unfounded statements and personal attacks.

" ' Fudge ! ' as Mr. Burchell said. I had nothing to do with their putting the article in the paper, and am in no way responsible for it. I presume it was put in to have me answer it, and make capital out of it. The best way is to let it alone, and to let it die out of itself. I have no opinion on the subject, except that I believe the fact of the motion ; what makes it, I have as yet no means of knowing."

To a former pupil, an instructor who had experienced some annoyance and ingratitude from his scholars : —

" I regret that you are thus troubled ; but things of this kind are good for us, if they work the fruits of righteousness. The case before you is painful, but not remarkably so. One of the commonest forms of trial to which we are subjected is the ingratitude and unkindness of those whom we disinterestedly intend to benefit. This is a source of pain which has followed me all my life. But who ever suffered so much from this source as the Captain of our salvation? It was his meat and drink daily. In our own case, the reason of it is evident. In attempting to do good, we are looking at the good to man, and are pleased with it, and so forget that we are the servants of God, and must do it for him. He removes the supports on which we were unconsciously relying, to teach us that we must look for our reward to him alone.

"But things being as they are, what is to be done? I reply, Gain piety and wisdom. In the first place, thank God for this very trouble. He saw that you needed it, and therefore sent it. Thank him for his faithfulness. But, then, how to use it? Gain victory over it. Leave no means untried to conquer every feeling of resentment towards everybody. Pray for them, love them, and look upon the thing without a single natural emotion; let all your feelings be Christ-like.

"When you have attained this elevation, you can look down upon the whole matter, and it will shrink in dimensions, so that 'the crows will look scarce so gross as beetles.' You will then be able to make up your mind on every point, as it comes up, with perfect equanimity and correct judgment. When we get into this atmosphere, everything stands in its true light, and we are not likely to err in judgment. Such are the principles I should suggest. The application of them to the particular case I cannot well make. If your manner needs correction, correct it. The order proper for a recitation I would maintain, or I would have no recitation."

To a son, then at Rochester : —

"June 22, 1853.

"I fear that you are calculating too much on our visit, and I feel troubled about it. When we set our hearts on anything, we are likely to be disappointed. Consider the uncertainty of life and health. I fear that your friends have exaggerated expectations of me. I am not eloquent, and it is very likely that my ideas will by no means be well received. I must tell them what I think, and that is not likely to be always acceptable. Bear these things in mind. Leave it all with God, and ask him to bless my coming, without allowing yourself to have any high-raised expectations about it. I know it results from your affection; but this may lead us astray."

To a candidate for the ministry : —

"October 2, 1853.

"In your last letter you speak of meditation on the Scriptures as the best means of understanding the Word. I hope you will keep this in mind. In every science there are central points, from which you can with ease behold the whole. In morals, moreover, it is necessary, in order to understand a doctrine or a law, that you be in the proper moral condition. Now, this is the case in theology especially. You do not get at the meaning of the Word by learning what men have dogmatically written about it. I would give more for a book of earnest devotion than a dogmatic treatise, in order to the understanding of the Scriptures. But this all leads to one point. The mystery of the cross is evidently the grand moral centre from which every other doctrine takes its departure. If a man were fully imbued with this, if he could look upon it as angels look, every doctrine would open to him as clearly as daylight. This, however, requires moral preparation — a heart in harmony with the cross. Let it then be your great effort to read the Bible with this view; to pray earnestly to understand this; and this key will unlock everything. Neander on John illustrates this. It is all about the work of Christ, and his relations to the Father; and it is remarkable to see what light it throws on everything else. Have this always in mind, and from time to time write down your thoughts; they will be the seeds of sermons."

To the same: —

"November 24, 1853.

"The sermon [Apostolic Ministry] will, I hope, be received as a true exposition of Baptist and New Testament sentiments. But only the power of the Holy Ghost can make it effectual in the hearts of men. I grieve to see the decline of our churches and numbers from the plan of Jesus Christ; but all is in the hands of God. Cultivate expository preaching. Nothing enriches the mind of the hearer and preacher like it. We thus come nearer to the thoughts of God."

To the same: —

"January 28, 1854.

"As to making sermons, the rule is, that any man of ordinary sense and advantages can do what other men do.

When you get into the work, and your mind is turned to it, it will aid you greatly. You will have at once truths which you see need to be enforced; and the necessity of doing a thing adds greatly to our power of doing it. I rejoice to hear of the appearance of good around you. Let me know more about it. Give yourself wholly to the work. You will learn more of the dealings of the Holy Spirit with man in this way than in any other. Observe the truths which affect men, the way in which they must be presented in order to affect them, and the various excuses and subterfuges of the human heart. A minister learns more from a real revival of religion, with prayer and reading of the Scriptures, than in any other way. But he must be thoroughly in it, and labor, not with the left hand, but *manibus, pedibus, unguibus et rostro.* As to your enterprise in carrying the gospel to a neglected part of the city, I hope you will urge it on to the end. If my sermon does no other good than to lead to this result, it will abundantly repay me for all the trouble of preparing it. You say that you feel inwardly moved to this. Always attend to these inward monitions. They are apt to proceed from on high, if they come to us when we are calm and unheated, and especially when they are at variance with our love of ease and self-indulgence. You will rarely find them deceive you, if duly mixed with prayer, and humility, and self-distrust, and faith in the power of the Holy Ghost. Try to follow the thing out as nearly as possible in the manner of the Acts of the Apostles."

To a candidate for the ministry : —

" I have let your questions as to study ' simmer ' (as Sir Walter has it) in my mind for a day or two. I am of opinion that I would read through the New Testament carefully, at least as far as the Revelation. You get thus the bearing and spirit of the whole, and form an opinion on each book. After that you may read theologians. But after you have read the New Testament through, you will be the better able to compare their proof-texts, and to judge for yourself. I am still of opinion that the New Testament, as it has been given to us, is the best book; and I would get hold of this first, before I went into the results of men's doctrines and theories in regard to it. This will strengthen your confidence in your own views of the truth as it was declared by Christ and his apostles. The New Testament is unlike any other book; the study of it, faithfully and humbly carried out, cultivates originality. The study of other books leads to authority. The great centre is Christ crucified. From this every other doctrine takes its bearing. If we have true views of this, everything else will take its place, and assume its true proportion."

To the same : —

". . . You can do nothing better than commence with Christ and his apostles. Why should you drink the truth diluted and adulterated by man, when you can go to the fountain?

" The preaching is weak, because at present men preach theology instead of the Scriptures. Nothing gives vigor to the mind, like deep contemplation of pure truth. Peter was an illiterate man, Paul a learned man, and yet 1st Peter will compare with any of Paul's Epistles for power of thought and rich, varied, and compressed exhibitions of truth. Keep to your idea of blending general culture with professional study, to enlarge and diversify your mental energies."

To his sister : —

" February 16, 1854.

" I regret I was not more conversable, as it is called, and more interesting when I saw you. But it is my misfortune. There is upon me a sort of habitual sadness, a want of interest, a kind of despair of ever effecting anything, and a feeling of inability to labor, which I think is unusual to me, at least unusual as a habit. I do not know whence it arises. My general health is good. I am inclined to attribute it to overwork, for two or three years, some time since. I see nobody except on business. I have no taste for society, as it is where I must see it, if I see it at all. I have no intimate companions. I incline to be alone, and when I am in company, am silent for the simple reason that I have nothing to say. I am never silent by design, but always by necessity. You must, therefore, excuse me for being so uninteresting, for I am not half so uninteresting to others as I am to myself. This looks like a Jeremiad; it is not. When I can get out more in the spring it will, I presume, pass off. The cares of college press me, and I have long wished to get rid of them. I am waiting for an opening of Providence."

To a former pupil, a lawyer : —

" You must, I think, be convinced of the effect which business is producing on your mind. You know, as well as I can tell you, that we are created with a moral as well as an intellectual nature, and that the former is by far the more important. You know also that every part of our nature develops by cultivation and exercise, and withers and grows inactive by neglect. Now, your present business occupies almost entirely the intellectual part of your nature. You are engaged in devising what, for yourself or others, is best for this world, and specially for one of the least important matters of this world — earthly possessions. There is nothing about it that lays hold of the moral elements of character. These are cultivated by prayer, adoration, repentance, striving after holiness, self-denial for the good of others, and devoting ourselves to the promotion of some good cause, some cause by which men will be made better for time and for eternity. You see how your present avocations tend (unless counteracted) to influence the development of character, and you see how the tendency must grow stronger by every day's exercise, until eternity, and all that relates to the moral character of man, will suffer a disastrous eclipse. You have referred this subject, time after time, to a later period. What later period can you conceive of, which will not be more unfavorable than the present?"

CHAPTER V.

THE NEBRASKA BILL. — THE BURNS CASE. — ADDRESS
AT UNION COLLEGE. — INTELLECTUAL PHILOSOPHY. —
CORRESPONDENCE. — NEED OF REST. — THE PRESI-
DENT'S RESIGNATION. — THE LAST COMMENCEMENT.

DURING the winter and spring of 1854, Dr. Wayland, was, in common with all good men, profoundly
moved by the proposed passage of the Nebraska Bill.
To his son he wrote, —

"I am glad to hear of your interest in the Nebraska
question. It is the most important that has occurred in
my time. We need to have the religious feeling aroused
on the subject. It is now intolerably torpid. Keep within a sound discretion, and go forward in the business."

At the meeting of the citizens of Providence, March 7,
1854, he was present and spoke. Waiving all incidental
and side issues, he opposed the bill on the broad ground
that it was designed to establish slavery throughout all
the territories concerned. He said, —

"I protest against this bill, in the first place, because it
proposes to violate the great elementary law, on which
not only government, but society itself, is founded — the
principle that every man has a right to himself. Second,
as an American citizen, I protest against this bill. Third,
as a citizen of a free state, I protest against this bill.
Fourth, I protest against it as a Christian."

His speech was published in full in nearly all the leading papers of the Northern States, both secular and religious, and was regarded as unanswerable. The National

Era declared that no such specimen of compact logic had been addressed to the American people since the death of Daniel Webster; and the south attested the power of his words by angry denunciation, and by the exclusion of his books from such of the southern institutions as had hitherto used them. He had never given up the hope that the iniquitous measure referred to would be disavowed and discountenanced by the good men and Christians of the Southern States, many of whom had by letter, and in conversation, expressed to him their sense of the evil of slavery, and their desire for its removal. It was with pain that he was forced reluctantly to abandon this hope. With great justice, an eminent Baptist minister in one of the border states, observed that the southern people would hear Dr. Wayland after they had ceased to hear any other northern man.

To his son, on the occasion of the Burns case in Boston: —

"June 2, 1854.

"Keep down your passions; pray for the country; try to look as patiently as possible upon wrong-doers. In the mean time, proclaim the principles of right, their obligation and supremacy, and nerve men to be willing to suffer loss in consequence of them. What is wanted is to extend and deepen the feeling of resistance to oppression, and of determination at all hazards to be free from participation in it. When this is universal, united, and moral, nothing can withstand it, and the agents to carry it on will soon appear. Do not allow yourself in strong excitement, but rather lift up the case with both hands, and all your heart, to the Judge of all the earth; plead his promises and his perfections, and wait for the indications of his providence. This seems present duty. Write, publish, inform the people, direct the present feeling in proper channels. This is all I see at present."

To a former pupil, a lawyer: —

"July 29, 1854.

"The times look grave. I hope that the spirit of the north is at last aroused. It seems to me that the thing to

be done is not to be committed to any rash or sudden
measure, but to deepen, extend, and unite the anti-slavery
feeling. I never before have been deeply moved by any
political question. May God direct it all to the advancement of truth and righteousness. Do not be anxious to
take extreme, but rather solid ground, and thus carry all
sober men with you.

" . . . I want the spirit of freedom and sense of right
extended in every direction, not by violence that cannot be
defended, but by showing the right, and keeping people
out of the wrong. I never knew anything so intensely and
cumulatively abominable. It is a matter of deep and anxious thought. You should study it carefully, and make
up your mind on all the points, so that, if a time comes
for action, you may be prepared with good reasons for yourself and others."

To the same : —

" Keep out of passionate excitement. Study the constitutional principles, and the slave laws, and think out for
yourself every case liable to occur, with all its termina-
tions. You may be called on in such a case. If so, it
will be of vast importance to be fully prepared in advance.
You may be invited to address an assembly. Any one can
advise them to resist, but a jurist should be able to show
them their constitutional position in all its bearings,
and the true ground for their conduct. From all 1 can
learn of the whole country, the feeling is such as I never
knew before. What we want is, to deepen it, place
it on fixed principles, extend it, and give unity to it. If
this is done at the north, we shall see some change. The
southern men are doing all we could desire in ripening
this state of public opinion. May God prosper the cause
of justice and humanity."

In reply to an inquiry about the Kansas and Nebraska
emigration scheme : —

" I do not see clearly enough through the business to
form any opinion. I do not think I have time at present
to think it through, and therefore should not dare to give
an opinion that would influence others to take so important a step. It is very painful to advise to a step which
turns out badly."

In reply to an invitation to preach at a distance from home : —

" I cannot make any promise. I am pressed very closely, and have (besides work at the Intellectual Philosophy, which must be done in time) to deliver an address at Union College, and one at the Institute of Instruction, which meets here in August. I am now doing rather beyond my strength, and cannot afford to lose a day or an hour."

To a minister : —

" What you say of free institutions is true and important ; but then I am opposed to uniting this, or anything else, with the preaching of the gospel. These other and more externally impressive ideas undermine and subvert the preacher as such. The Christian view is to look up to God, and to arouse the Christian feeling in men. To abolish slavery is a good thing, but it is not religion. Let the dead bury their dead, but go thou and preach the kingdom of God. Read the corresponding passages, and you observe that Christ places preaching the gospel above every other thing. I have no faith in any other means for curing the evils of this present. Northern men, if it were profitable, would themselves hold slaves in the present state of religion amongst us. What is needed is a general revival of religion in this country. Nothing else will save us. Since the bill has passed, I can only look to God to overrule it for the cause of righteousness. It will be a new event in the government of the universe, if such villany does not plague the inventors. God is infinitely wise and long-minded."

In reply to a letter from his son on his fifty-eighth birthday : —

" My days are fast gliding away. I feel the change produced by advancing years. My spirits are not so good as they once were. I am less able to meet difficulties. I cannot labor as much as formerly, and for the winter have barely been able to drag through my work. Age will claim its due. I am admonished that the night cometh."

Upon the 25th of July, 1854, he delivered an address

at Union College, upon the fiftieth anniversary of the presidency of Dr. Nott. Of the subject and spirit of the address we have already spoken. The scene was affecting when he reached the closing passage, and the aged instructor, weighed down with fourscore and two years, arose, surrounded by his graduates, many of them far advanced in years, and holding high civil stations, while one who had been his pupil forty-one years before, now on the verge of threescore, thus addressed him : —

"Venerable man! We rejoice to see that thine eye is not dim, though thy natural force is somewhat abated. We thank you for your care over our youth ; we thank you for those counsels which have so often guided our manhood ; we thank you for that example which has ever so clearly pointed out to us the path of earnest duty and self-forgetful charity. Long may you yet live to witness the happiness which you have created, and to cherish the genius which your inspirations first awakened to conscious existence. And when the Savior, in whose footsteps you have trodden, shall call thee home to receive thy reward, may death lay his hand gently on that venerated form, and gently quiet the pulsations of that noble heart. May thy fainting head recline upon the bosom of the Redeemer whom thou hast loved ; may thine eye open upon visions of glory which man may not utter ; and so may an entrance be abundantly administered to thee into the joy of thy Lord. Heaven will account itself richer, as it opens its pearly gates to welcome thy approach ; but where shall those who survive find anything left on earth that resembles thee?"

Returning home, he prepared the introductory lecture for the twenty-fifth annual meeting of the American Institute of Instruction, which assembled in Providence August 8th. In this address he reviewed the changes which had taken place in popular education in America since he last addressed the same body on the 19th of August, 1830. The progress already made seemed to suggest the possibility of yet further advances ; and he concluded with urging the consideration that we should

aim to render our system of education in the highest
degree useful, by basing it upon a study of the powers of
the human mind, and of the order in which these powers
are matured. In the portions of the discourse which
looked to the future, as in all his later utterances, it was
evident that in his view the method of education was an
open question, and that to use past experiences and suc-
cesses, not as a final resting-place, but as a means to new
discoveries and nobler conquests in the future, is one of
the first duties of the American teacher.

To Rev. Dr. Cutting, in reply to a request that Dr.
Wayland would write out, in detail, his views of a professional education for the ministry : —

"September 2, 1854.

"I really am unable to do anything in the premises at
present. Some time I may make a book about it. I am
now carrying through the press an Intellectual Philosophy.
I have a new Moral Philosophy, in my head in part, and
in part on paper, and a work on Evidences, two thirds
done. This is my line of present duty. The shadows in
my path begin to lengthen. The sun has long since passed
the meridian, and inclines to the west. I work as hard as
I can. I think I am able to do these things now ; in a
few years, even if I live, it may be impossible. It has
required some self-denial, and very steady work, to do my
duty in college and to discharge other important duties.
I have been constantly at my work all vacation, having
had only one holiday. . . ."

During the autumn of the same year, he published
The Elements of Intellectual Philosophy. This work
grew out of the lectures which he had for many years
delivered to his classes in the university. Its character
and purposes cannot be better explained than in a few
words from the preface.

"I have not entered upon the discussion of many of the
topics which have called into exercise the acumen of the
ablest metaphysicians. Intended to serve the purposes of
a text-book, it was necessary that the volume should be

compressed within a compass adapted to the time usually allotted to the study of this science in the colleges of
our country. I have, therefore, attempted to present and
illustrate the important truths in intellectual philosophy,
rather than the inferences which may be drawn from
them, or the doctrines which they may presuppose. These
may be pursued at any length, at the option of the teacher.
If I have not entered upon these discussions, I hope that I
have prepared the way for their more ample and truthful
development."

While the volume has not attained the preëminence and
circulation reached by the kindred treatise upon moral
science, yet it may be doubted whether any work is to be
found, better fitted by the absolute clearness of its statements, and by the training imparted to the mind of the
reader, to prepare a pupil for an extended course of metaphysical study. Without deeming it within the demands
of a biography like the present, to consider his character
as a metaphysician, or the relation that he holds to the
leaders in philosophy, we beg leave to direct the attention
of the reader to a most interesting and discriminating
discussion of these points, found in the North American
Review for July, 1855.

On the 1st of November he preached, at the ordination of his son in Worcester, the discourse upon " The
Church a Society for the Conversion of the World,"
which afterwards appeared among the " Sermons to the
Churches." And, during the period embraced in this and
the previous chapter, he prepared the greater part of the
sermons in that volume, as well as a large number of
others, intended for the regular service in the chapel, or
for special occasions.

To a minister recently settled : —

"October 8, 1854.

" I am greatly pleased at the indications mentioned in
your letter. Have the prayer meeting, and feel your way
for another. The singing is greatly important. We generally have two or three singers to do this portion of the

worship of God. It is totally destitute both of æsthetic and of devotional effect — a mere impertinence. Try for something else. Get the people to see that it must be accomplished, and then it will be. The effect of such music, with good tunes, in preparing the people to hear, is very great. I have seen a congregation solemnized by singing, so that preaching was like sowing on well prepared soil.

"I am working hard at my little book (Intellectual Philosophy), and then I trust that I shall write nothing more that does not bear directly on the kingdom of Christ."

To the same: —

"November 7, 1854.

"As to the day of fasting, I would take the greatest pains to have it a real thing, and to escape formality. The first meeting is better spent in trying to awaken confession and penitence; the second, in the exercise of faith and trust, and reliance on Christ. I would have an object, and strive to carry it out, not leaving it to mere random conversation and general prayers."

To the same, writing on the day devoted to fasting and prayer: —

"You and your people have been much on my mind to-day, and will be till I sleep. I pray that you and they may receive a Pentecostal baptism, and that from to-day a new era may commence, which may from you overspread our churches."

To the same: —

"I have just read Jay's Life. There is a good deal in it that is senile, but there is valuable instruction. His views were very much like mine. He determined to be a *preacher*. Commencing at sixteen, he maintained a high reputation until eighty-four. He was not only a highly esteemed, but a most useful preacher. It would be well for you to determine whether you mean to be a preacher or a reader of theology. The aims are different, and to be sought by different ways. There is nothing that I so much regret as that I did not make myself a preacher. I have too late come to the impression that I might possibly have suceeeded, if I had labored for it."

To a young minister : —

" It seems that you are about building. This is a great temptation. Men under such circumstances are strongly urged to preach so as to build up a society, and not to convert men. Be careful of this, and let it be your aim not to get men to take pews, but to enter the kingdom. If they do the last, they will certainly do the first. Do not build an expensive church. It will burden your friends, and render the establishment costly, and thus drive off the poor, to whom the gospel is to be preached. Have it neat, commodious, well ventilated, and plain. This best becomes Christians."

To his sister : —

" I am glad you like my book [the Intellectual Philosophy]. It has cost me many hours and years of thought, in one way and another. I have tried to make it plain. Whether I have succeeded or not, time must determine. At all events, it has all gone through my own mind, and is not made by the scissors. This is more than can be said of many books that have been published on that subject."

To the same : —

"You are very kind in inviting us to come to you. The fact is, I am just preparing to build a house, and until this is under way I cannot say anything, or I should have written to you before. I will come if I can, and shall make every effort to do so.

" I rejoice to hear you are all well and happy. It does not fall to my lot to enjoy much in this way. I wish it did. I am in the perpetual treadmill."

To a former pupil, a member of one of the earliest classes which President Wayland instructed in Brown University, recently elected to the United States Senate, who had first used his franking privilege to write, expressing his sense of obligation to his former instructor : —

"March 6, 1855.

" Your very kind letter arrived this evening ; and though it is late, and I have some work to do, I should not sleep soundly if I allowed it to be for a moment unanswered.

"As I read it, my eyes became moist, and my tongue grew thick, and I could easily have wept, though not much given to tears. Amid my many failures, and what I cannot but consider great want of success, it is more cheering than you can imagine, to know that my labors have not been in vain, or at least that one of my pupils, who has arrived at deserved distinction, is kind enough to take this view of them. I well remember the old chapel, and can see you rising to recite there, as though it were yesterday. If I then did you any good, I rejoice at it, for thus I did good to virtue and humanity.

"I have followed you year by year, ever since you left us. Few have marked every step of your upward progress with more sincere pleasure — I had almost said pride — than myself. More than all, I have been delighted to learn that as your influence increased, it was everywhere exerted in favor of virtue and religion. I always knew that when any question arose involving the interests of piety or humanity, you would be found on the side of Christ and his cause.

"And now a wider field opens before you. When I look at the position of this country, and the talent committed to it by God, and the power of the Senate over the destinies of humanity, I can hardly conceive of a more responsible position. Every important act of that chamber tells upon the civilized world — it may be for generations to come. My dear ——, may God baptize you with a spirit of power, and wisdom, and singleness of mind, and eloquence, and fortitude, and humility, and gentleness, and unfailing faith, and habitual prayer."

To a minister: —

"I am glad to hear of any seriousness among your people. Let me advise you to give yourself wholly to the work. Preach on the sinfulness, the helplessness, the accountability of man, his totally lost state, and the way of salvation by Christ. Do not, however, discourse upon these topics, as if you were preaching to the inhabitants of another planet, about what was going on here; but bring the truths down to the consciences and hearts of your people. Urge the evidences of piety, and arouse those that are asleep. Always, when you write, leave some three or four pages for the most pungent, personal, affectionate address and persuasion you can offer. Take high ground, as a messenger from God to sinners under his displeasure. This discoursing about things in general is ruining our churches and destroying the power of religion. Always remember that you make a blank failure, if your people do ñot go away obliged to make a personal application of all you say."

To a minister : —

"You wish that the work of God could be carried on without revivals. I wish so too. I wish that there were no special revivals; that there was no need of them, because the churches were always revived, that is, always in earnest. But if this is not the case, if they slumber for years, what but occasional revivals can prevent their sleep from becoming the sleep of death? I think you should labor not for a revival of six weeks, but for one of six years. Revivals show what God is willing to do always, if we are ready to receive his blessing."

To the same : —

" . . . We want to preach the truth, but we want to preach it so as to raise us in the estimation of men, attract the intelligent and wealthy, and make the gospel of the Son of God *respectable*. It is difficult to emerge from these influences, and to rely on the naked word, wielded by the right arm of the Spirit of God. Yet here is our strength. I would labor and pray to get all these things under my feet. I do not mean that a man is to speak carelessly, or foolishly, or awkwardly. These are not the teachings of the Spirit of God. It takes more pains and effort to get one's heart imbued with the Spirit than to write an intellectual sermon, as it is called. It is much more difficult to renounce self than to do the hardest work to please and glorify it.

"Get out of yourself so far as you can, and lie low at the feet of the Savior, perfectly willing to be everything, anything, if he will only give you souls for your hire. Humble yourself under the hand of God, and he will build you up. When *he* builds you up, you will probably stand."

To the same : —

"If you sincerely desire the salvation of the souls of

your people, and are laboring for this, you have all the promises of God to rely on. Jesus says, 'Lo, I am with you always, even unto the end.' God never causes such labor to be thrown away. You may plead all his promises, and freely claim all that he has said. But we must allow him to choose his own time and manner; and he is pleased when we, with child-like confidence, rely on his veracity; and if the vision tarry, wait for it. The promise of God cannot fail. Go on, then, cheerfully, not anxiously, knowing that it is yours to blow the trumpet, but that it belongs to Omnipotence to overthrow the wall. You may compass the city six times, and the walls remain solid as the hills; but on the seventh time they will fall down flat. God means to have all the glory himself, and he ought to have it; and surely we should rejoice in his carrying on his work in such a way that he shall secure it. Be, then, earnest, steadfast, enduring; but do all in faith, and trust in God."

In 1854 an eminent and learned college president in New England, in writing to acknowledge the receipt of the Intellectual Philosophy, had expressed what was the unavoidable sentiment of every one who remarked the results of Dr. Wayland's life.

"I wonder, my dear sir, how you find time to accomplish so much. It is but a few months since I read (and with great pleasure) your life of Dr. Judson; and now you have published another volume, which must be the embodiment of no small amount of laborious thought. I have considered myself a hard-working man. But I find it almost impossible to finish anything; and the *disjecta membra* of my toils as a scholar lie around me like the materials of a building which the carpenter can find no time to put together."

Alas! the explanation became in time painfully obvious. Like a steamer whose fuel is exhausted, he was supplying the motive power from the fabric of his own being. There has already been apparent, in many of his letters, a growing sense of weariness, which was indeed dispelled whenever a new call of duty was heard, yet which settled again upon him whenever the temporary demand had been answered. Ever accustomed to watch closely the phenomena of his own mind, he detected the imperious claim which nature, in various ways, was making for repose. His physician unhesitatingly told him that he must not longer remain pressed with the duties of his present office. His own convictions accorded with this opinion.

" I was convinced that I could not have discharged my duties for another year. . . . I was.treated with the greatest kindness by the corporation and by the Faculty. They desired me to continue with less labor. But I thought that no arrangement of this kind would be for the good of the university. So long as I was responsible, I could not help doing all that responsibility involved. If I did not act thus, the institution would suffer."

At a special meeting of the corporation, held August 21, 1855, President Wayland read the following letter : —

" BROWN UNIVERSITY, August 20, 1855.
" TO THE CORPORATION OF BROWN UNIVERSITY.
" Gentlemen : After more than twenty-eight years' service, the conviction is pressed upon me that relaxation and change of labor have become to me a matter of indispensable necessity. These, I am persuaded, cannot be secured while I hold the office with which you have so long honored me. I therefore believe it to be my duty to resign the offices of president of Brown University and professor of moral and intellectual philosophy. If it be agreeable to you, I desire that this resignation may take place at the close of the present collegiate year.
" In sundering the ties which have so long bound us officially together, I shall not attempt to express the sentiment of gratitude and respect which I entertained towards the gentlemen of the corporation of Brown University. For more than a quarter of a century we have labored together in promoting the cause of good learning, and specially in advancing the interests of this institution. Those who, like myself, were young men when I entered upon office, are with me beginning to feel the approaches of age. Yet during this long period, no spirit of dissen-

sion has either divided our councils or enfeebled our exertions. We have beheld this university, year after year, advancing in reputation and usefulness, and diffusing more and more widely the blessings of education. Let us thank God for giving us this opportunity of conferring benefits on mankind, and for crowning our labors with so large a measure of success.

"Permit me, gentlemen, to tender to each one of you the assurances of my grateful regard, and believe me to be,

With the highest respect,

Your obedient servant,

F. WAYLAND."

He writes to Rev. Dr. Bartol : —

". . . I am glad to see that you look upon my resignation as I have done, and, what is somewhat remarkable, for precisely the same reasons. Had you and I conversed together fully, and had you given my reasons in brief to another, you would not have altered a word from what you have written. The work was wearing upon me, and would in a few years have worn me out. It has become burdensome. It is almost entirely secular. A president is held responsible for what he cannot do, and this is sadly grinding to a man's conscience. I am happy to see that, now the thing is done, almost every one says that I have acted wisely. This, as you suggest, is a matter of substantial comfort, and adds to the great pleasure which I feel every moment when I reflect upon the fact that my work as president of a college has ceased — a comfort and peace which I have not felt for many years. I trust, therefore, that I have not acted unwisely. May God grant his blessing upon my doings, and render the remainder of my life useful to my fellow-men, and acceptable to him."

The corporation, convinced that his decision was fixed, accepted the resignation, and adopted a series of appropriate resolutions.

We quote from the Independent the following graphic delineation of the events of Commencement Day, 1855. The account appeared under the head of " Editorial Correspondence," and was, as we suppose, from the graceful

pen of Rev. J. P. Thompson, D. D., who, on the evening
preceding, had addressed the Missionary Society of the
University.

"PROVIDENCE, September 5, 1855.

". . . To-day there is but *one* Providence, and that is
the city on the hill, the light of whose university cannot
be hid; and there is but one name spoken in Providence,
and that is the name of the retiring president, which has
given to college and to city a world-wide fame. The
only use of railroads just now is to bring hither from
every quarter the sons of Brown and members of the
great fraternity of letters, to join in a parting testimonial
to Francis Wayland. . . .

"This day (Wednesday) is appropriated to the proper
Commencement exercises. After the degrees were conferred, the chancellor of the university, Dr. Tobey, presented to Dr. Wayland the resolutions which had been
adopted by the Board of Fellows and Trustees in accepting his resignation. Dr. Tobey is a member of the Society
of Friends, and, though not himself a graduate of any college, has manifested a lively interest in the cause of education. He is a man of generous culture and of handsome
address. He adheres to the strictness of Quaker phraseology, and expresses himself with that peculiar neatness
and taste which characterize the Friends, especially in
matters of compliment. In presenting the action of the
trustees, he said, 'President Wayland, I herewith present thee a certified copy of the resolutions now read in
thy hearing. Wilt thou be pleased also to accept from
me personally the assurance of my high regard for thee as
a citizen and an instructor of youth, with the desire that
Heaven may smile with prosperity upon the evening of thy
days?'

"The valuable document presented by Dr. Tobey, enu-
merating the various services of Dr. Wayland to the college,
was drawn up with excellent judgment and taste, and was
the more interesting from the quaintness of its style. The
Quaker chancellor did not scruple to give the retiring
president all his titles of vain and worldly pomp — D. D.,
LL. D., &c., while yet he accosted him with the familiar
thou.

" Dr. Wayland had the good taste not to attempt a speech. With evident emotion he said, —

" ' Mr. Chancellor, I beg you to accept, for yourself and for the gentlemen with whom you are associated, my grateful acknowledgments for the kindness with which you have been pleased to estimate my imperfect services.

" ' If the corporation of Brown University believe that I have faithfully endeavored to do my duty, I desire no higher earthly reward.'

" The whole scene — the ' unbaptized Quaker,' the representative of the extremest spiritualism, in his prim habit and with his precise and well-ordered phrase, contrasted with the sturdy Baptist, the representative of the intensest form of an outward ordinance, yet overflowing with spiritual emotion ; these two sects, whose forerunners were outlawed from the old Puritan colony of Massachusetts, now met in that shelter which Roger Williams founded for ' persons distressed for conscience,' and fraternizing in behalf of a sound and liberal Christian education — this was a scene which some painter's pencil or some poet's pen should have caught upon the instant to transmit to other generations. Will not Longfellow raise for us the spirit of Roger Williams to look upon the Providence of to-day?

" After these exercises came that indispensable conclusion of a Commencement, the public dinner. Tables were spread under a large tent in the college grounds, and several hundred sat down to the feast. At the close of the dinner, Judge Thomas, of Worcester, presented a series of resolutions adopted by the Alumni, highly complimentary to President Wayland. These he introduced by a happy and feeling speech.* . . .

" Dr. Wayland rose to reply, but said, ' his heart was liquid, and he could pour it out like water.' As, however, everybody demanded something from his lips, he proceeded to give the secret of that success which all agreed had been attained by Brown University in the last thirty years. I can only give an outline of the great thoughts and principles which Dr. Wayland uttered with a simplicity and candor which showed *the* secret of his power. I beg every one, — especially every young man, —

* The greater part of Judge Thomas' remarks has been quoted in a previous chapter.

whose eye may run over this letter, to ponder these weighty words of one of the wisest of teachers.

" Dr. Wayland referred to the fact, that when he entered on the presidency there were but three professors and two college buildings ; the library was small and seldom used, and there was no apparatus. There were no recitation-rooms, but recitations were held in the rooms of students, week by week, in rotation. Now, in its grounds and buildings, its library and lecture-rooms, its apparatus and professorships, Brown University is as well furnished as any college in New England. The secret of this success, so far as he was concerned, was as follows : —

" 1. *A resolute and honest consecration to the work to be done.* He had cut loose from whatever interfered with that work. He kept himself from amusement, — for which he had no taste, — and even from favorite studies, and gave himself to the work of building up the university.

" 2. *A dogged instinct to do his duty.* He had a fixed determination to go through with what he had begun, and to take up every duty as it came. No doubt, in the matter of discipline, some had thought him a ' regular old despot.' But God only knew the *agony* he had endured when called to inflict pain on any student or his friends. The pain *they* had suffered was nothing when compared with *his.* He had tried to avoid discipline, but could not. And now, as the rejected suitor appealed from Philip drunk to Philip sober, so he appealed from impetuous and excited young men to the men he saw before him, matured and subdued by experience. *They* must decide on his acts as an instructor ; and there was no pupil of his whom he would not be glad to meet anywhere, for he knew that towards all he had done his simple duty.

" ' 3. *Never to act for to-morrow, or next month, instead of to-day.* It has been my rule to do to-day what I have to do, as well as I know how. The way to prepare for to-morrow is, to do with a whole heart the duty of to-day. Sometimes young men take up teaching as a temporary employment, while preparing for a profession ; but their *heart* is not in it, and consequently they break down as teachers, and carry with them into their profession the reputation of men who have already failed. Do your

present duty, and never be mousing around for something
else.

"'4. *Adherence to general principles*. Have confidence in general principles. Our wisest men — for I take
it for granted that our politicians are our wisest men —
often mistake from want of confidence in principles.
Things follow their tendencies. Take a law of right and
carry it through, and accept the good and bad together.
You can't have the good of a principle without the evil.
But follow the principle. It will bring you into narrow
places, and up steep defiles; but keep on, and you will
see a glory beyond, that will repay the labor and toil of
the ascent. For myself, I am built railroad fashion. I
can go forwards, and, if necessary, I can back; but *I can't
go sideways.*

"'5. *Whatever of knowledge I have of men or mind,
I have gained from the New Testament of the Lord
Jesus Christ*. Study the Bible if you would be wise.
Count it your highest honor to be useful to your fellow-
men.'

"These remarks were received by all with deep emotion."

On Friday afternoon, when the bell rang for the opening exercises of the new term, Dr. Wayland was walking
through George Street, not far from the residence of the
late Professor Goddard. He stopped and listened. To one
of his former pupils, who was just passing, he said, —

"No one can conceive the unspeakable relief and freedom which I feel at this moment to hear that bell ring,
and to know, for the first time in nearly twenty-nine years,
that it calls me to no duty."

CHAPTER VI.

HIS NEW HOME. — THE OUTRAGE IN THE SENATE. —
"CHRISTIAN WORSHIP." — ELECTION OF 1856. — COR-
RESPONDENCE. — AN INTERESTING REMINISCENCE.

SEVERAL months previous to his resignation, Dr.
Wayland had commenced building a house at the
corner of Governor and Angell Streets. The lot was
beautifully situated, sloping eastward towards the Black-
stone River, with (at that time) nothing, save the trees, to
interrupt the view of the water.

His first care was to prepare the ground which was to
form the garden; and in doing this he put in practice the
principle which he had more than once urged on the farmers of Rhode Island — thorough tillage. The land was
subsoiled to the utmost possible depth, and all the stones
of any magnitude were removed. The effect of this labor
in relieving the ground alike from excessive drought and
excessive dampness, was marked and permanent. As
soon as the state of the ground admitted, he began to
set out fruit trees of all kinds. Probably there was not
a tree upon the place which his own hand did not plant.

In January, 1856, at the dedication of the Third Baptist Church in Worcester, he preached the sermon upon
"Christian Worship," afterwards included in "Sermons
to the Churches."

In this discourse he considers the radical idea of worship as existing under the heathen, the Jewish, and the
Christian systems. He then traces in each case the legitimate influence of the idea upon the outward form, and

particularly shows what should be the effect of the Christian theory of worship upon the construction of Christian edifices, and the conduct of Christian services.

His view of the several religious systems is searching and profound, and the sermon, while by no means wanting in directness and fidelity of personal appeal, is characterized, in a degree not usual in his later writings, by the graces of diction.

We quote a paragraph, not as by any means the finest passage, but as bearing perhaps, better than any other, to be severed from its connections.

"In the early ages of humanity, men, like children, think more readily through the medium of visible objects. Hence the idea of God is soon transferred to some representation of the Deity which can be seen and felt. Thus arose all the multiplied forms of heathen idolatry. Each nation, forming its own conception of the Supreme Being, embodied that conception in some material image. Then, again, the notion of the Deity became divided and subdivided, as some distinct supernatural being was supposed to govern some peculiar department of the visible creation. Thus every nation, and tribe, and city had its appropriate gods, to whom it specially looked for succor in calamity, and whom it adored as the author of every deliverance. Not only every trade and occupation, but every individual, had his supernatural friend, god, demigod, or deified hero, to whom his special service was due, and who was to him, in a peculiar sense, the giver of all good.

"It thus followed that a mutual intercourse was supposed to be established between the gods and men. The gods bestowed favors, and men made to them offerings of the things in which they specially delighted. The gods were present, either by representation or in person, and they received the sacrifices which the worshipper presented. But the common people were not worthy themselves to present their offerings to the gods. Hence a caste selected from the people, or holding their office by hereditary descent, was chosen by the god to mediate between him and men. And, again, since the gods were personally present, they must have a place of abode. At first the most beautiful and picturesque spots on earth were consecrated to their service. Thus, in Greece, the lofty hill-top, as it first received the rays of Apollo, the smiling valley, bearing on its bosom the rich gifts of Ceres, the solemn forest, as it whispered the praises of Jove, nay, every sparkling fountain, every mysterious cavern, every loud-resounding beach, had its presiding divinity. As wealth increased, men began to adorn and beautify their private residences. The deity must also have his appropriate dwelling-place. His house was the temple. This was his chosen abode, where, by his own appointment, he could be most acceptably worshipped. Hence he scattered blessings upon his friends, and hence he launched his thunderbolts upon his enemies. The splendor of the temple of the deity was the measure of the devotion of his worshippers. Hence the wealth of provinces was not unfrequently exhausted in providing a suitable edifice for the abode of the god. All that genius could conceive, or art elaborate, was poured out in profusion in honor of the patron deity. Hence arose those stupendous structures in India and Egypt, and those magnificent temples in Greece and Italy, the ruins of which cannot now be viewed without the profoundest emotions of grandeur and astonishment. The civilized world was dotted thickly with edifices and shrines, in comparison with which all that the Christian religion has done in the erection of forms of beauty and sublimity dwindles into insignificance.

"Of the moral results of the heathen temple worship, it is not my purpose here to speak. These may be best understood from the character of paganism delineated in the first chapter of the Epistle to the Romans."

In March, 1856, his residence being completed, he moved into it; we may suppose, not without many serious thoughts, as he looked forward to the events which, in the order of nature, the house would, in no very long series of years, witness.* Yet it was with many pleasant and cheerful anticipations that he became, for the first time

---

* It was worthy of note as an illustration of his conscientiousness, that, until he was a householder, he would not vote on any municipal question involving the expenditure of public money.

in his life, possessed of a home on which he might look as permanent, and found himself free from harassing avocations, and enabled to spend his time in the culture of his own soil, and in labors for the promotion of the happiness and holiness of mankind.

On the 7th of June, 1856, he took part in the meeting of the citizens of Providence, called out by the assault upon Senator Sumner. His appearance upon the platform was greeted by his fellow-citizens with a degree of enthusiasm, which was alike unexpected and grateful to him. In his remarks, as in his speech upon the Nebraska Bill, he put aside the incidental features of the matter under consideration, and sought to reach the grand principle involved. He alluded to the fact that there are but two forms of government — the government of law and the government of force. The recent assault he regarded as one of the steps in an effort to dethrone the government by law among us, and to inaugurate the government by force. He concluded thus: —

"The question before us is simply whether you, here and now, consent to this change in our form of government, and accept the position which it assigns to you, and whether you agree to transmit to your children this inheritance. For myself I must decline the arrangement. I was born free, and I cannot be made a slave. I bow before the universal intelligence and conscience of my country, and when I think this defective, I claim the privilege of using my poor endeavors to enlighten it. But submit my reason to the bludgeon of a bully, or the pistol of an assassin, I cannot; nor can I tamely behold a step taken which leads directly to such a consummation."

He was profoundly interested in the issue of the national election in 1856, and, it need scarcely be said, voted for the candidate of the Republican party. He was not, however, surprised at the result of the election, and had no doubt of the divine wisdom which permitted the event.

To Hon. C. G. Loring, Boston: —

"June 7, 1856.

" . . . Since I saw you, I have thought of but one subject — the condition of the Northern States. We have neglected the sighing of the captive, and said that slavery
was, after all, a small matter; and God is giving us a
taste of it, that we may see how we like it ourselves. The
iron already enters my soul. I feel that we are governed,
not by law, and the expression of the universal conscience
of the nation, but by bowie-knives, bludgeons, and the
lash. I hope that the conscience and love of liberty in
this people will be aroused.

" You mentioned a thought to me to which I attach great
importance; it is the formation of some plan of concert
among the free states. We must have concert, and *act
upon a plan*. It may require some time, and labor, and
sacrifice, but it is worth them all.

" But amidst all this confusion God reigns, and the
wrath of man shall praise him, and the remainder of wrath
he will restrain. I try to uphold my hopes for my country
by falling back on the character of God. There only is
our trust."

To a minister, during the Fremont campaign : —

"September 20, 1856.

" The business of a teacher of religion, I think, is to
press upon men the principles on which they should act.
When he applies these principles to particular cases, so
as to show men, as the minister of Christ, how they
should act, he mistakes his office; certainly, as a general
thing. You may on the authority of God urge his law.
To tell men that they must vote for Buchanan, Fillmore,
or Fremont, on the same authority, is to claim his sanction for your opinions. What is this but Romanism?"

To Dr. Bartol : —

" November 17, 1856.

" . . . Well, the election is over, and I am satisfied.
We have at last a North. It is an expression of decidedly
changed public opinion. We have now a basis of operations, and have only to be united, to keep alive the moral
sentiment of the people, to diffuse light, and to gain the
next tier of states, and the result is sure. If Fremont had

gone in with new and undisciplined men, and a Senate and House against him, we should have been broken up. Now I think the chances of freedom are good — God prosper the right."

To a minister : —

" . . . Let us try to do the work that seems set before us, looking to God for his blessing. He will take better care of the future than we can. I begin to distrust thoroughly all long-tailed human plans. God has not the least respect for them. The great power in morals is example, and no one can tell how far God will make this useful."

To his sister : —

" . . . The more I see, the more I am in love with the true Baptist principles. They are in accordance with the teachings of the Savior. This Abrahamic covenant, and hereditary membership, are the curse of the church. I think much more gravely of their effects than ever I did before.

" . . . You see the insidious nature of infant baptism. Manage it as you will, it leads to mingling the church and the world. It is the worm at the root of the spirituality of the church. . . ."

To a sister : —

" . . . The past year has been one of mercy to our family in general ; sickness has visited us, but death has not been permitted to invade us. We are all a year nearer to a change of worlds and to the judgment-seat. As I grow older, I am more and more impressed with those views of scriptural truth that were so dear to our beloved parents. I rejoice the more to hear them in the pulpit and to read them in the printed page. I deeply regret that they are no more dwelt upon by the ministers of the gospel. The present state of the churches shows the need of them, and until that need be supplied I have but little hope of any improvement in their condition. It has seemed to me that preaching is now directed to building up a society, as it is called, and not to making or improving Christians. May God send us a renewing, for all the influences of the Spirit are, as it seems, bestowed upon the heathen."

To the same : —

" . . . Your suggestion about society in your last bears
upon a difficult point. That we are social beings is true
and important. Columbus' idea of guiding a power which
he could not resist, does not, that I see, find an example
in the life of Christ. I do not see how we could guide
card-playing, polking, and waltzing to any good result,
any more than drinking champagne and whiskey, and
intoxication. These seem to be numbered among the
unfruitful works, with which we have no fellowship. If
we had the moral power to go among those engaged in
them, and reprove them, and mingle a prayer-meeting
with them, it would be another thing; but this would be
ill-bred, for we were not invited for such a purpose. I
take a different view of it. Why should not reasonable
and intelligent people have their own parties, and unite in
innocent and profitable intercourse. This is not ill-bred.
Let worldly people have their parties, and let us have
ours. It may be said this would not succeed. Well, it may
be tried. If it fails, then we can stay at home. It is very
useless to preach to other people to abandon the world
which we ourselves visibly cherish and pursue. So it
seems to me, but I am open to conviction. I know,
however, that I could not preach to people to die unto
the world, if I frequented such entertainments as are
common."

On his sixtieth birthday he writes to his son : —

" I thank you for your kind and filial expressions of
affection. As I grow older, I feel more and more the
need of kindness. I am not quite an old man, but am
approaching to it. Soon, if I am spared, feebleness will
come upon me. I hope to gather strength from my new
avocations and labors, yet this will be as God pleases.
But a small remainder of my life is left; and I desire to
spend it for the good of man and the glory of God. I
trust I have your prayers that this may be my course of
life until the end. I find myself getting more and more
unlike the men around me, and more solitary as I grow
older. I cannot be a partisan; and he who is not, will
have but few companions. I turn more and more to my
children and relations, and am glad to have their sympathy and succor."

During the summer of 1856 he attended Commencement at Yale College. The following incident, communicated by a gentleman of deserved eminence in literature and education,* is appropriate at this point : —

"I never spoke with Dr. Wayland, nor did I ever see him but once ; and I never heard him, except in a ten minutes' speech, off-hand ; and yet, in that speech he did more towards shaping my ideas and plans in life than any other person has ever done.

"I had just returned from a three years' tour in Europe, whither I went immediately after graduating at Yale. I was so situated, that I might reasonably be supposed to be beyond the need of much exertion. I had done and written some things which my friends thought warranted me in adopting a pleasant literary life. I was reading, and trying to enjoy myself in New Haven, yet not satisfied, and anxious to *do* something.

"Lounging about the edge of the crowd at the Alumni meeting at Yale, in 1856, I was attracted by hearing his name, as he was called on to speak. He rose, and his appearance made an impression upon me, such that I doubt whether those who saw him constantly, now carry in their minds a more vivid portrait of him than I do at this moment.

"He spoke of the possible rise or decline of this nation, of the duties of educated men, and said that he believed this country was fast approaching a ' switching-off place' towards good or towards evil, and added that, in determining which way the nation should be ' switched off,' the west held the balance of power, and that the west was the place for earnest men to work in, to influence the nation. That was all ; but it changed my whole life. I gave up law, literature, and politics, and thenceforward my strongest desire was to work anywhere and anyhow at the west in education."

---

* Hon. A. D. White, LL. D., president of Cornell University, New York.

CHAPTER VII.

VIEWS OF THE MINISTRY. — "APOSTOLIC MINISTRY." —
"NOTES ON THE PRINCIPLES AND PRACTICES OF THE
BAPTIST CHURCHES."—LETTERS FROM J. M. PECK, D. D.,
PRESIDENT ANDERSON, HON. W. LUMPKIN, R. ANDER-
SON, D. D., H. G. WESTON, D. D., DR. NOTT, J. W.
ALEXANDER, D. D. — EXTRACT FROM ARTICLE BY DR.
WILLIAMS.

WE will now retrace our steps in order to allude to a
topic, the full consideration of which has, for the
sake of unity, been deferred to this point.

In his sermon at Rochester, on "The Apostolic Ministry," Dr. Wayland, taking as his text the words of the
great Commission, asks, "What is the gospel? What
is it to preach the gospel? and, Who are to preach the
gospel?" To the latter question he replies, "Every one
who has heard and believed it." "Every disciple of
Christ must be a discipler." To the promotion of this
object, every endowment of every Christian should be
devoted; and those persons who are specially called by
the Holy Ghost, and fitted by peculiar qualifications, are
to consecrate themselves singly to this labor. "The minister does the same work that is to be done by every other
member of the body of Christ; but, since it is his exclusive business, he may be expected to do it more to edification." It was by acting on these principles that the early
disciples secured such triumphs for the gospel. Thus was
it that the nation of the Karens was evangelized. Thus,
too, have the German Baptists multiplied beyond prece-

dent; and such was the practice of our own denomination in America in its earlier days. He next considered the bearing of these doctrines upon Christian and ministerial education. The sermon closed with an appeal to the disciples of Christ, to exhibit a zeal proportioned to the demands of the nation, and the portents of the age.

In 1855 Dr. Wayland commenced, in the Examiner, (N. Y.), a series of letters, with the signature " Roger Williams," entitled " Notes upon the Principles and Practices of the Baptist Churches." Of their purpose he says, —

" The general design of these papers is twofold. In the first place, I have endeavored to present a popular view of our distinctive principles and practices, indicating, at the same time, their harmony with the precepts of the New Testament; and, in the second place, I have labored to impress upon my brethren the importance of a firm adherence in practice, to what they believe to be the truth." — *Author's Preface to the English Edition.*

He originally intended to prepare only eight or ten letters; but the subject opened before him; new topics suggested themselves to his mind, or were suggested by the letters of inquiry which reached him; and at last the series contained fifty-two numbers. The letters were commenced during the last year of his presidency, and were continued during a considerable portion of the following year. In 1856 they were collected and published in a volume. The " Notes," both as they appeared from week to week, and after their publication in a more permanent form, were favorably received. They do not bear the marks of elaboration, but resemble rather the familiar conversation of a man of large mind, extended experience, and elevated piety. Had the author consulted authorities more fully, he would have escaped some errors of detail; but it is doubtful if he would have preserved the singularly natural and transparent style which is one of the chief attractions of the book. He writes, —

" There was nothing in it which I supposed to be new.

It merely presents the views which have generally
been held by Baptists, as things taken for granted, and
which had never before been reduced to regular form.
Men were pleased to read in print what they had always
believed, but had never before seen collected together."
— *M S.*

The volume was republished in England as Vol. I. of
the Bunyan Library. In the Introduction to the English
edition, the editor, Rev. J. H. Hinton, offers some just
remarks upon the excellences and defects of the work,
closing with these words : —

" It is but simple justice to say, that the reader will find
the volume everywhere interesting, instructive, full of
sound judgment and wisdom, written in charming English, and never violating a Christian spirit."

Dr. Wayland's purpose in these letters, as indicated in
his words quoted above, unavoidably led him to consider
some of the particulars in which the practice of the Baptist churches had varied from their principles, and to urge
his brethren to " stand in the old ways." He was of
opinion that, adhering to their principles, they would not
fail to achieve great results for God, and especially to
gather large numbers of those holding neither the highest
station nor the lowest in society, the " middling interest ; " among whom, in his judgment, was always to be
found the most promising field for labors, looking to the
moral and intellectual elevation of man. But he thought
that he perceived a disposition to forget these principles,
and to seek, by conformity to other sects, to gain the more
aristocratic classes. This he regarded as a grave error.
He was convinced that the practice of the denomination
in regard to the qualifications and duties of the ministry
differed from the principles which the Fathers, adhering
to the divine standard, had held. An unwearied advocate of true progress, a radical in his views of education,
he yet could not regard anything as progress which varied
from the teachings and the spirit of the Bible ; and he

believed that the highest advancement of which man is capable is secured by obedience to the inspired wisdom. "The gospel is radical enough for me," he once said. And in proportion to this variation the ministry had lost in numbers and in power. He had already, in the "Apostolic Ministry," indicated some of the steps which would tend towards an increase in the numbers of the ministry. In the "Letters on the Ministry of the Gospel," published some years later, the increase of its efficiency is the leading theme. He devotes nearly a third of the volume now spoken of to considering both these points. The three productions really form one series.

He was deeply impressed with the fact that the number of Baptist ministers fell, by several thousand, short of the number of Baptist churches. He was of opinion that this want should be supplied, in part, by encouraging every Christian, whether ordained or not, to use all his powers for the service of Christ and the salvation of souls. Further, the number of laborers in the ministry would be enlarged, by encouraging persons engaged in secular business, yet possessing gifts of persuasive speech, to devote a portion of their time to evangelical labors. And the number of persons consecrating their whole time to the single work of preaching the gospel would be increased by removing any restrictions which had insensibly grown up (not warranted by Scripture, nor by the primitive usage of the denomination), and by allowing every one called of God to the ministry, to enter on the work of preaching, with such a degree of theological learning as the providence of God places within his reach. If he were able to devote a long series of years to preparation and study, let provision be made for him to do so. But if from age, or want of aptitude for study, or from poverty, or domestic circumstances, or from any other cause, such a course be out of his power, then let him diligently and conscientiously use such means of improvement and culture as God has made possible for him, and proceed in the work to which he has been divinely called, trusting in the promised aid of the Holy Ghost. That he was not mistaken in the opinion that the numbers of the ministry might thus be increased, would seem evident from a statement in his reminiscences.

" I have had several letters from ministers who had not had the advantage of a professional education, saying how greatly they had been consoled by this public declaration, that a man might be a called and accepted minister of Jesus Christ, without going through college or knowing a word of Latin or Greek. Others, who had given up all thought of the ministry in despair, had been encouraged to turn their attention to it."

An opinion has, we believe, gained some currency, that Dr. Wayland was opposed to the education of the ministry. That he regarded moral qualifications for this work as taking the precedence of all else, is, indeed, undeniable. But that he did not ignore or undervalue education, we will not undertake to establish by argument. If the record of his life and labors leave any room for doubt on this point, it would seem that it would be dispelled by the views advanced in the sermon on the Apostolic Ministry (pp. 46–57, as found in Sermons to the Churches). It would be difficult to find a more clear, terse, and unanswerable argument for Christian and ministerial education.

" I was said to be opposed to ministerial education, because I held that a man with the proper moral qualifications might be called to the ministry by any church, and be a useful minister of Christ, and that we had no right to exclude such a man because he had not gone through a nine or ten years' course of study. God calls men to the ministry, by bestowing upon them suitable endowments, and an earnest desire to use them for his service. Of those thus called, some may not be by nature adapted to the prosecution of a regular course of study. Many others are too old. Some are men with families. Only a portion are of an age and under conditions which will allow them to undertake what is called a regular training for the ministry, that is, two or three years in an academy, four years in college, and three years in a seminary. But does not every man require the improvement of his mind, in order to preach the gospel? I think he does. His faculties, all of them, are given him to be used in the service of God, and the more he can do to render them efficient, the more he will have to consecrate to that service. But this is to be conditioned by the circumstances under which he has been placed. A theological seminary should be so constructed as to give the greatest assistance to each of these various classes of candidates. Some may be able to take a smaller, others a greater amount of study. Let each be at liberty to take what he can, and then the seminary is at rest. It has done what it could. The rest is left to Providence." — *MS.*

Again, in the " Notes on the Principles," &c., he says, —

" If it be said that these views are opposed to an educated ministry, we reply, Is it opposition to an educated ministry to affirm that every man whom God calls to the ministry, should cultivate himself just so far as God has given him the opportunity? Is it opposition to an educated ministry to urge every minister to improve to the utmost his younger brethren, in whom he perceives gifts for usefulness? Is it opposition to an educated ministry to labor to improve the hundred instead of the ten? All that we propose is, that every one be encouraged to enter upon this work who possesses the qualifications which the Holy Ghost has established, and that every one who engages in it, be urged and aided to give himself all the means of improvement which the providence of God places in his power."

The writer of these pages once said to Dr. Wayland, " Is it your opinion that every candidate for the ministry should conscientiously secure just as high and complete an education as the providence of God renders possible?" Dr. Wayland replied, " That is exactly my opinion." A clergyman who, for a number of months, studied for the ministry under his instruction, says, —

" There cannot be a greater error than to suppose that Dr. Wayland had an inadequate or superficial notion of the preparation needed for the ministry. No one was ever more difficult to satisfy. An exegetical exercise, a sermon, or a plan offered for correction, that would pass muster almost anywhere else, he would criticise, exhibiting its short-comings, until the writer was glad to carry off the remains, and set himself to the task of re-writing it."

He was of opinion that the efficiency of the ministry might be increased, first, by admitting no one to ordination who had not given ample proof of a divine inward call, and of a personal adaptation and aptness to teach. Persons who entered the ministry under anything but the strongest and most unmistakable divine impulse, however complete their education, lowered its standard and reduced its power. Second, he would have the education for the ministry, whether in a seminary or under the advice of a settled pastor, so conducted as to be a moral rather than a mental preparation, and so as to lead the candidate as much as possible into a practical acquaintance with the duties before him. Third, he would have the entire ministry pervaded by a profounder spirituality, a larger acquaintance with the Word of God, and a more absolute forgetfulness of self, and consecration of every power to Christ; or, to employ his own words, —

" We need more prayer, more reading of the Scriptures, for our own spiritual improvement, as well as for public preparation; we need a more exclusive and entire consecration to our work; we need a victory over the world, which should trample under foot its applause, its wealth, its honors and distinctions, and be willing to become great by becoming little in the sight of men. The first thing for a minister of the gospel to attain, is conquest over himself; to be perfectly willing for men to say of him what they please; to bear the contradiction of saints and of sinners, if only he can, by preaching the simple truths of the gospel, be the means of converting men to Christ, and saving souls from eternal despair. When he has broken these fetters, and thus become a freeman in Christ

Jesus, he can enter upon his work, with a power of faith, with might in the inner man, which those who consent to bow down to the world, and do merely what those around them are doing, can neither attain nor understand." *

He was of opinion that the efficiency of the ministry would be greatly increased by faithful pastoral visitation.

" In such visiting, the pastor should make it his business to enter into the religious condition of every individual. With the Christian, he should converse on the evidences of personal piety, the motives to a holy life, the value of souls, and the importance of a life of entire consecration of ourselves to Christ. . . .

" He will pay particular attention to the children of every family, calling them to early repentance, and pressing home upon each one the gracious offers of mercy through the blood of the cross. . . . To the worldly and unrenewed in heart he will kindly, yet faithfully, speak of the vanity of the world, the hollowness of its pleasures, and the treachery of its promises, and will urge them without delay to seek for an interest in Christ."

He also believed that, by the relinquishment of manuscript sermons in the pulpit, and by the practice of expository preaching, the ministry would gain in power over the hearts and consciences of men.

The following corespondence is introduced as apposite in this connection : —

Dr. Wayland to Rev. Dr. Jeter, Richmond, Va. : —

"April 19, 1854.

" Your letter was really as cold water to a thirsty soul. It is now so long since I have heard from you, that I did not know but you had forgotten me. It was a great pleasure to converse in this way with you again. I am glad the Memoir pleased you. It was a very interesting labor. Dr. Judson rose in my estimation from the first to the last. He will take his place among the first missionaries of this or any age. . . . As to the sermon [Apostolic Ministry], I can say, with you, that the opposition of brethren to its doctrines has alarmed me. I did not know before, how

---

* Ministry of the Gospel, pp. 137, 138.

far Baptists in cities had swung from their ancient moorings. I do not think that there is a word in it that would not have been acknowledged by all Baptists when I was a boy. And yet, it is here considered as radically opposed not only to an educated ministry, but to all education. My brother, if the views which are held by many of our brethren be carried out, our denomination is done for. Let it be received as true, that a Baptist is not to preach the gospel without years of heathen learning, or, if he does, that he is nothing but a backwoodsman, of whom every one ought to be ashamed, and we are dead, plucked up by the roots. We leave the Acts of the Apostles, for the teachings of Presbyterians and Episcopalians. Look where you will, no denomination ever increased with this ministerial heresy. We began from nothing ; how God has blessed us ! But just as soon as we desert our principles, we cease to enlarge, and the Spirit of God is not with us. I hope that the brethren in Virginia will hold fast to the doctrine of the New Testament, and in this respect the distinguishing doctrine of the Baptists. It is most absurd for us to aim at the aristocracy ; they do not want our kind of religion. We are a *middling-interest* people, and there is no better interest. The Bible does not encourage us to aim for the rich. Jesus Christ did not, and we had better follow his example. . . .

"Well, my brother, I rejoice to unite with you, in love to all who love the Savior. There are, and will be, divisions of opinion; but there is one Redeemer, one hope through grace, and one heaven, to which all who love Jesus Christ are tending. I am sorely grieved at this Nebraska business ; but I love all my brethren in Christ, north or south, east or west; and I can rejoice with them in all that advances the kingdom of Christ. I shall always remember you with pleasure, and your visit here."

From the late Rev. J. M. Peck, D. D., of Illinois : —

"I regard your views pertaining to the Christian ministry, and especially the propagation of the gospel, not only as truthful, but as exceedingly important at this crisis in our denomination. Recently I have seen, in the Christian Chronicle, a report of your sermon, which confirms me the more in the correctness of your principles, and their adaptation to the exigencies of our churches. I am much gratified to learn that the sermon will go to press."

From President M. B. Anderson, LL. D., Rochester, N. Y.: —

" I have just finished reading your Memoir of Dr. Judson, and I cannot refrain from expressing the extreme gratification, which I have derived from the clear, comprehensive, and just delineation which you have given of the character of that great and good man. . . .

" By the remarks which you have interspersed with his letters, you have brought out the exact significance of his life, and the great moral lesson which it is divinely designed to teach. I have never felt more powerfully, than during the hours that I was reading these volumes, the glory of the simple gospel of Christ, when apprehended by faith, and honestly carried out into practice. I remember, when a boy, reading through the night the Memoir of Mrs. Ann H. Judson. I did not expect ever again to be so moved by the details of a life, with almost every part of which I had become familiar. I have, however, been more strongly moved than I was in my boyhood, but by a different class of emotions. I have felt crushed, under a sense of the inadequacy of my conception of the true ends of a moral being, under the government of God ; of my failure to seize, as I ought, upon the great elemental principles of our Savior's system of mercy.

" I see in your sermon on the ' Apostolic Ministry,' merely a transcript of the great lesson you have drawn from the facts in the life of Judson. There are some points in that sermon which I could wish otherwise ; but to the great fundamental idea developed in it *I adhere with all my soul.* I have tried, while an editor, to inculcate, with far feebler powers, a similar view of the gospel ministry. I have steadily refused to be ordained, while I had not the pastoral care of a church, so that I might be the better fitted to speak and act as a lay preacher. I have deliberately sunk the desire to attain distinction as a preacher (as the world at large understands the matter) in the desire to introduce among my brethren, and exemplify as far as my other duties would permit, the idea of talking about Christ to poor condemned sinners, not as a matter of professional skill, but as the spontaneous outpouring of a heart warm with the love of Christ. Though my ' talks ' have been necessarily ill digested, prepared often amid the noise and distraction of the streets of New York, while attending to business which exercised my body alone, they have given me great enjoyment.

"I know that it is only needful for pastors to lead off in work of this kind, and to enforce the necessity and obligation of it upon intelligent laymen, to accomplish in our larger cities a work for Christ which shall bring about a new era in the history of our Zion.   I have not a doubt, that, in and around the city of New York, a dozen large and vigorous churches might thus be gathered in two years' time.   When irreligious men see persons enter upon such labor, with no hope of reward, either in money or fame, it has a moral power over them which can hardly be exerted by the paid missionary.   Let laymen thus go forward and collect Sunday schools and churches, and God would provide pastors, as fast as the churches grew.

"I remarked incidentally that there were some things in your discourse that I could wish otherwise.   I ought to say that they are trifles, such as do not hinder me from doing all I can to circulate it, and inculcate its main principles. . . . I hope you will excuse me for obtruding these remarks on your time and attention.   I have written from the heart, because I have thought I should feel better for saying what I have.   I hope you will not feel under obligation to spend time in replying.   My main end will be accomplished, if I shall have said anything which may induce you to follow up the impulse which you have begun.   Can you not write a work on the propagation of the gospel in large cities, which shall point out in detail the practical working of the general principles which you have laid down?"

From Hon. Wilson Lumpkin, of Georgia : —

"I have read and re-read your discourse on the 'Apostolic Ministry,' with all the thought and consideration which I could bring to bear on the important subject.   I am so entirely satisfied with the value of the inestimable truths presented, that I dare not trust my limited range of thought to suggest a single modification of any paragraph contained in it.   I have been a member of the Baptist church for fifty-two years, and most of that time an acting deacon.   I have been deeply impressed, for many years past, with the conviction that the church of Christ was doing but a small share of what was necessary to be done, in order to hasten and secure the universal triumph of the Redeemer's kingdom on earth. Moreover, I have, for some time past, believed that the plans and efforts of our great and good men to regenerate and convert the world were deplorably deficient, and too much based on worldly wisdom and philosophy, without sufficient regard to the plain words of divine inspiration. I have felt that some great reform was needed in all denominations of our American church. But I have still worn the collar and worked in the harness prepared for me by others. I have looked in hope to our institutions of learning, including our rising theological seminaries, to furnish our destitute churches and people with a higher order of qualified men, to carry forward the work of the Lord. I have fully appreciated all the advances we have made in literary and religious culture; and yet I have been forced to see and feel that a greatly increased destitution in religious instruction pervaded many portions of our country. In direct proportion as the idea prevails that none are to preach a crucified Savior to a perishing race of precious immortals, unless they have come from the schools of the prophets, destitution spreads far and wide.

"But the question that has perplexed me most has been, What is the reform needed, and how shall it be brought about? For myself, although an old man, I felt that I was but a child in such great matters. In the first place, I had no well-defined plan of reform in my own mind; and, secondly, I had neither qualifications nor position for so great a work. But your discourse has revealed to me the great object which I have been in search of. It appears to me that it is imbued with the wisdom which comes from above, and is at the foundation of the reformation which can alone save the church from a downward tendency. Let the doctrines which you have advanced be inculcated and put in practice, and the Zion of our God will arise from the dust, and become the glory of the whole earth."

From Rev. R. Anderson, D. D: —

"Missionary House, }
Boston, February 13, 1854. }

" . . . You state, very clearly, under your first head, what the minister of Christ is to preach; but you lay yourself out mainly upon the preachers. The views you take are of the highest practical importance, and we shall never get the amount of gospel preaching we need at home, nor feel like sparing a sufficient number of our educated and able preachers for foreign missions, until your views are those of the public mind. I believe I agree with you to the full extent of your reasoning, provided the question be, how nominally Christian nations are to be evangelized. I sometimes feel no small apprehension as to whereunto it will grow, when I observe the. immense power exerted by our theological seminaries, on all questions relating to the creating and employment of the gospel ministry. I fear that the prevalence of a feeling that an uneducated ministry is worse than none (or what comes near to that), is a good deal owing to them. They have almost all the great batteries of thought in their hands. I am no enemy, but the firm friend, of these institutions, and would have them exist, and do all the good they can ; only I would by no means have the community shut up to them. Let your idea of the simplicity of gospel preaching be repeated in ten thousand forms, until it is understood ; and let all the preaching gifts that exist in the church be drawn into exercise, by men occupying high places of trust and influence, by churches and associated bodies of ministers, and, employed under their watchful and directing care. I no longer object to colporteurs, nor to lay missionaries in cities, nor to short courses into the home ministry when there is reason for it ; believing that an uneducated ministry (with an experimental knowledge of the gospel) is infinitely better than none. Your reasoning is conclusive, as it seems to me, in respect to home ministries for evangelizing the people.

" But I am not prepared to send many laymen, nor yet to send many uneducated ministers, on foreign missions. Nor do I think it well to attempt sending a very great number of foreign missionaries into any one heathen country not territorially large. It does not work well. Your theory comes in here. It is the simple gospel we wish to proclaim, — what every true convert understands, and can make known to others ; and I would rely chiefly on native force for evangelizing heathen nations ; and only a small part of this would I require to be in any sense learnedly educated. Our theological ideas, the result of our home system of

ministerial education, have gone too much into our foreign
missions, and we have found it difficult to get a native
convert ordained who had not been liberally educated.   I
have sometimes been almost reconciled to the scarcity of
missionaries for a time, if it only have the effect to break
down (as perhaps it is providentially designed to do) this
unapostolic notion.   I go for your discourse as regards
home ministries; but I am rather increasingly disposed
to send out a select body of foreign missionaries to be emphatically leaders and commanders of the people.   And
I see nothing in your discourse to induce me to think
that your views are not accordant with my own.   Go on,
my dear brother, without fear or shrinking, and believe
me as ever, respectfully and most truly yours."

Dr. Wayland to Rev. Dr. Anderson: —

"February 17, 1854.

"I am most happy to find that we agree in all that is
essential as to the gospel commission.   The point to
which you except, I confess I have not fully considered,
and will, therefore, hold my opinion in abeyance.   The
Moravians say that they do not desire for missionaries
highly educated men; they have not found them to do so
well.   One thing is, however, certain; heathen countries
must be evangelized by natives; no other plan is even
conceivable.   It is strange to observe, in our missionaries,
the most deplorable calls for aid from home, and the comparison of the relative proportion of laborers in heathen
and in Christian countries, and, at the same time, a settled
plan to keep out of the field of gospel labor all the natives, or to reduce the number of them as much as possible.   Some other views must prevail, and the churches,
wherever they are, must be looked upon, not as wheat
laid up in a garner, but as seed sown in a soil where it
must spring up and bear fruit, if it be planted and watered
by the Spirit of God.   We are all looking too much to our
own wisdom, and forgetting that there is any Holy Ghost.
We are making a difference between the times of Christ
and his apostles, and our own times, which I suspect does
not exist.   May God give us grace to understand his Word.
I would give infinitely more for a spirit to receive the
gospel as a little child, than for all the commentators,

divines, and decrees of councils that have existed from the beginning.

"But I am prosy. Can anything be done to put these things in a new light before the churches? I find good men everywhere are alarmed at our present tendencies."

From Rev. H. G. Weston, D. D. : —

"PEORIA, ILLINOIS, December 4, 1855.

"I can no longer deny myself the pleasure of thanking you for the views which you are presenting of our duty and danger as a denomination. Your sermon on Ministerial Education, and your articles in the Examiner, I have read with tears of gratitude, thankful beyond expression that such truth is set forth in such a manner, and from such a source. A short time since, a leading Presbyterian minister in this state remarked that your sermon at Rochester was *the* sermon of the age. I thought, if this is apparent to a Presbyterian, how can it fail of approving itself to Baptists?

"Views more needed and timely could not be offered to our churches. We have so long and with so much complacency congratulated ourselves upon the good work which we are doing in moulding the views and practices of other denominations (a work unacknowledged by them), that we have forgotten the (to us) more important fact, that they are wonderfully transforming us. For years I have desired to see a thorough exposition of the theme, 'The unconscious influence of other denominations upon the Baptists;' but the few to whom I have dared to make the suggestion have considered the very idea a slander. Nothing at the present time is so crippling our energies as our wholesale attempts to copy. Pedobaptists. The work to which God has called us we are leaving undone, and we waste our energies in vain endeavors to accomplish something which is not within our power. If, by any means, we can be induced to give up this vain attempt to combine things that are irreconcilable by nature, — this all-consuming endeavor to put new wine into old bottles, — if, by God's grace, we can be brought to understand our duty, and be content with it, our work will be already half done. We generally see clearly enough that the *theory* of the Baptists is radically different from that of the Pedobaptists; but alas! we lose sight of the inevitable consequence, that there should result an equally different *practice*. O that we could rid ourselves of this unwillingness to be singular in carrying out the grand principle of the New Testament! Would that we were content to be conformed to the principles, as we are to the ordinances, of the gospel, and that, in the one case as well as in the other, we esteemed it a very small thing to be judged by man or man's judgment!

"I will not weary you with expressions of gratitude for your exposition of the true nature of gospel preaching; but I could not resist the temptation of assuring you that thousands of hearts beat in warm response to yours, and that many prayers are offered that your efforts may be crowned with wonderful success.

"And now will you pardon the liberty I have taken, and believe me, &c."

From Dr. Nott: —

"I have read, with great interest, your book on the good old Baptist usages; and I sympathize more with its teachings than many of your own brethren seem to do. We, by our machinery, make ministers for cities and villages — I mean for what is called the 'upper crust' in them. But as to the great world, and the 'lower crust' of cities and villages, I know not what would become of these, but for the Methodists and Baptists. And of late, the Methodists and Baptists are following us, and we are following the Episcopalians, and they are following Rome, — at least in the outward aspect of our places of worship, and it will be well if not in the worship within. The Baptists, I am aware, are pretty far from Rome yet, and I pray that they may remain so."

From Dr. Wayland to Rev. J. W. Alexander, D. D.: —

"I have just completed your admirable Memoir of your father — now with God. A more charming biography I have never read. While you write as a son, it is as a son of Archibald Alexander. There is nothing filial that is not admirable, and not a word that could not be attested even more strongly by a host of witnesses. A more beautiful or noble specimen of Christian character can hardly be conceived. His gifts were great and abundant beyond

the common lot of humanity ; and God placed them where
they shone with a radiance that illumined the whole
church of Christ.   The moment I looked upon the portrait, I remarked its likeness to Wilberforce.   The latter,
of course, I never saw ; but I have seen his portrait by
Lawrence, and the resemblance is remarkable.   I saw
your father only on two occasions.   Once, about thirty
years ago, I spent a few hours in Princeton, and called
upon him.   He received me with a cordiality and kindness which I should have expected only from an old
friend, and showed me the place of repose of the mighty
dead.   He invited me to stay with him ; but I was unwell,
and was obliged to hurry home, fearing an attack of fever,
which I barely escaped.   I have seen hundreds of remarkable men since, whose impression on me has entirely
passed away ; but this interview with him is fresh and
green in my memory.   Many years afterwards I heard him
twice one Sunday, in Dr. Spring's church.   He preached
a sermon to Christians, admirable throughout, but not,
that I recollect, marked by any of those bursts of eloquence
of which he was so capable.   A high pulpit and a city
audience is not the place for those things.   An old Virginia church, or court-house, crowded around the windows, is the place for such eloquence.   Those magic
bursts of feeling must be rare among the conventionalities
and respectabilities of a city congregation.   The sound of
a bell depends as much on the quality of the metal as on
the vigor of the blow.

" I now see why Princeton has made good preachers.
I agree with your Presbyterian doctrine very well on most
points, especially on the marked prominence you give to
the work of Christ.   I differ from you in some respects.
You make the gospel system more rectangular and closely
articulated than I.   You see clearly, where I only have an
opinion.   But you make preachers.   The tendency of
seminaries is to become schools for theological and philological learning, and elegant literature, rather than schools
to make preachers of the gospel.   With every year their
general tendency is in this direction, as I think I have
observed.   I have thought this of Princeton.   As I would
have asked your father, so may I ask you, whether he
ever observed it, and feared for this tendency.   You will,
I trust, excuse this long letter.   I could not have satisfied

myself without writing, and I have written more than I intended."

From Rev. J. W. Alexander, D. D. : —

"NEW YORK, November 15, 1854.

"I should at any time have esteemed it a pleasure and honor to find myself in a correspondence with you; but this becomes peculiarly pleasant when I have to acknowledge such a letter as yours of the 10th. All your warm recollections of my honored father give me high gratification. Nothing can be more just than your remarks about his preaching. In the pulpit he was two different men, and least of all was he himself when he came into the cities to preach. When he got on his high horse, in conversation, he was indescribably delightful; this happened only once or twice in a month or two, and never ' upon compulsion.' Most heartily do I assent to your remarks about the literary tendencies of our theological seminaries. I feel it in my heart. Having left the desk for the pulpit, I feel it more. Alas, alas, that in an age and land demanding life, soul, activity, eloquence, fiery zeal, martyrdom, so many noble young men ' quite mistake the scaffold for the pile,' and come out *scholars.* Hall and Chalmers show us that great attainments need not spoil the preacher; but few learn it in America. In the somewhat senile gossip of dear good Mr. Jay (just out) there is some good talk on this. *He*, good man, was the *beau ideal* of the unlearned preacher. But give me this rather than the other. . . . In a great many discourses, tear off the text, and I wager no man living can tell whether he is reading a Commencement address, a sermon, or an article in the Bibliotheca Sacra. Indeed, I have known the same manuscript go through all three phases, literally. In many admirable, even masterly sermons (so called), in New England and New York, the idea of sermon, *qua talis*, seems to me to be wanting. This strikes our English friends most painfully. Such are not the sermons of the late Professor Scholefield, whom I heard at Cambridge, of McNeil, Stowell, Leifchild, Brock, or Binney. Yet this school of preaching, i. e., the true, always pleases, even in New England. Pardon my undue freedom of talk. I have been severely ill for a month, and am taking reprisals on my friends."

Dr. Wayland to Dr. J. W. Alexander : —

" Do not be alarmed. I am not apt to be so mercantile a correspondent. I do not always reply by return of mail. But your views so thoroughly accord with mine that I must add a few words to my last note. What you say of the pulpit is true to the letter ; and when to this style of preaching are added the indirect effect of Unitarianism, and the tendency to treat lightly and seldom the doctrine of depravity, and to generalize the atonement by Christ, until it fades away into an undefined and inoperative idea, what is to be expected? The pulpit is becoming of very small practical value, and the church of Christ is sinking into insignificance. Men do not preach to convert sinners, and subdue the world to Christ, but to ' build up a society,' to erect temples, and draw together the rich, practically excluding the poor. You feel this ; but what must be my feeling to see this overspreading my denomination, which by every principle of its nature is opposed to it, and to which it is certain death? It is good to find any one who reads the signs of the times as I am compelled to do. . . . How far is the evil owing to our seminaries? If it is not radical and necessary, can they be improved, or shall we return to some other mode of preparation for the ministry? I doubt if Princeton ever again makes as good ministers as when your father and Dr. Miller were the sole teachers. . . . I write in haste, but the subject weighs upon my spirit. It is overwhelming to see the glorious gospel of the ever-blessed God turned to such use, and something held out in its name from which all that is essential and awakening is excluded. Are there any men among you who feel this? Can anything be done in a better direction? It is sad to think of at home, and it is spreading to our *foreign missions.* I have asked all sorts of questions. Answer them or not, as you please or have time. It is at least a comfort to me to pour out my sorrows in the ear of a brother who mourns over the desolations of Zion."

From Dr. Alexander : —

"November 17, 1854.

" I will in the first place take my head from the series of remarks in your truly welcome letter. My belief is, that

the pulpit is sinking all over the country. It is worst in
towns and cities, and at literary seats. The sermon becomes an oratorical, æsthetic, or intellectual refection.
On this subject I cannot speak freely. *Peccavi!* I look
for the ' physican, heal thyself.' If you were to drop into
my church, you would find me sinning like others. The
proximate cause of the evil is this : a *selfish disposition to
gain character* for individual power, polish, ' mind,' and
all that. I have often preached worse than I could, because I wanted to preach (secularly) better. Though the
former of the two following reasons condemns myself, I
believe the main reasons of our failure are, 1. *Manuscript
sermons;* and, 2. The *absence of exposition,* as the great
matter of preaching. Pardon my resorting to an egotistic
way of expressing my thought. With a broken constitution I preach three sermons a week. The first I write
and read — it is my main achievement for the week ; the
second I preach from a page of hints — say a skeleton ; the
third, which for many years has been an exposition in
course, I deliver with no written helps at all. Now, my
impression is, that most of the good wrought by my means
is by 3 and 2, and very little by 1. But the grand cause
lies farther back ; it is want of fire, of faith, of feeling, of
love, of grace. If I had religion enough, all my sermons
would be like my expository lectures. I lament from the
bottom of my soul that I ever took ' the papers,' as the
Scotch say, into the pulpit. But even Scotland is going
into it. I sometimes go into a Wesleyan church to warm
up a little. Why ! — they are as genteel and formal as so
many Presbyterians.

" If I were not a poor feeble creature, whose work seems
nearly done, and who cannot exemplify what he teaches, I
would blow a trumpet of alarm. I think a revival of ministerial piety is the desiderandum ; an outbreak as abrupt
as that under Spener and Francke in Prussia, or the Wes-
leys and Whitefield in England. . . . This I say, being
preacher, in a Gothic pile, to one of the wealthiest assemblies in America ; I would, however, rather preach to
negroes — as I did for a long time.

" Remembering the entire history of Princeton seminary, I can speak confidently as a witness, though I wish to
be modest as a judge. On the whole, the difference between
the style of preaching of the first and last students is less

marked than I thought, till I came coolly to consider it ; and yet the tendency is decided towards learned, ele- gant, rhetorical sermons. *Present impression on hearers' souls* is not thought of enough. My father saw this ; he labored against it ; his own practice was against it. But I do not know that he ever ascribed the evil to seminaries. In my poor opinion, the evil cannot be laid at the door of seminaries, as such, any more than of colleges. It is a star- tling fact that, generally speaking, the type of the preacher is his *college type;* the gristle becomes bone, alarming- ly early ; seminaries and colleges both show the wide- spread atrophy and *anæmia* of the churches. Professors, specially, are tempted to be learned, rather than warm. The idea of returning to mere pastoral preparation, fright- ens all.

" Much might be done if men in high stations could more fully testify their conviction that the great end of preaching is to save souls, and if the curse of occasional sermons and great sermons could be wiped away. Invite a man a few months beforehand, and you never expect him to preach Christ. Our former revival excitements had some good results as to this point. People saw that min- isters were agreed, and were in earnest.

" My own particular mode of address is so cool and equable, that I am unfitted to stir up in this affair. Rich congregations like easy hearing. *Promiscuous* assemblies are what the gospel was made for. I deprecate all *chapel* preaching in colleges and seminaries. That *Baptists* should forsake their very strength, and come down to the poor level of ourselves, is amazing to me.

" If some author, preacher, and educator, like yourself, would adventure a small volume on this subject, it would have great weight. You and I, dear sir, must soon be gone. In what hands are we to leave the blessed gospel? It is a momentous question. You have brought this prolixity on yourself."

As these pages are preparing for the press, an honored Baptist minister, a theological instructor, has said to us, —

" When the Rochester sermon was published, I did not like it. But within the past five years I have read the New Testament carefully, with a view to seeing its bearing on the points touched upon in that sermon; and I have become a convert. I am convinced that the reason of our difference of opinion was, that he had read the New Testament more correctly than I."

Does not the recent liberal provision in the Andover Seminary, by which a theological course is opened for those persons who cannot command the time or means for a longer course of study, — does not the blessing of God resting on the labors of lay preachers, alike in the army, and at home — upon the labors of Stuart, and Durant, and Wilson, — do not these and kindred facts show that Dr. Wayland rightly read the demands of the times?

We may add, at this point, a paragraph from an obituary notice of Dr. Wayland, written by Rev. Abel Stevens, D. D., the historian of Methodism : —

" The *moral character* of this truly great man was the crown of his greatness. The practicality of his intellect characterized his moral life. Though evangelically orthodox, his extremely practical view of Christianity rendered him almost extremely liberal. A working religion was his ideal of Christianity. Dogmatics must give precedence to ethics ; this *doctrinaire* must stand behind the ' doer of the word,' the evangelist, the missionary, the Christian educator, the Christian philanthropist, the Christian statesman. Many of us remember the bold, practical, evangelical liberalism of his famous Rochester sermon. It was a resounding tocsin summoning American Christianity from its fields of speculation, polemics, and formalism, to its more legitimate fields of evangelical work — work on the highways, on the frontiers, in the suburban abysses of vice and poverty."

We do not know how we can better conclude this chapter than by quoting, from the columns of the Examiner, a portion of a notice of the "Principles," &c., in which there appear unmistakable traces of the affluent and polished diction of Rev. Dr. Williams.

" We rejoice to find a scholar and thinker, so justly eminent, far beyond the bounds of his own denomination, and of his own country, as President Wayland, setting

himself in the earnest, child-like simplicity which is one
of the surest marks of true greatness, to the task of putting
before this generation, in our churches, the ways of their
fathers, and of endeavoring to revive in the hearts of the
children the principles and practices of their spiritual
ancestry. He is, in the good providence of God, rarely
endowed for the work. His earlier volumes have taken
their rank ; and, as a thinker and writer, he cannot seem
to any, whom his suggestions may most displease, to have
criticised a culture that he did not himself possess, or to
have disparaged the use of powers which he could neither
understand nor emulate. Received in his visit to the
shores of Great Britain by men like Dr. Arnold, of Rugby,
Dr. Whewell, and the late Sir William Hamilton, as their
friend and compeer in the walks of philosophy and of the
highest education ; when in the maturity of his powers,
attainments, and honors, he sits down to say that in the
Christian ministry a regular and classic education is not
the first requisite, — nay, is often not a requisite at all, — it
seems to us that there is a glorious abnegation of all undue
honors for that professional education, by himself so long
and successfully dispensed, which should make his testimony doubly impressive, and which clothes that testimony, in all its simplicity and directness, with a noble
magnanimity.

"He was abundantly competent to have produced a
work of more form and pretension ; but he wrote for
the body of the ministry, and for the membership of the
churches. To attain his object in winning them as readers, these unstudied outpourings, as of a revered friend
holding us in a rich, free, and hearty conversation, were,
we think, the best form that he could adopt. He has
called his volume but 'Notes.' It is not elaborate, though
its views are often profound — the result, evidently, of long
and devout pondering. It is, in style of utterance, — to
use an image of Bacon's, — 'but the first crushing of the
clusters in the press, not the protracted twisting that leaves
the harsh taste of grape-skins and stems in the wine.'

"Our own denomination have, like our Methodist
brethren, been honored of God, in the times of our fathers,
to preach the gospel to the poor. Their converts and the
children of their converts have become very generally
advanced in worldly resources above the former level and

average position of their first membership; but both
Methodist and Baptist — and the last, perhaps, more than
the first — are not in our times displaying all the power
to win and hold the poor, which is the great need of
modern civilization, and which, largely displayed, is the
crowning earthly glory of the gospel. In endeavoring to
recall our churches to the simple tastes and more enter-
prising and aggressive piety of their forefathers, Dr. Wayland has made many suggestions as to sanctuaries, modes
of public worship, and forms of preaching, and views of a
divine call to the ministry, that deserve, not only from the
character of the writer, but from the present circumstances
of our people, very serious regard. . . .

"He would retain the due influence of the pulpit, but
would call to a more general recollection of the most scriptural positions taken by our fathers, as to the need of a call
from the Holy Ghost for entrance on the ministry. He would
dissuade from the undue reliance which some have had
upon a regular course of education as indispensable for the
modern preacher. If the friends of theological seminaries
construe these remarks of his as denying the advantages
of scholastic training, it seems to us that it would be an
unhappy misapprehension. He would, as we understand
him, but dissuade the exaggeration of the claims of such
education, an undue and unspiritual reliance upon its
power, and above all, such departure from the ways in
which God led and blessed our fathers, as would make it
an indispensable prerequisite to the ministry, that the man
had received certain secular instruction.

"Homage to the due and paramount sovereignty of the
Holy Ghost in taking his own workmen where he may
choose, provided the church see in them the experience,
holiness, and aptness to teach, that are among the evidences *externally* of his *internally* calling and qualifying
the men, — homage cheerfully and evermore rendered to
the perpetual presidency of the Redeemer in his own
modern churches, — is but simple loyalty to the Master.
This we suppose, although there may be divergencies
in the mode of expression employed, to be the great aim
of Dr. Wayland. If such be his meaning, it is, we think,
but a law of Christ that cannot, in our judgment, be abro-
gated, or even infringed, with impunity. Shall men, then,
it may be asked, no longer enter, and no more sustain,

theological seminaries? By no means. Let a man who has leisure, and youth, and helping friends, get, there or elsewhere, all the useful knowledge that he can. But let the door into the pulpit be kept open, not only for such younger brethren, but for the man of mature age and more slender training. And, above all, let the Paraclete choose his own tools."

CHAPTER VIII.

DEATH OF REV. DR. GRANGER. — ACTION OF THE
CHURCH. — THE WORK UNDERTAKEN. — THE PAS-
TOR'S SPIRIT AND AIM. — PREPARATION OF HEART.
— VISITING. — PERSONAL LABOR. — CHARACTER OF
HIS PREACHING. — THE VESTRY. — CORRESPONDENCE.
— PROGRESS. — DEATH OF MR. MOSES B. IVES. —
CRISIS OF 1857. — CORRESPONDENCE.

ON the part of any who might take exception to these
views of the ministry, the reply would not be altogether unnatural, " It is not difficult for one on whom the
labors of the ministry do not fall, to urge ministers to a
high self-forgetfulness, an earnest devotion, a renunciation
of fame, of ease, and emolument." Example, therefore,
though possibly more difficult, would be, after all, more
powerful.

On the 5th of January, 1857, Rev. Dr. Granger, pastor
of the First Baptist Church in Providence (a man of eminent ability, piety, and zeal), was removed by death.

At the request of the church and of the afflicted family, Dr. Wayland preached, on the 18th of January, a discourse suggested by this event, in which he expressed his
high estimate of the Christian character, and the religious
earnestness of the deceased pastor, and especially his
sense of his labors, and counsels as a minister of the
Deputation to the American Baptist Missions in the East
Indies.

Suddenly bereaved, the church acted in accordance with
the instinct of the community in any hour of perplexity.

On the 20th of February the joint committee of the church and of the society for the supply of the pulpit, —

" *Resolved*, that Rev. Francis Wayland, D. D., be earnestly requested to undertake the performance of ministerial and pastoral labors for the time being, and until it may be thought best to make some other arrangement; and that he be requested to devote his time and energies to these ministrations in such ways as may be best adapted to promote the highest religious interests of the church and society.

" *Resolved*, that the compensation for these services be twenty-five dollars per week." *

It may be remarked that the committee had previously asked him to undertake the supply of the pulpit only. He says, —

" This I was unwilling to do, for I thought that some time would elapse before a suitable candidate could be provided, and I believed that the church needed, not merely preaching on the Sabbath, but great and faithful labor from house to house."

The committee agreed with him, and thence resulted the invitation first alluded to.

He had now nearly completed his sixty-first year; he had not yet regained the strength which had been expended during his laborious years in college. He was preparing one or two volumes for publication, — one of which had been announced, — and he was proposing to complete the long-deferred work of revising and re-writing his Moral Science. He might, without difficulty, have pleaded excuses enough for declining to undertake a labor of the arduousness of which he had not a light conception; nor could he for such a decision have been " judged of man,

---

* The second of the above resolutions is inserted as an evidence (if any were needed) that a regard to compensation did not supply his motive or measure his exertions. He believed that "the minister is an agent, whose principal is, not the congregation, but Almighty God." — *Ministry of the Gospel.*

or of man's judgment." But it was to a higher authority that he held himself amenable. "With him, *ought* and *ought not* were the words most powerful of all that could be uttered." He wrote to his son,—

"I shall probably do it, and commence in a few days. This will confine me a good deal, but it seems an opening for usefulness, and I could not with a good conscience refuse. Should I do it, I pray God to grant us a revival of religion, and to build up his cause here."

In his reminiscences he writes,—

"The moment I assumed the duties of pastor, I relinquished every other engagement and occupation. I laid away my manuscripts, put aside all labor for myself, and devoted myself to the service of the gospel. . . . I had published my views of the ministry, of the kind of preaching needed, of the other labors (besides preaching) devolving on the minister, and of the necessity of making every other pursuit secondary to this, if we expected the blessing of God. From consistency, as well as from conscience, I felt under obligation to follow my own directions, or rather what I supposed to be the commands of our Lord and Savior. If I can speak of my own motives, I do not know that I ever commenced any undertaking from a more simple desire to do the will of the Master."

These words but inadequately express the completeness of his concentration of thought and effort. Not only did he give up all authorship, he relinquished all reading. He did not, we believe, even read a review during the period of his pastoral labors. He employed in studying the Bible, and in prayer, all the time not consumed in needful exercise, in preparation for the Sabbath, or in visiting the congregation.

"My first and most important effort was to gain victory over myself. I presume almost any preacher would understand my meaning. I had held some important offices of a literary character. I had published some things which were more than usually successful. I had had some reputation as a good writer. Now, all these antecedents would seem to point to a mode of preaching in harmony with them; elaborate, and calculated to commend religion to the taste and imagination; in fine, to a kind of preaching addressed to the ten, rather than to the hundred. I could not but feel that to preach otherwise would appear to many as a falling off, a sinking away; that it would, in a word, induce many persons to think less of me.

"On the other hand, I knew that such preaching as perhaps might be expected from these antecedents, though it may gratify the taste of the few, is without moral effect on the many; that hearers do not understand or follow it; and that it is, in fact, nothing more nor less than to use the awful truth of the coming of the Son of God upon earth, as a stepping-stone to the preacher's reputation. It it using the solemn realities of eternity, of redemption, and the atoning sacrifice of the Messiah, for the purpose of feeding the vanity of preacher and hearers, and making the preaching of no value to the mass of those who listen. How could a minister of the gospel render up his account at the day of judgment, in the presence of the Searcher of hearts, and in sight of those to whom he had accepted the office of religious teacher?

"There seemed, therefore, but one course to be taken. I strove to yield myself without reserve to the Savior, to preach whatever he bade me, and in the simplest manner possible, so that no one could fail to understand me. I was sent to labor for the conversion of men, and that not at some future time, but now, by means of every sermon. I saw that the preaching which has in view the exbibition of truth in such a manner as to convert men eight or ten years hence, is fatal to souls. It teaches men to put off attention to religion to a future period, and that period continues always a thing of the future, until death comes and ushers the soul into eternity, with the time for repentance as distant as ever.

"The minds of many members were pervaded by an idea of the greatness of the church, and a desire that it should occupy a high social position. I had myself an earnest longing for the conversion of my personal friends and their children; but this notion of the greatness of the church in the eyes of Christ seemed to me quite unfound-

ed and offensive to the Savior. I asked of God with im-
portunity for souls, *souls*, SOULS, let them be young or
old, friends or strangers, wise or unwise; I cared not who
or in what position; publicans and harlots were as good
as any. And I endeavored to inculcate this idea on the
minds of the members of the church."

It may be remarked, at this point, that the Rev. Dr.
Granger, the former pastor, had for many years been in
failing health; for two years he had been absent in the East
Indies; and during the entire period of his pastorate his
singular executive ability had led his brethren to lay upon
him many engrossing labors connected with the benevolent and missionary organizations (both state and national)
of the denomination. The church numbered about four
hundred members. The strong attachment felt by the
members to the church led them in many cases to retain
their relation to it, though living in very remote parts of
the city. The result was to give to the body an appearance of strength quite factitious, and to render a faithful
visiting of all the members peculiarly laborious.

Dr. Wayland writes, —

"I was well aware that the families of the church and
congregation were in need of real, pastoral visitation. This
had greatly gone out of use. Several of the families told
me that no minister had called on them for many years.
By the visiting needed among them, I do not mean a mere
call of civility to inquire into the health of parents and
children, and to manifest a neighborly regard for their
welfare. This is scarcely the business of men charged
with matters of grave importance. Such service is required of men in no other occupation of life.

"The visiting to which I refer is that which has for its
end exclusively the spiritual good of those to whom it is
made. This I attempted to carry on. I resolved that
I would visit no house without introducing the subject
of religion as a personal matter, and that in every case,
unless it was manifestly best to omit it, I would pray with
the family. I commenced this work immediately, and it
was nearly a year before I could complete it. Several

circumstances prevented my doing it in as short a time
as I expected. My house was so far from the centre of
the city, from which the residences of the members extended in all directions, that I was obliged to spend a large
portion of my time on the road. I found also that I had
not the physical ability to walk as I could some years
before. It will be asked, Why did you not ride? I answer, To do so would frequently have required the time
of another person; but most of all, I could not ride to
see poor persons who never ride. It would have an
appearance of social superiority, which is hostile to the
spirit of the gospel. Besides, it was very difficult to find
many of the persons whom I visited. It was on this account much easier to go on foot.

"I discovered that I could visit fewer persons in a day
than I at first supposed possible. One cannot begin this
work very early in the day, for no one cares to see you
until the household labor is completed. Then comes the
interruption of dinner, and for half the year the time between this and dark is very short. And, moreover, it takes
more time to make such a visit as I have spoken of than
an ordinary call. The condition of the parishioner's mind
must be ascertained, that you may know what kind of
truth is to be administered. If there are several persons
in a family to be seen, a considerable portion of time is
thus, of necessity (though most profitably), consumed.

"This kind of visiting, however, reached but a portion
of the parish — the mothers and daughters. The male
members of families were generally absent. It was necessary to follow them to shops, counting-rooms, or wherever
they were accustomed to spend the day. I talked to men
wherever I could find them alone, or could draw them
away for private conversation. Sometimes I would meet
them in the street, and accompany them far enough to
give the necessary warning. In this manner I believe I
held personal conversation on religion with by far the
greater part of the adults of the parish. I say this, of
course, in general terms, for accidents will prevent one
from seeing persons; and when they live at a great distance, the opportunity may not present itself for going so
far to see them again. And I will add that in all this
labor, which became more and more pleasant and easy to
me, I never once was treated rudely, or as if I was not

doing the business most appropriate to a minister. Some cases I found of persons steeped in worldliness, who evidently did not wish to be disturbed ; but by far the greater part were thankful, and were by this means personally attached to me and to the services of the sanctuary, and their hearts were opened to the instructions and warnings of the gospel. I record with sadness that in many cases, even of those who had been associated all their lives with professors of religion, I was told that I was the first one who had ever personally conversed with them on the condition of their souls.

" It will, perhaps, be thought that I had some natural aptitude for this kind of labor. Not at all. In the commencement of my ministry, it was as difficult for me as for any one. I gained upon it a little during my pastorate in Boston. I was in the habit, while in college, of seizing upon such opportunities as offered to converse solemnly with my pupils, though I confess with sorrow that I did not make these occasions as frequent as I might have done. When, however, I undertook this pastorate, I resolved, in the strength of God, that I would carry religion with me into every house I visited, and, so far as was in my power, edify saints and call sinners to repentance. Having resolved to do it, and having once commenced, the rest was easy. I found that it was of no use to begin afar off, and gradually come to it, through a long reach of indirect approach. If I tried this, I was in great danger of failing. My custom was, after the first incidental conversation, to address the persons directly, and inquire into the prospects which they had for eternity. It soon became known that this was my habit, so that sometimes, upon my saying to a family, ' I suppose you know what I have called for,' the ready answer would be, ' I suppose we do.' "

He carried this portion of his labor to the utmost limit of physical endurance ; indeed, he trespassed against the laws of health, in a manner that in another he would have reproved, and that can scarcely be commended in him. Setting out from his home as early in the forenoon as would allow time for the houses to be in order, he would continue visiting till noon. Sometimes he would accept an

invitation to dine wherever the noon found him, sometimes
he would eat something in a restaurant, and not seldom he
would continue his labors without any refreshment, sustained by meat which the world knew not of; for his meat
and his drink were to do the will of Him that sent him, and
to finish his work. And when the afternoon was ended,
if there was to be a meeting at the church in the evening,
he would go into the vestry, and would wait there till the
hour of service. A friend has said, —

"A number of times, on Wednesday evening, I went
into the vestry before the congregation had gathered; and
at first, thought there was no one there. But presently I
would see Dr. Wayland lying down on one of the seats;
he was worn out with the incessant visiting and talking of
the day, and was resting for a few minutes."

In his visiting he steered clear of the platitudes of religion, and while kind, sympathizing, full of charity, he
probed the conscience by his searching inquiries. "What
does your hope rest upon? How are you living?" And
he rarely failed to ask, to the confounding of many a com-
placent professor, "What are you *doing* for Jesus Christ?"
A visit from him was an event in the spiritual history of a
household, and the impression was deepened as it became
the topic of conversation with other families who had received a similar impulse.

He endeavored to proceed systematically, but was also
greatly guided by the intimations of the divine Spirit.
Sometimes he would say, "I must go and visit this or
that particular family;" and on being asked, "Why do
you go there, when you have been at work all day, and
are already tired?" he would reply, "I must go, for I feel
called there." Once he felt a peculiar call to visit a certain
family, though he was ignorant of anything in their circumstances calling for especial notice. He went, and
found the mother of the family sick of fatal disease. He
enjoyed a very solemn and profitable interview with her,

and it was the last occasion on which such a conversation could have taken place.

He referred any instance of successful labor to the same divine guidance. It was at one time strongly impressed on his mind that he must call and converse with Mr. S. He went to his counting-room, but failed to see him. On his return from this unsuccessful visit, he met Mr. M., and conversed with him. This conversation led to his conversion. "And then I knew," said Dr. Wayland, "that it was to Mr. M. that I had been sent, though I had supposed that it was to Mr. S."

He has said that he had no aptitude for introducing religious appeals in his conversation. Whether he had such facility naturally, we do not know; but no one could fail to remark, at this period of his life, that he was eminently wise in winning souls, and that the word spoken in season was like apples of gold in baskets of silver. This skill proceeded from a profound sense of religious realities, conjoined with a warm affection for those whom he addressed, and was perfected by many years of fidelity in the discharge of this duty. One can hardly say whether his earnestness in preaching the word out of season as well as in season, or his singular felicity in avoiding offence and in winning attention, was the more remarkable. Once he was spending the evening in a social party at the house of his neighbor, Professor ———. We imagine that this was before his pastorate began, as he rarely or never allowed himself even so slight a relaxation during that period. A young lady, whom he had often met, was present, who, though most amiable in character, was destitute of personal religion, and was in fact averse to evangelical views. He chanced during the evening to be alone with her, in a part of the room somewhat retired, and he said to her, "Emma, I am very glad to see you so happy; but you know that the birds want a cover to fly under when it storms." These kind words opened the way for a conversation. The next time he saw her, he sought to deepen the impression. Meanwhile he prayed for her without ceasing. She strove long against the influences of the Spirit, but at last yielded her heart to God, and became a very lovely and happy Christian. After a few years she was seized with sudden illness attended by delirium, and soon died. In writing to his son, and mentioning her death, Dr. Wayland said, "When all power of influence is lost and gone forever, it is a comfort to remember that you have tried to do good to one who has passed away." Very few circumstances in his life gave him more pleasure than the blessing which followed his word spoken out of season; and what shall we say of the hour when he, in his turn, was led to the enthroned Lamb, by those whom on earth he had guided to the Savior?

He was remarkable for perseverance in spiritual labor. One person says, "He was the only friend who ever talked with me. But he seemed determined that I should be converted, and that he would be the means. He took every opportunity to win me to Christ. When my children were very sick, and my heart was softened, he talked to me, and so he continued, until I was a new creature in Christ; all that there is in me of good, is due, under God, to him."

Meanwhile he had commenced preaching on the Sabbath, and in the vestry on Wednesday evening. He had, as he has said, gained a victory over himself, and renounced the desire of reputation and of literary distinction. "What things were gain to him, them he counted loss for Christ." But this renunciation was far from being synonymous with indifference to the character and adaptation of his discourses. He had drawers full of sermons; but to preach the gospel of Christ, in his estimation, was much more than to "supply the desk," or to "occupy the time." He felt that his sermons, prepared for another audience, expressing a state of mind far less earnest than he now experienced, and appealing with too little directness to the consciences of men, would not accomplish the end for which, with all his soul, he was striving. So he wrote always one, and often two, new sermons for the Sabbath, and prepared, without writing, entirely new discourses for the Wednesday evening service.

He made little use of adornment; if figurative language was employed, it was for the purpose of enlightening the conscience rather than gratifying the taste. He not unfrequently introduced illustrative anecdote, and with all the power of his great soul laid hold on the moral sense of his hearers. His sermons were not characterized peculiarly by logic, but by something — we know not how to name it — that bears the same relation to the conscience that logic does to the mind. He had, as he once said, little confidence in a moral truth that is reached by a long process of reasoning. He believed that the moral sense of men and the Bible were, by the Power that originated both, adapted to each other. Hence he believed, that if the truths of the Word of God were brought nearer to the soul, the effect must be felt. He would take a passage of Scripture, and would first very plainly show its meaning; then he would explain its bearing on the persons before him, considering them, perhaps, according to their station or calling in life, or according to their prominent traits of character. Much of his life had been devoted to the study of human character and motives. And now, using his power of moral analysis, — though it was always kept out of sight, — he read the hearts of men, revealed their motives to themselves, uncovered their subterfuges, and brought them face to face with their duty to God and man, so that a hearer must either say, " I will not do what I plainly see to be my duty," or else he must yield and obey. " His preaching was moral philosophy animated by the spirit of the gospel," a hearer has said of him. " There was one peculiarity in his preaching," said

Rev. Dr. Caswell, "in which he seemed to me to surpass all men to whom I have ever listened. It was in exposing the devices of the heart, and in hunting a guilty sinner from every subterfuge, from every refuge of lies, until he stood before himself in all the deformity of sin. He had deeply studied the laws and modes of action of the human conscience; and few, if any, of the world's great teachers have ever handled it more skilfully." Rev. Dr. Warren (of the class of 1835) once remarked, "No man ever ploughed through my conscience as Dr. Wayland did." "I never," said an experienced Christian, "knew any one make sin appear so hateful and so guilty." His ceaseless, prayerful reading of the Bible gave him topics; and his profound meditation took him out of the region of commonplace. As he dwelt on a text, new depths would open before him, until he almost lost himself in the greatness of his own conceptions. The writer was walking with him during the winter of which we speak, and Dr. Wayland alluded to a subject that had come into his mind for the next Sunday — "God our example." The sermon was afterwards published in "Salvation by Christ," with the text, "Be ye followers of God, as dear children." He spoke of the train of thought: "Example is the most powerful force in morals; this law God has established; and in his dealings with us he acts in accordance with it, setting us an example of the dispositions which he bids us cultivate. He bids us be benevolent, and he is ever conferring benefits on all his creation. He bids us show kindness to our enemies, and he is ever showering blessings on those who have done him all the injury in their power. He bids us sacrifice our all — ourselves — for the good of others." Here his voice fell, and he seemed overpowered; presently he said, "It is almost too much to say — one can hardly express it. He surrenders himself, sacrifices himself for us." When this sermon, which was among the earliest, was preached, a few hearers, of more than

usual discernment, recognized in it what was to be the
spirit of his ministry, and knew, with prophetic inspiration,
that his was to be a ministry of sacrifice.

Certainly, never in his life did his sermons contain more
of the divine ideas; and his constant intercourse with
his people, his daily, almost hourly, sympathy with their
anxieties, with their temptations, their dangers, gave to
his words a present power, a life that carried them home
to the bosoms of men. It was often remarked, that one
could tell by the preaching on the Sabbath what features
of character, what objections, what excuses, he had encountered during the week. The sins of common life he brought
into the pulpit, and held them up that he might warn men
against them — the frauds common in business, the ruinous example often set by professing Christians, the indulgence of disciples in worldly and sinful pleasures. He
often said, in public and in private, that many a professor,
blameless in his exterior and attendant on all the ordinances, was, by reason of covetousness, in as great a danger
of losing his soul as is the drunkard, the swearer, the gam-
bler. He was lifted by the divine Spirit above all fear or
favor. After reproving, as he only could do, some prevalent sin, " Pardon me," he said. Then recovering himself, " But no, I don't want your pardon for telling you
the truth." He once said, " I find, as I visit among you,
professors of religion, members of this church, who
rarely or never come to meeting, who do not pray, or
read the Bible, and all say that they have no enjoyment
in religion; and yet they would not give up their hope
for a thousand worlds. They are trusting that they will
yet be brought back to the enjoyment of the favor of God."
Then, with startling earnestness, " And who are you,
that God should work a miracle, and reclaim you while
you are living in the neglect of every means of grace
and every help to piety which he has revealed in his
word?"

He sought to undeceive those who entertained the impression that God had regard for any particular church or organization, otherwise than as it is peculiar for its good works, its piety, its faith, its humility, and its holy activity. His whole soul sympathized with the indignant exclamation of Chalmers (often quoted by him) in reply to those who suggested that his zeal was inflamed by a desire to build up the Free Church of Scotland. "Who cares for the Free Church, compared with the Christian good of the people of Scotland? Who cares about any church, but as an instrument of Christian good?"

We presume it need not be said that he was profoundly impressed with the truth of the distinctive principles of the Baptist denomination. On suitable occasions he exhibited these principles in his preaching; yet never as barren theories; always as principles vitally connected with practice. Thus, in a sermon from Acts viii. 36, 37, — "See, here is water; what doth hinder me to be baptized? And Philip said, If thou believest with all thine heart, thou mayest," — after exhibiting clearly the teachings of this and of kindred passages in regard to the mode and the subject of baptism, he thus closes: —

"Such, my brethren, is an outline of our belief on this subject. We think that we are in this matter following in the footsteps of our Lord and Savior. But let us, in closing, observe the course of conduct to which this belief of necessity pledges us.

"We believe that no one is a subject for baptism unless he is a truly regenerate person. We reject the opinion that every citizen has a right to this ordinance, or that uniting with a church is a means of grace which unconverted men may employ for their spiritual improvement. Our doctrine is all expressed in the words of the text, "If thou believest with all thine heart, thou mayest." Hence it becomes us to take all the pains in our power to discover whether those who present themselves as candidates for this ordinance give competent evidence that they are regenerate persons, the sincere disciples of Christ. If we fail in this respect, of what use is our belief? What is the value of correct principles if they do not govern our practice?

"But this is not all. Our belief in this matter involves our belief in the spirituality of the church. We hold that no one has any right to continue a member of a church, save so long as he exhibits in his life the evidence of discipleship to Christ. We often err in the reception of members. We have not the gift of discerning spirits. Hence we are liable to admit to the visible church those in whom the seed has sprung up, but in whom it has subsequently been choked by the cares of the world, the deceitfulness of riches, and the lusts of other things. Such persons may continue through life guilty of no breach of human law, and yet give not the slightest evidence of being governed by the law of God. They may neglect the worship and ordinances of the house of God; they may choose their associates from among the worldly and profane; they may neglect prayer in the family and in secret; they may be worldly, covetous, extortioners, unjust, lovers of pleasure more than lovers of God. Men frequently, by a gradual decline, fall as far as this from the character of discipleship, and yet the decline has been so gradual that at no particular time did there seem any opportunity for discipline. But, if such is the case, of what use is our belief in the spirituality of a church? If we allow Christ to be thus dishonored among us, our belief in the spirituality of the church will not save us. Let us, then, exercise a godly jealousy over each other. Let us watch over each other in the Lord. If a brother is wandering from the path, let us labor to reclaim him. If we cannot reclaim him, we must separate him from our company. If our principles be true, we must carry them out; for thus alone shall we make manifest their excellence. If, while we hold the truth, we do not put it in practice, what do we more than others? Nay, we hold up the truth to reprobation, by showing, in our practice, that it is utterly valueless."

His preaching might perhaps have been called severe, coming from any one whose tenderness of heart, wide benevolence, and profound sincerity, were less apparent.

It was often remarked, that from no one else would such absolute plainness have been endured.

Thus, by manifestation of the truth, he commended himself to every man's conscience in the sight of God; and men, as they listened, and as their hearts were revealed to themselves, felt as though they were standing face to face with the day of judgment.

Simple and scriptural as he was in the pulpit, he was even more so in the desk of the vestry. He writes,—

"The weekly lecture on Wednesday evening was, I think, a useful service. I spoke without notes, after reflection, on a subject which, at the time, seemed appropriate to the wants of the hearers. I endeavored to set aside all formality, and to bring myself in direct contact with the consciences of the people. The audience immediately began to increase in numbers and in solemnity. The attendance was large through the summer, and, indeed, continued so until the close of my temporary pastorate. I seemed to speak from my heart directly to the hearts of my hearers; and, sometimes (to use the words of the apostle), 'I think that I had the Spirit of the Lord.' Why could I not preach so in the pulpit on the Sabbath? The audience was mostly the same. I do not think that I was afraid. I generally wrote my sermons. The writing was a sort of screen between me and my hearers. I deeply regret that I did not overcome this foolish habit. I should have saved much time for other labors, and I believe that I should soon have learned to preach more effectually.

"Does the difficulty of which I speak grow out of anything in the construction of our houses of worship? or is it owing to the time of holding the service? Persons are always more susceptible to impressions in the evening. Can anything be done to afford a remedy in this matter? I have heard many persons relate the same experience, particularly that excellent preacher, Dr. J. W. Alexander. I do not know a better thing for the ministry than would be done, if we could only remove the vestry to the church. I, perhaps, did something in this direction. At any rate, I believe that I so preached that my hearers understood me, and knew that I was anxious for their salvation.

But (I know not why) I could not, or did not, attain to
the freedom, the nearness to the hearts and consciences of
the people, in the audience-room above, that I attained in
the vestry. Whether I am to recover my former health
I know not. If, however, I should be permitted to preach
again, I will certainly do what is in my power to learn to
preach directly to men, looking them in the face, and not
looking at the paper on the desk. Should I live to make
the attempt, may the Spirit of God enable me to do it
successfully."

The opinion which Dr. Wayland expresses, that the
Wednesday evening services in the lecture-room were
more productive of good than the public and formal utterances of the Sabbath, is probably correct. Some, at least,
of the reasons for this fact, every person accustomed to
public speaking will appreciate. The audience-room of
the church is very large (the house having been built, in
part, to accommodate the college Commencements), and is
not filled on any ordinary occasion. The pulpit is high
and massive. The singing, during most of the period of
his labors, was performed by a choir, the congregation
being listeners. There was as little as possible to bring
speaker and hearer into sympathy. The whole service suggested decorum and propriety. The lecture-room, capable of holding perhaps four hundred persons, while large
enough for comfort, is no larger than a speaker can easily
fill, while retaining his ordinary conversational tone. The
desk is low, and does not remove the speaker from the
audience. The singing was united and heartfelt. The
speaker could readily watch the faces before him, and
mark each varying shade of emotion. Every one felt at
home. The walls had been vocal with prayer, and the
sob, and the falling tear, were familiar. In the vestry his
language was unpremeditated, but the *matter* was the
result of prolonged and intense meditation and feeling.
When he stood before the audience in the lecture-room,
looking into the eyes of those, many of whom had been
his neighbors for thirty years, of those whose parents he

had known and loved, and, filled and inspired by the divine wisdom, poured forth all the emotion of his soul, he probably reached a point of impressiveness that he never elsewhere attained.

A few years previously, Dr. Wayland resumed the ladies' Bible class, referred to in Chap. XV. of Vol. I. But this exercise, with the needful preparation, consumed the greater part of a day. As his labors increased, he found it impossible to spare so much time, and was compelled to suspend it, until the cessation of his pastoral cares left him more leisure.

To Rev. Dr. Anderson : —

"January 11, 1857.

"My dear Anderson : Our brother Granger has been called up higher. . . . As our circle of intimate friends grows smaller, let us draw nearer together. I wish you and Mrs. A. could come, when it is pleasant, and see us. We have labored together a good deal : may we not, like the apostles, 'rest a while' here 'in a desert place'? In the midst of your business you have 'no leisure so much as to eat.'

". . . Come and see us if you can. You, Anderson, are one of the very few men left whom I knew intimately thirty years since, and our intimacy and love remain undiminished."

To Mr. and Mrs. W., on hearing of the death of their son : —

"March 22, 1857.

"My dear Friends : It was not until yesterday that I learned of your sore affliction. It is sorrowful beyond expression, and I can only think of you as crushed and overwhelmed. Of the dear and most lovely child I dare not speak. Were I with you, I feel as if I should, like the friends of Job, sit down for days without uttering a word.

"Yet still, there is a word that may be spoken — one word, which alone is sufficient to quiet the soul in the most frenzied agitation. It is GOD. In the immeasurable depth of his perfections we may find repose even in the tumult of the deepest sorrow. The God of infinite

wisdom and goodness, so good that he gave his only
begotten Son for us, is surely a Being to be trusted, even
though everything created fades away.   Nay, may we
not surrender a child to Him who gave his only begotten
Son for us?   Try and creep under the shadow of his
wing ; you will there find peace, and it is nowhere else
to be found.   Earthly helpers fail in all real sorrow ;
God alone can sustain us when support is truly needed."

To a minister : —

"March 4, 1857.

"You know I have undertaken the pastoral office *pro
tempore*.   I have preached twice, and am beginning to
do some visiting.   I intend to give myself to it as much
as I can.   The appearance of things is interesting.   We
hope for a revival.

"I am now laboring with the *church*.   I want, by
consecutive sermons, to fan the flame.   I am preaching
and visiting, and I have some faith that God will bless
my labor.   If he does not at this time pour out his Spirit
upon us, we may almost despair."

"April 10, 1857.

"I am rejoiced to perceive, by your letter, that you are
reading the New Testament with sufficient attention to
see the difference between the teachings of Christ and
those of his apostles.   Keep on studying it.   Bring your
own heart to it.   Preach your sermons first to yourself.
Realize them in your own soul, if you would realize
them in the hearts of your people.   An intellectually prepared sermon will reach the intellect ; a spiritually prepared sermon will reach the spirit.   May the good Lord
make you faithful in all things.   I am preaching as well
as I can, but without much visible result.   I endeavor to
say with entire plainness whatever is given me.   I do not
know if the people will bear it.   I must, however, deliver my message.

"I wrote to Mr. Finney a few days ago, and received a
reply.   It is remarkable that two men almost ignorant of
each other should see things so much alike."

To his son : —

"I pause in the midst of a sermon to congratulate you

on the anniversary of your birth. How old you are, I do not remember,* but at all events old enough to make me feel like an aged man. You are rapidly approaching the maturity of your intellect. You are now as capable as you will ever be, or very nearly so. Some things you will be able to do better, some more rapidly, and some more wisely; but for efficiency you are approaching very near to the table-land, the water-shed of your life.

" The ministry is a great work. Homer's highest conception of a man was, that he was αναξ ανδρων, or else a tamer of horses. The Christian conception is a converter of men. This is better than to be a political leader, or an eloquent orator, or anything else after which men may aspire. Try to be this in simplicity, and may the Holy Spirit lead you into all truth.

" I bless God especially for the unity of spirit and affection which he has given us all. That we are an undivided family is one of his richest gifts. I rejoice that I have entire confidence in the principles and in the affection of my children, and that, as I believe, they have confidence in me. May God increase and perpetuate it, so that when I am called away, they may be always on the side of truth, and abound in love to each other. I am glad that you come here when you can. Always do so when it is possible without neglecting any duty. I have always regretted that it was not in my power to visit my parents more frequently.

To a minister : —

" April 20, 1857.

" I have kept steadily at work since I commenced here, and have done nothing but labor for the First Church. There is, I think, a little improvement. I visit all I can, and have preached twice on Sunday and once in the week, without intermission. Frequently I write two and always one sermon for the Sabbath. I am, however, more and more satisfied that this is a useless labor, and I hope soon to begin to preach once a day without notes.

---

* This was one of his idiosyncrasies. He never remembered the ages of his children or other relatives, and probably could not have recalled his own age without calculation.

I see that I am in danger of becoming confined to them, and the writing consumes valuable time.

"There are some small indications of good."

To the same : —

"June 25, 1857.

"I am only pretty well. I have closed my Bible class for the summer. This will be some relief. I found that the services of Sunday oppressed me on Monday. My brain is growing old, and will not do as much work as it once did. I cannot well press it. I feel more and more that my opportunity of doing good to any one is short.

To the same : —

"July 6, 1857.

"I see with great pain, in to-day's paper, the death of W. L. Marcy, one of our best and ablest men. I rather think that as a negotiator and diplomatist he was superior to Webster, though most men would laugh at me for saying so. The fact is, that a large portion of Webster's mind was occupied with the thought of the presidency, and what was left was not superior to the minds of other able men. This shows the importance of having the eye single. Ministers fail more frequently from a want of this than from almost any other cause."

To his sister : —

"Poor, dear Marcy has been continually in my mind since his death. I had a very sincere regard for him. May it be, that he had been reconciled to God! Perhaps this is bad theology, yet I cannot but feel it."

He writes, —

"My labors were, at first, mainly confined to the church. I endeavored to set before them the character of the disciples of Christ, and the offence caused to the world if professors of religion manifested their godliness only on the Sabbath. I urged upon all, repentance and a return to the first works. The congregation increased, but for some time there appeared little change. At last there seemed some thoughtfulness. A few were baptized. This had a quickening effect on the church, and Christians became more prayerful. The female members, especially,

were awakened, and abounded in prayer. To their efforts
and prayers the progress of the church must, under God,
be principally ascribed. As two or three were, from time
to time, added by baptism, the flame which the Holy
Spirit had kindled was kept alive, and became more intense and pervading. This was, however, very gradual;
and, at the best, it was but a smouldering fire, leaving a
large part of the church very little warmed." — *MS.*

In the latter part of July, 1857, he went to Saratoga
Springs; but, after a few days' absence, he was recalled
by the circumstances of the parish, and especially by the
death of his friend, Mr. Moses B. Ives.* At the request
of the corporation of the university, Dr. Wayland prepared a discourse on the services of Mr. Ives, many passages in which afford a touching insight into his own
character.

"Again am I called upon, after too short an interval, to
commemorate the virtues of one of my friends. The men
who, on my coming to this city, received me with a
kindness which has never abated, and with whom, for
thirty years, I have labored in the cause of education and

---

* There were few of the citizens of Providence for whom Dr.
Wayland cherished a stronger attachment than for Mr. Ives; on
the other hand, no one was more untiring than Mr. Ives in his
public-spirited regard for the interests of the university, and in his
acts of personal friendship to Dr. Wayland. It is not too much to
say, that without his large-hearted munificence, the subscription
of 1850, and the reorganization of the university could not have
succeeded. A single circumstance illustrates the spirit in which he
discharged the office of treasurer, which he held from 1825 until his
death. He had invested six thousand five hundred dollars of the
funds of the college in a note of the Bay State Mills, indorsed by
Lawrence, Stone, & Co. The investment was regarded as not
only good, but eminently desirable. In course of time the makers
and the indorsers became bankrupt, and the paper was worthless.
Mr. Ives at once assumed the indebtedness, and put into the treasury his check for the whole amount. He never spoke of the act, and
it was only by accident that it became known to the president, by
whom it was communicated to the writer.

benevolence, have, for the most part, passed away. The good and the great, who were then the guiding lights of this city, have sunk beneath the horizon; and the memory of many of them is already fading from recollection. I seem to myself almost the representative of a bygone generation. And now another link that bound me to the earth is severed. The man who has so often cheered me in disappointment, and counselled me in success, lies low beneath the sods of the valley, and I shall meet him no more until the resurrection of the just. If Mr. Ives supposed a man to be honest and well intentioned, difference of opinion never arrested, for a moment, the genial flow of his kindly regard. On this subject I can speak from experience, as well as from observation. During the long period of our acquaintance, many questions arose in which our views were widely dissimilar. We were constitutionally unlike, he naturally looking upon the past, and I as instinctively turning to the future. Hence the lines of conduct which we pursued were sometimes divergent. I know that, for the moment, it pained him, that I should act, as he believed, unwisely; but I never perceived that these differences chilled in his bosom an emotion of kindness, or modified, in any respect, the friendship which so long subsisted between us." *

While the financial distress of 1857 was pressing upon the country, Dr. Wayland preached, on the 11th and 25th of October, two sermons, designed to impress and deepen the moral lesson of these disastrous days. Though prepared in the discharge of his ordinary parochial duties, the discourses attracted marked attention, from their singular adaptation to the wants of the public mind, and were published in compliance with the request of many citizens.

To a minister : —

" You speak of consecutive discourses for Wednesday

* Before opportunity offered for the public delivery of this discourse, the pecuniary embarrassments of 1857 had pre-occupied the public mind to the exclusion of every other topic. It was therefore published without having been pronounced.

evening. Some men succeed in such a thing. I never did. I would rather each week preach what seemed to be given me. And I would take less pains in *making out a discourse*, than in *imbuing my own mind with it, and feeding upon it myself.* We err in relying on our own intellect, rather than on the Spirit of God. . . . The prospect for winter is gloomy. There is danger of famishing among the poor. We are trying to economize all we can, to have something to give to the needy."

To a minister : —

"December 3, 1857.

" I am greatly rejoiced to learn that your mind is drawn in the direction you mention. You may be assured that we shall not receive the blessing of the conversion of men, unless we are wholly given to it. If we do a little in politics, a little in philanthropy, and a little in preaching, we shall accomplish but little in anything. The philanthropy which we need for our souls' good can be found in our daily duties. The more of this a minister does, the better, if it be personal ; but these associations I think less and less of. Try to forget yourself and the fear of all but Christ. If we have reputation with the Master, it is all that the servant can desire. Strive for the conversion of souls, strive for it wholly, looking not for the conversion of the rich and intelligent, but of all men, especially the poor. And you may be sure that the less you honor yourself, the more Christ will honor you."

To the same : —

"December 14, 1857.

" I am encouraged by your letters to hope that you will soon see the fruit of your labors. May God give you a simple desire to glorify him, and that he will certainly gratify. Get out of yourself, and, like Paul, be willing to be a fool for Christ's sake ; that is, let nothing connected with yourself prevent you from preaching so as to reach the consciences of men. Ask the Spirit of God what you shall say, and say it without regard to anything but the will of God. This will be the sure way of attaining a blessing. I am glad that you are carrying the gospel to the poor. This is the field which Christ cultivated, and on which his blessing is most apt to rest.

" There is little new here of any moment. There is some more earnestness in other congregations. On the first Sabbath I baptized two converts ; and a few other cases promise well. An old and leading church, or one so esteemed, can hardly stoop low enough to receive a blessing."

In June, 1858, he was invited to become permanently the pastor of the church, but did not accept the invitation, though he continued his ministerial labors.

CHAPTER IX.

THE   REVIVAL   OF   1858. — CORRESPONDENCE. — DR.
WAYLAND   IN   THE   REVIVAL. — PERSONAL   SOLICITUDE.
— CARE   FOR   THE   YOUNG. — PRAYER   MEETINGS. —
PREACHING. — RELIGIOUS   ENTERPRISE. — CONGREGA-
TIONAL   SINGING. — THE   GREAT   SOURCE   OF   HIS   INFLU-
ENCE. — CLOSE   OF   HIS   LABORS.

FOLLOWING the commercial reverses of 1857 came
the revival of 1858. We resume the narrative of Dr.
Wayland.

" In time, the revival which had overspread most of the
cities and towns in the Northern States, through the power
of the Holy Spirit, visited Providence. Prayer meetings
in the morning, noon, and evening were attended by multitudes. On one or two occasions, when these were held
with us, the lecture-room could not accommodate all the
the people. Persons of all beliefs, and of no beliefs, and
of all classes in society, attended. The solemnity was
deep and affecting, and I believe that the impression was
universal, ' This is the finger of God.' It was quite common for persons to rise and ask for the prayers of the congregation. Still more common was it for those who had,
as they believed, given their hearts to the Savior, to express their new-found hope, and their reason for it, and
to narrate the exercises through which they had passed.
The congregations on the Sabbath and on Wednesday
evenings were increased, and the solemnity which attended them was so great as to be by many persons
distinctly remembered up to this time. Several of those
converted with us joined other churches, being here
only temporarily for the purpose of education. During
my connection with the church I baptized fifty-one.

Several were baptized by the present pastor immediately after his coming. I think the number ostensibly benefited was not less than seventy."

To a minister : —

" I rejoice with you at the appearance of good among your people. God hears prayer, and blesses those who honor him.

" But you do not want any help from abroad, and I would not say that I did. You can do all the work yourself, with the aid of your best brethren and sisters. It will be a noble opportunity to develop the talent and piety of your church. As to yourself, all you need is the guidance of the Holy Spirit, which will be given abundantly, if you humbly seek it. Encourage the people to prayer, self-examination, conversation with sinners, abstraction from the world, and looking up to the Spirit alone for all the blessing. Do not aim at a great and temporary excitement; but pray and labor for a continual revival. The spirit of a revival should always be the spirit of the church. In a word, cast yourself on God for all, and read nothing but the Bible. Use this time specially to study the New Testament with the aid of the Spirit of God.

" Again I say, do not go to Egypt for help. Go to God with everything, and keep in his presence. You will learn more in this manner than in any other. It is not pleasing to the Master that we should ask others to do what he is willing and able to do for us.

" Try to keep your people low in the dust before God, prayerfully laboring for him. This will insure the greatest blessing. Have no revival expedients, that is, devices to commit people ; to hold them up before the congregation for effect. Be perfectly true, and do nothing for any other motive than you profess."

To the same : —

" I rejoice greatly in your prospect. God grant that the heavens may gather blackness, and there be a sound of an abundance of rain. I want you to gain all the good of it in your own soul, and therefore wish you to derive all your aid directly from the Holy Spirit. There is no opportunity for becoming acquainted with him like a revival. We had very bad weather for our Fast Day meeting on Wednesday. The attendance was small, but the aspect solemn. There is, however, no revival here, unless, perhaps, one is beginning in Mr. Bixby's church.

To his sister: —

" . . . I want much to see you, but I am let hitherto. My practical duties and responsibilities occupy all my time and thoughts, and, thus far, all to very little purpose. A few have been added, more come out to hear, and this is almost all that can be said. The church has called me to be the pastor. I have taken time to think of it, but I, as yet, see no light in that direction. I think I shall be guided aright, for I believe it is my desire to do what the Lord would have me. . . . There is considerable attention here among several of the churches, but nothing, as yet, of a powerful character. May God grant us some souls. Mr. Bixby, the missionary, has a greater blessing than any other of our ministers. The character of the persons converted is quite remarkable — mostly heads of families and those who will be very useful. He has simply proclaimed Christ, and God has blessed his labor. God will honor the preaching of the Cross. O that I knew how to preach it, so that he would bless it!"

To a minister: —

" A church must be in fault when there are not additions every month. I am glad that you are receiving accessions to your congregation from the poor. . . . Try to preach in entire simplicity: philosophical discussions in theology, which magnify ourselves, have little favor with God. Let us forget ourselves in striving to serve him."

To the same: —

" Were I visiting a place, and attending such meetings as we have had, I should have said, ' This is a time of revival.' But no apparent effect is produced, and there is no increase of attention. It looks as though all would pass away without result. . . . There seems something peculiar among our old churches here. Nothing moves them. All is dry as the mountains of Gilboa. It may be to illustrate the sovereignty of God that he withholds a blessing, or it may be because of our sinful formality and conformity to the world."

To his son : —

" I am now in my sixty-third year. Not many more
birthdays await me. I have, on a few occasions, used my
brain pretty hard, and I sometimes fear that it will never
be wholly restored to its former power. But this is all as
God wills. I have nothing to do with it.

" The attention here is on the increase. We had a
solemn meeting on Wednesday evening. The morning
prayer meeting to-day was encouraging. I have written
to Deacon Lincoln to suggest united prayer for members
of Congress. A revival in Congress would be a blessing
to the world, and would show to all people what God
could do. I feel just now more encouraged than ever before to hope that God is near. May you and I both do
our duty here, and, bringing many souls to glory, meet
with joy before the throne."

To a minister : —

" March 25, 1858.

" The interest here is increasing slowly. God evidently
means to do it all himself. Attention is very general.
All the prayer meetings are well attended. Conversions
are few, and grace is not largely poured out. The most
signal fact is the repentance of —— ——. At our meeting on Tuesday evening he was present, and made a
most humble confession, which dissolved the meeting in
tears. At the business men's meeting on Wednesday he
did the same thing. He seems a real penitent. It is producing a great impression. It is all encouraging, but we
hope for greater things, commensurate with the universality of the attention. Last evening our vestry was full.
God will, I trust, be glorified."

To his son : —

" April 2, 1858.

" I have had your letter lying on my table in full sight
ever since it came, watching for an opportunity to answer
it. Every evening of the week has been occupied, and
the day fully employed. I have read hardly anything but
the Bible, and have not had all the time I wanted for
that.

" There is, I think, some progress with us ; but the char-

acteristics remain the same — very general seriousness,
but, comparatively, a small number of conversions."

"April 7, 1858.

"With us the work has assumed a somewhat new aspect. The interest in the general meetings has declined,
I rather think, though I have not attended any since Monday. But there is more interest in the church. Confes-
sions of sin, and mournings over departure from God, are
of daily occurrence. We have had several meetings for
this purpose, and there was not sufficient time for all that
would have spoken. This is most encouraging. Conversions, however, do not as yet multiply. A few are brought
in, — some of the young, some old and hardened sinners.
What is to be the end I do not know; but if the church
arises in the beauty and power of religion, sinners will be
converted."

Probably there was not another minister or Christian
in Providence who would have written the reminiscences
and letters above quoted, and made no allusion to Dr.
Wayland's labors in the revival of 1858. During the year
preceding its appearance, the tone of spirituality in the
church under his ministry had been deepening. Members
of other churches would not unfrequently come to listen
to his fervent utterances, and carry back to their several
congregations something of the sacred flame.

His letters indicate that he had begun to grow conscious
of waning vigor at the commencement of 1858; but no
sooner did there seem a deeper interest, that offered more
than usual encouragement to labor, than he forgot everything but the salvation of his fellow-men. He had completed the pastoral visiting of his charge, but he now
recommenced it. If he heard of a case of inquiry or
interest at the north end, or out on the borders of Olney-
ville, he at once set out to visit and converse with the
inquirer, declining (for the reasons we have given above)
all invitations to ride. As he met his acquaintances
on the street, or in shops, he was ever pressing on

them the claims of eternity. Sometimes it would be only in a few words. Often, when he met young men of his acquaintance, he would address them tenderly, solemnly, briefly, and then pass on. A member of his family says, " I was walking with him down Thomas Street, when he said to me, ' There is a man who has been avoiding me for weeks. I want to speak to him ; ' and he left me standing there till he had done so."

His interest in the young was unceasing. However pressed with care, he almost invariably came into the Sabbath school for a little while before meeting, and usually said a few simple words to the pupils. At the young people's meeting, too, he was often present, though leaving the conduct of it to the superintendent, his friend, pupil, and associate, Professor John L. Lincoln. When it was over, he would often offer some suggestion of practical significance. " John," he would say to Professor Lincoln, " did you see that boy in the corner? He wanted to speak. He ought to be encouraged." And when not himself present at the meeting, he never failed to inquire how it went on, and who took part. The superintendent did not feel that he could go through with the work without consulting him as to the means to be adopted for increasing the interest in the school.

Many of the members of Mrs. Buel's Young Ladies' School, who attended the church, will always remember the paternal tenderness and wisdom with which he spoke to them of Christ. He called one day and asked Mrs. Buel to send to the parlor, one by one, those who were his parishioners. It was a memorable visit. The Spirit of God seemed to dissolve all barriers. One young lady was quite 'determined that he should not move her, nor even speak to her on religion, if she could avoid it. He seemed to have an insight into her feelings, and said to her, " My child, do you want me to talk to you about religion ? " She at once burst into tears ; her opposition was divinely removed, and he soon saw her a new creature in Christ.

It seemed as if the God whom he served gave him peculiar access to many persons not easily approached. His age, his station, and yet more the character which for thirty years had been patent to the community, entitled him to speak, without fear of giving offence, to men of whatever age and standing. He has related that in but a single instance was he repulsed. A young man replied to his appeal, that free-masonry was all the religion that he wanted.

In the business men's meeting, and in the other prayer meetings, he often charged the person presiding to apply to him the five minutes' rule; but the expressed wish of the audience often constrained him to complete what he was saying. As he rose, he looked, as he was, a tower of strength. His aspect, and voice, and manner were those of one who was living in intimate communion with heaven. All about him conveyed irresistibly the impression that to him spiritual things were a reality, more vivid and palpable than the objects of bodily sense; that he looked not "at the things which are seen, but at the things which are not seen, for the things which are seen are temporal, but the things which are not seen are eternal." His massive frame seemed fitly to body forth the momentum of his spirit and his words. To men of business he spoke with peculiar plainness. "You believe that there is a God; that you have a soul which must live forever. Is it not the plainest dictate of prudence now to secure its eternal happiness? Is it not the greatest madness to neglect it?"

Again he would take up the complaints urged against religion, and would so turn them as to make them the ground of a new and more urgent appeal. After alluding to the objection founded on the lives of many professors of godliness, — after stating it in its strongest form, and sorrowfully conceding all that could be said of the worldliness, the avarice, the sharp-dealing by which often the professions of piety are deformed, then, — "Gentlemen, did I ever ask you to become such Christians as this? This is not Christianity. We ask you to be something unspeakably better; to be the very reverse of all this; to be followers of Christ." How many persons in these meetings received impressions that changed their character for eternity, cannot be known in time. The following incident is one of many. Deacon K. says, —

"I was going out of the hall one day, when I chanced to look around, and saw an aged man, bowed down, and Dr. Wayland leaning over and speaking to him. I went back, and found that it was the venerable Judge P., overwhelmed with anxiety and sorrow. He was expressing his fear that for one so old, who had lived so many scores of years without God, there was no help. Dr. Wayland was most tenderly pointing him to the boundless mercy of God in Christ Jesus."

A few days later, Judge P., in one of the meetings, feelingly spoke of his change of heart and his hopes for eternity. The hoary head became a crown of glory; and he has since finished his course, and entered into rest.

Meanwhile, Dr. Wayland's sermons became even more direct than before, — more affectionate and solemn. He gradually relinquished the practice of writing his discourses. Indeed, it was a necessity. How he could find time for even the most imperfect preparation, when his days and evenings were so engrossed with meetings and conversations, it is hard to conceive. But his unwritten speech did not discover any falling away in continuity of thought, in terseness, and clearness of expression. Men of mature age, strong character, and high mental endowments listened eagerly; and a boy of nine years old said to his mother, with delight, "Why, mother, I can understand every word he says." Not all the proprieties of the sanctuary could exclude the bowed head and the weeping eyes of men not used to tremble or to shed tears.

In the crowded vestry, upon Wednesday evening, he spoke as he had never done before. An atmosphere of heavenly solemnity seemed to pervade the room. From the moment that he rose to open the service with prayer, every heart seemed rapt in devotion. "We have come to meet *thee*," was an expression that he rarely failed to use in the opening petition, and every heart expected to hold communion with Christ. During the period of the service, every worldly thought was excluded. When he pronounced the benediction, it was not a form; it was a tender, affectionate prayer that the favor of Jesus Christ might rest upon all who were present. And then they separated silently, reluctant to speak, lest they should mar and dissipate the heavenly spell.

"Those sermons were scathing to a man's conscience," said a constant and most intelligent hearer. "When he preached from the text, 'Escape for thy life; look not behind thee, neither stay thou in all the plain,' we seemed to see it all, — the burning city, the descending flames, — and we scarcely dared to look behind us as we returned home." Once he spoke from the words, "How shall we escape if we neglect so great salvation;" and "it seemed," says a hearer, "as if he knew what was in the heart of every one there. He appeared to be unconscious of himself, and to speak merely as the Spirit spoke through him." At another time, preaching from the words, "that like as Christ was raised from the dead by the glory of the Father, even so we also should walk with him in newness of life," he said that the contrast between the old unregenerate life and the new divine life is so great, that the Scriptures compare it to the contrast between Christ lying dead in the tomb of Joseph and Christ exalted, glorified with the Father. As he spoke of the gloom of the tomb where the body of Jesus lay, it seemed as if the darkness could be felt; as if one could see the words falling from his lips, so real, so palpable were they. Again he spoke from the words, "This day shalt thou be with me in paradise." He described what it must be to be with Christ in paradise, " and it seemed as if all the sweetness of all the poets was poured into his lips, so unearthly was his delineation of the heavenly state."

His reading of the Scriptures on these occasions, as always, was marked by a depth of feeling such as none of the schools could impart; such as nothing could give but his profound realization of eternal verities. One felt as he read, If a man really believed these to be the words of the living God, he would read them just as Dr. Wayland does. In the vestry he did not always select a long passage. He was guided by his feelings. One of the peculiar felicities of the place was, that he could rise above propriety — the grave of power. Once he read only three verses: " So, when they had dined, Jesus saith to Simon Peter, Simon, son of Jonas, lovest thou me more than these? He saith unto him, Yea, Lord; thou knowest that I love thee. He saith unto him, Feed my lambs. He saith to him the second time, Simon, son of Jonas, lovest thou me? He saith unto him, Yea, Lord, thou knowest that I love thee. He saith unto him, Feed my sheep. He saith unto him the third time, Simon, son of Jonas, lovest thou me? Peter was grieved because he said unto him the third time, Lovest thou me. And he said unto him, Lord, thou knowest all things; thou knowest that I love thee. Jesus saith unto him, Feed my sheep." While he was reading, there had been an attention, a suspense, almost breathless; no one thought of *him* at the time; but in remembering it afterwards, it seemed as if he were inspired while reading. The feeling could hardly have been more profound if the repentant apostle had been visibly present. When he closed the

Bible, there was plainly to be heard a sigh of relief from
the fixed and almost painful interest.

In these meetings the tenderness of his heart was as
affecting as his boldness of speech was heroic.   One
evening, when a person, who had been a backslider for
twenty years, was speaking of his wandering, and of his
repentance, Dr. Wayland sat in the desk, the tears flowing down his cheeks ; and when presently he arose to
pray for the returning penitent, some moments elapsed
before he could command his utterance.

During the closing part of his pastoral care, two movements greatly interested Dr. Wayland, connected with the
greater efficiency of the church, and the higher spirituality
of its worship.   He had but a very slight estimate of the
religion that is emotional only, and that ends in no practical efforts for the salvation of mankind.   That every disciple should be constantly seeking the increase of piety in
his fellow-disciples, and the conversion of the worldly,
was a lesson which he ever endeavored to impress by
his example, by his private conversation, and by his public teaching.   The existence of a church which is doing
nothing more than to enjoy the means of grace for itself,
and is in no way extending to others the blessings of the
gospel, seemed to him a monstrous contradiction in terms.
He often alluded to the fact, that one evening in the month
is devoted to hearing an account of the labors of Christian people in *heathen* lands for the conversion of souls,
and that this is usually the most interesting meeting.
" Why," he asked, " do we not meet to hear what we are
doing for the cause of God *at home?*   Why do we not,
at least once a month, learn from our own members what
labors they have engaged in to save their neighbors, to
reclaim the vicious and wandering, to comfort the forsaken ? "   Realizing that what is left to hasty impulses,
is usually done but imperfectly, and in time ceases to be
done at all, he proposed to the church to establish the following system of visitation : —

" The church and congregation shall be distributed, according to their places of residence, into twelve districts.

" A committee of two brethren and two sisters shall be appointed annually to the watch care of each district.

" It is expected of the committees, —

" 1. That they will make it their great object to call the unconverted to repentance ; to encourage their brethren and sisters to lead a holy and consistent Christian life ; to caution them against conformity to the world; to urge them to labor and self-sacrifice for the cause of Christ ; and to suggest to them appropriate fields of labor, so that every one may be a living member of the body of Christ.

" 2. That they will be in frequent communication with the pastor, and keep him informed of all matters in the several districts which require his special attention, particularly where there is sickness, affliction, or religious thoughtfulness and inquiry ; also that they will seek out strangers in the congregation, introducing them to the pastor, and promoting their acquaintance with others.

" 3. That the committee, or one of them, will visit every person committed to their charge at least once in six months.

" 4. That the several committees will meet on the evening of Tuesday after communion in October, January, April, and July, to confer upon the state of the church, and to devise means for its increase in piety and usefulness, the pastor presiding.

" 5. That they shall make report of their doings as often as the church shall direct, with such suggestions as they think proper for promoting the piety of the church and the advancement of Christ's kingdom.

" It is recommended that the members of the church in each district, if practicable, meet once a month, or from time to time, at some private house, for conference and prayer."

The plan was adopted, and continued for a number of years in active operation, with results (alike to those who put forth these Christian efforts, and to those in whose behalf they were exerted) the magnitude and the beneficence of which, eternity alone can reveal.

Nor was he satisfied to have the religious efforts of Christians limited to the single congregation with which they are associated. He was of opinion that every church should maintain mission schools and preaching stations in localities destitute of the gospel. He often dwelt upon the blessing which had attended such a system of evangelical effort among the German Baptist churches, who, beginning in feebleness and poverty, and under the positive prohibition of the civil magistrate, have increased almost beyond parallel. He felt, too, that every church, as soon as its numbers justify the step, should send out a colony, which would soon become a self-supporting interest; and he was equally of opinion that, in any such enterprise, those who feel moved to leave the spot endeared to them by many associations, in order to enlarge the facilities for preaching, and for hearing the gospel, ought to receive the cordial sympathy and aid of those who remain behind. These sentiments he often expressed, and he exemplified them in his own practice.

He had also long desired to see a reform in the service of sacred song. Though himself without any scientific acquaintance with melody, he knew what effect certain styles of music produced on him, he knew what belonged to moral impressiveness, and he thought he knew what manner of conducting this portion of worship was most conducive to devotion. That four persons, perhaps destitute of all pious feeling, should have in their hands this part of the service of God's house, introducing music utterly incapable of arousing a single religious emotion, holding themselves independent of all control, and rejecting any suggestions from the body of Christian worshippers, seemed to him utterly monstrous. He fully acquiesced in the remark of the late venerated Dr. Sharp, that the singing, as practised in most of our churches, is an abomination to God. He sometimes said, while acting as pastor, that often, when he had read a solemn and impressive hymn, the moral and devotional effect would have been greater to spend the time in perfect silence, than to have the hymn sung according to the prevalent method.

Holding these views, it will readily be understood that he was an advocate of *congregational singing;* and he ardently wished to introduce this mode of worship into the church for which he was laboring.

In urging the desired reform, he was not unfrequently met by the objection that there was not volume enough of voice in the congregation to carry it through. "So," he said, "one afternoon I gave out Old Hundred, and made the particular request that all would join in the singing; and you could have heard them at the top of Angell Street. That settled the question of the volume of voice." Finally, as the result of his repeated appeals, and no doubt in a great degree from personal regard to him, and from a desire to afford him gratification, the measure was adopted. Wishing to insure the successful inauguration of the reform, he invited Dr. Lowell Mason to come and address the people upon the method of carrying on this portion of worship. Dr. Mason accepted the invitation, and by his eminence in his profession, and his profound knowledge of the science of sacred music, removed many objections to the proposed change, and offered several most useful suggestions. Dr. Mason writes, —

"I well remember a remark which he made to me, after long and repeated conversations on sacred song, in reference to which we were fully agreed. 'Is it not strange,' he asked, 'that I, who am ignorant of music scientifically or artistically, should so exactly agree with one who has devoted half a century to its study, practically and theoretically, under such great advantages?' My answer was, in substance, this: 'Sir, your good common sense, and quick, intuitive perception of right, have done more for you than much study, experience, and observation can do for one less favored in these respects.'"

A few Sabbaths before the close of Dr. Wayland's la-

bors with the church, the voice of the whole congregation
was heard praising God.

In thus attempting a narration of Dr. Wayland's pastorate, we are aware that we have presented a most inadequate view of the sources and channels of the virtue
which went forth from him. The chief influence which
he exerted during those sixteen months of labor, during
those months of universal revival, was that of his own
character. " The great feature of his ministry," says a
hearer, " was not this or that particular measure ; it was
his absolute and undivided consecration to the work."
Another, an eminent practitioner of law, says, " It was
the most wonderful exhibition of goodness that I ever saw
or conceived of."

Since his death, two members of the bar were conversing, one of whom said, " I do not know how it is ; I never
felt so towards any one else, but I always had a strange
sensation of awe whenever I met him, or saw him. I do
not know what it was owing to." " Do you not know?"
said the other ; " why, you felt the influence of his almost
superhuman goodness."

It was his *character* which afforded to men a demonstration of the divineness of the faith he preached. It was
this which gave power to his words, and to his tone, as
he read the Scriptures or gave out a hymn ; to every
movement of his hand as he closed the Bible, or as with
a wave of his arm he seemed to put aside the excuses of
the procrastinating, and the objections of the caviller ;
and this it was which both exhibited to the Christian the
true standard of the religious life, and animated him to
its attainment.

" There is a force in the natural world which has
received the designation of catalytic. It is sometimes
called the power of presence. Bodies in which it resides
have the marvellous property of transmuting other bodies
by mere contact into their likeness. The force is too
subtle for analysis, and has hitherto defied all attempts at

224   LIFE OF FRANCIS WAYLAND.

explanation. Philosophers have contented themselves
with simply noting and naming it. The fact has its
analogy in the moral world. There are men who possess a similar power of presence. An influence goes out
from them equally controlling and alike incapable of
analysis or philosophical explanation. President Wayland presented a most striking example of this. It was
felt by all who came near him. His power as a speaker
and as a teacher depended largely upon it. The same
utterances might come from others, but how slight, comparatively, their effect! The same truths might be impressed by others, but how unlike their moulding influence! The same principles might be inculcated by others,
but how different their transforming power! Behind the
utterances, back of the teachings, was a living soul, from
which proceeded emanations entirely distinct and separate
from ideas, and quite independent of language. The subtle
influence poured through the eye. It streamed from the
features. It flowed through the voice. Gesture, posture,
and form were its silent vehicles. It emphasized thought.
It energized expression. It vitalized ideas. It awoke
aspiration. It kindled enthusiasm. It evoked power. It
was the direct efflux of spiritual energy by which a great
nature transformed other natures, in proportion to their
capacities, into its own likeness. It is the want of this
incommunicable power which is most felt by his pupils in
the perusal of his writings, and which makes them unwilling to admit that he has produced anything equal to
himself." *

But his ministry had one defect, a defect remediless and
daily increasing. It was the ministry of a man past threescore. In accordance with his life-long principle, while
he was charged with responsibility, he could not see anything remain undone for want of effort on his part. His
ideal of the work of the ministry was most exalted, and
was perpetually advancing. He toiled after its realization with an earnestness which was enkindled by the con-
straining love of Christ, and which, not improbably, was
intensified by his growing consciousness that the twelve

---

* Professor Chace's Address.

hours of the day in which he might work were far spent, and that night was at hand. It was a most instructive illustration of his estimate of the character of the work of the ministry, that while at the head of the college, he was always able, however engrossing his official cares, to find some time for outside work, for authorship, and various addresses. But after he assumed the care of the church, he had not an unoccupied hour, and did not even attempt anything outside of his strictly ministerial work, with the single exception — if it be an exception — of the address upon the occasion of the death of Mr. Ives. " His labors," says one gentleman, a member of the church, who observed him very closely, who is himself accustomed to intellectual toils, and eminent for industry, " were arduous beyond the power of expression."

And it became painfully obvious that while the inward man was renewed day by day, the outward man was inadequate to the demands of the soul. He grew visibly more wearied and feeble, and his physician again urged his speedy release from toil. Indeed, it is doubtful if he could have survived another year of such exertions.

Rev. Dr. Caldwell, having accepted the pastoral care of the church, Dr. Wayland preached, on the 30th of May, a sermon with which he designed to close his labors, from Acts xx. 32 : " And now, brethren, I commend you to God, and to the word of his grace, which is able to build you up, and to give you an inheritance among all them which are sanctified."

" More than a year and three months have elapsed, my brethren and friends, since I commenced my labors among you. Neither you nor I, at the beginning, anticipated so long a continuance of my services. The providence of God, however, directs all events in infinite wisdom. For a long time you have waited patiently and prayerfully for the coming among you of a pastor in whom you would all be united. Your prayers have been answered ; your patience rewarded. You have called to minister among you a brother beloved, whose praise is in all the churches, wherever he is known. You have done this, so far as I know, without a single dissenting, or even a reluctant voice. And he has informed us that very soon, perhaps on the next Sabbath, you may expect him to come among us to break to us the bread of life. My pastoral labors with you close, therefore, with the present Sabbath, and, in the words of the text, commending you to God and to the word of his grace, I commit you to the care of another."

The arrival of the pastor being delayed, he prepared and preached, on the following Sabbath, one more sermon, from the word (touchingly appropriate to his circumstances, and to the history of the past year), " He that goeth forth and weepeth, bearing precious seed, shall doubtless come again with rejoicing, bringing his sheaves with him." With this discourse, his services as pastor of the church were ended.

To a minister : —

"May 8, 1858.

" I am obliged, for the present, to continue laboring here, though I hope we shall soon have a pastor. I have next week meetings for private conversation on Monday afternoon and evening ; Tuesday, meetings at the Hospital and State Prison, and a meeting in the evening ; Wednesday evening, lecture ; Thursday, church meeting ; and meeting on Friday evening ; besides preparation for Sunday. I am rather jaded."

To his son : —

"June 1, 1858.

" I intended to write to you before, but I have not been able. On Thursday I had people calling upon me all the morning ; in the afternoon to attend a meeting of the committee ; in the evening a church meeting, to receive fifteen converts ; and on Friday and Saturday I wrote two sermons. On Sunday I baptized and preached twice. On Monday I called, as is my custom, on those baptized the day before, and attended meeting in the evening. To-day I have made a few needful calls. I feel that my work here is almost completed."

To the same : —

"June 15, 1858.

" Mr. C., the new pastor, preached last Sabbath very well, and the people are universally pleased. The church was never, since I have known it, in so hopeful a condition. This, so far as I have had anything to do with it, has been accomplished by steady *days' works*, and by putting aside everything that interfered with it. A year spent thus is worth ten of irregular, vacillating work, without plan or steadiness."

Exhausting as were these toils, consuming as were his solicitudes, and perceptible as was the draught on his strength, yet never were his consolations more abounding. In the " Letters on the Ministry of the Gospel," he observes, in allusion to this period, " I can truly say that no part of my ministerial life was so full of enjoyment as this; and upon no part of it do I look back with so much satisfaction." It was with a radiance brighter than that of noonday that the sun declined towards its setting.

CHAPTER X.

" SERMONS TO THE CHURCHES." — " SALVATION BY CHRIST." — CORRESPONDENCE. — WORK UPON THE MORAL SCIENCE. — VIEWS OF EUROPEAN AFFAIRS. — EXPOSITION OF EPHESIANS. — ATTACK OF ILLNESS. — BUST OF DR. WAYLAND. — ANNUAL REUNION OF HIS PUPILS. — HIS FEELING TOWARDS HIS PUPILS. — INSTRUCTION TO CANDIDATES FOR THE MINISTRY. — LETTERS.

DR. WAYLAND'S retirement from the pastoral care was succeeded, not by rest, but by change of labor. He immediately began to prepare for the press the volume entitled " Sermons to the Churches," which was published in August, 1858. It contained eight sermons, two of which had been previously published. The work is appropriately named, for the discourses were addressed peculiarly to professing Christians, and were designed to lead the people of God to emancipate themselves from subservience to the principles and examples of the world. A singular unity pervades the book ; indeed, the several sermons might have been chapters in a single work. But its most marked characteristics are overwhelming earnestness and the absolute simplicity of its appeals. It would seem impossible to use language with greater plainness. The preacher takes up courses of action which are all the more likely to escape observation, because they are so universal ; he exhibits them with such vividness that they appear novel, while yet the reader is compelled to confess that they are common — that they are his own. In none of his works has he excelled the presentation and enforcement here made of the ethics of the gospel.

In the following December was published, " Salvation by Christ," a collection of discourses, in the main, identical with those issued several years previously, under the title " University Sermons." Two, suggested by the revolutions in Europe, were omitted, and several new ones inserted, which had been prepared during his recent pastoral labors. A comparison of these with the sermons composing the original volume will substantiate the views presented in a previous chapter, of the change which the past few years had wrought in the character of his preaching.

In 1858 he was invited to accept the presidency of a university just established under circumstances of peculiar promise. He was informed that he would not be expected to put forth any large amount of personal labor, but only to give the weight of his name, and such supervision as he could exercise. We have alluded to the invitation only as introductory to the following extract from his reply : —

" I beg leave to express to the Board of Trustees my grateful acknowledgment for the honor which they have conferred upon me. I could not, of course, pretend to decide such a question without deliberate reflection. I have taken time for this purpose, and am obliged to say that it is not in my power to accept the appointment. I have overworked my brain, and it is not as good a servant as it used to be. I find that the labor of the pastoral office, which I occupied for sixteen months, has had an effect upon me from which it will take some time to recover. By manual labor and release from responsibility I am gaining ground ; but were I to embark in such an undertaking as that which the university of —— presents, I should break down in twelve months. I do not think I could have continued my former presidency a year longer. There is not, I am persuaded, a physician who has known me for ten years, who would not, on this ground, forbid my going. It might be said that I need not do much labor; but I cannot connect myself with such an undertaking on such terms. To see a cause of this nature fail from want of anything that I could do would be impossible. Nor is such a man the man you want. You cannot succeed unless he who has the office of leader performs, in fact, the hardest work. If I have had success in any undertaking, it has been simply from hard labor, and I could not act otherwise; but such labor I am not now able to render."

Extracts from letters to a minister, a former pupil: —

" I apprehend that when we give up the account of our ministry, one of our greatest failures will be found to be that we have so often neglected the Word of God. It looks strange that the Son of God has left heaven to teach us, and has promised his Spirit to accompany his Word, and has set us to preach it, and that we should have anything to preach that we like better, or that we should merely take a start from the Bible, and go on with our own imaginings."

" I have been astonished at the effect of a baptism on the spiritual condition of a church. If administered religiously, as a solemn thing, and not as a spectacle, the moral effect is most salutary."

" Above all, remember that you have accepted from the Savior the care of these souls, for whom you have engaged to give account. This is a very different idea from supplying the pulpit. It is not pleasing to God to have his service made a convenience of. Do your own work well, in the fear of God, and what is left, use for other good things; but do not cut off a piece of God's work to make anything else out of."

" A man, to succeed, must have a fort — some place where he stands strong, and is impregnable. This, to a minister, is his church and people. If he stands well there, he may laugh at everything else. . . . The Spirit of God is jealous; and if we do not receive his presence with thankfulness and renewed effort, he will withdraw. In spiritual things, make hay while the sun shines."

" . . . I heard yesterday Mr. ——. It was, I think, an attempted imitation of Mr. Beecher, but an unfortunate attempt. A sinner would hardly have been led to the Savior. I was saddened, for he used to be considered a very earnest and pious preacher. My dear ——, there is nothing but the glorious truth of the way of salvation by Christ that God will bless to the salvation of sinners. This is what Christ sends us to preach, and this alone he will bless."

" I have thought several times of the sermon you are to preach before the Association. The discourse will take its character from its object. What is that object? Is it to prove the truth of the text? I presume not, to ministers. Is it to confirm them in the belief of it? Hardly. What, then, is it? Here is a company of ministers, exposed, without knowing it, to the danger of being ashamed of the cross. You want to point out to them this danger, and so to affect them that, for the year to come, they may preach Christ more simply, earnestly, and effectually than ever before. Should they do this, no one can predict the result upon the churches, or the number of conversions that God would grant. It is possible that, with the blessing of God, from your sermon a revival may extend over the whole Association. I would labor and pray, and preach directly for that object; and it would, I doubt not, receive the blessing of the Savior, and cause joy in heaven over many a returning penitent."

" I have been reading several sermons in Spurgeon's new volume. I am struck with several things; first, the manifest truthfulness of the man, arising from his perfect belief in all that he says. The truths of religion are as much a verity to him as his own existence. Second, his intimate acquaintance with the whole Bible. It bubbles up everywhere as soon as he begins to speak. He uses it with great power to express his own ideas. Third, as a result of this, is his manner of making a sermon. He does not draw an abstract truth out of the text, but expands and illustrates the very text itself. It opens to him a train, or several trains of thought, which he illustrates from everything around him. It is owing to this that he has so great variety. Were he to deduce abstract propositions, he would of necessity often repeat himself. Fourth, he takes the very range of the thoughts of his hearers. They, therefore, all follow him. And then again, while he is accused of egotism, he seems to me to forget himself and his reputation more than any man I know of. He seems not to care what people say of him or do to him, if he can only convert them."

Upon the completion of the volumes named above, Dr. Wayland resumed his work upon the Moral Science. It had been his design entirely to reconstruct and re-write it, making it, in all but the general subject and spirit, a new book. With this view he prepared several hundred pages of manuscript. But he became satisfied that it would be a hazardous experiment to reconstruct a book, which, on the whole, had been so well received by the public in its original form. He therefore decided to revise it, re-writing only such chapters or passages as seemed susceptible of marked improvement. This labor engrossed him very constantly throughout the year 1859 and the early part of 1860. To his son he writes, —

"I am working at my book — sometimes doing a day's work, often only a fragment."

"I will try to come and see you; but it is difficult. I want to do something every day at my book, which is now advancing. If I leave it, even for a little while, I get cold in it, and it takes time to begin again."

"I am much engaged in my book, and am getting along slowly. I give up everything to it, and must do so in order to accomplish anything. I am thinking through a book at a time before I begin to write it, and it consumes more time than you would suppose. I sometimes come to a chapter which could, as it seems, be thought through in a day, and it takes a week or a fortnight. But this is no more than my ordinary experience."

". . . My health is, by the blessing of God, very good. I am rarely sick, but I feel that age is beginning to do its work upon me. I am not able to labor as I once could. My brain does not bear so long application. It is possible that I see as clearly, but my mind does not act as rapidly as formerly. I suppose I need recreation occasionally, but I have never learned to amuse myself, and have never had many intimate friends. I presume I must be unfortunately constituted in this respect, or else I have formed bad habits. I, however, keep on with my work, and am happy in it. Perhaps some good may come out of it."

The passages just quoted show, if we do not mistake, the singular control which he possessed over his powers. One who knew him for more than thirty years, and who is himself very observant of mental phenomena, has said, " I never knew any one who had such command over his mind. He made it obey his will perfectly." His mind had no freaks, no caprices. What he set it to do, it did, so long as the power to labor remained. When it failed to obey him, the failure was not the effect of insubordination, but of exhaustion and powerlessness.

During a part of the years 1859-60, his oldest son, with his wife, was in Europe. Many of Dr. Wayland's letters to them exhibit alike his comprehensive views on passing events, and the tenderness with which his heart yearned over those whom he loved, and from whom he was separated.

To his son, just previous to his embarkation : —

" And now, my dear son, I commend you and M. to God. I have a confident trust that he will watch over you, and return you both in safety. Keep it ever in mind that the first of all your relations is with God; that he is ever near to them that love and serve him; then try to make this journey a spiritual blessing to you both.

" I trust that I shall see you again. It may be otherwise. You know all I have so very imperfectly tried to teach you. You know that I have, first of all, desired that you should serve God, and be a high-minded, noble, disinterested benefactor towards man. God grant that you may be all this and more. May God bless and preserve you both to his heavenly kingdom."

" Strange as it may seem, things have gone on during your absence very much as usual, only a few families are always thinking of you, and frequently looking up to our common Father for his blessing upon you."

"Napoleon III. is almost a miracle. Having twice made himself the laughing-stock of the world, he has, at a single leap, shown himself the foremost man in it. His uncle said there was but a step between the sublime and the ridiculous. He, for the first time in history, has shown that there may be but a single step from the ridiculous to the sublime. He has astonished the world by his ability in war. So far as I can judge, in every case, the Austrians had the advantage before the fight, and in every case have been decidedly beaten by a man who had never seen a battle before. Every thing in Europe seems now to turn upon his moral character. If he should be true to principle, faith, and honor, and, after driving out the Austrians, should establish human rights in Italy, and then unite with England in promoting the best interests of man, he will overshadow the fame of his uncle. . . . Should he organize a great nation in the north of Italy, he will be able to attack England if he chooses. Their weakness is in their aristocracy in the army. Merit cannot rise. The very ablest men in India and the Crimea were discovered by accident and by the death of those above them. Aristocracy is good for many things, but it will not make great generals. War is a real business, and not a conventional arrangement. Skill and talent must command their proper position, or the requisite energy never will be developed. Napoleon III. has shown an unusual common-sense talent for it. He has commenced by making the individual soldier, whether officer or private, as distinctive a being as possible, and has given him, in the next place, the best means of distinction, and then has adopted the motto, ' The career open to talent.' If war is to be carried on, it is on these principles that it must succeed. If the English had learned the lesson taught them at New Orleans, they would not now be using the muskets of Ramillies and Blenheim."

"The news of the peace took us all, as it did the rest of the world, by surprise. No one knows how to understand it. It may be that the emperor tells the truth (not a common thing with emperors or diplomatists), that he was afraid of encountering all Germany, and of carrying on the war in the marshes of the Mincio and Adige in midsummer. But this he must have anticipated; and he says himself that he commenced the war in the face of all Europe. The other view taken — though I have not seen it fully stated — is this: He got the English into the Crimean war, and withdrew from the contest in order to secure the gratitude of the Emperor of Russia. He has played the same game with the King of Sardinia, and made the Emperor of Austria his friend. Here, then, are the three strongest military powers united, and the man of the greatest ability and boldness will use them. But still more: here are the three despotic powers, embracing the Greek and Catholic churches, together with the Pope, united as one man. Civil and religious despotism was never so powerful. There remain to Protestantism and liberty only Prussia and England. It looks as if a war of opinions would ensue, and the spirit of liberty triumph; or else despotism must press on the human race, how long, O Lord, how long? . Protestantism may have the aid of the free spirit of Italy and Hungary; but they are weak in opposition to such tremendous forces, united and upheld by the religious spirit of the Greek and Roman churches. I incline to this view, and I should be alarmed, were it not that God reigns, and that he is able to make the wrath of man praise him, while he restrains the remainder. He frequently allows his enemies to bring forth all their power for the sake of rendering his victory the more impressive. The view which I have taken corresponds with the gigantic ambition of the chief agent, and the love of glory and domination so characteristic of the French."

" Since I wrote you, I see new reasons given for the peace. It is said that Napoleon saw, that though the Sardinians were profuse in demonstrations, they did nothing in aid of the war, and he would soon have to meet Europe in arms, alone. This, however, is contradicted by all the previous accounts of the war, and of each battle. The only thing certain, I presume, is that, for reasons known to himself, he thought that he had carried on the war far enough, and made up his mind to put an end to it. The reasons will probably transpire in time. The Villa Franca convention is a very hurried and loose document, fixing hardly anything, and meaning simply, ' We will stop fighting.' I am glad they stopped, but care little about their reasons."

"I hope you will spend as much of your time in England as possible. There are brighter prospects and finer mountains elsewhere, but the men and women are in England, and at present it is the culminating point in modern civilization. . . ."

"You will have read in the papers all about Harper's Ferry and old Ossawottamie Brown. The results are yet to be seen. I believe they will be much greater than is anticipated. Every one perceives the madness or insanity of the attempt, and, so far as is known, the want of plan or forecast in the movement. But every one admires the bravery, coolness, and evident sincerity of the old captain. It will oblige millions to think of the subject, and will raise the tone of anti-slavery feeling several degrees higher throughout the North."

"We are greatly interested in your account of the revival in Scotland. Every one must say, with the magicians, 'This is the finger of God.' It is the work of the Spirit, as in the day of Pentecost; and it is sent, not to accompany preaching, nor to make much use of it. I sincerely hope that this power of the Holy Ghost is to be a general feature of our times, and that it will work a change in the minds of men as to the way of laboring for souls. All the recent manifestations have been in the direction which I have intended to indicate, so that I hope that I have not erred in my attempt to point out a more excellent way. But I seem to tread in the steps of that excellent old spinster, Cassandra, whom no one would believe. I have tried to be useful to my brethren, and have stood up for the rights and duties of the laity of Christ's people."

"I repeat what I said before: Make yourself acquainted with England. There is now, in their best circles, perhaps the highest state of civilization on earth. But more than this, in a general uprising of the human race, which is not impossible, Great Britain and the United States must stand together for the rights of mankind."

"Louis Napoleon is evidently a political economist and a statesman. His decrees are despotic, but they are wise and suited to the building up of a nation. If he would abandon the absurd idea of war and conquest, he

would show wisdom. But this, perhaps, is impossible.
France, largely intellectual, but wholly irreligious, can be
governed by nothing but a military despotism. With a
strong desire for liberty, they have no moral instincts to
direct them how to secure it. A despot is therefore a
necessity, and Louis Napoleon supplies that necessity.
Rigid as is his rule, it is better than anarchy, and the
majority uphold him. But granting a despotism, government is not a very difficult thing. It is all reduced to *Sic
volo, sic jubeo.* The government of France by a despot
does not require as much talent as the government of
England by the prime minister, if we consider the com-
plication of obstacles to be met and overcome at every
important movement."

"Every one in the civilized world is now looking towards
Italy and the French emperor. Whether he intended it
or not, his course has been directed with, apparently, great
wisdom. He went far enough to give the Italians room
and space to develop themselves, organize governments,
and get that taste of freedom so fatal to oppression ; and
now, united with them, his word can control Austria. He
has let the Pope amuse himself until the course of events
has rendered the return to the papal dynasty impossible ;
and now the Holy Father is in his power, and must really
ask of him leave to exist. At precisely the right moment
he has strengthened his alliance with England, not by a
treaty of combination, offensive and defensive, but by the tie
of mutual interest, which will make them in a few years
almost one people. There were never two nations, highly
civilized and so near together, whose products were so
dissimilar, and who would gain so much and be so
cemented by freedom of trade. All this looks well for the
liberty of man. Napoleon III. is a political economist,
which his uncle was not. It looks as if he was determined
to free France from the papal despotism. His letter to
the Pope is such a one as has never been sent before to
the Holy Father. It is plain, forcible, and ingenuous. If
he can control the priesthood of France, he will succeed.
I do not doubt that he will succeed if he has the people
with him, and I think he has. Priests are not so purblind
as not to know on which side their bread is buttered, and
few of them will prefer exile to a good benefice. If you

and M. make the acquaintance of the emperor and empress (and they will of course call as soon as they hear of your arrival), I hope you will treat them with every respect, and present them with my sincere regards, assuring them of the pleasure it will give me to have them visit us when they come to Providence. I think I shall not invite Cardinal Antonelli."

" I am glad that you have seen the ' city of the dead,' * as Scott calls it. It is worth a volume of history, and has shown you what the most cultivated nation on earth was at the time of Christ's appearing. Had he not appeared, what would have been the condition of the world? There was nothing to arrest a downward tendency to the deepest abyss."

" It now appears from all we can learn that both our friend Napoleon III. and Victor Emmanuel are held up before the world as being by no means such enthusiastic admirers of truth as we should wish to see. The latest information is, that the cession of Savoy was arranged from the beginning, although both of these excellent men had most steadfastly denied it. No one can henceforth trust either of them. It is, however, no disgrace for a Frenchman to lie. Louis Philippe would hardly shrug his shoulders when detected in a flat-footed falsehood. How it will affect a man in Italy, I do not know. It will, however, damage him in England. The Protestant religion forms a vastly superior national character to the Catholic."

" You can attend courts wherever you are, and will acquire new views by observing how other people than Yankees look at questions of right. Have you seen Macaulay's prophecy respecting this country? I confess it has made me tremble. It is according to all the wisdom of the past, and unless there are elements of safety in us that do not yet appear, or there be some wonderful display of divine power in our behalf, it will be fulfilled. A nation where everything can be bought and sanctified with money, is on an inclined plane, and nothing can arrest its progress."

" The Pope's bull has been issued, and it seems to have fallen to the ground, perfectly innocuous, — the thunder

---

* Pompeii.

without the lightning, — and that in Italy itself. The world has certainly advanced since the middle ages. This will give courage to Napoleon, and he will probably emancipate himself. This will be the beginning of the end of the papacy; for, if left to its moral power, what has it to hope for? But what then? It will make a struggle, and if a war of opinion is waged, it will be war to the knife, over every acre of that land. The French revolution will be child's play to it. The more, however, I look at these things, the more I am impressed with the vanity of human plans and the folly of human combinations. There sits upon the circle of the heavens One to whom all the nations of the earth are as the small dust of the balance, who is working out his own purposes, and will overthrow all wickedness, and bring out right and justice triumphant. Men's plans are all turned to dust, but the plan of God moves on, slowly, steadily, overturning nations, to establish a single principle, and making the wrath of man to praise him. You possibly may ask, When will all this be done? I answer, at the time appointed. God has plenty of time; a thousand years are with him as one day, and he, without regard to our calculations, takes a thousand years to accomplish what we would have done, if we could, in a day. The insects on a leaf, if the leaf dries up and falls to the ground, might think that the universe was coming to an end. They know not that the drying up of that leaf was to make way for a fruit-spur, and that from that fruit-spur will arise the seed of a mighty tree, that will furnish ten million such universes as their single leaf. Thus is it in the government of God. I reluctate from all plans, especially all wise ones. I incline to believe that our safest course is to do our personal duty, leaving all the planning to Him who sees the end from the beginning. I rejoice that over all this turmoil the Lord reigneth, and though clouds and darkness are round about him, justice and judgment are the habitation of his throne. It may be a geological epoch before all that is promised will be accomplished, but it will assuredly come."

"July 2, 1860.

" . . . There is a great deal of humbug about art. Not one in a thousand is willing to confess what he feels, but makes believe feel what he is told he ought to, and then sneers at those who do not repeat his words. They say when you put a pail of boiling water in a yard full of pigs, if one puts in his nose, and is scalded, and goes off grunting, another will follow, and do the same thing, and so on till every one has his snout scalded. So it is of pictures, and all this talk of high art. I know that there cannot be a greater number of pictures and statues than there are of poems and orations, that are worthy of commanding the admiration of all ages.

"Your letter of July 7, from London, gave me occasion to remember many of my own experiences. I am very glad that you saw Mr. Ingham. He is a very fine fellow, and was peculiarly kind to me. He has great weight of character from his honesty, intelligence, and disinterestedness. I was greatly pleased to find that the impression produced on your mind by the courts of justice and by Parliament were so similar to my own. The courts, I visited, as you did, with Mr. Ingham, when you were somewhat of a youngster. They presented to me the idea of a company of men, of the highest intelligence and most thorough learning, devoting themselves, in their different positions, to the simple purpose of administering justice. The decorum was perfect, as became men engaged in such a business. While the utmost deference was paid to the court, the court manifested almost fraternal courtesy to the bar, and seemed really to consider them as gentlemen who were aiding them to execute justice. One felt that he was in an atmosphere where slang, *ad populum* harangue, or personal altercation, could not breathe for a moment.

"*Mutatis mutandis*, the same remarks apply to Parliament. There was a collection of highly-educated gentlemen who had made statesmanship, not politics, their study, and had taken pains to render themselves acquainted with every subject that would come before them. As the subject opened, each one presented his views briefly, pertinently, in remarks rich in information, and bearing directly upon the point. Each sat down, when he had contributed his part to the discussion, to hear and learn from others. It was an appropriate national council for a great and free people.

"I want you to see all you can in London. What you see and hear there, will not greatly gratify the senses, but it will furnish you with facts, and principles, and recollections, that will build you up as a man of sense, and furnish you with matter for future judgments. Neither a view of a picture or a temple will aid you in conducting a difficult case, or give soundness to your opinion in an important political crisis; and who knows how soon such crisis may come!"

It had been the not unfrequent practice of the church of which Dr. Wayland was a member, to suspend the Wednesday evening service during the most oppressive portion of the summer, and more particularly during the vacation of the pastor. As the summer of 1859 approached, he expressed his opinion that it was undesirable to deprive those who remained in town of this means of grace, and he consented to bear the responsibility of the service. He accordingly gave, upon the Wednesday evenings of this summer, a series of expository discourses on the Epistle to the Ephesians. These expositions were characterized by his wonted simplicity of language, and secured a full attendance, even during the extreme heat of August. But those who remarked him closely could but observe, with pain and solicitude, the evident effort which these services cost him — the falling away from the abundant and unconscious power of other days.

Meanwhile he continued to labor upon the revision of Moral Science. In the winter of 1859–60, he wrote to his son, —

" I have just completed the first or theoretical part of my volume, and I think it is in straight lines, but I do not know. I have now but one heavy article before me — that on slavery. The rest is all familiar."

And again in March, 1860, he writes to his son, —

" I thank you most truly for all your expressions of affection. . . . I cannot express the yearning desire I feel for all my children, that they should accomplish their destiny, and return to the Master the talent which he has committed to them, improved and greatly increased. I fear that this interest sometimes carries me too far, and that I seem more earnest about your success and improvement than is proper. If I do, I trust you will pardon me, for you know my motive. I want you to be perfect in every good work, and I may seem to express myself to you in words much more direct than I should to any other person. . . .

"I am this day sixty-four years old. What remains to me, and how much, is known only to Him who will do all things aright. I should like to bear my testimony fully on human rights, and to labor at some other things that may be useful; but if I do not, some one else will be commissioned, who will do it better. I am in the midst of that subject now, and I ask your prayers that I may be enabled to treat it properly. I proceed slowly. It is difficult to state articulately truth that is so simple, and to state it so as to impress men. However, I make some progress. I hope I have been directed to do it, so as to aid Christ's little ones. The more I think of it, the more inextinguishable is my abhorrence of oppression, especially of our own slavery.

"God bless you, my dear son, and make you abundantly useful, and give you a bright crown to cast at his feet."

"I had labored for several years without any relaxation, and when I resigned, those who would have been most anxious that I should remain, were convinced that it was my duty to relinquish the position. My brain was tired out, and there was nothing to be done but to give it rest. I did not, however, long remain idle. My work as pastor, following so soon after my labors in college, had a bad effect on my brain. It kept up continual thought in one direction, without relaxation or diversion. During the period of my pastoral work, my strength had begun to fail. In fact, it had been so severely tried during my connection with the college, that I could no longer do what I had formerly done with ease. After publishing two volumes of sermons, I commenced re-writing my system of Moral Philosophy, and continued it until May, 1860. I wrote steadily, but not intemperately, — working every day, both morning and afternoon, and doing, as I supposed, no more than I could do with ease. I wrote in the attic room, away from noise. The room is small, and the roof of the house forms the ceiling. In the summer it was very warm, particularly in the afternoon, and in the winter it was very difficult to regulate the temperature. It was not easy to heat it sufficiently without rendering it too warm, and of this increase of temperature I could not readily be aware. I mention all the circumstances of the case which I can remember, not on account of their absolute importance, nor from senile garrulity, but because the knowledge of them, though apparently needlessly minute, may serve to guard my children from a similar misfortune."

As he proceeded with the chapter just alluded to, his soul became more and more deeply engrossed in the effort to vindicate the rights of man, and to exhibit the violation of personal liberty in the case of domestic slavery, until, unconsciously to himself, he had overtaxed his already strained energies. In his reminiscences he writes, —

"My habit in regard to sleep was to retire at eleven P. M., or a little later, and to rise in summer at half past five, and in winter at six. This did not give me sleep enough. I should have had one or two hours more. I found, when I put myself to work, that my mind did not act well in the morning. I was drowsy, and did not think readily or clearly. This was quite unlike my previous experience. I took exercise enough, but still did not improve.

"About the middle of May, as I was writing, I found my mind unusually dull, and not easily controlled by my will. The subject on which I was writing was one with which I was perfectly familiar ; yet I composed with unusual difficulty, hardly finishing one page when I should have finished three ; and on looking it over I found it badly done. I did not know what could be the cause, but I perceived that my thinking powers were in some way disordered. In the afternoon I attended my Bible class, without observing anything peculiar in the action of my mind. The only circumstance that seemed unusual was an incessant gaping, which I could neither control nor account for. So remarkable was it, that I was strongly inclined to apologize to the members of my class for the apparent rudeness.

" I retired to rest, and slept as usual. When I arose in the morning I found that my speech was affected. Some words I could not pronounce without effort, and my organs would not obey me without a special act of the will, and even then only imperfectly. My right leg was weak, and seemed to share in the general derangement. I went as usual to my dressing-room to shave, and my experience there was singular. Ordinarily, shaving is with me almost an automatic process, which proceeds regularly after it is commenced. But I found that this was not the case now. I had a sort of dialogue with my hand. It asked me, ' What shall I do next?' or, ' How shall I do it?' and I was obliged to answer by a distinct act of the will. I, however, completed the operation, though in constant danger of cutting myself.

" After breakfast it was necessary for me to answer a note. I found it impossible to write as usual, or in fact more than barely legibly. I could not keep on the line, nor command my hand so as to form the letters distinctly. My first attempt could not, I think, be understood. I tried a second time, and by writing slowly, and with constant attention of the will to every letter, succeeded a little better, but only a little. I at once perceived that something was the matter with my brain. I took medical advice. My pulse, and all that belongs to my physical system, was found to be in perfect health. I was advised to use entire quiet for the brain, moderate exercise, and patience. These I at once put in practice; and, indeed, they were necessary. I could not use my brain. It refused to work, and seemed to say to me, at the least attempt, ' I cannot do it.' I soon saw Dr. Jackson, of Boston. He told me, contrary to all my expectation, that it would take eighteen months or two years before I could be restored, and recommended the treatment just mentioned, with the additional prescription of a diet almost exclusively vegetable.

" I endeavored to conform to this medical advice, and very slowly improved. With regard to vegetable diet, I am not quite certain of its effect. I pursued it for a long time, and then returned to my usual diet, and have, for a season, again fallen back upon it. I think, in both cases, I have derived benefit from change. Which would be best for a permanent course I can hardly determine. I observe that medical writers of late, in general, advise, in similar cases, a full rather than a spare diet. I say a full, but of course not a feasting diet; merely generous living. It is now nearly three years since this attack, and I have only within a few months recovered the power of writing with my usual rapidity.

"One symptom that accompanied my disease, I have not seen noticed by physicians. It was disordered action in the sense of feeling on my right side (which was the most affected). Cold objects seemed to me warm. A glass of ice water, when held in the hand, had a tepid feeling. This symptom has not left me entirely at the present time.

"For a while I could read almost nothing; then easy narrative. What seemed impossible was original thinking — that is, thinking out a train of thought on any subject, or even following such a train of thought written by another. I have not yet regained the power of doing this. Perhaps it is only fancy; but my brain apparently refuses to do it, and says, 'I am not able to do it.' I do not like to pursue a train of thought in conversation, and in any given case had rather have the facts, and form an opinion spontaneously, than go through a process of reasoning to reach it.

"I have found it necessary to avoid all excitement. To become deeply interested in anything deprives me of sleep. I have been obliged to give up reading newspapers. I dare not attend public meetings, especially in the evening. It would be difficult for me to write a sermon, — so at least it appears to me, — or to think out the plan of a sermon. I can expound a passage of Scripture much more easily. Here the plan is laid out before me, and I can take up every separate point as it is presented, without thinking out the whole range of thought for myself.

"I am, however, through the mercy of God, slowly recovering. For some time (as I have said) I could read but little of anything. Afterwards I read that which required more thinking, but was obliged to use much care. On one occasion I read Macaulay's Essays with great pleasure, and pretty continuously. I found, however, that I had transcended my limits, and for a considerable time could read nothing of that character.

"After a while I attempted composition. The first thing which I undertook was this scattering collection of reminiscences. I was obliged to write but little at a time, say, for instance, two or three hours a day. If I did more than this, I was obliged to intermit for a number of days the work of composition. On several occasions I wrote too much, and was compelled to lay aside my pen for weeks together. I observe that I commenced these reminiscences in October, 1860. It is now April, 1863, and they have constituted my principal work, at frequently long intervals, since that time. It is a poor way of occupying one's self, yet I found the need of some mental exercise. I think that I improve by gentle use of the brain, but I suffer unless that exercise be confined within very exact limits.

" My means of recovery have been few and simple. I have devoted, during the summer, a large part of the day to labor in the garden. My diet has been simple, and almost entirely confined to two meals a day, at first with no animal food, and latterly with but little. I have taken more sleep, and find that I work more effectively the more I sleep."

In the account above quoted, the reader has undoubtedly remarked, if not the actual presence of paralysis, yet the evident tokens of its imminence. It was in this light that Dr. Wayland interpreted the symptoms he has delineated, although, probably from regard to their feelings, he rarely expressed to his family or to his friends his full apprehensions.

In August he wrote to his son, —

" I am gradually improving, gaining strength, and having a more natural mental feeling. I do not try to use my mind, but I think, with the blessing of God, I shall soon be able to do so. I have work to do which I should like to accomplish, if it be the will of God. But if he is pleased to devolve it on others, I am content; I think entirely so."

In September he wrote to Rev. Dr. Hoby, —

" You have me in your debt, as well as your excellent wife. I must confess it, but also add, that it has not been without reason. Since the spring I have been interdicted from mental effort and writing. Some time in May I was attacked with symptoms of overwrought brain, showing danger of paralysis, and demanding, most imperatively, rest; and rest I have taken. My illness was not severe, but only premonitory; and I at once laid aside my papers, and have not even looked at them since. So, you see, the troubles of advancing years affect us both. Soon the last will arrive — how soon God only knows; and I would not wish to ask him."

He was, of course, compelled to abandon many undertakings involving mental exertion, and to defer the execution of others. He had promised to deliver an address at the Andover Theological Seminary at the ensuing anniversary, and to give a course of lectures before the Lowell Institute. Both of these promises he was compelled to recall. And the Moral Science was laid aside for several years. In the fall of 1860 he prepared the Introduction to the "Life of Trust" (a condensed narrative of the dealings of God with George Müller).

This Introduction was written at the rate of six or eight pages a day, and was subsequently re-written.

The immediate effect produced on his mind by the attack lately referred to was seen rather in the diminished rapidity of his mental action, than in any want of accuracy in his judgment. He found himself, in time, able to think, and to express his thoughts, as clearly as heretofore. But he could not labor as continuously, nor as intensely. When formed, however, his conclusions were as just as they had ever been. Yet the attack acted, it is probable, indirectly, by abridging his physical power. He found it not easy to walk, and he grew more and more averse to travelling. He felt himself, he said, too clumsy for much motion. From this circumstance, and from the fact that he was compelled to avoid anything that excited him, may have resulted a greater degree of isolation than was favorable to his spirits, or to the soundest mental action.

During the summer of 1860 a circumstance occurred

which appropriately expressed the sentiments entertained towards Dr. Wayland by the successive generations of his pupils. For the following narrative we are indebted to Professor Gammell, who was active in the series of transactions of which he speaks.

" A desire to secure and transmit some memorial of President Wayland had long existed in the minds of very many of his pupils, and the matter had often been talked about among the graduates as they met each other ; but it was not until April, 1860, that any move was made for carrying into execution what was known to be a common wish. At that time a meeting was held of graduates residing in Providence. At this meeting, which was fully attended, it was determined to ask Dr. Wayland to sit for his bust, to be executed in marble by the best artist that could be procured. Several of those present were in favor of a statue in colossal size, either of marble or of bronze ; and they expressed a desire to see such a work placed in a conspicuous position on the college grounds. It was, however, believed that he was not likely to consent to this, even if it were solicited ; and it was at length generally agreed that a marble bust would be most appropriate, and on the whole most acceptable to his pupils.

" As soon as Dr. Wayland had given his consent, Mr. Thomas Ball, of Boston, was selected as the sculptor ; and he very soon came to Providence to commence the requisite preparations. This eminent artist was at the time just commencing his studies for the equestrian statue of Washington, ordered by the city of Boston, upon which, I believe, he is still engaged, while residing in Italy. He entered with great interest into the spirit of the work to which we invited him, and there presently sprang up a warm sympathy between him and his subject — a circumstance that, no doubt, contributed its full share to his ultimate success. The likeness has always been regarded as very excellent.

" It fell to me to conduct much of the correspondence with those of the graduates who lived at a distance, and I recall very distinctly the warm expressions of personal respect and admiration which often accompanied their contributions, and the evident pleasure which they felt in having an opportunity to unite in this testimonial. These expressions were particularly marked in the letters received from members of the older classes, and they often came from those who had scarcely seen him since they left the university, but who had felt his influence as a perpetual presence along all their way in life.

"The subscribers were all gentlemen who had graduated at Brown University under his presidency, with, I believe, but a single exception, that of Hon. William H. Seward, at that time a member of the United States Senate from New York. He had been a pupil of Dr. Wayland when the latter was a tutor at Union College, and, chancing to hear the matter spoken of by some of the graduates of Brown University in the Senate, he insisted on writing his name in the list of those who were thus expressing their gratitude to our president.

"The bust was formally committed to the custody of the corporation at Commencement, 1861."

As the Commencement of 1860 approached, Dr. Wayland conveyed, through the Providence Journal, an invitation to his former pupils to call upon him, after the usual annual dinner. In response to this invitation, many of the graduates changed their plans of business or of pleasure, that they might visit him in compliance with his request. The invitation was renewed, with one or two exceptions, during each of the succeeding years of his life.

It was a source of peculiar gratification to Dr. Wayland to meet his former pupils, in an unofficial way, on the ground of friendship; and he felt grateful to any who afforded him this opportunity. It was a matter of regret and of mortification to him, that he was unable in every case to recognize them by name, particularly when the progress of years had both effaced something of the vividness of his recollections, and had changed their lineaments of countenance.

A gentleman of deserved professional and literary eminence writes, —

"For several years, as I afterwards learned, 1 entirely

misinterpreted Dr. Wayland in one respect, and I am quite sure that others, at one time or another, made the same mistake. During my college course I had no *special* occasion to come in contact with the president. I was always regular in my performance of college duties, and never asked permission to be absent for a single day, nor needed to be excused for any delinquency. It was only in the presence of others that I saw him, in the chapel, or the recitation-room, until the very close of our course, after the last lesson had been recited. Of course I had had very little opportunity to know him as a personal friend. For three years following my graduation I had been unable to attend Commencement; and in the mean time, although I had seen him several times, he had not spoken with me. On one or two occasions he *seemed* to pass by me without recognition, as if not wishing to know me. When I remembered that no student had ever passed through college with a fairer record as to attendance and a faithful performance of college duties, I was grieved by this apparent slight. More than once I put myself in his way, and saluted him respectfully, that he might be sure of my desire to be recognized. But, although he always returned the salutation, he did it as if he did not care for me, and in no instance uttered a word. Subsequently, I made a more deliberate attempt to attract the president's notice, but failed utterly. He cast a glance at me, and then passed on, as if he could have no concern with me. This troubled me not a little. I did not like to be so completely ignored by a man whom I respected so highly, and to whom I had sustained such a relation. I could not help believing that he thought me guilty of some wrong, which made him unwilling to recognize me.

" But on the day on which he retired from the presidency of the college, you remember, perhaps, that he said he should be glad to have his pupils take him by the hand, if they felt any interest in his welfare, and that there was not one among them all for whom he did not cherish a feeling of fatherly kindness. I resolved at once that he should have no reason to doubt my confidence and respect. Seizing the earliest opportunity, I extended my hand, reminding him, by way of apology, of what he had said in the tent after Commencement dinner. What was my amazement on his asking my name, and seeming to be surprised when I gave it. He spoke pleasantly, cordially, and evidently knew my name and history much better than my face. I had abundant confirmation afterwards of his personal good will, and have no doubt that he supposed he had not seen me since the day of my graduation.

"I afterwards learned two facts, which were unknown to me before; first, that his memory in reference to facts and incidents was not good, — that he was utterly unable to tell in what year he was baptized; and, second, that he had far more personal interest in those who had been his pupils than he seemed to them to have. He knew where they had been; he rejoiced in their prosperity; his great heart was glad when they were honored. Most of his pupils never knew the depth of his affections, nor suspected the warmth of his generous nature. Those who went to him in trouble — especially if they sought religious counsel — learned how tenderly he could speak to them, and with what loving earnestness he could pray with them. But most of the students knew him only as the stern president, whose imperial presence awed them, and whose commanding spirit claimed their respectful obedience. Repeatedly, during the last years of his life, I saw the most convincing evidence of a warm and generous nature under his somewhat severe exterior, and in the assurance that he was my friend, and recognized me as his friend, I found ample compensation for years of apparent, but not intended, neglect."

It has already been said that Dr. Wayland was, for a time, prevented from any composition requiring exact or original thinking. He could, however, converse without difficulty upon subjects which were familiar to him, and this single talent he as heartily consecrated to the service of the Master as he had done the fulness of his powers. Two candidates for the ministry, who had known him through his works, requested him to give them some stated instruction suited to their future work. He consented to do so, and accordingly, during the summer, they met him twice a week for this purpose.

One of the gentlemen referred to writes, —

"During the revival of 1858, while Dr. Wayland was

pastor of the First Church in Providence, I attended his
meetings, and watched his course very closely; for I saw
that a new way of doing things had come over that conservative church, and that I could learn much which
would be of great use to a minister. I read also his book
on ' The Principles and Practices,' &c., which produced
a strong impression on my mind. . . .

"After he consented to give us some instruction, it was
decided that, as our time was so limited, our attention
should be given wholly to the matter of homiletics and
pastoral work. I remember well his first remark to us
at the opening of our brief course. I have never seen it
in any work on homiletics. 'When you have selected
your text, spread your Bible before you, and, kneeling
down, ask God to show you just what the Spirit means
in the words.' That came in his mind before the consultation of commentaries. How many times have I thought
of his direction, given, not to save research in the original,
or hard mental toil, but that a minister's mind might be
brought *en rapport* with the Spirit, and might find the
glow and unction so much needed in preparing for the
pulpit, which nothing but prayer will bring; that he might
experience the insight which a young convert feels when
he first opens the Bible after his conversion, and reads
again familiar passages. No better sentence for the title-
page of a work on sermonizing could be given, than his
opening remark to us on the first Thursday of July, 1860.

"How often he charged us to stick to our text, and to
the exact shade of thought in the text — advice which
has been of incalculable value to me, and has always
provided me with fresh subjects for my people. He had
given me this text, on which to present a plan — ' The
love of Christ constraineth us.' I brought in a plan which
pleased me somewhat, and which he thought would
make a good sermon. He took his Greek Testament,
and looked at the original, and remarked on the word
translated ' constraineth.' ' Brother ——, you could make
a sermon that would be admired from that plan; but you
have no συνέχει in it. Try again, and put in a large
charge of συνέχει.' I did try again, and heard his 'Admirable!' His remark has put the συνέχει into a great
many sermons of mine since, and I have asked myself
again and again, as I have come from the pulpit, ' Did I

aim to have some one *do* something, as well as admire the truth and enjoy its presentation?'

"This leads me to mention another remark of his concerning sermons, which I often think of when I am writing my text. Reading my plan, he would ask, 'Now, ——, what is the precise thing you are aiming at in that sermon? What is *the* thing you wish to accomplish?' I would state it, and then he would go on with his criticism. I think it a remarkable test to apply to a sermon. Is it not true that very many sermons are preached each Sunday in evangelical pulpits that are as aimless as the lives that are lived about us? 'What do you want to accomplish? Are you driving at anything?' he would say. If I have in any degree the power of driving at one thing in a sermon, I owe it to him.

"You cannot conceive how invaluable were his suggestions concerning the pastoral work of the ministry. He had lately been putting his own principles to a practical test as pastor of the First Church, where they had proved themselves to be powerful in upholding God's cause, in converting souls, and in giving him access to men whose hearts had been closed.

"Over and over again he insisted on the value of a personal application of religion to the individual soul. I remember his saying, 'There will be no time when you cannot drop a word for Jesus. In the social gathering of your church, a word in the ear of the sinner will not be lost.' He insisted that it was ever my duty, as a minister of Jesus, to have the souls of my people always before me, and to be ever planning, as well as praying, to bring the truth to bear in the right direction. Always I was to remember that souls were going to hell, and many of them through the neglect of the Lord's people. I cannot forget an illustration which he quoted from a shrewd minister, much to my, as well as his own, amusement. It was to exhibit the character of the minister's work, according to the circumstances under which it is performed. A man sits down to fill a large number of bottles, which are ranged before him on the floor. Taking up a water-pot, he waves it over them; but much more water falls upon the floor than into the narrow mouths of the bottles. Tired of that, he takes a bottle at a time in his hand, and just pours the water in; and soon the bottle is filled, for the water must go in.   So take a sinner, as it were, by the neck, and the truth must go in.   It is not lost.

" ' And then, when you visit them, remember that you are a minister, and that conversation on other topics, *to the exclusion of religion*, is wicked.   Your business is religion, and men, as well as God, expect you to attend to it.'

" When I was settled, it was his intention to preach my ordination sermon ; but he was prevented.   I used to write to him occasionally, though not so often as I wished to ; for his time was so much occupied that it seemed presumption in me to be always asking questions.   I sought to make an application in practical life of the principles he so closely held, and I found them wonderfully powerful in moving men and influencing the churches.   The Association was composed of a number of weak churches, almost too weak to live ; and among them I was accustomed to do much of the work of an evangelist.   I never visited Rhode Island without reporting to him, and spending three or four hours in his study.   I remember calling once when he was busy with some distinguished visitors ; but he would not let me retire, and I apprehend that his guests thought me something more than a simple country minister, from the reception he gave me.

" It may be well to sum up what I consider to be his influence upon my ministerial work.

" First. He led me to feel that the ministerial life which is not saving souls, is, in the view of the gospel, a comparative failure.   In this balance he weighed us all, and it was here that he first began to doubt the faithfulness of the ministry.   He realized, O, how intensely ! the value of the soul, and the danger of its eternal loss.   In August, when I last saw him, I was telling him of a letter which I had just received, informing me of the very sudden death of one of my friends, occurring only one week after the man's conversion, during a visit which had long been contemplated — a visit which had almost persuaded him to delay attention to his soul's salvation until his return. Dr. Wayland's eyes filled with tears, and his voice trembled, as he said, ' O, how near that man came to losing his soul!'   It was this feeling that made his great heart burn with holy indignation as he saw so many of God's ministers engaged in everything besides saving souls.

" Second. I felt the influence of his estimate of the importance of the work of the ministry. I refer to his opinion that the Christian ministry was exalted above every other calling under the sun.

" Third. I have very decidedly sympathized with his views concerning the ministry as a mere profession. Under the influence which I brought away from my repeated conferences with him, I have endeavored to look upon my work, not as a way of getting a living, but as God's way of saving men, and building up his cause.

" Fourth. I have been greatly influenced by him in my preaching. Tempted at times into the use of a word or phrase which I knew that very few of my congregation could understand, I have drawn my pen across it, as I have thought of his remark, ' Say what you mean in language that the commonest mind will not fail to understand.' And as I already remarked, he helped me incalculably by his homiletic instructions.

" Fifth. He gave me new views of a Christian church, and of its duties, which have been of great benefit to me. He longed to see the unused talent of the church brought out, and the inactive members led to duty and earnestness. I have tried to accomplish this, and have been so far favored that in my young church I have a hundred whom I can depend on in a prayer meeting. I have sought, too, to impress each one with the duty of laboring personally for the salvation of others, so that our weekly reports are full of interest, and souls are constantly coming to Jesus.

" A word as to his views of the ministry of the present day. Some have said that he seemed to be growing sour in his old age ; that he was querulous, and in his dotage ; whereas I know that during the five years of my acquaintance with him — which, I hope, it may not be presumption on my part to call an intimate one — he seemed to grow even more tender and more affectionate, to yearn with more depth of piety for the salvation of souls, to sigh with more heartfelt pain over the languishing condition of Zion, and to speak of the Baptist ministry with more and more concern. And his family knew how false the charge that his heart was growing acrid, when every month showed him increasing in love to Christ, and to those whom he loved as his own.

"He had no prejudice against the ministry (why should he have?), and no desire to be a fault-finder or accuser. He did not believe that the ministry was a failure; that all, or that any, utterly failed in the performance of their duty. He was met with the declaration of faithfulness, of devotion, and of the possession of all that he thought wanting in the ministry, from those whose congregations were waning, and whose people were dissatisfied and complaining. He was very forbearing, and went away to pray when some men would have taunted and tried the *argumentum ad hominem*, with an effect that would have closed many mouths that had been loudest in condemnation.

"His views of the ministry, which have excited the most severe comment, may be expressed in one sentence: The ministry of the day is wanting in a passion for the salvation of souls. In details he was at times in error, — I mean in appearing to charge all with neglect, when some felt that they had been peculiarly faithful. But in the general charge — absence of the flame, the fire, the zeal, the συνέχει — he was, alas! too true.

"May God speed the day when all of us shall realize that we build up and edify the church and all believers, when we are on fire for the salvation of souls. Whoever takes this stand-point, will admit all, and more than all, that Dr. Wayland has said of the failure of the ministry in earnestness."

To the same: —

"I am glad you had a pleasant gathering of your parish. I would have them at your house as often as they will come. People like society; it is natural, and they will have it. Society of this kind is innocent, and it binds them together, and may be made an instrument of good. When we had our gathering here, I had a very good and long talk about religion with a person whom I should not have seen elsewhere."

To the same: —

"You write about faith. It is manifest, if we suppose the existence of an all-perfect Creator, and a dependent moral creature, that there must be a feeling required from the creature towards the Creator. This is evident from other cases. You have certain feelings, it may be to a rock, to a brute, to a good or to a bad man, to a relative, a son, &c. So, in the same way, there is a feeling towards the Creator, properly called forth by the exhibition of his perfections. Power in the Creator calls for the feeling of dependence; holiness, for the feeling of awe and adoration; goodness, for that of love and confidence; and, in general, paternal affection calls for the feeling of filial love. Now, this feeling, which is due towards God, in what form soever exhibited, is faith. Sin broke up this feeling, and sinners look upon God without any responsive emotion, unless it be dread. Hence sin is often spoken of as death; that is, a state in which the natural moral causes produce no effect, as ordinary agents that move the living exert no influence on the dead body. And this death is eternal without some power to new-create.

"Repentance is an accidental affection, for sin is an accident not provided for in the original constitution, since that was made for a holy world. It is merely a true sorrow for what is past, and a surrender of the heart to God on the part of one who has rebelled against him. In virtue of the atonement, when a sinner does this, God receives him back again, and puts a new life in him, by virtue of which this responsive emotion begins to act again, and a man is rightly exercised in view of the perfection of God.

"Faith in Christ is a similar feeling towards the Redeemer, God manifest in the flesh. To man, in his fallen state, Christ is a root out of a dry ground; but when the soul is vivified, he is the chief among ten thousand, and every manifestation of his love creates a corresponding action in the soul.

"This all shows the necessity of the work of the Holy Spirit, without which no soul could ever be converted. This agency is taken for granted.

"You see I have here merely sketched out the thought; by reflecting on it you will easily fill it up for yourself. Faith is thus a temper of mind, varying with every attribute of God to which it responds. Hence the variety of ways in which it presents itself. *I am not sure* that God does not always recognize it even in unregenerate men. Samson may have exercised it in a certain way by trusting to the word and promise of God, without any other emotion; so of Rahab and others."

To a minister: —

"There is no reason, that I can see, why it should not be given to Christians to work miracles. Miracles are variations from the ordinary laws of cause and effect. Is not Müller's establishment a miracle? The conversion of a soul is a standing miracle, which nothing but omnipotence can effect. It is God's witness, and will always be, to the end of the world."

To his son, after the election of 1860: —

"Since the evening of the 6th I have breathed more freely. It is plain that the only constitutional party is the Republican. Nothing would be acceptable to the south but our entire submission — that we should become slaves. This we are not yet ready for. It is a question, not of black, but of white slavery."

To a minister: —

"About the day of fasting and prayer [for the country] let me say, I would have it a real day of fasting and prayer, as solemn as I could — as if I really believed in prayer. I would not preach politics, but, looking on this as a day of trouble and danger, would ask God to help us. I would set the people's sins before them, and ask for forgiveness and deliverance; that God would overrule all things for the glory of his holy name, for the spread of the gospel, and the overthrow of oppression; that he would give oppressors better minds, would forgive and bless them, and would unite all our citizens in love of liberty and right. I would not discuss, but honestly strive to lead the people to pray. If I preached in the morning, I would have a prayer meeting in the afternoon. It is a crisis in which nothing will do us so much good as real prayer."

To a minister: —

"Seek for simple reliance on God, and trust him. Was any one that trusted in him ever confounded? Strive to go beneath the mere exegetical view of a text, and realize in your own soul the whole depth of its meaning. The Spirit will grant you this."

To a young man, a relative : —

" As to your being distinguished or great, my dear
——, I have no wish about it. I want you to do your
duty, and the rest I willingly leave. I would rather, immeasurably, have you a God-fearing, honest man, doing
your duty, than have you Choate or Webster. If I could
make you such as either of them by dotting an i or crossing a t, God forbid that I should do it."

To Rev. Dr. Withington : —

" You ask me about Müller and his book. The book
has, I think, many imperfections : cases are set down as
answers to prayer which can as well be accounted for in
other ways ; and some things are published which might
better have been left between God and his own soul. My
son (and I agreed with him) did not feel authorized to do
anything else than condense the book, leaving it to make
precisely the impression which Mr. Müller intended.

" But leaving out these doubtful cases, as we should do
when a new law is to be set forth, there is enough to turn
a thoughtful man's mind in a new direction. The question is simple. We go to God in all special cases, and
ask for, and believe we receive, an answer. Why not in
every case? for we can never tell whether the most trivial
thing may not be special. Or, in general, what is the
relation of Creator and creature, and especially of the creature to God in Christ? Is it not that of a *little* child to
a kind and wise parent? Is not that a model child who
will do nothing without asking the parent's consent, and
confiding itself always to his care? Is not this the type
of the most exalted piety? Is not this the fruit of the indwelling Spirit which the Savior promises? This would
be living as though God were everywhere present, and to
be called upon, not by an outcry like that of the priests
of Baal, but addressed to one so near that he could hear
the faintest whisper."

CHAPTER XI.

DR. WAYLAND'S VIEW OF WAR. — FEELINGS AT THE
OUTBREAK OF THE REBELLION. — TRUST IN GOD. —
THE HAND OF GOD RECOGNIZED. — MEEKNESS INCUL-
CATED. — WEST POINT. — GENÊRAL MITCHELL. —
LOVE, THE UNIVERSAL SOLVENT. — THE ELECTION
OF 1864. — CONDUCT OF ENGLAND. — THE ASSASSI-
NATION. — THE CHARITIES OF THE WAR. — FREED-
MEN. — THE CHRISTIAN COMMISSION.

THE reader of these pages will, perhaps, be interested
in observing the impression made on Dr. Wayland's
mind by the series of unparalleled events which crowded
closely upon each other during the war for Liberty and
Union.

Of war he entertained the opinion which, as we suppose, prevails among the great body of enlightened Christians. He thought it an evil of enormous magnitude,
destructive of wealth, life, happiness, and prejudicial
to morality. He sought to promote the bloodless settlement of all international disputes. He was, for several
years, president of the American Peace Society. We have
already remarked the abhorrence with which he regarded
the invasion of Mexico by the United States.

But he did not look upon war as universally and absolutely wrong. To be enslaved was, in his opinion, worse
than war.

In 1861 he writes to a minister, —

"Your question admits, I think, of an easy solution.
Civil government is an ordinance of God, and its object

is to punish evil-doers, and to protect the innocent. It has authority to do this. The magistrate beareth not the *sword* in vain. The sheriff is the organ of society in the county, and he arrests and hangs evil-doers. He acts, not for himself, but for society ; and has the right and author- ity to summon to his aid the whole community. When the violence is done or intended by a part of a commu- nity, the sheriff cannot act, but the community must act for itself; in other words, it must resist iniquitous force by innocent force, that is, there must be war.

" Such being the case, a Christian may exert himself for the support of a just government. He is called on to do it. He prays for it, and, as in any other case, must act in accordance with his prayers. He cannot ask other men to do for him what he cannot properly do for himself ; and if he neither acts nor encourages others to act, no gov- ernment would stand against wicked men for an hour.

" —— ——, I believe, is going as chaplain to one of the regiments, and I have advised it. Here are men who need the consolations and principles of religion. It is our duty to offer them to both parties alike, and to aid Christian men in resisting the influences of the camp. Religious men may, I think, do great good by going."

Some months before the actual outbreak of hostilities, he wrote to a friend who was deeply interested in the issues at stake, —

" I advise you to make yourself fully acquainted with the principles of military science. A knowledge of these often enables a commander to accomplish his objects with the smallest possible waste of life."

From the firing of the first gun, the struggle, in its vari- ous aspects, took precedence of all else in his thoughts. He found it impossible to read the accounts of battles. They affected him so painfully as to deprive him of sleep. Once, after receiving from a son a letter describing an en- gagement, he kept it, for several days, unread. He could not, he said, endure the thought that one dear to him was exposed to such peril. But there was no such bar to his carrying every issue to God in prayer. He regarded the war as an event in the moral history of man and in the providential government of God, and hence he looked upon it perpetually in its highest relations. He prayed incessantly for the country, for the soldiers, and for the enemies of the republic. He searched the Word of God for promises, for revelations of the divine character, which might strengthen his own faith, and which he might use in pleading with the Hearer of prayer. He perpetually sought, by every form of private and public appeal, to extend and intensify the spirit of supplication. In anticipation of the national day of fasting, September 26, 1861, he prepared, at the request of the executive committee of the American Tract Society at Boston, a tract, appealing to all the disciples of Christ to unite, upon the approaching day, in persevering intercession for the country.

The following extracts from his letters in 1861–5, copied nearly in the order of their dates, require, we imagine, no introduction or explanation : —

To Senator Foster : —

"January 18, 1861.

" . . . It is one of the most wicked things, I fear, that God ever looked upon. It is a legitimate effect of slavery. The prostitution of conscience in one thing leads to its universal prostitution. . . . Well, what is to be done? I dare not pray for any one thing, only that a just and holy God would glorify himself, and deliver the oppressed, and show himself in favor of justice, by giving strength to right and to those who preserve it. In looking for this I have not forgotten you. . . .

" Can it be doubted on which side God will declare himself ? Can we doubt that, if we look to him in faith, he will bring forth judgment unto victory? If you want to see how God looks upon oppression, read the ninety-fifth psalm. I hope all our friends will continue firm, and sacrifice no principle for a present advantage. The best place to meet a difficulty is just where God puts it. If we dodge it, it will come in a worse place. May God grant you wisdom. Look to him, and lean upon him in confidence and earnest faith."

To his son: —

"January 5, 1861.

". . . God is about to bring slavery forever to an end. He has taken it into his own hands, and allowed the 'south to have their own way. They proclaim slavery as a most religious thing, for which they are willing to die. God is taking this way to free us from complicity, and to let them try it by themselves. Greater madness never existed. But 'the Lord is known by the judgment which he executeth; the wicked is snared in the work of his own hands.'"

To the same: —

"January 8, 1861.

"The slavery question is all in a nutshell. 1. No one can establish slavery unless he makes it the law of humanity. This will authorize the intensest oppression, and will justify any man in enslaving any other man; this would destroy society.

"2. No one can affirm that Jesus approved of slavery, unless he affirm that he approved of it as then practised in Rome and elsewhere; how that was we all know.

"3. No one can affirm that Jesus approves of it now (so as to be of any use in the argument), unless he affirms that the Lord approves of it as it now exists in the Southern States, — which would be blasphemy. It is horrible. I wish I could get out my Moral Science. I go into the subject thoroughly. But I must wait the decision of Providence.

"Slavery all falls into fragments before generalization. Just say, 'If this is true, it is universally true,' and see where it will lead you."

To a friend: —

"I have been this afternoon to two flag-raisings; on Wednesday I addressed the troops, and marched with them to the wharf; our flag goes up to-morrow or Monday. Mrs. Wayland cannot sew, but she and I have been making bandages. The state of the country was the theme of every sermon yesterday. At this moment, probably, seven hundred Rhode Island troops are in the presence of the enemy."

To his son : —

" I should be glad to take the journey you speak of, but I fear I cannot meet the expense. I will pay my debts, and then I can decide better. I have been trying to secure a little money, but the sale of my books is very small, and I must have something for my country and her defenders besides my regular charities. I must, therefore, hold the journey in abeyance, until I see my way more clearly."

To a member of Congress : —

" I have thought frequently of you of late, in connection with the subject which agitates every bosom ; and specially do I think of you now, when the destinies of this country, and of the race, are so palpably in the hands of you and your brethren in Congress. It is a time when, if ever, you need the wisdom which Omniscience alone can confer, and which every one of his perfections is pledged to grant us abundantly, if we ask it. . . . Do your duty, my friend, and humbly look to God for the wisdom of his Omniscience and the strength of his Almightiness. Live and think as ever in his sight, and plead his love for our race in becoming incarnate to save sinners.

" Why could not you, and one or two whom you might know, meet in private for prayer? I do not think much of prayer meetings for such objects, in such a place, where it may be for Bunkum, though I would encourage calling upon God in every reasonable and devout form ; but for myself I enjoy such things most with a congenial few in a private chamber, the doors being closed."

To a chaplain in the army : —

" I think of you and your comrades almost constantly. I read the papers but little ; I strive to ask our Father in heaven to overrule all to his glory and the good of mankind, to preserve you from evil, and to bring to confusion all the devices of the adversary. . . . The wrath of man worketh not the righteousness of God. Our Master loved and prayed for those who were murdering him, and committing the greatest crime in the history of our race. Try to imitate him, and to cherish no feeling that would prevent you from praying for those whose wickedness you abhor."

To the same, at the sailing of the Sherman expedition : —

" Your officers are well spoken of. These things give me a little comfort, for God is more likely to use wisdom than folly in the accomplishment of his purposes. But I strive to commend you, and the expedition of which you form a part, to his care. You are safe only in his hands. There I, without ceasing, commit you.

" . . . War is intensely demoralizing. Doing nothing in the intervals of the strongest excitement can hardly continue long without something to occupy the attention. Gambling, licentious conversation, and profanity spring up naturally in such a soil. . . . The grace of God, however, can go anywhere, and can bless the faithful proclamation of the message of salvation to any sinners under any circumstances. When we see the amount of wickedness perpetrated by man in a day, and think of the elements of atrocity in a single sin, and remember the centuries during which this earth has raised to heaven the smoke of awful transgressions of a holy law, how it shows us the magnitude of the atoning sacrifice, which is sufficient to change this whole race, to expel sin from the earth, and to justify God in pardoning the ungodly ! May you be able to present this truth in such a manner that hundreds may receive it, and be rescued from eternal death."

In allusion to the wedding of a relation, he writes, —

" We stay at home for a very vulgar reason. We cannot afford the journey ; we could not go without taking the money from charity, already so small that I think of it with pain. However, the blessed Lord accepts according to that a man hath, and not according to that he hath not."

To a chaplain : —

" I think that you do right in having the communion whenever it can conveniently be arranged. It is of great consequence that Christian men, under such circumstances, should learn to testify publicly for Christ, and that all who are disciples should unite in the service. . . . I would also form Christians into a sort of church, an association, for the purpose of watching over each other, and building up the cause of Christ. I would unite together all who seem to love the Lord Jesus, and they will form the leaven to leaven the whole lump. They will be the more energetic for being thus associated."

To his sister : —

" If we look upon God's dealings, as recorded in the Old Testament, there is great reason to tremble. I do not suppose that Israel did worse things than surrounding nations. Yet they alone knew God's will, and were the more guilty. ' Thee only have I known of all the nations of the earth ; *therefore* I will punish you for your iniquities.' There has been, I think, too much confessing other people's sins, and not enough confessing our own. Slavery is a very wicked thing ; but I know not that it is any worse than idolatry, and shutting God out of his own universe. I do not feel guilty on account of slavery, but I do on account of my forgetfulness of God, and disobedience. He has made use of the slavery question to bring about his judgments. He will chastise and humble us ; and then he will pour out his wrath upon those who, in addition to sins in common with us, must answer for the sin of slavery, and for laying it at the door of the Holy One "

To a chaplain : —

" Let no opportunity escape you to learn and record every fact respecting the condition of the slaves — physically, intellectually, and morally. . . . My impression has been, that a fair and true photograph of slavery, just as it is, would deprive it of the support of all moral and honorable men, to say nothing of Christians. . . . I derived more material for the formation of a judgment on our relations with the south, from Olmsted's volumes than from anything else I ever read. I came deliberately to the conclusion that the opinions and civilization of the south must change, or we must of necessity separate before many years ; but I had no idea that the thing was so nearly upon us.

" May God give us success in bloodless victories, change the minds of our deluded fellow-citizens, and restore peace to our once happy land. And, what is of more consequence than all, may he so order things that his great name may be glorified, and that his perfections may be displayed as never before. It is surely a time in which we may expect God to work. Moral issues of the most signal kind are at stake. His truth and justice, his hatred of sin, of lust, of oppression, of treachery, are all involved in the termination of this struggle. I cannot but hope that he will appear for us in such a way that all may see his hand, and, above all, that his Spirit may be poured upon all our land as never before. This is my only prayer."

"February, 1862.

" The temper of the south in this war has been about as bad as it can be, and in the professors of religion worst of all. If they were hungry, I would feed them; if thirsty, I would give them drink; if sick or in prison, I would visit them; but beyond this, *I eschew them. Selah.*"

To a chaplain : —

" . . . A great step has been taken in the right direction by the abolition of slavery in the District of Columbia. The number of the enslaved was small; but this is a declaration of the sentiments of the north, to go before the whole world. And it will change the character of Congress. . . . Let us thank God and take courage. I believe that he will remember us in mercy, in that we, as a nation, have done and suffered something for disobedience to his commandments. This is all we hope. Almost everything takes place contrary to our calculations."

To his sister : —

"April 9, 1862.

" . . . As to public matters, I have very little to say, except it be to bless God for his repeated appearances in our behalf. I dare hardly read newspapers; in fact, for several years I have not seen the time when I read them so little as now. I am always apprehensive of defeat and slaughter; or, if victory is given to us, the death of men who have made themselves enemies, but to whom I have no feeling of enmity, is sad beyond anything that I can express. I cannot get these things out of my mind, and they prevent me from sleeping. I say, ' Lord, how long? Shall the sword devour forever? Say to the destroying angel, It is enough; put up thy sword into its sheath.' I beseech you pray without ceasing for this beloved country, for friends and enemies; that God would give these latter better minds. . . ."

To a chaplain : —

" . . . But in order to accomplish this, we must be filled with the love of Christ, and strengthened with might by his spirit in the inner man. We must strive earnestly after a deeper, more pervading, spiritual life; we must gain victory over the world in all its forms, and not let it get inside of our hearts. The danger is imminent in your case. The army, and the victories and operations of the army, are liable to enter in and possess the heart, and to drive the Holy Spirit out of it. This danger is increased by the necessary association with men who do not know the grace of God, and by the imperfect opportunities of being alone. God must be *first*, and other things will then assume their proper position. The country may be loved, the army may be loved, but God must be loved before all. These are small things in comparison with the love of Christ, and are really valuable only as they promote the cause for which he took upon him our flesh. What is this whole war good for, but as it prepares the way for the reign of Christ, by removing various forms of evil which oppose his cause? He was manifested to do away with, or overthrow, the works of the devil, and I trust he is thus doing it. If we are carried safely at last through this trial, what glory will God have conferred upon our country ! "

To the same : —

" I have lately seen two colored people from Virginia. They represent that the negroes have very generally been praying for this event, at least for deliverance; and when their children were taken away and sold, they quelled their natural vindictiveness, and left their judgment with the Lord. . . . This forms, in my view, a most important feature in the case. If they are laying aside the weapons of the flesh, and taking hold on the promises and faithfulness of a God of holiness and truth, everything in the book of God teaches us that at some time their prayers must be answered. I know that we are an ungrateful and wicked people; but prayer in faith, without wrath, breathing the breath of forgiveness, waiting solely upon God, never, since the morning of creation, failed of entering the ear of the Lord of Hosts. God will help us, and that right early. Events of every kind, prosperous and adverse, all turn to the same end. God will be glorified, and will rebuke the foul slander which asserts that he is the author of this system, that he loves oppression, and approves of shutting up the Bible from our fellow-men, that we may make them the more profitable beasts of burden. But this destruction of human life weighs on me.

" . . . I do not see how the war could have been averted, except by surrendering ourselves and all we hold dear to the rule of men who have displayed nothing less than the heart of demons. Under such a government as they would establish, we could not have existed. God has called us to this conflict, sad as it is, and I trust and believe he will carry us through it."

To a chaplain : —

" I have great faith in the prayers of the poor, down-trodden Africans, held in bondage, deprived of the privilege of reading the word of salvation, who cry day and night unto him. Fenelon asked a person in affliction, whom he was consoling, to pray for him, adding, ' I have great faith in the prayers of the afflicted.'

" Duty is ours. Success, in just the way he sees best, is God's. He can keep us in safety amid the greatest peril, as he kept you, through mercy, in that disastrous battle. I think of you and look up for you many times in the day."

In the summer of 1862, Dr. Wayland was appointed a member of the Board of Visitors to the West Point Military Academy.

In his reminiscences he writes, —

" I accepted the appointment with some reluctance, for I doubted whether I was able to discharge the duties. I found, on reaching West Point, that the members of the board had delayed their organization until my arrival. They immediately elected me chairman. I could not, under these circumstances, decline the office, although it imposed on me additional duties, especially the labor of writing the report. I discovered, to my surprise, that the mental exertion did not oppress me, but that I was really better for it. Indeed, my health perceptibly improved while I remained at West Point. . . .

"My visit was agreeable in many respects. The gentlemen associated with me were all moral, and a large proportion of them religious, men. I am happy in the belief that nothing was said or done that would tend to set a bad example to the young cadets. There was not a member of the board whom I should not be glad to meet again. Mrs. Wayland and my son were with me for a few days, and this added greatly to the pleasantness of the occasion.

"Some of the visitors were very able men. Of these I cannot forbear to mention the name of Judge Christiancy, of Michigan. I formed very agreeable intimacies with Judge Biddle, Mr. Knox, Dr. Batty, Rev. Dr. Scott, Mr. MacPherson, General Rodgers, and others of the board. We separated with mutual regret; such, indeed, on my own part, as I have rarely experienced after so short an acquaintance. Immediately before our final adjournment we united in prayer. Every member of the board appeared to join fervently and solemnly in this religious service."

That the friendly feelings which Dr. Wayland entertained for his associates were warmly reciprocated, will appear in the following letter from Judge Christiancy, dated November 11, 1865 : —

"I had known President Wayland by reputation for many years prior to 1862. I was familiar with his writings, and esteemed them very highly. But much as I had revered him, I discovered, on personal acquaintance, that I had not half appreciated the excellence of his character.

"Our intercourse at West Point was as free and familiar as if we had been members of the same family. With a powerful and massive intellect, he combined the frank simplicity of a child and the tenderness of a woman. His whole bearing exhibited the transparency of truth, and we felt as much attracted to him by the purity and amiability of his character as by the greatness of his mental powers.

" Although our acquaintance had lasted less than two weeks, I left him with a greater reverence and a warmer attachment than I have ever felt towards any man I have met in the course of my life. No one could be in his company without acquiring higher notions of the dignity of human nature, and its susceptibility of progress and improvement. When I heard of his death, I felt as though I had lost a father."

To his son Dr. Wayland writes, —

" This morning has brought to us the news of the death of General Mitchell — to human appearance an irreparable loss. We must turn to the Lord and be devout, and open not our mouths, because he has done it. General Mitchell's last letter to me breathes the spirit of a Christian soldier. I have had several long talks with him on the subject of religion, and believe him to have been a truly pious man."

To a home missionary, laboring at the south : —

" I imagine that your position is one of peculiar difficulty, one in which you will especially need the presence and direction of the Spirit of all wisdom. Try to keep near to him, and rely, not on your own wisdom, or on that of any one else, but simply and earnestly trust in him. One thing I would suggest : the universal solvent is love. This can melt the hardest hearts. It was this that God used to bring back to himself our lost and ruined race. I would try the effect of this in the position in which you are placed."

To a relative in England : —

" . . . As to public affairs, I try to think of them as little as possible, except to pray that God would deliver us. One of the worst trials we have to bear is the conduct of England. The kind, fraternal feeling that welcomed the prince a few years ago, may have been extravagant, or even childish, but it signified the good will of our people to England, and our respect and love for your queen and her consort. That kind feeling will never again be seen by any man now living. To think of your welcoming Semmes, of the Alabama, who, after fitting himself out in British waters, had done nothing but burn and destroy non-combatants, and had thus put the carrying trade into your hands!"

To C. G. Loring, Esq. : —

"September, 1864.

"As to the coming election, to beat the Copperheads is nothing. They ought to be crushed. We have all the argument, the honesty, the character, the patriotism, and power of appeal to the American heart. God grant us success. All is in his hand, and I look up to him with confidence and hope."

To George Bemis, Esq., Boston : —

"I have re-read with deep interest your article, which you have enlarged from the Advertiser, on our relations with England. I thank you for it in my own behalf and in behalf of our country. I hope that you will, from time to time, give us the results of your investigation and logic upon this great question. It is a source of unmingled joy that our own record is so clear, as you have shown before, and that now it holds that of Great Britain in so disgraceful contrast. It looks as if we should defeat them in diplomacy, as we have defeated their friends, the rebels, in the field. But this is not all. We are making laws for the nation, and establishing the principle, that nations, as well as individuals, must submit to justice. And it is a great thing that we ourselves set the example and hold to the principle.

"It is most astonishing that men who have a reputation and who are supposed to have a character, should be as reckless of dates as you have shown them to be, and of facts, as Mr. Adams has demonstrated. Earl Russell must, with true aristocratic spirit, have relied more on his blood than on facts. If he were not of the house of Bedford, I should suppose that he would be mortified. But the same stigma rests on their most eminent jurists. It looks as if there were a selfish meanness lurking in the national character, which believes in the rights of others only where their cannon cannot reach."

To Senator Foster : —

"March 22, 1865.

"I sympathize with you entirely on the question of retaliation. It is awful to know that our fellow-citizens were starved to death. It is abhorrent to every feeling to visit the same treatment on mere brutes. I hardly know what I should do. But how thoroughly are the southern people doing all in the power of men, or devils, to eradicate from our bosoms every feeling of respect or kindness!"

On the morning of the 15th of April, Dr. Wayland opened his paper, and read, as millions were reading at the same moment, the tidings of the murder of Abraham Lincoln. Late in the afternoon of the same day, a gentleman called, in behalf of the citizens of Providence, to request him to attend and address a public meeting in the evening. Dr. Wayland was compelled to decline this invitation, feeling his strength at that time inadequate to the effort. The committee then said, " Will you address them if they will come to your house." This request he could not refuse. Accordingly, not far from nightfall, a body of citizens, numbering about fifteen hundred, proceeded in order, to the sound of appropriate music, towards his residence. Regardless of the pouring rain, they gathered silently about a platform which had been hastily erected near the corner of the house. Prayer was offered by Dr. Caswell. Then, —

" Dr. Wayland arose to address, for the last time, as it proved, his assembled fellow-citizens. It is the same noble presence which many there had, in years long gone by, gazed upon, with such pride and admiration, from seats in the old chapel. It is the same voice whose eloquence then so inflamed them, and stirred their·young bosoms to such a tumult of passion. The speaker is the same ; but how changed! That hair, playing in the breeze, has been whitened by the snows of seventy winters. That venerable form is pressed by their accumulated weight. The glorious intellectual power that sat upon those features is veiled beneath the softer lines of moral grace and beauty. It is not now the Athenian orator, but one of the old prophets, from whose touched lips flow forth the teachings of inspired wisdom. The dead first claims his thoughts. He recounts most appreciatively his

great services, and dwells with loving eulogy upon his un-
swerving patriotism, and his high civic virtues.   Next the
duties of the living, and the lessons of the hour, occupy
attention.   Then come words of devout thanksgiving, of
holy trust, of sublime faith, uttered as he only ever uttered
them.   They fall upon that waiting assembly like a blessed benediction, assuaging grief, dispelling gloom, and
kindling worship in every bosom.   God is no longer at
a distance, but all around and within them.   They go
away strengthened and comforted." *

To his son : —

"April 18, 1865.

" The event is overwhelming.   The crime is atrocious
beyond expression.   It seems as if God has given over
the south and their friends to work all iniquity with
greediness, and to make themselves an insufferable abhorrence to the civilized world.   The moral sense of mankind rises against them.   They stand without a defence
to meet the condemnation of humanity.

" But I never felt more sure that God has taken all this
work into his own hands.   He has left the rebels to work
out the wickedness of the human heart, intensified by the
practice of slavery.   And he will glorify himself out of
this overwhelming disaster.   The mind of this whole
people, even of the thoughtless and irreligious, has been
brought to acknowledge God, and to believe that he has
done it.   They have never before wept or prayed so much
or so earnestly.

" Is not God thus preparing us for a universal revival
of his work?   He has swept over the whole land in a
few hours, so that all men had but one thought.   Now,
why should not his Holy Spirit, as a rushing mighty
wind, visit the soil thus prepared for his influences?
How would God be glorified, and all heaven rejoice!
Cease not to pray for this.   Urge others to pray for it.

" . . . Let us lay aside all malice and all revenge, and
let us firmly *do justice* to the high as well as the low.
Let the moral principle of this people be strengthened.
God has made us the leading nation in the world.   Let
us act as it becomes us.   Let our example lead other nations in the way of peace and holiness."

---

* Professor Chace's Address.

To Rev. Dr. Hoby:—

"All is now swallowed up in the overwhelming news which, before this letter arrives, will have reached you. For some months past the Almighty Ruler of nations seems to have made bare his arm, and to have moved like a God. Our presidential election was most astounding; in an election among more than twenty millions of people, from the Atlantic to the Pacific, over the whole country, there was not so much *rowdyism* as you have at the election of a single member of Parliament. Such an election, after four years' war, was never heard of; and what is remarkable, the people seemed with one voice to acknowledge it as the work of God. Then came victory after victory. At last Richmond itself was abandoned; and in a week after, Lee, with his army, capitulated. The entire country was in a frenzy of joy; the burden and anxiety of four years were cast off. Then, on Friday, April 14, Lincoln was assassinated, and the nation awoke on Saturday morning to a grief that has rarely, if ever, had a parallel! I have not since seen a smile on the face of a man. Old men in the streets wept like women, and women sobbed at home. All loved him for his kindness, revered him for his patriotism, honored him for his honesty of purpose, and rejoiced in him for his success. He was emphatically the man of the people."

It will readily be believed that Dr. Wayland's whole soul was enlisted in the grand charities which grew out of the war. In the efforts for the elevation of the emancipated negroes he sympathized profoundly; but his benevolence was as wise and discriminating as it was sincere.

To E. L. Pierce, Esq., then at Port Royal, he writes, in 1861,—

"To free the negroes, and pay them wages for their labor, will be hardly a blessing, unless you teach them the responsibilities of freedom. If they begin by having such wages as they never dreamed of, and besides this, have their clothes *given* to them, they will be ruined. They will expect it, and be idle, loafing beggars, without an atom of self-respect. I would not give away a rag except in cases of sickness. I would make every one pay for his shirt, or her petticoat; if not able at once, at any rate by weekly instalments. No one knows how long this war will last; and we shall want so much for real destitution that it is not best to bestow charity in such a way as to render the necessity perennial."

To Rev. S. Peck, D. D., Beaufort, S. C. : —

" I look upon Beaufort District, just now, as one of the most interesting spots on the face of the earth. There, under our own eyes, is going on an experiment which may either confirm, or consign to universal contempt the statements which southerners have made concerning the character and capabilities of the colored people. They have said that the negroes are incapable of being taught, or of taking care of themselves, and are unwilling to work except under the stimulus of the lash, and that efforts to change this character were entirely thrown away.

" Now, if it can be practically shown that they are just like all the rest of Adam's children; willing to work for compensation; capable of taking care of themselves, if they only have an opportunity; as eager to learn as any others who have for years been forbidden to use their brain; willing to give every effort to the acquisition of some little learning, — they will stand forth before the world, calling, with a voice that must be heard, for sympathy and aid from every philanthropist and every Christian. . . .

" You must teach them the responsibilities, as well as the blessings, of freedom. This is absolutely necessary to the success of the experiment. . . . If we pay them fair wages, and begin by giving them clothing and schooling, they will expect it as a part of freedom. It has been found, by the most successful laborers among outcasts in London, that it is of the most questionable benefit ever to *give* to a person who is able to work. The dresses, shoes, &c., are all paid for, and in advance; the poor person paying the price by the day or week, in instalments, as best able to do it, and the account being kept and the article delivered when its price has been received. The prospect of obtaining it at the end of a stated period quickens the disposition to work; thus the labor bears visible fruit, and the

association is at once formed between the sweat of the
brow and the convenience which it brings. All this is
new, and needs to be established in what some philosophers
call the, ' negro mind.' Labor and the rewards of labor
have never before had any connection. I would extend
this to schools, and everything else. Of course moral laws
are not cast iron, or unsusceptible of variation. There
may be sick persons, widows with children, and orphans,
whom God evidently casts upon us for support. A man,
however, with full health and plenty of work, may need
a loan, but never charity. It will be no fair experiment,
and of no value to the south, unless we carry it on upon
sound political principles. I beg you to think of this. I
would let them pay for everything, schooling included ; I
do not say that they should pay the full price at first, but
something, that they may see that all their blessings are
the result of their own labor. Nothing will do more to
elevate them into self-dependent men."

To a chaplain : —

" It seems to me important that the negroes should be
taught to instruct each other. This will spread education
indefinitely, and will give it the habit of spreading. If
you teach twenty men A, B, C, D, you have twenty teachers of these four letters, who can teach them as well as
you can. If each of these teaches ten others, you will
thus teach two hundred, each of whom might be a teacher
in turn. They would thus impress the lesson on their
own minds, and would be proud of their office.

" Of one thing I am pretty sure — that the black people
need, more than anything else, good superintendents, to
keep them at work, and to show them the connection between labor and comforts ; to explain to them that without
work they shall not eat, and that the more they work the
better shall they eat, and the more desirable things there are
in possession or in prospect. We are in danger of relying
too much on book learning. I doubt if any book learning, such as it is possible for them to acquire, would elevate and expand their minds so much as a good superintendent, who would set them steadily at work, show them
the reasons of things, and teach them their duty, *viva
voce*. I think that nothing would make them desire reading so much. . . . I fear the government err egregiously in
supporting them in idleness."

Dr. Wayland was filled with sympathy for those who were exposed to the hardships of war. To a member of one of the regiments stationed on Morris Island he writes, —

"I have thought of you much in respect to the weather, and when it has been unseasonably cool here (the thermometer at 50°), I rejoiced that, although it was unpropitious for us, it was a source of relief to you all on Morris Island. It is a most merciful providence that you are so well, and have been able to endure your unparalleled labors."

To Senator Foster he writes, —

"December 10, 1863.

"This note will be presented to you by Lieutenant-Colonel Palfrey, late of the Massachusetts Volunteers. Colonel Palfrey visits Washington on an errand of mercy, justice, and humanity. He wishes to promote the views of those citizens in this vicinity who desire the organization of a competent ambulance corps. He will explain our views to you. But the thing is at once beyond argument. Our fellow-citizens go into battle in defence of all that we hold dear. The result of battle is death or wounds of the most terrific character. How can we answer it to our own consciences, if we do not provide every alleviation in our power?"

But it was for the souls of those who were exposed to peculiar temptations and in hourly peril of death that he felt most deeply; and accordingly his whole heart was enlisted in the work of the Christian Commission, which sought to promote the bodily comfort and the eternal salvation of the soldier. Mr. Stuart, the noble apostle of this grand charity, writes, —

"During the four years of work of the Christian Commission, I met few men who took such an *intense* and abiding interest in that organization. When I was in Providence, he came to see me repeatedly, with respect to the work in which we were engaged, and expressed, with every evidence of heartfelt sympathy and love, his earnest desire for its success. He presided at our last public meeting in Providence, and also at a meeting held for the organization of a Ladies' Christian Commission. I was deeply impressed with our last conversation, when he said to me, ' I am looking forward to the most glorious revival of religion, at the close of the war, that this country has ever seen. In all efforts to secure it, your Christian Commission work will be largely instrumental. I may not live to see it, but I hope you will.' "

CHAPTER XII.

"HOW TO BE SAVED." — A LAWSUIT. — "LETTERS ON
THE MINISTRY OF THE GOSPEL." — CORRESPONDENCE.
— MEMOIR OF CHALMERS. — NEIGHBORHOOD PRAYER
MEETING. — CORRESPONDENCE.

WE have said that, during the continuance of the war,
the welfare of the country had the first place in the
thoughts and prayers of Dr. Wayland. But he did not
withhold his hand from any duty which the providence
of God seemed to indicate.

He prepared, in 1861, a tract entitled " How to be
Saved," which was published by the American. Tract
Society, Boston, and was widely circulated. A year or
two later, an honored minister, residing at the west,*
wrote to him, —

" I was lately at B., Ill., on a Sabbath, when a man
and his wife were baptized, and united with the Baptist
church. I learned that they owned a farm out upon one
of the prairies, and attended no place of worship, feeling
no interest in religion. Our excellent sister F. gave the
woman a copy of your tract ' How to be Saved,' and it
was blessed of God to the conversion of herself and her
husband. I have heard of many similar cases."

During the years 1861–3, probably for the first time
in his life, Dr. Wayland was involved in a lawsuit. Miss
Eliza Angell, a benevolent Christian lady, residing near
Providence, having no near kindred, had bequeathed
her property to trustees (of whom Dr. Wayland was

---

* The late Rev. L. Porter, D. D.

one), for the erection of two Baptist meeting-houses. The will was contested, and three trials were had before the jury agreed upon a verdict. The needful preparation for these trials, and the attendance upon the daily and protracted sessions of the court, — held at the court-house which has since been indicted by the grand jury for its wretched accommodations and its want of ventilation, — were a severe draught on his time and health. He constantly carried the cause to the throne of grace ; and at the family altar — and no doubt in his secret devotions — he pleaded with God that justice might prevail, and that the humane and pious purpose of a Christian woman might not be frustrated. After the conclusion of the trials, and the overthrow of the will, he writes to his son, " Personally it is a relief to me, but I am sorry to have lost so much valuable time."

He had been gaining in strength ever since the attack of 1860, and found himself gradually becoming able to apply himself to original composition. His mind continued deeply impressed with the need of a revived spirituality and an increased efficiency among the ministry. Fully convinced of the power of the gospel of Christ to regenerate the world, yet seeing that in a country blessed with absolute religious freedom, it failed to produce its legitimate results, he was compelled to believe that there was need of much searching of heart on the part of those charged with the proclamation of the gospel, to learn whether the responsibility lay in any degree at their door. The result of these impressions was his little work, published in 1863, entitled " Letters on the Ministry of the Gospel."

This volume was, by some persons, severely criticised as a distorted picture of the state of religion, and as proceeding from a morbid condition of mind. On the other hand, it was welcomed by Christians of eminent piety and wisdom, members of various denominations, as truthful, and urgently demanded by the aspect of the times.

The work may be open to criticism in some incidental features. When Dr. Wayland believed anything, he believed it fully. When he arrived at a view, or embraced a general truth, he sometimes may have overlooked the exceptional cases and the modifying circumstances. Yet, when all just concessions have been made, as to the incidental and superficial defects of the book, must it not also be said that its excellences are radical, are essential, and that no one can read it, candidly and seriously, without being aroused, quickened, and profited?

In one of the " Letters " he expresses his conviction that he had erred in leaving the work of a pastor for that of an educator. Probably very few persons, and perhaps none of his pupils, would agree in this view; yet it strikingly illustrates his candor and his exalted estimate of the work of the minister. It is certain that no one of his writings was the result of a deeper conviction of duty; never did he less than on this occasion seek to please men, or to confer with flesh and blood.

He writes to Rev. S. Peck, D. D., —

" I wrote the ' Letters ' under a solemn sense of responsibility. I did not dare to do otherwise. I endeavored to say the. truth, and I labored faithfully to avoid giving unnecessary offence. . . . I look back upon my ministry with pain. I tried to preach the truth, but I did not proclaim the whole truth as it is in Jesus. If I should ever be able to enter the ministry again, I hope that I shall preach Christ and him crucified, and nothing else. Is it not true that our orthodox preaching is frequently such that you would not read the sermons on the Sabbath, because not sufficiently religious? Is it not the fact that a sinner might attend many of our churches, and never learn what he must do to be saved? "

We may appropriately quote, at this point, from a letter written in October, 1865, to the St. John's (N. B.) Christian Visitor, by Rev. William L. McKenzie (pastor of the Friendship Street Baptist Church), a much valued friend of Dr. Wayland.

" As I was sitting with him one day, not long since, in
his study, he conversed very freely, with the tears rolling
down his face, concerning the ungracious reception which
had been accorded by the ministry to his honest and earnest attempts to raise the type of piety among his brethren,
and to bring about a more thorough preaching of the
gospel. Never can I forget the tone of amazement and
sadness in which he raised his voice, at the same time
lifting his clasped hands and tearful eyes heavenward, and
exclaimed, ' My God, thou knowest *all* things — thou
knowest I have spoken the *truth* in regard to the condition of religion among us ; but my dear brethren will not
receive it from thy unworthy servant.' Then suddenly
turning to me, with the smile peculiar to him, he said,
' But, my son, we must not expect to be above our Lord.
Perhaps, when I'm in my grave, God will show them that
I was right.' He was charged with painting a gloomy
picture of the present piety and activity of the churches
and the ministry. But they are not few in number, nor
weak in influence, who fully concur with Dr. Wayland in
his view of the condition of the ministry and the churches
in this land. Instead of attempting to deny, or to explain
away the statements of this holy man and devout servant
of God, we had better look facts in the face, and pray
God to roll upon our souls the burden of sorrow which
oppressed the great heart which has now ceased to beat.

" It is true, as it has of late been frequently and emphatically asserted, in order to weaken the force of his statements
respecting the condition of religion in our churches, that
Dr. Wayland had not mingled much in actual life. But
he nevertheless knew all that was going on, far and near.
And his estimate of the degeneracy of this age was formed
in a region of purer air and light than is to be found in
actual life. He was preëminently a *praying* man. He
walked with God. He dwelt under the shadows of the
eternal. throne, and measured human life by the exalted
standard of divine revelation. It was in his habitual and
intimate communings with God in prayer that he opened
his eyes and gazed out upon the field around him, and saw,
with a vision clarified, the real condition and necessities
of that field. It was from the *mount of prayer* that he
looked down into the vale below, and saw the disciples,
destitute of faith and independent of prayer and fasting,

attempting to exorcise demons from human hearts, but ever failing, and bringing into disrepute the power and glory of the religion they *proclaimed* as divine and efficacious.

"I have said that Dr. Wayland was a man of *prayer*. In this service he was as simple as a child. Any one who has heard him pray, can never forget the *pleading* intonations of his voice and the simplicity of his language. His *public* prayers were like those which Christians are wont to offer in the privacy of closet devotions. During the past year he has frequently sent me notes through the post office, requesting me to meet him in his study, for special and mutual supplication at the throne of grace for the descent of the Holy Spirit. To the latest day of life shall I remember that great frame bending at my side, and that *beseeching* voice, and that *importunate* pouring forth, from the depths of his soul, such prayer as he only could frame. How humble, how earnest, how familiar, he was, not only in his study, but when he prayed in public! He *talked* with God. But not one tone of his voice, not one syllable of his supplications, indicated any of that lack of reverence which we sometimes hear from human lips addressing the Majesty of heaven."

The following letters are taken from a considerable body of similar correspondence, called forth by the publication of the "Letters on the Ministry of the Gospel."

From the late Rev. J. H. Kennard, D. D., Philadelphia: —

"I read your letters on 'the Ministry of the Gospel' with the deepest interest. On closing the book, I gave thanks to the adorable Head of the church, that your attention had been called to the subject, and also for the fearless but kind spirit that pervades its pages. The book cannot fail to do good. Our churches and ministers have occasion to consider the whole matter seriously and prayerfully. You do not speak too strongly of the growing departure from the simplicity of New Testament churches and their Christ-like ministers.

"For forty-six years, I have aimed to live and labor in accordance with the views you have so ably presented. I began preaching when very young, and without the advan-

tage of a liberal education. This led me more earnestly to
read the Word of God with prayer, and to depend on the
Master's aid with a child-like faith. I believed that he
would help me, and he has helped me. Allow me con-
fidentially to speak of the last twenty-five years of my
ministry, the period of my labors in the church I now
serve. Our twenty-fifth anniversary occurred in January
of this year, we having been dismissed from the Fourth
Baptist Church in 1838. Our number was one hundred
and sixty-one ; we had little wealth, but there was a mind
to work. A plain house was soon erected, capable of
seating more persons than several recently built at double
the expense. The Lord, from the beginning, prospered
the work of our hands. Revival succeeded revival, to
the praise of his grace, for many years. A narrative read
at our late anniversary showed the following results : —

" ' Our number had increased from one hundred and
sixty-one to twenty-three hundred and seventy-five, of
whom fourteen hundred and fifty have been baptized,
or an average of fifty-eight each year. Five churches
have been successfully established in this city, and twenty
brethren sent forth to preach the gospel, many of whom
are now useful pastors. Your plan of outpost labor and
visitation has been our plan from the first. The five
churches planted grew out of Sabbath schools, accompanied with preaching. We have also had meetings of
the church to revive our spiritual state and labors. The
pastor has a report on the general state of the church.
Other reports follow, on the Sabbath school, on collections for benevolent societies, &c., accompanied by prayer
and praise. To encourage the church to abound in such
labors, I read a few pages of your book, and they were
much pleased with the agreement between your plan and
our practice.' "

Dr. Wayland to Bishop McIlvaine, of Ohio : —

" September 7, 1863.

" I thank you much for your Charge on ' Preaching
Christ.' I have read it twice, and should be reading it
the third time were I not writing to you.* I have read it

* Dr. Wayland circulated the Charge among his friends, and
those who, he thought, would sympathize in its devout sentiments.

with great pleasure, and I hope, spiritual profit. You have succeeded in striking at the very point of divergence from the simplicity of the gospel of Christ, which has led New England, and I fear our whole country, so far from the great truth of God manifest in the flesh. This is really the great effect of Unitarianism and its kindred errors. It has made the Cross, the great work of the Son of God, an offence, and men want to preach so as not to disaffect the rich. It has created a desire among ministers to appear as members of the *élite*, and not subject to such old-fashioned dogmas as *Christ crucified, the only hope of a perishing sinner.* Hence we have *societies*, rather than *churches;* handsome buildings, but few conversions; sermons which might as well be preached in one place as in another; and the truth so disguised by generalities that no one understands it. I unite with you in prayer that God will make your Charge greatly useful; that it may be an arrow that shall reach the heart of every one who shall read it.

"I do not know whether you ever come eastward. If you do, it will give me great pleasure if you will visit me. You and I are both growing old, and I should like very much to see you while we are on this side Jordan."

From Bishop McIlvaine: —

"Reverend and dear Sir: I had no doubt that the views in my Charge would find a most cordial response in your heart and mind. I read your late book on the ministry with great pleasure, and more especially because it points out evils and departures from the 'old paths,' which I have long marked with great pain. The impression of sad decline in the real preaching of the gospel as identical with the person and work of our Lord Jesus, within the

---

He sent a copy to an eminent layman of a Congregational church in Boston (Abner Kingman, Esq.), who was so impressed with the value of its teachings, that he caused to be printed and circulated four or five thousand copies. Is it not thus, by Episcopal prelate, and Baptist minister, and Congregational layman, uniting to spread the knowledge of Christ crucified, that the prayer of our Redeemer is fulfilled, "that they all may be one, as thou, Father, art in me, and I in thee, that they also may be one in us"?

last thirty years, has long been a burden on my mind.
When the ' truth as it is in Jesus' is substantially preached,
there is so often a dress put on it, robes of philosophy,
trappings of man's speculation, language studiously as far
from the simplicity of the Scriptures as possible, that one
gets the impression that the preacher is rather a lecturer
on Christian abstractions, a sort of baptized philosopher,
than a follower of St. Paul, a seeker of souls for Christ,
a sower of seed taken from the Scriptures. Sensational
preaching, the overwrought inculcation that ministers
must be intellectual according to the demands of an intellectual age, all fostering the ambition of men to be thought
wise, and learned, and great, rather than simple teachers
and preachers of Jesus Christ, have perverted and effemi-
nated much of the work of the pulpit in our time.

" Be assured, dear sir, that, should I be in Providence,
it will give me sincere pleasure to visit you. As you say,
we are both nearing the end of our work and of our days
on earth. We are closing our pilgrimage in awful times,
and most affecting as concerns our country. One would
like, if God please, to live to see this wicked rebellion put
down, and peace and union restored. But we must leave
such things with God. It is sweet to think of being so
near the rest, and holiness, and glorious communion of
the people of God in their everlasting home, and in the
immediate vision of Christ. May grace be given us to
become more and more meet for that inheritance."

A Presbyterian clergyman presented a copy of the
"Letters" to each member of the graduating class at
Princeton ; and a layman of the same denomination (Hon.
William E. Dodge, of New York) sent one to each mem-
ber of the Auburn and the Union Theological Seminaries,
accompanied by the following letter : —

" NEW YORK, September, 1863.

"My young Friend : In presenting you with a copy of
' The Letters of President Wayland on the Ministry of the
Gospel,' let me request you to read and carefully ponder
each letter, and prayerfully ask yourself if you have properly considered the importance of the work you have
undertaken. I have felt for years the need of just such a

book as this. I fear that many enter the ministry who have little idea that the great object is to rescue souls from hell by leading them to Christ.

"Each Letter is full of valuable suggestions; but let me call your especial attention to the sixth, 'On the Manner of Preaching,' each part of which I commend to your careful consideration.

"I might suggest, that while I approve of all the author says about extemporaneous speaking, yet a carefully written sermon once a week might be best for a few years; but if you would reach the hearts of your hearers, they must feel that your own heart is so full of the love of Christ that you can tell them of it without a written manuscript.

"For many years I have made the subject of the *voice* and *manner* of public speakers one of especial interest, and have been pained to see how little attention has been given to it in our theological seminaries. Many of our students come out good scholars, can write well, are fervent in spirit, and are anxious to be useful; but having neglected the cultivation of the voice and the manner of delivery, they enter upon their work sadly deficient in grace and ease of action, and in well-developed, clear intonations; and for lack of these they never attain any considerable standing as preachers, and much of what they have acquired avails but little, for want of ability to present it with attractiveness.

"When a youth, I resided in a New England village, where there was no place for evening meetings but a school-room, in which we held frequent meetings, and enjoyed several revivals. At times we would have, perhaps, a Methodist preacher with but little theological education, but good natural talents, and a fine, full, clear voice, who, without notes, would deliver a plain gospel sermon fresh from the heart, and secure the attention of all present; and I was often ashamed at the contrast when one of our young men from New Haven or Andover would come along to preach, and I would have to take a bandbox and cover it with a towel, and place it on the table with candles, that he might read off his sermon, generally to a sleepy and inattentive audience.

"I hold it to be the duty of every man, who is preparing to deliver God's message to dying sinners, to see to it that in tone and manner it be done in the best way to secure attention.

" A person intending to make public singing a profession will study for years to cultivate the voice, to give it strength and volume, so that, if necessary, he can interest the largest audiences. Let me beg of you to consider the vast importance of a full, clear, pleasant voice, properly modulated, and without any unpleasant tone. A beautiful piece of music, performed upon a harsh, discordant instrument, loses all its effect.

" The man who becomes confined to his notes can never make an attractive speaker. The times demand an easy, off-hand style of address.

"'Don't wait until you can enter the pulpit before you learn to speak, but in the prayer meeting and Sunday school acquire an easy, familiar style of public address. If you would give the trumpet a certain sound, you must learn to use it.

" May God bless you, and prepare you for turning many to righteousness, is the earnest prayer of
Your friend,
WILLIAM E. DODGE."

During the winter of 1863-4, wishing to neglect no opportunity for religious usefulness that lay within the limit of his physical powers, Dr. Wayland taught a class in the Sabbath school of the colored church on Meeting Street, near his residence.

Shortly after the publication of the volume last alluded to, Dr. Wayland chanced to open the Life of Chalmers, which he had not read for several years; and becoming interested in it, he re-read it throughout. He was profoundly impressed with the fact that the life of this eminent servant of God presented a striking example of the earnestness and devotion which he had himself endeavored to awaken in his Christian brethren. Believing that an exhibition of his distinctively Christian and evangelical labor could not but be useful, he prepared for publication " A Memoir of the Christian Labors, pastoral and philanthropic, of Thomas Chalmers." The volume is, of course, drawn mainly from the large standard work of Dr. Hanna. It is not, however, an abridgment, but is made up by selecting, arranging, and, in some cases, condensing the portions which exhibit a single aspect of the life and character of Chalmers. This work was published in 1864.

If we are not mistaken, there is a striking resemblance between the character of Dr. Wayland and that of Chalmers. In power of commanding an audience, and of inspiring his hearers with his own enthusiasm, the Scotch divine stands alone. But in profound earnestness, and in consecration of large intellectual endowments to the unselfish promotion of simple Christianity, they were clearly akin. We apprehend, also, that Dr. Wayland sympathized deeply with the feelings of Chalmers, as thus delineated on pages 192, 193 of the Memoir : —

"With all his social cheerfulness and beaming joy, there were tokens not a few of an internal conflict — glimpses of an inward desolation — which told, unmistakably, that, like David, he felt himself to be a stranger on this earth. 'I would not live always' was a sentence which he often uttered. 'What a wilderness this world is to the heart, with all it has to inspire happiness! I am more conversant with principles than with persons. I begin to suspect that the intensity of my own pursuits has isolated me from living men, and that there is a want of that amalgamation which cements the companionships and closer brotherhoods that obtain in society. I have a great and growing sense of desolation.' These are perhaps the feelings which arise, in advanced life, from the necessity of the case, and belong to a mind of originality and independence, oppressed with that sense of responsibility which withdraws instinctively from all ambiguous or useless associations."

During the winter of 1864–5, Dr. Wayland invited his neighbors to unite with him, each Friday evening, in a prayer meeting at his house. His design was to promote the spiritual good of those who found it difficult to attend the evening meetings of the various churches, and also to engage his neighbors in prayer in behalf of the suffering and imperilled country. These meetings, which were often attended by thirty or forty persons, he conducted with his wonted, or even more than his wonted simplicity, tenderness, and devotion. One who was often present says, " Sometimes, as he sat with his eyes closed, his hands clasped, and the Bible open before him, while the words of eternal life were flowing from his lips, we knew something of the feelings of Peter, when on the Mount he said, ' It is good to be here.'" Many persons, who were not accustomed to frequent prayer meetings, attended these from personal regard for him. The young, even, won by his kindness and sincerity of manner, longed for Friday evening to arrive. Professors of religion who had lost the ardor of their piety were revived, and impressions were made upon the careless that proved a permanent blessing. Nor was the influence limited to those who were actually present. Months after Dr. Wayland's voice had ceased to be heard among men, a candidate for admission to a church in the city, relating her religious experience, said, —

" I was living in the neighborhood of Dr. Wayland, and he invited me to come and attend the prayer meeting held at his house. I did not want to go, and did not mean to ; but I told him that I would come, and should be glad to do so. I did not go, however. Some time afterwards, he asked me again if I would not come ; and again I told him that I would, but still without meaning to attend. As I thought of it afterwards, it made me feel wretchedly to think that I had *lied* to *Dr. Wayland*, and the more I thought of it, the more ashamed I felt ; and I had no rest until I sought from God the pardon of that and of all my other sins."

In January, 1865, Dr. Wayland published in the "American Presbyterian and Theological Review" an article suggested by the celebrated letter of John Foster on the Duration of Future Punishment ; and in the July number of the same Quarterly, an article on " the Ministry of Brainerd."

We quote from his letters written in 1861–5.

To Mrs. O'Brien : —

"1861.

"... Has God ever been unfaithful to you, even in a single instance? Then why should you ever distrust him? You speak of assurance. Why, what is the ground of assurance? Is it not the temper of our heart, the bias of our desires? Do you not want, above all things, to be holy? Do you not want to be like Christ? Does anything give you joy like the light of his countenance? Does anything torment you like sin? Who has wrought this in you? Man, yourself, Satan, or God? You know that these are the gifts of the Holy Spirit. You say your faith is weak, and that you have many imperfections. You will have them, as all others do on this side of Jordan. But take just such a soul, with just such desires, and tell me, was it ever lost? You think much about death. Is not this a conquered foe? I talked lately with a departing saint, who said, 'God has dying grace, which he gives only to the dying.' You have it not now, but you will when you need it. Why should we not trust Christ in advance?"

To Dr. James Jackson : —

"1862.

"I should have answered your letter immediately, but I had not a copy of my photograph in the house. I was able to procure one this morning, and I enclose it immediately. It is, I think, the best I have had taken, though much inferior to yours. This, however, is as it should be.

"In your letter you refer to the doctrine of original sin. I am not going into an argument, for you cannot dislike controversy more than I do. Permit me, however, to say that, in my view, the Scriptures fully teach the doctrine of the universal sinfulness of man. As to the mode in which the race became sinful, I am not sure that they teach us. It may be accounted for, or, in other words, referred to a general law, in either of two ways. It may be by hereditary descent. Much, both of good and of evil, comes to us in this way. Or, again, it may be owing to the entrance of such a being as an infant into a sinful world, at enmity with God. He would inevitably take the type of character which existed universally around

him. The general law is, that much which we suffer, or
enjoy, comes to us through those with whom we have no
direct connection. You and I both know how much our
probation has been rendered favorable by good parents.
The contrary, also, we see every day. This law is necessary to our present state, or our race would be at a perpetual stand-still. I hope I make myself intelligible; but I
do not know. My impression is, that the Bible deals with
the fact, and this may be accounted for in either of these
ways, or perhaps in others.

"May God, my dear friend, lead us into all necessary
truth, and prepare us for his heavenly glory. To me, the
plan of salvation made known in the New Testament
seems evidently one of the ideas of God. Man did not
frame it.

"I forgot to say how much I am obliged by your sun
picture. I have given it an appropriate place in our al-
bum. It faces that of Florence Nightingale."

To a minister : —

"I will merely turn your attention to John viii., from
the twelfth verse, and also John x. Has it ever occurred
to you that nothing more sublime can be conceived than
when that poor barefooted Jewish peasant stood on our
earth and declared, "I am the light of the world; whosoever believeth in me shall not walk in darkness, but shall
have the light of life"? He declares that whatever he
does is done by God ; that, like Him who appeared to Moses, he is the "I am," and that none shall pluck out of his
hand those that believe in him ; that he is the only way of
access to the eternal God. What overpowering and astonishing words ! a little too good and important for ministers to use as a theme for an essay, and people to hear
for an intellectual diversion. O my Savior, has it come
to this, that the message thou didst bring from heaven
should be used as an instrument for building up a reputation among men ! May God forgive us."

To Mr. Loring : —

" . . . I have read Mill on "Liberty" once, and had re-
read the first half the second time, when I was taken sick.
It is a strong book, and by an able thinker. Most of his
points are good, though I think that they might have been

stated more simply. His treatment of the rights of the individual might have been better by setting out with the simple principle, ' Every one has a right to himself,' and, of course, to all the legitimate use of himself, that is, of all his powers. As this belongs to every one, it excludes interference. His style is not easily understood, at least by stupid fellows like me. He does not believe in the Christian religion, as I do, but apparently thinks it of human origin; nor does he set forth the fundamental principle of its morality. He seems to consider absolute obedience to God as slavery. But such obedience is evidently necessary to the condition of a creature ignorant of the future. In my opinion he exaggerates the obedience to custom, and the want of independence in man; at least, I do not find it as he states it, in my own consciousness. Men do not commonly long hold to a custom, unless they find it, by practice, to be convenient. You wear pantaloons not simply because every one else does. I presume you remember when your father wore small-clothes. I know mine did. The reason of the change is, that pantaloons have proved more comfortable and convenient."

To his son : —

" I have read Herbert Spencer through, and some of the essays twice, and have read his volume on education. . . . His book will do much to change the opinions of the civilized world. I hope it will be widely read here and in England. . . . As to the worth of knowledge, he is very strong. Here, he and I are aiming at the same thing. I did not expect to see, in my day, any one with whose views I could so sincerely sympathize. . . . He speaks to the common sense of humanity, and hates sham; and he will triumph, though it will take some time first. The ruts are deep, the crust is old and strong, and a generation will pass away before a change comes. However, it will come. Democracy must prevail, but can be a blessing only by the intellectual and moral education of the people. This education must be a reality, and must not consist in spending years in hammering on Horace and Virgil, and Græca Majora. Revelation may follow revelation, each coming nearer to the truth, until the benevolence of the gospel makes every one the helper of his brother; and then democracy will stand."

To his son, — after alluding to the sudden death of his friend, Rev. Henry Jackson, D. D. : —

"March 10, 1863.

" My summons may be as sudden. When I am called to leave you, live in love ; seek each other's best interests ; bear with each other's infirmities, and strive to present each other faultless before the throne. Let each esteem the other better than himself. Live so as to please God. Think the same things. Contend lovingly for the faith once delivered to the saints."

To a former pupil : —

" . . . Is it wise to take so much upon one's self? After doing the things that you mentioned, what time is there left for things of at least as great importance? I have thought of this of late, frequently, in connection with you. You know that the word failed to bring forth fruit on some soil, being choked with the cares of the world and the deceitfulness of riches. You will say, I have no time to attend to my soul's concerns. But what was your time given for? If God gives it to you, and you use it for something else, on what principle can you say, I have no time? He gave you time for this very purpose."

To his son : —

" Have you ever seen the hymn commencing, ' I worship thee, sweet Will of God,' in the Plymouth Collection? I think it will be useful to you. I admire it very much."

The hymn referred to is from the Lyra Catholica.

> I worship thee, sweet Will of God,
>   And all thy ways adore ;
> And every day I live, I long
>   To love thee more and more.
>
> Man's weakness, waiting upon God,
>   Its end can never miss ;
> For men on earth no work can do
>   More angel-like than this.
>
> He always wins who sides with God ;
>   To him no chance is lost ;
> God's will is sweetest to him when
>   It triumphs at his cost.

Ill that God blesses is our good,
  And unblessed good is ill;
And all is right that seems most wrong,
  If it be his dear will.

When obstacles and trials seem
  Like prison walls to be,
I do the little I can do,
  And leave the rest to thee.

I have no cares, O blessed Will,
  For all my cares are thine;
I live in triumph, Lord, for thou
  Hast made thy triumphs mine.

In writing to his sister, Dr. Wayland alludes to the hymn just quoted, and says, —

"I cannot yet say that I have attained; but this is the spirit after which I am striving, and towards which I hope that I make some feeble approach."

To Hon. L. H. Morgan, Rochester: —

"Dear Sir: I have just completed reading, for the second or third time, your 'League of the Iroquois.' I cannot forbear the pleasure of thanking you for it. It is the most remarkable book of the kind I have ever seen. The plan of social organization is original, unlike any other I have ever known of, and exhibits a power of statesmanship such as I do not remember to have seen equalled. It was a great man who devised it, a most powerful man who persuaded men to adopt it at first, and a most self-governed and sagacious people who received it. And then their religion was the purest and best theism that men unblessed with revelation have ever arrived at. Their dresses show a refinement of taste such as a barbarous people almost never attain. It is in all respects, to me, a most surprising book, and ought to be in every public library in the world. Men ought to know that such a race as this has lived."

To Professor W. D. Atkinson: —

"I thank you for your discourse on the schools of Great Britain. I have read it with much interest. The lessons which it suggests are of great importance, but I fear they will not be heeded as they deserve. Your motto is significant — *Mutato nomine, de te fabula narratur.* We, I apprehend, are following in the same course. It is now supposed that the only way to build up a college is, not to teach well what it is important to teach, and thus make the success of an institution depend on the skill and power of the instructors, but to collect money, to found scholarships, and endow professorships, and thus make the teachers wholly independent of their own labor. . . . In this country public opinion may discover a corrective, but what it is I know not. I thank you for placing before us the facts in the case."

To Rev. Dr. Hoby : —

". . . I have had some sad, very sad, hours and days : there was no refuge but GOD. A train of thought like this has given me consolation — God is omniscient! He knows everything about us, and is able to do everything for us. He is all love — such love that he gave his Son for us. He is as faithful to his promises as he is full of love and power. I know that nothing can happen to me that has not been appointed by the perfect will of a God of love. And more than this, he has promised that he will receive as his child every one who comes to CHRIST. Have I thus come? Do I now take him for my Savior? Do I long for holiness more than for anything else? Are the marks of a child of God upon me? I try myself — I must believe that Christ has given me new life, and that I am a child of God. All the promises are mine, and our God has never, through eternity, been unfaithful to his word. He will do all, and more than all, that he has promised. All things will therefore work together for my good — pains as much as pleasures, sickness as well as health. On these things I try to rely, and when I find my faith failing, I cry in anguish, Lord, increase my faith.

" I have lately read the Bible more than ever in my life, in the same space of time, and at every new reading I find more to love and admire. O, how much have I lost by not reading it more! I have reason to bless God for setting me apart, on a side bench, at school, alone, to read his Word and call upon his name. Sometimes I think how much better I might have lived, how much more good I might have done, if, eschewing everything but Christ, I had lived above the world, and laid myself a living sacrifice on his altar.

"It is a great comfort to me to know that 'The Life of Judson' has been a blessing to you. There is no labor which we perform that yields so delightful a result, as that undertaken to promote the cause of Christ, and do good to the souls of men."

To a clergyman : —

"I received a letter, some days since, from Mr. T., with a prospectus of the new monthly magazine [Hours at Home] which he proposes soon to issue, and to which he asks me to become a contributor. He mentions you as one of the stated contributors. It is not in my power now to engage in the undertaking; but it seems to me to be a matter of great importance. The social literature of this country is almost wholly in the hands of those whose religious opinions are entirely dissimilar to ours : the best are merely neutral on those points which we esteem of vital importance, and the others tend to a position at variance with the doctrines which we hold dear. It seems to be time to establish something which shall be popular and useful, and which shall maintain boldly, on all suitable occasions, the doctrines of the cross. I believe it can be done. Let us engage in it with our whole thought. We are liable to let the truth become obscured or forgotten by our silence. I am for uniting good men of all denominations in the effort."

CHAPTER XIII.

HIS HOME. — THE MORNING HOUR. — THE GARDEN. —
THE STUDY. — THE TABLE. — VISITORS. — THE YOUNG.
— THE DAY CLOSED. — THE SABBATH. — THE HOUSE
OF GOD.

AT no time had the life of Dr. Wayland been diversified by startling adventure, or marked by sudden inspirations. One day greatly resembled its fellow. But during the latter portion of his life, his employment of time afforded a better index to his character than when his occupations were closely prescribed by his external circumstances and his official duties.

The hour before breakfast was always given to secret prayer and reading the Scriptures. During this hour he read the Bible for devotion, not at all for criticism. He highly estimated the value of communion with God before the mind has become pre-occupied or distracted with other thoughts. From his study he came, when summoned, to lead in domestic devotions, which were invariably brief, never tedious.

Breakfast over, he was ready for exercise. He seemed to take as much pains to provide himself with physical labor as many persons to avoid it. He sometimes walked; but this did not fully satisfy him. It was scarcely active enough; and moreover he wanted his work to have a result, to show what had been done. In the winter he shovelled the snow from the walks, if there was opportunity. If this could not be done, he continued his practice of sawing and splitting wood. There seemed something of heroism in his victories over the gnarliest logs; and beyond the tamer toils of the axe and saw, he valued the conquests won by the beetle and wedges.

But joyful was the season when he could lay aside the saw, and could take the spade and rake. Gardening was to him what pictures, statuary, travel are to another. He loved his garden, because it afforded him exercise diversified in character; because it was a productive form of labor, and because it combined thought with toil. He was never weary of working in it, of walking through it, of talking about it. He seemed to establish personal relations with all his plants. He would go out many times a day to visit them, as a fond parent would visit the chamber of a sick child. " I think that my garden knows me," he sometimes said; and it seemed as if every tree and shrub would put forth peculiar efforts, and at his instance would do what no one else could prevail on them to achieve. His tenderness was like the love of woman. Once, when the house was building, it was found that a cherry tree, then in full blossom, must be moved. He had it taken up with every care, and transplanted. He watched over it, watered it, sheltered it, and it lived for perhaps a year, though its constitution never recovered from the shock. He was training a grape vine by the porch, and a branch, about which he was very hopeful, had become cracked in the effort to give it a symmetrical curve. He at once made a sort of splint of sponge, and wound it around, and kept it moist for days, coming out from his study every hour or two to watch it.

He was keenly alive to his honor as a gardener. In the following, to Mr. F., of New Haven, he expressed the pleasure he felt at a compliment from a professional horticulturist: —

" I thank you for the line by Mr. H. I showed him all my plantation. He gave me a fair character as a gardener, with which I was much pleased. He is a rare man. I admire him exceedingly."

He did not like to be surpassed. When he was out-stripped by those who could afford the luxury of a green-house, he was not perturbed, for that, he said, was capital. But he would not willingly be inferior to any who had only the advantages of sun and air, common to all. In gardening, as in all else, nothing satisfied him but perfection. Nothing was done so long as anything remained to be done. Wishing to gather wisdom from past experience, he kept, during the latter portion of his life, and after he felt that he could spare time for the employment, a garden diary. Some extracts, embracing a few weeks in the spring of 1863, will give an idea of its character : —

"*March* 22. Commenced labor in the garden. Sowed peas in A. 1, east of asparagus bed. Hoed spinach.

" 27, 28, 30. Scraped and washed trees. At the south end of the bed, sowed Tom Thumb peas. At the north end, early Philadelphia, for seed, if they prove good. The rest are Daniel O'Rourke.

"*April* 1. Prepared hot-bed.

" 2. Planted elm tree on Governor Street.

" 6. Sowed celery and lettuce in hot-bed. Planted elm tree at end of the lot.

" 8. Prepared another hot-bed.

" 10. Planted early June potatoes, put salt in three rows, lime in the others, with manure over all; salt in three western rows.

" 11. Buckeye potatoes treated as above, two rows east salt, others lime.

" 13. Uncovered rose-bushes and raspberries; sowed onions and some beets. Weather at night cold.

" 14. Warm and pleasant day. Treated raspberries with vegetable manure made from refuse rubbish of the last year. Planted more onions.

" 15. Finished raspberries.

" 16. Rained incessantly and violently all day.

" 17. Set out cauliflowers and lettuce from Mr. Nesbit. Warm and pleasant.

" 20. Hoed and raked strawberries — not hoed, but loosened with the hoe. Weather cold and cloudy.

" 21. Sowed Champion of England peas.

" 22. Planted white apple potatoes. Cold last night; white frost. Gathered spinach for the first time. Treated potatoes with lime.

" 23. Raked the grass on plats.

" 24. Rain.

" 25. Rain, cold and dreary. Set out in the hot-bed plants from Mrs. Sprague.

" 27. Raked borders. Cut spinach; it is growing well.

" 28. Sowed carrots on upper border. Planted early beans and cotton seed. Raked borders. Loosened the ground round early peas. Weather warm and sunny. Strawberries show buds.

" *May* 1. Warm and pleasant. Asparagus begins to appear. Early potatoes are breaking ground.

" 2. Very warm. Grafted Easter Beurre and St. Michael's, the former with the Glout Morceau, the latter with Belle Lucrative and Rostezer. Planted melons. Cut about half a pound of asparagus.

" 4. Rained almost all day. No work done, excepting the setting out of Silesia and California lettuce.

" 7. Rain continues. Easterly wind and cold. Nothing done in garden. There is fear lest the seed sown some days since may rot in the ground. Blossoms do not advance.

" 8. Planted pole beans. Continued spading. Cherry blossoms begin to appear.

" 9. Sowed parsnips and carrots. Set out tomatoes. Spinach gone. Cherries begin to bloom. Gooseberries in full bloom. Some blossoms on strawberries. Onions and beets, the first planted, are up.

" 10. This and the two preceding days warm and pleasant. To-day cherries in bloom. Cut two and a half pounds of asparagus. Hoed peas. Planted melons. Finished spading upper side of C. 1. Sowed mignonette."

In writing to his friends, with whom he had any horticultural affiliations, he would always ask and give the news of the garden; thus, " Strawberries will be ripe in a few days; peas are well formed, but do not yet fill. Nothing else deserves notice but the gooseberries, which thrive finely." " Beans picked to-day, beets in a day or two; strawberries fail since the dry weather." And again, " I

must acknowledge that you beat us in Hubbard squashes."
He always delighted in the exercise of reciprocity among
the craft, in giving and receiving plants.

We know not whether the cause was material or spiritual, but somehow, when he could not walk without fatigue,
he could be on his feet in the garden, working from breakfast until two o'clock, and was not conscious of weariness.
It was truly wonderful to see him, almost up to his latest
summer, toiling under the sun of July, his hair drenched
in perspiration, distancing his sons, and exhibiting hardly
any falling away from the vigor of forty years.

His labor was not devoted to the useful merely. Perhaps he loved the beautiful quite as truly. He was exceedingly fond of flowers. Of a Wisteria in full bloom
he said, "It is the prettiest thing in town." Especially
he liked to combine beauty with use, to train his pear trees
and grape vines in graceful lines, and to cultivate fruit
that was fair to the eye as well as pleasing to the taste.

Self-control seemed to be powerless when he went into
the garden. Here alone he did not keep his resolution.
He often went out intending to stay only a few minutes;
but, fascinated by the spell of nature, he would expand the
minutes to hours. Sometimes Mrs. Wayland would urge
him to relinquish his toils, and he would promise to work
only half an hour more; but one moment led to another,
until some imperative call summoned him to the house.

During one year only was his garden neglected. In the
spring of 1858, he was so engrossed with gathering in
sheaves from the Master's fields, that his grounds had
little care. He writes in July, "I was so much engaged
with the church that I put the garden off on the man, and
nothing has prospered. Everything in gardening depends
on the work in spring. If this is badly done, it is difficult
to repair the damage."

The morning did not often pass away without the cows
receiving a moment's attention. For horses he did not

profess admiration, nor had he any thorough knowledge
of them ; but cows he understood and loved.   He had
studied the theory of Guenon, and knew the points of a
good cow.   He was much amused, and probably not at
all displeased, when a stranger, who was proposing to exhibit some fat cattle or extraordinary stock in Providence,
called to ask him for a line of commendation in behalf of
his exhibition.   He urged that "everybody told him that
Dr. Wayland knew more about stock than anybody else
in town."

When the work of the garden was over, he bathed, and
soon was dressed for the remainder of the day.   He then
spent a little while in prayer in his chamber ; and at this
time he would lay before God any event affecting the
household, any unusual care or embarrassment.   If a servant were needed, he did not fail to tell Him who watches
the fall of the sparrow, and he would say, "We must wait
and see what God will do for us."   He *believed in prayer*.
He believed that God is a rewarder of them that diligently
seek him.   In one of his last years, when a young friend
asked him, "Can you always feel, when you pray, that
prayer is a reality?" he said, "Almost always I can ; and
the older I grow, the more fully I am convinced that it is
a real thing to ask God for blessings, and to receive them
in answer to prayer."

Then, if the morning were not already past, he went
to his study.   The view from this room is not marked.
Its attractions were within.   Upon the walls were two
portraits of Napoleon, one as at Milan, in command of the
army of Italy, and the other, as at Fontainebleau, on the
eve of his abdication.   Separated from these by a window,
was Wellington.   Elsewhere were Dr. Nott, and Sir Robert Peel, and Dr. J. M. Mason, and Humboldt in his study,
and Algernon Sidney, and Cromwell, the Protector, conversing with Milton, the secretary of the commonwealth.
On two sides were books ; and on the study table were

those in most constant use. Chief of these was the Greek Testament. Of late years he used Bagster's edition, on account of the distinctness of the type ; but he found many misprints, and one page of the fly-leaf is covered with his errata. Robinson's invaluable Lexicon was ever beside him. He did not greatly affect commentators, but relied rather on prolonged meditation and on prayer for divine illumination. When a gentleman, about commencing a Bible class, asked him, " What is the best commentary ? " he replied, " Your own eyes, first of all." The annotated Paragraph Bible of the Religious Tract Society he valued extremely, for its brief notes and its full references. Of exposition, he most enjoyed Dr. Brown on I. Peter, preferring him even to Leighton, his early favorite. Of the English Bible his reading was mainly in a very plain, leather-covered quarto, which he had procured in 1824. With each year he seemed to spend more and more time in reading the Scriptures. No sense of duty urged him ; in the wisdom imparted, and the hopes revealed, he found a perpetual reward. Can his children ever forget, how, entering the study, they would find him in the rocking-chair, opposite the door, with his Bible open on his knee, and his eyes filled with a strange liquid light, and how, becoming conscious of earth, not without an effort and a perceptible lapse of time, bringing from heaven its gentle benignity, he would put his spectacles back upon his forehead, and, leaving his silk handkerchief as a mark in the Bible, would say, " Well, my son ? " and then would flow forth the utterings of affection, of experience, of human counsel, and of divine wisdom, but all spontaneous, all natural, never preceptive.

On the table was the long, narrow note-book, in which he made minutes of the trains of thought that he wished to follow out. Sometimes he worked on a subject ; not seldom a subject came to him, and he put down his spontaneous thoughts, to be used hereafter.

Thus the hours passed until dinner. He was usually an " honest eater," despising with all his heart an epicure, or gourmand, yet enjoying without disguise the blessings of Providence, particularly the fruit of his own labor. Scarcely less keen was his gratification when some product, redolent of the forest or the deep, or of the garden or orchard, served as a token of the remembrance of valued and perhaps distant friends. Thus he writes, —

"Yesterday a box of prairie chickens arrived, all in excellent order. To-day we invited a pair of them to dine with us, and they discharged their duty admirably. ——, who is here, pronounced them first rate. I thank you for your kindness. We shall be all the while wishing that you were with us."

And again, after an arrival from Florida, in 1863, —

"The box of oranges reached us, as you had foretold. We thank you very much. They are thinner-skinned than is usual, and are the most juicy I ever saw. They substantiate what you say — that we need not go out of the United States for oranges, or indeed for any tropical fruit. Besides being delicious, they are in remarkable preservation."

His readiness to be pleased with any well-meant kindness was always touching.

It is probable that, in his later years, from 1860, he erred on the side of undue abstemiousness. It seemed to escape his attention that an attack, like that which he had experienced, might result either from too high living or from too intense labor, and that the treatment, in cases so widely diverse, must needs be as different as are the two sources of the disease. He dieted, as if his attack was the result of excessive indulgence, and allowed himself by no means (in our opinion) the nourishment needed for his great frame and his protracted physical exercise — drawing upon his will to supply the needed energy.

After dinner there was often some public business to transact, or meeting to attend. If not thus called from his home, he spent the afternoon in reading, or in writing letters. After 1860 he confined his severe mental exertions to the forenoon.

His reading, during the most laborious portion of his life, especially during the later years of his presidency, had been very limited, embracing few books that were not directly in the line of his duties, or required for immediate use. He had, however, always read the leading reviews, particularly the English quarterlies, with regularity, and had thus " kept himself abreast of society." And his singular faculty of wise questioning, his power of extracting from others the result of their studies or experiences, made him well informed on many subjects that were apparently out of his line.

During his temporary pastorate, as we have seen, he relinquished all secular reading. He did not, of course, think this the duty of every minister, nor of himself under ordinary circumstances. He felt that the demands upon him were for the time so pressing that all his spiritual and mental energies must be turned into a single channel. But after he was released from official care, he read more, probably, than he had ever done since he entered public life. His intellectual sympathies were almost as broad as his moral. He read universally, in all departments.

Few days passed without some visitor, perhaps one of his old friends, — with every year growing fewer, — or one of his former colleagues in instruction, or a colaborer in benevolent enterprises. Not unfrequently one of his younger brethren in the ministry, always welcomed, came to tell him of the progress of the work of God, or to ask his counsel. Or perhaps some stranger, visiting Providence, would have a desire to see the ex-president, and the author of the Moral Science.

With many visitors, strangers till then, he enjoyed delightful interviews, conversing upon the great interests of the world, and the brighter glories of immortality. In

July, 1861, Dr. Tobey called with Mr. John Hodgkin, an eminent English barrister, and a leading member of the Society of Friends. Mr. Hodgkin had declined high station under the British government that he might engage in a religious mission to America and other countries. He had a long and deeply interesting conversation with Dr. Wayland; and their views of the spirituality of worship, and the duty of alienation from the world, were remarkably coincident. After leaving him, Mr. Hodgkin said, " That man has a *bruised brain*." Perhaps no words could more justly express the results of the violent strain to which Dr. Wayland had long subjected his mental powers.

On the following day Dr. Wayland met Mr. Hodgkin again, and they enjoyed a further delightful conversation. Not long before leaving town, Mr. Hodgkin said, " I must see Dr. Wayland once more." He went to the house, and found him in the study, alone and at leisure. After conversing a little while, they " fell into silence." Presently the spirit of prayer being given, Mr. Hodgkin knelt, and at once Dr. Wayland knelt beside him. Mr. Hodgkin offered a touching petition for the advancement of religion, for the welfare of the church of God, and especially for the aged disciple at his side. Tears were flowing from the eyes of each. Then Dr. Wayland prayed, asking peculiar blessing for Mr. Hodgkin; and then they separated, with the most tender Christian feeling, after Dr. Wayland had given to Mr. Hodgkin a letter of commendation to Christians in America, of all denominations.

From Mr. Hodgkin to Dr. Tobey : —

"August, 1866.

" . . . How peculiarly does he live in my memory and in my heart ! There was a grandeur, and yet a simplicity, about him that were almost apostolical. Rarely have I known a man in whom intellectual power and culture were so harmoniously combined with love, and faith, and every Christian grace. It was, moreover, a very unusual

feature in one who had ruled and taught with chief
authority more than a quarter of a century, that he was
so totally devoid of all approach to dogmatism, either in
thought, expression, or manner. Instead of laying down
the law, he conferred, and reasoned, as one who sought
to learn; and he held communion with those who were
his inferiors, as showing that he and they sat at one
table, where all are brethren, and where one is our
Master even our omnipotent yet all-gracious Lord and
Redeemer."

Often he received visits from some of his young friends,
whom he had guided to the Savior. When perplexed in
questions of duty, they came and confided all to him. He
was often enabled to remove clouds, and doubts, and anxious cares. To one who was much troubled with the fear
that she had assumed too great responsibility in the advice she had given to another, he said, —

"Did you ever see a person rolling tenpins, who, after
he has rolled a ball, and while it is on its way, will sway
his body and twist himself about, as if to influence the
movements of the ball? But it all does no good. You
are doing just so. But you acted in the fear of God.
You have rolled your ball; now, dismiss it from your
mind."

Sometimes religious inquirers would visit him, either
brought by their Christian friends, or urged by their own
feelings. He was remarkable for the simple directness,
mingled with tenderness, with which he relieved them
from all embarrassment. He would see, as by intuition,
the errand which had brought them; and, "Well, my
child, you have come to talk with me about religion —
have you not?" he would say. In removing obstacles
from their pathway, he was, as he has hitherto said,
greatly aided by the remembrance of his own religious
experience.

It was wonderful to see how the youngest and most
timid found themselves able to talk without constraint
with one who had often been regarded as the embodi-

ment of all that was stern and awe-inspiring. While charged with the discipline of the college, and compelled almost always to stand in antagonism to something or somebody, he could not venture to exhibit the tenderness which was in his heart. Nor was the change merely in his aspect; but as he grew older, and drew nearer to the world of love, he was perpetually more gentle, more considerate, more patient, more ready to bear with everything, in the hope of being useful. Once in his later years, while he was visiting a friend for a few days, and had to see a good many rather commonplace people, a member of his family, when alone with him, said, "This must be very tiresome to you." He replied, " I am very willing to do it. Seeing people in this way is a means of doing good."

The thought of awakening a sensation of fear seemed painful to him. When one, who had known him very well, brought with her a young friend who knew him only by name, he walked with them a portion of the way home, and at parting said to his new acquaintance, " Now, I am not so very terrible — am I?" A lady, brought up in sentiments opposed to the evangelical belief, was invited by a friend to attend his Bible class. She says, —

" I continued to go for many weeks, and I more and more wanted to talk with him; but I did not venture to. At last I went to him one day after the class, and asked him if I might call and see him. He was exceedingly kind, and urged me to come. I went a great many times. It was very hard for me to understand about the doctrines of religion. I had never had any idea of such a thing as a change of heart. I could not believe in the atonement; and I told him so. I could not say that I saw, until I was more than sure that I did see. He was unwearied in his patience. I said to him once, that I at first believed that his kindness would wear out, when he found how slow I was in believing as he did, and that he would show his severer side. He laughed, and said, ' Well, S——, you haven't seen it yet — have you?'"

His parental care of the young disciples, for whom he had been interested, never ceased. Meeting one of them on the street, he said, "Who was that I saw you walking with the other day?" She replied, "That was Miss ——." He asked, "Is she a Christian?" "O, yes." "That is right," he said: "you know, if you put one coal of fire out on the hearth by itself, it soon goes out; but if you put a good many together, they keep each other warm."

He was walking by the High School, when he met a young girl, a pupil, who was on her way home. He asked her about her studies, and presently said, "When are you going to be a Christian?" She answered, "I ought to be now; I hope I shall be some time." He replied, "I am sure that you will be. I am praying for you." These simple, tender words could not be forgotten. His prayers were not in vain.

Persons sometimes wondered that he, with his broad experience, lofty ideas, and severe sense of duty, should awaken such confidence and attachment in the young, the ignorant, the impulsive, the often erratic, and that he should be able to make so large allowance for them, and to bear with them so patiently. It was owing, in part, to the unaffected benevolence of his nature, to which nothing of human interest could be indifferent; in part to his universal power of sympathy; and in part to the clearness of all his conceptions and the simplicity of his teachings. His singular power to attract the young, and to elevate them, in some degree, to his own spiritual level, was not the only feature in which he resembled the Man of Nazareth. It was not by humoring them that he won their regard. Rather he held them most rigidly to the one standard — the perfect law. Says one of his young friends, —

"I would tell him of some fondly-cherished ambition. He would listen patiently to the close, and then say, 'Well, my child, you have given yourself to the service of the Lord. Would the cultivation of this talent, the gratification of this taste, help you to serve him better? Would it tend to his glory? If you are sincere in your Christian profession, you must carefully consider, and abide by the decision.' He never would consent to a compromise. There were only two paths — one right, and one wrong. There must be a choice between the two. He believed that a Christian had no right to call anything his own. If he had truly given himself to the Lord, he could not say, 'Here, Lord, this proportion of my time, or wealth, or energies, shall be devoted to your service, and the rest shall be devoted to my own use.' And yet, the religion that he inculcated never seemed to me gloomy. Often he taught me self-sacrifice, which it was hard to make; but then he made the service appear so sweet and sacred, that the burden was taken away in the thought of the dear Savior for whom it was performed.

"Once when he asked me how I was employing my time, I told him of one of my occupations, at which a strange expression appeared in his face. I inquired, 'Do you not think it right?' I told him that it was with my mother's approval. He said, 'Then it is all right; but it seems trifling, when life is so short, and there is so much to be done.'"

He did not shrink from reproving; but as affection attended the motive' of the reproof, so it governed its spirit.

The following letters illustrate the tone of his intercourse with his young friends, some of whom had been converted under his ministry, others of whom had been pupils in his Bible class.

"My dear —— : . . . The best of all, however, is what you tell me of yourself. You have done something for Christ, and he has rewarded you with his richest blessing, by giving you more grace. You must have acquired more government over yourself. You have learned to *swim* in the place of *drifting*. Go on in this strength, my dear ——, and he will aid you abundantly. . . .

"Seek for consistency of character; that is, let the love of Christ *rule* in your heart, and that will accomplish

what I recommend. If the love of Christ does not rule,
but only shares with other things your best affections, your
likes and dislikes, your character will not be consistent.
Never think, 'How far may I go? I will obey just up to
the line,' as though you were a slave; but as a dear
daughter, act from love, and think, not, How far may I go
in the course of worldly pleasure without forfeiting my
Christian hope; but, What can I do, or from what can I
refrain, that will most please the Savior who died for me,
who loved me, and whom I love. You know from experience that this is the happy way of living, and that we
do not surrender anything for Christ without receiving
abundantly from him. The reward for sacrifices for
Christ is, you know, a hundred fold. Form your character on the highest and most noble principles, and you
will be the loveliest —— in the world."

"... Your letter deeply interested me, and made me
wish you could be here in my study for an hour or two, to
talk over the things which concern our spiritual interests.
How many hours we have spent in such happy conference, gaining strength to resist the world and to follow in
the steps of the blessed Savior! I know it is pleasant to
you, and, am sure it is to me, to remember those interviews,
and to recall the hour when, at last giving up all the world,
you surrendered your heart to the Savior, and felt in your
own soul that he had received you, that he loved you, and
had given you a new heart. And then remember the day
of your baptism — that bright and beautiful morning in
May, when you publicly took Christ for your Savior, when
you died to the world, and rose again to a new life, and on
the evening of that day, for the first time, partook of the
memorial of that body which was broken and the blood
that was shed for you. It is sweet to recall those days.
Has the world ever yielded you anything so satisfying, so
delightful in the recollection?

"Dear ——, I fear that you have changed somewhat from
the 'little girl' of those days. I fear that worldly pleasure,
and amusement, and society, have taken possession of a
portion of your heart, and that it has become divided.
The struggle is now going on between Christ and the
world; and for some time past the world has gained
strength, and the love of Christ has grown weaker. Is it

not so, my dear child? But if it be so, you have made a poor exchange, and you feel it to be so. You long for the days when the candle of the Lord shone round about you, and when by his light you walked through darkness. If you have wandered from him, he has not cast you off; he still loves you; he still hears your feeblest cry for his presence, and is waiting to fold you again in his arms. Look back and see when, and where, and how, it was that you began to forsake his path, and resolve to return to him. Think how he followed you when you were determined to have nothing to do with him. He is grieved that you should cherish anything in comparison with him; and yet he loves you, and pleads with you to be reconciled to him.

"My dear ——, if I loved you less, I should not have written thus. But my time is short: soon I must give up my account, and it would be very wrong if I did not seek first of all your best good. You will know how to understand it."

"My dear ——: It gives me great pleasure to learn that you have marked out a path of duty for yourself, and are becoming decided to walk in it, and thus to be a consistent Christian. The Savior calls us to take up the cross, and follow him, denying ourselves. Sometimes the cross is in one shape, and sometimes in another. It may be in the form of persecution. Parents may persecute, brothers and sisters may be unkind, the world may sneer, imprisonment may threaten, nay, life may be in danger, for doing the will of Christ. Or the cross may take another form. The opera may open its doors, company may invite, balls and parties may induce, dress may attract, ease may beckon, intellectual vanity may whisper, — all tending to withdraw us from simple obedience to the commands of Christ. Pleasures sought for themselves appeal powerfully to the young, and do not allow them time to reflect that the pleasures which God has prepared are all blooming on both sides of the path of duty. My dear ——, remember that if we deny ourselves, and take up the cross for Christ, one form is as pleasing to him as another. It may be as hard a thing for a young person to bear the reproach of being too precise, as it was in old times to be whipped or imprisoned; and the blessing of the Savior rests on one as much as the other."

"My dear ——: ... But what you say of yourself deeply interests me. You look upon yourself very much as I do. I have thought and told you that there seemed to me undeveloped powers of doing good in you, and that you would not be very happy until they were called into exercise. You are surrounded by the kindest of parents and friends, and seeing and loving them takes up all your time. You have not object enough to call forth and strengthen your energies. You need some active pursuit in which you can *labor* to do good. You are in danger of getting into a miscellaneous life; this is unprofitable. You say you love teaching. That is a beautiful and useful talent. God gave it to you for something: see that something comes out of it. Do not drizzle away your time. You tell me that you would like to go to the *west*. Do you not fix your eyes there because there is no prospect of your being wanted here? The world is round, and it is all west. You say that there are some ten or twelve young persons around you who ought to be taught. Begin and teach them. If this be a seed which God plants, he will water it; and who knows how large a tree it may become!"

When visitors called, if the weather was suitable, he often took them into the garden; using, like his Master and example, nature as a means of leading the soul to God and heaven. Many of his young friends, who were pupils at Mr. Buel's school, will remember the afternoon when, after he had shown them all that the garden contained, clothing its commonest features with attractiveness by the love he bore it, there was spread before them a table crowned with his own melons and grapes.

It was not easy to say whether he took more delight in the labor of cultivating his garden, or in bestowing its products upon others. When he heard that visitors had been at the house during his absence, "Did you take them into the garden," he would ask, "and give them some fruit and flowers?" Once, when he asked, "Did you give them some pears?" and received the reply that there were none in the house, and that there was hardly time to take the visitors into the garden, "You should have a plate of them always at hand," he said. "We do not realize how persons value these things, when they cannot raise them for themselves."

By five o'clock he usually went out again for exercise, walking or working in the garden. But walking became wearisome to him in time.

After tea he often sat a little while in the parlor with the family, conversing, or reading a magazine for a few minutes, or looking over some volumes of humorous sketches by Leech, extracted from Punch, in which he found great amusement. But after a few minutes, he would seem to hear the call of duty, and would return to his study.

He received many letters from persons quite unknown to him, often persons in remote places, propounding questions of conscience, of church discipline, of moral science, and of Christian doctrine.

How lovingly he wrote to his kindred, particularly when any anniversary awakened affectionate remembrances, or when their circumstances, temporal or spiritual, called for a word of cheer or of wisdom, need not be told to any one who has read the preceding pages.

Of his tenderness to the members of his immediate family, to his wife, to his children, we know not how to attempt any description. Perhaps in no instance was it more marked than in his relations to his youngest son, an invalid for many years. It might with truth be said that "whatever touched him touched the apple of the father's eye." As this son was rarely absent from his home but few letters were addressed to him. From those which have been found, we make the following extracts: —

"1852.

"I write to you the first letter with the pretty pen and handle which you gave me. I am much obliged to you for it, my dear boy, and shall think of my little son very frequently when I am using it. I hope that you may have a great many birthdays, and that you may grow every year wiser and better.

"... We thought frequently of you, my dear son, yesterday, and remembered that it was your birthday. We wished we could have been with you, and have made a little party for you. You are now in your thirteenth year, and getting to be a large boy. We hope that God will restore your health, and especially that he will give you a new heart, and make you a religious boy."

"1858.

"... I am rejoiced to hear of your good health and happiness during your visit. I hope you will return much stronger than you were when you went away. Nothing is growing much, and you will see but little change on your return. The cold rain keeps everything stationary. I hope, my dear son, you are improving in piety, as well as in health. All these changes are trials of our religion, which always gains strength with every effort to do right and to keep ourselves in the love of God."

He writes to the same: —

"The chapter of events in your department is as follows: —

"1. Jerry [the horse] is as well as usual.

"2. Ned [the terrier] has killed several rats; the last time, three in one morning.

"3. The top-knot pullet is dead.

"4. Eggs to-day, four; yesterday, six.

"5. Two mice caught in the trap this morning; one small, the other very large.

"I do not remember anything else of consequence."

Sometimes the little family circle was enlarged by the presence of relatives, always welcome to his home. At Thanksgiving, 1860, his family was united. His three sons were present, one just returned after a year's absence from the country, and with them the wives of his two older sons, whom he had taken to his heart, making them, not only daughters-in-law, but daughters in love. And in the third generation he saw his children's children, and peace upon Israel. His intercourse with them did not, indeed, afford any confirmation of the popular belief, that grand-parents are the ruin of children. Yet with what a wise affection he was endowed, the little grandson will not forget, who, while attending school for a short time at Providence, was wont to bring home his cards marked " Good boy," or "Excellent," and to receive from a drawer in the study-table a welcome reward if the report was favorable, and to meet a grave, grieved look if no approving testimonial was at hand; and who, at a later day, used to sob himself to sleep at the thought that he should never see his grandfather again.

On the Thanksgiving of which we speak, Dr. Wayland was in unusual spirits. He was recovering slowly from the attack of the spring. He had received an enforced release from toil. The country had just declared for liberty by the first election of Lincoln; nor did any one anticipate the madness that would take occasion from the election to reveal itself.

He was cheerful, even mirthful, keenly enjoying the humor of others, and contributing his share to the common hilarity.

Persons who knew the earnestness of his mind, and the grave character of his pursuits, often supposed him to be wanting in a sense of humor. We learn from Rev. Dr. Hoby, that while Mrs. Emily C. Judson was in England, on her return from Burmah, allusion having been made to Dr. Wayland as a suitable biographer of Dr. Judson, she expressed her entire satisfaction in all but a single respect. She feared that Dr. Wayland would not appreciate the lighter aspects of Dr. Judson's character — his refined sense of the ludicrous, his keen wit. Never was there a greater mistake. His humor was not, indeed, trifling and flippant. It was earnest and practical, like all his faculties. But his appreciation of wit in others was quick, and his drollery was often irresistible. It gleamed in his conversation, sometimes in his letters; not often in his public discourses or printed works.

Sometimes he went, at the call of affection, to visit his kindred in Boston, or one of his sons in New Haven or Worcester, or his sisters in Saratoga. As a guest he was the most easily entertained of mortals. In fact he did not want to be entertained at all. Nothing could be too simple for him, nothing too quiet. He made allowances for everything; the youngest, the most inexperienced housekeeper need not fear him. He would not permit any of the ordinary engagements of life to be neglected on account of his presence.

The few visits which he made he enjoyed keenly. He was exceedingly appreciative of the kindness shown him on such occasions, and added immeasurably to the pleasure of his hosts by his readiness to be pleased. After visiting a friend and former pupil, he writes, —

" We both enjoyed ourselves extremely, and are quite invigorated. My mind, old as it is, is quickened by your conversation ; and your constant kindness has brightened the links which bind me to humanity. It will be long before your home and its surroundings grow dim in my recollection. It is all delightful to think of, as it was more delightful to enjoy."

A member of a family, at whose hospitable house he was an occasional and welcome visitor, says, —

" I often used to walk with him, and ever found him a delightful companion. I think he never failed to talk to me about religion, but it was always naturally. He was very sportive, but his mirth was never such that religious conversation was out of consonance with it."

No doubt it would have been greatly to his advantage if he had allowed himself more frequent journeys and visits, in which his mind might be removed for a time from its accustomed employments, and become quickened by contact with differing yet sympathetic spirits. But he had no faculty for relaxation.

To Mr. Loring he writes, in 1864, —

" . . . Through life I have had no recreation. I do not know how to *amuse* myself; and it has been one of my greatest misfortunes. I suffer from it to-day, and have all my life. By the way, were you not astonished at Chalmers' two or three hours a day of labor, and the mighty results he accomplished? Should we not all learn a leaf out of his book? I am satisfied that with us we keep the brain too long at work at a time. I think this, and too little sleep, and no recreation, lead to softening of the brain."

Almost the only thing he could not do was to amuse himself. It was only when he bade his mind rest, that it disobeyed him. Once, on his return from a journey which he had enjoyed very much, but which had been less extended than was expected, he said that, after being away from home and from his work a little while, he seemed to hear a voice say, " What doest thou here, Elijah?" and he felt that he must hasten home, and be doing something. It was strange that he did not apply to himself the lesson which he taught to others. In " Salvation by Christ" (sermon upon " A day in the life of Jesus of Nazareth ") he has said, —

" The religion of Christ is merciful, and ever consistent in its demands. It requires of us all labor and self-sacrifice ; but to these it affixes a limit. It never commands us to ruin our health and enfeeble our minds by unnatural exhaustion. It teaches us to obey the laws of our physical constitution, and to prepare ourselves for the labors of to-morrow by the judiciously conducted labors of to-day. . . . We sometimes meet with the industrious, self-denying servant of Christ in feeble health and with an exhausted nature, bemoaning his condition and condemning himself because he can accomplish no more, while so much yet remains to be done. To such a one we may safely present the example of the blessed Savior. When the apostles had toiled to the utmost of their strength, — although the harvest was great and the laborers few, — he did not urge upon them additional labor, nor tell them that, because there was so much to be done, they must never cease from doing. No; he tells them to turn aside and rest for a while. . . . The Savior addresses the same language to us now. When we are worn down in his service, he would have us rest, not for the sake of self-indulgence, but that we may be the better prepared for future effort."

He by no means ignored, nor under-estimated, the need of relaxation for ministers, and for all persons, although it must be confessed that he did not highly value the amount of reinvigoration, bodily, mental, or spiritual, that is gained at fashionable watering-places and European capitals. He wrote to a minister who was setting out on a pedestrian excursion to the White Hills, —

"I think highly of your 'tour to the Hebrides.' It will add greatly to the vigor of your constitution. Begin slowly, and walk only ten or fifteen miles the first day, gradually increasing the distance. It will do more for you than much more extended travel in the ordinary manner. Try and have some sort of good to do on the way. This will add interest and profit to the excursion."

And again to the same: —

"I hope that you have returned with increased health. I advise you to go on these expeditions as often as you can get company. You will gain more in every way than in a railroad car, and will confirm your health and extend and intensify your love of nature greatly. You will also see much more of mankind. I would stay at private houses as often as possible."

But we have wandered from the story of a day. At about nine he rejoined the family in the parlor. After prayers were his own devotions, and those who occupied the room above the study heard his voice last at night, as it had been the first sound in the morning. Through the greater part of his life he had worked till far into the night; but in later years, convinced of his need of more sleep, he always went to bed at ten. Unless his mind had become absorbed in some subject or event of unusual interest, he slept soundly, or if, for a moment, aroused, was soon again asleep.

The Sabbath presented features less marked than would have been the case had not the employments of each secular day been so largely spiritual. He was not legal in his spirit, and did not constrain himself, nor others, by rigid Sabbatical rules. His life was the expression of duty, modified by the spirit of Christian liberty. It was from love, it was for his pleasure, that he spent the day in exercises of devotion. He read nothing but the Scriptures, and books tending directly to spirituality. The religious newspapers and periodicals (except the Herald and Magazine) he did not read on the Sabbath. In his manner, in his conversation, as he came from his study on that day, there was a calm seriousness, not a sadness, as of one who had been looking on eternal realities.

In the house of God he longed for simplicity, for sincerity, first of all; for life, fire, zeal; for the truths of the Scriptures, urged in the spirit of the Scriptures, and enforced by the words of the Scriptures. He was habitually charitable in his judgments, and this charity seemed to grow more pervading as he advanced in years. But if there was any instance in which he approached the verge of harshness, it was in his estimate of sermons that had in them no power to save or sanctify the soul; that were made up of cold, formal, and fruitless exhibitions of doctrine, however orthodox, of brilliant rhetoric, metaphysics, political economy, or kindred material. But when the *truth* was presented with warmth, with earnestness, with an evident desire for the salvation and edification of the hearer, he was satisfied and gratified, however homely the garb. We quote again from Mr. McKenzie's Christian Visitor: —

" Coming down the aisle of my church one day, after closing the services, I met him with his hand extended;

and without letting go of my hand, he drew me to his side in a pew, and said, — ' My son' (thus he was in the habit of addressing me), — ' my son, I have been pained and grieved with your preaching here to-day. It has been evident to my mind that you have been pleased and proud over your finely-wrought and finished discourse. Those sermons were, as sermons, very creditable to your ability as a preacher, but very discreditable to you as an ambassador of Christ. There was too much learning and too little of Christ in them. Go home, my son, and burn them up, and on your knees weep over your delinquency.' All this was said with a tenderness and affection which put to silence any disposition to rebel under the stroke which my proud ambition had received. On another occasion he said, ' My son, you preached the gospel to-day, and may God bless you. You did me good. I feel that I am a poor hell-deserving sinner, but that Jesus Christ is my Savior. When a preacher makes me feel thus, I know he is proclaiming the truth, and that God is with him.' "

CHAPTER XIV.

HUMANITY. — FOREIGN MISSIONS. — HOME MISSIONS. —
SLAVERY. — INDIVIDUAL EFFORT. — TEMPERANCE. —
THE " SOCIAL EVIL." — EAST TENNESSEE. — THE SYRI-
AN CHRISTIANS. — PROVIDENCE AID SOCIETY. — BUT-
LER HOSPITAL FOR THE INSANE. — RHODE ISLAND
HOSPITAL. — PROVIDENCE REFORM SCHOOL. — RHODE
ISLAND STATE PRISON. — EMPLOYMENT OF MONEY. —
PRIVATE BENEFACTIONS.

THE reader of the preceding pages does not need to be
informed that, as the love of God was the controlling motive of the life we have sought to delineate, so
its great aim was to manifest the fruits of that love by
deeds of unselfish benevolence to man.

Dr. Wayland's private kindness, and his public labors;
his patient watchfulness over the young, and his toils in
the pulpit and in the pastoral office; his efforts for the
enlargement and liberalization of high education, and for
an increase in the numbers and in the efficiency of the
ministry, — were simply the expression of his desire for
the elevation and happiness of humanity.

Believing, as he did, that the gospel of Christ contains
a remedy for every human woe, it was natural that he
should desire to see mankind enlightened by its teachings
and informed by its spirit; and hence his devotion to the
cause of Christian missions. His opinions upon the true
method of conducting missions are indicated in the Memoir of Judson, in his report on " the relative proportion of time that should be devoted by missionaries to

teaching, translating, and other occupations, apart from preaching the gospel," presented in 1854 to the Missionary Union, and republished by the A. B. C. F. M., and in the following extracts from letters.

To Rev. Dr. Anderson, who was about to visit the Eastern missions of the American Board: —

" I have just received your letter, and answer it immediately, for I presume your time is short, and you want the points before you as soon as possible.

" The general movement of Christianity has been this. It begins among the poor. Persecution keeps it there, and makes every man a minister, or preacher, or exhorter, or propagandist. Thus it spreads, and nothing can withstand it. Soon it silences persecution, and is then ashamed at finding itself among the poor and middling classes. It aspires to take its place among the rich, wise, learned, and worldly. This leads to the casting pearls before swine ; that is, a surrender of principle to expediency, which is the meaning of that much abused passage. Hence results the doctrine that a man must be learned in order to be a minister. This separating the ministry from the people leads to the distinction of clergy from laity, and ends, in its last result, in Puseyism and Romanism, and, in various forms, to the sanctity of the office, and the idea of a quasi or real priesthood. Arrived at this point, the church stands still, becomes one with the world, and dies out in formalism, until some new development breaks forth and pursues the same course. In this country, Congregationalism and Presbyterianism advocated a learned ministry. They did not increase, except by hereditary succession. The Baptists began on the other principle, and overran the country in spite of all opposition. The Methodists followed, and did the same thing. They both now are aiming at a learned ministry, and they are standing still, except in new parts of the country, where these ideas do not prevail.

" The same is true among missionaries. In this country and in India, the whole effort is to dress up Jesus Christ so that we may not be ashamed of him when we meet him in respectable society. But he will not be so introduced. He still cleaves to his old friends, the publicans and sinners; and if we will not meet him in such company, he turns away from us. I have, of course, no objection to education in the ministry; but I object to giving it a place not authorized by Jesus Christ, and making it a *sine qua non;* thus establishing a ministerial caste. I think that these ideas lie deeper than has been commonly believed. Look at the example of Jesus Christ. He took the lowest place, and so long as his disciples kept there, the cause of Christianity prospered. He put the ploughshare in the lowest stratum, and kept the point down. We raise the point, and it flies out of the ground; then it moves very easily, and the horses caper off with it; but it turns up no soil; the ground bears no fruit; and, plough over as much as we will, it is all barren as the plain of Sodom. But I did not mean to make an allegory; I only suggest this for you to think of. It concerns your mission; and were I going on such an errand, I should like to have every suggestion, even were it but of the smallest value."

To the same: —

" I rejoice that you are succeeding so well with your debt. I thought that the Jubilee would lift you over. Let us thank God and take courage.

" In reading your last Missionary Herald, I was somewhat impressed with the thought that you are relying too much on intellectual cultivation in the preparation of your native ministry. I fear you will fall into the New England error. Give the Holy Spirit some freedom of action, and see if he is not able to do something by himself, if he will."

To the same: —

" I read your Memorial Volume some time since, and intended to read it a second time before writing to you. This, however, may detain me for a week or two, and so I will not wait.

" It is throughout a noble volume. Dr. Hopkins' sermon, with which it commences, is very able, and a fitting introduction. The work accomplished, of which it gives an account, is really wonderful, and is the mere forerunner of greater things to come. It commenced when Napoleon was at the zenith of his power, and all the Continent of Europe was at his feet. Compare the two.

" It is a branch of the stone cut out of the mountain without hands — that is, if stones have *branches.*

" But the idea that you have developed is worth all the labor of fifty years, — and without that labor it could not have been consummated, — that the business of the foreign missionary is to sow the seed, establish a church, and then go on to regions beyond, thus following in the steps of the apostles. This puts a wholly new aspect on the work, and breaks up effectually the tendency to make every station a little Christian city, with translators, periodicals, presses, schools, and every element of European civilization.

" It is a delightful work to set forth thus the labors of half a century, of which you can say with Æneas, ' All which I saw, and part of which I was,' and to show at what cost of talent and labor such a work was accomplished. *Tantæ molis erat Romanam condere urbem.* You see how you put me in mind of Æneas again. I rejoice that you have been spared to do what no one but you could have done. It is the most important volume on the subject of missions that I have ever seen. God be with and bless you."

We also insert the following from Dr. Anderson, written in 1866 : —

" His reliance for the conversion of the heathen world, so far as means are concerned, was upon agencies strictly spiritual. I think I may say that he had no confidence in any system of missionary operations which went upon the ground of placing much reliance upon purely secular agencies, even though the result of relying upon spiritual agencies was, that ' not many wise men after the flesh, not many mighty, not many noble, are called.' We ever agreed that the solution of the great problem, how the rich, and great, and noble, shall be reached, will be in some way consistent with a determination not to know anything, among the heathen, save Jesus Christ, and *him* crucified. And we had a common anxiety that missionaries descended from the Puritan stock should carry this principle out at all hazards. On the great practical points in the working of foreign missions, I am not aware that we differed. I speak of the *foreign* field, for I think that I was obliged to dissent from some of his later speculations on what may be called the *home* department of the foreign missionary work. I recollect saying as much to him, but am not able now to lay my hand upon the pamphlet containing these views."

We presume that, in the closing words of the above paragraph, Dr. Anderson refers to the sentiments which Dr. Wayland put forward in 1859, in a little tract, entitled " Thoughts on the Missionary Organizations of the Baptist Denomination." In this pamphlet he proposed that the existing missionary bodies, with their large and cumbrous machinery, should be laid aside, and that each association of Baptist churches should undertake, for itself, the conduct of missionary affairs, on a scale proportioned to its resources.

While, however, Dr. Wayland had definite views of the best means of promoting missions, and while he deemed it right to express them, he did not adhere to them with anything like pertinacity or pride of opinion.

To a minister he writes, —

" I have no trouble about your views of organization, &c. I do not care a fig about the question. Only let missions prosper, and I care not how it is done.

" The feelings of personal regard, which you so kindly express, I cheerfully reciprocate. I have cherished a sincere attachment to you ever since I knew you, and have rejoiced in your prosperity and usefulness. I have dissented from many of your views, and I presume you have from mine ; but this is only what is likely to happen with men differently constituted. May God go with you, and grant you much of his presence and blessing."

With many laborers in the missionary field Dr. Wayland maintained an interesting correspondence. We had hoped to present some of his letters to these brethren ; but, from causes which we are unable to explain, they have failed to reach us. The following letters contain passages of interest bearing on his personal feelings towards his missionary brethren.

To a minister : —

"I do not look at Mr. Vinton as you do. There were various things in his communication which I am disposed to wish had been modified. But, at the same time, I must make allowance for the feelings of a man who had been travelling for years in the pestilential jungle, laboring for souls, while we had been living at home in our ceiled houses; who had given his life, not to us, or to the committee, but to Christ and the perishing Karens; who had labored like *two* men, while others were sitting at ease. I would unloose the shoe-strings of such a man. He will have a bright crown when his Karens meet him before the throne.

"As to the question on which we differed in opinion: when I am asked whether this paper is white or black, I look at it, and must give such an answer as is consistent with truth. If a man *comes* to me, and declares, 'If you say that it is white, Mr. —— will go to New York, and therefore it will be better for the cause that you call it gray,' I reply, 'I must say what it is, and nothing else.' If I am asked whether I want Mr. —— to go to New York, I will answer that question by itself; but I will not answer one question when I am asked another. Such has always been my rule in all business transactions. I may very likely have erred; but I have found the rule to work well, to say just what I mean, and nothing else.

"In all these matters I look at the Karens, and the souls of the perishing, and the brethren who are laboring for them. We at home are doing a small work in comparison with them — some of them, at least. I think that the missions are in a bad condition. . . . If you do not think so, you ought to say so; but if this is my opinion, I am not called upon to withhold it because I cannot see things as others do. In these matters we must all exercise the right of private judgment, and act according to our individual light.

"May God overrule all to his glory and the good of souls.

"We expect too much of missionaries. We do not allow them enough relaxation in the way of revisiting their homes. We ought to bring them back statedly once in ten years, if they need it. We lose continually our best men in the very meridian of their usefulness. We

judge otherwise of pastors at home. We send them abroad in pursuit of health; and we destroy our foreign pastors in the hour of our greatest need. We must make some change in this matter."

We have seen that Dr. Wayland was eminently an American. He loved his country. Its privileges awoke his gratitude, its real glories kindled his patriotic pride, and its many defections from perfect rectitude saddened him. When he was in a foreign land, the happiest hours he spent were those passed in thinking of his home and preparing for his return. To a relative who was travelling on the Continent he wrote, —

" As to this country, with all its faults, I would hardly talk with a man who should compare it with France. Our curse is, that we do not know our own blessings. *O fortunatos nimium sua si bona nôrint!* was the reflection ever in my mind when I looked upon Europe and thought of my own country."

He was very jealous for the honor of his native land, and did not concede to any foreign nation the right of moral censorship over America.

To Rev. Dr. Hoby, 1852 : —

" The country is prospering, and we manage our affairs not very well, but at least as well as you. You are greatly excited about the Cardinal and Puseyism, which we do not intermeddle with. Slavery is bad, and we labor with it as well as we can; but it cannot be cured yet. We thank you for your labors in our behalf, but would excuse you if you could find anything as valuable to do at home, or in Poland, or Italy, or Hungary."

From his profound patriotism, and his religious ardor for the diffusion among all men of the gospel of Christ, sprang his zeal for home missions — a zeal that grew more animated as he advanced in life. With his later years, while he never for a moment dreamed that too much had been done for the conversion of the remote heathen, he deeply felt that the wants of our own land had been overlooked. In 1854 he remarked, in a sermon, that very many professing Christians were, apparently, more deeply interested for the heathen of distant continents, than for the ignorant, destitute, and perishing of the next street.

He did not scatter his sympathies over far-off territories, forgetting his own neighborhood. He was deeply interested in the work undertaken by state conventions, of caring for weak churches, and for localities destitute of gospel privileges.

" He used to say," remarks Dr. Caswell, " ' Look over Rhode Island, and see these feeble churches. We have lived here thirty years, and they are feeble still. Something must be done to raise them up.' "

Longing to see all the inhabitants of his own country practising the precepts of Christ's gospel, and attaining to the highest happiness and elevation of which they are capable, there could be no doubt as to his estimate of American slavery.

In 1854, in his speech on the Nebraska Bill, he said, —

" Taking Christ for my example, and striving to imbibe his spirit, can I do otherwise than take to my bosom all the oppressed and down-trodden children of humanity. Jesus Christ, my Master, is not ashamed to call them brethren ; and can I have any partnership in an attempt to trample them under foot? The Union itself becomes to me a thing accursed, if I must first steep it in the tears and blood of those for whom Christ died."

In 1857, in his letter to the investigating committee of the American Tract Society, he urged the duty of the society to bear its testimony, through its publications, in regard to the sinfulness of enslaving, buying and selling human beings, and the numberless sins of which slavery is the parent.

In a previous chapter we have exhibited the profound and deepening abhorrence of slavery which possessed him as he was re-writing his Moral Science.

To a minister, who wrote informing him that, in the state where he resided, every citizen was compelled, on becoming a voter, to take an oath to support the constitution and laws of the United States, and inquiring whether he could properly take that oath while determined not to obey the Fugitive Slave Law, he wrote, —

" In all such cases of conscience as that to which you refer, I think the proper direction is that of the apostle, ' Whatsoever is not of faith is sin.' That is, what we cannot do with a clear conscience, do not at all, for we greatly injure our conscience whenever we in any manner put a blind before its eyes. I did not know that voters were obliged to take any oath. I never was thus called upon. If you cannot do it with a clear conscience, you must abstain. You can express your views on the subject; you can say which party is, in your opinion, right, and which wrong, and give your reason for not voting. Consistently adhere to right, calmly and lovingly, and all men will esteem you more in the ' long run.'

" I have always declared that I would never aid to arrest a fugitive, or do a thing to return him to slavery. I would make no opposition to the government, but would patiently endure the penalty. This I have a right to do, on the principle that I must obey God rather than man. Whether this applies to the oath to obey the constitution and laws, I do not see clearly, and would advise you to consult the best judicial authority as to the meaning of the oath. Is it intended to express agreement to every particular, or, as the old Puritans had it, to the general scope and tenor? It is easy to show your love for the constitution and laws in other ways besides voting."

One of his sons having sheltered and aided a fugitive slave, and having given him a letter to Dr. Wayland, the latter wrote, —

" I gave him money, clothes, mittens, and shoes. It is a clear case of humanity, and I was happy to give him shelter. . . . I am glad you sent the poor fellow."

When slavery had gained supremacy over all departments of the government, and was aiming at conquests

yet greater, he not unfrequently expressed his conviction
that a crime of dimensions so vast, and of character so
atrocious, God would take into his own hands, and would
punish with an overthrow so marked, that none could fail
to recognize the divine hand, although the particular
agencies through which this result would be reached, he
could not predict.

On his entrance upon active life, Dr. Wayland entertained a high estimate of the good to be achieved by organizations. But the experience of many years gradually
impressed him with the belief that too much confidence is
liable to be placed in combined action, to the neglect of
personal, individual exertion. In speaking of the efforts
for the removal of slavery, he often cited the example of
that eminent and pious Friend, John Woolman, who went
individually to slaveholders, setting before them the commands of God, and inducing many of them to emancipate
their slaves. He was of opinion that a similar course of
fidelity and religious labor, if pursued by Christian persons, would have produced the most benign results, at the
smallest possible expense of human suffering.

The same remedy suggested itself to him for the evil of
intemperance. If Christian men would go personally to
the drunkard and to the rum-seller, and would converse
with them, appealing to their consciences, and pleading
with them to abandon their ruinous courses, accompanying
every effort with prayer for the aid of the Holy Ghost,
he believed that it could not fail to receive the divine
blessing. He had often heard persons in Providence
speak of one ——, a dram-seller, whose shop was notori-
ous for the number of young men who had there been
led to ruin. Dr. Wayland determined to converse with
him ; but his efforts were for a long time in vain. The
man seemed to have an intuitive knowledge of Dr. Wayland's design, and carefully avoided him. But at last they
met. Dr. Wayland conversed with him fully, kindly,

plainly ; plying every motive by which a moral being could be influenced. Mr. —— replied, that it was all true ; that he knew how he was despised and hated by the good, and that he could but despise himself. Often, he said, he was on the point of giving up a traffic so fraught with misery. He subsequently became much changed in character, abandoned the liquor trade, and when he died, his friends had hopes of his salvation.

In 1860 Dr. Wayland writes to a minister, —

" I am much perplexed about the Maine Law question, and do not see my way clear. All our efforts thus far seem failures, and I fear we are on the wrong track. What is the use of trying to punish Irishmen for selling liquor, when mayors, judges, and the highest men in social standing make people drunk at parties? No law can be effective which does not strike all alike. The ' rummies ' (I mean the poor ones) have the best of the argument. I do not know what to do. Church members are as much in the wrong as others. In such a case, what can law effect? Hence I doubt. If you, however, see your way clear, act according to your conscience, but weigh the matter well."

The " vice of great cities," and the means of staying its frightful devastations, greatly enlisted the attention of Dr. Wayland. For years he rendered all the moral encouragement, and all the pecuniary aid in his power, to a woman who had taken on herself the work of rescuing the fallen, and seemed singularly fitted by boldness and address for this service. But he had reason, subsequently, to believe that he had been deceived in her character. We do not know that he saw any light as to the means of removing this hideous stain upon our civilization.

His hand was ever ready for the relief of distress. In 1864, when a movement was made to send supplies to the destitute in East Tennessee, he was conversing with two gentlemen, one of whom expressed some doubt as to the character and worthiness of the recipients. " But," said the other, " they are starving " Dr. Wayland said, very emphatically, " That is enough. There is no need of saying any more."

He could not with indifference hear of suffering in regions however remote. In 1860, when news reached this country of the massacre of the Syrian Christians (so called) by the Druses, and of their distress, he wrote at once to R. Anderson, D. D., —

" I read your circular in part before our monthly concert. I also read a letter on the same subject from Mr. Johnson, our consul at Beyroot, which I received the day before. We appointed two gentlemen to take charge of the subject, and coöperate with other churches and associations who might become interested in the matter. Would it not be well for you in Boston to have a central committee, that we might act through you, and try and send a ship-load of provisions as soon as possible to those starving sinners? I say sinners, for there is apparently little to choose between them, only one sect has fallen among thieves, and is stripped, and wounded, and left half dead. If you have anything to suggest, please do so. It is a matter in which we must act in concert, and secure *provisions*. Money at a place where food is at famine prices, would be of small value."

A few days later he writes, —

" I wish you would use the enclosed $—— in such manner as will do the most good to the Syrian sufferers. I cannot wait for our committee."

He was increasingly impressed with the belief, which we suppose is now universal among all intelligent philanthropists, that to help the poor to help themselves, is to give them the truest relief. During the prevalence of the panic of 1857, when labor was paralyzed, and starvation was imminent, he originated the conception of the Providence Aid Society, whose main design was to supply work to the destitute by opening an office, where all needing employment and those able to furnish employment could be brought together. With this design was united the plan of districting of the city, and the efficient action of district committees, who should personally investigate and judiciously relieve all cases of want coming under their notice. Of this organization he was president from its origin to his death, and was rarely absent from the monthly meetings of the board.

His name and his labors were prominent alike in the foundation of the Butler Hospital for the Insane, and in every movement for its increased efficiency. He was for a long time a member of the board, and even during the years when he was most engrossed with labor, he never failed in the discharge of the duties imposed by this trust.

To quote from the annual report for 1865, —

" For many years he labored as a trustee of this hospital with a zeal and fidelity exceeded by no one, giving us the benefit of his clear, practical views and matured judgment. It is not for us to dwell upon his world-wide fame as a teacher and an author, a philanthropist and a Christian; but as connected with this and other institutions and societies, whose object is the relief of human suffering, we may testify to his remarkable individual exertions to promote the end sought to be attained. To do his duty was his only concern; self-sacrifice was of no account with him. The cause which he knew not he searched out, and the blessing of those that were ready to perish rested upon him."

Perhaps the noblest charity of the state, alike in the beneficence of its purposes and in the magnitude of its endowments, is the Rhode Island Hospital. In the inauguration of this enterprise, Dr. Wayland was able to render a service of extreme delicacy and of great moment. In June, 1863, when the people of Providence were intensely interested in everything which related to the proposed scheme, at a public meeting, designed to stimulate into increased activity the generous purpose of the community, a gentleman of high standing presented an offer, from a number of persons (not named), to give one hundred thousand dollars, upon various conditions, one of which was, that the interest of twenty-five thousand dollars should be devoted to the support of the chaplain of the institution, who should be, through all time, a clergyman of the Protestant Episcopal church. In case this condition was declined, the sum of seventy-five thousand dollars was offered.

The subject was referred to a committee, of which Dr. Wayland was the chairman; and to him was assigned the delicate and responsible task of drawing up the report. He accepted the appointment with sincere regret, both because he was reluctant to tax his brain with new duties, and also because he feared that his convictions would compel him to propose a course that would inflict pain on those who had been his warmest friends. He presented a report, which, while accepting the other features of the offer, recommended that the condition in question be declined, in accordance with the predominant sentiment of the community. But the recommendation was made in such terms, and the report was instinct with such a spirit, as to avoid the difficulties which had been feared, and to unite all humane and public-spirited citizens in the proposed charity. The report was adopted, the people of Rhode Island were enthusiastic in their support of this truly noble and Christian enterprise, and the gentleman by whom, as was supposed, the previous offer was made, has ever been its most munificent benefactor.

Upon the establishment of the Providence Reform School, Dr. Wayland (though never a member of the Board of Trustees) visited it every week; constantly advised with the efficient superintendent, Mr. Tallcott; for a long time knew personally each of the boys, and understood his disposition, his temptations, his history. He was always ready to address the lads. Mr. Howland, who, for ten years, had charge of providing the speakers at the Sabbath services, says, —

"I once engaged two young gentlemen to speak, and also Dr. Wayland. The day proved frightful. There was a foot of snow on the ground, and it had been, and was still, raining. The snow was all slosh. The two young gentlemen did not appear; but, punctual to the hour, there was Dr. Wayland."

He said to Mr. Tallcott, —

" Remember, the boys must always have their Thanksgiving service, as well as their dinner. I would rather go without my dinner than that they should not have some one to speak to them."

He rarely failed to address them six or eight times in the year; and (what may create a little surprise) there was no speaker, out of five or six hundred, whom the boys were more glad to hear. He did not often tell them stories; he spoke quite slowly; at times it was not easy to hear him; yet somehow he reached their hearts. When the question was asked them, " Whom do you want to have speak to you?" the two names most often uttered in reply were, Gilbert Congdon * and Dr. Wayland.

His words became proverbs. Years after, the boys who had left the school would write back to the superintendent, " As Dr. Wayland said to us once;" and would quote some remark that had become " like a nail fastened in a sure place."

Upon the day of Public Fast, observed after the murder of Abraham Lincoln, he spoke to the boys from the words, " As for our Rock, his way is perfect." " And when is anything perfect?" he asked. " Why, it is perfect when it cannot be made better. If you have done a thing perfectly you cannot improve it." Then he showed how God's way, throughout the war, had been perfect; how all our defeats had been for our good. Then he told them of Abraham Lincoln, of his boyhood and his early hardships. He showed him toiling in the flat-boat, and mauling rails. As he spoke, the boys leaned forward to listen. Then he carried Mr. Lincoln through all his life, and drew the lesson that even in this event God's

---

* A highly esteemed minister of the Society of Friends.

way is perfect, and that all would be for our good. He was full of the subject, and spoke for an hour and a half; but there was not one weary hearer.

A year and a half later, a gentleman, visiting the Reform School, said to one of the lads, " Do you remember Dr. Wayland?" "O, yes." "What do you remember that he ever said?" "Well, he said that if anything is perfect, you can't make it any better."

Not more than a week before Dr. Wayland's last sickness, he called at the school just at dusk, and said to Mr. Tallcott, "Is not this your evening for meeting?" Mr. Tallcott replied, "No, this is not the regular evening; but we will have the boys together in five minutes, if you will say a word to them." So they were assembled; and he spoke to them, in the September twilight, for the last time.

The reformation of convicts was an object that lay very near Dr. Wayland's heart. He was for many years president of the Prison Discipline Society. Later in life, having, as we have seen, become impressed with the need of individual effort for the successful achievement of the various objects of Christian reform, he began to labor as a Sabbath school teacher in the Rhode Island State Prison. But he soon was satisfied that the external condition of the inmates was such as to preclude any bright prospects of their moral amendment. In June, 1851, Governor Allen offered him an appointment upon the board of inspectors, to whom the care and government of the state prison and of the Providence county jail are committed. Dr. Wayland inquired if any salary attached to the office; and on hearing that the labor was entirely gratuitous, he at once accepted the appointment. The new board elected him chairman, and devolved on him, for many years, the preparation of the annual report.

Both the prison and the jail had been, from the commencement, a source of annual loss to the state. In 1846, the expense exceeded the revenue seven thousand five

hundred and sixty-three dollars; in 1848, five thousand
four hundred and sixty-two dollars. This outlay would
not be worthy of mention had it been the price paid for
the proper results, physical and moral, of imprisonment.
But the prison was, probably, in all essential particulars, the worst of any in New England, perhaps in any
of the northern states. The state prisoners were confined in cells erected in 1837. These cells are " constructed of solid blocks of split granite, with the external faces exposed to the cold blasts of winter, and the
internal faces devoid of furring and covering. During the
cold weather, the crystals of frost remain upon the interior
surfaces of the cell walls, sparkling in the light, and chill-
ing the shivering prisoners. These stone dungeons are
imperfectly ventilated as well as lighted." * The air was
close and almost insufferable. It was not without difficulty, at times, that visitors, unwonted to the atmosphere,
could avoid violent nausea upon entering the prison.
The result was a great prevalence of rheumatism, pul-
monary diseases, and diarrhœa, as well as the peculiar
malignity of contagious and epidemic complaints. Nor
was any hospital provided for the sick.

The moral effects were even more discouraging. The
number of cells being less than the number of inmates,
two or more were confined together, and each corrupted
his comrade. No chapel was in existence, and the efforts
of the chaplain and of other benevolent persons were conducted under every disadvantage. There was no library,
or other means of useful relaxation. The female convicts,
from ten to twenty in number, were crowded into two or
three cells, the young and erring catching contagion from
the utterly depraved. And while such was the condition
of the *prison*, that of the *jail* was vastly worse.

The institutions did not answer a single purpose for
which they were designed. They did not reform, they

* From a report of the board.

did not awe ; indeed, they did not even restrain and confine the convicts, as appears from the fact that in September, 1847, twelve made their escape in a single day.

The legislature, in the same month in which Dr. Wayland and his associates entered on their duties, made an
appropriation to erect a new wing for the state prisoners.
This building, under the direction of the board, was constructed upon the most approved plans, and in accordance with all the teachings of modern intelligence and
humanity. The cells are well warmed and lighted, affording ample security, yet inflicting no needless suffering. And, while the unwholesome and every way hideous cells of the old wing cost eighteen hundred and fifty
dollars each, the new cost but two hundred dollars each.

The report for 1852 states that the female convicts
were all employed in useful labor, under the care of a
suitable matron.

In the report for 1853 it is stated that a library of four
hundred volumes had been provided, to which all the
prisoners had access, with excellent results upon their
character.

In 1854 the board were able to report that, for the
first time since its establishment, the income of the
prison had exceed its outlay by one hundred and twenty-
five dollars, and that this revenue was not secured at the
expense of humanity and moral reform, for the physical,
mental, and moral condition of the inmates was higher
than ever before.

" The health of the prisoners has been remarkably
good since they were removed into the new wing. They
spend most of their leisure in reading ; their moral character is manifestly elevated, and a large portion of them
leave the prison better prepared to become useful members of society than when they entered it."

But the condition of the jail still remained little amel-
iorated. The inmates had been removed into the old
cells before described. Three or four were confined in a

single apartment. No adequate provision was made for the constant employment of the prisoners. "A prison of this character thus becomes a very expensive nursery of vice."

While such was the condition of the male prisoner, that of the female inmates of the jail was incomparably worse. In each of three small cells, ten feet by twelve, six or eight females were confined night and day.

"The atmosphere, in spite of every effort, becomes intolerably offensive. The physician expresses his apprehension that it will generate jail fever. Is the General Assembly of Rhode Island willing any longer to perpetuate a system so utterly useless, expensive, and inhuman? The convicts, although they have done wrong, are men and women, entitled to the privileges of humanity. They have a right to a comfortable abode, pure air, and the opportunity of moral improvement. When the law sentences them to imprisonment, it does not sentence them to breathe an atmosphere which exposes them to pestilence and death. When the law sends them to a house of ' correction,' as it is termed, it surely does not mean to place them in circumstances where reformation is impossible, and where the only result of our treatment must be to render them more depraved and hopelessly vicious."

Moved by these appeals, and not uninfluenced, we may believe, by the evident self-forgetfulness and public spirit of him, who, with his associates, was devoting time, labor, and wisdom to the interests of humanity, the General Assembly made an appropriation; and in 1855 the report states that a wing, calculated to afford accommodation for thirty male and thirty female prisoners, was approaching completion. They also report that the income of the *prison* exceeded its expenses — fourteen hundred and thirty dollars. Although this revenue was more than swallowed up by the expenses of the *jail*, yet a proof was afforded that, under favorable circumstances, no reason existed why such an institution should not be self-supporting.

The reports, not confined to a bare exhibition of the internal state of the prison, offer, from time to time, important suggestions, bearing on the jurisprudence and legislation of the state. At one time the evil effect, as well as the expensiveness to the state, of very short sentences, is indicated. At another it is estimated that the amount annually paid by the county of Providence alone, for imprisonment for intoxication, if divided among the several towns of the state, would purchase for each a library worth two hundred dollars. At another time it is stated that the people of Rhode Island are taxed, in connection with the jail, five thousand seven hundred and fifty-one dollars a year to support the rum-shops of the city of Providence. In 1853 the report suggests that, —

" The interests of the prison have been injuriously affected by the too frequent exercise of the pardoning power, where no new facts in the case are elicited. If the laws are unjust, they ought to be amended. If they are just, they should be administered without respect to persons. It, however, frequently happens, that convicts who have respectable friends, or who have reserved from the avails of successful villany a sufficient amount to employ earnest counsel, are pardoned ; while the friendless, and those who have surrendered all, serve out the full time of their sentence. This creates in the minds of the prisoners a feeling of injustice, and deprives the law of its moral effect on the criminal. It seems unreasonable for the state to employ its highest talent and integrity in the detection and trial of crime, and then to set aside the whole proceeding on the pleading of counsel."

In 1856 the inspectors report that the prison had earned over its expenses, two thousand and thirty-one dollars, although this balance was again swallowed up by the expenses of the jail. They also report, —

" Probably no workshop in the city employing the same number of men, has suffered so little from illness as the state prison. The moral character of prisoners is, so far as we can discover, improving. . . . Some of those whose term has expired are now at work in the city, and have secured the confidence and respect of their employers. . . . The library is diligently and extensively read. The fees for the admission of visitors enable us to make large additions to it annually. . . . The prison has, during the past year, been lighted with gas, in order to afford the inmates better facilities for mental improvement. The inspectors are happy to report that the state prison has now become what the General Assembly has always intended to make it — a valuable means of reformation. Men who have been seduced into habits of vice have here the opportunity of acquiring the means of self-support, a taste for intellectual improvement, and a knowledge of their duty from the Word of God."

The report urges the total removal of the old prison, and the erection in its place of a wing, on the plan of those already constructed.

The chaplain * reports, in 1856, that the completion of the new chapel afforded greatly increased means for the religious instruction of the prisoners, and that "in no year has the improvement in the physical, mental, and moral condition of the inmates been more decided and cheering." The completion of the new wing also afforded room for the establishment of a hospital.

The report for 1857 states that the prison had earned twelve hundred and fifty-six dollars over its expenses, and that the annual deficit in the jail accounts had been lessened. With this report was transmitted a catalogue of eight hundred and fourteen volumes, composing the library.

In 1859 the inspectors report that the earnings of the prison over its expenses had more than balanced the expenses of the jail, and had left six hundred and thirty-five dollars returned to the state treasury from the two establishments. "The state prison and jail have, therefore, for

* Rev. William Douglass, to whom we are greatly indebted for much valuable information with reference to Dr. Wayland's labors in behalf of the prison.

the first time, paid their own expenses and exhibited a balance in favor of the state. For this result the Board of Inspectors have earnestly labored, and they congratulate the Assembly on its final accomplishment." The volumes in the library amounted, at this time, to nearly a thousand.

The report just alluded to is the last, we believe, prepared by Dr. Wayland, although he remained for several subsequent years a member of the board.

The report for 1860 exhibits a revenue from the prison of twenty-eight hundred and seventeen dollars, and (after deducting a loss of two hundred and thirty-four dollars for the jail) a profit to the state of twenty-five hundred and eighty-three dollars. The improvement in the character of the prisoners still continued.

For 1862 the board, for the first time, reported that the prison and the jail had *each* earned more than its expenses. The same fact is stated in the reports for the two following years.

It is not, probably, too much to assert, that the prison became as well managed, as healthful, as favorable to moral reform, as any similar institution in America. It is proper to add, that in efforts for these results the whole board faithfully coöperated. Rewarded only by a sense of good done to mankind, they did not withhold any sacrifice of time or labor. Their attendance at the meetings was regular, and their regard for the interests of the institution was, in many cases, more exact than they would have paid to their own.

But we apprehend that we do not err in saying, that of all these movements Dr. Wayland was the informing and animating spirit. His name and his character assured the public, and especially the legislature, that no private interest was to be advanced; and his unwearied activity inspired all his associates. In his labors he fixed his attention upon three objects. He desired to promote, within proper bounds, the *comfort* of the prisoners. He care-

fully watched the character of their accommodations and
of their provisions. When complaint was made of the
beef served out to them, he examined it, ate of it, was satisfied that it was not suitable, and caused it to be changed.
He sought to *economize* the resources of the state, — with
what success has already been shown. And he desired
to attain, as the great end, the *diminution of crime*. In
reaching this result, he was of opinion that the chief
agency is the production of a change in the moral character of the criminal. We are thus led to remark another
aspect of his labors.

His relation to the prisoners was not merely official.
He stood to them not alone as inspector to convicts, but
as man to his brother man; or, rather, shall we not say,
as the disciple of Christ to sinning, suffering, immortal
beings. His labors for the spiritual good of the prisoners
were unceasing. He conversed with them personally in
their cells; he frequently preached to them on the Sabbath; and always he was present at the more familiar
exercise of the Sabbath school, of which he was superintendent, in addition to teaching a class. "It was truly
wonderful," one gentleman says, who was associated with
him as a teacher,* "to see him standing among them, and
to see them talking as freely, as familiarly, as if he were
their friend from childhood." The marvellous power of
illustration, the faculty for simplifying difficult truths, the
knowledge of the Word of God, that had held scholars in
rapt attention, were now put into requisition to draw to
Christ these outcasts from society. "I have never," said
a convict, "believed that there was anything in religion;
but when I see Dr. Wayland come here to talk to us, I
know that religion must be real." Nor was it, on his part,
a matter of duty and of constraint. He loved to be there.
During a year or more previous to his pastoral labors in
the First Church, he not only attended the Sunday school,

* Professor Chace.

but remained during the morning service, and listened, with interest and edification, to the practical, evangelical sermons of his former pupil, Mr. Douglass, the chaplain. Often he said to Mr. Douglass, " I never enjoyed religious worship more than in this place and with this congregation ; " and once he remarked, " If the Savior were to visit the city of Providence, I do not know any place where he would be more likely to be found than here." At another time, in speaking of his Bible class, he said, " I love to present the gospel to these poor fellows in all its precious promises. How adapted it is to meet the wants of just such men ! "

These labors were not ineffectual. On more than one occasion there were indications of religious interest. During the fall of 1856, several of the inmates seemed deeply impressed, and many appeared changed in heart.

He writes to his son, —

" November 17, 1856.

" I spent the morning and afternoon of yesterday at the prison. Instead of the Bible class before preaching, we had a conference meeting, and invited the prisoners to speak. Five arose and gave quite interesting accounts of their religious hope, and several more would have spoken if there had been time. I asked one to pray, and he prayed with much fervor, appropriateness, and simplicity. I think that as many as seven or eight give us reason to hope for them, and others are deeply anxious. Some of them speak of a joy in religion that is wholly inexpressible. Their manifestations of gratitude to those who have labored to be useful to them are very touching. I went over in the afternoon and had an individual conversation with most of them. It was a very edifying occasion. I do not know how it is, but some how or other, all my instincts lead me to labor among the poor and forsaken. I enjoy worship vastly more among these poor prisoners than among the rich, and well dressed, and intelligent. That prison chapel is much more pleasing to me than the —— high steeple, or any of our quartette choir congregations. It seems to me vastly more like the true worship of the Master."

It was probably at the meeting referred to in the above letter, that a lad arose, — Pat Cassidy by name, — who had been a pickpocket in New York, had come to Rhode Island to rob, and had been arrested and found guilty of a larceny in Woonsocket. After speaking of his past life, he said, —

"A week or two ago, I was sick, and afraid I should die. Mr. Douglass came, and asked me if I was prepared to die. I asked him how that was going to be. He taught me this prayer : ' God, be merciful to me a sinner.' He made me say it over and over, till I had it by heart. Well, as I said that prayer, I thought of that ' *me* a sinner.' I felt worse and worse. I walked up and down my cell, feeling as if the floor would split and let me into hell entirely. And I tell yez there is a hell. And so I walked with the sweat dripping off of me, till, at last, I remembered the words I heard Dr. Wayland say here : ' The blood of Christ Jesus, his Son, cleanseth us from all sin ; ' and as soon as I thought of that, says I [clapping his hands], ' Pat, my son, that is for you.' And then in a minute don't you think but I was ready to fly ? "

Pat continued to give every proof of being a Christian. After serving out his time, he went to Fall River, and joined the Second Baptist Church. He was afterwards employed on board a vessel sailing to New Orleans. In that city he caught the yellow fever and died ; and in the opinion of a pious man, the master of the vessel, who was with him, he died in hope.

During the same period of religious interest, W. H., who had been sentenced for life for murder committed in a state of intoxication, gave evidence of being converted. Some years later (having been in prison fifteen years), he was pardoned, and has ever since maintained an irreproachable character. We mention these as examples. Some persons, of course, there were, in whom Dr. Wayland and others found themselves deceived. It is impossible to say whether they were self-deluded ; whether they really meant well, but were afterwards led astray; or whether they were intentional deceivers.

Dr. Wayland's solicitude did not cease when those who had been inmates of the prison were no longer under his official care. On their departure, he counselled them, tried to secure employment for them, and, in one instance, when a released prisoner thought that, with a little capital, he could perfect an invention which he had devised, Dr. Wayland loaned him fifty dollars, which, we believe, still remains as a permanent investment.

And they felt a pride in their relation to him, in being Dr. Wayland's pupils, that went far to restore the self-respect which imprisonment is so apt to obliterate, and without which reform or high character is impossible. A gentleman, who was a fellow-teacher, relates, that once, in the south part of Rhode Island, he saw a number of men at work in an oat-field, one of whom said to him, " How do you do, professor? How is the doctor?" The gentleman seeming not at once to recognize him, he said, " I used to see you at the institution, and I used to be in the doctor's class." Another gentleman relates a similar incident as happening to him in the interior of Massachusetts. Their pride and their fondness for " the doctor " seemed to overmaster the reluctance with which they would naturally recall the circumstances under which they knew him.

The view which we have given would be defective and erroneous, if we did not add that in his sympathies and benevolent efforts there was nothing of weakness or maudlin tenderness; there was no " coddling " of the prisoners, nor — during the latter part of his experience — any want of understanding of their character. He knew them to be depraved, designing. He was convinced, as he once said, that the word of a convict is utterly worthless when he sees the least possibility of securing a release by any representations which he can make. He realized fully

how unspeakably difficult is the work of reforming crim-
inals.

Yet, though often painfully disappointed by the inherent
wickedness of those whom he had believed to be reformed,
he was never disheartened. If not as hopeful, he was still
as unwearied, as ever. Partial or complete failure did not
paralyze his efforts, for he knew that a deed done for God,
and from love to Christ, must bear some fruit. " I do not
know what will be the result," he once said, when com
mencing a very arduous undertaking; " but I know that
if I do my duty, God will be glorified." Ingratitude did
not chill his humanity, for it was not inspired by any desire for gratitude. Kindled by no human motive, it could
by no human power be quenched. It was the love of
Christ that constrained him. The same unwearied tenderness that had been shown towards him, a sinner, by one
who loved him and gave himself for him, he gladly exercised towards his fellow-sinners. Whatever the result
of these efforts on earth, he knew that nothing could rob
him of the heavenly reward promised in those unspeakably
divine words, " I was in prison and ye visited me," —
words which were often music in his thoughts, as he went,
laden with years and with growing infirmity, from his
home to the prison ; as he entered the iron door ; as he sat
down beside murderers, and forgers, and burglars, and told
" the poor fellows " of the blood that cleanseth from all sin.

He felt a peculiar pleasure in applying the gospel to
the hearts of these men, because he was sure that this was
just what they needed ; that this could save them, and
this alone ; and also because he felt that the gospel gains
new trophies and testimonies of its power by the renova-
tion of such hearts.

We have thus far referred mainly to the amount of time
and labor bestowed by Dr. Wayland upon the numerous
benevolent enterprises in behalf of which his feelings were
enlisted. But he was quite as prompt to expend money

in aid of every deserving charity as to offer advice, or to express sympathy. He never urged upon others a liberality which he did not enforce by his own example.

Indeed, it would be impossible to give a just idea of his character, without alluding to his pecuniary contributions in answer to the private or public calls of humanity. He regarded almsgiving as a duty, placed by the divine Teacher on a level with the practice of prayer and a holy life. And how he should secure the means of discharging this duty, and of cultivating the graces which flow from it, often occupied his thoughts. Inheriting nothing from his parents save their prayers, he could gain the means of benevolence only by the exercise of industry and economy.

He desired, in the first place, to keep out of debt. His experience at Andover, his weeks of dependence, burned into him a hatred and horror of indebtedness that ever remained. He often quoted, as expressive of his view of the use of money, the lines of Burns : —

> "Not for to hide it in a hedge,
> Not for a train attendant,
> But for the glorious privilege
> Of being independent."

"One of the first elements of freedom," he once said, "is to be out of debt." And in writing to a former pupil, just entering in life, "I am glad you see the day-star of competence. It tells of yet better things, if anything can be better."

He once said that when he began his life in Boston, he expended up to the limit of his income. But one of his deacons asked him, after a year or two, "Are you saving anything?" On his replying that he was not, the deacon said, "You ought every year to lay up something. Now begin at once. I want you to lend me some money, and to lend me some every year." Acting on this suggestion, he laid up something (though often very little) every year. One result of this wise frugality was, that he was able to say, "I never had a bill presented to me twice, nor have I ever had a note discounted."

Next to being independent, his desire was to be able to respond to the claims of benevolence. When he was twenty-one years old, it will be remembered that he rejoiced in the prospect of his tutorship, because it would enable him to have something for charity. And in 1856 he wrote, "I must work in order to have something to give away. I have been losing by bad investments."

A gentleman, always active in every scheme of philanthropy that appeals to the citizens of Providence, has said, "I never liked to go to Dr. Wayland in regard to any charitable object, for he always gave more than I felt that he ought." In 1863 the committee charged with soliciting donations for the Rhode Island Hospital were agreed that Dr. Wayland ought not to be called on, for they felt that he was not able to give anything. But meeting a member of the committee, he said, "Why have you not called on me?" His friend replied, "We did not feel that it was right to ask you to contribute." Dr. Wayland said, "I could not sleep if this thing were going on and I had done nothing towards it;" and he put down his name for a sum that in proportion to his means was munificent. The gentleman with whom he held the conversation was afterwards reminded by other members of the committee that they had agreed not to ask Dr. Wayland for anything. He replied, "What could I do? I could not help myself. He *would do it.*"

In 1862-3, owing to the advance in prices and the diminished sale of his books, he found that he was in danger of being without the means of benevolence; and, in order to have something for charity, he gave up housekeeping, and all the pleasures associated with his home, and boarded for several months. Later, during the war, he heard a friend speak of the expensiveness of tea, and the good that might be done with the cost of this article. He at once resolved to forego this, one of his few luxuries, and for several months continued to do so.

It was about this time that he received a letter from a brother in the ministry, not personally known to him, who wrote expostulating with him on his inconsistency in inculcating the duty of Christian self-denial while living in luxury. He read the letter with thoughtful attention, seeing in it the sincere utterance of a conscientious man, and feeling only the kindest sentiments towards the writer. But probably Dr. Wayland did not see, and certainly those about him could not discover, any particular in which he could live with more plainness, with less self-indulgence.

He had a religious horror of waste. He once expressed the opinion that, in the millennium, people would so conduct their cooking, and all their household arrangements, as to secure perfect economy. All these things, which would have been petty if their end had been selfish accumulation, were ennobled by the object which he had in view. It was by economy only that he was enabled to practise benevolence.

He was never wealthy. Those who thought otherwise were deceived by the largeness of his donations. During many years he gave away more than half of his entire income. After his salary as president ceased, the amount of his contributions was necessarily diminished. With his later years he inclined to bestow his benefactions without the intervention of a society, " seeking out the cause that he knew not," and enhancing the value of the gift by the sympathy which accompanied it.

It would be unjust did we fail to add, that, in all his plans of benevolence, from his marriage in 1838, his wife coöperated with a largeness of heart and an openness of hand akin to his own. During twenty-seven years of a life united by the holiest ties, neither cherished a desire for the relief of woe, or for the promotion of the welfare of mankind, that did not find in the other a full and absolute sympathy.

CHAPTER XV.

THE REVISED MORAL SCIENCE. — THE CUSHING INSTI-
TUTE. — THE WARREN ASSOCIATION. — SICKNESS AND
DEATH. — MEETING OF THE GRADUATES. — FUNERAL.
— THE PUBLIC. — PROFESSOR CHACE'S ADDRESS.

THE chief labor of Dr. Wayland, after the publication
of his Memoir of Chalmers, was the revision of his
Moral Science. He urged forward this work with an earnestness that was, perhaps, intensified by the remembrance
of the repeated interruptions that had already prevented
its completion — an earnestness that probably led him
again to transcend the limits of his endurance.

The proof-sheets of this volume were corrected during
the summer of 1865, and the work was issued from the
press in October.

In 1854, Thomas P. Cushing, Esq., of Boston, a native of
Ashburnham, Worcester County, Mass., a brother-in-law
of Dr. Wayland, had died, providing in his will for the
establishment of an academy of high order in his native
town. Dr. Wayland was named as an executor, and
subsequently was, by the act of incorporation, made one
of the trustees of the " Cushing Institute." The first meeting for the permanent organization of this educational
enterprise was to be held at Ashburnham, on Wednesday,
the 6th of September, 1865.

Although much enfeebled by the almost unparalleled
heat of the past summer, and by the literary labor to which
we have just alluded, Dr. Wayland could not neglect this
opportunity of testifying his unabated interest in the cause

of popular education. Accordingly, leaving his home on the 5th of September, and spending one night in Fitchburg, he reached Ashburnham at the time appointed for the meeting. He was elected president of the Board of Trustees, and, at the request of his associates, presented, in brief, his views as to the course of studies that should be pursued in the Institute.

" He mentioned particularly reading, spelling, penmanship, music, grammar, rhetoric, geography, arithmetic, geometry, algebra, trigonometry, natural philosophy, botany, physiology, agriculture, drawing, book-keeping, intellectual and moral philosophy, political economy, and the science of government. In this plan neither ancient nor modern languages found a place.

" The scholars were to be carefully instructed in the use of their mother tongue. He would have no classes preparing for college, on the ground that an arrangement of that kind might foster distinctions, excite jealousies, and produce an unhappy effect on those students who should confine themselves to English studies. Besides, he had observed that in schools where the classics are taught, they receive undue honor and attention. On this point he spoke at length and with great earnestness. He believed that the Cushing Institute would better subserve its design by giving instruction in the English branches only." *

At the conclusion of the meeting of the trustees, Dr. Wayland returned to Fitchburg, and on the following day proceeded to Providence. We are favored with a letter from Lewis H. Bradford, Esq., of Fitchburg, from which we quote : —

" The evening previous to the meeting at Ashburnham, having heard that Dr. Wayland was at the Fitchburg Hotel, I called upon him, with one of the trustees. We found him intensely interested in the proposed institution. He

---

* For this statement of Dr. Wayland's views, as expressed to the trustees, we are indebted to Rev. A. P. Marvin, of Winchendon, Mass., who was present at the meeting, and made careful minutes of the remarks of the chairman.

remarked that the light which it might shed upon this part of the country was of incalculable importance.

" On the evening of the following day, he attended the prayer meeting of the Baptist church in Fitchburg. In the course of a brief address, he exhorted us most affectionately to be faithful followers of the Lord Jesus, and then united with us in prayer. No one but myself knew the name of the speaker, but all felt the power of his presence and the weight of his counsels.

" I gave him my arm at the door of the church, and as we walked to the hotel, he said, ' Brother Bradford, we do not pray enough ; we lack faith in God.' Arrived at the hotel, he kindly insisted that I should go to his room, where he conversed with me at some length with regard to the future of the Institute. One idea which he expressed I shall never forget — that its object should be to make *men* and *women*, rather than *graduates;* of the latter, he said, we had an abundance.

" I took this opportunity to thank him, in behalf of our Baptist church, for his generous contribution towards the erection of our first place of worship."

Dr. Wayland writes to his sister, on the 16th of September, 1865, —

" There has been a long time of silence, and I presume that I am in fault. The truth is, that I have been, for the past four or five weeks, daily receiving proof-sheets, and have been obliged to read them carefully. Work of this kind consumes a great deal of time. When this was finished, I made a visit to Ashburnham — quite a journey for me. But it is now all over, and I am at rest. And yet, I hardly know why, — perhaps because travelling, or the hot weather, has had an unfavorable effect upon me, — I have felt dizzy and ' powerful weak ' since my return. I hope to be revived by the rain and cool weather, which may now be reasonably expected. During the whole summer we have been but moderately well. I have been the best of the three, and from this you may judge of the average."

On Wednesday and Thursday (September 13 and 14) the " Warren Association " met, with the " Central Baptist Church," in Providence. Dr. Wayland manifested a

peculiar interest in this meeting, and was present at all
of its sessions, excepting those held in the evening. He
was appointed chairman of the committee on the " state
of religion in the churches," but requested his friend,
Rev. W. L. McKenzie (a member of the committee), to
prepare the report. Towards the close of the morning
session on Thursday, the regular business of the association having been completed, the question arose whether
the body should adjourn until its next annual meeting, or
should spend the afternoon in a conference upon the facts
presented in the report just named. Rev. Dr. Lincoln,
chairman of the committee of arrangements, said to Dr.
Wayland, " Will you address the association, if we decide
to hold an afternoon session?" Assent to this proposition
having been secured, there was no objection to a temporary adjournment.

During the intermission, Dr. Wayland seemed to look
forward with profound interest to the afternoon meeting.
As his own home was at a considerable distance from the
church, he dined with a friend. His meal was hastily
finished, and saying to his host, " I must not fail to be at
the afternoon meeting in season," he hurried away. He
was in his seat among the very first, before the meeting
was called to order.

When the introductory services were concluded, he arose
and addressed the congregation.

" The sentiments and emotions expressed by this servant of God, ' this prophet of our captivity ' (as one has
styled him), were a most solemn reiteration of what, for a
few years previous, he had been proclaiming through the
press, and uttering in private. . . . In his public addresses,
in the pulpit, in the prayer and conference-room, in his
personal interviews with numerous visitors in the retirement of his study, in books, tracts, and letters, everywhere and in every way, he had been sounding an alarm;
faithfully reproving and warning, earnestly inviting and
beseeching the churches and the ministry to awake and

cry mightily unto God to pour forth his Spirit, and revive his sinking cause." *

His words were earnest, affectionate, instinct with truthfulness, and profoundly impressive. They could hardly have been more so, had he and his brethren been aware that he was soon to put off this tabernacle, and that they all, among whom he had gone preaching the kingdom of God, should see his face no more.

Dr. Wayland was followed by Rev. Dr. Swain, of the Congregational church, who gave some account of the state of religion in his denomination, inviting his brethren to contend earnestly for the common faith of evangelical Christianity. Addresses were also made by other ministers and by laymen. The entire service produced a deep and quickening effect upon the minds of all who were present, and, we are warranted in believing, made itself felt in a higher spirituality, in a more absorbing zeal, and in more fruitful labors during the succeeding year.

For some months previous to the time of which we write, Dr. Wayland had seemed conscious of a growing sense of weariness. It was with increasing effort that he performed even the slightest labor. He had written to his son in August, "We are living by main strength;" and, still later, "We are only middling. . . . I work in the garden three or four hours a day; but this is all. I crawl about, accomplishing very little." Yet, except as he felt the depression natural to this enforced inactivity, he was cheerful, and probably looked forward to several years of labor in the service of his Master.

On Friday, the 22d of September, he found himself exceedingly weak. He took his accustomed walk in the afternoon, with a relative who was visiting the family, but seemed unusually silent. After tea he went to his chamber much earlier than was his habit. On Saturday, for the first time in many years, he did not leave his bed.

---

* Rev. W. L. McKenzie, in the Christian Visitor.

His debility was extreme. He had occasion to sign his name, but the signature bore little resemblance to his ordinary writing. His physician was summoned. He prescribed entire rest, and some simple remedies. With an intimate Christian friend, who sat by his bedside for an hour on Sunday evening, Dr. Wayland conversed freely and fully. He said, —

"I feel that my race is nearly run. I have, indeed, tried to do my duty. I cannot accuse myself of having neglected any known obligation. Yet all this avails nothing. I place no dependence on anything but the righteousness and death of Jesus Christ. I have never enjoyed the raptures of faith vouchsafed to many Christians. I do not undervalue these feelings, but it has not pleased God to bestow them upon me. I have, however, a confident hope that I am accepted in the Beloved."

Monday was a bright September day; and in the course of the forenoon, while he was alone, he arose, dressed himself, and went into his garden. Did he know that it was for the last time? and did he desire to bid farewell to the cherished objects of his care? or was he rather testing his remaining strength? It was not without considerable difficulty that he returned to the house, and regained his room.

On Tuesday morning, when his breakfast was brought to him, Mrs. Wayland observed that he used only his left hand. She said, "Shall I not feed you?" and he consented. Alarmed at this acknowledgment of weakness, she called Dr. Miller in consultation; but he did not recommend any remedies in addition to those already prescribed. At about ten o'clock, Mrs. Wayland left the room to write a telegram. Returning, she found her husband lying across the bed, motionless, helpless. Apparently he had attempted to rise, possibly hoping to repeat the experiment of the previous day; or, perhaps, wishing to see of how much effort he was capable. The fatal blow had fallen! He was placed in a more natural position, and lay unconscious except when aroused, his eyes closed, his right side paralyzed. His oldest son arrived in the evening, and said to him, "Do you know me, father?" He responded by a look of affectionate intelligence, and distinctly articulated, "Yes," but immediately relapsed into unconsciousness. All hope was gone. The disease was steadily drawing nearer and nearer to the sources of life; it was only a question of time.

On Thursday, his two sisters (now, with him, the sole surviving children) arrived; and on Friday morning his second son, summoned by the sad tidings from his home in Michigan, took his father's hand. But it returned no answering pressure, nor did eye or voice give token of recognition. On Saturday afternoon, September 30, 1865, at twenty minutes before six, his wife, his three sons, his sisters, and the wife of one of his sons, stood by his bedside. It was apparent that a change was at hand. His daughter, seeing that the end was near, gently laid her hand upon his cheek. He opened his eyes with an expression of entire consciousness, — the same, exactly, that his children had so often seen on his face in the study, as he looked up from his Bible, — and of perfect intelligence, but an intelligence not of this world. Then he closed them, and all was over.

Throughout all the week, when any one, known to be a friend of the family, was seen upon the street, he was constantly met with the inquiry, "How is the doctor to-day? Is there any hope?" On the morning of Sunday, the tolling of the bell of the First Baptist Church from eight to nine o'clock smote heavily on a thousand hearts, telling them that the servant of God and the friend of man was no more on earth. In the prayers offered in all the sanctuaries of the city, the bereavement was noticed. When Mr. Douglass said to the convicts in the state prison, assembled in the chapel, "You will never see your friend Dr. Wayland again; he is dead," he was interrupted by their sobs.

Monday's issue of the Providence Journal contained
an obituary article from the pen of Professor James B.
Angell,* the fidelity and gracefulness of which could not
be surpassed. On the same day, the Baptist ministers of
Boston and New York, at their accustomed meetings,
passed resolutions commemorating the event. On Tuesday afternoon the graduates of the college met at Manning Hall. Hon. H. B. Anthony was called to the chair.
A series of resolutions was read by Professor Chace.
A silence of several minutes ensued, broken at last by
Chief Justice Bradley. He was followed by A. Payne,
Esq., E. H. Hazard, Esq., President Sears, Rev. Dr.
Caswell, and Rev. Dr. Lincoln. Dr. Caswell, overcome
by an emotion unspeakably more eloquent than words,
was unable to complete his remarks.

Meanwhile the deceased lay, resting at last, within his
chamber, the windows of which looked forth over the
garden, down the slope, towards the gleaming river. But
he saw now a brighter river, trod greener fields, beheld a
more beautiful paradise. No painful traces of sickness
and infirmity were visible. All was calm, majestic repose. To borrow his own language, "Death was a conquered foe, and had been able to erect no trophy over the
mortal tabernacle that had been the scene of conflict."

On Wednesday, at half past nine o'clock, after prayer
had been offered with the family, the body was removed
to the First Baptist Church. It was placed in front of
the heavily-draped pulpit, and for an hour all who desired passed in order, and looked for the last time upon
those well-remembered features. The corporation and
Faculty of the University, the delegates chosen by the
Baptist ministers of Boston, gentlemen of eminence in
literature, in science, in political station, citizens of Rhode
Island, and residents of remote states, joined in the sad
procession. But profounder and more significant was

---

* Now president of the University of Vermont.

the emotion manifested by the young disciple whom he had guided, the aged saint whom he had consoled, the poor whose sufferings he had relieved, and the members of the long down-trodden race who had enjoyed his earliest and almost his latest Christian labors.

Rev. Dr. Caldwell, pastor of the church, read passages of Scripture and offered prayer; Rev. Dr. Caswell made an address most appropriate and comforting; and Rev. Dr. Swaim closed the services with prayer. The remains were then borne to the " North Burying Ground." In this ancient cemetery are the graves of many of the friends with whom he had loved to labor for the welfare of mankind; of Nicholas Brown, and Professor Goddard, and Moses B. Ives, and of others honored in the history of Rhode Island for their private worth and public services. There, on a knoll which receives the last rays of the setting sun, in a spot selected by himself, where were resting the remains of his early-lost wife, and of his infant daughter, he was buried.

For many weeks and months the ground had been parched with drought. During the dry season Dr. Wayland had prayed daily, at the family altar, for two things: for showers to refresh the thirsty soil, and for an outpouring of the Spirit of God. As he was laid in the grave, the rain fell in torrents — a promise of spiritual blessings, of answers to prayer yet to be realized.

On the following Sabbath, commemorative sermons were preached from many pulpits in Providence, Boston, New York, and in other parts of the country. These discourses were delivered, not alone by clergymen of his own denomination; professors of faiths widely differing from his paid a tribute of reverence to a great soul and a noble life.

A committee, appointed by the graduates of Brown University, requested Professor George I. Chace, of the class of 1830, to deliver an address commemorative of

"the virtues and services of Francis Wayland." On
Tuesday, September 4, 1866, the alumni of the college
assembled in the First Baptist Church. After prayer by
Rev. Dr. Fisher, of the class of 1847, the following ode,
composed by Hon. Thomas Durfee, of the class of 1846,
was sung : —

> Early to him the Spirit came,
>   His soul with love and light to fill,
> And touched with consecrating flame
>   His mighty mind and lordly will.
>
> It called him to a noble task —
>   To teach the Fair, the Good, the True:
> With pious heart he did but ask
>   To do what God would have him do.
>
> From near and far his pupils flocked,
>   Drawn by report that told how well
> His keen analysis unlocked
>   The wisdom hid in learning's shell.
>
> Year after year, and day by day,
>   O'er them he watched, for them he wrought,
> To lead them in the wisest way,
>   To teach them that which best were taught.
>
> Yet for themselves he bade them think,
>   Regarding reason more than rule,
> And freshly from experience drink
>   The truths untaught by book or school.
>
> And as they clomb the path he showed,
>   Before them, luminous and pure,
> His genius, ever towering, glowed
>   To guide and keep their feet secure.
>
> Meanwhile, with tireless tongue or pen,
>   He toiled to spread the gospel light,
> And kindle in the hearts of men
>   The love of freedom and of right.
>
> No caste or color, clime or creed,
>   The fervor of his zeal allayed;
> He strove to realize in deed
>   The life of love for which he prayed.

The convict, in his lonely cell,
  The slave by cruel fetters bound,
The heathen, with his fetich fell,
  In him a benefactor found.

For his belief was no mere word,
  Which, uttered, dies upon the lip;
But faith, co-working with the Lord,
  In meek and loving fellowship.

He sleeps in death: its darkness hides
  The grandeur of his form and face:
The lesson of his life abides,
  A blessing to the human race.

Professor Chace encountered an unavoidable embarrassment; for those to whom he spoke had known so well the life and character which were to form the theme of his discourse that he could hardly hope to equal the demands of their recollections, or of their conceptions. Yet such were the keenness of his analysis, the justness of his portraiture, the heartiness of his appreciation, and the felicity of his diction, that the most enthusiastic were satisfied, and the coldest were kindled into sympathy.

THE END.

APPENDIX.

The following list of the published writings and addresses of Dr. Wayland, although necessarily imperfect, will perhaps be of some value for purposes of reference: —

1823. Discourse on the Moral Dignity of the Missionary Enterprise.
1825. Discourse on the Duties of an American Citizen.
1826. Discourse on the Death of the Ex-President.
1828. Report on System of Public Schools in Providence.
1830. Murray Street Discourse — Certain Triumphs of the Redeemer.
1830. Discourse before the American Sunday School Union at Philadelphia, on Encouragements to Religious Effort.
1830. Inaugural Address before the American Institute of Instruction.
1831. Moral Efficacy of the Doctrine of the Atonement — Sermon preached at the Installation of Rev. William Hague (Boston).
1831. Phi Beta Kappa Oration (Brown University) — Philosophy of Analogy.
1831. Address before the Providence Temperance Society.
1832. Sermon at the Ordination of Rev. John S. Maginnis (Portland) — Objections to the Doctrine of Christ crucified, considered.
1832. Sermon at the Installation of Rev. William R. Williams (New York).
1832. Sermon on the Abuse of the Imagination.
1832. Sermon before the Howard Benevolent Society, on Motives to Beneficence.

1832. Volume entitled "Wayland's Discourses," comprising most of the public addresses above mentioned.

1834. Missionary Sermon on the Moral Conditions of Success in the Propagation of the Gospel.

1835. Discourse at the Dedication of Manning Hall, on the Dependence of Science upon Revealed Religion.

1835. Elements of Moral Science.

1836. Elements of Moral Science, abridged.

1837. Elements of Political Economy.

1837. Elements of Political Economy, abridged.

1837. Two Discourses on the Moral Law of Accumulation.

1838. A Discourse at the Opening of the Providence Athenæum.

1838. Limitations of Human Responsibility.

1840. Introduction and Notes to the Pursuit of Knowledge under Difficulties.

1841. Address before the Rhode Island Society for the Promotion of Domestic Industry.

1841. Discourse on the Death of Nicholas Brown.

1842. Discourse on the Affairs of Rhode Island.

1842. Thanksgiving Discourse on the Occasion of the Close of the Rhode Island Rebellion.

1842. Discourse on the Claims of Whalemen (New Bedford).

1842. Volume entitled "Thoughts on the Present Collegiate System in the United States."

1843. Article in Bibliotheca Sacra (1st series), on the Doctrine of Expediency.

1844. Articles on the Debts of the States, in North American Review and Christian Review.

1845. Article on the Life of Dr. Arnold, in North American Review.

1845. Domestic Slavery considered as a Scriptural Institution — Discussion with Rev. R. Fuller, D. D.

1856. Address before a Meeting of Citizens of Providence, on Occasion of the Assault upon Hon. Charles Sumner.

1857. Letter to the Investigating Committee of the American Tract Society (New York).

1857. Discourse on the Death of Rev. J. N. Granger, D. D.

1857. Discourse on the Death of Moses B. Ives, Esq.

1857. Two Discourses on the Present Crisis.

1858. Sermons to the Churches.

1858. Salvation by Christ.

1858. Revised Edition of Sabbath Hymn and Tune Book, for the Use of the Baptist Churches.

1860. Address at a Meeting auxiliary to the American Tract Society (Boston).

1861. Introduction to the Life of Trust.

1861. Tract, on Prayer for the Country.

1862. Tract, entitled " How to be Saved."

1863. Letters on the Ministry of the Gospel.

1864. Memoir of the Christian Labors of Thomas Chalmers, D. D., LL. D.

1865. Article entitled "John Foster on the Duration of Future Punishment," in the American Presbyterian and Theological Review.

1865. Article on Choice of Companions, in Hours at Home.

1865. Article on the Ministry of Brainerd, in the American Presbyterian and Theological Review.

1865. Address to the Citizens of Providence on the Assassination of Abraham Lincoln.

1865. Revised Edition of Elements of Moral Science.

In addition to the foregoing were various contributions to the Baptist Magazine, the Macedonian, the Christian Watchman, the Christian Reflector, the Examiner, the Christian Review, the Providence Journal, and the Michigan Christian Herald.

INDEX.

Barnes, D. H., Mr., I. 26.

Bartol, Rev. C. A., D. D., I. 405, 424; II. 52, 62, 81, 94.

Bemis, George, Esq., II. 272.

Bereavement, views of, I. 363.

Bible Class, College, I. 289.

Bible Class, Ladies', I. 342.

Bible Society, I. 335.

Birmingham, II. 12.

Bradley, Hon. C. S., I. 240, 308.

Brown University, becomes president of, I. 203.   Condition of in 1855, II. 108.   Final resignation, 145.

Brown, Nicholas, I. 393; II. 46.

Burritt, Dr. E., I. 37.

Burns case, II. 134.

Bust of Dr. Wayland, procured by Alumni, II. 248.

Butler Hospital, II. 336.

Candidates for the ministry, gives instruction to, II. 251.

Caswell, Rev. A., D. D., I. 300, 337; II. 7.

Catholicity of spirit, I. 83.

Chace, George I., LL. D., I. 270, 309; II. 365.

Chalmers, Rev. Thomas, D. D., I. 100; II. 39.   Memoir of, 39, 40, 289.

Christiancy, Judge, II. 270.

Christian Commission, the, II. 274.

" Christian Worship," II. 151.

Church music, II. 139, 221.

" Churches, Sermons to," II. 228.

Clarke, Sir James, II. 30.

Clifford, Hon. J. H., LL. D., I. 207, 221.

College course, I. 31.

Collegiate education, present system of, open to examination, II. 69, 83.

Commencement exercises, II. 146.

Controversy, dislike for, I. 400.

Conversational powers, I. 395.

Conversion, I. 49.
Convention, Triennial, I. 126, 176; II. 58.
Coquerel, Rev. A. L. C., II. 17.
Cornelius, Rev. E., D. D., I. 58.
Courts of law in London, II. 28.
Crane, William, Esq., I. 66.
Cromwell, Oliver, I. 399, 425.
Cushing Institute, II. 355.

Davis, Hon. Isaac, LL. D., II. 43.
Debts of the states, articles on, II. 54.
Discipline, church, I. 147.
Discipline, college, I. 261.
Dispensary, Providence, I. 336.
Doctrines, views of, I. 121.
Dodge, Hon. William E., II. 287.
Dormitories in college, II. 70.
"Duties of an American Citizen," I. 170.

Economy, conscientious observance of, I. 407; II. 353.
Education, ministerial, II. 163.
Education, kind of, demanded by people of United States, II. 102, 137.
England, our recent relations to, II. 271, 272.
Evening prayer meetings, II. 290.

Faculty of College, relations to, I. 293.
Faith, Christian views concerning, II. 257.
Family affection, II. 317.
Family meetings, fondness for, II. 407.
Federal Street Church, call to, I. 423.
Foreign missions, interest in, II. 329.
Foster, Hon. L. F. S., II. 262, 272, 278.
Foster, John, II. 42, 45, 74, 291.
Freedmen, interest in, II. 275, 277. How to be assisted, 276, 277.
Fugitive Slave Law. II. 332.

Religion in America
Series II

An Arno Press Collection

Adler, Felix. **Creed and Deed:** A Series of Discourses. New York, 1877.

Alexander, Archibald. **Evidences of the Authenticity, Inspiration, and Canonical Authority of the Holy Scriptures.** Philadelphia, 1836.

Allen, Joseph Henry. **Our Liberal Movement in Theology:** Chiefly as Shown in Recollections of the History of Unitarianism in New England. 3rd edition. Boston, 1892.

American Temperance Society. **Permanent Temperance Documents of the American Temperance Society.** Boston, 1835.

American Tract Society. **The American Tract Society Documents,** 1824-1925. New York, 1972.

Bacon, Leonard. **The Genesis of the New England Churches.** New York, 1874.

Bartlett, S[amuel] C. **Historical Sketches of the Missions of the American Board.** New York, 1972.

Beecher, Lyman. **Lyman Beecher and the Reform of Society:** Four Sermons, 1804-1828. New York, 1972.

[Bishop, Isabella Lucy Bird.] **The Aspects of Religion in the United States of America.** London, 1859.

Bowden, James. **The History of the Society of Friends in America.** London, 1850, 1854. Two volumes in one.

Briggs, Charles Augustus. **Inaugural Address and Defense,** 1891-1893. New York, 1972.

Colwell, Stephen. **The Position of Christianity in the United States,** in Its Relations with Our Political Institutions, and Specially with Reference to Religious Instruction in the Public Schools. Philadelphia, 1854.

Dalcho, Frederick. **An Historical Account of the Protestant Episcopal Church, in South-Carolina,** from the First Settlement of the Province, to the War of the Revolution. Charleston, 1820.

Elliott, Walter. **The Life of Father Hecker.** New York, 1891.

Gibbons, James Cardinal. **A Retrospect of Fifty Years.** Baltimore, 1916. Two volumes in one.

Hammond, L[ily] H[ardy]. **Race and the South:** Two Studies, 1914-1922. New York, 1972.

Hayden, A[mos] S. **Early History of the Disciples in the Western Reserve, Ohio;** With Biographical Sketches of the Principal Agents in their Religious Movement. Cincinnati, 1875.

Hinke, William J., editor. **Life and Letters of the Rev. John Philip Boehm:** Founder of the Reformed Church in Pennsylvania, 1683-1749. Philadelphia, 1916.

Hopkins, Samuel. **A Treatise on the Millennium.** Boston, 1793.

Kallen, Horace M. **Judaism at Bay:** Essays Toward the Adjustment of Judaism to Modernity. New York, 1932.

Kreider, Harry Julius. **Lutheranism in Colonial New York.** New York, 1942.

Loughborough, J. N. **The Great Second Advent Movement:** Its Rise and Progress. Washington, 1905.

M'Clure, David and Elijah Parish. **Memoirs of the Rev. Eleazar Wheelock, D.D.** Newburyport, 1811.

McKinney, Richard I. **Religion in Higher Education Among Negroes.** New Haven, 1945.

Mayhew, Jonathan. **Observations on the Charter and Conduct of the Society for the Propagation of the Gospel in Foreign Parts;** Designed to Shew Their Non-conformity to Each Other. Boston, 1763.

Mott, John R. **The Evangelization of the World in this Generation.** New York, 1900.

Payne, Bishop Daniel A. **Sermons and Addresses,** 1853-1891. New York, 1972.

Phillips, C[harles] H. **The History of the Colored Methodist Episcopal Church in America:** Comprising Its Organization, Subsequent Development, and Present Status. Jackson, Tenn., 1898.

Reverend Elhanan Winchester: Biography and Letters. New York, 1972.

Riggs, Stephen R. **Tah-Koo Wah-Kan; Or, the Gospel Among the Dakotas.** Boston, 1869.

Rogers, Elder John. **The Biography of Eld. Barton Warren Stone, Written by Himself:** With Additions and Reflections. Cincinnati, 1847.

Booth-Tucker, Frederick. **The Salvation Army in America:** Selected Reports, 1899-1903. New York, 1972.

Satolli, Francis Archbishop. **Loyalty to Church and State.** Baltimore, 1895.

Schaff, Philip. **Church and State in the United States** or the American Idea of Religious Liberty and its Practical Effects with Official Documents. New York and London, 1888. (Reprinted from *Papers of the American Historical Association,* Vol. II, No. 4.)

Smith, Horace Wemyss. **Life and Correspondence of the Rev. William Smith, D.D.** Philadelphia, 1879, 1880. Two volumes in one.

Spalding, M[artin] J. **Sketches of the Early Catholic Missions of Kentucky;** From Their Commencement in 1787 to the Jubilee of 1826-7. Louisville, 1844.

Steiner, Bernard C., editor. **Rev. Thomas Bray:** His Life and Selected Works Relating to Maryland. Baltimore, 1901. (Reprinted from *Maryland Historical Society Fund Publication,* No. 37.)

To Win the West: Missionary Viewpoints, 1814-1815. New York, 1972.

Wayland, Francis and H. L. Wayland. **A Memoir of the Life and Labors of Francis Wayland, D.D., LL.D.** New York, 1867. Two volumes in one.

Willard, Frances E. **Woman and Temperance:** Or, the Work and Workers of the Woman's Christian Temperance Union. Hartford, 1883.